Matt Mendelsohn

About the Author

DANIEL MENDELSOHN was born on Long Island
and educated at the University of Virginia and at
Princeton. He is a frequent contributor to the *New
York Review of Books* as well as the *New York Times
Magazine* and the *New York Times Book Review*, and
is a contributing editor at *Travel + Leisure*. His first
book, *The Elusive Embrace*, was named a *New York Times*
Notable Book of the Year and a *Los Angeles Times* Best
Book of the Year. He teaches at Bard College.

"Remarkable. . . . Mendelsohn's book shows how partial and fragmentary our knowledge of the past must always remain. . . . Mr. Mendelsohn insists on searching and writing. More than just an act of familial piety, this kind of recuperation is one of the distinctive ethical acts of our time."

—Adam Kirsch, *New York Sun*

"A grand book, an ambitious undertaking fully realized."   —*The Forward*

"Daniel Mendelsohn has written a powerfully moving work of a 'lost' family past in tones reminiscent of the richly expansive prose works of Proust and the elusive texts of W. G. Sebald—a remarkable achievement."

—Joyce Carol Oates

"A spectacular trail of discoveries, disappointments, and staggering coincidences. . . . Mendelsohn constructs an artful, looping narrative. . . . The technique pays off, showing how the Holocaust continues to affect people who had no direct experience of it."   —*The New Yorker*

"A magnificent and deeply wise book. . . . Mesmerizing. . . . Mendelsohn's accomplishment is enormous."   —*Los Angeles Times Book Review*

"A sad, wise, compelling book. . . . A poignant, powerful, and ultimately lasting tribute to the lives of six of the six million."

—*Raleigh News & Observer*

"Engaging and poignant. . . . Despite its considerable length, *The Lost* doesn't seem too long, thanks to the author's fine-tuned sense of drama and deft prose style. . . . Harrowing, absorbing, and supremely intelligent, the book amounts to an eloquent Kaddish, a prayer for the dead of Bolechow."

—*San Francisco Chronicle*

"*The Lost* is an extraordinary book, and in its breadth and uniqueness of vision, is one of the exceptional books of this year."

—*Pittsburgh Tribune-Review*

"Riveting. . . . Recalls the recent work of Jonathan Franzen or early Joan Didion. . . . A brilliant, steely-eyed personal history." —*Newsday*

"Amazing. . . . Breathtaking. . . . *The Lost* is completely engrossing. . . . Through meticulous, even obsessive, scholarship and detective work, Mendelsohn unearths and reconstructs the lives of six people in his own family." —Maureen Corrigan, NPR's *Fresh Air*

"An intimate and unforgettable portrait. . . . Mendelsohn . . . personalized past horrors by investigating them in the present. It is a detective story, shockingly all true." —*St. Louis Post-Dispatch*

"A masterpiece. . . . Daniel Mendelsohn is an astonishing writer. . . . This book, for better or worse, makes the Holocaust new again." —*Jerusalem Post*

"Extraordinary. . . . A charming, elegant, suspenseful book. . . . Mendelsohn's search for his family story is in fact a way to communicate the pathos of the Holocaust." —Gideon Lewis-Kraus, *The Nation*

"A brave and wise book. . . . Mendelsohn, a nonobservant, secular Jew, manages to script and conduct his own ceremony on a scale that is epic but in a voice that is personal, warm, and intimate." —*Buffalo News*

"Moving. . . . Proves that there are limitless ways of looking at that most inexplicable of human moments." —*Entertainment Weekly*

"Mendelsohn plunges deep into the heart of the Holocaust, deep into the heart of his family, deep into his own heart. . . . This is dense, rich, riveting reading; as Mendelsohn travels the globe to 'find the six,' he manages to find, and give voice to, a lost world, a lost family." —*San Diego Union-Tribune*

"*The Lost* is a remarkable accomplishment. . . . The narrative of the search provides the basic structure, but it is the reflections on memory, family, and the human condition, interwoven skillfully into the travelogue, that give the book its multidimensional power." —*The Globe and Mail*

"A stirring detective work in its own right, *The Lost* is set in the context of stories of the enigmatic interventions of God in human affairs, and deepened by reflections on the inescapable, incomprehensible part that chance plays in history."   —J. M. Coetzee

"Enough cannot be said about *The Lost*. It is among the best of books about the Holocaust, and its special virtue is that Mendelsohn is successful in rescuing his lost family from the anonymity of the mass graves and crematoria."
                                                —*Philadelphia Inquirer*

"A stunning achievement. . . . Extraordinary. . . . An unspeakably sad and yet also triumphant and therefore joyful project of recovery. . . . It accomplishes what many of us would do if we had both the skill and obsession required to recover our own nameless lost."   —Rebecca Goldstein, *New York Observer*

"It is the aspect of the quest that gives *The Lost* its particular character—a peeling away of the obscurities of time, a penetrating into the depths of knowledge. And that pool of knowledge is every year diminishing."
                                                —*Boston Globe*

"Gripping. . . . A page-turning mystery, a lesson on how history is written, and a work of religious scholarship. This is a book that you start and think: I have never read a book like this one before."   —Salon.com

THE LOST

A Search for Six of Six Million

DANIEL MENDELSOHN

PHOTOGRAPHS BY

MATT MENDELSOHN

HARPER ● PERENNIAL

NEW YORK ● LONDON ● TORONTO ● SYDNEY

HARPER ● PERENNIAL

Grateful acknowledgment is made to the following institutions and individuals for permission to reproduce photographs and to quote from documents in their possession:

Beth Hatefutsoth, The Nahum Goldmann Museum of the Jewish Diaspora, Tel Aviv, Permanent Exhibition (pp. 338 and 341); the Jewish Museum in Prague (p. 284); Yad Vashem, the Holocaust Martyrs' and Heroes' Remembrance Authority, Jerusalem (pp. 208-10, 227-29; p. 351); Lane Montgomery (p. 484); Henryk Jaronowski (pp. 290 and 292); and State Archive of the Russian Federation (GARF) (p. 510).

A hardcover edition of this book was published in 2006 by HarperCollins Publishers.

HarperCollins books may be purchased for educational, business, or sales promotional use. For information please write: Special Markets Department, HarperCollins Publishers, 10 East 53rd Street, New York, NY 10022.

FIRST HARPER PERENNIAL EDITION PUBLISHED 2007.

Designed by Joseph Rutt

The Library of Congress has catalogued the hardcover edition as follows:

The lost: a search for six of six million/Daniel Mendelsohn.
p.   cm.
ISBN: 978-0-06-054297-9
ISBN-10: 0-06-054297-7
1. Mendelsohn, Daniel Adam, 1960–   2. Mendelsohn, Daniel Adam, 1960–   —Family.
3. Jews—United States—Biography—Anecdotes. 4. Jaeger family.
5. Jews—Ukraine—Bolekhiv—Biography—Anecdotes. 6. Holocaust, Jewish
(1939–1945)—Ukraine—Bolekhiv. I. Title.

E184.37.M48L67   2006
973'.049240092—dc22
[B]   2006041096

ISBN: 978-0-06-054299-3 (pbk.)
ISBN-10: 0-06-054299-3 (pbk.)

07 08 09 10 11   NMSG/RRD   10 9 8 7 6 5 4 3 2

To

FRANCES BEGLEY

and

SARAH PETTIT

sunt lacrimae rerum

The Family of Shmiel Jäger

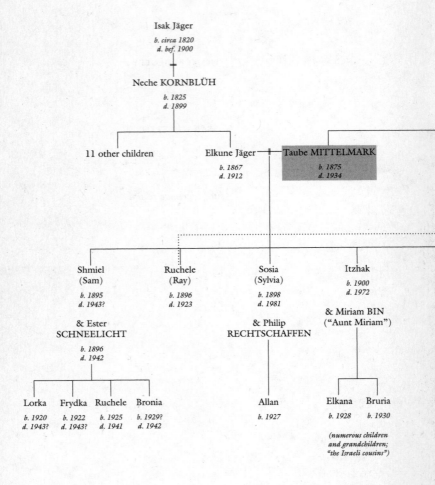

JÄGER

Isak Jäger
b. circa 1820
d. bef. 1900

Neche KORNBLÜH
b. 1825
d. 1899

11 other children

Elkune Jäger
b. 1867
d. 1912

Taube MITTELMARK
b. 1875
d. 1934

Shmiel
(Sam)
b. 1895
d. 1943?

& Ester
SCHNEELICHT
b. 1896
d. 1942

Ruchele
(Ray)
b. 1896
d. 1923

Sosia
(Sylvia)
b. 1898
d. 1981

& Philip
RECHTSCHAFFEN

Itzhak
b. 1900
d. 1972

& Miriam BIN
("Aunt Miriam")

Lorka
b. 1920
d. 1943?

Frydka
b. 1922
d. 1943?

Ruchele
b. 1925
d. 1941

Bronia
b. 1929?
d. 1942

Allan
b. 1927

Elkana
b. 1928

Bruria
b. 1930

*(numerous children
and grandchildren;
"the Israeli cousins")*

MITTELMARK

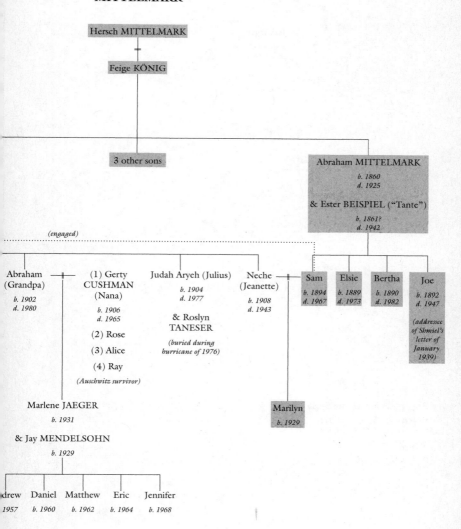

Hersch MITTELMARK

Feige KÖNIG

3 other sons

Abraham MITTELMARK

b. 1860
d. 1925

& Ester BEISPIEL ("Tante")

b. 1861?
d. 1942

(engaged)

Abraham
(Grandpa)

b. 1902
d. 1980

(1) Gerty
CUSHMAN
(Nana)

b. 1906
d. 1965

(2) Rose

(3) Alice

(4) Ray

(Auschwitz survivor)

Judah Aryeh (Julius)

b. 1904
d. 1977

& Roslyn
TANESER

*(buried during
hurricane of 1976)*

Neche
(Jeanette)

b. 1908
d. 1943

Sam

b. 1894
d. 1967

Elsie

b. 1889
d. 1973

Bertha

b. 1890
d. 1982

Joe

b. 1892
d. 1947

*(addressee
of Shmiel's
letter of
January
1939)*

Marlene JAEGER

b. 1931

& Jay MENDELSOHN

b. 1929

Marilyn

b. 1929

drew   Daniel   Matthew   Eric   Jennifer

1957   *b. 1960*   *b. 1962*   *b. 1964*   *b. 1968*

PART ONE

Bereishit,

or,

Beginnings

(1967–2000)

WHEN WE HAVE PASSED A CERTAIN AGE, THE SOUL OF THE
CHILD WE WERE AND THE SOULS OF THE DEAD FROM WHOM
WE HAVE SPRUNG COME TO LAVISH ON US THEIR RICHES
AND THEIR SPELLS. . . .

Marcel Proust,
In Search of Lost Time
(The Captive)

THE FORMLESS VOID

SOME TIME AGO, when I was six or seven or eight years old, it would occasionally happen that I'd walk into a room and certain people would begin to cry. The rooms in which this happened were located, more often than not, in Miami Beach, Florida, and the people on whom I had this strange effect were, like nearly everyone in Miami Beach in the mid-nineteen-sixties, old. Like nearly everyone else in Miami Beach at that time (or so it seemed to me then), these old people were Jews—Jews of the sort who were likely to lapse, when sharing prized bits of gossip or coming to the long-delayed endings of stories or to the punch lines of jokes, into Yiddish; which of course had the effect of rendering the climaxes, the points, of these stories and jokes incomprehensible to those of us who were young.

Like many elderly residents of Miami Beach in those days, these people lived in apartments or small houses that seemed, to those who didn't live in them, slightly stale; and which were on the whole quiet, except on those evenings when the sound of the Red Skelton or Milton Berle or Lawrence Welk shows blared from the black-and-white television sets. At certain intervals, however, their stale, quiet apartments would grow noisy with the voices of young children who had flown down for a few weeks in the winter or spring from Long Island or the New Jersey suburbs to see these old Jews, and who would be presented to them, squirming with awkwardness and embarrassment, and forced to kiss their papery, cool cheeks.

Kissing the cheeks of old Jewish relatives! We writhed, we groaned, we wanted to race down to the kidney-shaped heated swimming pool in back of the apartment complex, but first we had to kiss all those cheeks; which, on the men, smelled like basements and hair tonic and Tiparillos, and were scratchy with whiskers so white you'd often mistake them for lint (as my younger brother once did, who attempted to pluck off the offending fluff only to be smacked, ungently, on the side of the head); and, on the old women, gave off the vague aroma of face powder and cooking oil, and were as soft as the "emergency" tissues crammed into the bottom of their purses, crushed there like petals next to the violet smelling salts, wrinkled cough-drop wrappers, and crumpled bills. . . . The crumpled bills. *Take this and hold it for Marlene until I come out,* my mother's mother, whom we called Nana, instructed my other grandmother, as she handed her a small red leather purse containing a crinkled twenty-dollar bill one February day in 1965, just before they wheeled her into an operating room for some exploratory surgery. She had just turned fifty-nine, and wasn't feeling well. My grandmother Kay obeyed and took the purse with the crumpled bill, and true to her word she delivered it to my mother, who was still holding it a number of days later when Nana, laid in a plain pine box, as is the custom, was buried in the Mount Judah Cemetery in Queens, in the section owned (as an inscription on a granite gateway informs you) by the FIRST BOLECHOWER SICK BENEVOLENT ASSOCIATION. To be buried here you had to belong to this association, which meant in turn that you had to have come from a small town of a few thousand people, located halfway around the world in a landscape that had once belonged to Austria and then to Poland and then to many others, called Bolechow.

Now it is true that my mother's mother—whose soft earlobes, with their chunky blue or yellow crystal earrings, I would play with as I sat on her lap in the webbed garden chair on my parents' front porch, and whom at one point I loved more than anyone else, which is no doubt why her death was the first event of which I have any distinct memories, although it's true that those memories are, at best, fragments (the undulating fish pattern of the tiles on the walls of the hospital waiting room; my mother saying something to me urgently, something important, although it would be another forty years before I was finally reminded of what it was; a complex emotion of yearning and fear and shame; the sound of water running in a sink)—my mother's mother was not born in Bolechow, and indeed was the only one of my four grandparents who was born in the United States: a fact that, among a certain group of people that is now extinct, once gave her a certain cachet. But her handsome and domineering husband, my grandfather, *Grandpa,* had been born and grew to young manhood in Bolechow, he and his six siblings, the three brothers and three sisters; and for this reason he was permitted to own a plot in that particular section of Mount Judah Cemetery. There he, too, lies buried now, along with his mother, two of his three sisters, and one of his three brothers. The other sister, the fiercely possessive mother of an only son, followed her boy to another state, and lies buried there. Of the other two brothers, one (so we were always told) had had the good sense and foresight to emigrate with his wife and small children from Poland to Palestine in the 1930s, and as a result of that sage decision was buried, in due time, in Israel. The oldest brother, who was also the handsomest of the seven siblings, the most adored and adulated, the *prince* of the family, had come as a young man to New York, in 1913; but after a scant year living with an aunt and uncle there he decided that he preferred Bolechow. And so, after a year in the States, he went back— a choice that, because he ended up happy and prosperous there, he knew to be the right one. He has no grave at all.

OF THOSE OLD men and women who would sometimes cry at the mere sight of me, those old Jewish people with the cheeks that had to be kissed, with their faux-alligator wristwatch bands and dirty Yiddish jokes and thick black plastic glasses with the yellowed plastic hearing aid trailing off the back, with the glasses brimful of whiskey, with the pencils that they'd offer you each time you saw them, which bore the names of banks and car dealerships; with their A-line cotton-print dresses and triple strands of white plastic beads and pale crystal earrings and red nail varnish that glittered and clicked on their long, long nails as they played mah-jongg and canasta, or clutched the long, long cigarettes they smoked—: of those, the ones I could make cry had certain other things in common. They all spoke with a particular accent, one with which I was familiar because it was the accent that haunted, faintly but perceptibly, my grandfather's speech: not too heavy, since by the time I was old enough to notice such things they had lived here, in America, for half a century, but still there was a telltale ripeness, a plummy quality to certain words that were ripe with *r*'s and *l*'s, words like *darling* or *wonderful*, a certain way of biting into the *t*'s and *th*'s in words like *terrible* and (a word my grandfather, who liked to tell stories, often used) *truth. It's de troott!* he would say. These elderly Jews tended to interrupt one another a lot on those occasions when they and we would all crowd into somebody's musty living room, cutting off one another's stories to make corrections, reminding one another what had really happened at this or that *vahnderfoll* or (more likely) *tahrrible time, dollink, I vuz dehre, I rrammembah, and I'm tellink you, it's de troott.*

More distinctive and memorable still, they all seemed to have a second, alternate set of names for one another. This confused and disoriented me, when I was six or seven years old, because I thought that the name of (say) my Nana was Gertrude, or sometimes Gerty, and so I couldn't figure out why, in this select company, in Florida, at large family gatherings that took place forty years after her husband's bossy and self-dramatizing family had disembarked at Ellis Island to remake themselves as Americans (while never ceasing to tell stories about Europe), she became *Golda*. Nor could I understand why my grandfather's younger brother, our Uncle Julius, a famous giver-out of inscribed pencils, who had married unusually late in life and whom my swaggering, well-dressed grandfather always treated with the kind of indulgence you reserve for ill-behaved pets, suddenly became *Yidl*. (It would be decades before I learned that the name on his birth certificate had been Judah Aryeh: "lion of Judah.") And who, anyway, was this *Neche*—it sounded like *Nehkhuh*—whom my grandfather would sometimes refer to as his darling youngest sister, who, I knew, had dropped dead of a stroke at the age of thirty-five in 1943 at (so my grandfather would tell me, by way of explaining why he didn't like that holiday) the Thanksgiving table; who was this *Nehkhuh*, since I knew, or thought I knew, that his beloved baby sister had been Aunt Jeanette? Only my grandfather, whose given name was Abraham, had a nickname that was intelligible to me: Aby; and this added to my sense that he was a person of total and transparent authenticity, a person you could trust.

Among these people, there were some who cried when they saw me. I would walk in the room and they would look at me and (mostly the women) would put both twisted hands, with their rings and the knots, swollen and hard like those of a tree, that were their knuckles, they would put these hands to their dry cheeks and say, with a stagy little indrawn breath, *Oy, er zett oys zeyer eynlikh tzu Shmiel!*

Oh, he looks so much like Shmiel!

And then they would start crying, or exclaiming softly and rocking back and forth with their pink sweaters or windbreakers shaking around their loose shoulders, and there would then begin a good deal of rapid-fire Yiddish from which I was, then, excluded.

OF THIS SHMIEL, of course, I knew something: my grandfather's oldest brother, who with his wife and four beautiful daughters had been killed by the Nazis during the war. *Shmiel. Killed by the Nazis.* The latter was, we all understood, the unwritten caption on the few photographs that we had of him and his family, which now lie stored carefully inside a plastic baggie inside a box inside a carton in my mother's basement. A prosperous-looking businessman of perhaps fifty-five, standing proprietarily in front of a truck next to two uniformed drivers; a family gathered around a table, the parents, four small girls, an unknown stranger; a sleek man in a fur-collared coat, wearing a fedora; two young men in World War I uniforms, one of whom I knew to be the twenty-one-year-old Shmiel while the identity of the other one was impossible to guess, unknown and unknowable. . . . *Unknown and unknowable*: this could be frustrating, but also produced a certain allure. The photographs of Shmiel and his family were, after all, more fascinating than the other family pictures that were so fastidiously preserved in my mother's family archive precisely because we knew almost nothing about him, about them; their unsmiling, unspeaking faces seemed, as a result, more beguiling.

For a long time there were only the mute photographs and, sometimes, the uncomfortable ripple in the air when Shmiel's name was mentioned. This was not often, when my grandfather was still living, because we knew this was the great tragedy of his life, that his brother and sister-in-law and four nieces had been killed by the Nazis. Even I, who when he visited loved to sit at his feet, shod in their soft leather slippers, and to listen to his many stories about "the family," which of course meant *his* family, whose name had once been Jäger (and who, forced to give up that umlaut over the *a* when they came to America, over time became Yaegers and Yagers and Jagers and, like him, Jaegers: all of these spellings appear on the gravestones in Mount Judah), this family who for centuries had had a butcher store and then, later, a meat-shipping business in Bolechow, *a nice town, a bustling little town, a shtetl,* a place that was famous for the timber and meat and leather goods that its merchants shipped all over Europe, *a place where a person could live, a beautiful spot near the mountains;* even I, who was so close to him, who as I grew older would ask him so often about matters of family history, dates, names, descriptions, places, that when he responded to my questions (on thin sheets of stationery from the company he'd owned long before, in blue ink from a fat Parker fountain pen) he'd occasionally write *Dear Daniel, Please don't ask me any more questions about the mishpuchah, because I'm an old man and I can't remember a thing, and besides are you sure you want to find more relatives?!*— even I felt awkward about bringing it up, this dreadful thing that had happened to Shmiel, to his very own brother. *Killed by the Nazis.* It was hard for me, when I was a child and first started hearing that refrain about Shmiel and his lost family, to imagine what exactly that meant. Even later, after I was old enough to have learned about the war, seen the documentaries, watched with my parents the episode of a PBS series called *The World at War* that was preceded by a terrifying warning that certain images in the film were too intense for children— even later, it was hard to imagine just how they had been killed, to grasp the details, the specifics. When? Where? How? With guns? In the gas chambers? But my grandfather wouldn't say. Only later did I understand that he wouldn't say because he didn't know, or at least didn't know enough, and that the not knowing, in part, was what tormented him.

And so I didn't bring it up. Instead I would keep to safe subjects, the questions that would allow him to be funny, which he liked to be, as for instance in the following letter, written to me just after I turned fourteen:

May 20/74

Dear Daniel

Received your letter with all your questions, but sorry I havent been able to give you all the answers. I noticed in your letter where you are asking me if you are interruptin my <u>busy</u> <u>schedule</u> with all your questions, the answer is <u>NO</u>

I noticed that <u>you</u> are very happy that I remembered HERSH'S wife's name. I am also happy, because <u>Hersh</u> is my Grandfather and <u>Feige</u> is my Grandmother.

Now about the dates of Birth of each one I don't know because I was not there, but when the <u>MESSIAH</u> will come, and all the relatives will be Re-United I will ask them . . .

An addendum to this letter is addressed to my sister and youngest brother:

Dearest Jennifer and Dear Eric,

We thank you both for your wonderful letter's, and we are especially happy because you have no questions about the <u>Mishpacha</u>

DEAR JENNIFER
I WAS GOING TO SEND YOU AND YOUR BROTHER ERIC SOME
MONEY, BUT AS YOU KNOW THAT I AM NOT WORKING AND I HAVE NO
MONEY. SO AUNT RAY LOVES YOU BOTH VERY MUCH, AND AUNT RAY
IS ENCLOSING TWO DOLLARS ONE FOR YOU, AND ONE FOR ERIC.
LOVE AND KISSES
AUNT RAY AND GRANDPA JAEGER

Dearest Marlene
Please be advised that Tuesday May 28 is YISKOR . . .

Yiskor, *yizkor*: a memorial service. My grandfather was always mindful of the dead. Each summer when he came to visit, we took him to Mount Judah to visit my grandmother and all the others. We children would wander around and look blandly at the names on the modest headstones and low footstones, or at the giant monument, in the shape of a tree with its branches lopped off, which commemorated my grandfather's older sister, who had died at twenty-six, *a week before her wedding,* or so my grandfather used to tell me. Some of these stones bore little electric-blue stickers that said PERPETUAL CARE, nearly all of them boasted names like STANLEY and IRVING and HERMAN and MERVIN, like SADIE and PAULINE, names that to people of my generation seem quintessentially Jewish although, in one of those ironies that only the passage of a certain amount of time can make clear, the fact is that the immigrant Jews of a century ago, born with names like SELIG and ITZIG and HERCEL and MORDKO, like SCHEINDEL and PERL, had chosen those names precisely because to them the names seemed quite English, quite un-Jewish. We would wander around and look at all this while my grandfather, always in a spotless sport coat, crisply creased slacks, boldly knotted tie, and pocket square, would make his meticulous and orderly progress, stopping by each stone in turn, his mother's, his sister's, his brother's, his wife's, he had outlived them all, and would read the prayers in Hebrew in a kind of urgent mumble. If you drive along the Interboro Parkway in Queens and stop near the entrance of the Mount Judah Cemetery, and look over the stone fence by the road, you can see all of them there, can read their adopted, slightly grandiose names, accompanied by the ritualistic labels: BELOVED WIFE, MOTHER, AND GRANDMOTHER; BELOVED HUSBAND; MOTHER.

So yes: he was mindful of the dead. It was to be many years before I realized just how mindful he was, my handsome and funny grandfather, who knew so many stories, who dressed so famously well: with his smoothly shaven oval face, the winking blue eyes and the straight nose that ended in the barest suggestion of a bulb, as if whoever had designed him had decided, at the last minute, to throw in a hint of humor; with his sparse, neatly brushed white hair, his clothes and cologne and manicures, his notorious jokes and his intricate, tragic stories.

MY GRANDFATHER WOULD come each year in the summer, since in the summer the weather on Long Island was less oppressive than it was in Miami Beach. He would stay for weeks at a time, accompanied by whichever of his four wives he happened to be married to at the time. When he came to stay he (and, sometimes, the wife) would occupy my little brothers' room, with its narrow twin beds. There, on arriving from the airport, he would hang his hat on a lamp shade and neatly fold his sport coat over the back of a chair, and afterward he'd set about taking care of his canary, Schloimele, which is Yiddish for *little Solomon:* settling the cage on a tiny oak child's desk, sprinkling the little bird with a few drops of water *just to refresh a little.* Then, slowly, meticulously, he would remove his things from his carefully packed bags, gently placing them on one of the two tiny beds in that room.

My grandfather was famous (in the way that certain kinds of Jewish immigrants and their families will talk about someone being "famous" for something, which generally means that about twenty-six people know about it) for a number of things—his sense of humor, the three women he married and, except for the one who outlived him, divorced in rapid succession after my grandmother died, the way he dressed, certain family tragedies, his Orthodoxy, the way he had of making waitresses and shopkeepers remember him, summer after summer—but to me the two salient things about him were his devoutness and his wonderful clothes. When I was a child and then an adolescent, these two things seemed to be the boundaries between which his strangeness, his Europeanness, existed: the territory that belonged to him and no one else, a space in which it was possible to be both worldly and pious, suave and religious, at the same time.

The first among the things that he would remove as he unpacked was the velvet bag that contained the things he needed to say his morning prayers— to *daven*. This he did every day of his life from the day in the spring of 1915 when he was bar mitzvahed to the morning before the June day in 1980 when he died. In this satin-lined bag of burgundy velvet, on the face of which was embroidered, in gold thread, a menorah flanked by rampant lions of Judah, were his yarmulke; an enormous old-fashioned white and faded-blue tallis sewn with its tickling fringes, in which, in conformance with the instructions that he meticulously dictated to me one hot day in 1972 when I was twelve, a year before my bar mitzvah, he was buried that June day; and the leather phylacteries, or *tefillin*, that he bound around his head and left forearm each morning as, while we watched in mute awe, he davened. To us it was a sight both bizarre and majestic: each morning after sunrise, murmuring in Hebrew, he would wrap his arm with the leather bands, and then wrap a single thick leather band around his skull, attached to which was a leather box containing verses from the Torah that nestled in the center of his forehead, and would then put on the huge, faded tallis and the yarmulke, and then taking out his *siddur*, his daily prayer book, would mumble for about half an hour, his words completely incomprehensible to us. Sometimes, when he was finished, he'd say to us, *I put in a good word for you, since you're only Reform.* My grandfather was an Orthodox Jew of the old school, and it was for his sake, more than anything else, that we had any religion at all: went to services on the holidays, got bar mitzvahed. As far as I know, my father, a scientist who did not see eye to eye with his garrulous father-in-law, went to the little synagogue we belonged to exactly four times: on the mornings of his sons' bar mitzvahs.

As exacting and meticulous as the ritual of the davening was, so too the way in which my grandfather would dress each morning: precise and orderly, just as much of a ritual. My grandfather was what used to be called a "snappy dresser." His brushed and polished appearance, his fine clothes, were merely the external expression of an inner quality that, for him and his family, characterized what it was to be a Jäger, something they would refer to as *Feinheit:* a refinement that was at once ethical and aesthetic. You could always count on his socks matching his sweater, and he preferred to wear soft-brimmed hats in whose bands you could spot a rakish feather or two, until the last of his four wives—who had lost her first husband and a fourteen-year-old daughter in Auschwitz, and whose soft, tattooed forearm I used to love to hold and stroke, when I was little, and who because she had lost so much, I now think, could not abide anything so frivolous as a feather in a hat—started to pluck them out. On a typical summer day in the 1970s, he might wear the following: mustard-yellow summer-weight wool trousers, crisply creased; a soft white knit shirt under a mustard-and-white argyle sweater-vest; pale yellow socks, white suede shoes, and a soft-brimmed hat that, depending which year in the 1970s it was, did or did not sport a feather. Before stepping outside to walk around the block a few times, or to the park, he'd splash some 4711 cologne on his hands and slap it onto the sides of his head and beneath the wattles of his chin. *Now,* he would say, rubbing his manicured hands together, *we can go out.*

I would watch all this very carefully. (Or so I thought.) He might also wear a sport jacket—this, to me, seemed incredible, since there was neither a wedding nor a bar mitzvah to attend—into which he would slip, invariably, both his wallet and, in the inside breast pocket on the other side, an odd-looking billfold: long and slender, rather too large in the way that, to American eyes, certain items of European haberdashery always look somehow the wrong size; and of a leather, worn to an almost suedelike smoothness, which I now realize was ostrich skin, since I own it now, but which then I merely thought amusingly pimply-looking. I would sit on my little brother's bed as he talked, watching him and admiring his things: the argyle vest, the white shoes, the sleek belts, the heavy blue-and-gold bottle of cologne, the tortoiseshell comb with which he slicked back the sparse white hair, the worn, puckered wallet that, as I knew even then, contained no money, unable as I was to imagine at that point what might be so precious that he had to carry it with him every time he dressed himself so impeccably.

THIS WAS THE man from whom I gleaned hundreds of stories and thousands of facts over the years, the names of his grandparents and great-uncles and aunts and second cousins, the years they were born and where they had died, the name of the Ukrainian maid they had had as children in Bolechow (Lulka), who used to complain that the children had stomachs "like bottomless pits," the kind of hat his father, my great-grandfather, used to wear. (Homburgs: He'd been a courtly man with a goatee, my grandfather liked to boast about his father, and was something of a bigwig in his small but bustling town, known for bringing bottles of Hungarian Tokay to prospective business associates "to sweeten the deal"; and had dropped dead at the age of forty-five of heart failure at a spa in the Carpathian Mountains called Jaremcze, where he'd gone to take the waters for his health. This was the beginning of the bad years, the reason, in the end, why nearly all of his children eventually had to leave Bolechow.) Grandpa told me about the town park, with its statue of the great nineteenth-century Polish poet Adam Mickiewicz, and the little park across the square with its allée of lime trees. He recited for me, and I learned, the words to "Mayn Shtetele Belz," that little lullaby-like Yiddish song about the town quite near the one he grew up in, which his mother had sung to him a decade before the *Titanic* sank—

Mayn heymele, dort vu ikh hob
Mayne kindershe yorn farbrakht.
Belz, mayn shtetele Belz,
In ormen shtibele mit ale
Kinderlakh dort gelakht.
Yedn shabes fleg ikh loyfn dort
Mit der tchine glaych
Tsu zitsen unter dem grinem
Beymele, leyenen bay dem taykh.
Belz, mayn shtetele Belz,
Mayn heymele vu ch'hob gehat
Di sheyne khaloymes a sach.

My little home, where I spent
My childhood years;

Belz, my shtetl Belz,
in a poor little cottage with all
the little children I laughed.
Every Sabbath there I would go
With my prayer book
To sit down under the little green
tree, and read on the river's edge.
Belz, my shtetl Belz
My little home, where I once had
So many beautiful dreams . . .

—learned these words, which I recently had the bizarre experience of hearing again, for the first time since my grandfather's death twenty-five years
ago, at a Sixties "theme" party at a club in New York City, and when I asked
the DJ where he'd found this particular song he handed to me, without ceasing to gyrate to the strange music, the worn cover of a 1960 album, made by a
famous Italian-American pop singer, titled *Connie Francis Sings Jewish Favorites.*
From my grandfather I learned, too, about the old Ukrainian woodsman who
lived in the hills above Bolechow but who, on the night before Yom Kippur,
watching the unusual and, to him, frightening stillness settle along the glinting
towns beneath the Carpathians' timbered foothills as the Jews of the shtetls
prepared for the awesome holiday, would make his way down the mountain
and stay in the house of a kindly Jew, such was this Ukrainian peasant's fear, on
that one night each year, of the Jews and their glum God.

The Ukrainians, my grandfather would say now and then with a weary little
sigh, as he told this story. *Oo-krah-EE-nyans.* The Ukrainians. Our *goyim.*

So he would come each summer to Long Island and I would sit at his feet
as he talked. He talked about that older sister who'd died *a week before her wedding,* and talked about the younger sister who was married off at nineteen to
that older sister's fiancé, the hunchbacked (my grandfather said), dwarflike
first cousin whom first one and finally the other of these lovely girls had had
to marry because, my grandfather told me, this ugly cousin's father had paid
for the boat tickets that had brought those two sisters and their brothers and
mother, brought all of my grandfather's family, to the United States, and had
demanded a beautiful daughter-in-law as the price. He talked bitterly about
how this same cousin, who was of course also his brother-in-law, chased my
grandfather down forty-two flights of steps in the Chrysler Building after the
reading of a certain will in 1947, brandishing a pair of scissors, or perhaps it

was a letter opener; talked about that mean aunt of his, the wife of the uncle who'd paid for his passage to America (the same aunt my grandfather's older brother, the prince, had had to live with during his brief stay in the United States in 1913, and perhaps it was her meanness that had resulted in his decision to go back to Bolechow to live, the decision that seemed so right at the time); my grandfather talked about that aunt of his, *Tante,* who in the few remaining photographs of her is a huge, doughy, sour-faced matriarch whose fat arms settle around her torso like opulent robes of state, a woman so formidable that even today, in my family—even among those of us born a full generation after she died—it is impossible to hear the word *Tante* without a shudder.

And he talked about the pleasing modesty of Old Country bar mitzvahs as compared (you were meant to feel) to the overdressed and officious extravagance of the ceremonies today: first the religious ceremonies in cold, slope-roofed temples and, afterward, the receptions in lavish country clubs and catering halls, occasions at which boys like myself would read the *parashah,* the Torah portion for that week, and uncomprehendingly sing their *haftarah* portions, the selections from the Prophets that accompany each *parashah,* while dreaming of the reception to come and the promise of furtive whiskey sours. (Which is how I sang mine: a performance that ended with my voice cracking, loudly, mortifyingly, as I chanted the very last word, plummeting from a pure soprano to the baritone in which it has remained ever since.) *Nu, so?* he would say. *So you got up at five instead of six that morning, you prayed an extra hour in shul, and then you went home and had cookies and tea with the rabbi and your mother and father, and that was that.* He talked about how seasick he was on the ten-day crossing to America, about the time, years before that, when he had to guard a barn full of Russian prisoners of war, when he was sixteen during the First World War, which is how he learned Russian, one of the many languages he knew; about the vague group of cousins who would visit every now and then in the Bronx and who were called, mysteriously, "the Germans."

My grandfather told me all these stories, all these things, but he never talked about his brother and sister-in-law and the four girls who, to me, seemed not so much dead as lost, vanished not only from the world but—even more terrible to me—from my grandfather's stories. Which is why, out of all this history, all these people, the ones I knew the least about were the six who were murdered, who had, it seemed to me then, the most stunning story of all, the one most worthy to be told. But on this subject, my loquacious grandpa remained silent, and his silence, unusual and tense, irradiated the subject of Shmiel and his family, making them unmentionable and, therefore, unknowable.

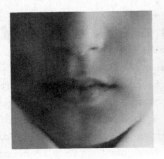
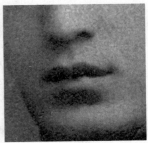

Unknowable.

Every single word of the Five Books of Moses, the core of the Hebrew Bible, has been analyzed, examined, interpreted, and held up to the scrutiny of rigorous scholars over many centuries. It is generally acknowledged that the greatest of all biblical commentators was the eleventh-century French scholar Rabbi Shlomo ben Itzhak, who is better known as Rashi, a name that is nothing more than an acronym formed from the initial letters of his title, name, and patronymic: Ra(bbi) Sh(lomo ben) I(tzhak)——Rashi. Born in Troyes in 1040, Rashi survived the terrible upheavals of his time, which included the slaughters of Jews that were, so to speak, a by-product of the First Crusade. Educated in Mainz, where he was the student of the man who had been the greatest student of the renowned Gershom of Mainz (because I have always had good teachers, I love the idea of these intellectual genealogies), Rashi founded his own academy at the age of twenty-five and lived to see himself recognized as the greatest scholar of his age. His concern for each and every word of the text he was studying was matched only by the cramped terseness of his own style; it is perhaps because of the latter that Rashi's own commentary on the Bible has itself become the object of some two hundred further commentaries. One measure of Rashi's significance is that the first printed Hebrew Bible included his commentary. . . . It is interesting, for me, to note that Rashi, like my great-uncle Shmiel, had only daughters, which was, as far as these things go, more of a liability for a man with a certain kind of ambition in 1040 than it was in 1940. Still, the children of these daughters of Rashi carried on their grandfather's magnificent legacy, and for that reason were known as baalei tosafot, *"Those Who Extended."*

Although Rashi stands as the preeminent commentator on the Torah——and, hence, on the first parashah *in the Torah, the reading with which the Torah begins, and which itself begins with not one but, mysteriously, two accounts of the Creation, and includes the story of Adam and Eve and the Tree of Knowledge, and which is for that reason a story that has attracted particularly rigorous commentary over the millennia——it* is important to acknowledge the interpretations of modern commentators, such as the recent translation and commentary by Rabbi Richard Elliot Friedman, which, in its sincere and searching attempts to connect the ancient text to contemporary life, is as open-faced and friendly as Rashi's is dense and abstruse.

For instance, throughout his analysis of the first chapter of Genesis—the Hebrew name of which, bereishit, literally means "in the beginning"—Rashi is attentive to minute details of meaning and diction that Rabbi Friedman is content to let pass without comment, whereas Friedman (who is, admittedly, writing for a more general audience) is eager to elucidate broader points. An example: Both scholars acknowledge the famous difficulties of translating the very first line of Bereishit—bereishit bara Elohim et-hashamayim v'et-ha'aretz. Contrary to the belief of millions who have read the King James Bible, this line does not mean, "In the beginning, God created the heavens and the earth," but must mean, rather, something like "In the beginning of God's creation of the heavens and the earth . . ." Friedman merely acknowledges the "classic problem" of translation, without going into it; whereas Rashi expends quantities of ink on just what the problem is. And the problem, in a word, is that what the Hebrew literally says is "In the beginning of, God created the heavens and the earth." For the first word, bereishit, "in the beginning" (b', "in," + reishit, "beginning") is normally followed by another noun, but in the first line of parashat Bereishit—when we refer to a parashah by name we use the form "parashat"—what follows the word bereishit is a _verb_: bara, "created." After an extended discussion of the linguistic issues, Rashi eventually solves the problem by invoking certain parallels from other texts in which bereishit is followed by a verb rather than a noun, and it is this that allows us to translate these first crucial words as follows:

> In the beginning of God's creating the skies and heavens—when the earth had been shapeless and formless, and darkness was on the face of the deep, and God's spirit was hovering on the face of the water—God said, "Let there be light."

The key issue, for Rashi, is that the wrong reading suggests an incorrect chronology of Creation: that God created the heavens, then the earth, then light, and so forth. But this is not how it happened, Rashi says. If you get the small details wrong, the big picture will be wrong, too.

The way in which tiny nuances of word order, diction, grammar, and syntax can have much larger ramifications for the entire meaning of a text colors Rashi's commentary overall. For him (to take another example), the infamous "double opening" of Genesis—the fact that it has not one but two accounts of Creation, the first starting with the creation of the cosmos and ending in the creation of humankind (Genesis 1:1–30), the second focusing from the start on the creation of Adam, and moving almost immediately to the story of Eve, the serpent, and the Expulsion from Eden—is, at bottom, a stylistic issue, easily enough explained. In his discussion of Genesis 2, Rashi anticipates readers' grumblings—the creation of man has, after all, already been dealt with in Genesis 1:27—but declares that, after having himself consulted a certain body of rabbinic wisdom, he has discovered a certain "rule" (number thirteen of thirty-two, as it happens, that help explain the Torah), and this rule says that when a general statement or story is followed by a second telling of that story, the second telling is meant to be understood as a more detailed explication of the first. And so the second telling of the creation of mankind, in Genesis 2, is, so to speak, meant to be taken as an enhanced version of the first telling, which we get in Genesis 1. As indeed it is: for nothing in the first chapter of Genesis, with its dry, chronological account of the creation of the cosmos, the earth, its flora and fauna, and finally of humankind, prepares us for the rich narrative of the second chapter, with its tale of innocence, deceit, betrayal, concealment, expulsion, and ultimate death, the man and the woman in the secluded place, the sudden and catastrophic appearance of the mysterious intruder, the serpent, and then: the peaceful existence shattered. And at the center of all that drama—for Rashi goes to no little trouble to explain that it does indeed stand at the center—the mysterious and somehow moving symbol of the tree in the garden, a tree that represents, I have come to think, both the pleasure and the pain that come from knowing things.

Interesting as all this is, when I immersed myself in Genesis and its commentators over a number of years recently, I naturally came to prefer Friedman's general explanation of why the Torah begins the way it does. I say "naturally," because the issue that Friedman is interested in having his readers understand is, in essence, a writer's issue: How do you begin a story? For Friedman, the opening of Bereishit brings to mind a technique we all know from the movies: "Like some films that begin with a sweeping shot that then narrows," he writes, "so the first chapter of Genesis moves gradually from a picture of the skies and earth down to the first man and woman. The story's focus will continue to narrow: from the universe to the earth to humankind to specific lands and peoples to a single family." And yet, he reminds his readers, the wider, cosmic concerns of the world-historical story that the Torah tells will remain in the back of our minds as we read on, providing the rich substratum of meaning that gives such depth to that family's story.

Friedman's observation implies, as is certainly true, that often it is the small things, rather than the big picture, that the mind can comfortably grasp: that, for instance, it is naturally more appealing to readers to absorb the meaning of a vast historical event through the story of a single family.

BECAUSE SHMIEL WASN'T much talked about, and because when he was talked about it tended to be in whispers, or in Yiddish, a language my mother spoke with her father so that they could keep their secrets—because of these things, when I did learn something, it was usually by accident.

Once, when I was little, I overheard my mother talking to her cousin on the phone and saying something like, I thought they were hiding, and the neighbor turned them in, no?

Once, a few years later, I heard someone saying, *Four beautiful daughters.*

Once, I overheard my grandfather saying to my mother, *I know only they were hiding in a kessle.* Since I knew by then how to make adjustments for his accent, when I heard him say this I simply wondered, What castle? Bolechow, to judge from the stories he told me, was not a place for castles; it was a small place, I knew, a peaceful place, a little town with a square and a church or two and a shul and busy shops. It was only much later on, long after my grandfather was dead and after I had studied more seriously the history of his town, that I learned that Bolechow, like so many other little Polish shtetls, had at one time been owned by an aristocratic Polish landowner, and when I learned this fact I naturally fitted the new information to my old memory of what I'd overheard my grandfather saying, *I know only they were hiding in a kessle.* A castle. Clearly, Shmiel and his family had managed to find a hiding place in the great residence of the noble family who'd once owned their town, and it was there that they were discovered after they had been betrayed.

At some point I heard someone saying, It wasn't the neighbor, it was their own maid, the *shiksa.* This I found confusing and upsetting, since we ourselves had a cleaning lady who was—I knew this was what *shiksa* meant—a Gentile woman; a Polish woman, in fact. For thirty-five years, my mother's Polish cleaning lady, a tall, heavy-hipped woman whom we eventually considered to be, and acted like, a third grandmother, a woman who, as the 1960s turned into the 1970s, and the 1970s into the 1980s, came to have the same body type that (as it is possible to see from the few photographs of her) Shmiel's wife, Ester, once had, came each week to our house and vacuumed and dusted and mopped and slopped and, in time, advised my mother about which bric-a-brac to put where. (*Iss the junks!* she'd scold about this or that bit of porcelain or crystal. *Throw him in garbage!*) After Mrs. Wilk and my mother had become friends, and the weekly visits to the house devolved, over time, into increasingly long lunches of hard-boiled eggs and bread and cheese and tea at the kitchen table, at which the two women, whose worlds were less far apart than might at first seem likely (it was Mrs. Wilk to whom my grandfather, when he'd come to visit us, would tell his scandalous off-color jokes in Polish); after the years of Tuesdays when they would sit for hours and complain and share certain stories—for instance, the one that Mrs. Wilk eventually confided to my mother about how, yes, she and the other Polish girls of her town, Rzeszów, had been taught to hate the Jews, but they didn't know any better—and also would gossip about the *pani,* the rich neighbor ladies who did not share their meals with their cleaning ladies; after this time, during which the two women became friends, Mrs. Wilk started to bring to my mother jars filled with Polish delicacies she'd cooked, of which the most famous, as much for the amusing sound of its name as for the sublime aroma they exuded, were something she pronounced "gawump-kees": spiced ground meat wrapped in cabbage leaves, swimming in a rich red sauce . . .

This, and I suppose the fact that I did not grow up in Poland, is why I found it painful to think that Shmiel and his family had been betrayed by the *shiksa* maid.

Another time, years later, in a phone conversation, my mother's first cousin Elkana in Israel, the son of the Zionist brother who had had the good sense to leave Poland in the Thirties, and a man who, more than anyone else alive, reminds me now of his uncle, my grandfather—with his air of omniscient authority and sly sense of humor, his largesse with family stories and family feeling, a man who, if he hadn't changed his family name to conform with Ben-Gurion's Hebraizing policies in the Fifties, would today be known still as Elkana Jäger, the name he'd been given at birth and, with minor variations in spelling, the same name that had once been borne by a homburg-wearing forty-five-year-old who fell over dead one morning in a spa in a province of an empire that no longer exists—my cousin Elkana said, *He had some trucks, and the Nazis wanted the trucks.*

Once I heard someone saying, *He was one of the first on the list.*

So I would hear these things, when I was a child. Over time, these scraps of whispers, fragments of conversations that I knew I wasn't supposed to hear, eventually coalesced into the thin outlines of the story that, for a long time, we thought we knew.

Once, when I was a little bit older, I had the boldness to ask. I was about twelve, and my mother and I were walking up a flight of broad, shallow concrete steps toward the synagogue we attended. It was autumn, the High Holy Days: we were going to the Yizkor, the memorial, service. At that time, my mother was obliged to say Kaddish, the prayer for the dead, only for her mother, who had died so unexpectedly after entrusting a twenty-dollar bill to her (and she has it still: the bill is safely tucked in the red leather purse at the bottom of a drawer in her house on Long Island, and sometimes she will take it out and show it to me, along with my grandfather's glasses and hearing aid, as if they were relics)—"only for her mother," since everyone else was still alive: her father, his sisters and brothers, all of those who had come over from Europe, fifty years before, all of them except Shmiel. We were slowly ascending those shallow steps that evening so my mother could mourn her mother. Perhaps it was because I had blue eyes, like her and her mother, that she took me that day. The sun was setting and it had grown suddenly cool, and it was for this reason that my mother decided to turn back to the parking lot in order to get a sweater out of the car, and during that brief extra time before the (I thought) scary prayer began she started talking about her family, her dead relatives, and I brought up the ones who had been killed.

Yes, *yes,* my mother said. At that time she was at the acme of her good looks: the high cheekbones, the strong jaw, the wide, photogenic movie-star smile with its sexy prominent incisors. Her hair, darkened over time into a rich chestnut that retained some blond highlights that were the only sign, now, that she had been a towheaded girl, as her mother and grandmother had been, as my brother Matthew once was (Matthew, Matt, who had the slender, high-boned, somewhat elongated face of an icon of the Orthodox Church, oddly feline amber eyes, and a shock of platinum blond hair of which I, with my mass of kinky, unmanageably wavy dark hair, was secretly jealous)—my mother's hair flicked in the stiffening autumn wind. She sighed and said, Uncle Shmiel and his wife, they had four beautiful daughters.

At the moment she said this a small plane passed loudly overhead and for a moment I thought she'd said not *daughters* but *dogs,* which threw me into a small turmoil since, although we knew so little, I'd always thought that at least we knew this: that they had four daughters.

My confusion lasted only a moment, however, since a few seconds later my mother added, in a slightly different voice, almost as if to herself, They raped them and they killed them all.

I stood there stock-still. I was twelve years old, and a bit backward for my age, sexually. What I felt, when I heard this shocking story—the more shocking, it seemed, for the almost matter-of-fact way in which my mother let this information slip, as if she were talking not to me, her child, but to an adult who had ingrained knowledge of the world and its cruelties—what I felt was, more than anything, embarrassment. Not embarrassment about the sexual aspect of the information I'd just been made privy to, but rather embarrassment that any eagerness to question her more about this rare and surprising detail might be misinterpreted by my mother as sexual prurience. And so, strangled by my own shame, I let the comment pass; which, of course, must have struck my mother as even odder than if I had asked her to tell me more. These things raced through my head as we once again climbed the steps to our synagogue, and by the time I was able to frame, elaborately, a question about what she had said, framed it in a way that didn't seem inappropriate, we were at the door and then inside and then it was time to say the prayers for the dead.

IT IS IMPOSSIBLE to pray for the dead if you do not know their names.

Of course we knew *Shmiel*: apart from everything else, it was my brother Andrew's Hebrew name. And, we knew, there had been *Ester*—not "Esther," as

I later found out—the wife. Of her I knew virtually nothing at all for a long time besides her name, and, later, her maiden name, *Schneelicht*, which, when I was studying German in college, I was obscurely pleased to know meant "Snow-light."

Shmiel, then; and *Ester* and *Schneelicht.* But of the four beautiful daughters, my grandfather, in all the years I knew him, all the years I interviewed him and wrote him letters filled with numbered questions about the *mishpuchah,* the family, never uttered a single name. Until my grandfather died, we knew the name of only one of the girls, and that was because Shmiel himself had written it on the back of one of those photos, in the forceful, sloping handwriting that I would later become only too familiar with, after my grandfather had died. On the back of a snapshot of himself and his stout wife and a little girl in a dark dress, my grandfather's brother had written a short inscription in German, *Zur Errinerung;* then the date, *25/7 1939*; and then the names *Sam, Ester, Bronia,* and so we knew that this daughter's name was Bronia. The names are underscored in a blue felt-tip pen, the kind my grandfather preferred, in his old age, to write letters with. (He liked to decorate his letters with illustrations: a favorite was a sailor smoking a pipe.) This underscoring interests me. Why, I now wonder, did he feel it necessary to underline their names, which clearly he knew? Was it something he did for himself, as he sat in the nights of his old age, who knows when and for how long, contemplating these photos; or was it something he meant us to see?

This German formula, *Zur Erinnerung,* "as a remembrance of," appears, sometimes misspelled, always written in Shmiel's energetic hand, on nearly all of the photographs that Shmiel sent to his siblings in America. It is there again, for example, on the back of the snapshot in which Shmiel is posing with his drivers next to one of his trucks, the image of the prosperous merchant, a cigar in his right hand, his left hand thrust into his trouser pocket, pulling the jacket away just enough so that you can see his gold watch-chain gleaming, his small, prematurely white mustache, in the toothbrush style made famous by someone else, neatly trimmed. On the back of this picture Shmiel wrote *Zur Errinerung an dein Bruder,* "to remember your brother by," and then a slightly longer inscription that features the date: the 19th of April 1939. To his siblings Shmiel wrote only in German, although it was never the language they used to speak to one another, which was Yiddish, nor was it the one they used to speak to the Gentiles of their or other towns, which was Polish or Ukrainian. For them, German always remained the high, official language, the language of the government and of primary school, a language they learned in a large single schoolroom where once (I have learned) there had hung a large portrait of the Austro-Hungarian emperor Franz Josef I, which was replaced, eventually, by one of Adam Mickiewicz, the great Polish poet, and then by one of Stalin, and then of Hitler, and then of Stalin, and then—well, by that point there were no Jägers left to go to the school and see whose picture might be hanging there. But it was German they learned, Shmiel and his brothers and sisters, in the Baron Hirsch school, and it was German that remained in their minds as the language in which to write of serious things. For instance (four decades after those siblings first learned their *Du*'s and *Sie*'s and *der*'s and *dem*'s and *eins-zwei-drei*'s), *What you read in the papers is barely ten percent of what is going on here;* or, still later, *I for my part will write a letter addressed to President Roosevelt and will explain to him that all my siblings are already in the States, and that my parents are even buried there, and perhaps that will work.*

German, the language for weighty things, was a tongue in which they read and wrote with only rare errors in spelling or grammar, perhaps only a few lapses into Yiddish or, even more rarely, Hebrew, which they also learned by rote when they were boys and girls during the reign of the emperor whose empire was so soon to be lost. Lapses such as one in the letter in which Shmiel wrote, *Do what you can to get me out of this* Gehenim. *Gehenim* in Hebrew means "Hell," and when I read this letter for the first time, in a year as far distant from Shmiel's writing of it as his writing of it was from his own birth, I caught a sudden vivid whiff of something so tenuous as to have been almost completely lost: a fleeting but intense moment, perhaps, from his and my grandfather's childhoods, the way, maybe, their father might have lapsed half angrily, half humorously into Hebrew when he was scolding his children or complaining about what a *Gehenim* they'd made his life, little guessing in 1911 what kind of Hell his little town would become.

So German is the language they wrote in. But the only time I ever heard my grandfather actually speak German was long after Shmiel had become nothing more than the earth and weather in some Ukrainian pasture, when my grandfather, grudgingly preparing for the annual trip to the spa, Bad Gastein, that his fourth wife forced them to make, said to this woman (who had a number tattooed on her forearm and who, having been, a lifetime and many régimes ago, a well-bred Russian, disdained to speak Yiddish) as they finished packing their many bags and the special provisions for Schloimele, *Also, fertig?*—So, ready?—which may be why I would forever after associate German, even after I myself learned to read and speak it, with elderly Jews being forced to go places they didn't want to go.

Zur Erinnerung, To remember me by. That picture, with its inscription, is the reason why, until much later, Shmiel was the only one of the six whose birthdate and year we knew. April 19 was his forty-fourth birthday, but he didn't write "on the occasion of his 44th birthday"; he chose instead "in his 44th year," and as I read this I am struck by the fact that the word I am translating as "year" is *Lebensjahr,* which means, literally, "year of life," and this diction, although of course it was casual and there's no doubt in my mind that he didn't give it a second thought when he wrote it, strikes me as noteworthy, perhaps because I know that, on the spring day this picture was taken, he had exactly four of those life-years left to live.

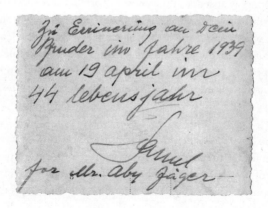

HENCE WE KNEW a few names, and one date. After my grandfather died, certain documents pertaining to Shmiel, along with some other photographs that none of us had ever seen, came into our possession, and it was only when we found these documents and looked at these photographs that we finally learned, or thought we learned, the names of the other girls. I say "thought we learned" because, as a result of certain peculiarities of Shmiel's old-fashioned handwriting (for instance, his way of adding a tiny horizontal line to the tops of his cursive *l*'s, or of making his final *y*'s the way we today might make final *z*'s, if we bothered to write longhand letters in proper cursive), we had, I later learned, been misreading one of the names. This is why, for a long time, in fact for over twenty years after my grandfather died, we thought the names of Shmiel and Ester's four beautiful daughters were as follows:

Lorca
Frydka (Frylka?)
Ruchatz
Bronia

But that, as I've said, came after my grandfather died. Until then I thought that all we would ever know about them were the one date, *19 April,* and those three names, *Sam, Ester, Bronia;* and of course their faces, looking out from the pictures, solemn, smiling, candid, posed, worried, oblivious, but always silent, and always black, and gray, and white. As such, Shmiel and his family, those six lost relatives, three of them nameless, seemed to be wildly out of place, a strange, gray absence at the center of all that vivid and noisy and often incomprehensible presence, that talk, those stories; immobile and unspeaking ciphers about whom, amid the mah-jongg and red nails and cigars and glasses of whiskey drunk over punch lines in Yiddish, it was impossible to know anything very important, except the one salient fact, the awful thing that had happened and that was summed up by the one identifying tag, *killed by the Nazis.*

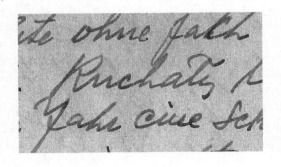

LONG BEFORE WE knew any of this, in the days when the mere sight of my face was sufficient to make grown-ups weep, long before I started pricking up my ears at whispered phone conversations, long before my bar mitzvah, the truth is that I was, at best, no more than a bit curious, not particularly interested in him, in them, except perhaps for some vague resentment that this resemblance made me more of a target for the grasping, clutching old people into whose mildewy apartments we would enter, during those summer and winter vacations, bearing boxes of chocolates and candied oranges that were yellow and green and red as well as orange, which was wonderful.

Most of them were harmless, and some were great fun. On the lap of my great-aunt Sarah, my father's mother's sister, I would contentedly sit, when I was six or seven or eight, playing with her beads and secretly but intently trying to see if I could see my reflection in the shiny surface of her Chinese Red nails as she played mah-jongg with her three sisters, who were very close. I have a dim memory of the house she lived in, in Miami. In this memory I was perhaps five. Inside, the adults and the old people were talking about whatever adults and old people talked about: family stories, whispered tales of earlier marriages; the names of relatives to whom we weren't any longer speaking. I had gone outside to get away from the grown-ups' talk, and was playing on a little lawn with my older brother, the one whose Hebrew name was *Shmiel,* a fact of which I was jealous. Andrew and I were playing on the lawn with the plastic military dolls then popular, called G.I. Joe, and I was very enthralled with an accessory my parents had just bought, no doubt to keep us boys quiet while they talked about whatever it was they talked about. This accessory was a gray plastic submachine gun, mounted on a little plastic tripod. I carefully lined up my submachine gun at the edge of a little ditch and started firing away at my brother's G.I. Joe; at first my brother played along and I must admit that the sight of his doll falling into the ditch gave me an obscure sense of power, which I enjoyed since he was, after all, older and I was unused to getting the better of him. But then my brother and I began to fight over the plastic machine gun. Suddenly he yanked it out of my hand—he was eight, I was only five—and threw it down a sewer grating nearby. Wailing, I ran inside to where the adults were, and my great-aunt Sarah took me on her lap and I was soon comforted.

But some of these old Jewish people, we children knew, young as we then were, were to be avoided at all costs. There was, for instance, Minnie Spieler, the photographer's widow, with her nose and clawlike fingers and the strange

"Bohemian" clothes she wore; Minnie Spieler, for whom, in our family cemetery in Queens, a blank sandy rectangle was waiting, with a tin sign stuck in the ground that said RESERVED FOR MINA SPIELER, which used to spook us when we went there every year to put rocks on the graves of dead relatives, and I would wonder, resentfully, what she was doing in our family cemetery anyway. Minnie you didn't want to talk to; she would take your arm in her crablike hands at these gatherings and look into your face intently, like someone who had lost something and hoped you might be able to help her find it; and on realizing you weren't what she was looking for, would suddenly turn aside and stalk into the next room.

So there were people like Minnie Spieler, who after a while stopped coming to family reunions—she had, it was said, moved to Israel—which is why it never occurred to me to ask about her again.

But the old person to be avoided most of all was the man we knew only as Herman the Barber. At those gatherings at which, occasionally, I could make people cry, this Herman the Barber would appear, tiny and shrunken, hunched over, unimaginably old, older even than my grandfather, and try to whisper things to you—or, I should say, to me, because I always felt that it was on me that he would bear down, if you could describe his slow but intent shuffle as "bearing"; it was toward me that he used to move, trying to grab a hand or arm and smiling and clacking his teeth, which I now realize were not his, and murmuring things in Yiddish when he got near that I couldn't, then, make out. Of course I would move away as soon as I could squeeze out from between him and the wall and run into the arms of my mother, who would give me a perfect green semicircle of candied orange, while in the other corner Herman would be laughing with one of the other old Bolechowers, the Jews of that town where my family was from, pointing at me and smiling indulgently and saying what *a frische yingele,* a fresh little boy, I was. I would escape from him and join my brothers, and we would play our silly games, games that consisted, occasionally, of making fun of the odd words that would sometimes rise into the air above their whispered, contentious conversations, the words with their odd, wailing, Old Country diphthongs that made us embarrassed and which we'd mock. *TOOOIIIIPPPPP,* we would shout, running in a circle and giggling, TOIP TOIP TOIP! I grew up hearing my mother speak Yiddish with her parents, and some words and phrases I was able to figure out early; but others—like *vaihrbinishgrafpototskee,* which my grandfather would say with an amused smile if you asked him for, say, a nickel to buy a piece of bubble gum, or *toip!*—sounded so silly that all we could do, we *frische yingelach,* was to laugh at the funny sounds.

Fresh we may have been, but in these instances I was never chided. Nobody yelled at you for trying to avoid Herman the Barber, ever since, in his confusion, he had given my brother—the one who'd yanked the whiskers of some other old man—a whole roll of Tums, thinking that it was candy, and my brother threw up for two days. To the other old people, you had to be nice; but Herman the Barber you were permitted to avoid, and after a few more trips to Florida, a few more summers and winters, he wasn't there anymore when we came, and we never had to worry about him again.

CREATION

I T WAS ON the day of my bar mitzvah that the search began.

Like every other Jewish child I knew, I had had some religious training. This was mostly to appease my grandfather, although, since the Reform Jewish education I was getting was so watered down, so denatured in comparison to the rigorously Orthodox *heder* learning he had acquired in Bolechow a lifetime ago, I and my three brothers may as well have been educated by Catholic priests, as far as he was concerned. This education, the aim of which was to prepare us for the day of our bar mitzvah, something else we did primarily to satisfy my mother's father, was divided into two stages.

At the age of about nine or ten we had to start Sunday school, a weekly class that was held in the basement of a local motel, which later became infamous, at least locally, as the place in which the famous Italian-American pop singer Connie Francis had been raped in 1974 after performing at a local concert hall. In the basement of this unappealing building a tall and much-liked man called Mr. Weiss taught us Jewish history and Bible stories, the names and significance of the holidays.

Many of these holidays, I had by then realized, were commemorations of narrow escapes from the oppressions of various pagan peoples, peoples whom even then I found more interesting, more alluring and potent and, I suppose, more sexy than my ancient Hebrew ancestors. When I was a child in Sunday school I was secretly disappointed and vaguely embarrassed by the fact that the ancient Jews were always being oppressed, always losing battles to other, mightier, and bigger nations; and, when the international situation was relatively uneventful, were being victimized or punished by their glum and unappeasable god. When you are a certain age, or a certain kind of child—odd, perhaps; perhaps the kind of child whom other, bigger kids pick on—you do not want to spend your free time reading about victims, about losers. Far more appealing to me, when I was a child and then an adolescent, were the civilizations of those other ancient peoples, who seemed to be having a lot more fun, and who, as it turned out, were the oppressors of the ancient Hebrews. When we read about Passover and the narrow escape from *eretz Mitzrayim*, the Land of Egypt, I dreamed of the Egyptians, with their playful love-poems and transparent linens and jackal-headed death gods and caskets of pure gold; when we read about Purim, about Esther's triumph over the wicked Persian vizier Haman, I closed my eyes and thought of the superb refinements of the Medes, of the bas-reliefs at Persepolis, with their hypnotically repetitive depictions of innumerable and obeisant vassals wearing fine robes and sporting crimped, perfumed beards. When I read about the miracle that is commemorated each year at Hanukkah, the holy oil of the Temple miraculously preserved and increased over the course of eight days after the defilement of the holy place by a Hellenistic Greek ruler, I would think of the wisdom and potential benefits of Antiochus IV's Hellenizing policies, of how they might have brought stability to that always-troubled region.

At the time, that is what I thought. But now I can see that the real reason I preferred the Greeks, above all the others, to the Hebrews was that the Greeks told stories the way my grandfather told stories. When my grandfather told a story—for instance, the story that ended *but she died a week before her wedding*—he wouldn't do anything so obvious as to start at the beginning and end at the end; instead, he told it in vast circling loops, so that each incident, each character he mentioned as he sat there, his organ-grinder baritone seesawing along, had its own mini-history, a story within a story, a narrative inside a narrative, so that the story he told was not (as he once explained it to me) like dominoes, one thing happening just after the other, but instead like a set of Chinese boxes or Russian dolls, so that each event turned out to contain another, which contained another, and so forth. Hence, for example, the story of why his beautiful sister had been forced to marry her ugly, hunchbacked cousin began, necessarily from my grandfather's point of view, with the story of how his father had died suddenly one morning in the spa at Jaremcze, since after all that was the beginning of the hard time for my grandfather's family, the dire years that ultimately necessitated his mother's tragic decision to marry her eldest daughter off to her brother's hunchbacked son in return for the price of passage to America to start a new but, as it turned out, equally tragic life. But of course, to tell the story of how his father had suddenly died one morning at Jaremcze, my grandfather would have to stop himself to tell another story, a story about how he and his family, in the rich days, used to vacation at certain beautiful spas at the end of each summer, for instance at Jaremcze, high in the pre-Carpathian foothills, unless of course they went not south but west, to spas in Baden, or to Zakopane, a name that I loved. But then, to give a better sense of what his life was like then, in the golden years before 1912 when his father died, he would go further back in time to explain just who his father had been in their little town, about the respect he commanded and the influence he wielded; and that story in turn would, in the end, take him back to the very beginning, the story of how his family had lived in Bolechow since the Jews first came there, since *before there even was a Bolechow*.

One by one, the Chinese boxes opened, and I would sit and gaze into each one, hypnotized.

As it happens, this is precisely how the Greeks told their stories. Homer, for instance, will often interrupt the forward motion of the *Iliad,* his great poem of war, spiraling backward in time and sometimes space in order to give psychological richness and emotional texture to the proceedings, or to suggest, as he sometimes does, that *not* knowing certain stories, being ignorant of the intricate histories that, unbeknownst to us, frame the present, can be a grave mistake. The most famous example of this is, perhaps, an encounter that takes place toward the beginning of the poem between two warriors named Glaucus and Diomedes: as the Greek and Trojan prepare to fight, each launches into a long story intended to highlight his military prowess and his family prestige, and the genealogies they retail are, as it happens, so long and detailed that it soon emerges that there are important family ties between them, and with cries of joy the two men, who only minutes before would gladly have killed each other, clasp hands and declare eternal friendship. Similarly (to move from poetry to prose), when the historian Herodotus, centuries after Homer, composed his grand history of the Greeks' improbable and total victory over the vast Persian empire at the beginning of the fifth century before Christ, he, too, resorted to this old and mesmerizing technique. Hence it seems only natural to him that to tell the story of the Greek-Persian conflict, he must narrate the history of Persia itself, which involves digressions both great and small, from the famous story of a certain Eastern potentate's desire to have another man see his wife naked (the arrogant sin, we are meant to understand, that set in motion a great dynasty's downfall), to an entire chapter dedicated to the history, customs, mores, art, and architecture of Egypt, since after all Egypt was a part of the Persian empire. And so on.

But then, every culture, every author tells stories in a different way, and each style of storytelling opens up, for other storytellers, certain possibilities that he may not otherwise have dreamed of. From a certain French novelist, for instance, you might learn that it is, in theory, possible to devote the better part of a substantial novel to a single conversation that took place over one particular meal; from a certain American novelist (born, however, in Poland), that dialogue can be made to appear interestingly, dangerously, indistinguishable from the narrator's point of view; from a German writer you admire you may realize, with some surprise, that under certain circumstances pictures and photographs, which you may have thought inappropriate to or competitive with serious texts, can add a certain dignity to some sad stories. And of course those Greeks, Homer and Herodotus, demonstrated that a story needn't be told in a straightforwardly chronological, this-happened-then-that-happened, way—the way that, for instance, Genesis tells its story, which after a while, it must be said, can seem tedious and flat. And indeed, although I wasn't aware of it at the time, I now see that a certain ringlike technique of storytelling, which for a long time I thought my grandfather had invented, was the real reason—more than pagan beauty and pleasure, more than pagan nudity, more than pagan power and authority and victory—that the Greeks, rather than the Hebrews, gripped my imagination from my earliest childhood, from the beginning.

Which is how it came to pass that my grandfather, who to me represented Jewishness itself, created in me my lifelong taste for the pagans.

The history that we learned in Sunday school, the history of the Jews and the Jewish holidays, was, therefore, a history that set me at odds with myself, since I was a Jew who admired the Greeks. This ambivalence may have been the reason that I failed so woefully to satisfy the requirements of the second phase of my Jewish education, which was called Hebrew school, and which we began at the age of twelve. Hebrew school classes were held on Wednesday afternoons in the dark-pewed, gabled synagogue my family attended, and focused solely on preparation for the bar mitzvah. Conducted by a plump little man who prefaced his name with the title "Doctor," in the exacting way a certain kind of Central European person might do (although this man was from Boston), these two-hour sessions were primarily devoted to the study of the Hebrew language itself. But by the age of twelve I was already studying ancient Greek, and had advanced far enough to read certain simplified passages: a racy story about a god and a nymph, a passage from Herodotus about the crocodiles in the Nile, subjects that held far greater appeal for me than did the monotonously grumpy outpourings of the Hebrew prophets that furnished the texts of the *haftarah* portions that, on the day of the bar mitzvah, you had to chant after reading from the Torah itself, or the bizarre prohibitions about eating and lovemaking to be found in Leviticus. For this reason I studied my Greek but not my Hebrew, and hence although I learned the Hebrew alphabet well enough to read long passages fluently, as I would eventually do at my bar mitzvah, I had no knowledge of the language itself, apart from how to read and write the phrase *aba babayit,* "Father is at home."

IT WAS ONLY much later, long after I had devoted my studies to the Greek and Latin classics, that I bothered to go back to Hebrew and study it with greater seriousness. This was not because I felt any more religious at the age of twenty-five than I had at the age of thirteen. I wanted to study Hebrew again because, in my mid-twenties, just before I entered graduate school, I was greedy to know languages, the way my grandfather once had known so many, and it bothered me that I'd squandered that early opportunity to learn one. And so I bought a thick volume called *Introduction to Biblical Hebrew,* and for about a year I slowly made my way through it. After a while, during those months in 1985, I started to be able to read biblical passages, and eventually I went back to the bookstore and bought some more books, not language guides but books that explained to me what I should have learned half a lifetime earlier; explained what, now that I had some expertise and interest in old literatures and sacred texts, I was eager to read about, not because I believed what they said, but because I was able, now, to understand them as products of ancient Mediterranean cultures.

And so for a few months I immersed myself in my Jewish education, and learned something about the composition of the *Tanakh,* the Hebrew Bible, the names and themes of its various books, and of the different *parashot,* the weekly readings from the Torah, the Five Books of Moses, how and when each *parashah* was read, and what it meant.

I learned, for instance, how *parashat Bereishit,* the first formal section of the book of Genesis, was about the beginnings of things, how out of the undifferentiated murk, gradually, the forms of things became clear: oceans, skies, heavens, earth, and later animals, plants, fishes, birds and, finally, humans. I learned how certain of its stories were allegories for the way the world is: for instance how the Adam and Eve story explained, among other things, why women must endure the labor of childbirth; how the story of Cain and Abel, which disturbed me so much when I was a boy that I never bothered to learn it properly in Sunday school and hence for a long time afterward was never clear whether it was Cain or Abel who was the "bad" one, explained why there is violence and murder and war in the world. I learned about *parashat Noach,* the section of Genesis that includes the story of Noah and the Ark, of his terrible wanderings across the face of the earth—which once again would become an undifferentiated mass of water, since God had decided to wash away his own Creation in a fit of annihilating rage that would not be his last—but also includes a genealogy of Noah's descendants, focusing, with increasing intensity as the narrative progresses, on one family in particular, and then on one man, Abram. I learned how Abram's trek across the known world in search of the land that God has promised to him, an epic wandering that is recounted in the *parashah* called *Lech Lecha* ("Go Forth!"), forces him, in the end, not only to pass through strange new geographies but to confront the extremes of human evil and goodness, as is recounted in *parashat Vayeira*, "And He Appeared": for there we see how, in Sodom and Gomorrah, he encounters total rejection of God's moral law, and on Mount Moriah he himself is called upon to submit to a total acceptance of God's law, even if that law must cost him his own son.

I must admit that I never got beyond *parashat Vayeira* in my Jewish homeschooling program. But of course I know the ending of the five books I started to read, twenty years ago: how Joseph, the favored descendant of Abram, was rejected by his brothers, was abandoned and ultimately led off into Egypt, where, eventually, his tribe prospered—although Egypt was, in the end, to become the land from which this family, that tribe, would make its long, arduous, unimaginable journey back to a "home" that, since none of them actually knew it, must not have felt like home at all.

As I have said, the first thing that happens in parashat Bereishit *is not, as many think, that God created the heavens and the earth, but rather that at the* beginning *of his creation of the heavens and the earth, when everything had been a stupefying void, he said, "Let there be light." This is, in fact, the first act of creation that we hear about in* Bereishit. *But what is interesting to me is that every creative act that follows—light and dark, night and day, dry land and oceans, plants and animals, and finally man from* dust—is described as an act of separation. What did God do when he saw that the light was "good"? He separated it from the darkness, and then proceeded to go on separating until the component parts of the cosmos assumed their pleasing and rightful order.

Rashi devotes relatively little space to this fact, and his concerns are essentially the moral ramifications of this initial separation of light from darkness: "According to its simple meaning," he writes of God's separation of light from darkness, "explain it as follows: He saw that it is good, and it is not proper for it and the darkness to be functioning in a jumble, so He assigned to this one its sphere during the day, and to this one its sphere during the night." And why does God do this? Because light, as Rashi says, "does not deserve that the wicked use it, and He set it aside for the righteous, to [be used by them in] the future." The moral implications of being able to "separate" in this way come to a narratively satisfying conclusion, of course, at the end of Genesis, chapter 3, which is the culmination of the story of Creation: the story of Adam and Eve and their eating of the forbidden fruit of the Tree of Knowledge. The story begins with Creation, which as we've seen is the story of acts of distinguishing one thing from another; it ends by alluding to the most crucial distinction of all, the distinction between Good and Bad, a distinction that becomes apprehensible to humans only by eating of the Tree of Knowledge, a tree about which the Torah tells us that it was (like light) "good," that it was a "delight to the eyes" of Eve, and that it was "desirable for comprehension," and it was because of this goodness, this delightfulness, this desirability that Eve ate of it.

I want to linger for a moment by this strange Tree, whose fruit, though so good, was, as we know, to prove poisonous to mankind; for the eating of it is what, according to Bereishit, caused humans to be expelled from Paradise, to be forced, ultimately, to experience death. But it is the pleasure and delight of the Tree of Knowledge that I want to explore briefly, because the connections, in Bereishit, between creativity, distinguishing, knowledge, and pleasure are, for me, utterly natural. As a child, I already had an oddly scholarly bent: the desire both to know and to order what I knew. This, I have no doubt, was the by-product, or perhaps I should say the fruit, of my father's intellectual gifts—he is a scientist—and my mother's passion for order, the taste for rigorous neatness and organization that she would only half-jokingly attribute to her "German blood." It's my German blood, she would say, the once-blond product of families that had fully German—not German-Jewish—names, names like Jäger and Mittelmark (the latter, as I have learned, being the name of a county in Prussia); she would say this, sometimes with a laugh and sometimes not, whenever she remade a sloppy bed or reorganized a shelf full of our schoolbooks or tried to impose order on things that properly belonged to my father's somewhat sloppier sphere of influence, with sometimes comical results, as for instance when she finally gathered together all of the various broken objects, toys and *light fixtures and small gadgets, that he had laconically promised to fix but had never managed to get around to, and put all these orphaned objects in a box that, using a heavy navy blue Magic Marker, she labeled, in her bold, loping handwriting,* THINGS TO BE FIXED *ALEVAY——"alevay" being the Jewish word that expresses a sort of hopeless, battered optimism:"it should only happen (but it won't)."*

So my father loved knowing things, and my mother loved organizing things, and perhaps this is why I, at an early age, discovered in myself an acute pleasure in organizing knowledge. It wasn't merely reading about (say) the ancient Egyptians and, later, the Greeks and Romans, about archaeology and the Romanovs and Fabergé eggs that gave me pleasure; the pleasure lay, more specifically, in the organization of the knowledge I was slowly accumulating, in the making and memorizing of lists of numbered dynasties and vocabulary charts and hieroglyphic tables and chronologies of numbered Catherines and Nicholases and Alexanders. This, I now realize, was the first expression of an impulse that is, ultimately, the same as the one that drives a person to write——to impose order on a chaos of facts by assembling them into a story that has a beginning, a middle, and an end.

If an early, though admittedly eccentric, pleasure of mine lay in the ordering of hitherto messy masses of information——a combination of my father's and my mother's natures——then it was also true that I felt a kind of pain, a form of anxiety even, when confronted by masses of information that seemed resistant to organization.

IT WAS MY bar mitzvah, at any rate, my bar mitzvah that Saturday afternoon when my voice so excruciatingly cracked, the bar mitzvah that was the culmination of the spotty Jewish education I'd had, that made me curious about my Jewish family, made me begin to ask questions. Naturally I'd always been curious: How could I not, I whose face reminded certain people of someone long dead? But the fervent interest in Jewish genealogy, which became a hobby and, much later, almost an obsession, began on that April day. This, I have to add, had nothing to do with the ceremony itself, with the ritual for which I'd been preparing for so long; it was, rather, the reception at my parents' house that was the beginning of everything. For as I was passed from relative to relative to be kissed and slapped on the back and congratulated, the confused mass of unknown and similar-looking faces bothered me, and I began to wonder how it was I came to be related to all those people, to the Idas and Trudys and Juliuses and Sylvias and Hildas, to the names Sobel and Rechtschaffen and Feit and Stark and Birnbaum and Hench. I began to wonder just who they were, what their connection to me could possibly be, and it was because I didn't like being confronted with this undifferentiated mass of relations, was irritated by the mess, that I thereafter devoted hours and weeks and years to researching my family tree, to clarifying the relationships and ordering the branches and sub-branches of genetic connection, to organizing the information I eventually gathered on index cards and charts and in folders. It is of course silly to think that anybody "becomes" a man at the age of thirteen, but it is probably fair to say that, however inadvertently, my bar mitzvah made me more aware of what it was to be Jewish than any comprehension of the words I was saying, that day in April 1973, could have done.

And so the questions I began to ask, immediately following my bar mitzvah, were about not just the mysterious Shmiel, but about all of them. These questions led me, at first, to write letters to the relatives who were, in 1973, still alive—a number that was already far smaller than it had been six or seven or eight years earlier, when I'd go with my family to Miami Beach. I would write to these old relatives in Queens and Miami and Chicago and Haifa, and sometimes the replies frustrated and confused me. (*I'm not telling you the exact date I was born,* my grandfather's unhappy sister Sylvia told me one afternoon in 1974 over the phone, *because it would have been better if I'd never been born.*) But more often, these elderly people were gratified that someone so young was interested in something so old, and they answered eagerly and told me whatever they knew in reply to my questions. My father's aunt Pauline, for instance (always "Aunt Pauly"), banged out nearly a hundred letters on her rickety old Underwood between June 1973, when I first shyly wrote to her, and June 1985, when her formidable brain, which had furnished me with so many crisp and critical details about my father's side of the family (*I also seem to remember someone saying the name of a town called . . .*), collapsed on itself. By the end, the *a*'s and *o*'s and *e*'s of her ancient manual typewriter were completely indistinguishable, a parallel, maybe, for what was taking place in the confused and hardening tissues to which I owed so much.

Or there was my great-aunt Miriam in Haifa, the wife of my grandfather's brother Itzhak, the woman who, because of her lusty Zionism, had persuaded her husband that, despite the fact that their butcher business was prospering so greatly, the future of Jewry lay in Palestine, which is why she and he and their two small children escaped the fate that swallowed Shmiel and the others. I came to write often to her, and she had much to say on the subject of Bolechow as it once had been, before she left it. I would welcome the sight of her flimsy aerograms with their exotic Israeli stamps, the tissue-thin blue paper bearing a distinctive, old-fashioned European script written in blue ballpoint pen and covering every centimeter of each flap of the weightless document. From an English whose syntax and spelling were as difficult for me to decipher as her crabbed handwriting was, I learned a lot, the pleasant life of the old town, the flattering things her father used to say about my great-grandfather, Elkune Jäger; the two men, she wrote, had belonged to the same social club in Bolechow, a detail (club?) that forced me to reassess what I thought I knew about life in little Galician towns at the turn of the century. I was particularly interested to know about my great-grandfather, since by that time I was old enough to understand that family history could be more than just tables and charts, could in fact help explain how people—my grandfather, say—became who they were. About Elkune she wrote:

> The Elkana Jager I don't remember but my father tell me that they was a member in the same synagogue and also in the club and he say me that he was a very fine and good fellow he like to spend money for the poor familys, and he have a very good opinion and sympatie in the Christians cytycions and this was very important for him and all the town. But he died very young in the century he was with Rachel to take a rest and became a heart attake this was a tragedi for all the town and family.

It took me some time to realize that *cytycions* was *citizens*. *Rachel,* I realized with a thrill, was my grandfather's older sister, the one who'd died *a week before her wedding,* died because, I later learned, she too had had a bad heart.

Because I knew that Miriam and her husband had remained in Bolechow until the 1930s, I was emboldened to ask her about Shmiel, too. I remember the dark thrill when I wrote the letter in which I asked her what exactly had happened to them, a letter I did not tell my grandfather about. But on this subject Aunt Miriam was more tentative, and could only give me the following, in an aerogram dated January 20, 1975:

> The date of Onkel Schmil and his family when they died nobody can say me, 1942 the Germans kild the aunt Ester with 2 daughters. The oldest daughter was with the partisaner in the hills and died with them. Onkel Schmil and 1 daughter Fridka the Germans killed them 1944 in Bolechow, so say me one man from Bolechow nobody know what is true.

If this turned out to be not quite true, as she herself (as I now see) was warning me might be the case, it was hardly her fault. She was only repeating what she had heard.

Somewhat later, when I had learned not to expect too much from the responses, and was beginning to pride myself on being an efficient researcher, on having developed a certain method, I began to write, too, to institutions and agencies, the kind of letters in which you were instructed to enclose "SSAE"s, letters to the New York City archives containing money orders in payment for official copies of birth or death certificates (five dollars each, then), to cemeteries (a favorite) with names like Mount Zion and Mount Judah ("the gravesite reserved for Mina Spieler remains unclaimed at this time"), to places with names like The Hebrew Orphan Asylum, to grim-sounding archives with acronyms like AGAD in countries that were, then, blocked by the Iron Curtain, and from whom you never heard back although you'd enclosed the international postal money order; questions that led me, two decades later, to more sophisticated tools. Now there were Internet searches on genealogy Web sites, on the Social Security Death Index and on genealogy.com and jewishgen.org, on the Ellis Island database, which is where I learned the precise date of Shmiel's arrival in 1913 in New York City, a place he decided wasn't lucky for him; now there were FamilyFinder boards; now I had lengthy correspondences with total strangers, unimaginably different from those toilsome aerogram exchanges I'd pursued when I was in my teens, e-mail queries to people in California and Colorado and Wales and Denmark that promised total fluency and complete instantaneity. These, finally, led me to travel, over the course of a year, to a dozen cities from Sydney to Copenhagen to Beer Sheva, to embark on airplanes and ferries and trains packed with Jewish boys and girls in uniforms with guns strapped to their narrow bodies; to go, in the end, to Bolechow itself and there talk to the few remaining people who had seen what had been done.

As TIME PASSED, when I was a young man in my twenties, I would occasionally dip back into the files I'd made, push my research a little farther, write a few new letters to this or that archive, learn a few more facts. By the time I was in my thirties, late thirties, it seemed clear that I knew everything there was to know about my family history: about the Jägers most of all, since in addition to the documentary evidence, the material obtainable from archives and libraries, there were all those stories; and, over the years, about my father's family as well, the taciturn Mendelsohns. The only gap, the only irritating lacuna, was Shmiel and his family, the lost ones about whom there were no facts to pencil in on the index cards, no dates to enter in the genealogy software, no anecdotes or stories to tell. But as time went on it hurt less and less to think that we'd never know anything more about them, since with each passing decade the entire event receded, and with it they, too, grew dimmer, blunter, not only those six but all of them; and as decade followed on decade they seemed more and more to belong not to us but to History. This, paradoxically, made it easier not to think about them, since after all so many people were thinking about them—if not them specifically, then about a kind of generic *them,* those who had been killed by the Nazis, and for this reason it was as if they were being looked after.

Still, every now and then it would happen that some reminder would rise to the surface of things and make me wonder if there might still be something left to learn.

For instance:

My grandfather preferred to tell stories that were funny, since he himself was so funny, and since people will love you more if you amuse them. I remember—or rather, my mother told me—how he once made my great-aunt Ida, my grandmother's sister, pee in her pants at the Thanksgiving table one year, a long time ago, so funny was the story he was telling. We don't know which of his many funny stories it was, since the story of how he made her pee her pants has now eclipsed the story itself—has become a funny story of its own, one that now gets told in order to illuminate, or perhaps to preserve, a certain aspect of my dead grandfather's personality. To me in particular he loved to tell his stories about the town in which he was born, and where his family, that family of prosperous butchers and, later, exporters of meat, had lived "since," he would say, clearing his throat wetly in the way that he did, his eyes huge and staring, like a baby's, behind the lenses of his old-fashioned black-plastic glasses, "there was a Bolechow." *BUH-leh-khuhv,* he would pronounce it, keeping the *l* low in his throat, in the same place where he caressed the *kh,* the way that people will do who are from that place; *BUHlehkhuhv,* the pronunciation that, as I found out much later, is the old, the Yiddish pronunciation. The spelling, too, has changed: Bolechow under the German-speaking Austrians, Bolechów under the Poles, Bolekhov during the Soviet years, and now, finally, Bolekhiv, under the Ukrainians, who had always wanted the town, and now own it. There is a joke that people from this part of Eastern Europe like to tell, which suggests why the pronunciations and the spellings keep shifting:

it's about a man who's born in Austria, goes to school in Poland, gets married in Germany, has children in the Soviet Union, and dies in Ukraine. *Through all that,* the joke goes, *he never left his village!*

That I was mispronouncing the name of the town in which my mother's family had lived for over three hundred years was something I didn't know until I met an old woman in the late 1990s, the mother of a man with whom I had recently become friends. After knowing him for some time I learned that he, who is of my parents' generation, was born in the town next to Bolechow— a small city, really, once called Stryj, now spelled Striy, which I have since visited, a place where today tall trees grow luxuriantly in the middle of the roofless ruin of what used to be the city's main synagogue. When I discovered the strange geographical coincidence that linked our families, I mentioned it to my friend, who like me is a writer and who, knowing of my interest in the history of that small and now forgotten part of the world, offered to introduce me to his mother, a woman then nearly ninety years old; perhaps she would share with me her memories. His mother. Mrs. Begley. *Begley:* another name that, like the names of the towns where people like her once lived, had subtly altered; for the name had in fact been *Begleiter,* which in German means "companion" or "escort." Of course I eagerly accepted my friend's invitation, since by then, when I was nearly forty, there had been a small number of strange coincidences, odd reminders of Bolechow, or Shmiel, or our family's specific past, that had surfaced improbably in the present, tantalizing us with the possibility that the dead were not so much lost as waiting . . .

A FEW YEARS AGO, FOR instance, I read somewhere that, sixty years after the event, it was still possible to submit to the International Red Cross the names of Holocaust victims to be traced. And so one day I walked to the local Red Cross office, which is in a large, rectangular, rather impersonal building not too far from my apartment. On the front of this building is a large red cross. Inside, I duly filled out a set of six Missing Person forms. I did so with the barest flicker of optimism, knowing what the odds were; but even so, I told myself, you never know.

And you never *do* know. Maybe fifteen years ago my youngest brother, who at that point was a costume assistant on Woody Allen movies, was shopping for fabrics in a dimly lighted store, a place filled with rolls of fabrics, located in the Garment District in New York City. He noticed that the elderly man at the counter bore a tattoo on his forearm, and struck up a conversation with this man. During this conversation, my brother mentioned that our own relatives who had perished in the disaster were from Bolechow, at which point the old Jew in the garment shop clapped his hands together in a kind of ecstasy and exclaimed, Ach, Bolechow! They had the *most* beautiful leather!

There was the time when, after I posted an inquiry in an Internet genealogy site, an old man called me to say he'd once known someone called Shmiel Jäger. Before I could respond, he added that this Shmiel Jäger had come from Dolina, a small town near Bolechow, and had fled eastward, when the Germans came in the summer of 1941—fled, as it turned out, deep into what was then the Soviet Union. *I heard he married an Uzbek woman, he even had children with her!* this old man, who was hard of hearing, shouted into the phone. Amused at the thought of a shtetl Jew roaming as far as Uzbekistan, I thanked him for getting in touch and hung up, thinking, So there's nothing to be excited about.

And yet it was odd: like the unexpected touch of a cold hand.

Or there was the time that another one of my brothers—Matt, the one born just after me, with whom for a long time I had no great intimacy (unlike the youngest, who like me was thought to be artistically inclined and to whom I always thought I was very close); Matt, with whom I felt, while I was growing up, an obscure but ferocious competitiveness, and to whom, in a moment of fury, I once did something physically very cruel—Matt called me to say he'd stopped by a big international gathering of Holocaust survivors in Washington, D.C., where he lives. Matt is a photographer, so perhaps he was shooting a story about the convention; I don't know, I can't remember. At any rate he called me up to say that at this gathering he had run into someone who said he had known Shmiel Jäger.

What? I said.

Not *Uncle* Shmiel, Matt said, hurriedly. He then related what this man at the Holocaust survivors' convention had told him: that the Shmiel Jäger he'd once known had been born with another name, but during the war, when he'd joined a band of partisans operating near Lwów, he'd taken the name Shmiel Jäger since, for safety's sake, these partisans would sometimes take the names of dead men they had known.

I listened and thought, *The oldest daughter was with the partisaner in the hills and died with them. Onkel Schmil and 1 daughter Fridka the Germans killed them 1944 in Bolechow.*

So you never know. It was for this reason that I filled out the Red Cross forms, not hoping for much, and gave them to the person at the desk, and went home that day. About four months later I received a thick envelope in the mail from the Red Cross. My hands were shaking as I tore open the packet. Immediately, however, I saw that much of the bulk was due to the fact that the Red Cross was returning to me copies of the six forms I'd filled out. On a seventh piece of paper was a letter stating that there was no known information about the fates of Ester Jäger, Lorka Jäger, Frydka Jäger, Ruchatz (as I still thought) Jäger, or Bronia Jäger, inhabitants of the Polish town of Bolechow.

With respect to Shmiel Jäger, the letter concluded, his case was considered to be "still open" . . .

FOR THIS REASON, THEN, I was eager to meet my friend's mother, this Mrs. Begley who had lived so close to my dead uncle and aunt and cousins. It wasn't that I thought I'd learn anything from her; I just wanted to have the experience of talking to someone of her vintage and provenance, since it seemed incredible to me that there might still exist anyone who'd even walked the same streets as they did. That is how accustomed I'd grown to thinking they and everyone of their era belonged utterly and irretrievably to the black, white, and gray world of the past.

And yet it is also true that when I heard about the existence of this very old woman, of Louis's mother, I was flushed with a fantasy so intense that it almost shamed me, the way that adolescents are shamed. I wondered if it could be possible that, even though this woman had lived in Stryj and my relatives had lived in Bolechow, perhaps . . . they had met? Perhaps she might remember them? Shmiel's wife, I knew (from where? I can't remember), came from a Stryjer family. Her brother ran a photography studio there, and indeed one of Shmiel's daughters would, as I found out only because of an accident after my grandfather died, end up working there, briefly; and so when Louis offered to introduce me to his formidable mother—or so I thought of her, having read some years previously Louis's first book, which seemed to be a novelized account of how he and his mother survived the Nazi years, outwitted the Germans and the Ukrainians as my own family had not—when Louis offered to introduce us, my mind began to race. I envisioned a scene in, say, October 1938, when Louis (then Ludwik) and his mother might well have come into the Schneelicht Studio in Stryj to have a picture taken to celebrate this only child's fifth birthday. I imagine Shmiel's daughter, my mother's first cousin Lorka, a tall, good-looking, somewhat aloof girl of seventeen, carefully taking Mrs. Begley's coat as she enters the atelier (it will have a fur collar, I think, since her husband, as an ancient Ukrainian woman would recall to me on a street corner sixty years later, *was the biggest doctor in town*), and, her natural reserve dissolving, saying something charming to the little boy, who is wearing a woolen cap from beneath which strands of his fair hair, which may or may not help save his life later on, escape. My fantasy is that the sudden warming of this serious-looking girl makes an impression on the Mrs. Begley of 1938—she is herself a serious and deeply shrewd woman—and because of that impression, Mrs. Begley will remember her, remember the murdered girl Lorka Jäger, remember her so many years later and in that way will help me rescue her.

But what happened was this:

I finally met Mrs. Begley for the first time in 1999, at a reception for one of Louis's sons, who is a painter. The party, which was held in an upstairs room at an impressive-looking uptown gallery in New York City, was noisy, and Mrs. Begley was sitting, very erect, with an expression that mixed a grandmother's prideful pleasure and a deaf person's isolated irritation—she had a bad enough time hearing in general, she told me soon after we met, without all that *noise*—in a chair at the back of the room.

So you had family there? she said to me after I'd taken her hand and crouched down to talk to her, slightly disoriented by the way in which she'd spoken, as if we'd been in the middle of a conversation, and not quite sure whether "there" meant eastern Poland or the Holocaust.

Yes, I replied, they lived in Bolechow.

BUH-leh-khuhv is what I said. This Mrs. Begley had a long, intelligent face with a high, clear forehead, the kind of face a person of another place and generation would have described as *the face of a Rebecca*, a soulful beautiful Jewish woman's face; crowned by an immaculate coif of pure white hair, it was dominated by a tenacious, wry, covert gaze that was not diminished by the fact that it emanated from one eye alone; the other was opaque, and slightly hooded, and I never asked why. This gaze would hold your own and not let go during conversations, a gaze that even after I'd known her for a while struck me as unnerving, not least because it always seemed as if the eye, watchful, remote, assessing, was reacting not to the conversation that was taking place, but to a hidden conversation, a conversation about what happened to her and what she lost, a loss so great that she knew I would never understand, although she was sometimes willing to talk to me about it. On the night I met her, she was sitting there, elegant in a black velvet pantsuit, grasping the head of a walking stick in one hand and leaning toward me, partly to suggest she was interested and partly because of the terrific noise, and when I said that my family was from Bolechow—*BUH-lehkhuv*—her good eye flickered with amusement, and for the first time she smiled.

What, *BUH-lekhuhv?* she said, disdainfully.

The first word sounded like *vawt.*

She shook her head and I flushed like the teenager I was when I first became obsessed with this place. With a sour expression she said, You must say *Buh-LEH-khooff.* It's a *Polish* town. You say it the *Yiddish* way!

I found myself embarrassed and defensive, having suddenly detected a whiff of long-dead gradations of class and culture that are of no importance to anyone, anymore: the condescension, perhaps, that the secular, urban, assimilated Jews of a certain era in a certain place, Jews who grew up in a free Poland and spoke Polish at home, displayed to the countrified Jews of the rural shtetls, Jews like my grandfather, who although not even ten years older than this Mrs. Begley had grown up in a wholly different world, Austrian, not Polish, who spoke Yiddish at home, and for whom a trip to even a small city, like Stryj, was something of an event.

In any case, because of all this, of the way I pronounced or mispronounced Bolechow, my secret fantasy suddenly was ashes in my mouth. Which is why, when Mrs. Begley asked me what my relatives' name had been, after she'd corrected my pronunciation, and I'd replied *Jäger,* and she had shaken her head and told me she'd never heard the name, I couldn't bring myself to mention the photography atelier of the family Schneelicht, my great-uncle's in-laws who had lived in her city, in Stryj, where perhaps, once before, there had been the smallest chance that they and she would have met. A chance that, for me, would have been a way of connecting the remote past, in which my relatives seemed to be hopelessly, irretrievably frozen, to the limpid present in which this meeting was taking place, the transparent moment that, as anyone could see quite clearly, held me and the old woman with her white hair and her cane, held the noise and the party and an ordinary early evening in autumn in a city that was at peace.

DESPITE MY OCCASIONAL errors, however, I learned a lot, over the years of letters and queries and interviews and Internet searches, a lot about Bolechow that wasn't mistaken. For instance: *They were there since before there was a Bolechow!* How long was that, exactly? It is possible to know almost to the day.

If you are an American Jew of a certain generation, the generation that, like mine, had grandparents who were immigrants at the beginning of the twentieth century, you probably grew up hearing stories about the "Old Country," about the little towns or shtetls from which your grandpa or grandma or nana or *bubby* or *zeyde* came, the kind of little town celebrated by Yiddish authors like Isaac Bashevis Singer and in *Fiddler on the Roof,* the kind of place that no longer exists; and you probably thought, as I thought for a long time, that they were all more or less alike, modest places with maybe three or four thousand inhabitants, with a vista of wooden houses clustered around a square, places to which we are, now, too willing to ascribe a certain sepia charm, perhaps because if we thought about the Ping-Pong games and the volleyball and skiing, the movies and the camping trips, it would be that much more difficult to think of what happened to them, because they would seem less different from us. The kind of place so ordinary that few people would have found it worth writing about, until of course it and all the places like it were to be wiped out, at which point their very ordinariness seemed to be worth preserving.

This, at any rate, is what I thought of Bolechow. Then, one day not too long ago, my older brother, Andrew, sent me as a Hanukkah gift a very rare volume, published by the Oxford University Press in 1922, called *The Memoirs of Ber of Bolechow.* (I say "Hanukkah gift" but as I write this I am aware that the words are not really true, and certainly not as close to the truth as my grandfather would have liked: since my two sisters-in-law are not Jewish, and my nieces and nephews are enjoying the kind of eclectic religious upbringing now very common, the gift I received was something I undoubtedly thought of at the time as a "holiday" gift. No: let me be really honest. I'm sure I just thought of it as a "Christmas present." The fact is that in my own house, when we were growing up, we didn't have a really thriving Hanukkah tradition. What I remember mostly was my mother, whose Orthodox upbringing clung to her despite the erosive force of my father's disdain for religion, putting a kitchen towel or a doily on her head in our kitchen, the first night of Hanukkah, and as we kids gathered around the table somewhat self-consciously, singing the half-remembered blessing over the candles in Hebrew. When her memory as to the exact words failed her, she would lapse, with no embarrassment at all, into Yiddish filler: *Yaidel-daidel-daidel-dai,* she would say. The brass menorah she used was tiny and old-fashioned and plain, and had belonged to her mother; at some point her father gave us a more imposing one with rampant lions of Judah supporting the central candle. That was after most of us had gone off to college, and so I imagine that there was a time when my mother performed her annual ritual in front of this imposing object alone; although while my grandfather was still alive she would, I remember, call him in Florida just as she was getting ready to light the candles, and she would sing the blessing over the phone to him, so in a way she wasn't really alone after all. . . . But for the rest of us, as I was saying, it wasn't really a very big holiday, and the giving of gifts dwindled away after we were very small children. So I was surprised and impressed when my older brother started sending carefully chosen gifts to all of us, a few years ago.)

The Memoirs of Ber of Bolechow is the first English translation of a manuscript of some ninety-five sheets crammed with a good Hebrew cursive script, typical of educated Jews of the eighteenth century, that was written at the turn of the nineteenth century by a Polish Jew called Ber Birkenthal, an inhabitant of Bolechow. Reb Birkenthal, who lived from 1723 to 1805, a tumultuous period in the history of Poland and, as his memoirs show, of Bolechow itself, was a remarkable man—a sage of great repute whose grave, in the Bolechow cemetery, would become the site of pilgrimages. Ber was the son of a forward-thinking, broad-minded wine merchant who encouraged his son's precocious intellectual appetites from his earliest childhood—even allowing the boy to study Greek and Latin with the local Catholic priests, an unheard-of thing that would later cast suspicion, briefly, on Ber's allegiance to his religion. The precocious boy grew up to be a precocious man: a successful wine merchant but also a scholar of enormous breadth and depth, a man who could read easily in Polish and German and Italian, as well as in Hebrew and Greek and Latin, a man who delved as happily into the great Italian work of world history known as the *Relazioni universali,* first published between 1595 and 1598 (which he began to translate into Hebrew), as he did into the arcane Kabbalistic texts that fascinated him, such as the *Hemdat Yamim*, by Natan Ghazzati, the so-called prophet of the false messiah Shabbtai Zvi. Ber of Bolechow, therefore, was a man who exemplified the liberal, worldly energies that helped to create the *Haskalah,* the great Jewish Enlightenment movement, during the eighteenth century, a movement that flourished, as it happened, under the philosopher Moses Mendelssohn, the grandfather of the composer.

From the twentieth-century editor of Ber Birkenthal's memoirs, a man called Vishnitzer, we learn that the town of Bolechow, where Ber was born, is situated in the eastern part of the province known as Galicia, which stretched from Kraków in the west to Lemberg (now L'viv) in the east. This part of Galicia is quite close to the Carpathian Mountains, which constitute a formidable natural barrier to Hungary, which lies to the south. (One that, however, can be breached, as I learned from an old woman who, as a young girl in 1943, walked barefoot over the Carpathians from Bolechow to Hungary, where the local Jews, to whom war had not yet come, found it hard to believe the reasons for this girl's desperate flight.) The specific plot of Galician land on which the town of Bolechow was established had been owned by a Polish nobleman called Nicholas Giedsinski; in 1612 Giedsinski laid the foundations of the town and granted it a charter. In this charter the Polish lord laid down the laws that were to govern the three communities that coexisted in the place: Jews, Poles, and (as the charter puts it), "Ruthenians," which is what Ukrainians used to be called. Vishnitzer points out that Jews had settled in this area before the place became a proper town, but a regular community arose only after 1612, when the charter granted by Giedsinski provided equal rights and liberties for the Jews.

Vishnitzer goes on to describe the rare privileges the Jews of Bolechow enjoyed upon its founding almost four hundred years ago. They were, he writes, allowed to acquire landed property in the center of the town and to build houses there. (*It was right there on the Ringplatz,* my grandfather would say to me when I was a boy, referring to his family's store: right there on the main square.) The town's Jews were ceded a plot of land for the erection of a synagogue and, across the little river that runs through the town, a plot for use as a burial ground. If you go there today, one of the first things you see, as you hop across a little creek onto the grounds of the cemetery, is a big headstone on the back of which is written the name JAGER.

The Jews of Bolechow, the author of this book goes on, could vote in the election of the Burgomeister (who, on taking office, had to swear to protect the rights of all three nationalities who lived in Bolechow) and of the aldermen of the Municipal Council. They enjoyed legal protections: the Polish municipal court could not settle a dispute between a Jew and a Gentile without the assistance of representatives of the Jewish community. (My grandfather told me that his father had once quietly intervened with the Austrian authorities, with whom he apparently enjoyed excellent relations, perhaps because of all those bottles of Tokay, in order to help an impoverished Jew get out of jail. *A word from him was worth something,* my grandfather told me.) So it is no wonder that, as Vishnitzer puts it, "harmony prevailed in the relations between the Jews and their Gentile neighbours."

Not surprisingly, given his scholarly enthusiasms and his success as a merchant, Ber Birkenthal's memoirs oscillate between the arcane and (far more frequently) the mundane. There are, to be sure, learned allusions to biblical verses. "One night," he writes, "a sentence from the Bible came into my head. It was from Psalm 58, verse 5: 'Their poison is like the poison of a serpent: they are like the deaf adder that stoppeth her ear; which will not hearken to the voice of charmers. . . . As a snail which melteth, let every one of them pass away: like the untimely birth of a woman, that they may not see the sun.' " But more often, Ber goes on about ordinary things, from politics ("After Poniatowski had been appointed Commander-in-Chief . . ."), business irritations ("I was very disappointed at not being able to obtain any of the old wines. I discussed the matter with my partner on our way from Miskolcz, as I had no other opportunity of doing so, because I had to return to Lemberg . . ."), local dramas ("With great difficulty, and by dint of tireless efforts and many intercessions, they were released from prison . . ."), and domestic matters. ("When my sister and sister-in-law, Rachel, learned of my desire to marry this widow, they talked to Yenta, so that the match might soon be made.")

An ordinary life, in other words, despite the extraordinary intellect of the memoirist. Still, it must be said that by the time Ber of Bolechow was prominent in Bolechow, the world was a less stable place than it had been a century and a half before, when the foundations of the little town were laid down by the Polish nobleman. Political instability was rife throughout Poland during the eighteenth century, and incursions of Russians and Tatars and Cossacks inevitably wreaked havoc on the Jews of the little town. And so it was that, in July 1759, Ber Birkenthal of Bolechow dreamed a terrible dream, a dream of pain that turned out to be a premonition: a dream, he writes with anguish, that his wife had gone into "severe labor." He knew this to be a sign, and sure enough he learned, the next day, that twenty-eight Ruthenian ruffians had descended from the timbered hills above the town and, taking the Jewish neighborhood by surprise, laid waste several Jewish homes and killed a man. Ber's property and family were not exempt from the destruction, which Ber himself vividly describes in his memoir. Given the existence of this eyewitness account of events that are so distant from anything I could ever have experienced, and which therefore I have a difficult time "imagining" or "envisioning," I prefer to avoid paraphrase and instead will simply cite his description:

> In the meanwhile two other robbers had entered my house and found my wife Leah still in bed. They demanded a large sum of money, whereupon my wife gave them a ducat and 20 gulden, apologizing that she had not another farthing in ready money. One of them hit her cruel blows with an axe on her arm and back,

so that the flesh and skin remained black for a long time. They commanded her to hand over to them the golden ornaments and pearls. Some said that the Gentile inhabitants of our town had informed the robbers that they would find such things in my house. My wife had to hand over all her precious things: two necklaces of fine and beautiful pearls, one of four rows and the other of five rows, a head-dress of great value and beauty, and ten gold rings set with magnificent and rare diamonds. The value of all these things amounted at that time to 3000 gulden. Besides this the robbers took away the furniture, and burnt the house.

The surprise attack, the Gentile informer, the robbery and the violent assault, the greedy appropriation of rare diamond rings: all this would happen again. (The Polish nickname for *Leah,* the name of Ber's wife, is, I should mention, *Lorka.*) But there were, too, unexpected and inexplicable kindnesses. Ber goes on to commend the thoughtfulness of a Gentile maid who stayed behind to rescue her master's books from the conflagration. "She took pity on the books," he writes, "because she knew that I was fond of them." Such acts would also be repeated, centuries later.

But the terror Ber describes in this passage, while not unknown in Bolechow and other Austro-Hungarian towns, was not the rule. *The Memoirs of Ber of Bolechow* is not especially literary, and the minutiae of business deals and court cases, to say nothing of the esoterica of early modern publishing, are unlikely to win many readers; but the very ordinariness of the life that this strange, forgotten book records is, it now seems, knowing what we know, quite precious.

After all, the only other book, to my knowledge, that had ever been written about Bolechow and its Jews until very recently is a book titled *Sefer HaZikaron LeKedoshei Bolechow,* or "Memorial Book of the Martyrs of Bolechow," edited by Y. Eshel and published in 1957 by a group calling itself the Association of Former Residents of Bolechow. It is, in other words, what's called a Yizkor book: one of the hundreds of books compiled after World War II, filled with the reminiscences of people who'd left before the war and the witness statements of those who hadn't, in order to memorialize the communities—little towns, big cities—that were destroyed, and of course to commemorate, inasmuch as was possible, a way of life that had been lost. I own a copy of this book, which my grandfather used to own; it's bound in blue cloth, now very faded, and the text is in Hebrew and Yiddish. I used to wonder, when I was a boy and my grandfather would, very rarely, let me handle this precious object, why they published it in a language that (as I then thought) only the victims could understand. My grandfather would show me the photographs in the book, and on a piece of stationery from the company he used to own—my grandfather also had a great impulse to save things, to preserve—which he later placed between the pages separating the Hebrew and Yiddish sections, he wrote the numbers of all the pages on which his family were mentioned. This is what he wrote, sometimes in block capitals, sometimes in his loping script, very occasionally letting slip an error in spelling:

44—BARON HIRSH JEWISH SCHOOL
67—BOTTON CITY HALL *right*
67—*Bottom our store Left*
110—THE CENTER OF TOWN HAD A FIRE
282—ISAK *and* SHMIEL my two brothers
189—*The public School I attendet*

The underlining is, uncharacteristically, the only emphasis. It is, indeed, odd to see my grandfather's writing, which I knew so well—to hear his voice, as it were—describing something so laconically, so devoid of the snaking cadences and the ornate enhancements and additions that once made all those stories about his world, his childhood, this town, so memorable to me. At the bottom of this piece of paper is the printed motto of his company: TRIMMINGS ALWAYS MAKE IT LOOK BETTER.

And there is something else I see: I notice, now, the way that my grandfather, who when talking to me always called his older sister Ruchele "Ray" and his younger sister Neche "Jeanette" and his brother Yidl "Julius," always referred, as he did while writing this list, to the lost brother as Shmiel. Which is to say, not by the public, "official" name, *Sam* (which is, I learned much later, the way he referred to himself), the name that corresponded to the Rays and Jeanettes and Juliuses, but only by the Yiddish name: *Shmiel*. I think this is because for him, the others had two identities, the one that belonged to a lost childhood in an empire that no longer existed, a time when you spoke Yiddish, and the other that belonged to his adulthood, when the names of so many things had shifted. But of course the last time my grandfather saw his older brother was in 1920, when he, an adventurous eighteen-year-old, left Bolechow forever, and his failure to think of this brother as anything but Shmiel, his consistent use of that Yiddish name, suggests to me how truly lost this murdered brother must really have been, like an unsmiling face in a picture that has lost its caption.

The interesting thing, for the present, is the answer to the question first raised by my grandfather's bold statement that his family had lived in Bolechow since *before there was a Bolechow to live in*. How long was that, then? Between them, our two books give us the answer. From the first book, the memoirs of Ber Birkenthal, the sage of Bolechow, we learn when it all started; from the last book, of course, we know when it ended. The Jägers lived in Bolechow for the entirety of the three and a half centuries during which it existed as its founders had intended, a community in which Jews, Poles, and Ruthenians would live in relative harmony. Which is to say, from the year 1612, when the fair-minded Count Giedsinski laid the foundations, until 1941, when the Germans came from the west, and the Ruthenians descended again.

AND SO, FOR a long time, the sum total of our knowledge was this:

We knew a great deal about my Jäger relatives, going back to the names of my great-great-grandparents, Hersh and Feige Mittelmark and Isak and Neche Jäger. We knew about the businesses they ran, the kind of town they lived in, the names of their children and grandchildren and great-grandchildren and, in the cases of many of these, their dates of birth and death and marriage. We knew about the history of Bolechow, where it was on the map. We knew what the faces of many of these people looked like from the old photographs carefully tended in my mother's album. We knew a great many stories.

And about the lost we knew, at least, this:

We knew that Shmiel Jäger and his wife, Ester, and their four daughters, who I then thought were called Lorca, Friedka, Ruchatz, and Bronia, lived in a house somewhere in Bolechow, as Jägers had been doing for three hundred years. Their address, I learned from a copy of a 1929 Polish business directory, was 9a Dlugosa Street.

We knew that in September 1939 the Nazis invaded Poland, but the Jews of eastern Poland were given a reprieve in the form of the Molotov-Ribbentrop Pact, which assigned the region that contained Bolechow to the Soviet Union. What Shmiel and his family endured under the Soviets, nobody knew.

We knew that the Nazis broke the pact in the summer of 1941, and soon after, at the beginning of the summer, they invaded eastern Poland. Soon after that, they arrived in Bolechow.

We knew that Shmiel owned a truck. (Trucks?) We'd heard that the Nazis wanted the trucks.

We'd heard that he was one of the first on the list. (List?)

We'd heard that at some point they went into some kind of hiding place. Perhaps it was the old castle belonging to the Polish counts, the Giedsinskis who had once owned the town when it was a private holding. My grandfather had, after all, said that *they were hiding in a kessel.*

Anyway, they were hiding. Or some of them were hiding.

We'd heard that the neighbor betrayed them and turned them in,

(or)

that the Polish maid, the *shiksa,* betrayed them and turned them in. Which was it? Impossible to know.

We'd read in Aunt Miriam's letter that in 1942 the Germans killed Ester and two of the daughters. This must have been Ruchatz and Bronia. Were they in the same hiding place as the others? Impossible to know.

Aunt Miriam had said that Lorca somehow escaped and fought in the hills with the partisans, with whom she was later killed. Which hills? Which partisans? When? How? Had she been hiding, too? Impossible to know.

She'd written that Uncle Shmiel and Frydka were killed by the Germans in 1944. Were they in a different hiding place? How and why had they been separated? Impossible to know.

And for a long time, that's what we knew. It wasn't a great deal, but it was a great deal more than *Killed by the Nazis.* For a long time, it was as much as we ever thought we'd know; and given the extent of annihilation, given how many years had passed, given that there was, now, no one left to ask, it seemed like a lot.

The beginning chapters of Bereishit, *the part that begins with the creation of the cosmos and narrows, over time, to the story of Adam and Eve and their fatal expulsion from Paradise (which is, too, the beginning of all of human history) tells us much about the pleasure to be had from the Tree of Knowledge: We know that it was good, it was a delight to the eyes, it was something "desirable for comprehension"—in other words, necessary for making distinctions, for, ultimately, creating. (For it is only after eating of the Tree that Adam and Eve go on to procreate.)*

And yet we all know, too, that the Tree confers pain as well as pleasure. For the pleasurable knowledge that comes from eating the fruit of the tree is conjoined with great pain—expulsion from Paradise, labor, childbirth—and leads, indeed, to the greatest pain of all, which is death.

In my ongoing search for the helpful meanings that may be found in parashat *Bere-*

ishit, which is after all the beginning of Torah's vast explication of the meanings of Jewish history, I have yet to discover an answer to a question I have had since I was a small child, when I first read this story in Sunday school. Why, I used to wonder, should Knowledge come from a tree? Why not from a rock, a cloud, a river—a book, even? The trees I was familiar with, then, offered no answers. The front of our house was guarded by a horizontal line of tall pin oaks, which didn't seem particularly wise, while in the back there stood, for a while, enormous, sulky willows, one quite close to the house—its farthest fronds used to brush, creepily, against the windows of my brothers' and my bedrooms during storms—and the other at the far edge of our property, in a corner next to the compost heap, which my industrious father hoped, each year, would become "established." Under one of these, years after I stopped attending Sunday school, I would overhear my parents and their parents reveal a secret about my father's father that startled me, and which drew me more passionately into a study of his family than I had ever thought likely. Another of these would come crashing down during a hurricane that improbably hit the New York area in August 1976, the tops of its (luckily) tender upper branches squashed softly against the big window of my mother's kitchen, so that when she walked into the kitchen the morning after hearing something go "crash" in the night, she screamed on seeing this monstrous mass looming in the window, looking for all the world as though it was about to devour the window, on the broad sill of which she would meticulously display some favorite tchotchkes: blue and white Delft candlesticks, vaguely modernistic Israeli utensils made of aromatic olive wood, brightly colored Italian ceramic jugs and vases filled with the plants that flourished so exuberantly in her care. It was on the day before this storm felled our willow tree, in fact, that the wife of my grandfather's brother Julius, the one who never seemed quite to fit into the family, the one who had no Feinheit, refinement, had to be buried, having dropped dead suddenly the night before, in an elevator in their apartment building in the Bronx. Dutifully, my parents assembled us children and we all drove out, in the day of obliterating rain that preceded the hurricane itself, to Mount Judah, where poor Roslyn, dead at only fifty-eight, would be buried where all the other Jaegers, Yaegers, Jagers, and Jägers of Bolechow were patiently waiting. And of that sodden funeral, my mother tells one of her favorite stories: the story of how, as we Mendelsohns waited for the rest of the funeral party to arrive, in a downpour so furious that it punched holes in our umbrellas and half filled the open grave with muddy water in a way that made me, for the first time, wonder just what happened after the grave was sealed, she suddenly had the idea that we should all wait in the relative comfort of a nearby mausoleum, and how when one of us, terrified, resisted, my mother said, "Oh, come on, how bad could it be? It's just nice old Jewish people in there!"

So the willow tree didn't seem particularly wise, since it couldn't even save itself. There was one more tree on our property that I liked to look at, when I was growing up and wondered, briefly, about what a "Tree of Knowledge" could possibly be. This was the great, twisted apple tree that stood in the corner of our backyard opposite the corner that was, for a time, occupied by the weeping willow. This tree had a claim to distinction that I didn't know about until I was, I think, in high school: on its trunk, when it was young, there had been grafted the branches of seven kinds of apples, so that in its maturity it produced seven kinds of fruit—fruit that we, being suburban and not trusting anything edible that didn't come from supermarkets, never ate, and which instead fell on the ground and rotted until someone, either we boys or the gardeners my parents eventually hired once we'd grown up, raked them away. The only person I ever saw eating from this tree was my uncle Nino—not a blood uncle, of course, since he was Italian, but rather my father's close friend from work, a man who had considerable glamour for me, when I was a child, since he drove a sports car, served foods we never laid eyes on elsewhere, and talked about faraway places he'd been, and who for all those reasons reminded me, pleasantly, of my grandfather; although the wordly confidence with which Uncle Nino plucked green apples off this tree and ate them had, in my eyes, something distinctly un-Jewish about it, and for this reason, I now realize, was obscurely connected to my later desire to study the culture and language not of the Jews, the people to whom I belonged, but of the Greeks and Romans, the Mediterraneans of whom Nino himself was so obviously one. . . . It was my grandfather, I should say in this context, who under that same tree chased me in circles one day, when I was perhaps ten, threatening to beat me black and blue—if I remember correctly, he was holding an empty milk bottle as he did so—because I had been setting model cars afire under the tree, and as he chased me he kept saying, A fire you're lighting, a fire? Do you want to kill us all? At that time, I had not yet learned the story of how his childhood home in Bolechow had been hit and set afire by a Russian shell in World War I, or indeed the one about how he had watched, during another shelling in the same war, as a school friend of his had been burned, or perhaps the better word is boiled, to death when the river that ran through Bolechow was set afire.

We know that the Tree of Knowledge in Bereishit was neither an oak nor a willow nor an apple, but a fig; and we know this, or at least infer it, from the fact that after Adam and Eve eat of the tree and acquire the shameful knowledge that they are naked, they cover themselves with the leaves of a fig tree. To this Friedman has fairly little to add, apart from the fact, which is admittedly interesting, that the improvised coverings the first two humans made for themselves were not actually "clothing," but crude coverings, since it is God, in Genesis 3:21, who makes the first clothing for them. But Rashi explores the detail of the fig leaves more searchingly, and derives from it (as he does *so often) a moral conclusion. "By the very thing through which they came to ruin," he writes, "they were corrected."*

To my mind, this progress from ruin to correction is intimately connected to the nature of knowledge itself, which is, at best, a process: from ignorance to awareness, from intellectual "ruin" to its "correction," from indistinct chaos to orderly scholarship. Knowledge, therefore, encompasses at once the starting point, which is empty, harmful, painful, and the end point, which is pleasure. To my mind, it is this quality of process, of development, which can only take place over time, that answers, finally, the question of why Knowledge must come from a tree. For a tree is a thing that grows; and growth, like learning, can only happen over and through time itself. Indeed, outside the medium of time, words like "grow" and "learn" cannot have any meaning at all.

And it is time, in the end, that gives meaning to and makes sense of both the pleasure to be had from knowledge, and the pain. The pleasure lies, to some extent, in the pride in accumulation: before, there was void and chaos, and now there is plenty and order. The pain, on the other hand, is associated with time in a slightly different way. For instance (because time moves in one direction only) once you know a thing you cannot unknow it, and as we know certain things, certain facts, certain kinds of knowledge are painful. And also: while other kinds of knowledge bring pleasure precisely as I have described above, filling you with information that you wanted to have, allowing you to make sense of what once looked like a disordered jumble, it is possible to learn certain things, certain facts, too late for them to do you any good.

Listen:

MY GRANDFATHER DIED in 1980. In the middle of the night, although he was very weak—at most one or two weeks, my mother had told me, away from dying of the cancer that was eating him alive—he got out of bed, wearing his immaculate white pajamas, and somehow had the strength to sneak past his sleeping wife, the one who had hated his feathers, the one who had been in Auschwitz, and to leave the apartment and press the elevator button "L"; found the strength to walk through the marble lobby of the Forte Towers and out the back doors to the swimming pool, into which he then found, finally, the strength to jump, although he knew that he could not swim.

That is how great the pain was. Now I ask myself, which pain?

Because my grandfather had committed suicide, I worried secretly—I was then twenty, but with respect to my grandfather I always seemed to be about eleven—if he would somehow get in trouble, whether the exacting details of the funeral arrangements he had dictated to me, the washing of his body, the plain wooden box, the grave site in Queens that was, of course, waiting for him because he was a man of Bolechow, and had paid his dues—would be denied to him. But everything went according to plan, and my grandfather was buried in New York. During the weeks afterward, my mother flew down to Miami Beach several times to settle his affairs. (Even when anticipating his own death, he was funny. When she opened the safe-deposit box containing his papers, she found a note at the very top, written in the unmistakable handwriting of my grandfather, who knew my mother would only ever read this note upon his death. "Now Marlene," it began, "first, you'd better stop crying because you know how lousy you look when you cry. . . .") As she had done in the case of her mother, she gave away most of his things to Jewish charities, but there were of course many things with special private and family significance that she brought home to Long Island.

Among these, for instance, was the faded-blue book called *Sefer HaZikaron LeKedoshei Bolechow,* the "Memorial Book of the Martyrs of Bolechow." Seeing it, that summer day in 1980, I remembered having seen it in his apartment one day years before, when I'd come alone to visit him. I was fifteen at the time, and already somewhat officially the family historian, a fact in which my grandfather took great pride, however much he liked to tease me about my importunate questions. During that previous visit, he'd wanted my help in cleaning out a lot of old boxes of "useless things," as he called them, and I sat next to him for a few hours one day, tossing things he was handing me—packets of letters wrapped in rubber bands or string, old driver's licenses, articles from *Reader's Digest* that he'd torn out—into a tall kitchen garbage pail lined with a white plastic bag. At one point, he went to the bathroom and I quickly sneaked a look at one of the packets of letters, which turned out to be his correspondence with his third wife, a lady called Alice. I scanned the letters quickly, and the occasional phrase caught my eye—for instance, *I don't care, frankly, about your $400,000, I have money of my own.* (I naturally assumed that this particular missive came from the period of their divorce.) I berate myself, now, for not having crammed the whole packet into my suitcase; my grandfather would never have noticed. But I am also aware that at that point, I wasn't interested in the marriages my grandfather made after my grandmother so unexpectedly died, because I thought of them as "recent" history and hence not of any real interest. Of course, his marriage to Alice in 1970 is farther from me now as I write this than Shmiel's days as a businessman in

Bolechow were from the day I sat there combing through my grandfather's useless correspondence.

Anyway, that was the day my grandfather took out the *Sefer HaZikaron LeKedoshei Bolechow,* "Memorial Book of the Martyrs of Bolechow," and showed it to me, and I wonder if that was also the day when, perhaps that night after I'd gone to sleep, my grandfather went through this book and wrote down for me (I like to think) on that piece of his company stationery, which he had carefully preserved and had not tossed away, all the information I needed to know about who was who and what pages their pictures could be found on, looking ahead to the time when he wouldn't be there to tell me himself.

My mother brought back other things, too, things of sentimental value to her (his glasses with the attached hearing aid, for instance), bank documents, his photo album with those black-and-white pictures that I would later come to know so well, even if I knew so little about the people in them.

There was something else she brought back, too, something I'd seen many times since I was young, but to which I hadn't ever given a second thought. It was that funny wallet, the long, slender one with the pimples, that he'd often carefully put in the breast pocket of one of the jackets he liked to wear. I recognized it, of course, but I could never have guessed what was inside it.

For when we finally opened the wallet, what we found was this: many folded pages covered in writing, writing in an even, forceful, elegant hand, writing in German. My mother had studied some German, long ago, although not with great success—she liked to tell the story of how her high school German teacher, expecting great things from a girl whose name was, after all, *Marlene Jaeger,* had been bitterly disappointed—and so she put the sheaf in my hands, when we discovered them, since by that point I was in college and had been studying German myself. *Lieber Teurer Bruder samt liebe Teure Schwägerin,* I read: "Dear darling brother and dear darling sister-in-law." *Liebe Jeanette und Lieber Sam,* I read: *Dear Jeanette and dear Sam. Lieber Cousin,* I read. I read, on three separate letters, *Lieber Aby.* Dear Aby.

Aby. My grandfather.

I read the dates: *Bolechów 16/1 1939.* I read, randomly, from the pages. From the opening of one: *Ich lebte einige monate mit der Hoffnung mich mit Euch meine Teure persönlich sehn zu können, leider wurde mir der Traum verschwunden.* "For a few months I lived in the hope of being able to see you in person, my dears, but my dream vanished." (For a long time after I first saw it, I couldn't stop thinking of this sentence: Why had Shmiel allowed himself to dream this hopeful dream, and why had it vanished? Who had given him false hope? I think about this a lot, knowing as I do how brothers, for reasons that no archival document can ever illuminate, can fail each other.) From page 2 of another (all the pages are carefully numbered at the top): *Man hält mich in Bolechów für einen reichen Mann* . . . "People in Bolechow consider me a rich man . . ." *Du machst vorwürfe mein l. Frau warum sie wendet sich nicht zu ihr Bruder und Schwester.* "You upbraid my d[ear] wife for not having turned to her brother and sister." *Wass die Juden machen hier mit, dass ist aber ein hunderster teil wass ihr weisst* . . . "What you know about what the Jews are going through here, is just one one-hundredth of it." *Die liebe Lorka arbeitet in Stryj bei einem Fotograf.* "Dear Lorka is working in Stryj at a photographer's." *Die kleine Bronia geht noch in Schule.* "Little Bronia is still in school." . . . *in ständiger Schreck ergriffen,* "gripped by constant terror." *Gebe Gott dass Hitler verrissen werden soll!* "God willing, Hitler should be torn to bits!" And I read, of course, the signature, again and again: *Ich grüsse und Küsse Euch alle vom tiefsten Herzens, dein Sam.* "I bid you all farewell and kiss you all from the bottom of my heart, your Sam." *Von Euer Treuren Sam,* "from your faithful Sam," *von Euer Sam,* "from your Sam." Sam. *Sam.*

Shmiel.

So this is what my grandfather had been carrying with him, all those years. The letters Shmiel had been writing, in the last desperate year while he could still write, when he thought he could find a way to get out. It had been there, right in front of my eyes, all that time, those summers when I'd idly look at the odd wallet, impatient to go outside and hear my grandfather's stories, never dreaming of the story that he was carrying in his left breast pocket. It had been there, right in front of me, and I hadn't seen a thing.

Listen:

YEARS AFTER MY grandfather died, I decided to try out the Jewish gene-alogy Web site's FamilyFinder page. To use this, you list all of your family names, along with the towns those names were associated with; then you list your own contact information—the idea being that someone looking for people with your names from your towns is bound to be related to you, and will want to be in contact with you.

So I listed my family's names. When I did so, I decided to err on the side of thoroughness, and so listed not only the names and cities of origin of my three foreign-born grandparents (MENDELSOHN, RIGA; JAGER JAEGER YAGER YAEGER, BOLECHOW; STANGER, KRAKOW), but the names of every single person I could think of who was related to my relatives, so to speak: and so my entries included RECHTSCHAFFEN, KALUSZ (my great-aunt Sylvia's husband), BIRNBAUM, SNIATYN (my paternal great-grandmother's relatives), WALDMANN, BOLECHOW (my grandfather had told me, when I was about thirteen, that his father had had a sister named Sarah who'd married a man named Waldmann), BEISPIEL, KALUSZ (relatives of "Tante"), MITTELMARK, DOLINA (the family of my grandfather's mother), KORNBLÜH, BOLECHOW (the family of my grandfather's paternal grandmother). And although I knew it was pointless, I also entered SCHNEELICHT, STRYJ. *Snowlight*. Maybe it was snowing that day.

And what happened was, a few of them worked. Almost immediately I was contacted by a nice lady from Long Island whose father was the grandson of that Sarah Jäger who'd married a man named Waldmann, and although it probably sounds foolish and sentimental, and the relationship is a very distant one, I was exultant about this discovery for weeks. Then, about a year later, an even more remarkable find: we discovered an entire lost branch of my father's family, because I'd noticed that someone else was looking for BIRNBAUM from SNIATYN. (And how nearly we missed it: originally I'd put BIRNBAUM from KRAKOW, because I seemed to remember that this is where my grandmother's parents had been from. Then, about a year after I'd first posted this, I was digging through some old letters from my Aunt Pauly and saw that in one of them she'd written, *I think they came from Cracow, but I also seem to remember someone saying the name of a town called Sniatin or Snyatyn, maybe that will help you.* That is how close a call it was—how nearly we missed finding the wonderful couple from Colorado who had, on their end, posted BIRNBAUM from SNIATYN, and who are our cousins.)

But the strangest response of all was the one I never expected, the response to SCHNEELICHT, STRYJ. I happened to be visiting my older brother at his home in the Bay Area a few years ago, and while there I retrieved a message on my answering machine in New York City from a man who said he'd seen my posting and wanted to talk to me about the name Schneelicht from Stryj. I was sufficiently excited that I didn't wait to get back to New York, but instead called him from my brother's house that evening. He lived in Oregon. He told me that his late father—the gentleman had died only a few years earlier, in 1994, at the age of 103—had been born Emil Schneelicht, in Stryj, and had lost several of his six siblings in the Holocaust. He said that his father's parents names were Leib Herz Schneelicht and Tauba Lea Schneelicht, names that, of course, meant nothing to me then. Then he told me the names of his father's siblings. They were:

Hinde
Moses
Eisig (his father)
Mindel
Ester
Saul
Abraham

I listened, and when he said the name *Ester* I actually gasped. She had seemed to belong so utterly to the remote and untouchable part of our family's past, my uncle Shmiel's wife had, that to be talking to someone who had a closer connection to her than I did—to her nephew, in fact, to the first cousin of the girls whom I'd grown to think of as being wholly "our" cousins—talking to someone who might have knowledge of the lost gleaned because of a relationship that I hadn't dreamed even existed (how could I, knowing so little about her, not even knowing if she'd had brothers or sisters?)—to be talking to this person was both thrilling and, in a way, startling. I started to wonder, then, how many other traces she had left behind, how many other clues might be out there, floating in Internet postings and buried in archives that I wouldn't even know were relevant because I had so little to go on, that I wouldn't even know were relevant even when I saw them.

Still, maybe I was jumping to conclusions: after all, there might have been more than one Ester Schneelicht born in the 1890s, from Stryj. But as I was thinking this, the man on the other end of the line said something else. He was telling me that certain of these brothers and sisters of his father's, who for all I knew were the brothers and sisters of my great-aunt Ester, had had nicknames, which of course was something I knew well from my own family history: his father *Eisig*, for instance, he told me, was also known as *Emil*. I was taking notes while he was speaking, and on the piece of paper I had in my hand I wrote EISIG = EMIL. Then he said that one of the aunts, Mindel, or Mina, had not, in fact, perished in the Holocaust, but had come long before to the States and lived in New York with her husband. He was a photographer.

Mina, this voice on the other end of the line repeated. They also called her Minnie.

I was starting to write MINDEL = MINA = MINNIE, when my hands grew sweaty and my heart started thudding.

Wait, I said. Wait.

I cleared my throat, and then said, She was married to a photographer, and her name was Minnie?

Yeah, the man said. Her husband was Spieler. Jack or Jake. Spieler. They were my aunt and uncle. Jack and Minnie Spieler.

Listen:

SOON AFTER I began to use the jewishgen.org site regularly, I made contact with a woman who, like me, had a family connection to Bolechow. This woman, who, after I finally met her, turned out to be as lively, outgoing, and generous as her e-mails at first suggested, and whose opulent masses of reddish ringlets, when I finally went down to Greenwich Village to meet her one March morning in 2001, somehow seemed to express these qualities, had volunteered for the Web site's Yizkor Book Project. (Many of the Yizkor books, including the *Sefer HaZikaron LeKedoshei Bolechow,* are in Yiddish or Hebrew or both, and jewishgen.org has sponsored a project to translate them into English and post the texts on the site.) The woman, whose name was Susannah, had also made a trip to Bolechow—even though, as she would later tell me, none of her immediate family, no one she'd actually known, was from there, a detail that moved and impressed me—and had posted photographs of the town on ShtetlLinks. I'd e-mailed her to say how much I'd enjoyed her postings, and we began a correspondence, during which she gave me two crucial pieces of information.

First, she put me in touch with a young Ukrainian researcher named Alex Dunai, who'd been her guide in Bolechow—or, as it must now be called, Bolekhiv—and who, she told me, also did archival research in the various local offices. As a result of this tip, I e-mailed Alex and asked him to explore the Jewish archives of Bolechow, which, miraculously, had not been destroyed during the war, and about two months after I'd first contacted him I received a bulging package from Ukraine containing over a hundred documents: photocopies of the originals, along with Alex's painstaking, typed translations. Of these I will say, for the present, that the earliest surviving records of the Jewish community of Bolechow, now stored in the L'viv Municipal Archives, date from the beginning of the nineteenth century, and that among these earliest records is a death certificate, dated the twenty-sixth of November 1835, that records the death at the age of eighty-nine of a certain Sheindel Jäger, on the twenty-fourth of that month. This Sheindel, the widow of the late Juda Jäger, had died (the certificate perhaps unnecessarily notes) of "old age," at an address given as House 141; for administrative purposes, all the houses in the village were numbered, and these numbers, rather than the names of streets, were used for official documents, although I can tell you, since a woman who knows told me a few years later as we were having lunch in Tel Aviv, that the street was called *Schustergasse*, Shoemaker's Way. She was, we may therefore deduce, born in 1746 or, possibly, 1745, which makes her my family's oldest known ancestor, for she was the mother of Abraham Jäger (1790–1845), who was the father of Isak Jäger (ca. 1825–before 1900, which was the year my grandfather's Zionist brother, Itzhak, who was named for him, was born), who was the father of Elkune Jäger (1867–1912), my great-grandfather who dropped dead at a spa, thereby setting in motion a string of events that would, at its farthest, least imaginable reaches, result in the deaths, by shooting, beating, and gassing, of his son, daughter-in-law, and four granddaughters; and who in turn was the father of Abraham Jaeger (1902–1980: Grandpa); who was the father of Marlene Jaeger Mendelsohn (born 1931), who is my mother.

It is not without a certain bitter irony, I am aware, that the reason I know all of this was, ultimately, that there exists something called the *Sefer HaZikaron LeKedoshei Bolechow,* or "Memorial Book of the Martyrs of Bolechow." For it was because of this book that I found Susannah, and it was Susannah who put me in touch with Alex, a gregarious young Ukrainian whom I would eventually meet myself, and it was this Ukrainian, who makes his living now by taking American Jews to the blighted settings of their own family stories, who found for me the documents that chart the path of my Jäger relatives beginning with an unimaginable eighteenth-century woman—a woman who could very well have known, and is almost certain to have laid her (blue?) eyes on, Ber Birkenthal of Bolechow, a woman who, like every one of her descendants, from her son to her great-great-grandson, my grandfather, was born and lived in the same house, house number 141 of a town called Bolechow in the vicinity of Lemberg (later Lwów, later L'vov, presently L'viv) in the province of Galicia in the Imperial and Royal Empire of the Dual Monarchy of Austria-Hungary.

That was the first thing that Susannah did for me. The second was something I hadn't imagined possible, once.

We'd been corresponding about her trip to Bolechow in 1999, since by now I was considering going there myself. I thought, then, that I might write an article about what it was like to return to an ancestral shtetl, two generations later, and to talk to the people who now lived there: to find out what, if any, faint traces still remained of the life that had been. On a Thursday in January 2001 I wrote Susannah an e-mail asking her whether, based on her experience of the place, she thought there was anyone now living in Bolechow, in Bolekhiv, who had clear memories of the pre—World War II period—people I might interview for the article I thought I might write. Perhaps, I wrote, I should get Alex to help me put ads in the local papers.

She replied on Tuesday the thirtieth, providing, almost as an aside, some information that was astounding to me. Apropos of old Bolechowers who might be of interest to me, she wrote, there was a very elderly Jew who'd only recently moved, with his equally elderly wife, from Bolechow to New York City: an eighty-nine-year-old man called Eli Rosenberg. He was, as Susannah put it, "the last Jew of Bolekhov," who had once been the town's hatmaker. (In the years that followed this exchange, I would meet the last Jew of Stryj, too, and the last Jew of a tiny town outside Riga. His name was Mendelsohn.) This Bolechower Jew, she explained, had survived the war years because in the summer of 1941, when the Germans arrived, he'd fled east into Russia with the retreating Soviet army. On returning to the town after it was liberated in 1944, he found that none of his original family had survived, but had decided to stay. Except for that last detail, it was a story I would hear again, later.

I looked at my computer screen, at the cursor blinking on the word *returned* in the sentence *Returned home after the war to find no one left from his family or from the entire Jewish community*. I'd grown so used to thinking of Bolechow as a mythical place (because it had existed for me only in my grandfather's stories), and had grown so used to thinking of the present-day Bolechow, Bolekhiv, as hopelessly distant from its wartime past (because six decades had passed and because almost none of the original population, whether Jewish, Polish, or Ukrainian, remained there), that the existence of an old Jew of Bolechow, alive today in New York City, a person who could bridge the distance between the place I'd always heard about and the place that existed on the map, between Bolechow and Bolekhiv, seemed to me as improbable as the existence of extraterrestrials.

At the end of her e-mail Susannah asked whether I lived in the New York area, and, if so, whether I wanted someday to go with her to meet the Rosenbergs, who lived in Brooklyn. They spoke only Russian and Yiddish, she explained, but she herself had been studying Yiddish seriously for some time and could act as an interpreter. I enthusiastically wrote back to accept her invitation. My enthusiasm was, I should say, motivated only in part by my desire to discover whether this Eli Rosenberg could shed any light on Shmiel and his family. The last Jew from Bolechow who'd spoken Yiddish in my presence had been my grandfather, dead now for twenty years. I wanted to hear it again.

Susannah replied soon after. The "great news!!!" was that she had called Mr. Rosenberg, or rather had spoken with his son, and they'd arranged a date for our meeting—my first and, I then thought, probably my last meeting with a Jew from Bolechow who could tell me something, anything, about what had happened there before, or during, or after the war. The date was set for Sunday, March 11. I was to meet Susannah at her apartment downtown and then she'd drive us to Brooklyn. She warned me that Eli spoke very softly, was quite weak physically, and that the death of his wife, Feyge—which Susannah hadn't known about until her recent communication with Eli's son—had been a serious blow.

By the time we drove to Brooklyn, I was extremely tense. Once again, as had been the case with Mrs. Begley at that reception two years earlier, the idea of proximity to someone from the place and time I was interested in was almost too tantalizing, too powerful, to bear: my leg was shaking as I sat in Susannah's car and watched Manhattan drop behind us. As we navigated the unfamiliar streets, Susannah peering at the street signs and I scrutinizing an oversized road atlas, I was, once again, prey to fantasies so intense, at once so vivid and so embarrassing in the mundaneness of the information this meeting could yield—*had Shmiel once bought a hat from this man?*—that, after we parked and found the tiny, dark apartment in an enormous, rather Soviet-looking stone-and-brick complex, I didn't trust myself to speak. I was lucky, I thought, that Susannah was going to do the talking.

But in the end there wasn't that much talking to be done. As we sat in the Rosenberg apartment, which was sparsely furnished and quite dark, listening to the thumping of basketballs resounding in the little courtyard of the housing project, it became clear that Mr. Rosenberg's condition had deteriorated quite seriously since the last time he and Susannah had been in touch. Susannah introduced me in Yiddish, and I told her to tell him that I was hoping he might have known my grandfather's brother, Shmiel Jäger.

Shmiel Jäger, Shmiel Jäger, Eli Rosenberg said in a soft, rather high-pitched voice, his mouth open. But nothing followed, except that he raised his hand high above his head, as if to indicate a tall person. Susannah said something to him and he nodded vigorously and said something back to her, and she turned to me.

He says he was a very tall man, Susannah said.

A very tall man, I thought to myself, my heart sinking. He didn't look very tall in the photographs I'd seen; no one in my family was very tall, to tell the truth.

Then Eli Rosenberg looked at Susannah and asked her who I was. His son, a very dark, rather Slavic-looking man in his forties, offered us tea and cookies. A game show was playing very loudly on the TV set. Susannah explained to Eli, again, that I was the grandson of the brother of Shmiel Jäger, who had the butcher shop in Bolechow. She told him again that I wanted to know if he had known Shmiel.

Shmiel Jäger, Shmiel Jäger, Eli said again, nodding in a way that seemed, for all that this impression was completely misleading, endearingly sage. Then he looked up—at me, not at Susannah—and said, *Toip,* and then nodded again, as if pleased with himself. I had no idea what he was talking about. Susannah talked to him some more, as it to make sure she'd heard correctly, and then turned to me.

He says Shmiel Jäger was deaf. *Toip.*

I looked from Susannah to Eli Rosenberg, who was nodding and cupping a hand to one ear, miming deafness. Then he asked Susannah, again, who I was and what I wanted.

My heart sank again. If Shmiel had been deaf, I'm sure my grandfather, or someone, would have mentioned it. It was the kind of detail salient enough, and harmless enough, to have escaped the unofficial censorship that my grandfather had imposed on any stories having to do with Shmiel. I began to wonder what other neighbor from two lifetimes ago, some tall deaf person wholly unrelated to me, this Eli Rosenberg was conflating my lost great-uncle with, and suddenly I felt defeated. All the energy, all the secret anticipation that had carried me through the agonizing slowness of these exchanges in a language I hadn't heard in two decades, all the stoked fervor of my hopes that he might say something big, something important, something about how they had died, about the last day he'd seen them, *something*—all this had, I realized, somehow exhausted me, left me empty. At that moment I wanted only to leave this dark, depressing apartment, and go home to look at my photographs, which at least I knew to be of them, knew to be authentic.

Then the son said he thought his father was getting tired. I was relieved. We all got up and shook hands—Eli's was surprisingly firm—and Susannah and I began to turn in the direction of the door. Looking at no one in particular, Eli said, again, *Shmiel Jäger, Shmiel Jäger*. A shiver of embarrassment coursed through the room, and the son, apologetically, explained that his father hadn't been doing so well since his mother died last year.

It's too bad you didn't come a couple of years ago, he said. He could have told you a lot.

Since then, I've heard those words, or variations on them, many times; but at the time, because it was fresh, the phrase hurt me. It was painful to think of how much more it would have been possible to know, if only I'd started two years, even a year, earlier.

I was thinking this, nodding at the son and making a sympathetic face, when suddenly Eli Rosenberg looked straight at me and said one more thing, one single word that had, somehow, in that final moment, been able to get past the ruined axons and blasted synapses and rise to the surface before sinking back forever, and what he said was:

Frydka.

Listen:

THE EARLIEST KNOWN photograph of Shmiel is the picture in which he is sitting in his Austrian army uniform next to that other man, the standing figure whose identity seemed destined to remain a mystery. In this picture Shmiel is remarkably handsome, as we have all been told he was: ripe jaw, full lips, even features, the beautiful hollows of his eyes, deep-set, blue . . . well, I know they were blue, even if this picture can't tell us that. Shmiel came of age at a time when, if you were this handsome (and often if you weren't), people would say, *You could be in pictures!* or *You should be an actor!* and that's what we always heard about him: that he was a prince, that he looked like a movie star. This picture is much more studied and, despite the wear of nine decades, of a much finer quality than the others we have, and indeed it's obvious that it was taken in a photographer's studio—perhaps the one that belonged to the family of the girl he would marry, once the war ended and the empire he'd fought to defend had vanished, the nation whose emperor, Franz Josef, people always said, was good to the Jews, and hence was rewarded by those grateful, grateful Jews, who always had their official names and their Yiddish names, Jeanette and Neche, Julius and Yidl, Sam and Shmiel—was rewarded with Yiddish nicknames of his own: *untzer Franzele,* "our little Franz," or *Yossele,* "Joey."

In this photograph, Shmiel is seated, stiffly posed on a chair, wearing the uniform of the Austro-Hungarian army, the artificiality of the setting and the pose made immaterial by the softness, even sensuality, of his looks. Dreamily, as if distracted during the long and tedious process of making this picture, he's looking off to the left, while at his right is standing the other soldier. This man is much older, plain-looking, stolid but not unpleasant-looking, wearing a mustache (Shmiel hasn't got his yet). Although when I first looked at this picture a long time ago I knew that this other soldier must have had a life, a family, a history, it seemed to me then, as it does even now, that he is in that picture to serve an almost aesthetic purpose, the way a commercial photographer today might wittily place a diamond on a piece of coal in a jewelry advertisement: I feel that he is there to make Shmiel look more beautiful, and therefore to conform more perfectly to the legend of his own good looks. Still, this other man, while not attractive, while clearly older than Shmiel, seems kindly: his thick arm rests in a friendly way on his younger companion's right shoulder.

For years I knew this picture through a photocopy I had made in high school: my mother kept the original, which had come from her father's precious album, along with others like it, in a sealed plastic baggie in a carton stored in a closed cabinet in our basement. On the carton she had written, in Magic Marker, the following:

FAMILY: <u>ALBUMS</u>
Jaeger
Jäger
Cushman
Stanger

Cushman was the maiden name of my mother's mother; Stanger was the maiden name of my father's mother, Kay, and of her sisters Sarah, the one with the long red nails, and Pauly, the writer of so many letters.

The original of the wartime picture of Shmiel was in these boxes, but I myself kept only the copy of the obverse, of the image itself. It was that photocopy that I subsequently took and pasted into an album of old family pictures that formed the basis of what would become a rather large archive relative to my family history. This is why, for a long time, I had in my possession only the image of the two men itself, but not the inscription that I knew had been written on the back.

I know, however, that I must have looked at that inscription at some point, for the following reason:

The only time I can remember being allowed to handle the original was when I was doing a presentation for my tenth-grade history class, in a unit devoted to European wars. I can't remember now whether it was World War I or World War II we were studying, but either way the picture would have been appropriate to bring into that class. I know for a fact that I must have brought the original photograph into class to display, this stately picture of my youthful great-uncle in his Austro-Hungarian uniform from World War I, because for a long time afterward my mind's eye retained an image of what had been written on the *back* of the photograph by my grandfather, in his looping cursive hand, in red felt-tip pen. I remembered what had been written because I so clearly remembered the reaction to those words of my high school history teacher, who when she read what my grandfather had written clapped a hand to her handsome, humorous face, when I brought the original into class that day thirty years ago, and exclaimed, "Oh, no!" What my grandfather had written on the back—or at least, what I long remembered of what he had written—was this:

Uncle Shmiel, in the Austrian Army, Killed by the Nazis.

That much, at any rate, I would remember, not least because I was a little shocked by Mrs. Munisteri's reaction, so used was I to knowing about what had eventually become of the beautiful young man in the picture, so inured had I become to the phrase *killed by the Nazis*. And that is what subsequently lodged in my memory, after my mother swiftly replaced the photograph in the labeled boxes of family documents and photographs from which it was briefly allowed to escape, for the purpose of making a strong and necessary point in a high school class.

So for a long time, possessing just the photocopy of the front of that picture, I could only scrutinize Shmiel's face, and maybe as I looked at it— I am sure, in fact, that this happened—it would occur to me how easy it is for someone to become lost, forever unknown. There, after all, was Shmiel, with that face, with a name that people still uttered, however infrequently, with some kind of history and a family whose names we knew, or thought we knew; and yet just next to him was this other man about whom nothing could ever be known, as good, it seemed to me as I looked at the picture, as if he'd never been born.

And then, many years after I'd been pinched and petted in the living rooms of long-dead Miamians, many years after I first photocopied that picture, when I'd only been interested in completing my classroom assignment; many years after I first felt that I had to know whatever it was possible to know about Shmiel, about the man with whom I shared a certain curve of brow and line of jaw, and for that reason had once made people cry, and because I had to know would spend an entire year, decades later, traveling—I the writer traveling with my younger brother the photographer, the one with his words to write and inscriptions to decipher, and the other, who had unwittingly gone into the family business, with his photographs to pose and to print, the two of us, two brothers, the writer and the photographer, traveling to Australia and Prague and Vienna and Tel Aviv and Kfar Saba and Beer Sheva and Vilnius and Riga, and then Tel Aviv again and Kfar Saba again and Beer Sheva again, to Haifa and Jerusalem and Stockholm and, finally, those two days in Copenhagen with the man who had once traveled even farther than we had, and who had a secret waiting for us; spent a year, summer and fall and winter and a spring that was also a fall, time itself seeming to fall out of joint as the past rose out of its ashes and its dirt and its old paper and powder and whiskey and violet salts, and surfaced once more like the almost illegibly faint script on the back of an old photograph, rising to compete with and confuse the present; spent a year tracking down people who are now far older than the old people who'd pinched my cheeks and offered me pencils in Miami Beach had been at the time, tracking down people who knew Shmiel only as the grand, impressive, and somewhat remote father of their schoolmates, those four daughters, all lost; flew across the Atlantic and the Pacific to talk to them and glean whatever bits still remained, whatever weightless puffs of information they might have to tell me—: then, many years after all that, when I was getting ready to sit down and write this book, the book of all those travels and all those years, and had persuaded my mother to let me see the original photograph once more, the obverse that I knew so well, yes, but also the reverse; then, only then, was I able at last to read, now in its entirety, the original inscription, read the words that my grandfather had written on the back, telling me something that, I now realize, like so much else that he had underscored for me, he thought was crucial, wanted me to know and think about. (But how could I see that then, when all I needed was a picture to go with a classroom presentation? In the end, we see what we want to see and the rest falls away.) What he had actually written, as I can now tell you since I've looked very recently, was this, in blue ink, in capital letters: HERMAN EHRLICH AND SAMUEL JAEGER IN THE AUSTRIAN ARMY, 1916. It was in red Magic Marker that he had added the words that I'd always remembered: KILLED BY THE NAZIS IN WORLD WAR 2.

Ehrlich? I asked my mother, when we were going through the boxes that day, stumped by a name that I had never seen before, despite all my research.

She seemed impatient. *You* know, she said. He was married to Ethel, they were my father's cousins. His sister was that Yetta Katz, she was big and fat and pretty and was the most marvelous cook.

But still I was confused. I turned over the picture and again looked at the two figures, the one so utterly familiar, the other so hopelessly unknown. Then, to be helpful, my mother added something.

Oh, *Daniel,* she said, You *knew* him! Herman Ehrlich. Herman the *Barber!*

AT NIGHT, I think about these things. I'm pleased with what I know, but now I think much more about everything I could have known, which was so much more than anything I can learn now and which now is gone forever. What I do know now is this: there's so much you don't really see, preoccupied as you are with the business of living; so much you never notice, until suddenly, for whatever reason—you happen to look like someone long dead; you decide, suddenly, that it's important to let your children know where they came from—you need the information that people you once knew always had to give you, if only you'd asked. But by the time you think to ask, it's too late.

About the rest of the family, I had of course long known everything there was to know; for a long time I had thought that I knew everything there was to know about the six who'd been lost, too. For in my mind, the word *lost* referred not only to the fact that they'd been killed, but to their relation to the rest of history and memory: hopelessly remote, irretrievable. At the moment when my mother said *Herman the Barber* I realized I could be wrong, that traces of those six might still remain in the world, somewhere.

So it was a kind of guilt, as much as any curiosity; guilt, as much as a desire to know what had really happened to them in whatever detail still remained to be known, that ultimately moved me to go back. To leave my computer, to leave the safety of books and documents, their descriptions of events so clipped that you'd never guess that the events were happening to real people (for instance, the document that recorded this fact: *During the march to the train station in Bolechów for the transport to Belzec, they were forced to sing, particularly the song "My Little Town of Belz"*); to forego the coziness of the records office and the comfort of the Internet, and to go out into the world, to make whatever effort I could, however slight the results might be, to see what and who might still remain, and instead of reading the books and learning that way, to *talk to them all,* as I'd once talked to my grandfather. To discover if, even at this impossibly late date, there might still be other clues, other facts and details as valuable as the ones I had allowed to slip away because, while the people who knew them still lived, the time wasn't ripe for me to ask my questions, for me to want to know.

And so, eighty-one years after my grandfather left his home in a bustling town nestled among pine and spruce forests in the foothills of the Carpathian Mountains, and twenty-one years after he died in a swimming pool surrounded by palm trees; three-hundred and eighty-nine years after the Jägers arrived in Bolechow, and sixty years after they finally disappeared from it, I went back.

This was the beginning.

TEXT OF A LETTER FROM ABRAHAM JAEGER, DATED 25 SEPTEM-
BER 1973, FOUND BY THE AUTHOR IN A STACK OF OLD PAPERS ON
6 JUNE 2005:

Dearest Children and Elkana and Ruhtie and Grandchildren

*It is almost Yom Tov so we wish you all a Happy and <u>Healthy</u> New Year please
give this picture to Daniel for the family album. Standing is Herman the Barber,
and sitting down is my Dear Brother SHMIEL in the Austrian Army, this picture
was taking in 1916.*

Ethel gave me this picture.

Happy New Year

> *Love*
> *Daddy——Grandpa*
> *Ray sends her Best*

PART TWO

Cain and Abel,

or,

Siblings

(1 9 3 9 / 2 0 0 1)

IN THE COMMUNITY HOUSE THERE WAS A PARCHMENT WITH A CHRONICLE ON IT, BUT THE FIRST PAGE WAS MISSING AND THE WRITING HAD FADED.

> Isaac Bashevis Singer,
> "The Gentleman from Cracow"

I

THE SIN BETWEEN BROTHERS

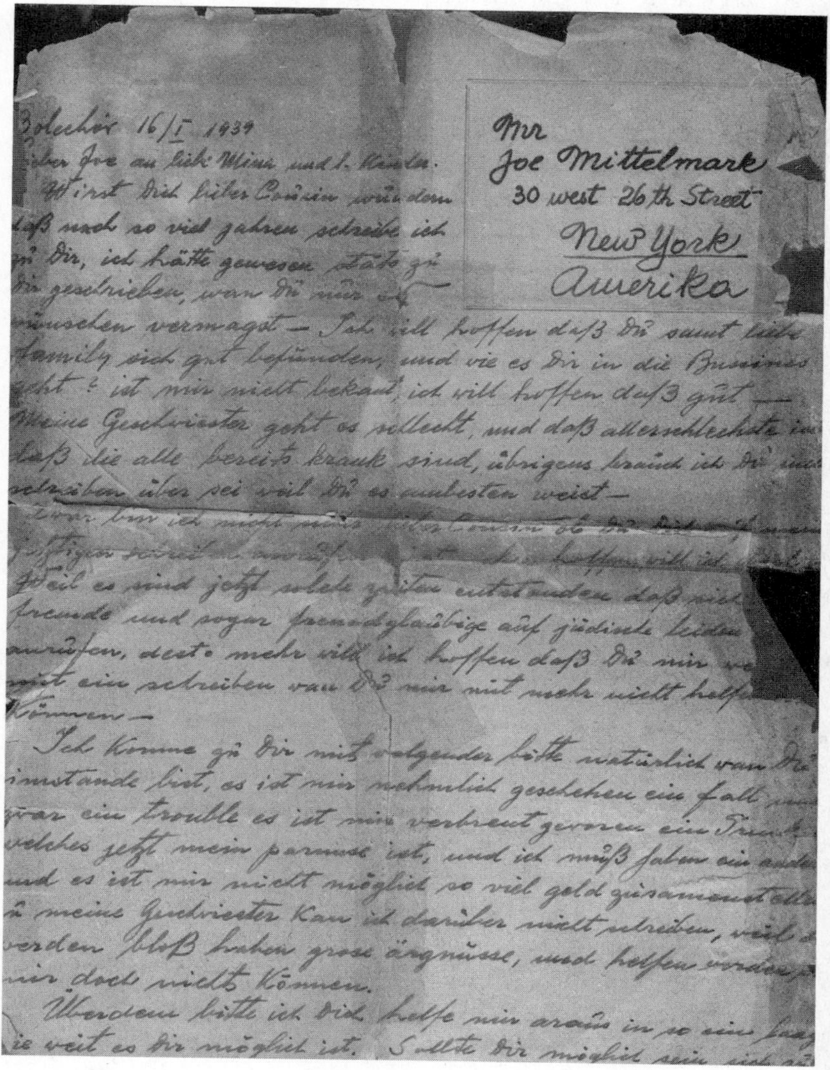

Mr
Joe Mittelmark
30 west 26th Street
New York
Amerika

Bolechów 16/I 1939
[illegible] Joe an liebe Mina und l. Kinder.
Wirst Dich lieber Cousin wundern
daß nach so viel jahren schreibe ich
zu Dir, ich hätte gewesen stets zu
Dir geschrieben, wan Du mir [illegible]
wünschen vermagst — Ich will hoffen daß Du samt liebe
family sich gut befünden, und wie es Dir in die Business
geht ? ist mir nicht bekant, ich will hoffen daß gut —
Meine Geschwister geht es schlecht, und daß allerschlechste ist
daß die alle bereits krank sind, übrigens brauch ich Dir [illegible]
schreiben über sei weil Du es ambesten weist —
[illegible]
[illegible]
Weil es sind jetzt solche zeiten entstanden daß [illegible]
fremde und sogar fremdglaubige auf jüdische leiden
anrufen, desto mehr will ich hoffen daß Du mir [illegible]
mit ein schreiben van Du mir mit mehr nicht helfen
Können —
Ich Komme zu Dir mit volgender bitte naturlich van Du
imstande bist, es ist mir nehmlich geschehen ein fall [illegible]
zwar ein trouble es ist mir verbrent gewesen ein [illegible]
welches jetzt mein parnose ist, und ich muß haben ein ander
und es ist mir nicht möglich so viel geld züsammenstellen
zu meine Geschwister Kan ich darüber nicht schreiben, weil [illegible]
werden bloß haben grose ängnüsse, und helfen werden [illegible]
mir doch nichts Können.
Überdem bitte ich Dich helfe mir araus in so ein [illegible]
[illegible] weit es Dir möglich ist. Sollte Dir möglich sein [illegible]

On August 12, 2001, two of my brothers and my sister and I climbed out of a cramped blue Volkswagen Passat and our feet touched the wet earth of Bolechow. It was a Sunday, and the weather was bad. After six months of planning, we had finally arrived.

Or, I suppose, returned.

Almost exactly sixty years earlier—on August 1, 1941—the civil administration of what had once been the Habsburg district of Galicia, a region that included the town of Bolechow, was transferred to the German authorities, who, after breaking the Molotov-Ribbentrop Pact, had turned around and invaded eastern Poland two months before and were now, finally, putting things in order. Not long afterward—perhaps later that same August, certainly by September 1941—plans for the area's first Aktion, or organized mass murder of Jews, began taking shape. These actions were scheduled for October. The Bolechow Aktion took place on October 28 and 29, 1941. In it there perished approximately a thousand Jews.

Of those thousand, there is one in particular who interests me.

On January 16, 1939, Shmiel Jäger sat down to write a desperate letter to a relative in New York. It was a Monday. There were other letters that Shmiel wrote to his family in the States, but it is this letter, I later realize, that contains all of the reasons we went back to Bolechow. More than anything else, it is what connects the other two dates: the plans that reached their fruition in August 2001, the plans that were set in motion in August 1941.

When I think now about that Sunday when we finally reached Bolechow, the climax of a trip that required months of planning, many thousands of dollars, painstaking coordination among a large number of people on two continents, all for a journey lasting barely six days, of which only one, really, was spent doing what we had come to do, which was to talk to people in the crucial place, in Bolechow, the town about which I had been hearing, thinking, dreaming, and writing for nearly thirty years, a place that I thought (then) would be the only place I could go to find out what happened to them all—when I think about all this, I feel ashamed at how casual we were, how ill-prepared and naive.

We had come, after all, having no idea what we might find. Months earlier, in January, when the idea for this trip was first taking shape, I had e-mailed Alex Dunai in L'viv, asking if there might be anyone left in Bolechow old enough to have known my family. Alex wrote me back to say he had talked to the mayor of the town, and the answer was Yes. The town was tiny, he said; if we came to visit, all we'd have to do was walk around and talk to a few people in order to find those who might have known Shmiel and his family, who might be able to tell us what really happened. Because I was determined to go anyway—because this had been my obsession from the beginning, simply to go there, as if the air and soil of the place could somehow tell us something concrete and true—this was enough for me. It was on this slimmest of possibilities—the possibility that we might, just might, stumble onto a chance encounter on a Sunday afternoon with a Ukrainian who was not merely old enough to have been an adult sixty years before, which was already asking a lot, but who actually knew them—that I committed myself, and my brothers and sister, although at the time I did not tell them just how slim the possibility was, to going there.

And so at the core of this trip, which seemed like a symbol, almost a cliché of family unity, there was a hidden deceit.

Still, we did end up finding out what happened to Uncle Shmiel and his family—by accident; and for that reason it's perhaps unnecessary to feel guilty even now, as I sometimes do, for having led my brothers and sister on a trip that would very likely have been our sole and, basically, unsuccessful fact-finding journey if it hadn't been for my mother's first cousin Elkana in Israel . . . Elkana, the last male on earth to be born a Jäger of Bolechow, who had abandoned the family name, taking a Hebrew surname and thereby sealing the extinction, in a way, of a certain part of my mother's family heritage, although of course the fact that there were Jägers in Israel at all, by whatever name, had ensured the survival of something more primitive, more biological, which is the family's genes. Elkana, the fabulous, storied cousin who (we knew) was some kind of big *macher* in Israel, who had blown up bridges in the War of Independence and, on his rare trips to visit us on Long Island, would get the local police department to fly him over our house in a helicopter, much to our delirious glee and to the secret envy of other children on the block. Elkana, who had retained the family's high sense of its own significance, its confidence in the appeal of its narratives and its dramas, and for that reason shared the news of our trip to Bolechow that summer with certain others, who told others, who told others . . . DNA is not the only thing that runs in families. But then, I am aware that the story of what happened to Shmiel would never have existed, would never have been worth telling, if that same innocuous self-aggrandizement had not led Shmiel to stay in Poland, led him to insist on being *a big fish in a small pond*, as my grandfather once put it, and so to remain stubbornly, perhaps even resentfully behind after his three brothers had moved on.

Or at least, those are the emotions that I, who know something about tensions between siblings, attribute to him.

In August 1941, the fate of Bolechow's Jews fell officially into the hands of the Germans.

In August and September of that year, most of the Jews of Bolechow, including my great-uncle and his wife and four daughters, were unlikely to have a clear idea of what was being planned for them. There were, to be sure, rumors of mass killings in cemeteries farther west, but few people credited them—protecting themselves, as people will, from knowledge of the worst. It is important to remember that many of the Jews of Bolechow, that early autumn, had already weathered the severe deprivations of two years of grim Soviet occupation; as difficult as it is to remember, for those who enjoy the benefit of hindsight, many Jews, as the Soviets fled before the Germans, were hoping that there would be some way to adapt to the harsh new status quo. And indeed, while drastically changed in certain respects, everyday life in the first few months of the German occupation rather surreally maintained certain features of everyday life from before. For instance, Jews were not prevented from attending synagogue on the Sabbath. A man I talked to sixty-two years after the German takeover remembered quite clearly attending Yom Kippur services in 1942. They knew they were going to kill us all anyway, he remarked. So why bother stopping us?

And so, in September 1941, the most pious Jews of the town maintained the traditions of their ancestors. As September melted away, so did the old Jewish year. In 1941 Rosh Hashanah, the NewYear, was scheduled to fall in the middle of September, and some of the Jews of Bolechow prepared themselves. Among the things that happen when a new year begins, for Jews, is that the weekly cycle of rereading the Torah also begins again. The parashah *for the first Sabbath of that new cycle is, naturally,* parashat Bereishit, *which begins with God's formation of the heavens and earth and ends with his decision to exterminate humankind by means of the Flood. It is a portion, that is to say, that travels a magnificent and dreadful arc from inspired creation to utter annihilation.*

In the year 1941, the reading of parashat Bereishit *took place on Saturday, October 18. The following week, on October 25,* parashat Noach, *the account of the Flood itself and of the survival of a very few, would have been read. I have to wonder how many of Bolechow's Jews went to shul the following week, since between Saturday, October 25, and Saturday, November 1, there occurred in Bolechow the first of the mass annihilations of which there would be so few survivors—the first Aktion, which began on Tues-*

day, the twenty-eighth, and ended the following day. So it is possible, perhaps even likely, that the last parashah that many of the town's Jews ever heard was Noach, that tale of divinely ordained extermination, one among several that we find in the Torah. But even if certain Jews of Bolechow had stayed home on Saturday, the twenty-fifth, perhaps out of indifference, perhaps out of fear, even if the last reading from the Torah that they would ever hear in the grand old shul on the Ringplatz or in any of the town's many smaller shuls and little prayer houses was the first of the year's readings, they would have had cause to ponder. For parashat Bereishit not only includes themes that are of great interest in general—Creation to be sure but also expulsion and annihilation and, in particular, lies and deceptions, from the serpent's seductive half-truths to the self-serving deceits that circulate among families, starting with the very first human family in Creation—but has as its very center the story of Cain and Abel, the Bible's great narrative of original fratricidal sin, its most comprehensive attempt to explicate the origins of the tensions and violences that hover not only within families, but among and between the peoples of the earth.

Comprising the first sixteen verses of chapter 4 of Genesis, the tale is by now familiar: how Adam knew Eve, who became pregnant and gave birth to Cain, an event that prompted her to boast, "I have created a man with YHWH!"; how she then gave birth to the younger brother, Abel. How, curiously, it was the younger brother who had the more pleasant task of tending the flocks, while the older brother toiled as a worker of the ground, and how when the brothers made their offerings to God, the fruits of the earth and the firstborn of the flock, God acknowledged the offering of the younger, but not the offering of the older boy, and how this greatly upset Cain, "whose face was fallen." How God chided Cain, warning him that sin "crouched in the threshold," that he must "dominate" it; and how Cain did not, in the end, dominate his sinful urge, but called his brother out into a field, and killed him there. How all-knowing God demanded to know of Cain where his brother was, the question to which Cain made his famous answer, replete with the sullen cheekiness all too familiar to parents of guilty children: "Am I my brother's keeper?" How God cries out, then, that Abel's blood "is crying from the ground," and curses Cain to be a roamer and rover on the earth. Then Cain's anguish, the expulsion, the mark upon his brow.

Despite its archaic stiffness, it is a story that, to anyone who has a family—parents, or siblings, or both; which is to say everyone—will be eerily familiar. The young couple, the arrival of the first child; the arrival, entailing more complex and compromised emotions, of the first sibling; the seeds of an obscure competition; the parental disapproval, the shame, the lies, the deceits. The violence in a moment of—what?

The departure that is both an escape and an exile.

ON A MONDAY in January 1939, Shmiel Jäger, who was then a forty-three-year-old businessman with a wife and four children, sat down to write the first of those letters. It is true that nearly every aspect of my grandfather's relationship with his oldest brother must be a matter of conjecture, since Shmiel's mind long ago became the molecules and atoms in the air above the little town of Belzec, while the matter that made my grandfather who he was has long since crumbled and gone back into the earth of that small portion of Mount Judah Cemetery in Queens that is reserved for the Jews who came from Bolechow. But there are certain aspects of this letter, concrete things, things the letter actually says and which, therefore, I do not have to surmise, that force me to think about family quarrels, about proximity and distance and "closeness" that are not temporal or spatial but emotional.

The letter begins with a date, which Shmiel has written as follows: 16/I 1939. January 16, 1939. I know that the sixteenth of January fell on a Monday in 1939. Naturally this fact is verifiable in all sorts of ways, since there are now Web sites that, within tenths of a second, are able to provide the most casual researcher with endless amounts of calendrical, geographical, topographical, and other kinds of data. For instance, there are a number of sites that tell you on what date in any year in the past century the ritual reading of a given *parashah*, or weekly Torah portion, took place, or can tell you in fractions of a second which *haftarah*, the selection from the Prophets, was read on which date.

In this context it seems worth noting that one explanation for the practice of reading the *haftarah* portion in addition to the Torah portion each week is that it evolved during a period of Greek oppression of the Jews during the second century B.C. as a kind of rabbinic subterfuge, since the Jews' Greek overlords at the time had banned the reading of the Torah. In response to this interdiction, the rabbis of the Second Jewish Commonwealth replaced weekly reading of the *parashot* with readings from the Prophets—texts that were not forbidden. These excerpts, however, were carefully chosen so that the *haftarah* portion to be read on any given week had strong thematic connections with the unreadable *parashah* for that week. (For instance, a Torah portion about sacrifices made by the High Priest for the purposes of atonement—a *parashah* about ritual scapegoats—might be replaced by a *haftarah* portion about the purging and subsequent redemption of the people of Israel: my *parashah*, my *haftarah*.) In this way, the weekly reading on the Sabbath, during this very early period in the oppression of the Jews, created a kind of parallel narrative world, in which what was being read was being read precisely because it vividly called to mind that which was not being read, that which had, for the time, become unsayable.

So there are many ways to ascertain specific, concrete kinds of information on the Internet, information that will tell you when certain things happened. And yet the method I use to ascertain certain kinds of dates is, oddly enough, although as infallible as the vast archival data that go into creating those online databases, based on a single human memory.

I have a young friend who has the odd ability to tell you instantly the precise day of the week on which any date over the past two millennia that you care to name happened to fall. This is most useful for people who, like me, are interested in histories that vastly predate the era of newspapers or wall calendars. My young friend can, for instance, tell you that July 18, 1290—the day on which the entire Jewish population of England was, by an edict of King Edward I, given until the first of November that year (a Wednesday) to leave the country, on pain of execution—was a Tuesday (this Tuesday coinciding with the observance, that year, of the fast of the ninth day of the Hebrew month of Ab, a ritual that commemorates a variety of disasters for the Jewish people, including the destruction of the Temple); and despite the fact that one group of fleeing Jews was, infamously, left to drown by the captain of the ship they had engaged (*Cry to Moses*, he told them as he sailed away, *by whose conduct your fathers passed through the Red Sea:* a cruel deceit for which the evil captain was hanged on order of the king, who was shocked by this crime against innocent men, women, and children), England's Jews did indeed depart, most of them making their way to safe haven across the Channel in France. . . . But then, Nicky can also tell you that the respite of these English Jews lasted only until a Friday sixteen years later, since on July 22, 1306, by edict of King Philip the Fair (whose treasuries had grown perilously depleted), all of the Jews of France, numbering perhaps some hundred thousand men, women, and children, were expelled from that country, after which their houses, lands, and movable goods were sold at auction, and Philip the Fair, undeterred, apparently, by scriptural sensitivities against usury, brought himself to assume title of the loans still owed by Christian Frenchmen to the now-absent Jewish moneylenders. (Six centuries later, France was still uneasy about its Jews. On October 15, 1894—a Monday—a Jewish officer of the French army, Alfred Dreyfus, was arrested on fabricated charges of betraying secrets to the Germans; the ensuing trial, to say nothing of subsequent revelations of a high-level governmental cover-up intended to protect anti-Semitic officials, was one of the most explosively divisive scandals of French and indeed European modern history, its confrontational and internecine mood summed up in the famous two-word challenge—*J'accuse!*, "I Accuse!"—offered by the novelist Émile Zola to the president of the Republic on the front page of a literary newspaper called *L'Aurore* in its issue of January 13, 1898, which was a Thursday. Newpaper coverage of the affair was, in fact, extensive throughout Europe, a fact perhaps worth mentioning here because among the foreign reporters covering the trial was a young Austrian journalist called Theodor Herzl, who went on to become the founder of the modern Zionist movement and who indeed later claimed that it was his experience of the Dreyfus case, his exposure to the official anti-Semitism that was made evident in the proceedings, that had galvanized his conviction that the only solution to the problem of European anti-Semitism was for the Jews to have a homeland of their own—a place, that is to say, from which they could not be expelled.)

Still (to return to the fourteenth century), there were other places to go, and it is entirely possible that some of the Jews who were expelled first by the English and then by the French decided to make their way across the Pyrenees to, say, Spain. And it is entirely possible that they would have flourished there, although it must be said that this respite did not last, and indeed there are two more dates of interest in this regard, which is to say March 30 and July 30, 1492, the former being the Friday on which the edict of expulsion signed by Ferdinand and Isabella, well known to American schoolchildren as the patrons of Columbus but less well known, I suspect, as the authors of this particular legal document, was issued, the latter being the Monday on which it took effect, thereby condemning some two hundred thousand Jews to exile— although it should be said that tens of thousands were murdered as they tried to leave, some by greedy Spanish ship captains who threw them overboard after collecting exorbitant sums for safe passage, others by greedy Spaniards who, having heard that the Jews had swallowed gold and jewels, murdered the Jews on the road. Still, we know that many of the fleeing Spanish Jews eventually fared well, having been invited by the canny and tolerant Ottoman sultan, Bajazet, to enhance his kingdom. (*How can you call Ferdinand of Aragon a wise king, this same Ferdinand who impoverished his own land and enriched ours?* he is reported to have said.) And indeed, many of those who stopped short of Istanbul fared just as well. Yet one must note that nearly all of the descendants of the fleeing Sephardim who eventually settled in Thessalonica, the great Byzantine and later Ottoman city in what is now northern Greece—nearly all of the sixty thousand who were the direct descendants of those particular Jewish refugees, and who were alive at the beginning of the 1940s—perished, inevitably, as the direct result of the entry of the German armed columns into that city on April 9, 1941, a Wednesday. (The first transport of about twenty-five hundred, which was a fairly modest number as these things went, left the railway sidings in Salonica on the morning of March 14, 1943. A Sunday.) And my friend can tell you that the twenty-ninth of October in that same deadly year of 1941, which, as we would learn after we went to Bolechow, was the date on which was killed one of the Jägers who, at least in part because of Shmiel's desire to be *a big fish in a small pond*, were still living in Bolechow after the Second World War began, was a Wednesday.

So it is remarkable how certain human memories will be fallible, while others seem as reliable as machines.

IT WAS ON a Monday that Shmiel sat down to write the letter.

Bolechów, 16 January 1939

Dear Joe and Dear Mina and dear children,
    You'll be wondering, dear Cousin, why I'm writing to you after so many years; I'd have written you continuously if you'd only wished it. . . . I'll hope that you and the dear family are well, how are things in the business? I don't know, and I'll hope that the answer is "good"—my siblings aren't doing well, and the worst

of all is that all of them are sick; anyway I hardly need to tell you what you yourself know best.

Since by now the times that have arisen can only be called strange, if not indeed hard to believe, with respect to the troubles of the Jews, I'll hope all the more that you'll be able to help me if only with a letter in response, if you can't help me with anything else—

Naturally, I come to you with the following entreaty only if it's something you're able to do; an accident—no, a disaster—has recently befallen me, namely one of my trucks has been burned, the one for which I had a permit, and I simply must have another and it's not possible any more for me to get so much money together, and I can't write to my siblings, since they'll only get terribly worried, and at any rate they won't be able to help me out.

On the one hand I'm not even sure, dear cousin, that you'll respond to this letter of mine, but I'll hope you will. And so I'm begging you: help me out of this, as far as it's possible for you. & if possible get in touch with my Schneelicht brother-in-law and get him involved in helping, too.

I will note for you that in the event that I don't buy another Truck by March 1st, 1939, my state permit [to be in business] will be taken away, and also that I'm the only Jew in our community business board who even had a permit for a truck.

I won't write to you a whining letter about how until now I had a permit, and am the head of a beautiful household, and have four well-brought-up beautiful daughters, don't let me go on about all that, I just want to go on working and not be a burden to anyone.

Consequently, since I know that an American businessman doesn't have time to read so much, I won't write too much, and will hope that you and your dear wife have understood me here, and I'll wait for a call from you, my dears—to whom should I turn in times of need but to my own?——I embrace you and kiss you and dear Mina and the dear darling children.

My wife and dear children hug and kiss you many times over,
                                    Your Cousin
                                    Sam

It's clear from the first line that this letter cannot have been easy to write. This was not because Shmiel had a hard time expressing himself in writing: he was, after all, fluent in four languages and competent in two more, and his letters suggest that he was not a little vain about his expressive powers, as he was about many things, his fine house, his wife, his four good-looking daughters, his high status in the small town where his family has lived for hundreds of years, his flourishing business. The German that he has chosen to write in flows fairly easily from the nib of his pen. It is not his native tongue, nor, indeed, that of the recipient, but as we know it was the written lingua franca of the family. The problem was that he barely knew the man to whom he was writing and from whom he now had to ask for a substantial loan.

This fact alone suggests, rather poignantly, the extent to which, still early in a year that would prove terrible, Shmiel was worried about his business, the flourishing meat-shipping concern that he proudly built up after inheriting the butcher shop that had been in his family for centuries, carefully husbanded by generations of Jägers who, as it is now possible to see by shrewd examination of the surprisingly numerous surviving vital records of Bolechow Jewry, enhanced whatever business acumen they may have had (a quality to which birth or marriage or death certificates cannot, naturally, attest) with strategic marriages to other families in either the same or related businesses . . .

For instance:

In the birth register entry for my grandfather's uncle Ire Jäger, who was born in house number 141 in Bolechow on August 22, 1847, a fact that is attested to by a document known as birth record number 446 for the year 1847 for the town of Bolechow, the following notation is made in the "comments" section, in German, in a fine, cobwebby hand: *Der Zuname der unehel: [ichen] Kindes Mutter is Kornblüh [Kornbuch?]*: "The surname of the illegitimate child's mother is Kornblüh [Kornbuch?]." What excited my attention, on seeing this piece of paper for the first time—it was one of the hundred or so documents that Alex Dunai had unearthed for me from Ukraine—was not, as someone might think, the adjective *unehelich,* "illegitimate"—the offspring of all Jewish marriages were considered to be illegitimate by the State authorities who kept these records, since the marriages had not taken place in the Catholic Church and the Jews, as often as not, didn't bother paying the exorbitant fees necessary to legitimize their children's births—but the name Kornblüh, a name that, on reading it here, seemed somehow familiar, a name I had vaguely remembered my grandfather using although in what context I couldn't, any longer, remember. But now, when I saw that forgotten name reappearing on this document, I realized that at some point he must have told me that it was his own grandmother's maiden name. With this in mind I went online to www.jewishgen. org and called up the online database known as the 1891 Galicia Business Registry, which is a searchable transcription of a musty tome, of impossibly small interest to the vast majority of people in the world, titled *Kaufmannisches Adressbuch für Industrie, Handel und Gewerbe, XIV: Galicia*, first published in Vienna by L. Bergmann & Comp., in 1925, and existing, now, as a photocopy in the British Library: which is to say, a printed version of the official 1891 directory of all business owners in Galicia, the Austro-Hungarian province of which Bolechow was then considered a part. I had searched this database before, and so I already knew that there were Jägers from Bolechow here—their names are given as Alter, Ichel, and Jacob—although for reasons that are, simply, impossible to know now, my great-grandfather Elkune Jäger does not appear in this index, although on the 1890 birth certificate of his first child by his first wife he is certainly listed as being a *Fleischer*, a butcher. (First wife, first child: I only recently and quite accidentally found out, during a search of some records made newly available online, that my great-grandmother Taube was Elkune's second wife; that Elkune had had another, first wife, who along with their two infant daughters had died early in the 1890s. Her name was Ester Silberszlag. I started tracing the Silberszlag family tree online, had added many Silberszlags to my family tree file, the fruit of many hours online, until I realized that I was wasting days on documenting a branch of my family that was, like certain first marriages you can read about in the Torah—Abraham's, or Isaac's—a dead end.) On a hunch I entered the name KORNBLUH and, after the computer whirred for a few moments, the search result, expressed in five columns—FAMILY NAME; GIVEN NAME; TOWN; OCCUPATION; OCCUPATION IN ENGLISH— was exactly what I had expected:

KORNBLUH CH. BOLECHOW FLEISCHER, FLEISCHHANDLER BUTCHERS, MEAT AND SMOKED MEAT

KORNBLUH JAC. MAJER BOLECHOW FLEISCHER, FLEISCHHANDLER BUTCHERS, MEAT AND SMOKED MEAT

KORNBLUH SCHLOME BOLECHOW FLEISCHER, FLEISCHHANDLER BUTCHERS, MEAT AND SMOKED MEAT

And so it seems clear to me that, very likely just before his death on May 7, 1845, my great-great-great-grandfather, Abraham Jäger, arranged a profitable marriage between his son, Isak, who was then around twenty years old, and Neche Kornblüh, a daughter of a family that was also involved in the business of processing the meat that came from the cattle that grazed on the rolling green pastureland that surrounded this idyllic hamlet. My suspicion, moreover—

judging perhaps erroneously from the terse but suggestive entry in volume fourteen ("Galicia") of the *Kaufmannisches Adressbuch für Industrie, Handel und Gewerbe,* is that my Jäger ancestors had made the slightly more advantageous match, since after all these Kornblühs seemed to have their mercantile fingers in many more pies.

But then, judging from this precious if rather abstruse resource, what a rich little commercial life Bolechow must have had in the mid-nineteenth century! Although I was preoccupied, on this particular day, with Kornblühs and Jägers—and was satisfied with what my search turned up, since it seemed to provide a reasonable back-story for the tantalizing entry on my great-great-uncle Ire's birth record—I decided to enter, simply, the name of the town itself in the search field of the 1891 Business Directory, and this search yielded a list of all the merchants in Bolechow who bothered to list themselves on some long-ago day at the end of the 1800s. As I read the names and occupations, which ran an opulent gamut from the familiar to the hopelessly lost, I tried to imagine these long-dead neighbors of my Jäger ancestors. JACOB ELLENBO-GEN, BUSINESS AGENT seemed to me to be a prosperous fellow: I pictured him with a broad, somewhat Slavic face, his eyes narrow and evaluating, full of testy humor and impatience, sleek in clothes he's brought home from Lemberg or even Vienna, impatient to make the next deal. The entry devoted to ABRAHAM GROSSBARD, BAKER, because it made me think of how good fresh bread smells, permitted me to dream of a person of great goodness and patience; the kind of person who knows you have to wait, to let things rise. BERL REINHARZ, the *Getreide- und Produktenhandler,* the grain and produce dealer, who was based in Skole, the little resort spa near Bolechow, must surely have come to town every Monday, which I have subsequently learned was market day: a slender, pleasant man (I told myself), quiet and industrious. The otherwise anonymous GOLDSCHMIDT, FISH-DEALER was surely big, broad, and not without a certain self-deprecating sense of fun. (Life is smelly, but what's the alternative?) GEDELJE GRÜNSCHLAG, on the other hand, is all business, with his flourishing *Baumaterialienhandlerei,* his building-materials firm, twinned with his *Holzhandlerei,* his lumber business—the opposite, in a way, of EFRAIM FREILICH, a *Hadern-und Knocheshandler,* a rag-and-bones man. Of course I knew nothing about poor Efraim, but I couldn't help thinking, and of course I could have been completely wrong, that his *nebuchl,* his pitiable, profession had made him tough; perhaps he was the kind of person who'd do a lot, maybe too much, to push his family forward, to get ahead, to leave his rags and bones behind . . .

But this, of course, was a fantasy, an indulgence. Much more probable was the other hypothesis that this directory yields, which was that the family business that Shmiel Jäger inherited, the butcher shop whose growth into a meat-shipping business eventually necessitated the purchase of a few trucks, a few trucks that were eventually to be the cause of no little trouble—that this family business was one that his ancestors (which is to say, my ancestors) had carefully tended in many ways. . . .

So it is the tending of the family business that now, in January 1939, preoccupies Shmiel Jäger, too, all too obviously. What, exactly, has happened to this truck, on which his business, the business of shipping meat, depends? It is impossible to know, now—although naturally the imagination yearns to supply a dramatic explanation. In this case, history lends a helping hand. For we know that, by January 1939, the anti-Semitic Polish government then in power had enacted restrictions on Jewish businesses that were severe, though not of course on a par with those enacted across the border by the anti-Semitic German government. Indeed, after 1935, when the autocratic but (relatively) moderate leader Josef Piłsudski died, the government of Poland veered sharply to the right; admiring of Hitler, who of course would soon destroy Poland altogether, the country's right-wing leaders were quite clear and open about their aims to reduce drastically what was perceived as Jewish influence on the faltering economy—even as the Polish political elite, with its lofty sense of the refinement of Polish civilization, denounced actual violence against Jews. "We have too high an idea of our civilization," one 1937 government proclamation stated, "and we respect too strongly the order and peace which every state needs, to approve brutal anti-Semitic acts. . . . At the same time, it is understandable that the country should possess the instinct compelling it to defend its culture, and it is natural that Polish society should seek economic self-sufficiency." This kinder, gentler anti-Semitism was reflected in the call by Prime Minister Sławoj-Składkowski for "economic struggle" against the Jews "by all means—but without force."

Still, the economic legislation against Jews that was subsequently enacted had brutal effects on businessmen like Shmiel Jäger. Between 1935 and 1939 the government of Poland made war on Jewish businesses, which citizens were encouraged to boycott: Christian-owned businesses were warned not to engage in commerce with Jewish-owned businesses; Christians were discouraged from renting property to Jews; anti-Semitic agitators appeared on market day in Polish towns warning Gentiles not to do business with Jews. Jewish stalls in marketplaces and at fairs were often destroyed, and Jewish shopkeepers in small towns were often terrorized by government-sponsored hooligans. And, in the most cunningly calculated attack, one aimed not so much on Jewish businesses as on an entire Jewish way of life—although its effect specifically on businesses like the one owned by Shmiel Jäger can easily be imagined—the Polish government banned *shkite,* the ritual slaughter of animals. Already crippled by the Great Depression—as far back as 1934, fully one-third of the Jews of Polish Galicia had applied for economic relief of some kind—the economic security of Poland's Jews was devastated by the boycott. It is in this light, then, that we must read Shmiel's letters, which are filled with mournful references to "troubles"— although of course his real troubles had not, in 1939, even begun. And indeed even if the disaster to Shmiel's business, this trouble with the trucks, had somehow been accidental, certain references in the letter—*the troubles of the Jews, my permit will be taken away, I am the only Jew who even had a permit*—suggests the apparently concrete fact that whatever his previous prosperity, however much he may have achieved his goal, at least for a while, of being a big fish in this particular small pond, Shmiel, like nearly all the other Jews in that little pond, has been reduced to dire straits.

And so on this January day he sat down to write a letter.

> *You'll be wondering, dear Cousin, why I'm writing to you after so many years; I'd have written you continuously if you'd only wished it. . . . I'll hope that you and the dear family are well, how are things in the business? I don't know, and I'll hope that the answer is "good". . .*

The reason that this letter makes me think about closeness and distance again is that, although it is written to a close relation—to his first cousin Joe Mittelmark, the son of his mother's oldest brother—a certain rather embarrassing stiffness immediately makes itself felt. Note the odd progression: the ostensibly warm salutation with its three repeated "dear's" (picked up yet again in the first line of the letter proper) followed by a marked defensiveness (*I'd have been writing you continuously if you'd only wanted*), which is itself followed by a certain forced casualness. In part, this stiffness, this awkwardness of tone, undoubtedly owes something to the fact that Shmiel has to ask for money, which is never a pleasant thing. But I happen to know that there are other reasons for the awkwardness, the distance, the failure in feeling that are detectable in this letter. You have the *Mittelmarks'* hair, my mother would sometimes hiss when I was a boy, thereby exiling me from my identity as someone who shared certain crucial traits of her family, of the Jägers and Jaegers, those self-dramatizing and grandiose Austro-Hungarian Jews for whom—because their handsome, high-browed faces and unusually blue eyes in their unusually deep sockets were merely the physical manifestations of the qualities of intelligence, artistic talent, culture, and refinement that they believed characterized them as a family, and which were summed up by the German word *Feinheit,* "refinement," which they used of themselves a great deal and denied to those of whom they disapproved for whatever reason—the way you looked and who you looked like was of particular importance. *I hate it when you're so mean,* she would say, glancing at my kinky hair. *It's the Mittelmark in you.*

The fact is that I know very well why Shmiel felt so awkward, that Monday in January, writing a letter to this man named Joe. For the Joe to whom Shmiel Jäger was writing, on that long-ago Monday, the "dear Cousin" to whom he addressed his mortified entreaty, was a Mittelmark; and even then, in January 1939, the bad blood between the Jägers and the Mittelmarks was already a generation old.

The story of this bad blood looks, at first, like a story about feuding cousins. My grandfather and his siblings had, after all, been beholden to, uncomfortably indebted to, their wealthy Mittelmark uncle, who'd paid for their steamship passages to America; and then there was the awful fact that this debt had been paid off (as my grandfather saw it) in human flesh, in the flesh of two of the three Jäger girls, my grandfather's sisters: the eldest, Ray, *Ruchele,* betrothed to that uncle's unappealing son, Sam Mittelmark, her first cousin; and, after she died *a week before the wedding,* the youngest, Jeanette, *Neche,* married off to this same Cousin Sam after she'd had time to grow old enough to wed. Throughout his life my grandfather blamed that cousin for what he insisted were the unhappy lives, and what we know to have been the premature deaths, of those two girls, one at twenty-six, the other at thirty-five; and it is hard not to think that this poisonous resentment wasn't shared, to some extent, by his other siblings as well, even far-off Shmiel.

So it looks like a story of bad blood between cousins. But if you read carefully between the lines—if you are, at least, a person who's grown up in a certain kind of family, a family, for instance, with five siblings—you realize that it must have started out as a story about poisonous feelings among brothers and sisters. When I was growing up, my grandfather would tell this story about the arranged marriages of his two sisters to their cousin, and as he related this irresistibly tragic tale he would linger above all on the anguish that these matches had caused his mother, who at the age of thirty-seven had found herself, suddenly, a widow with seven young children, and who after eight years of widowhood in Bolechow, of hardship and poverty and then a terrible war, was reduced, finally, to selling off—for surely this was the right way to put it—first one and then another of her lovely daughters to her rich brother in New York: the price she was forced to pay for tickets to America and a new life for her family. When I was growing up, my grandfather would tell this story and he would say, *It broke her heart!* And I would listen and think, How dramatic, how tragic, these bartered brides, these brides of death! But now, when I think about this story, I think, What kind of brother would compel a sister he loved to consent to such a marriage in the first place? And I wonder about the relationship between my great-grandmother Taube and her brother.

But then, between siblings there can be trouble. Between siblings there can be small and ostensibly meaningless things that can simmer under the surface when you grow up together, many, perhaps too many, children in one small house, and then explode into rage or violence or both. Now when I ponder, Who would do that to his sister? I think of other things in my family history, things from the distant past and things more recent. I think of how, when I was ten and he was eight, I broke my brother Matt's arm, just snapped it in a fit of rage during a fight one day out in the yard behind our parents' house, the way you might snap a twig, and now I know that whatever the immediate reason for my violence was, the real reasons were murkier: the color of his hair, the fact that he had the middle name Jaeger, which I thought I deserved more; the fact that he liked sports and had friends at school, the fact that he was born too soon after I was. Close in age, we were not close in other ways: I can't remember ever seeking out his company, when I was a child, and I am sure he didn't want mine. I much preferred the company of our youngest brother, Eric, who like me was interested in (and, as soon became clear, more talented at) painting, drawing, art, and whom when I was around ten and he was only six I was trying to teach about ancient Egypt, a passion of mine just then, only so I'd have someone to talk to about it. In our basement, I would make myself costumes: pharaonic crowns made out of empty bleach containers, broad collars, kilts with cardboard fronts, the outfit of the oppressors of the Hebrews. In my room upstairs, I would put on my pharaonic regalia, hold my crook and flail, and, with the egotism of the older sibling, and no little vanity of my own, would make Eric recite aloud the names and dates of dynasties, which he gladly did because (I now realize, too late) he wanted me to love him, whereas all I wanted was not to be alone with my strange hobbies. So there we would be, me sitting on a child's oak desk chair wearing a plastic crown painted blue, Eric kneeling before me, stumbling through names and dates about which he cared nothing at all, trying to please me.

To Matthew, whose arm I snapped in two, I was, I now realize, less cruel. Perhaps that is why it was Matthew who would, against all odds, become my companion and partner in the search for Shmiel: for all of the many hundreds of photographs of our trips, first to Bolechow and then to Australia, Israel, and Scandinavia, and finally Ukraine one last time were, first, images that passed through his tawny eyes, eyes set in a face like that of one of the icons to which, for generations, the members of his wife's Greek Orthodox family prayed. And perhaps that's why Eric, the brother whom I, in my vanity and arrogance, my self-centered belief that what interested me must interest him, my desire to make him a moon circling the planet of myself, I had thought my companion, was the brother who, after years of this heedlessness on my part, I had estranged.

Those murderous silences between brothers run through my family as surely as do certain genes. I think of my father, who for thirty-five years didn't speak a word to his older brother, to whom I knew he had once been close, my Uncle Bobby whom my father, as a child growing up in the Bronx, had (I learned only after Bobby died) watched silently each morning as Bobby strapped the cumbersome braces to his pencil-thin legs. Bobby, whose polio, as so often happens, returned late in his life to kill him, and at whose funeral, a few months before I and four of my five siblings went in search of my grandfather's unknown brother, my father read a eulogy of such poignancy and naked emotion that I realized only then that the reason he hadn't spoken to him all those years was that the feelings were too strong, rather than too weak. I think of how, as in some bizarre zero-sum equation, as soon as my father had resumed talking to Bobby, he lost touch with his other brother, a gentle man, tall and bearing well into his adulthood and even old age the now almost-invisible traces of a terrible acne, who shared my brother Matt's birthday, and who, an accomplished amateur photographer himself, was the first person to encourage Matt in the hobby that would eventually become his career.

I think, too, of my grandfather, of how imperious and condescending he'd been to Uncle Julius, who'd committed no greater sin than to be unattractive and coarse in his manners, to lack *Feinheit*. I think of my grandfather and Shmiel, and wondered yet again what might have passed between them, what upsurge of unacknowledged and unknowable emotion that, in me, had led me one day to break my brother's arm, might have led my grandfather to do something far more terrible, something I began to worry about only when Shmiel's letters were discovered.

FOR WHEN, ON that January Monday in 1939, Shmiel sat down to write his letter, he needed money to save his truck; by the end of the year, he would be begging for money to save his life. Between January 1939 and December 1939, when the last letter got through, my grandfather's brother wrote again and again, asking for money from my grandfather, from their younger sister, Jeanette, money this time not for trucks or repairs but for papers, affidavits, emigration papers for (at first) the four daughters, for (a little later on) two daughters, perhaps (finally) for one daughter, "the dear Lorka," as he playfully called his eldest girl, whose given name, I know from a birth record sent to me a few years ago by the Polish State Archives, was Leah.

> *Should the time of crisis not end immediately it will be impossible to endure things. If it were only possible for dear Sam [Mittelmark] to manage an affidavit for dear Lorka, then this would all be a little easier for me.*

I realize, on rereading these letters, that what makes them so uncannily moving is the second person address. Every letter, after all, is addressed to a "you"—"I bid you farewell and kiss you from the bottom of my heart," is Shmiel's favorite valediction—and because of this it is difficult, when reading letters, even letters addressed to other people, not to feel implicated, not to feel vaguely responsible. Reading Shmiel's letters, after we found them, was to be my first experience of the strange proximity of the dead, who yet manage always to remain out of reach.

As the requests for money get more strident, so too the references to the "troubles" Shmiel keeps mentioning. In the early spring, he writes my grandfather a bitter letter that begins "I turned 44 years old on 19th April of this year, and so far haven't had a single good day, each time it's something different." He goes on:

> How happy are the people who are lucky in that respect—although I know that in America life doesn't shine on everyone; still, at least they aren't gripped by constant terror. The situation with the truck-permit gets worse from day to day, businesses are frozen, it's a crisis, no one has any business, everything is tense. God grant that Hitler should be torn to bits! Then we'd finally breathe again, after all we've been through.

A little later on, though, in a letter to his sister Jeanette, it's plain that the "time of crisis" refers to more than business headaches:

> From reading the papers you know a little about what the Jews are going through here; but what you know is just one one-hundredth of it: when you go out into the street or drive on the road you're barely 10% sure that you'll come back with a whole head, or your legs in one piece. Work permits have all been taken away from the Jews, etc.

Here, then, is an escalation: the physical violence from which the Polish government liked to think itself aloof was clearly a reality for the already economically oppressed Jewish merchants of Galicia. And indeed we know, from contemporary newspaper accounts, that in the late 1930s in Poland, the number of violent attacks against Jews rose sharply: in 150 towns, between 1935 and 1937, nearly thirteen hundred Jews were injured and hundreds were killed by . . . well, by their neighbors: the Poles, the Ukrainians with whom they'd lived side by side more or less peacefully, "like a family" (as an old woman in Bolechow put it to me, later) for so many years . . . until something was unleashed and the bonds dissolved. *The Germans were bad*, my grandfather used to tell me, describing—from what authority, from what sources, from what hearsay I do not and cannot know—what happened to Bolechow's Jews during World War II. *The Poles were worse. But the Ukrainians were the worst of all.* A month before I went to Ukraine with my own siblings, I stood in the stifling lobby of the Ukrainian consulate on East Forty-ninth Street in New York, waiting for a visa, and as I stood there I would look around at the people standing next to me, who were all talking animatedly and often exasperatedly in Ukrainian to each other, yelling at the solitary officer behind the bulletproof glass, and the line *the Ukrainians were the worst* would go through my head, over and over, acquiring its own kind of rhythm.

It is in these later letters that Shmiel's tone becomes panicked. In a letter to my grandfather, written probably in the fall of 1939—in it, he asks my grandfather how he spent his summer—he talks about the possibility of sending even one of his four daughters abroad, once again hinting at his difficult financial situation:

> *If only the world were open and I'd been able to send a child to America or Palestine, it would be easier, since today children cost a great deal, particularly girls—*
>
> *Dear God should only grant that the world should be quiet, because now it's absolutely clouded. One lives constantly in terror.*
>
> *Don't be broyges [Yiddish:"angry"] with me, my dears, because I write you so many letters in this pessimistic vein, it's no wonder—in life now there are so many opportunities for people to be so evil to each other—*
>
> *I've now written to you so many times dear Aby . . .*

It is difficult to miss the tone of reproof in that last line.

It is clear that, by late in 1939, Shmiel was obsessed by the idea of getting his family out of Poland. In that last letter to his sister Jeanette and his brother-in-law, Sam Mittlemark, his mind is racing:

> *Anyway this is my mission: it's now the case that many families can go, and have already emigrated, to America provided that their families there put down a $5000 deposit, after which they can get their brother and his wife and children out, and then they can get the deposit back; and I'm of the opinion that they also take securities and perhaps you could manage to advance me the deposit; the idea is that with the money in custody I won't, once I'm in America, be a burden to anyone. Otherwise I wouldn't have had to contact you with no money. If I have to*

sell everything that I'm able to I'd have about $1000 left, not including costs, to
bring to America, but of course as long as there's a possibility that I could save all
of us in so doing, then there's no question of doing that, as you know.

Shmiel has been a businessman all his life; this is why, at first, he's all business, all facts and figures. But soon a note of desperation creeps in. What follows is the part I always find hard to read:

You should make inquiries, you should write that I'm the only one in your
family still in Europe, and that I have training as an auto mechanic and that I've
already been to America from 1912 to 1913—

(here he is referring, of course, to the disastrous visit that he made, as an eighteen-year-old boy, to his uncle Abe's apartment, the trip that convinced him that going back to Poland was his ticket to success)

—perhaps that might work. . . . For my part, I am going to post a letter, written
in English, to Washington, addressed to President Roosevelt and will write that
all my siblings and my entire family are in America and that my parents are even
buried there . . . perhaps that will work. Consult with my sister-in-law Mina and
maybe she can give you some advice about this, as I really want to get away from
this Gehenim with my dear wife and such darling four children.

My sister-in-law Mina: Minnie Spieler, whom I used to make fun of and ignore.

Shmiel spells the president's name *Rosiwelt,* and spells the name of the capital city *Waschington,* and for some reason this has the effect of dissolving the scholarly calm with which I try, whenever I read these texts, to decipher Shmiel's train of thought. I think of this man. I think of him writing that letter of pleading and cajoling, that letter to "President Rosiwelt" in "Waschington," and then I think of everything Shmiel was, and of what he thought of himself in the world; I think, indeed, of how he closes this particular letter with a reassertion of his native pride—

but I emphasize here to you all that I do not want to leave here without
something to live on . . . life is the most precious thing of all, as long as you've got
a roof over your head and bread in your mouth and all is safe and sound. I'll now
close my letter for today, and await a swift answer to the whole question & what
you have to say about it

—I think of all this, and I can't help wondering whether, as some clerk in Washington, D.C., opened a certain letter with a strange postmark, sometime in 1939, a letter written in stilted, high school English, he bothered to read it, or simply dismissed what was, after all, just another indecipherable missive from some little Jew in Poland.

IN ALL OF the stories I used to hear about how Shmiel and his family died, there was the terrible crime, the terrible betrayal: maybe the wicked neighbor, maybe the unfaithful Polish maid. But none of these betrayals worried me as much as did the possibility of one that was far worse.

Because Shmiel's home, and his belongings, and eventually his life were all taken from him, the only letters that survived are the ones from, not to, Poland. And so we have no way of knowing how, or whether, the others who were close to Shmiel—not the Polish maid or the Jewish (or Polish, or Ukrainian) neighbors, but the cousin, the brother, the sister, the brother-in-law to whom he'd written so frantically—ever responded. Or if they did respond, how fervently? I have read these letters many times, and I worry now whether enough had been done for them. Really done, I mean. It's true that in one letter, which was addressed to my grandfather, Shmiel refers to some money he'd received—eighty dollars; so there was some response. But what about the affidavit? Why, given the frequency and intensity of Shmiel's letters to his siblings in New York, is he always complaining that he doesn't hear from anyone? In the fall of 1939:

Dear darling Brother and dear darling Sister-in-Law,
   Since it's been so long since I've had a letter from you, I'm hurrying one off to you to remind you to let me know how you all are doing and especially how the whole dear family is. It's also been a pretty long time since I've had a letter from Jeanette, Why? I have no idea . . .

or:

Write me more often, it's like giving me a new life and I won't feel so alone.
   Dear Ester will write you a postscript of her own. I hug and kiss you with all my heart and wish for you longingly,
      From your
      Sam

or, the most damning:

Dear Aby,
   I was just about to send this, when at that very moment I received your letter.
You upbraid my dear wife for not having turned to her brothers and sisters. And so
I write to you saying that you're out of your mind. She already wrote to them, and
never got an answer. What should she do?

Of course there is no way to know what exactly transpired between the siblings
here. What seems, on a cold reading of the words themselves, like callousness
on my grandfather's part could, after all, have been something more innocent.
Perhaps, amid the treasures buried in the attics and sewers of the houses, still
standing, that once belonged to the Jews of Bolechow, there is a cache of letters, stuffed with some photo albums and jewelry and wrapped in blankets and
squashed into a leather valise that was sunk into the murk beneath an outhouse,
among which can be found a letter with an American postmark, which begins
*Dear Brother, We exhausted every possibility here, but cannot raise the sum you refer to.
Has Ester tried writing to her siblings here in the States?* . . . Perhaps. Because all of
the letters that my grandfather and Jeanette and Joe Mittelmark wrote (or may
have written) to Shmiel have long since crumbled to dust, we cannot know.

   Still, I tried. The month before we left for Ukraine, I convened a conference of my mother and her cousins—the surviving children of Shmiel's siblings—to ask them what memories they had of that time, just before the
war, when Shmiel's letters would have been arriving. These three cousins had
all grown up together, occasionally in the same apartment buildings, in the
Bronx; they all knew the same things. We sat one afternoon in June 2001, on
my mother's cousin's patio in Chicago, and they reminisced. But they weren't
old enough, weren't close enough to what had happened, to know for sure; all
they had was an adamant certainty that everyone had adored Shmiel, and that
everything possible had been done for him. I wanted hard facts, details, some
story or anecdote that had the uncomfortable asymmetry of truth, but what I
kept getting was the smooth sound of comforting platitudes.

   My mother's cousin Allan, the host, said, firmly, They would have done
anything possible to get them out.

   Allan is the son of the middle sister, the one who once wrote to me *I'm not
going to tell you when I was born because it would have been better if I'd never been
born*, and I never wonder why he became a psychologist.

   Everyone else enthusiastically agreed.

I remember when the news came, after the war, that they'd died, my mother's other cousin, Marilyn, drawled.

Marilyn is a couple of years older than my mother, but has a smooth, almost translucent fineness of brow and nose and jaw that, she unnecessarily confides to me, she gets from her mother, my mother's favorite aunt, Jeanette. (It was her *skin* that was so beautiful, but you can't tell from the *pictures,* she said at some point during that weekend, in the surprisingly deep Southern accent that she had acquired during her years away from the Bronx. *Picshuhs.* I have many pictures of Marilyn's mother—one in the opulent lace wedding dress her rich cousins, now her in-laws, bought to adorn their trophy bride, the other taken just before her death at thirty-five; in the latter, my mother tells me, Jeanette was mute, unable to speak because of the first of the strokes that would eventually kill her—and I am forced to agree, for none of the legendary beauty I have so often heard about is evident in these photographs of what looks to me to be a merely pleasant-looking Jewish lady of the earlier part of the last century. I wonder now whether the reason I was oddly relieved to hear from her daughter, one day almost fifty years after she died, that she was in fact beautiful, was that at this point I was still unwilling to entertain the idea that so many of my family's stories might be embellishments or even fabrications.)

Anyway, Marilyn was now responding to my question about what was or was not done for Shmiel by her parents, who after all are the addressees of at least two of those letters, but while she was unable to remember ever hearing them discuss Shmiel's pleas before the war, Marilyn had vivid memories of the day, months after the war had ended, when they got the news that he and his wife and children had been killed along with all the others.

I remember when the news came, this attractive Southern lady told me, fixing me with her wide-eyed, slightly surprised blue gaze. There wasn't just crying—there was *screaming*.

Who knows what went on between those siblings, seventy years ago? Impossible to say. At one point, during the Chicago conference of cousins, I took out the photocopied translations I'd made of Shmiel's letters to their various parents, and handed them out.

No, no, no, my mother said, vaguely pushing her copy across the table. I don't want to read them, it's too sad.

Then she made the slightly sibilant, sad, clucking noise with her tongue that she has always made when she's about to utter the Yiddish word *nebuch,* which means something like *what a terrible pity*.

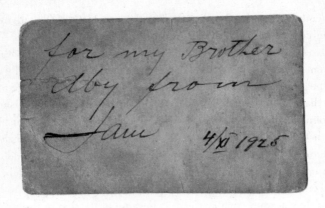

When Cain sulks over the fact that God has preferred his younger brother's offering to his, God chides him: "Why are you upset, and why has your face fallen? Is it not that if you do well you'll be raised, and if you don't do well then sin crouches at the threshold? And its desire will be for you. And you'll dominate it."

Rashi is very concerned to explain the striking if rather mysterious image of sin, like a female animal, crouching at a threshold. Where is it crouching, we wonder; at the threshold of what, exactly? "At the entrance of your grave," Rashi replies; there "your sin is preserved." But of even greater import to the meaning of this passage, for him, is the precise antecedent of the word "its" in the line "its desire will be for you." The Hebrew text here is, in fact, rather vexed. "Sin," in Hebrew, is hatâ't, a feminine noun, and hence grammatically we would expect the text to say, literally, t'shukâtâh—"her desire." And yet the Hebrew gives us a masculine rather than feminine possessive here: t'shukâtu, "his desire." Which is to say that when you read this line, it seems to say "his desire," in which case the "his" would most likely refer, if anything, to Abel. Hence the meaning of the line would seem to be something like "his desire is for you"—i.e., for reconciling with you, for maintaining good relations with you, his brother—"but you will rule over it"—in other words, you will reject this surge of brotherly goodwill, or perhaps even more accurately, you will repress any goodwill of your own that rises, however unwittingly, in response.

Yet Rashi, for whatever reasons, is eager to rule out this reading. And so he states, of the words "its desire," that the reference is to something not actually in the text—a phrase that is, in fact, a paraphrase of the word "sin" here, yêtzer hârâh, "drive toward evil." Because this phrase is, grammatically speaking, masculine, Rashi thus gets around the problem of the text's masculine possessive by supplying a masculine antecedent that is not actually in the text. Since this is a bit of a stretch, by any standard of textual emendation—and since Rashi's ruse entails further interpretive difficulties, not least of which is the fact that Cain patently does not "dominate" his sinful impulses, which is how Rashi's effortful reading would require us to read the text—it is worth wondering why he is so eager to rule out the most natural reading, which happens to be the reading that requires us to think, among other things, about the tortured dynamics of aggression, guilty shame, and tentative forgiveness between quarreling brothers.

But then, who does not find ways to make the texts we deal with mean what we want them to mean?

THE SOUND OF YOUR
BROTHER'S BLOOD

BY THE TIME we drove into Bolechow, my brothers and sister and I, on that Sunday in August 2001, we had been in Eastern Europe for four days, and our mood was not good. We four siblings—Andrew, Matt, Jennifer, and I—were traveling together for the first time since—when? I think it must have been 1967, during the famous "only" family vacation to Ocean City, Maryland, less famous in my mind for the inverted commas than for the fact that it was during that vacation that the final episode of the TV series *The Fugitive* aired, and even though I had begged my parents to make sure I was awake for the finale, they, thinking they knew best, let me sleep through it, with the result that I never did learn, or at least learn with a thoroughness of detail that satisfied me, the precise manner in which the true killer was revealed, never did see the satisfying moment in which the one-armed man was apprehended, the guilty party caught and the innocent victim finally, after so many years of being hunted, freed . . . I believe it had been that long, three and a half decades, since all of my parents' children, or at least a significant percentage of us, had traveled together. We grew up in a modest split-level, my brothers and sister and I, the four boys sleeping two to a room; but since those days we have grown unused to being together in close quarters for any period of time.

Because I am a classicist, I know that the word "intimate" comes from the Latin *intimus*, which is the superlative form of the adverb *in*, which means the same thing in Latin as it does in English—the comparative form being another familiar English cognate, *interior*. *In, interior, intimus:* inside, more inside, the most inside. I know that to many people who have families, these words will map out a self-evident emotional truth: that those who grow up *in* the same family will, because they shared the same inner space, *interior*, will feel closer, more *intimate*, to one another than perhaps to any other people, including their own spouses. But I also know, from my own and others' experiences, that being so intimate, having too much access to what goes on inside those closest to you by blood—"inmost" is how my Latin dictionary defines *intimus*—will sometimes have an opposite reaction, causing family members to flee one another, to seek more—we use the literal and figurative terms interchangeably, these days—"space."

This, I suspect, is at least part of why my brothers and sister and I haven't spent more time vacationing together. As I write this I think of the bitter if suggestive joke my youngest brother once made—the one who didn't come with us, perhaps because of an excess of intimacy—about how we relate to one another. *We're close in the way that people who were in the same concentration camp were close,* he cracked.

We are told that Abel changed his life and became a herder of flocks while Cain remained a tiller of the ground—the commentator Emes LeYa'akov has much to say about the different verbs "to be" used of each of the brothers—and Rashi thinks we should ask our-selves why. Why? Because, Rashi says, the earth had been cursed by God, and hence the younger brother "separated himself from its work." There is, in fact, an ongoing tension throughout the Torah between those who work the earth and those who tend flocks— just as there is, famously, an ongoing motif, even more striking, of murderous conflict between older and younger siblings. In light of the latter, it is worth noting that it is always the younger sibling who manages to endear himself to the father- or authority-figure, and subsequently to find himself the more prestigious line of work (shepherding, say, or advising Pharaoh), a phenomenon that, we cannot help thinking, is part of the resentment on the part of the older brother that fuels his fatal rage. (Even here, in Gen-esis, so early in our narrative, certain readers will be struck by Abel's fastidious choice of a job that—as Rashi's comment suggests—he cannot help knowing will win him

the approval of God, with whom, to me at least, it seems clear Abel is trying to ingratiate himself.) Indeed Rashi also remarks that Cain's offering to God was "from the
poorest"—a deduction based, in fact, on what is not in the text, i.e., any description
whatsoever of Cain's offering; whereas Abel's offering is described as being the choicest.
Perceptively, Rashi goes on to note that God not only reacted to these offerings, one agri-
cultural, the other ovicultural ("He turned . . . He did not turn"), but must have registered His reaction, somehow, to the two brothers, since it is clear that Cain knew that
God had rejected his offering.

But what's striking here is the tension between the workers who are tied to the
accursed ground—the farmers—and those whose livelihood derives from movable chat-
tels, like flocks of sheep. I think of how resentful Cain is—of how envious certain farmers must be of those others who, although born of the same soil, the same country, seem
to be luckier, because they enjoy the luxury of being able to go far afield, and because
their wealth seems to increase of its own accord, and because this wealth is movable, too.
I think of how the natural tensions between siblings, between those who grow up in close
quarters and know one another too well, can be exacerbated by these economic resent-
ments and envies. I think of certain brothers who stay put, trying to make a living off the
resisting ground, and of other brothers who take their chances far away.

And I think of other kinds of siblings, too, those who grew up in close quarters and
know one another too well, some forced to work the land, the others, seemingly luckier, more blessed, able to wander here and there with their (seemingly) ever-increasing
wealth. I think, naturally, of Ukrainians and Jews.

AS I HAVE said, it had been raining from the start of our Eastern European
trip—a cold, steady, wet drizzle, enough water to be irritating without ever
providing the giddy relief of a downpour. After the months of anticipation
about this dramatic family trip—the return to the ancestral shtetl was by
now so cliché that we half-mocked ourselves even as we made the elaborate
plans necessary to get four adults with careers onto the same plane at the
same time—the unrelentingly miserable weather, since the Thursday morning when we had landed in Warsaw and then transferred to the short flight to
the Kraków airport, where the big, blond Alex Dunai was waiting, beaming,
at the arrivals area holding a small cardboard sign that said, forlornly, MEN-
DELSOHN, seemed to be mocking the whole enterprise: the idea of the family
return to its roots, the enforced family togetherness necessary to make it happen, and most of all the expectations of what we would find.

The latter in particular had, even before the trip had really begun, started to feel oppressive. There was a good deal of bickering. We had no idea what, if anything, we were going to find here, and the unspoken but oppressive sense, as persistent and irritating as the constant drizzle, that we might well have made this difficult and expensive trip to this sodden and impoverished place all for nothing made us irritable. Because I had organized it all, because I was the one who had always wanted to come back, because it was I who had the notion, a deeply sentimental one I admit, that the return to the ancestral village should be a family affair involving as many of the siblings as possible, because I thought that one day I might write about this trip—because of all of this, I felt not only a grim responsibility to my siblings, but, even more, a terrible pressure to find someone who could tell us what happened, who could tell us the dramatic tale we were all hoping for. And so those first three days, during which we visited Auschwitz, toured what was left of the old Jewish quarter in Kraków, drove the five hours east to L'viv, spent a day in L'viv touring what was left of the old Jewish life there, too, were gloomy. Every decision—where to eat, what time to leave the hotel, where to go and what to see first—somehow became an argument. *I just don't understand why he's always so pissed off at me,* Andrew fumed one night, back at our hotel, about Matt. Since Matt had always been an enigma to me, too—we are closest in age, but during family get-togethers didn't, for a long time, have much to say to each other—I had nothing to say in response.

We started in Poland rather than going directly to Ukraine, to Bolechow, partly because of something I wanted, and partly because of something Andrew wanted. I had wanted to begin this way because I was eager to travel through what had been Galicia, the province from which so many American Jews come. If we started in Kraków, the westernmost city in Galicia and the city where my father's mother, my grandmother Kay, was born (a woman who, like my mother, raised four sons, certain of whom do not speak to certain others), and then drove east to L'viv, we'd traverse the whole province. I was, as I kept reminding myself, interested in the life of the Old Country, not merely its death, and I wanted to see what Galicia looked like, what the topography was, what kinds of trees and animals and people lived there. What kind of place my family had come from.

But we had also come here first because from Kraków it is only an hour or so to Auschwitz, and Andrew in particular wanted to see Auschwitz. Although he hadn't always been interested in family history, as I had been, Andrew had enthusiastically signed on for this trip, and before our departure had spent months immersing himself in the literature of the Holocaust, books about the Jews of Eastern Europe and about Polish and Ukrainian history. This was not surprising. His interests have always been many; more, I think, than those of any of the rest of us. Perhaps because he has the firstborn's sense of limitless possibility, he has thrown himself into everything, from raising species rhododendrons to building furniture to collecting Japanese prints, with unlimited enthusiasm. He is tall, dark-haired, fair-skinned, and has a face not unlike the one described on an old family passport, dated 1920: *face: oval, complexion: fair, nose: straight*. He plays, at a high level, the piano, the harpsichord, the recorder, tennis. As often happens in large families, we children early on adopted, or were given, what I thought of for a long time as "labels." I, with my kinked dark hair and blue eyes above their dark circles, was *Bad at Math but Good at English and French;* Matt, blond, yellow-eyed, with a wide grin usually reserved, during his combative adolescence, for people outside our family, and already something of a hero in high school for the photos he took of the soccer team, the students, the teachers, was *Secretly Sensitive Rebel;* Eric, with his mop of brown hair and watchful brown eyes, the sheafs of macabre and delicate drawings that he was already producing at the age of twelve and thirteen, with their unsettling captions ("Stop Following Me Or I'll Have My Maid Strangle You"), was, as everyone knew, *The Artistic One,* although he also happened to be *The Funniest Person in the Family.* And Jen, the youngest, the long-awaited only girl, vivid, dark, and petite, with her eyes like (the old Jewish relatives would say) *black cherries,* the valedictorian, the cellist, the writer, was *The Star.* But to me, who spent the first fifteen years of my life sleeping two feet away from him, listening to him listen to his hockey games, wondering how anyone could be that good in math, science, English, and sports, Andrew was simply *Good at Everything.* So it was no surprise that he knew as much about Bolechow as I did by the time we left for L'viv; it was he, after all, who gave me the precious gift of *The Memoirs of Ber of Bolechow.* During the months that led up to the trip, that August, he was constantly e-mailing me with the names of books he'd read and thought I should acquire: *Bitter Harvest: Life and Death in Ukraine under Nazi Rule,* say, or *Masters of Death: The SS-Einsatzgruppen and the Invention of the Holocaust.* Of course I bought them.

And so, because Andrew wanted to go, and because Andrew rarely asks for anything; and because Matt thought he could get some interesting pictures; and because Jennifer, who had, lately, been making her own private study of Jewish life and religion, and who would soon be the only one of my siblings to marry a Jew, was interested also: because of these things, which were important to my siblings, we went to Auschwitz, that first day we were in Poland.

I alone hadn't wanted to come. I was leery. To me Auschwitz represented the opposite of what I was interested in, and—as I started to realize on the day I actually did go to Auschwitz—of why I had made this trip. Auschwitz, by now, has become the gigantic, one-word symbol, the gross generalization, the shorthand, for what happened to Europe's Jews—although what happened at Auschwitz did not, in fact, happen to millions of Jews from places like Bolechow, Jews who were lined up and shot at the edges of open pits or, failing that, were shipped to camps that, unlike Auschwitz, had one purpose only, camps that are less well known to the public mind precisely because they offered no alternative to death and hence produced no survivors, no memoirs, no stories. But even if we accept Auschwitz as the symbol, I thought as I walked its strangely peaceful and manicured grounds, there are problems. It had been to rescue my relatives from generalities, symbols, abbreviations, to restore to them their particularity and distinctiveness, that I had come on this strange and arduous trip. *Killed by the Nazis*—yes, but by whom, exactly? The dreadful irony of Auschwitz, I realized as we walked through the famous rooms full of human hair, of artificial limbs, of spectacles, of luggage destined to go nowhere, is that the extent of what it shows you is so gigantic that the corporate and anonymous, the sheer scope of the crime, are constantly, paradoxically asserted at the expense of any sense of individual life. Naturally this is useful, since even now, even while the survivors live and tell their stories to people like me, there are, as we know, those who want to minimize the extent of what happened, even to deny that it happened at all, and when you walk around a place like Auschwitz, wander the enormous, vertiginously broad plain where the barracks once stood, and trudge over the great distance to the place where the crematoria were, and from there to the place where the many, many memorial stones wait for you, representing the countless dead of scores of countries, it begins to be possible to understand how many people could have passed through there. But for me, who had come to learn about only six of six million, I couldn't help thinking that the vastness, the scope, the size, was an impediment to, rather than vehicle for, illumination of the very narrow scrap of the story in which I was interested.

There was, too (I thought as we walked, on a humid morning whose air was filled with aggressive mosquitoes, through the yawning entrance of the guardhouse past a group of Scandinavian tourists), the problem of overexposure. As we walked around, we remarked that everything looked so familiar: the gatehouse, the siding, the barracks, the electrified barbed wire with its warnings signs in German still intact, and most famous of all, the sign—surprisingly small, as is curiously the case with so many famous monuments when you finally see them up close—that reads ARBEIT MACHT FREI, which although a deception of the sardonic sort so beloved of the Nazis, proved at Auschwitz to be potentially more accurate than similar signs at, say, Belzec, a place where there was only one destination after you got off the cattle car. All of this has been reproduced, photographed, filmed, broadcast, and published so often that by the time you go there, you find yourself looking for what it is difficult not to think of as the "attractions," for the displays of the artificial limbs or glasses or hair, more or less as you'd look for the newly reconstructed apatosaurus at the Natural History Museum.

And so as I walked around Auschwitz I struggled with the question of why one goes as a tourist to places like this. Not, in a general way at least, to learn what happened there; for anyone who comes to Auschwitz and the many other sites like it already knows what happened. And certainly not to get a better idea of "what it was like," as if by beholding the architecture or feeling the dimensions of the place, knowing how long it took to walk from point A to point B, one could understand significantly better the experience of those who came to this place not in air-conditioned tour vans but in cattle cars. No. Perhaps it's because I am the child of a father who was a scientist and mother who was the product of an emotional and nostalgic family, but it seems to me that there are two reasons to go to a place like Auschwitz. The first of these is scientific and juridical: one reason to go to Auschwitz is that the entire site is a gigantic piece of evidence, and in this respect seeing the piles of eyeglasses or shoes themselves, as opposed to merely knowing about them or seeing photographs or videos of the piles of eyeglasses or shoes or luggage, is more useful in conveying what happened. The second is sentimental. For the other reason you go to Auschwitz is the reason you go to a cemetery, which is something that Auschwitz also happens to be: to acknowledge the claims of the dead.

This is what I was worrying about after I left the indoor museum of hair and shoes and artificial limbs and stood in a fine drizzle waiting for my siblings. A gaggle of tall blonds—Swedes? Norwegians?—all with backpacks that had little bottles of water sticking out of them, was approaching the spot where I was standing, just outside the women's barracks, and it was then—as I was reading a plaque that told of the summary shootings that used to take place in what now seems like a not particularly menacing courtyard that wouldn't look out of place on the grounds of most American elementary schools—it was then that a young woman next to me muttered, If I don't get a bottle of water, I'm going to *pass out!*

So Auschwitz was, for me, always just the prelude. We knew, as we looked that first afternoon at the famous barbed wire, of which it is possible to make beautiful artistic compositions, and at the famous vista of the railway sidings that disappear, in those famous images, with the same reasonable inevitability of space and distance that you find in the perspectives in Renaissance paintings—*The School of Athens,* say—through a roofed, openmouthed gatehouse toward a vanishing point that was indeed a vanishing point; at those piles of shoes and eyeglasses and artificial limbs, all carefully preserved behind their glass panels; and then, as we looked the next morning at the empty synagogues of the Kazimiersz quarter in Kraków, the old Jewish quarter where my father's mother was born in another, unimaginably teeming world and where today the politely attentive German and American and Swedish tourists, wandering among life-size cardboard cutouts of Jews propped up in attitudes of rigidly pious devotion while recordings of Hebrew prayers droned in the background, reminded me of childhood trips to see the dioramas of dinosaurs at the American Museum of Natural History; and then, as we looked on the third day at the self-satisfied if somewhat dilapidated residential architecture of the city I still can't help thinking of as Lwów, and even sometimes Lemberg, but never L'viv, the solid blocks of Habsburg-era apartment buildings, indistinguishable from comparable blocks of apartment buildings in Vienna or Budapest or Prague, their Neoclassical windows, some topped by pediments and others by shallow arcs, looking across at their neighbors from above heavy ground-floor rustication that, if my memories of an architectural history course are correct, were intended to make their owners feel safe—we knew, as we looked at all these things, at the whole history of European Jewry crammed into two and a half days, the teeming ghetto, the failed assimilation, the successful annihilation, that as interesting or poignant or boring as all this may be, we were just biding our time. The whole point of this six-day trip, we knew, was Bolechow: everything—the planning, the expense, the effort, the bickering, the article—everything depended on whether, would be justified if, we could only find something there, find someone who knew them, who could tell us what happened, or who could tell us, at very least, a story good enough to be true, to repeat. This was the whole point of the trip, this Sunday when we would finally go to Bolechow.

And so it was on the fourth day that we finally drove to Bolechow. When our car pulled up in the tiny, unkempt square, there wasn't a single person there.

FROM THE LITTLE crest in the road that you go over just before entering the town, Bolechow doesn't look like much: a cluster of fat, steep-gabled houses grouped among a tangle of streets so dense that the little open square in the middle feels like a sigh of relief, the whole thing nestled in a depression among some hills. As I looked down from where we'd stopped to take pictures—Matt, who had been sniping back and forth with Andrew in the car, wanted to get out and photograph a horse standing next to the ugly sign bearing the name of the town in Ukrainian, *Bolekhiv*—I thought of course of how vulnerable it looked: how easy to enter, how isolated. We got back in the car and went down.

There, in the tiny town, we found three people, each of whom brought us a little closer to them, to Shmiel and his family, even as each reminded us of how distant they really were.

We found Nina first. Alex had parked the Passat wagon in the ragged, unpaved town square, a little ways down from the brightly painted, onion-domed Ukrainian church where services were going on, and just across the house that stood on the spot where my family's house had once stood. (A few months earlier, Alex had found a nineteenth-century surveyor's map of the town and had located "our" house, House 141.) On the same side of the square as the church was the old town hall, next to which my family's store once stood. Opposite the town hall was the large synagogue where my grandfather had been bar mitzvahed; after the war ended and there were no more Jews to be bar mitzvahed, or anything else, it became a leatherworkers meeting hall. With everyone in church, as far as we could tell, it was a pretty desolate spot, although a peaceful one. As we strolled around, treading wetly on the damp grass and gravel, we could hear the sound of liturgical chanting from the church. A goat was wandering around, untethered.

Suddenly a jolly-looking woman passed briskly by. Thickset in the way that is common among women of a certain Slavic provenance (as are the flowered print dresses, tightly stretched across their vast bosoms), she was, I guessed, around fifty. She looked at us standing awkwardly in front of this house, and with a mixture of small-town curiosity and something else, something lighter—the local person's generalized amusement about out-of-towners—asked who were were and what we were doing. Alex explained at some length, and it occurred to me that he must be telling her that we were American Jews who had come back to this, the town of our origin; and while he went on and on in Ukrainian all I could hear was the phrase *the Ukrainians were the worst*.

The woman's face cracked into a huge smile, and some rapid-fire Ukrainian ensued.

This is Nina, Alex explained. She is inviting us into her house. She herself was born after the war—

(I thought to myself, This is going to go nowhere)

—but her neighbor Maria is much older, and she thinks maybe this Maria will remember your family.

Well, I thought; perhaps it wouldn't be so bad. And so we walked the short distance to Nina's flat, which was on the first floor of a drab block of concrete modern apartments, located in back of the old synagogue. The apartment block reminded me of the dormitories of certain American universities. The approach to the apartments was from the back, and as we went around the building I was surprised to see, in stark contrast to the dinginess of the building itself, that the back of the lot was filled with quite elaborate, obviously well tended flower gardens, which at that time of year were abloom with roses, daisies, hollyhocks.

We went up the few concrete steps to Nina's front door. Outside the door, on a mat, several pairs of shoes were lined up. Matt gave me a sidelong, mischievous look.

So this is where Mom got it! he said. I knew what he was talking about: When we were growing up, we always had to remove our shoes at the door, a rule that infuriated and embarrassed us at the time; it was, among other things, humiliating to ask our friends to take off their shoes whenever we'd have someone over. There were, to be sure, other things that made us seem a little foreign to our school friends and neighbors. When I was about eleven or so, I had a friend who lived down the block who used to like to come call for me to play very early on weekend mornings. One summer morning when my grandfather was up from Miami Beach, the doorbell rang at around eight in the morning. I knew at once that it was Lonnie, and I raced down the stairs of my parents' house to get the door before the noise of the doorbell irritated my grandfather, who was *davening,* murmuring the Hebrew words and pacing slowly back and forth in my mother's spotless living room, enfolded in his vast, old-fashioned tallis, his leather *tfillin* wrapped around his arm and his forehead. It was not at all unusual for my grandfather to be able to have rudimentary conversations *while* he was davening: you could ask him, for instance, if he wanted Cream of Wheat for breakfast and some prune juice, and he would look at you and give an assenting glance while raising the volume of his murmuring in a way that suggested *yes*. I mention this because when I opened the door to Lonnie, my grandfather made his way over to the banister and, never abandoning his Hebrew text, raised a leather-encircled arm in a gesture that was partly incredulous and partly threatening, and simultaneously he raised his voice in a way that suggested that no one in his right mind paid social calls at eight in the morning. Then he turned his back and walked back into the living room, my eyes following him with secret delight: my exotic, funny grandpa. When I turned back around to whisper with Lonnie, he'd already fled down the front steps and disappeared.

And *that,* my grandfather would say later on, telling this story, was the last we ever saw of *that* one!

So we had these strange family habits, among which were my grandfather's davening, and my mother's insistence that shoes were to be lined up on a mat just inside the front door of the house. I thought of this, as Matt obviously had, too, as we stood at the threshold of Nina's apartment, and it occurred to me that perhaps my mother as a girl had absorbed this rule from her father, who had had to follow it a half century earlier, because he had lived, as Nina lived a century later, in a country town where simply walking a hundred yards was likely to cover your shoes with real filth—dirt, mud, or worse.

The apartment was tiny. Much of the small living room was taken up by a large sofa, on which nearly all of us—the four Mendelsohns and Alex—somehow managed to squeeze, our legs tucked out of the way of the little coffee table in front of us. Off the living room were a small kitchen and a bedroom of some kind, which was occupied, as far as I could see, by a piano. As we sat on the sofa, Nina, who was banging around the kitchen, chattered loudly in Ukrainian with Alex, who looked amused, and also pleased that perhaps we had found what we were looking for. Finally Nina came back from the kitchen, a small plate in her hand. On it were slices of local sausage. She then went to the credenza and took down a dusty bottle of what she described as Soviet-era champagne—how odd to think of the Soviets making champagne, we said, but she countered that it had once been a big business farther east, in one of the indecipherable "-stans"—

and, after uncorking it, poured us each a little celebratory glass. Then she made each of us a cup of Nescafé, which was clearly considered something of a treat.

It is a big honor, Alex told us, giving us a warning look.

Matt, sitting next to me, muttered that he didn't like Nescafé.

Andrew and I gritted our teeth and said, simultaneously, Drink the fucking coffee, Matt.

I wondered what Alex himself was thinking. Alex is a heavyset, gregarious blond in his mid-thirties with a broad, ready smile cushioned among pink dimples. Since the dissolution of the Soviet Union, he'd made a career of taking American Jews around the old shtetls of Eastern Europe, near his home town of L'viv, where he proudly showed us around. (During that tour he'd assured me that there was no castle near Bolechow that had once belonged to a Polish aristocrat.) During the past ten years he'd come to know more about the history of Jews in Galicia than most Jews do. He was the first Ukrainian I'd ever had extensive dealings with, and when we finally met, at the Kraków airport the day we first arrived, we were all taken with his warmth and natural expansiveness, which easily carried us through the inevitable awkwardnesses. It was during the long drive from Kraków to L'viv, the day after our trip to Auschwitz, that we'd asked him how a young Ukrainian, formerly of the Soviet army, had come to this career escorting American Jews around their ancestral shtetls, and he had replied, a shade guardedly, I don't tell most people what it is I do, I don't think they'd understand.

Now, Alex was clearly delighted that Nina was rolling out the red carpet. As she fluttered and bustled away, my brothers and sister and I gave one another sidelong glances, and it was clear we were all thinking the same thing: *some Ukrainians aren't so bad*. As we did so, Nina's husband, a thin, affable man who was wearing a bathing suit and flip-flops, banged out tunes on the decrepit piano in the closet that, we were told, was his study. "Feelings" was followed swiftly by—presumably in our honor, and certainly to show us his multicultural goodwill—"Hava Nagilah." We looked at each other again. Then he played "Yesterday."

IT WAS ONLY after we had drunk the Soviet champagne, sipped the Nescafé, and eaten the local sausage—which was quite good, and which seemed appropriate since, after all, we had come from a long line of Bolechow butchers and meat-merchants—that Maria appeared at Nina's doorstep, smiling

shyly. Again, there was a long introduction: who we were, what we were looking for. Maria was a beautiful woman in her seventies, soft white hair, a broad
face with high, slanted bones; the characteristic look of the area, as I'd come
to realize. She looked pensive when we mentioned the name Jäger, and nodded. I hoped that finally, this would be it—the explosion out of generalities
into something specific, some hard piece of knowledge, the start of a story.

Yes, yes, Alex told us, translating, she knows the name. She knows it.

I felt, right then, very close to them. This woman would have been a teenager during the war; she could indeed have known them. My siblings and I
exchanged glances.

Then Alex said, But she didn't really know them.

Still hoping for something—and feeling, suddenly, how absurd this whole
expedition was, how mightily time and space and history were against us,
how unlikely it was that anything of them could still remain—I took out the
sheaf of photographs I'd brought with me and showed them to her. Photographs of Shmiel in his thirties and early forties, wearing a fur-collared overcoat, taken in the photography studio in Stryj that his wife's brother owned;
pictures of three of the girls (which three? impossible to know) as children, in
lace dresses; a studio head shot of one of the girls as a teenager, with a broad
smile and, I can't help noticing, the same kinky Mittelmark hair that I had as
a teenager. Maria looked at them, shuffling the old prints slowly. Then she
shook her head with an apologetic little smile, the kind of smile you can fashion with your lips framing a frown, as my mother's mother used to do. She
said something to Alex.

She doesn't remember them, Alex told us. She says she was young, just a
child, during the war. She didn't know them herself. It's too bad, she says,
because her husband was much older, he would have known, but he died three
years ago.

As I looked at the ground, Alex exchanged a few more words with Maria.
Ah, he said. He told us that Maria had just said that her husband's sister, Olga,
was still alive; she lived just down the road. Perhaps this Olga would be able
to tell us something.

We all got up, with Nina bossily leading the way—she had clearly adopted
both us and our search—and marched down the road to Olga's.

The road we walked down to get from Nina's apartment to Olga's house
was, we later found out, the road that leads from the center of town to the
cemetery, past the old lumber mill. Now we walked down this road, and before
Maria left us, we asked her how the Jews and Ukrainians had gotten along,

before the war. We had, of course, done our research, and so we already knew about the centuries of economic and social competition between the Jews and the Ukrainians: the Jews, nationless, politically vulnerable, dependent on the Polish aristocrats who owned these towns, and for whom so many of the Jews inevitably worked as stewards and moneylenders, for their security; and the Ukrainians, who for the most part were workers of the land, who occupied the lowest rung of the economic totem pole, a people whose history, ironically, in so many ways was like a mirror image, or perhaps a negative image, of that of the Jews: a people without a nation-state, vulnerable, oppressed by cruel masters of one description or another—Polish counts, Soviet commissars. It was because of this strangely precise mirroring, in fact, that in the middle of the twentieth century it evolved, with the precise, terrible logic of a Greek tragedy, that whatever was good for one of these two groups, who lived side by side for centuries in these tiny towns, was bad for the other. When, in 1939, the Germans ceded the eastern portion of Poland (which they had just conquered) to the Soviet Union as part of the Molotov-Ribbentrop Pact, the Jews of the region rejoiced, knowing they had been delivered from the Germans; but the Ukrainians, a fiercely nationalistic and proud people, suffered under the Soviets, who then as always were determined to stamp out Ukrainian independence—and Ukrainians. Talk to Ukrainians about the twentieth century, as we did so often on that trip, and they will tell you about their own holocaust, the deaths, in the 1930s, of those five to seven million Ukrainian peasants, starved out by Stalin's forced collectivization. . . . So the miraculous good luck of the Jews of eastern Poland, in 1939, was a disaster for the Ukrainians of eastern Poland. Conversely, when Hitler betrayed the Molotov-Ribbentrop Pact two years later and invaded the very portion of eastern Poland that he'd given to Stalin, it was, of course, a disaster for the Jews but a blessing for the Ukrainians, who rejoiced when the Nazis arrived, having been freed from their Soviet oppressors. It is remarkable to think that two groups inhabiting such close quarters for so many years could be so different, suffer and exult over such different, indeed opposite, reversals of fortune.

It was knowing all this that we asked Alex to ask Maria how the Jews and Ukrainians had once treated each other.

Everyone got along, for the most part, he replied after speaking for a moment with Maria. She says the children often played together in the square, Ukrainians and Jews together.

It was because I knew well what playing together can lead to—how beneath the closeness, the knowing each other, can be a knowing too well—that I asked what seemed to me to be the next logical question. Were there Ukrainians who were happy when the Jews were taken away? I asked.

They talked for another moment. Yes, Alex said after a pause. There were some, sure. But there were some who tried to help, and for that they were killed. She repeats that this was a small town. Everyone knew each other. The Jews and the Poles and the Ukrainians, it was many people in one small place.

Maria smiled her beatific, translucent, hopeful smile, and murmured something else to Alex. He turned to us and said, She says that it was like a big family.

All commentators try to wrestle with the bizarre problem of what, if anything, Cain said to get Abel to go out into the field with him, the field where Cain planned to kill his brother. The strict translation of the Hebrew of verse 8, vayomer Qayin el-Hevel ahchiyv vay'hiy . . . , yields what seems, at first, like nonsense: "And Cain said to Abel. And when they were in the field . . ." Which is to say that the Hebrew text tells us merely that Cain said something to Abel, and that in the field Cain rose up and killed Abel; but we are never actually told what one brother said to the other. The authoritative Hebrew text remains silent; it is only the Septuagint, an Alexandrian Greek translation of the Hebrew Bible made in the third century B.C., and the Vulgate, the Latin translation of the Hebrew and Aramaic Bible made by Jerome (later Saint Jerome) between A.D. 382 and A.D. 405, that tweaks the text to give it more ostensible sense, and it is their translations, inaccurate but more satisfying, that most of us know: "And Cain said to Abel, 'Let us go into the field . . .'" Naturally, the impulse to maneuver the text so that it tells us what we want it to say is nothing new, either—as we have already seen—in biblical scholarship, or anywhere else.

Friedman, the modern commentator, seems less perturbed by this than Rashi is, and in keeping the brisk, good-natured twentieth-century practicality that characterizes his approach, supplies a perfectly reasonable explanation for the odd syntax of the text here: "Cain's words," he writes, "appear to have been skipped in the Masoretic Text"— the Hebrew texts represented by copies dating as far back as the 900s—"by a scribe whose eye jumped from the first phrase containing the word 'field' to the second." To anyone familiar with the study of manuscript traditions, this seems a likely enough explanation: some ancient scribe, as he sat before a venerable and now-lost manuscript of the Torah that he was dutifully copying, and as he was about to write the now-lost phrase, "Let us go out into the field," the remark made by one brother to another, shut his eye in a moment of weariness; so that, when he moved his tired hand to write once more, the tired eye, now reopened, was already focused on what was, in fact, the second occurrence of the word "field"—that is, the word as it appeared in the line that we do have, the line that was not lost: "And when they were in the field . . ." And because he was tired, because he was, after all, only human (and we know what lapses human memory is prey to), this is the line he actually wrote, having never actually written the line that said "Let us go out into the field"(or something very much like that); and because of this tiny lapse, that one line, which if it actually existed would eliminate a troublesome reading from this most authoritative of all texts, was irretrievably lost.

And yet the loss of this line does not seem to bother Rashi that much; or at least, he has an equally cogent explanation at hand—although his explanation is psychological rather than mechanical. His comment on the ostensible half-sentence that we translate as "And Cain said to his brother Abel" goes as follows: "He entered with him into words of quarrel and contention to find a pretext against him, to kill him." To Rashi it is quite clear that the actual words that Cain said are immaterial, since they were false, merely a pretext; the commentary here indicates that Rashi knows well that, between brothers, there are darker forces lurking that need the barest excuse to rise to the surface and erupt into violence. What is of interest are the forces, not the pretext.

IT WASN'T FAR to the house of Maria's sister-in-law, Olga, from the point at which Maria had turned back, in the middle of the road, leaving us in Nina's broad and energetic hands: just a couple of hundred yards farther away from the town square on the narrow unpaved road that was lined with the steep-gabled wooden houses typical of the region, houses of one story, with a few large windows, that were not at all unlike those that my grandfather would draw, with his blue Parker pen with the nib that he would lick before writing, when I would ask him to show me what his house had been like, in the Old Country. We reached an isolated, very pretty old house standing on the bend of the road where it curves suddenly to the right, toward the cemetery. Alex knocked—not on the door but, as he likes to do, on a side window. A small dog barked from somewhere inside. Outside, there was a big yard with chickens and more dogs bustling about; there were plum trees in bloom. Alex knocked again. Finally, a tiny, solid old woman opened the door. She peered over Alex's shoulder and then looked at us; then she looked back at Alex. This Olga was very old, plump but with the cool, translucent skin of extreme old age, and for some reason everything about her made me think about food: her face was as round as a loaf of bread, her two bright blue eyes peering out between fat cheeks, like raisins baked into a cake. Alex started his little speech, and she suddenly seemed to relax—without, however, smiling—and motioned us in.

Again we filed into a strange living room. The house was a comfortable one, with several airy rooms whose large windows were hung with exquisite lace curtains; on every available wall elaborate rugs, weavings, and tapestries were hung. Dishes and glasses glistened in substantial-looking, glass-fronted cupboards. Again chairs were fetched, again we sat down; but this time something was different. (For one thing, I noticed that no food was being offered, and this struck me as numinous.) Alex was talking, and once again I heard the name *Jäger*, and she said something twice, and before Alex even translated, I knew it would be different, because she was saying, very emphatically, *Znayu, znayu*, making an impatient little gesture with both hands, as if it were plain what she was saying.

I know, I know.

That much Ukrainian I had picked up, in the days since we'd arrived, the days of disappointment and bickering and rain. Olga nodded vigorously and said it again, and then started talking animatedly to Alex, who was trying to keep up as best he could.

She knew these Jägers very well, he said. It's not just that she's heard the last name, but she knew this family very well. They had a . . . butchery?

I nodded and said, hoarsely, *butcher shop*. At this point Alex interrupted himself to assure us that he hadn't provided her with that detail, the information about what kind of business they had had. He knew how frustrated we'd been, and wanted to guarantee the authenticity of this particular memory of them and their lives.

She knows, he went on. She remembers.

It was the sudden and vertiginous sense of proximity to them, at that moment, that made my sister and me start crying. This is how close you can come to the dead: you can be sitting in a living room on a fine summer afternoon, sixty years after these dead have died, and talk to a plump old woman who is gesturing vigorously, who, you realize, is exactly as old now as Shmiel's eldest daughter would have been, and this old woman can be this far away from you, a yard away; that's how close she can be. In that moment, the sixty years and the millions of dead didn't seem bigger than the three feet that separated me from the fat arm of the old woman. I was crying, too, because it was a moment that brought me closer to others of my dead. I felt intensely the presence of my grandfather, who before this moment had been the last living person I'd talked to who had known them, and suddenly the twenty years since he had died seemed to shrink, too. And so I sat there, the tears bathing my eyes, thankful that Jennifer was crying as well, and listened to Olga talk. She said the name again, and looked at my pictures, and kept nodding. Alex went on.

She said that they were very nice, very cultural people, very nice people.

Even through my emotion I smiled to myself, because I knew that my mother, with her family's vanity, the Jäger self-importance, would love the fact that Olga has remembered this one quality above all. Nothing too specific, but something just specific enough, if you are the kind of person who believes the stories you hear, to ring true.

But here again, as close as we've gotten, there was the inevitable distance.

She doesn't know what happened to them, Alex went on after a brief exchange with Olga. Not to this particular family. She knows that they, like others, other Jews, they suffered very much.

It is of course possible to learn about the sufferings of the Jews of Bolechow without having to go to a town that is now called Bolekhiv and track down elderly ladies who witnessed certain of those sufferings. You can, for instance, check in the Holocaust encyclopedia and learn there that the Germans entered the town on July 2, 1941, and that the first Aktion, the first mass liquidation, took place in October of that year, when approximately one thousand Jews were rounded up, confined in the Dom Katolicki, the Catholic community center house, and, after being tortured there for a day in various ways, they were brought to a mass grave and shot. You can read that the Jewish population of the town, which had been about three thousand at the beginning of the decade, swelled by thousands who were brought in from small neighboring villages. You will learn, further, that the second Aktion took place about a year later, when, after a three-day manhunt, a few thousand were herded into the town square outside of the city hall building—the place where we'd parked our car when we got to Bolechow, the place where the goat had been wandering around—and that there five hundred people were murdered on the spot, with the remaining two thousand deported on freight trains to the camp at Belzec. According to the Holocaust encyclopedia, moreover, most of the remaining Jews were killed in December 1942, leaving only about a thousand by 1943, of whom most were eventually murdered, with "only a few" escaping into the nearby forests to join the partisans.

But the information that you'll get from the Holocaust encyclopedia is, for all its detail, impersonal, and if you're a person who grew up listening to elaborately detailed stories, it won't satisfy your hunger for the particulars of what happened to your relatives, which is of course what I was hoping for when, in my senior year of high school, I'd written to Yad Vashem, the Holocaust memorial museum in Israel, to find out what information they had on the Jews of Bolechow, and they sent me back a photocopy of the "BOLE-KHOV" entry in the Holocaust encyclopedia, which is one place you can get the details I've just mentioned. For instance, that photocopy will not be able to tell you what Olga told us that day—particulars not of the deaths of my relatives, it's true, but other particulars, details that make you think about things differently. A quarter century after I'd heard back from Yad Vashem, I sat in this old woman's living room and listened to her give this generic story a new specificity. I had wondered, when I was eighteen, what "being tortured for twenty-four hours" might mean. She told us that the Jews had been herded into that Catholic community center at the northern edge of the town, and that there the Germans had forced the captive Jews to stand on each other's shoulders, and had placed the old rabbi on the top; then knocked him down. Apparently this went on for a good many hours. (It was much later, in Australia and then Israel and then Scandinavia, that I learned the rest, the kinds of details you would know about only if you'd been inside.)

"Brought to a mass grave and shot"? The thousand or so Jews who perished in the Dom Katolicki Aktion of October 1941 were shot in the Taniawa forest, a couple of kilometers outside of town. But during one of the "small" Aktions that took place in 1943—by which time there were only about nine hundred Jews alive in Bolechow, working in improvised labor camps—groups of Jews, a hundred or so here, a couple of hundred there, were taken to the cemetery and shot there in mass graves, although these mass graves could not compete in size with the one in Taniawa where, we were told two years after we talked with Olga, the earth continued to move for days after the shootings, because not all of the victims were actually dead when the grave was filled in. Still, a certain detail that Olga gave us about one of the "small" Aktions has stayed in my mind ever since, perhaps because of the way it marries the utterly mundane and accessible with the absolutely horrible and unimaginable, and because of that improbable link permits me, in some very small way, to imagine the scene. Olga told us that the sound of the machine-gun fire coming from the cemetery (which was, after all, just up the road from her house) was so terrible that her mother, then a woman in her forties, took down a decrepit old sewing machine and ran the treadle, so that the creaky noise would cover the gunfire. The gunfire, the sewing machine.

Whenever Olga described some particularly horrible incident, like this one, she would squeeze her eyes shut and make a downward-thrusting motion with her fat hands—an eloquent gesture of literal repulsion. It was the kind of gesture my grandmother or mother might have made, while clucking her tongue and saying *nebuch*.

It strikes me as strange that Friedman, the modern, the product of the century of Freud, shows no psychological interest in the missing (or immaterial) words that Cain said to Abel, and is instead deeply preoccupied with a detail that might strike us as unworthy of extended analysis: "it was while they were in the field." "What," Friedman asks, "is the significance of informing us that they are in a field at the time?" In order to arrive at a satisfactory explanation, Friedman rehearses the extensive history of violent sibling conflict that runs throughout the Bible, from Cain's murder of Abel to Solomon's execution of his brother Adonijah, of internecine rivalry between brothers both real and metaphorical: between Jacob and Esau, between Joseph and his brothers, between Abimelek and his ("killing seventy of his brothers," Friedman remarks), the wars between the tribes that made up the people Israel—Benjamin against all the others; Israel against Judah—the conflict between David's sons Absalom and Amnon. Friedman goes on to make a fascinating observation: that the word "field" recurs repeatedly, as a kind of leitmotif, in these stories of sibling violence. Esau is a "man of the field"; Joseph begins the story of the dream that so offends his brothers with the detail that they were binding sheaves "in the field"; a woman attempts to persuade King David to pardon Absalom for his act of fratricide by inventing a story about one of her own sons' murder of the other—a crime that took place "in the field"; the story of the conflict between Benjamin and the other tribes (narrated in Judges 20 and 21) twice refers to "field."

What Friedman deduces from all this is surely correct: that "the recurring word, therefore, appears to be a means of connecting the many instances of brother killing brother." And yet there is, to me, something about this that is, once again, unsatisfyingly concrete. Indeed, even though he does go on to speculate about the psychological implications of the well-known fratricide motif—"it recognizes that sibling rivalry is felt by nearly all humans, and it warns us to be sensitive to keep our hostile feelings in check— and to be sensitive to our siblings' feelings as well"—it seems, to me at least, that there is not merely a literary but a psychological resonance to the detail of all that violence taking place in the field; and Friedman's failure to speculate about it leads me to wonder whether the commentator has any siblings. For it strikes me as psychologically natural (and we know that it is historically true) that if you are going to do something terrible to your sibling, to vent your rage for the resentment that has smoldered so long, you plan carefully to do it outside, someplace where you think nobody can see you.

TWENTY MINUTES INTO our talk, Olga's husband, Pyotr, arrived home from church. A small, surprisingly fit and muscular man of nearly ninety wearing thick glasses and a worker's cap, he was dressed in an old suit of indeterminate color and a tight vest: a peasant in his Sunday best. He, too, immediately recognized the family name, and he told us things, too. That anyone who tried to help the Jews would be shot, for instance, which of course we knew—Nina had told us, and Maria had, too, and Nina had made sure to remind Olga as well, apparently, as we began talking to her. "Some Jews were employed in the local tanneries," the encyclopedia had said. "Later, Jews were employed in lumber work at a special labor camp." What Pyotr told us was that when, as a worker at the lumber mill, he tried to use some Jews to fill a workers' quota, the Germans had threatened him. *Do you really need Jews?* he remembered them saying. *Do you really want trouble?* And as he said this I was torn between wanting to believe him, wanting to believe that the openness and friendliness that every Ukrainian we'd met on this trip had shown us, knowing that we were Jews, knowing what we were looking for, would have been shown in the past as well; and trying to be dispassionate—trying to remember, as these two and everyone else said how much the Ukrainians had tried, or at least wanted, to help the Jews, even as we sat across from these people, as we'd sat across from others who'd welcomed us so generously, even lavishly into their houses, as we'd sat across from Maria and Nina, that nobody has ever told a story without having some kind of agenda.

We sat and listened to Olga and Pyotr, and for the first time I was glad not to have specific information about my relatives, because now that I was there I wasn't sure I wanted to know which of these things they had endured. I thought of those people in the Dom Katolicki, forced to form a terrible human pyramid. Who were they? Whoever they were, they were not nameless supernumeraries; each was a someone, a person—a teenage girl, say—with a family, a story, a cousin, maybe, in America whose children might one day return and find out just what happened to her and try to restore her identity to her, if not for her sake then certainly for their own peace of mind . . .

And then, as our conversation came to a close, and I realized that we'd get no closer to knowing anything specific about Shmiel and his family, that by being here in person we still hadn't come any nearer to some fact, some detail that could either prove or disprove the stories we'd always heard (was there a castle nearby? I'd asked everyone we met, remembering what I'd over-heard my grandfather saying, ages ago; and the inevitable answer came again, as I always knew it would, that there was no castle, no place to hide)—as our conversation came to a close we heard a final detail. *Brought to a mass grave and shot.* Pyotr recalled the final Aktion, when the Jews were marched to the cemetery and shot in a mass grave.

Where was the road they walked on? my brother had asked.

Olga hoisted herself up vigorously, pointed out the window, and said, Here! and Nina clapped a hand to her mouth in astonishment, apparently hav-ing never heard this story before, as if she couldn't believe that something at once so enormous and so remote had happened right *there*. But it was, in fact, still that close. It was the same road we had walked to get to this house, the road where Maria had left us.

Pyotr remembered further that in the last of the Aktions, as their neigh-bors the Jews of Bolechow were being marched, nearly naked, on this road— the few remaining Freilichs and Ellenbogens and Kornblühs and Grünschlags and Adlers, or whoever they may have been, the last of those generations of Bolechower Jews, the butchers and rag-and-bone men and timber mer-chants whose presence there, so completely unimaginable now, is nonetheless attested in the meticulously inked entries in long-forgotten censuses and business directories and now, however improbably, however bizarrely, available to anyone who owns a computer—that as the last of the Jews of Bolechow walked naked, two by two, to the deaths whose date and precise location appears on no official record, they called out in Polish to their neighbors—that is, to Olga, who was still standing and pointing out the window, and to the others—"Stay well," "So long, we will not see each other anymore," "We'll not meet anymore."

As Alex translated Pyotr's description of the death march of his neighbors, I remembered the exact timbre of my grandfather's voice on the telephone when he would say "So long": those opulent liquid *l*'s of the Polish Jews, a pronunciation that has, now, nearly vanished from the earth. But this wasn't why the anguished farewells stuck in my mind, and were the most terrible of all the details we heard that day. It was only later, after I'd returned to the States, that I realized that that single detail connected what we had heard, that one day in Bolechow, the day on which everything depended, to something I'd remembered from Shmiel's letters: the self-conscious leave-taking, the unthinkable good-bye. *I bid you farewell and kiss you from the bottom of my heart.*

SO LONG, WE will not see each other anymore.

It is a matter of recorded fact that many of the most violent savageries carried out against the Jews of Eastern Europe were perpetrated not by the

Germans themselves, but by the local populations of Poles, Ukrainians, Lith-
uanians, Latvians; the neighbors, the intimates, with whom the Jews had lived
side by side for centuries, until some delicate mechanism shifted and they
turned on their neighbors. Some people find this strange—not least, the Jews
themselves. More than one survivor I interviewed, in the years following that
first trip to Bolechow, expressed bemusement, or anger, or rage that the people they had considered to be neighbors could, in the next moment, become
killers.

Cannibals, a women in Sydney would spit. I call them *cannibals*. We lived
next door to them for years—and then *this*.

Another of the Australians I later came to know consistently and rather
casually referred to the Ukrainian collaborators as *butchers,* the way you might
say that so-and-so is a real *operator* or someone else a real *go-getter*. One afternoon he said to me, Strutinski was a well-known butcher, he killed many people. And there was a butcher, Matwiejecki, who boasted that he personally
killed four hundred Jews himself. There was also a family known as Manjuk—
a family of Ukrainians, they spoke a perfect Yiddish, and two of the brothers
turned against the Jews in the Holocaust and they killed many Jews, too.

They spoke a perfect Yiddish? I asked, bemused. This man in Australia nodded and explained to me that sure, many of Bolechow's Gentiles, Polish as
well as Ukrainians, spoke perfect Yiddish: that's how close they all had been.

With a rueful grin he said, We were the first multiculturals.

It seemed to me that behind the rue, the bitter disbelief of the people
I talked to, to say nothing of the incredulity with which most people confront the fact that near neighbors can easily murder one another, given the
right combination of circumstances—a thing that we have seen, of course,
more recently than 1941—that behind the bitterness and disbelief there is
an assumption, rather generic and perhaps optimistic, that it is harder to kill
those to whom you are close than it would be to kill total strangers. But I am
not so sure. The crook and the flail, the broken arm, the iron leg braces, the
terrible forced marriage, *I write to you saying that you're out of your mind*. The
only time I ever had the boldness to ask my father why he'd stopped speaking
to his brother, an annihilating silence that lasted the better part of my entire
life, he replied, Sometimes it's easier to deal with strangers.

In, interior, intimus. Closeness can lead to emotions other than love. It's the
ones who have been too intimate with you, lived in too close quarters, seen
too much of your pain or envy or, perhaps more than anything, your shame,

who, at the crucial moment, can be too easy to cut out, to exile, to expel, to kill off.

It is perhaps worth noting that our medieval commentator, Rashi, is more interested in explicating God's famous question, "Where is Abel your brother?" whereas our modern commentator focuses on Cain's equally famous reply, which he translates as "Am I my brother's watchman?" Rashi wonders why the all-knowing God bothered to ask Cain a question the answer to which God must have known. Here once again, his primary interest is psychological rather than literary. Why does God question Cain? "To enter [into a conversation]," Rashi says, "with words of calm" as an inducement to the guilty brother: "Perhaps he would repent and say, 'I killed him and sinned against You.' " For the French commentator of the Middle Ages, God's question has nothing to do with curiosity——how could it?——but instead reflects a touching psychological nuance: God's desire to give Cain a chance to admit his guilt. When I read this I am reminded that apart from being a great sage, Rashi was a parent.

*Friedman rightly refuses to render Cain's words in their best-known form: "Am I my brother's keeper?" He does so because the English word "watchman" nicely recapitulates a repeated motif in the Hebrew, which is an ongoing play in Genesis on the root of the word "watch," sh-m-r. Thus man is placed in the Garden of Eden to work it and "watch over" it, ul'*sham'rahu*; after man's fall, the cherubim are assigned to "watch over" (*lish'm'or*) the way to the Tree of Life; and later on, God promises to uphold his word to Abraham and his descendants because Abraham "kept my watch" (wayyi*sh'mor*). So the phrase is associated with loyalty——and, of course, disloyalty. It is in this context, Friedman argues, that we must understand Cain's reply to God: "Now the first human to murder another questions cynically his responsibility to watch out for his brother." It is only in the context of Genesis's ongoing preoccupation with the idea of "watching over," in other words, that we can fully appreciate the extent of Cain's failure as a brother.*

AFTER WE TALKED to Olga and Pyotr, we left Bolechow and returned to L'viv. Because I felt we had gotten something concrete, something specific, and hence was satisfied, and because we were all feeling somewhat drained, I was almost afraid when, as we were getting into the car, a group of old Ukrainian women ambled past through the square and Alex, trying to be helpful, shouted across the grass to them, asking whether they'd known a family called Jäger. The women looked small, framed against a large, two-story house that,

Alex told us, had undoubtedly once belonged to some Jews, as had most of the houses that fronted the Ringplatz. The three of them talked rapidly among themselves, and even from perhaps a dozen yards off we could see their silver dental crowns flashing. One of them, after consulting with the others, finally turned and shouted back at Alex, shrugging her arms in the universal gesture of innocent ignorance. She talked for a minute or so. Then Alex nodded to them and turned to us.

They knew no one called Jäger, he said. They only remember one Jewish family called Zimmerman. It means something to you?

No, I told him, I who knew the entire family history, the intricate genealogical trees; it meant nothing to us. We all got in the car, obscurely relieved, and started the drive back to L'viv.

On the drive back we were all quiet, trying to absorb what we'd heard—the details that, at last, we had about what happened, even if they weren't the specifics of what happened to our relatives—which, it must be said, suddenly seemed less vital to have, now that we knew what we knew. But once we returned to our hotel a reactive volubility set in, and we all sat in the hotel lounge and talked late into the night about what we had seen and heard. Then we went back to our rooms. The conversation I had that night with Andrew, after we returned to our room, was very different from the one we'd had the night before, when we were still anxious and irritated and worried that we'd find absolutely nothing once we actually got to Bolechow. The night before, we had lain in the narrow twin beds of our hotel room, venting our minor irritations with each other and with the other siblings, something Jen had said that annoyed me, Matt's glum irritation with Andrew, and at some point Andrew had said, Maybe you just can't have a relationship with siblings.

Now, something indefinable had changed, and the air had cleared. Now we were excited. The trip to the town, the ebullience and hospitality of Nina, the translucent politeness of Maria, trying so hard to place a photograph of a face that, if she'd ever seen it, had disappeared off the earth two lifetimes ago, the cautious effusiveness of Olga and Pyotr—we had, after all, found something here; not exactly what we'd come for, perhaps, not *that* detailed: but we had made contact.

And so, filled with renewed energy at last, we all decided that we'd go back the next day, too—not to do more interviews, since we doubted we'd find anyone else, but to see the cemetery, to make at least a token visit to the place where members of my family had been buried for three hundred years.

We had no hope of finding specific graves. The headstones, we knew, would all be in Hebrew, eroded, and difficult to decipher; and besides, we knew that in these old Jewish cemeteries, family names were rarely used, since the custom was still the biblical one: here lies so-and-so, son or daughter of so-and-so. And we knew, too, from an earlier visit Alex had made, that there were hundreds and hundreds of them. Another haystack; more needles. Still, we went.

The hour-and-a-half drive from L'viv to Bolechow seemed shorter the next day; we were all in high spirits, still talking about our discoveries of the day before. Our luck had changed. And indeed, as we pulled up alongside the little creek that runs along one side of the ancient cemetery, Matt started shouting.

Stop! Stop! Sima Jäger! Sima Jäger! he said, over and over, pointing off to the right.

Over where he was pointing there was one solitary headstone, there at the top of the hill. It had Roman rather than Hebrew characters, and what they said was: SIMA JAGER. Because I had been studying these people since I was thirteen, I knew right away that this was my grandfather's great-aunt. We parked the car and scrambled up the weedy hill. We spent a great deal of time there, photographing headstones, videotaping them, and as we left, I did what Jews do when they visit cemeteries, which is to put a rock on top of the tombstone. I found a rock and placed it on Sima's headstone, and took some other rocks from that place, too, to put on my grandfather's grave once we returned to New York. Off in the distance, over by the edge of the cemetery where the procession of listing stones came suddenly to a halt, blond Ukrainian children were swinging in an old rubber tire from the arm of a great old oak. They were beautiful children, and Matt, who more than anything loves photographing children—although because of this trip, and the many others he and I would take together, for a long time he did nothing but photograph the very old—couldn't resist pausing to take pictures of the towheaded, slender-faced boys and girls as they played among the graves of forgotten Jews. In one of these photographs, one of the boys has clambered atop a particularly large and solid-looking stone—clearly the monument of someone of no little stature. Long after we returned home, I noticed for the first time that the name on the stone was KORNBLUH. The inscription elaborates: it's the grave of a girl who died before she could be wed . . .

We stood there, watching Matthew take his pictures. The largish patch of

earth over which the tire arced back and forth with its cargo of squealing children was subtly discolored and very hard, as if it had been tamped down on
purpose, long ago.

*A notorious problem of translation arises in the Cain and Abel story. What the Hebrew
actually says at one point is "the voice / sound your brother's bloods are crying to me
from the ground." Because* kol, *"voice" or "sound," is singular yet both the word for "blood,"*
d'mây, *and the form of the verb "to cry out,"* tso'akiym, *are plural, a way must be found
to resolve the two when translating God's statement. One way, followed by most translators,
is simply to ignore the grammar and to translate the sentence like this: "The voice of your
brother's blood is crying . . . " But this is clearly incorrect, since a singular noun, "voice,"
cannot have a plural verb, "are crying." The editors of Rashi's commentary, in their own
translation of this passage, convey the odd syntax while making sense of it: "the sound
of your brother's bloods, they cry out to Me from the ground!" In other words, the phrase
"The sound of your brother's bloods" becomes, essentially, a slightly jagged interjection,
but still, strictly speaking, syntactically disconnected from the actual statement, which
is that there are things that are crying from the ground. (Rashi, incidentally, explains
the strange plural "bloods" in two ways, one rather figurative and the other quite lit-*

eral. Rashi first thinks poetically: he imagines that the plurals refer to "his blood and the blood of his offspring." He then thinks practically, the way a man would think who meant to do murder:"Alternatively, because [Cain] made in [Abel] many wounds, because he did not know from where his soul would depart.")

Friedman's translation is far bolder and, I cannot help thinking, far more effective: "The sound! Your brother's blood is crying to me from the ground!" Here, he makes no bones about wresting that disturbing singular noun, The sound! from the rest of the sentence entirely, so that it stands isolated as a pure exclamation of horror. The effect of this is twofold. First, it is both moving and somehow disturbing to think that the sound of blood shed in violence could be so terrible to hear that even God can react no more articulately than to cry out as a mere human might, as if clasping his hands to his ears: The sound! But what is really uncanny about this way of handling the strange Hebrew of the text is that it suggests, quite vividly, that even after it is shed, screams of innocent victims do not cease to issue from the earth where their blood was spilled.

WE LEFT THE cemetery behind and walked back to the center of town. There, we stopped in front of the house that stands on the site of Shmiel's house, to take some pictures. As we did so, a tall young Ukrainian, with the blond crew cut and icon's long face that you see all over this area, emerged from the spacious house and asked us, not without a kind of aggressive suspiciousness, who we were and what we were doing. Again, Alex talked; again, the same story. And again, the unexpected welcome. The boy's face—he couldn't have been more than twenty-five—split into a huge grin, and he motioned us all inside.

He says it's a big honor, Alex said, not for the first time that day. He says, Please come in.

And so once more we filed in, and the boy, whose name was Stefan, begged us to sit in the living room, where among the few decorations there was a modest reproduction of *The Last Supper*. He disappeared into the kitchen, and we overheard an urgent, whispered conversation between Stefan and his pretty blond wife, Ulyana. Soon after he emerged with a bottle of cognac and said something to Alex.

He's inviting you all for a drink, Alex explained. We all made polite noises of refusal, until it became clear that to refuse would be rude. We let him fill our glasses, and we drank. We drank toasts to my grandfather, who was born somewhere very near the spot we were sitting on; we drank toasts to America, and to Ukraine. It wasn't even noon yet. The high emotion and extreme improbability of the long morning was beginning to take its toll; we were all a bit silly. Ulyana bustled in the kitchen, and before long Stefan emerged holding two dried whitefish by the tails, explaining to Alex that he wanted us to take them home with us. He insisted on another round, and again we drank toasts. Stefan said we all looked alike, and I replied that this certainly reflected well on the honor of our mother. Laughter, more toasts.

Then, thinking of the long and spacious property outside, which ran a good ways down the road toward the church, and which had orchards of apple and plum and quince trees, too, I asked Alex to ask him how they'd come to live in this particular house. Stefan replied, with a smile, that it had belonged to his wife's father, who'd acquired it after the war. From whom had his father-in-law gotten it? we asked. The boy spread his hands in a gesture of bemusement, and smiled the same frowny smile that Maria had given us twenty-four hours earlier, when I'd asked about the castle.

He doesn't know, Alex said, although I already knew what *nye znayu* meant. Even if I hadn't known that this towheaded boy with the long, high-boned face of a beautiful Orthodox icon was saying *I don't know*, I'd have expected it anyway. No matter: if Olga was the closest in time that we'd come to what we were searching for, surely the half hour we spent in that house was the closest in space. On that very spot, they had all lived; and, for all we knew, died as well. It wasn't until Sydney that we realized how wrong we were.

As we walked outside toward the car, Stefan suddenly rushed up to us with a basket. It was filled with apples, tiny green unripe apples that he'd shaken from one of the trees. He held up the basket and thrust it in our direction, saying something to Alex.

For your mother, Alex said. So she will have fruit from the house that would have been hers!

It was a kind and touching gesture. But I knew that it wasn't, in fact, the house where my family had lived and my grandfather had been born, hadn't been the house where Shmiel wrote those letters. We had already been told that that one had been torn down, either during the war, at the Germans' behest, or immediately afterward, to make way for the larger, more modern ones constructed by the Ukrainians who, freed at last from the Poles and the Jews who, some of them had always felt, had overshadowed them, oppressed them, exploited them, were, at least until their own turn came, finally the sole inhabitants of the town.

When Cain's crime is discovered, God announces his punishment: Cain, he says, will be more cursed than the earth that drank his brother's blood; the earth will no longer be bountiful to him; he will wander the earth a perpetual exile. Much depends on whether we interpret Cain's response to this dire news as a question or a statement. Does Cain declare, "My crime is greater than I can bear!" or does he wonder, "Is my crime greater than I can bear?" And is it "I shall be hidden from your presence" or "Shall I be hidden from your presence?" Friedman, writing for his modern audience, takes the text at face value—that is, as an abject statement: Cain has no idea how he will bear his guilt and his exile. Rashi, typically, worries about the hidden implications of the text.

For Rashi, a chastened Cain is asking a resigned, rhetorical question that assumes a negative response: he knows well that no, his crime is not greater than he can bear, that he will be able, somehow, to endure his sin, since (as Rashi points out), if God bears "the higher realms and the lower realms," how could it be that one man cannot bear his punishment? And he knows full well that no, he will not be hidden from God's presence: for how, knowing God's great power, could he ever be hidden from God? (A question, of course, that begs the perhaps more difficult question of why, if no crime is hidden from God, God allows the crimes to be committed in the first place.) For many people it will be difficult not to prefer this older reading, because it suggests that, at least in retrospect, Cain realizes that however far off he might go, into whatever seemingly remote fields and hidden places, the criminal will still be seen by the eyes of God.

THERE WAS ANOTHER house that had preoccupied me during our trip.

This house, which is located in Striy, formerly *Stryj*, the small city between L'viv and Bolechow, still stood; the problem was finding it. It had belonged to Mrs. Begley, my friend's mother, the one who kept correcting my pronunciation of the names of Polish towns. Despite my bad Polish accent, however, she was intrigued by my interest in her own vanished world, and soon after that first meeting, Mrs. Begley had me to tea at her apartment on the Upper East Side. At first she seemed skeptical about the intensity of my interest, but soon she was showing me things: old photographs, the Yizkor book from Stryj. She is not a sentimental woman—when she said not to bring any house gifts, that first time I went to her home for tea, in January 2000, and I brought a bunch of flowers, she was actually annoyed; or so it seemed then to me, who hadn't yet learned to read her complicated signals—but she cried, a tiny bit, on that first Saturday at her house, when she was showing me the Yizkor book.

Seventeen, she said, embarrassed and annoyed by her tears as she pointed to a blurry photograph of some vanished boy—a nephew, a cousin, I can't remember now. *Seventeen* he was, he almost made it out.

Then she made an impatient gesture and made me sit at the table, with its fresh white cloth and its dish of pickles, its tray of slices of black bread and lox, the white plate with its formations of cookies and pastries. Her maid, Ella, a soft blond Polish woman in, perhaps, her fifties, nervously approached with a teapot.

You shouldn't have done all this, Mrs. Begley! As I spoke I suddenly felt as if I were twelve years old, repeating, dutifully, the reflexive courtesies of my Long Island upbringing.

She gave me a look that wasn't adorable. What do you want me to do? she said, a tone of voice that mixed irritation and indulgence. I'm a Polish Jewish lady. This is what I do.

I ate the salmon, the cookies.

And so it went over the next few months. There was something very formal, almost ritualistic, about these visits; until fairly recently she refused to call me anything but *Mr. Mendelsohn*. The phone would ring and a voice would say, *Mr. Mendelsohn, why don't you come for tea next week, Friday would be good, yes, Friday, all right, I'll see you then.* When I arrived she would be waiting in the narrow front hall, upright and elegant in one of the midnight-blue velvet hostess dresses she favored. I would proffer the flowers I'd brought, and ignoring them, she'd shake my hand instead and say, as Ella took the flowers away, Come have something to eat. The two of us would walk slowly down the hall into the dining room, and there we would eat the salmon and cookies and drink the tea, which depending on the weather was either hot or iced, and talk about my children or her children and grandchildren and great-grandchildren. Sometimes, after eating, we would go off into the living room, with its dozens of framed photographs of her son and his children and grandchildren, its deep sofa and fresh flowers, with that slightly stale air common in rooms in which there is not a great deal of swift movement, the air of contemplation rather than of activity, the atmosphere of a museum or a memorial, and she would sit in her chair in the corner, high-backed and authoritative, and I would perch on the edge of the deep soft sofa, and talk some more. Then, after not too long, she'd reach for her stick and, rising, as queens or prime ministers do when they want gently but firmly to indicate that the audience was now over, she would say *All right then, so good-bye and thank you.* She would offer me her knotted, cool, paper-dry hand, the way a deposed empress might give hers to a courtier who had known her before the revolution, and I would go.

By the time these visits were taking place, my grandfather, whose stories and secrets and lies I have spent a good part of my life preserving and unearthing and untangling, had been dead a quarter of a century, and with him all the others. And now here I was, having tea every month with this woman, who had been born only eight years after my grandfather was born, who was of his generation and his culture. This is why I felt, when I first started visiting Mrs. Begley, that something had been unexpectedly restored to me, that I had cheated death just a little, just as she had. I had missed so much, when those elderly Jews who had surrounded me when I was a boy, and who had, it turned out, known so much that I now needed to know, were alive. This time, I told myself in the months when I was first getting to know Mrs. Begley, at the onset of the new millennium, I would not let anything slip by, I would be conscious of every word, I would forget nothing. By knowing her, I thought, I would make a restitution for all those others whom, because of youth or stupidity or both, I had ignored.

And so, immediately before I left for Ukraine, that summer in 2001, I had promised her that we would go to Striy and look for her house. A week or so before I rendezvoused with my siblings at Kennedy Airport I went to her apartment. She had things she wanted to tell me before I went, she had told me one day over the phone. So I went one Friday to her place. She was sitting ramrod straight in her chair in the living room, wearing a velvet gown, with her hand on her cane. We were all business that day: there was only iced tea in the living room as she dictated to me the names of the places I must see when I was there. *Morszyn,* she told me, pronouncing the name of a spa resort for which she still had promotional brochures, in Polish and French, from sixty years before. *Skole.* Then, her hand shaking almost imperceptibly, she drew on a piece of paper a map meant to indicate the location of the house she'd lived in when she was a girl in Rzeszów, a small city halfway between Kraków and L'viv. (I am holding the paper now.) Then she made me write down the address of the house in which she and her husband and then her son, my friend, had once lived in Striy. She was sitting there, austere, ancient, enjoying the fact that she was dictating to me, and pretending not to be excited.

In front of the house we had the *most* wonderful lilacs, she was saying. The most wonderful, you can't imagine.

I'd noticed that she often said *you can't imagine* when she wanted to evoke some positive, pleasant memory of her past, as if there were no point in trying to use more concrete, more descriptive adjectives for what had been good in the past, since after all, it was all gone. When she said this about the lilacs, I silently resolved to bring her back flowers from the garden of the house where she had lived so long ago. These flowers, I thought to myself, she would accept.

The day after we went to Bolechow for the first time, the day we drove back to see the cemetery, I told Andrew and Matt and Jennifer and Alex that I really wanted to stop in Striy. At first everyone enjoyed the challenge of finding Mrs. Begley's house, and of course it was impossible to resist the idea of doing a favor for an old Jewish lady, a Holocaust survivor, back in New York. (They hadn't met her, and I was amused to think what they would think if confronted with this particular old lady, so different from the effusive, adoring old ladies we knew from our childhood.) But the search soon disintegrated into frustration. The problem with this house was, in a way, the inverse of the problem with the house that now occupies what used to be lot #141 in Bolechow. There, we found the location but the house itself had been destroyed—it was the same place, but a different structure. Here, we were told that the house still stood—*a big house on the main avenue of the town,* everyone knew of it—but we couldn't find it. *Number Five, Third of May Street,* Mrs. Begley had told me when she'd given me that list of places to see in Galicia; but history, I have learned, has a way of making a mess of local geography, and Third of May Street had changed names so many times that it was difficult to know which of the streets and houses we saw in front of us corresponded to the streets and houses on a prewar map of Stryj we had managed to obtain . . .

. . . Now WE HAD obtained this map in the following way: When I told Alex that we wanted to stop in Striy, he told us that there was someone there that we'd certainly want to meet, given our interests—Josef Feuer, known far and wide as the last Jew of Striy. On the day we ended up spending so much time looking for Mrs. Begley's house, Alex drove us to a decrepit block of apartments on the outskirts of town, and we walked up a few flights of dank concrete steps to Feuer's apartment. The old man, stooped but dignified, with a short white beard and a scholar's air, beckoned for us to enter the cramped room, and the four of us shuffled in and took seats at the wooden table in the center of the room. For a while we chatted with Josef Feuer who, in a mixture of German, Yiddish, and Russian, from which I tried to provide a running translation for my siblings, told us the story of his survival, which was similar to the one I'd heard about Eli Rosenberg earlier that year: the narrow escape, the flight east into the Soviet Union, the service with the Soviet army, the return to a desolated town. Like Rosenberg, Feuer had married and stayed in his hometown, but unlike Rosenberg he'd done something else, too. As we sat there listening to his story, it was hard not to gawk, for the entire apartment had been turned into a private archive, a museum of an extinct culture, in which Feuer himself had assembled whatever fragments of Striy's lost Jewish life he could get his hands on: old prayer books, maps, yellowing documents, municipal surveys, photographs of people he knew and many he didn't, Yizkor books, boxes bulging with his various ongoing correspondences with Yad Vashem or the German government. It was from this moldering archive of old papers that he produced, when we told him why we'd come to Striy that day, several large old maps of the town; and it was from the fat mass of more recent papers that he took a recent exchange of letters that, he said, would provide us with an amusing story. He had, he said, written quite recently to the German government about getting them to erect a memorial at the site of the great Aktion in the Holobutow forest outside of the city, where in 1941 a thousand Jews were taken and shot; the site, he said, was overgrown and wild, and bones could be seen thrusting up from the ground.

As he told us this story, Feuer held up a copy of the letter he'd written, in German, to Berlin. Then he picked up another, bearing an official-looking governmental seal. The Germans, he said, had responded with great alacrity, and had proposed the following: that if Mr. Feuer and the other members of Striy's Jewish community could raise a certain amount of money toward the landscaping of the site at the Holobutow forest and the construction of the memorial on it, the German government would be more than pleased to match the amount.

At this point Feuer brandished a third paper: his response to the Germans' proposal. It's difficult, now, to remember the gist of it, since the opening of his letter was so distracting. It said, *Dear Sir, All the other members of the Stryjer Jewish community are in the Holobutow forest.* This fact, the accuracy of which we had no reason to doubt, was surely what led this scholarly and gentle man to turn to us, as he was leading us down the gray steps of his building when our interview had ended, and say to Matt, who at that moment snapped his picture, *Tell them that I am the Last of the Mohicans . . .*

. . . So it was Josef Feuer's map that we used to determine where Third of May Street must be. On the street that seemed the likeliest candidate, Alex stopped an extremely old woman wearing a head scarf. He begain to explain in Ukrainian what we were looking for, and then with an apologetic grimace on his wide, easygoing face, interrupted himself and turned to me.

The name of your friend in New York again?

Begley, I said, and then shook my head and corrected myself: *Begleiter.*

Ah, *Doktor Begleiter*! the woman exclaimed, before Alex had a chance to translate. She smiled broadly and said something to him in rapid Ukrainian. Then he turned to us and said, She says he was a *very* big doctor here.

Sixty years, I thought to myself, thousands of miles, and we'd managed to run into this woman on this street, who out of the blue had pulled this fact, the one that we wanted. Still, the concrete object itself, the house where the big doctor had lived, was impossible to retrieve. For nearly an hour we walked up and down this long avenue; at one point we videotaped a house that bore the number 5, although immediately afterward we were told that this particular part of the street hadn't, before the war, been part of Third of May Street proper. After a while my brothers and sister began to grumble, and so rather than continuing to look, I started taking pictures of every single house on the street that, we were assured, had once been Third of May Street. When I sheepishly showed these pictures to Mrs. Begley soon after our return from our trip to Ukraine, she made a face and shook her head wearily.

Achhh, it's *very* disappointing, she said while we were eating the elaborate lunch she'd prepared to celebrate my homecoming. She had looked at the slides I'd made, and as she did so all she kept saying was, I'm telling you, that wasn't my street.

Still, she hungrily peered at every photograph, every slide, every minute of the videotape we'd made of the streets of Striy, including the stark images of the city's once-great synagogue, now fallen in ruins, enormous trees growing out of its gutted interior and reaching easily for the sun, since there was no roof. *Look,* Mrs. Begley said as she and Ella and I rather uncomfortably perched on the foot of her bed across from the TV. She pointed and said, That was my life. After the video was over, we went into the dining room, where Mrs. Begley looked at the slides again and shook her head once more rather severely as Ella brought in an enormous tureen. I made this myself! Mrs. Begley said. Then she offered me stuffed cabbage and told me I was looking too thin.

WE SPENT THE day after the fruitless search for Mrs. Begley's house sight-seeing in L'viv. That evening, our last in Ukraine, Alex and his wife, Natalie, a doctor, hosted us all at a sumptuous dinner at their apartment. *The Ukrainians were the worst,* my grandfather had always told us. *Cannibals,* the lady in Sydney would hiss, later. *They were only nice to you because you're Americans, because to them you're more American than Jewish,* someone I would come to know well in Israel told me, when I described how generous, how gracious and kind all the Ukrainians had been to us during our six-day return to the Old Country, our two days in Bolechow. Knowing what I now knew—a very tiny part of what I would come to know—and seeing what I'd seen, the mass grave there in Bolechow, the roofless synagogue of Striy, it was tempting to believe them. But I knew other things, too, and had seen other things. Of course there were the terrible betrayals; but there had been the rescues, too, the unimaginable, risky acts of kindness. How, after all, do you know how people are going to behave?

The next day, a Wednesday, we all flew back to New York. The flight was long, we were exhausted, but we'd done and seen a lot, in the end, and we felt we had learned something; the trip had been a success after all. After our plane landed we all crammed into a taxi and raced toward Manhattan. Andrew was going to be spending the night in New York City before flying home to California the next day, but Matt and Jen, who both lived in Washington, D.C., were trying to make the eleven P.M. train back home. For some reason there was a lot of traffic heading into town from JFK, and we pulled up in front of Penn Station with just a minute or so to spare before the train was to leave. I can't tell whether it was because of relief that we'd made it just in time, or something else, that Matt, as he raced toward the station, suddenly turned around and said, Bye, I love you! as my cab started to pull away. Then they disappeared into the night.

AS IT TURNED out, it was not until many months after our return from Ukraine that we began to learn, finally, the details of what had happened to Shmiel Jäger and his family.

On a cold February night in 2002 I was sitting in my apartment in New York City. I had had tea that day with Mrs. Begley, who still refused to call me anything but *Mr. Mendelsohn;* I'd been showing her another batch of photos of our trip that I'd only that day received back from the lab. So when the phone rang that evening, not three hours after I'd returned home, and a deep Central European voice said, Mr. Mendelsohn? I shot back, without missing a beat, Mrs. Begley?

Once again the voice said, Mr. Mendelsohn? and I realized it wasn't she. Flustered and slightly annoyed—I was embarrassed—I asked who it was.

My name is Jack Greene, the voice said, and I'm calling you from Sydney, Australia. I heard on the grapevine that you're looking for people who knew the Jäger family in Bolechow?

The line hissed softly. Immense distances.

Ye-e-e-ss? I said, stalling as I scrambled around my desk for a pen and then started to write GREEN(E?). AUSTRALIA → BOLECHOW. GRAPEVINE??? on a piece of paper.

Well, this voice from the other side of the planet was saying, in a plummy accent that admixed with pure Polish the unmistakable consonants and vowels of a Yiddish-speaker, You should know that I dated one of Shmiel Jäger's girls, and I'd be happy to talk to you.

And that is how we began, at last, to find them. Not on the trip itself; but, in a way, from having gone on the trip.

When we returned from Bolechow, we made tapes of the videos we'd taken there, which included videos of our interviews with Nina and Maria and Olga, and had sent copies to the remaining Jäger cousins, including Elkana in Israel. This turned out to be the beginning of the grapevine: Elkana had in turn invited some of the few remaining former Bolechowers over to watch the tape. One of these survivors was Shlomo Adler, the leader of the ex-Bolechower community in Israel, who during a flurry of e-mails much later on told us not to believe Pyotr, who may have convinced himself (Adler wrote) that he'd tried to help the Jews, but it was very unlikely, and told us not to bother trying to erect a memorial to the dead in the mass grave, because the stones would be vandalized and the construction materials stolen, and asked us, too, whether we'd noticed that there is no reference to the town's Jews in the little museum in Bolechow. Most important, it was he who had mentioned our trip to Jack Greene, who had been born *Grünschlag* and who now lives in Sydney, very near his younger brother, with whom, miraculously, he had survived the war, and who dated one of the Jäger girls, and who knew them, and who was the first of what eventually turned out to be the twelve remaining Jews of Bolechow who told us, in time, what had happened.

When Jack Greene said *I dated one of Shmiel Jäger's girls*, I had the same vertiginous feeling I'd had when Olga in Bolechow had said, *Znayu, znayu.* All that distance, all those years; and then there she was, right there across the table, there he was, chatting with me on the phone, there they were, still out there if you knew where to find them: remembering them.

Because his nighttime call had caught me by surprise, I asked Jack Greene after a few breathless minutes whether he wouldn't mind if I called him back later that week, so I'd have time to prepare an interview.

Sure, he said. Feel free to contact me whenever you like. For me it is as precious as it is to you.

A day or so later I called Australia and talked to Jack Greene for a long time on the phone, and it was from him, really, that we started to learn about Shmiel and his family, how they lived and how they had died. And smaller things, too. It was in this conversation that I learned that the "Ruchatz" of Shmiel's letters was really *Ruchele,* sometimes written *Ruchaly. Now the first thing I have to say to you*, Jack said that night, *was that the third daughter of Shmiel was Ruchele, spelled R-U-C-H-E-L-E.*

I protested that I was sure that Shmiel had written R-U-C-H-A-T-Z, and Jack laughed. No, no, he said, sometimes you would make a line across the *l,* and that's a *y,* not a *z.* When he said this I felt suddenly foolish and ashamed. I had been brought up to be deferent to old Jewish men, after all.

But he merely laughed and said, Look, I used to go out with her, so I know this. *Ruchele.*

ROOKH-eh-leh, I repeated to myself silently. I listened to him correcting me and thought, How could I get something as basic as a name so wrong? And yet despite the shame, the adolescent embarrassment, there was now this, another precious nugget of new information to add to my growing hoard: this Ruchele had been the third of the four. We had never known for sure what the order of the children was.

As Jack talked I listened intently, making sure that the little red light on my voice recorder was on, occasionally typing notes into a file I'd opened on my computer whenever he said something that struck me as particularly noteworthy. A lot of what he told me was undramatic—for instance, that young teenagers in Bolechow would go to see movies in the Catholic community entertainment center, the Dom Katolicki, although perhaps "undramatic" is inappropriate since it was in the same entertainment center that some of those teenagers were forced, only a few years later, to entertain their tormentors before being killed. He told me about the American movies they would see (Wallace Beery, he recalled) and about the meetings of the Zionist organization that he attended in order to see Ruchele, and about Shmiel's business, and about how Bronia *looked like her mother, exactly* and Shmiel had the first telephone in town, and that the boys and girls would take walks in the park in the evening, and that Ruchele did not have her father's showy personality.

She was a very placid girl, he said. Blond hair. In my eyes she was a *beautiful* girl.

Then he paused and, as if just then remembering, said, Frydka was a *very* good-looking one.

For reasons I would learn a few minutes later, the thought of Frydka led Jack Greene to the subject of the war years, and this is when he told me what he'd heard about our relatives' fates, although he emphasized that this was merely what he'd heard, since of course after a certain point he himself had been in hiding.

I can tell you, he began, that Ruchele perished on the twenty-ninth of October 1941.

I was startled, and immediately afterward moved, by the specificity of this memory.

I said, Now let me just ask you, why—because you remember the date so specifically—why do you remember the date?

As I wrote down RUCHELE → OCT 29 1941, I thought to myself, He must have really loved her.

Jack said, Because my mother and older brother perished on the same day.

I said nothing. We are each of us, I realized at that moment, myopic; always at the center of our own stories.

Then Jack went on.

He said he could only surmise that Shmiel, his wife, and the youngest daughter were taken in the second Aktion, early in September 1942, but that he knew for a fact that Frydka, the second girl, about whose employment prospects Shmiel had worried in a letter to my grandfather, had managed to get work in the barrel factory—one of the local industries that had been appropriated for the German war effort—and was still alive after that Aktion.

Thirty years after I'd started asking questions and making notations on index cards, I was finally able to write this: SHMIEL, ESTER, BRONIA, KILLED 1942.

I know I saw Frydka there in the factory after that Aktion, Jack said. Those who had positions as forced laborers had at least some chance of surviving, he said.

I wrote, BARREL FACTORY. FORCED LABOR → SURVIVE.

The idea was to get yourself a job for the war effort, this voice, which sounded so much like my grandfather's voice, said over the phone. And that gave you some feeling of security—that they wouldn't take you tomorrow. They might take you in three months, but not *tomorrow*.

A little later on he added that he'd heard that when it became clear that the few hundred remaining Jews in the town were going to be liquidated, Frydka and her older sister Lorka had escaped from Bolechow to join a group of partisans operating in the forest outside of the nearby village of Dolina. Unlike some local partisan groups, he said, this group was happy to take Jews. The group had been organized by two Ukrainian brothers, he added, named Babij.

Jack said, B-A-B-I-J, and I wrote, FRYDKA / LORKA $\rightarrow$ BABIJ PARTISANS.

Then I wrote DOLINA, and after a moment added TAUBE. The Mittelmarks were from Dolina; my great-grandmother Taube had been born there. It was in Dolina that she had played, and perhaps fought bitterly, with her older brother.

You see, Jack said, there were three Polish fellows, not Jews, and the boys were assisting the partisans, or they were in contact with them. And one night—I wasn't in Bolechow at the time, I was in hiding, but I heard this later—the boys were found out, and the Germans took the three Polish fellows and they shot them in town. That was exactly—well, more or less at the same time they wiped out the Babij group in the forest. I think there were maybe four survivors.

Four? I said.

Jack made a noise on the other end; wry amusement, perhaps, at my naïveté. Well, he said, think of Bolechow. Of six thousand Jews, we were forty-eight who survived.

Again I said nothing. I looked at my computer screen. FRYDKA / LORKA $\rightarrow$ BABIJ PARTISANS. I typed, BOYS HELPING WERE KILLED.

That night in February 2002, little guessing how far this story would end up taking me, how many miles and continents we would travel to find out what had really happened, who had really been helping and who had been found out and killed, I was more interested in the girls than in the boys, and so I said, I see. But by this time the girls were in the forest, no?

That's right, Jack said. The boys were in contact with the people in the forest, they used to visit them, they used to supply them, I don't know if with ammunition or with food, I don't know. They were killed because they were supplying them with something.

Right, I said. I typed the words SUPPLYING SOMETHING into the file I'd opened.

You see, the Germans implanted spies, Jack continued. That means, Jews who ran away, they were spying on the group and revealing everything. I imagine they were being forced or blackmailed into betraying them, somehow, something.

This made me snap up in my seat. As I typed JEWS → BETRAYED!!, I had a sudden idea of what must have happened, of how the story I was hearing now could have been connected to the stories, the fragments, that I'd heard long ago. Clearly (I thought), the betrayal of the Babij partisans had gotten garbled in translation somewhere between the event itself and the point at which someone told my grandfather and his siblings what had happened to Uncle Shmiel and his family; and somehow this sole element of the story, the *betrayal*, had gotten itself woven, over time, into my family's private narrative. My grandfather and his siblings and the others, all of them, had willingly believed this story, as we ourselves had in time, this story that my brothers and sister and I had traveled halfway across the world to confirm, because we wanted to believe that there *was* a story; because a narrative of greed and naïveté and bad judgment was better than the alternative, which was no narrative at all.

At the same moment that Jack Greene told me about the spies who ratted out the Babij group, and I realized what the origins of our family story had been, I remembered my mother's cousin Marilyn in Chicago as she recalled the reaction to the news of Shmiel's death—I remembered her using the word *screaming*—and I realized that I'd made the trip to Chicago, too, in the hopes of finding a drama. I saw then that I'd wanted to unearth something unpleasant in the history of my grandfather's and great-aunts' and -uncles' relationships with Shmiel, something that would confirm my private, suspicious narrative about a closer, more terrible betrayal of siblings by siblings, which was, after all, something I knew about, and something that could provide a coherent motivation for their failure to save Shmiel—if, of course, there *had* been such a "failure." My desire to have that narrative was no different from my grandfather's desire to believe the stories about the Jewish neighbor or the Polish maid. Both were motivated by a need for a story that, however ugly, would give their deaths some meaning—that would make their deaths be *about* something. Jack Greene told me something else that night: that like Shmiel, his own parents had been hoping to get their family to safety, hoping to get visas; but that by 1939 the waiting list for papers was six years long. (And by then, he said, everyone was already dead.) Because I am a sentimental person, I would like to think—we will, of course, never know—that my grandfather and his siblings did everything they could for Shmiel and his family. What we do know is that by 1939, nothing they could have done would have saved them.

All during our trip, I had been disappointed because none of the stories I'd known about was confirmed by what we heard and saw; all during the trip, I'd wanted a gripping narrative. It was only when I listened to Jack Greene that I realized I'd been after the wrong story—the story of how they'd died, rather than how they had lived. The particulars of the lives they had led were, inevitably, the kinds of unmemorable things that make up everyone's day-to-day existence. It is only when everyday existence ceases to exist—when knowing that you'll die in three months rather than tomorrow seems like an oasis of "security"—that such lost details seem rare and beautiful. The real story was that they'd been ordinary, and had lived, and then died, like so many others. And once again we learned that, of certain ordinary lives, and deaths, there is, surprisingly, still much more evidence than you might guess at first.

This is why, when I began to think that there was only so much I could get over the phone from this rich and unexpected new source of information, and when, as if reading my thoughts, Jack suddenly said that what I should *really* do was to come to Sydney and spend some time with him and his brother and, he now told me, a couple of other Bolechow survivors who lived there, I knew that I would go. They had been there, they had known them, and I knew that I had to see them. This man who had surfaced from nowhere to tell me in one phone call more than my family had ever known, this man who sounded like my grandfather when he spoke, had dated little Ruchele; and his mother had been killed on the day that she had been killed. We were bound, now, to Jack by bonds of both love and death.

There was another factor, too:

So I should really come to Australia? I asked Jack at the end of our conversation that night.

Don't hesitate, he said—

(OK, I won't! I interrupted: wanting to please him, the way I'd have tried to please my grandfather)

—because I won't last long.

So Australia was our next stop. And it was in Australia, when we met with Jack Greene and the four other Bolechower Jews who after the war had chosen to settle on that remote continent, as far as it is geographically possible to get from Poland, that the contours of the story came into focus at last, and we began to get the kind of concrete details that we'd wanted, the specifics that can transform statistics and dates into a story. What color the house was, how she held her bag. And then Australia led to Israel, where we met Reinharz and Heller, and Israel led to Stockholm, where we met Mrs. Freilich, and Stockholm led to Israel again, and Israel led to Denmark, where we met Kulberg, with his remarkable tale.

In the end, we got our story.

But there was one particular, one concrete fact that I already knew about one of the Bolechow Jägers even before we went on those other trips and met those other people. We knew, as I have said, that Ruchele Jäger, Shmiel's third daughter, died in the first Aktion, on either October 28 or October 29, 1941. We don't, and can't, know for sure exactly how old she was: for some reason, the Polish National Archives in Warsaw, while it possesses the birth certificates of her two elder sisters, cannot find those of Ruchele and her younger sister, Bronia. Jack Greene thinks she was sixteen, and this is probably true. But I do know one thing for certain, know it for a fact, and don't need any archive to tell me it's true: I know that Ruchele had to have been born after September 3, 1923.

I know this because that was the day on which another young woman named Rachel, *Ruchele,* died. Because Eastern European Jews only name their children after the dead—I and my four siblings are named after dead relatives, just as my grandfather and his six siblings were, and because of this practice people who are interested in Jewish genealogy have a remarkably reliable method of determining certain dates, if the information is otherwise lacking—I know for a fact that Shmiel's daughter Ruchele Jäger had to have been born after the death of her father's and my grandfather's sister: the first Rachel Jäger, born in 1896, the doomed bride whose tragic and unexpected death, also horribly premature, would later become, over the course of many years, my family's greatest story, a mythic narrative at whose heart, or so I believe, stands an even older legend about closeness and distance, intimacy and violence, love and death, that first of all legends, first of all myths about how easily we come to kill those to whom we are closest.

Although he punishes history's first murder severely, God declares that anyone who kills Cain will be avenged sevenfold. Here again, the medieval and modern commentators offer radically different interpretations of the text. The crux is the nature of the punishment of those who would kill Cain, expressed in the word shiv'ahthayim, *which literally means "sevenfold." Rashi once again goes to great lengths to get around the most natural reading of the verse; instead, he wants us to read it as being made up of two discrete elements. The first, he insists, is the half-sentence "Therefore, whoever slays Cain . . . !" Adducing syntactical parallels from elsewhere in the Hebrew Scriptures, Rashi insists that this half-sentence be read as an implied but unspecific threat against anyone who might be tempted to harm history's first murderer: "This is one of the verses which cut short their words," he argues, "and made an allusion, but did not explain. 'Therefore, whoever slays Cain' expresses a threat— 'So shall be done to him!' 'Such and such is his punishment!' But did not specify his punishment."*

This manipulation of the text leaves Rashi with a two-word fragment, shiv'ahthayim yuqqâm, "will suffer vengeance sevenfold." Rashi insists, however, that the implied subject of this statement is not, as we may be tempted to think, whoever might be tempted to slay Cain, but rather Cain himself. What God is saying here, according to Rashi, is, "I do not wish to take vengeance from Cain now. At the end of seven generations I take My vengeance from him, for Lamech will arise from among his children's children and slay him"—as indeed happens in Genesis 4:23.

Why is Rashi so eager to avoid a reading of the text that would suggest that a killer of Cain would be punished "sevenfold"—would, in other words, suffer seven times as much pain as the pain that he inflicted? (It is a question we are tempted to ask all the more since Friedman calmly accepts the more natural reading of this verse, as his translation indicates ["Therefore: anyone who kills Cain, he'll be avenged sevenfold"] and, even more, as the lack of any comment on his part seems to suggest.) A footnote to my translation of Rashi's commentary on this verse tells us why: "[T]he verse does not mean that God will punish him seven times as much as he deserves, for God is just and does not punish unfairly." As I read this, it occurs to me that perhaps the discrepancy between Rashi's and Friedman's approach stems from the difference between the eleventh and the twentieth centuries. I wonder if it is easier for us than it was for Rashi to imagine that maybe, after all, God could punish unfairly.

THE SIN BETWEEN brothers is now burned into our family story permanently, the recurrent theme of the past grafted, now, onto the future. On August 11, 2002, almost exactly a year to the day after we entered Bolechow, and precisely sixty years after the mechanism that would end up destroying my grandfather's brother and his family was set in motion, my sister, Jennifer, was married. As I have said, she is the only one of my siblings to have married a Jew. It is, of course, purely a coincidence—but a poetic one, nonetheless, one that couldn't be any more artistic if you'd made it up, had created it as a symbol for the fiction you were writing—that the family name of the man she married is *Abel*.

PART THREE

Noach,

or,

Total Annihilation

(March 2003)

The stream of Time, irresistible, ever moving, carries off and bears away all things that come to birth and plunges them into utter darkness, both deeds of no account and deeds which are mighty and worthy of commemoration. . . . Nevertheless, the science of History is a great bulwark against this stream of Time; in a way it checks this irresistible flood, it holds in a tight grasp whatever it can seize floating on the surface and will not allow it to slip away into the depths of Oblivion.
I . . .

Anna Comnena, *The Alexiad*

THE UNIMAGINABLE JOURNEY

A peculiar if structurally satisfying aspect of parashat Bereishit *is that this particular portion of Genesis, which begins with an account of Creation, concludes with God's decision to destroy much of what he'd invented at the beginning of the story. His dissatisfaction with humankind in particular starts out innocuously enough—the first sign is his decision to drastically limit the span of a human life, from nearly 1,000 years to a mere 120—but ends dramatically, with the deity's realization that the proliferation of the race itself has led to a proportional increase of vice and sin. "I regret that I made them," God says; "He regretted that He made them," the narrative echoes. This decision, taken at the end of* Bereishit, *is what sets the action of the next weekly reading,* parashat Noach, *in motion.* Noach, *the story of the Flood, is among the first sustained attempts in literature to present an image of what the total annihilation of a world might look like.*

I say "total annihilation," although to be strictly accurate the Hebrew word that God uses to describe his plans for mankind and all land-based life-forms—sea creatures are, interestingly, exempt—is more nuanced. What God says he plans to do to his own Creation is that he'll "dissolve" it: ehm'cheh. *Rashi anticipates confusion on the part of the reader who, he knows, expects some more conventional verb, such as "destroy" or "annihilate." (Friedman translates the word as "wipe out" without any comment, but he has much of interest to say about the elaborate and beautiful wordplay on the strong root-letters of Noah's name, N and H, that is threaded throughout the Flood narrative:* <u>N</u>oa<u>h</u> masa'<u>hen</u>, *"Noah found favor";* wayyi<u>nn</u>a<u>h</u>em, *"he regretted";* <u>nih</u>amtî, *"I regret";* watta<u>nah</u>, *"and the ark rested"; and so forth.) The medieval French commentator* reminds us that since humans were made of earth, God's act of dissolution, which will take the form of a terrible deluge that pours from the seas and falls from the skies, is akin to pouring water on figures of dried mud. When I read Rashi's remark, it occurred to me that, as any child who has played in the mud knows, water is necessary to the creation of such figures, too; Rashi's observation about the watery means of God's annihilation of mankind thus returns us to the moment of Creation——a nice complementarity.

This subtle linkage between opposites——creation, destruction——recurs throughout Noach. For instance, just as the destruction narrated in Noach is linked to the prior act of creation described in Bereishit by the medium of earth (or, so to speak, mud), a further detail in the Flood narrative suggests, in turn, that we should see a link between the enormous destruction caused by the Flood and the next act of "creation"——that is, the new beginning of life, among the few survivors, that follows the Flood and reestablishes humankind on earth. For we are told in various midrashic commentaries that the waters of the Flood, the torrents that obliterated all living things from the face of Creation, were hot and sulfurous; but we are told in the Torah itself, at the beginning of Noach, that the ark, the vehicle of rescue and redemption from those sulfurous torrents, was made of a wood known as gopher——a name, Rashi comments, derived from gaf'riyth, "sulfur." There is, therefore, a complex linkage between acts of creation, acts of destruction, and acts of revival in Genesis, suggesting that these distinct and seemingly opposed acts are, in fact, coiled in an infinite and intricate loop.

This interconnectedness suggests in turn another, larger point that the text wants us to be aware of. For if Noach were merely a tale of total annihilation——destruction without any survivors, without any new "creation"——it would soon lose our interest: it's the existence of those very few survivors that helps us, ironically, to appreciate the scope of destruction. Conversely, to appreciate the preciousness of the lives that were saved, it is necessary to have a thorough appreciation of the horror from which they were so miraculously preserved.

DEPENDING ON HOW you want to think about it, on how anxious you are about losing time, the trip from New York City to Australia takes either twenty-two hours or the better part of three days.

The journey is divided into two legs. The first of these, according to the stewardess on the Qantas 747 that took me and Matt to Sydney in March 2003 to meet Jack Greene and the other Bolechowers there, is the "short flight," although it constitutes what most people would think of as a significant journey in itself. We flew out of New York at 6:45 in the evening on the nineteenth, the day a war began——although, because we were in the air for so long, through the night on which the ultimatum expired and for most of the next day, too, we couldn't be sure we were at war until a day and a half later——and then made our way across the continent, to Los Angeles. This took about five and a half hours. Then there was a stopover of about an hour's duration in L.A., during which the plane had to receive a fresh crew because of, we were told, "industry regulations": no single crew, a stewardess explained, is permitted to work through both legs of the flight——to work, in other words, for the entire length of time we were going to be flying. This information lent an air of emergency to the proceedings.

Anyway, after we received our fresh crew, we all trundled back onto the plane, groggy and resentful, and then took off again. For the next sixteen hours, there was nothing beneath us but the Pacific Ocean. I had flown many times over the Atlantic, and had never really thought much about the size of oceans until I went around the world, to Australia, to meet five elderly Jews who had once lived in Bolechow and now lived there, five of what turned out to be twelve people still living who had once known Shmiel Jäger and his family, and who could tell me things about them. The Atlantic I had grown used to, and had come, I suppose, to seem manageable. The Pacific is vast.

It is during the second leg of this long flight that you are most likely to become disoriented with respect to time. For the better part of a day there is nothing beneath you but water, indistinct and undifferentiated; the neutral quality of what you are able to see, when you look out of your window, reflects the quality of the time you are passing as you fly, which also is indistinct and undifferentiated. It is time that has no quality at all. If you make this journey, a journey I had not imagined I would ever make, the extremely pleasant Qantas stewards and stewardesses will bring you your meals from time to time and, handing you a tray with some steaming sealed dishes on it, will tell you that it is breakfast, say, or dinner; but after a while it's difficult to tell whether these evenly spaced mealtimes are meant to correspond to those in the time zone you flew out of, or those over which you are flying, or perhaps some totally abstract, "virtual" time zone that exists in, and is particular to, the plane alone but nowhere else. In the end you must take their word for it, because you have no real sense of what time it really might be.

As I SAT in this plane, looking out the window and occasionally flipping through a dire-looking pamphlet about how to avoid something called "vascular thrombosis," a circulatory crisis that can occur if you spend too long in a commercial jetliner's pressurized cabin——which, of course, is precisely what Matt and I were doing——as I sat in this plane, hour after hour, I realized that the way in which the meals on board the plane had made me aware of a certain quality of time (or lack of quality) was reminding me of something from my childhood, something that had similarly connected mealtimes and the agonizing passage of bland hours.

As I have said, my mother grew up in an Orthodox household, ruled over by her grand and domineering father, in whose elaborate observance of all the various holidays his wife, my grandmother Gerty (or, depending on who was addressing her, and under what circumstances, *Golda*), was an expert accomplice, cooking for him the superb and strictly kosher meals for which she was justifiably "famous," in the tiny world that was her apartment building in the Bronx, even if my grandfather took pleasure in withholding the acclaim that everyone else gave her. (*So, how is it, Aby?* she would anxiously ask him after serving him a bowl of her soup, soups being her specialty; and he would answer, *Soft!*) She made her famous soups, my grandmother did, and her *kney-dlach* and *latkes* and, every Hanukkah, her *matzo brei,* crisp on the outside and mushy within, dusted with confectioners' sugar, and kept a kosher house. Scrupulously, Nana kept the *fleyschadikh* dishes, the dishes reserved for meals of meat, separate from the *milkhadikh* dishes, those that were reserved for dairy meals. Even the dish towels had to be kept strictly apart: one set (my mother has told me) bearing blue stripes, the other red. With equal scrupulousness, she strictly segregated from both of those sets of dishes the *Peysadikh* dishes, the Passover service, an ornate Bavarian service the colors of whose long-discontinued pattern ("Memphis"), even more than the images themselves (a stylized phoenix, perched atop a bower of orientalizing blossoms, grandly lofting one wing heavenward from the rim of each dinner plate, salad plate, bread plate, soup bowl, covered butter dish, soup tureen, creamer, sugar bowl, gravy boat), summon to mind another era entirely. For who now, really, cares to eat off such lavenders, citrines, turquoises, ivories, teals, oranges?

Hence my mother's family was, as they would have said, *frum,* deeply religious. But my father's family, as I have also mentioned, was just as profoundly irreligious. It was because my father grew up in a household that was in many ways the diametric opposite of the one in which my mother was raised, a household unbound by traditions, by Judaism, by Europe, that we did not observe the Jewish holidays when I was growing up in the 1960s and 1970s to the extent that my mother had done when she was growing up in the 1930s and 1940s. Yom Kippur, however, was an exception. This had less to do with the august status of this holiest of holy days on the Jewish calendar than with the fact that it was the only Jewish holiday that had any intellectual or (as I always suspect) aesthetic appeal to my father, who is after all a scientist, a person who likes the idea of rigor, of absolutes, even of hardship. He enjoyed the self-denial, the abnegation of Yom Kippur. And so it was that every year, although he almost never set foot in the tiny, strange synagogue to which my mother took me and my brothers and sister over the years, the synagogue where, one day as she and I were walking into the Yizkor, or Memorial, service that comes toward the close of the Yom Kippur observances, she told me that her uncle Shmiel had had four beautiful daughters who had been raped before they were all killed by the Nazis— although my father never set foot in this place for Yom Kippur services, he always strictly fasted. He would, in fact, keep a careful eye on the clock to make sure that no one broke fast until precisely twenty-four hours had elapsed.

Most of those anguishingly slow-moving twenty-four hours, I should admit, were not usually spent by any of us, including my mother, in the little synagogue we went to. And yet because of some obscure flavor of uncanniness and, slightly, of scariness that clung to this one day of the year in our family (very likely because of the stories about it that my grandfather liked to tell, such as the one about the woodcutter), the twenty-four hours of fasting were, it was understood, not to be spent doing anything "frivolous." Playing with toys was considered frivolous; so was watching TV. Go *read,* do something *serious,* my mother would tell us, absentmindedly, as she checked, with supreme self-control (it seemed to me then) the pans of roasting lamb or chicken, the potatoes, the vast, hotel-sized electric coffee urn that everyone pretended to be shocked by but secretly enjoyed, when they saw it churning away ("so many people this year!"), the sweet and savory noodle casseroles or *kugels,* the platters of smoked salmon and sable and whitefish that awaited the onslaught of the thirty or forty or so guests who, each year, would descend on my parents' small split-level house for the breaking of a fast that most, but not all, of the guests kept. (An aunt whom I loved, petite, redheaded, foulmouthed, and pretty in, everyone used to say, a *goyish* way, would sit on my parents' living room sofa and say, *I'm just having some coffee, because coffee doesn't count!*) So we children would go do serious things. But between not being able to eat and not being able to watch our regular after-school TV programs, which were the most reliable markers of time when I was a kid, the day of the fast, that one day of the year, felt impossibly long, without any character at all except a feeling of anticipation, a day stripped of all the recognizable features that on every other day made, and make, the passage of time bearable.

It was exactly that feeling, that association between meals and unbearable ennui—brought on, in the case of our trip to Australia, by a surfeit rather than a dearth of food——that came to mind as I sat on the plane that was taking us to the other side of the world.

The trip from New York to Sydney takes twenty-two featureless hours, then. But of course when you fly to Australia from New York City you are, in a way, making a much longer trip. We left on a Wednesday in the early evening; but because of the change in time zones, because, when you fly from New York to Los Angeles and then across the Pacific, you are crossing the international date line, we arrived late on Friday morning. And so when you make this trip, as Matt and I did, that March of 2003, in order to recuperate a tiny fragment of the past, you are actually, literally, losing time: a Thursday of your life simply disappears. And there is something else, too. When you make this trip, you are flying from the Northern to the Southern Hemisphere, and so in a way you lose much vaster stretches of time. We left New York as spring was beginning, and arrived in Sydney at the onset of autumn.

So what did we lose, when we flew to meet Jack Greene, as he insisted we should that day exactly a year earlier when he and I talked about Bolechow, about the day in October 1941 when my mother's cousin Ruchele had gone for a walk and never come back? What did we lose? It depends: a day, three days, six months.

LIKE MANY GRANDCHILDREN of immigrants, I grew up listening to stories of strange and epic journeys.

There was the story of my father's father, a small, slightly shrunken and taciturn man, bald like my father, who had once been an electrician and who, every now and then, would cry out, as we ran up and down the stairs of my parents' house when he and my grandmother Kay were visiting, that we had to *take it easy, fellas!* because we were *bothering the wiring!*; a man who had been (we were always told, so that the phrase resounded in my mind long afterward like a slogan, or a chapter title) *born on the boat,* the boat that had carried the Mendelsohns from Riga to New York at some point in the 1890s. And not only that: my father's father had always insisted that he had had a twin who'd died in infancy. But precisely when that birth, that voyage had taken place, or what the other twin's name had been, or what boat it was, no one ever seems to have known, or cared enough about to remember: not my father, not his older brother to whom, for a long time while we were growing up, he was on such friendly terms, not the other brother, with whom, for such a long time, he had nothing to do, but to whom, much later, he once again grew close, before the polio returned, one last time, to end that tortured conversation permanently. My father's family always seemed to me to be a family of silences, and what little I was able, in time, to learn of them helped to explain why: my grandfather's father, the violinmaker who, because he could not sell enough violins, made shoes as well, and earned too little from that, too; the mother who would die at thirty-four, exhausted from her ten pregnancies, three of which resulted in twins; the numerous siblings who never grew up, felled in infancy or childhood or adolescence by this or that illness, by tuberculosis, by the great Spanish flu epidemic in 1918, leaving my grandfather alone to grow to adulthood, an adulthood in which he preferred never to talk about that depleted past. A family, then, raised in silences, of which those grim, empty stretches between brothers, silences that lasted decades, were just the most extreme examples.

Because they were so quiet for so long—because they lived in their American present rather than their European past—there are, now, fewer stories to tell about them. It was only by accident that I learned, because I happened to be sitting unnoticed under the willow tree in my parents' backyard one day in 1972 while my father's parents were up from Miami Beach on a visit, that my grandfather Al had had a wife before he married my grandmother Kay, and that our family existed only because this first wife had died in the Spanish flu epidemic; and indeed that my father in fact had a much older half brother to whom (for reasons I was successful in excavating only much later, while my grandfather Al was dying) my father had not spoken since this lost half-uncle had left home, decades earlier. Once again I was reminded that our line was the result of an accident, an untimely death; once again I was put in mind of the Hebrew Bible's preference for second wives, for younger sons. Why, I thought at the time, had we never heard this dramatic tale before? But then, this same grandfather had never thought to mention to anyone, even after my sister, Jen, was born in 1968, that among his many dead siblings there had been a girl called Jenny.

When I was growing up, I would look at my father's father, and then look at my mother's father, and the contrast between them was responsible for forming, in my childish mind, a kind of list. In one column there was this: Jaegers, Jewishness, Europe, languages, stories. In the other there was this: Mendelsohns, atheists, America, English, silence. I would compare and contrast these columns, when I was much younger, and even then I would wonder what kind of present you could possibly have without knowing the stories of your past.

THERE WERE OTHER stories of difficult journeys in my family. My mother's mother was the only one of my grandparents who was born in the United States, but her mother, my great-grandmother Yetta, was not. Yetta Cushman (or *Kutschmann* or *Kuschman,* depending on which documents you unearth), who in the only extant photograph of her, taken shortly before her untimely death in the summer of 1936—while sewing the neck of a chicken she pricked her finger, and died days later of blood poisoning, which was the source of the terrible emotional shock on which my mother's father thereafter blamed the onset of his young wife's diabetes—stares forlornly out at you, an exceedingly plain, almost cross-eyed woman of indeterminate age. Yetta, sometimes Etta, is the relative for whom my brother Eric is named. She was Russian. RUSSIA, it says on her death certificate, under COUNTRY OF ORIGIN, although neither RUSSIA nor COUNTRY OF ORIGIN can, it must be said, suggest the nature of or reasons for her awful emigration, about which I eventually heard from this exhausted and homely woman's son-in-law, my grandfather, a story that is, for someone of my generation and background, simply impossible to imagine.

What did my grandfather tell me? He told me that his mother-in-law, for whom I gathered he had no particular fondness but no particular antipathy, either (*You know,* he said to me one day with a little shrug, *in-laws!*) had come to America after her entire family had been burned to death in a pogrom in, or near, Odessa, from which fate she was saved only because she happened to be in the outhouse when the Cossacks, or whoever it was, came that day (they had, of course, come many times before); that, utterly alone at the age of fifteen, she walked across Europe to get to the place where the boat was that would take her to America, a place where she had a relative who helped her, and that upon her arrival early in the 1890s she did what must be done, which was to find a husband immediately, and that in this case the husband she found was a crippled widower with grown children who, after he married this homely traumatized young woman of nineteen or so, would torment their father's new wife by hiding smelly socks deep, deep under the beds, which she had to make each morning, a story her daughter, my grandmother, would later tell *her* daughter, who would later tell me.

From this pathetic woman my diabetic grandmother whom I loved so much inherited the golden hair that was my mother's, too, which is why my brother Matt (of whom I, with my kinky, inky adolescent frizz, was once so jealous) had such beautiful white-blond hair when he was a boy; why I have always thought that he looked, with that hair and his slightly Tatar, slanted eyes and the austere planes of his face, both like the figure in an icon and like the Slavs who would have worshipped it. The Slavs, that is to say, who on some unknowable day in the 1880s descended on a town near Odessa and raped, and pillaged, and burned the houses of some insignificant Jews to the ground, which is why my great-grandmother came to America, and which was, indeed, how some of my family had come to have such blond, blond hair in the first place.

BUT THE BEST of all the stories were, naturally, the ones told by my mother's father, since after all he was the only one of my relatives who'd made the remarkable trip to America and had been old enough at the time to have anything to remember about it. *How was the trip to America, you want to know?* my grandfather would repeat, chuckling softly, when I interviewed him about his life. *I couldn't tell you, because I was in the toilet throwing up the whole time!* But of course this self-deprecating joke, meant to suggest that there was no story to tell, was part of the story of his coming to America, a story, as I knew, that had many chapters. In no particular order, I remember, now, these stories: the one about how he and his sister, my glum Aunt Sylvia, whom he always called *Susha,* and whose name appears on the passenger manifest, now available online through the Ellis Island database, as *Sosi Jäger,* had traveled "for weeks" to get from Lwów to Rotterdam "where the boat was waiting," he would say, and being a child with little knowledge of the world, I would be impressed, back then, to think that such a big boat would wait for these two young people from Bolechow, a false impression that my grandfather did little to correct; and then how, after the long trip on the train, from Lwów to Warsaw, then Warsaw through Germany to the Netherlands, they almost missed the boat, because the girls had such long hair.

Because the girls had such long hair?! I would exclaim. The first time I heard this story, which was so long ago that I can't remember when it might have been, I asked this question because I was genuinely perplexed; only now do I understand how sophisticated a storyteller my grandfather was, what a brilliant tease *because the girls had such long hair* was, how it was intended to make me ask just that question, so that he could launch into his story. Later on, I asked it simply because I knew he wanted me to.

Yes, because the girls had such long hair! he would go on, sitting there in the webbed garden chair on the broad stoop outside the front door to my parents' house, surveying the neighborhood, as he liked to do when he visited, with an expression of lordly satisfaction, as if he were somehow responsible for the split-level houses in their many odd colors, the neat lawns, the spiral topiaries pointing to the clear summer sky, the silence of this weekday noon. And then he would tell me how, before boarding the big boat that took him and my perennially disappointed aunt to America, all the steerage passengers had to be inspected for lice, and because the girls, including my twenty-two-year-old great-aunt Sylvia, had such long hair in those days, these preboarding examinations took a very long time, and at a certain point my grandfather (who today, I suspect, we would describe as suffering from severe anxiety, although in those days people just said he was "meticulous") panicked.

So what did you do? I would ask, on cue.

And he would say, So I yelled *Fire! Fire!* and in all the confusion, I took your aunt Susha's hand and we ran up the gangplank and got on the boat! And that's how we came to America.

He would tell this story with an expression that hovered between self-congratulation and self-deprecation, as if simultaneously pleased and (now) slightly embarrassed by the youthful audacity that, if this story is not a lie, had won him his trip to America.

THERE WERE, TO be sure, other stories about this trip to America, stories I often heard when my grandfather came to visit and I would hang quietly about the house in the hopes that he'd decide to sit down and talk to me, waiting for him to finish reading the paper, maybe the *Times* or, more likely, *The Jewish Week* (to which, after my mother married my father, he had bought them a subscription because, he said, he was afraid she'd *forget how to be Jewish*). He would read his paper slowly, letting his large head move down the left side and then jerking it up and to the right as he took in the print on the opposite side. Silently watching him read—for you never, ever interrupted my grandfather, no matter what he was doing—I would wait for him to finish and hope he'd be in the mood to tell me stories . . . Or I would wait for him to finish drinking his prune juice, which, he liked to say, *was good for the machinery,* or to finish quietly talking to my mother as she did her nails at the kitchen table in front of the big bay window, or, standing in the "big" bathroom, which was tiled in pale blue, to finish taking, with great precision, one or more of the many, many pills he carried with him in a pale brown calfskin attaché case. My grandfather was a hypochondriac, we all knew, and evidently his various doctors humored him; each night and some mornings he'd stand in my mother's gleaming bathroom and line up a bunch of pills and, one by one, swallow them in turn with a matter-of-fact smile. Since my father disapproved of medicines, pills, and even doctors in general, about whom he had great suspicions and toward whom, as a group, great if vague animosity (and why not, given what he'd spent his boyhood watching?), he would sneer, not so secretly, at my grandfather's rituals with the pills. But we children loved to watch Grandpa take his medicines when he visited, a ritual that, like so much else, he made somehow funny. *Tonight,* he'd say, looking at the long row of pharmacist's bottles in mock confusion, like a housewife confronted by a daunting array of detergents or breakfast cereals, *maybe I'll take a blue one and a red one.*

So I waited for him to finish doing whichever of his routines he happened to be doing and tell me these stories about his many travels and many adventures. The one about How Crowded the Boat Was, the one about How Afraid He and Aunt Sylvia Were of Being Robbed and So They Hid Their Money Wrapped in a Kerchief, or, worse, How Seasick He Was, how it made him never want to travel by ship again. How, after two weeks on the boat, the famous two weeks of being sick, they had arrived in New York and tried to make their way to the location of the rendezvous their Mittelmark cousin had designated, and how everyone he talked to had replied to his queries with blank stares. He would, he told me, approach people and utter the name of this place with an interrogatory tone of voice: *Timmess skvar? Timmess skvar?* and it wasn't until he wrote it down on a piece of paper that someone finally laughed and pointed him in the right direction: *Times Square.* And from Times Square my grandfather and great-aunt, accompanied by their English-speaking cousin, went to the Lower East Side, to East Fourth Street, to live in the apartment of their uncle, Abe Mittelmark, a red-haired man whose estrangement from, or resentment toward, his only sister, my great-grandmother, was responsible, as I like to think, for the cruel matrimonial deal-making that would set the Jägers against the Mittelmarks for generations to come; and which was not the only instance of internecine sibling conflicts in my family.

Now, when I think of that trip, I whose longest journey was twenty-two hours in a business-class seat on a 747, I am impressed by the audacity he had to have simply to make the trip in the first place. As I write this I am looking at his Polish passport, the one with which he made that unimaginable journey, and although he is dead now and can no longer tell his stories, the document has its own tales to tell. By deciphering the elegant official handwriting with which its blanks are filled in, scrutinizing the visas and stamps, I can, with far greater precision than my grandfather was ever concerned with when he told his stories, reconstruct his trip to America.

I can, for instance, tell you that the passport ("DOWÓD OSOBISTY," "identification paper"), number 19272/20, was issued to him at Dolina, the small village to the south of Bolechow that was the administrative center for the region, and where my grandfather's mother's family, the Mittelmarks, once lived, on the ninth of October 1920. Affixed to it is a small black-and-white photograph of my grandfather, the earliest known image of him. He is standing, it seems, against a wooden wall of some kind; the familiar face is smooth, serious, the nearsighted eyes very deep-set, the hair, still very thick, swept back from the high widow's peak that I would inherit. The ears stick out ever so slightly, something I do not remember. The collar of his white shirt is narrow and uncomfortable-looking, and the extremely high, narrow lapels of the jacket he is wearing seem impossibly antique. The passport also provides a written description: stature "medium," face "oval," hair "dark," eyes "blue," mouth "medium"—precisely what this means I cannot say—and nose "straight."

As I read this description now, having heard certain stories in which straight noses and blue eyes are elements on which the outcome depended, I wonder, not for the first time, how my sly, blue-eyed, straight-nosed grandfather would have fared, if he, like his older brother, had decided not to make the trip during which he used this passport. It is something my brother Andrew and I have discussed, when reminiscing about my grandfather and his tricks.

I bet he would have survived, Andrew once said, knowing well that there were other stories of my grandpa's ingenuity, the times he bluffed and stonewalled people into giving him what he wanted, deals and breaks and, the one time I was a witness to his special kind of dexterity, when I was fourteen, a free wide-screen television from a savings bank—not for him, the account holder, but for my mother, which was, technically, against the rules. I, too, like to think that my grandfather, had he not made his long journey to *Timess skvar* in 1920, would have somehow used his talent to get what he wanted, to survive . . .

. . . As I know, for instance, that Mrs. Begley, to whom I sometimes spoke about my grandfather and who also was lucky enough to be blond and blue-eyed, survived.

You see, I was fair, and I spoke German, she told me on one of my first visits to her apartment on the East Side, perhaps the first, in January 2000, when I was afraid she wouldn't want to talk about the past, especially the war, but she surprised me by talking of little else, by even weeping, suddenly, at one point, as she pointed out to me the name, in the Yizkor book for her town, Stryj, of that seventeen-year-old boy who didn't survive: whether a relative or a family friend, I couldn't remember until I recently found the Stryj Yizkor book, the *Sefer Stryj*, online, and located the page on which she had showed me a list of names of the dead, a page bearing the Hebrew heading *Sh'mot shel Qidoshei Striy*, "Names of the Martyrs of Stryj." (It's perhaps worth stopping here to note that the Hebrew word *qidush*, "martyr" or "sacrifice," is derived, as is the word for "sacrifice" in certain other languages, from the word "holy," *q-d-sh*. The use of *qidush* in this way is consistent with the concept in Judaism known as *qidush HaShem*, which refers to dying in the name of a Jewish cause, the idea being that through the process of dying, you sanctify, or make holy (*qdsh*) God's name—*HaShem* meaning "the Name." The traditional example would be Hannah and her seven sons, who all died at the hands of Antiochus—this would have been Antiochus IV, the Hellenistic monarch of the Hanukkah story—because they wouldn't eat pork or bow down to idols. But the use of the phrase also extends to Holocaust victims, who died based on the fact that they were Jewish.)

"Names of the Martyrs of Stryj" was, in any event, the page on which Mrs. Begley's late husband, the very big doctor from Stryj whose name an old Ukrainian woman had instantly recognized six decades later, had caused to be entered the following text:

BEGLEITER-BEGLEY EDWARD DAVID Dr.
commemorates:
BEGLEITER SIMON, Father
BEGLEITER IDA, Mother
SEINFELD MATYLDA, Sister

SEINFELD ELIAS, Brother-in-law
HAUSER OSCAR & HELENA, Parents in law
SEINFELD HERBERT, Nephew

This Herbert Seinfeld, she told me as her low, deliberate voice broke, this Herbert Seinfeld had already had his emigration papers but failed to get out in time.

A boy of *seventeen,* she had said that day, weeping a little. He almost got out, but he didn't make it.

I had said nothing, feeling embarrassed by this unexpected display of emotion. It was my fault: I'd asked her to show me this Yizkor book from Stryj because I wanted to see if Shmiel and his family were listed there among the names of the victims; his wife, Ester, as we knew, had been from Stryj. (And Minnie Spieler had been from Stryj, too.) And indeed there they were:

SCHNEELICHT EMIL
commemorates:
SCHEITEL HELENE, Sister
SCHEITEL JOSEPH, Brother-in-law & 3 child.
SCHNEELICHT MORRIS, Brother
SCHNEELICHT ROS, Sister-in-law & 5 child.
JAEGER ESTER, Sister
JAEGER SAMNET, Brother-in-law and 4 child.
SCHNEELICHT SAUL, Brother, wife & 5 child.
SCHNEELICHT BRUNO, Brother
SCHNEELICHT SABINA, Sister-in-law

This is why I had wanted to look at the *Sefer Stryj,* and it goes without saying that if I had located this book years ago, I would have known that my great-aunt Ester had had a brother Emil who had not perished, and perhaps would have found him sooner than the day in 1999 when his son had called me out of the blue from Oregon to tell me, among other things, that Minnie Spieler was Ester's sister.

So I looked at the names of my dead—noticing, for how could I not, that Shmiel's name, SAMUEL, had been grossly misspelled, perhaps because of the same peculiarity of handwriting, the crossed lower-case *l,* a tic, now lost but once widespread among a certain echelon of people from a certain place, that had transformed Shmiel's "Ruchaly" into "Ruchatz" in my eyes—I looked at these names, whose presence on the page seemed obscurely like a confirmation of something, perhaps of the fact that these people for whom I was searching existed outside of my family's private memories and stories of them, and for that reason was satisfying to me. But as I looked I suddenly felt foolish for having asked Mrs. Begley to look in her book for my relatives, whom I never knew and who meant something rather abstract for me at that point, when so many of hers, so much closer to her, were there, too.

You see, she repeated, pulling the book away from me slightly to run a cool, translucent hand over it, I was fair, and I spoke German. I could pass. My mother was very beautiful, but in a *Jewish* way. She was what they called a real *Rebecca*, a beautiful Jewish woman.

She stopped speaking for a few moments and simply looked across at me, steadily but warily, from beneath her hooded eye, the good one—whether to compose herself for the next story or (more likely, I suspect) because she doubted I could appreciate what she was telling me, I cannot say. I sipped my tea in silence. Then she took a breath that was also a sigh, and started telling me her own stories of slyness and survival, and other stories, too. Of, for instance, how, successfully hidden herself, she had bribed someone to bring her parents and in-laws to a certain place from which she would take them to safety, during the great roundup of Stryj's Jews in the fall of 1941, and how when she arrived at this rendezvous she saw a wagon filled with dead bodies passing by, and on top of the pile of bodies were those of the elderly people she had come to rescue.

You see, she said, I recognized my father-in-law by the shock of long white hair that he had.

And then she added this: Because she herself was in danger, was "passing" at that point, she couldn't allow herself to betray any emotion when she saw the bodies of her family passing by in the wagon. . . .

. . . So when I hear about slyness, and survival, and the color of one's hair or eyes, I think of Mrs. Begley, and I am also tempted to think of my grandfather and wonder whether he would have survived, too. But then, as I know, many clever people did not.

What else can my grandfather's passport tell us, apart from the fact that at the age of eighteen he was fair, blue-eyed, and straight-nosed? I knew from his stories that he arrived in November 1920. (This element of his story is one that can be confirmed by the Ellis Island Web site: he did indeed arrive on the seventeenth of November 1920, on the SS *Nieuw Amsterdam*, accompanied by a sister to whom the records refer as "Sosi Jäger" from "Belchow, Poland," the latter being a name that I know to be inaccurate but which someone else might, at this moment, be carefully writing down on a notecard somewhere). But what, exactly, happened between the ninth of October, when he received his passport, and the seventeenth of November, when we know he arrived? The passport fills in many blanks of this particular journey. For instance, I know that on the twelfth of October he was in Warsaw, where he visited the Dutch and American consulates. I know that on the fourteenth of October he went to the German consulate, where he received a transit visa for passage through Germany en route to the Netherlands. I know from various border stamps that he and Aunt Sylvia entered Germany at Schneidemühl on the eighteenth of October, passed through that country, and exited the next day, the nineteenth, at Bentheim, whence they passed across the German-Dutch border to Oldenzaal, at the eastern border of the Netherlands, and that from Oldenzaal they then proceeded west to Rotterdam, where, after perhaps ten days of waiting in the Netherlands, on the fifth of November 1920—having yelled *Fire! Fire!* because he was afraid of missing the boat—my grandfather and his sister finally boarded the SS *Nieuw Amsterdam,* a seventeen-thousand-ton, fourteen-year-old, single-stack liner of the Holland America Line, six-hundred and fifteen feet long and sixty-eight feet wide, accommodating 2,886 passengers in total (of whom 2,200 were, like my grandfather and great-aunt Sylvia, relegated to steerage), and commanded by P. van den Heuvel, who, on arriving in New York Harbor twelve days later, signed an affidavit stating that he had "caused the surgeon of said vessel . . . to make a physical and mental examination of each and all of the aliens named in the foregoing Lists or Manifest Sheets, 30 in number, and that from the report of said surgeon . . . no one of said aliens is of any of the classes excluded from admission into the United States."

Oh yes: we knew about the physical examination which, Captain van den Heuvel naively believed, all of his passengers had passed. *The girls had such long hair.* But the passenger manifest, which is the extant official record of my grandfather's arrival, can't possibly suggest just how it was that he got to America, how all the stories began.

But there is an odd gap. For the passport tells us nothing about what happened between the nineteenth of October 1920 (which, my friend Nicky assures me, was a Tuesday), and the fifth of November, which, according to the ship's manifest now accessible through the Ellis Island Web site, was the day the ship sailed . . .

About those lost seventeen days, my grandfather told a certain story. In

Holland, he used to say, he and Aunt Sylvia ran out of the money their mother had given them for their journey; just how this happened, he never said. And *so,* he would say, he *spiffed himself up* and took himself to the various consulates and official offices in Rotterdam—of which there were many, it being a major port of embarkation for America during that period of intense immigration— and offered his services as a translator. Now his passport states that he spoke Polish and German, but I know that he spoke many other languages as well: the Russian he learned as a fifteen-year-old, guarding Russian war prisoners in Bolechow after the tables had turned and, briefly, the Austrians had the upper hand against the Russians who had, night after night, so cruelly bombarded the town (*they blew up the center of town!*); the Hungarian he grew up learn- ing in school, until after the war, when his town no longer belonged to the Austro-Hungarian empire. *And so I got myself a job at a Hungarian office, translat- ing from Hungarian into German and back,* he would say.

Really!? I would say, when I was thirteen or fourteen. The first time I said this, I was really amazed; thereafter I was, once more, merely doing my job, prompting him, being the straight man. You must have really known Hungar- ian fluently! I would exclaim. So say something to me in Hungarian!

At which point he would smile his special punch-line smile and say, *You know, I can't remember a single word!* And I would marvel, then—truly, not as a pretense, and indeed even today I marvel—that you could know an entire lan- guage well enough to translate it, and subsequently forget every single word. How could you forget so much, I wondered then, when I was eleven and twelve and thirteen, when I had nothing, really, to remember yet; how could you forget something so utterly?

Anyway, it was in March 2003 that we made our long and remarkable trip to Australia, another family saga of long voyages, to find out what five Jews, every one of them far older than my grandfather was when he started telling me the stories of his epic travels, could remember about my relatives who had disappeared from history sixty years before.

Rashi's analysis of the text of parashat Noach *suggests that the noun that God uses to describe what he's planned for men and animals, which we generally translate as "Flood"—the Hebrew* mabool—*is a word with subtleties far greater than the English translation can convey. Alert as ever to the nuances of etymology and diction, the great scholar toys with the components of the Hebrew—the letters m-b-l—and muses on three possible verbs, all containing the b-l cluster, each of which adds to our understand- ing of the shades of meaning that* mabool *could have (apart from "flood"). These are* n-b-l, "to decay"; b-l-l, "to confuse"; and y-b-l, "to bring." Rashi then remarks that all three of these words associated with mabool, "flood," are apposite "because," he writes, "it decayed everything, because it confused everything, because it transported everything."

It is worth pausing here to note that Rashi's linguistically subtle interpretation is enthusiastically seconded by the great sixteenth-century Bohemian scholar and mystic Judah Loew ben Bezalel (1525–1609), for many years the chief rabbi of Prague, who wrote that the Torah deliberately uses the resonant word mabool to describe God's annihilation of mankind in order to convey simultaneously all three of the meanings that Rashi detected in those related verbs. This remark may be found in Rabbi Judah's learned commentary on Rashi's commentary on the Torah—a "supercommentary," as scholars call it; the work is known to scholars by a title that puns on the rabbi's German surname, which means "Lion": Gur Aryeh al HaTorah, "The Lion's Cub on the Torah." It should be said, however, that Rabbi Judah owes his considerable fame, both within and outside Jewish circles, to another by-product of his intimacy with Jewish scripture: the Golem, the Frankenstein-like creature that the rabbi is said to have created from the mud of the Vltava River, using powers gleaned from his knowledge of the Creation story. This creature, meant to protect the embattled Jews of Prague from attacks fomented by hostile courtiers of the Habsburg monarch Rudolf II, ultimately ran amok, and in the end the rabbi had to destroy his own creation by removing from its mouth the shem, a tablet covered with mystical inscriptions. He is said to have then buried the lifeless clay in the attic of the Prague synagogue.

In any event, it is clear that both Rashi and his distinguished early modern commentator, who knew a thing or two about creating and destroying himself, agreed that the result of God's dissolution of his Creation in parashat Noach was this: Decay, confusion, and vast movements over watery spaces. These, it would seem, are necessary for life to begin anew.

2

THE STORY OF THE FLOOD

I T TOOK MATT and me a full day to get over the immense change in time and season, once we arrived in Sydney. We spent most of the day after we landed in bed, although occasionally we'd leave the hotel and walk on the sunny waterfront promenade, across from which, as if to confirm that we were, indeed, in Australia, stood the famous Sydney Opera House. Like many iconic monuments I've seen in photographs before ever laying eyes on them in person—San Marco in Venice, Stonehenge on the Salisbury Plain, the gate at Auschwitz, the little Habsburg-era townhall or *Magistrat* in Bolechow, across the street from which my family's store had once stood—the Opera House was much smaller, much more human-scaled, than I'd imagined. As it happened, the little balcony of our hotel room looked right across a patch of clear water at the Opera House, and as Matt and I rather dazedly walked around that Saturday, trying our land legs after so many hours in the plane, after so many time zones, we'd go out onto the balcony every now and then and check to make sure that the Sydney Opera House was there, that we had really made it all the way here. We would stumble across the carpet of our hotel room, and gratefully we would look at the landmark: small, indifferent, *there.*

That was Saturday, a lost day. It was on Sunday that we met the people we'd come all this way to talk to.

In the weeks before we arrived, Jack reminded me that he wasn't the only Bolechower who'd ended up in Australia. Apart from his younger brother, Bob, with whom he'd survived the war, there were some others "of interest," he told me, whom I would want to meet: a woman who had been a friend of Frydka's; a very elderly relative of hers who, amazingly, was old enough to have known my grandfather when he still lived in the town; a man who had been Shmiel's neighbor. And so Jack had invited everyone to his place in Bellevue Hills, near Bondi Beach—about a twenty-five-minute drive from our hotel in downtown Sydney. *Bondi Beach* meant nothing to me, but Matt repeated the name, clearly impressed, when I first forwarded him the fax Jack had sent me with information about local hotels and driving directions.

Bondi Beach! Matt said. It's incredibly famous for its surfers! People come from all over the *world* to surf there!

Well, I retorted, we've come from all over the world to talk to the Bolechowers there. I had a sudden dread that he'd want us to go surfing; he had been on the track team in high school, had jumped out of airplanes. But no, he was just amused: he loved the fact that a bunch of old Polish Jews had come to settle near a surfer paradise.

So on Sunday, we went to Bondi Beach. A taxi left us in front of Jack's luxurious-looking apartment complex, and we took an elevator up to his floor. Look, Matt said with a sly grin, pointing out a metal plate affixed into the floor of the elevator on which the name of the manufacturer, SCHINDLER, could be read, We're in Schindler's Lift!

I rolled my eyes and said, Oy *vey*.

Jack greeted us at the door when we rang. He was a smallish, wiry man with a long face that was at once kindly and, maybe, a little sad: a prominent chin was offset by wary, melancholy eyes. A thatch of thinning gray hair was carefully combed across the sides of his head. He motioned with his right hand for us to come in. The apartment was attractive and comfortable, filled with sunlight that came in through floor-to-ceiling windows that opened onto a flower-filled balcony. The living room was all cream and blue; off to one side some glass-and-brass tables gleamed. There was a kind of careful neutrality about the pleasant taste of this home, something I had noticed, too, in Mrs. Begley's apartment, with its spotless 1950s and 1960s china and blond-wood furnishings, the sleekly "contemporary" metal menorah. I had wondered about this, during my increasingly frequent visits to Mrs. Begley's house, and only now, standing in the entrance to Jack Greene's comfortable apartment on the other side of the world, did it occur to me that of course their homes bore no traces of the heirloom pieces you can see, for instance, in my mother's house, the heavily framed old family photographs and antique marble inkwells and ancient brass menorahs (such as the one, with rampant Lions of Judah, that my grandfather left to my mother), the tiny paper bride and bridegroom that had stood atop my mother's parents' wedding cake in

1928. Of course there were no traces of the European past, of family history. They had all been destroyed.

We shook Jack's hand and went inside. Waiting there were his wife, Sarah, a pretty, sweet-faced blonde with a gentle manner, and his daughter, Debbie, who I guessed was about my age or so, and who had Sarah's open, pleasant, and pretty face with what I imagined had once been Jack's dark coloring. I was struck by the fact that she had come to hear us interview her father and his friends, although she had, I guessed, heard their stories many, many times. But then, this I could understand: I too had been happy to hear certain stories over and over again, once.

Debbie told me that her husband and daughter would come later. *Lighter*, it sounded like to my American ear. I was just getting used to Australian accents—or rather, still getting used to the idea of Jews with Australian accents. Of course we knew that there wasn't a country on earth that didn't have its Jews, but that abstract knowledge was somehow different from being confronted by the reality of other people. Where I grew up, Jews had either Old Country accents—Polish, German, Russian, Yiddish—or rather pronounced New York accents. But now we were in Australia, where the Jews of my generation had Australian accents, just as they have English accents in England and French accents in France and Italian accents in Italy. The world is so much bigger than you can possibly imagine, if you grow up in a provincial place: a New York suburb, a Galician shtetl, it doesn't really matter. Then you start to travel. My grandfather had known that. Now I knew it, too.

Also waiting for us in Jack and Sarah's apartment, already seated at the dining room table, which had been laid with a white lace cloth, and on which Matt and I started, rather awkwardly, to unload all of our recording and photographic equipment, was Jack's brother Bob. Bob I had already met. The previous summer, he'd been in New York and had looked me up, and over an iced tea at my place he had given me some details about how he, Jack, and their late father, Moses, had survived, by hiding in an underground, foliage-covered bunker in a forest just outside of Bolechow. Bob told me that they had escaped to this place, aided by a Ukrainian peasant, just before the final liquidations in 1943. It was a story, I knew, that they had told often, first in a book that had been written by a German journalist named Anatol Regnier (who was, more than one of the Australians would point out at various times, not without a certain incredulity, *married to a popular Israeli singer!*), and then in a documentary that had been made by a German television station on the occasion of Jack and Bob's return to Bolechow in 1996.

Like Jack, Bob was of medium height, but he had a wiry, sporty presence. He struck me as a person who spent a lot of time outside, and I wasn't surprised to hear, later, that he took brisk daily walks on the beach. I had spoken to Jack on the phone several times by the time I met Bob, and what struck me was the fact that whereas Jack, who was born in 1925 and hence was nineteen when the Nazi occupation ended in Bolechow, speaks with a pronounced Polish-Jewish accent, Bob, who was born in 1929 and was therefore barely a teenager when the war ended for him, sounds almost completely Australian. This difference in the way they speak took on, for me, greater resonance as my visit went on. Jack struck me as, maybe, more a citizen of the former world, maybe more Jewish; he liked to sprinkle his conversation with Yiddish and sometimes Hebrew expressions. Bob, by contrast, came to strike me over the next few days as someone determined to be free of the past. Perhaps the erosion of the accent, of the patterns and sounds that had once characterized his speech, hadn't been an entirely natural process. He was clearly not very religious.

But then, Bob had retaind the family name, Grunschlag, whereas Jack had anglicized it. Things can be strange, between brothers.

So there were Jack, Sarah, Debbie, and Bob, waiting there for the Americans to come interview them. When we had made our way into the apartment, we saw that an elderly man was already sitting at the table, too. Jack had told me about him: Boris Goldsmith, who was eighty-nine, and who had lived across the street from Shmiel and his family. Jack had warned me that Boris was rather hard of hearing—throughout the afternoon he would keep reaching up to his ear to adjust his hearing aid—but when I met him he seemed clear and robust, and had a humorous, solid presence. He was wearing a tan-and-black houndstooth check sport coat, and when he said hello and shook our hands, I noticed his mouth gleamed with metal. It was a look that I had, by then, come to associate with Eastern Europe.

Matt and I set up for the interview while we all waited for the appearance of the final guest, Meg Grossbard, who like Jack, like Bob, like the others, had made the improbable journey from Bolechow to New South Wales after the war. (You see, Jack had told me on the phone a year earlier, when he first called me, a lot of us had thought about fleeing to Australia before the war. So we kept the idea even afterward and ended up here eventually.) I would later learn that of Meg's family—twenty-six people in Bolechow alone—only Meg, her husband, and his much older brother had survived the war. Meg and her husband had settled in Melbourne, where, as in Sydney, there was a substantial population of survivors; her brother-in-law, Salamon Grossbard, had settled in Sydney. He had never remarried after his wife and child were killed. Now ninety-six, he was, Jack told me, too frail to attend the reunion in Jack's apartment that day. But Meg had flown in from Melbourne for the occasion, and was staying at her brother-in-law's apartment.

She will be here shortly, Jack told me.

I hope she won't be too late, I said.

With an opaque expression Jack said, She's very much her own person.

I was particularly anxious to meet this Mrs. Grossbard. This was only partly because Jack had reported to me that Meg (who had taken this English-sounding first name on arriving in Australia) had been Frydka's best girlfriend; if I wanted to know about Frydka, he said, I should talk to her, since he himself could tell me only about Ruchele. But as interesting and crucial as this was to me, I was even more eager to get to Mr. Grossbard, even though Jack had told me that he was one of those who'd been taken east by the retreating Soviet troops that summer in 1941, and would therefore be unable to tell me anything about what may have happened to my family during the war: he had been deep in the Soviet Union the whole time that Bolechow was suffering under the Germans. It was during this time, indeed, that his wife and small son had been killed.

But I had my reasons for wanting so badly to meet this Mr. Grossbard. Born in 1908, he belonged to an earlier generation than that of Jack and Bob and Meg, who were, after all, the friends and schoolmates of Shmiel's children, my mother's lost first cousins. Nineteen-hundred and eight was the year in which my grandfather's youngest sister, Neche, Jeanette, the doomed bride of their first cousin, had been born: and yet she'd been dead so long, seemed to belong so totally to the past, to the world of stories and family legends, that it was impossible for me to think of her, when I heard about Mr. Grossbard, as someone who could, conceivably, still be alive. This ancient man was the last Bolechower alive of my *grandfather's* generation. Just as I had fantasized, when I first heard about Mrs. Begley, that she might once have known or even just met one of those lost Jägers, now I fantasized that perhaps this old, old man had, as a child, known one of the Jäger children, perhaps in the Baron Hirsch school, perhaps at *cheder*, Hebrew school, perhaps at play in the unpaved streets of the town; and if he even just remembered the name of one of them—my grandfather, perhaps, or hopeless Uncle Julius or maybe Jeanette—he would not only restore them, if only for a moment, to the present, but would, in a way, restore to me something even more precious. If I had begun to think of my travels in search of Shmiel's family as a kind of rescue mission, to salvage from the past some shards of their lives, their personalities, then I also thought of this particular trip, with its possibility that I could talk to this old, old Mr. Grossbard, as a mission to rescue something of my grandfather.

So I secretly hoped. If things went well with this Mrs. Grossbard, I thought to myself, I would find a way to persuade her to let me talk to her brother-in-law.

AS WE WAITED for Meg's arrival, we all sat down at Jack and Sarah's dining table, laid with its lacy cloth. On it Sarah had placed many cups and plates, ready for coffee and cake; when Meg arrived, we would begin to eat, and to talk. In the meantime Jack looked through the photographs I'd brought, both old family pictures and pictures of our trip to Bolechow.

You know, he said, we used to have Yiddish nicknames for every town in the area.

Nicknames? I repeated.

Sure, Jack said. (He used the word emphatically and often, as he also used *That's right,* a phrase he tended to utter with a slight Polish inflection, *det's rhight,* while giving an emphatic downward nod of his head.)

For instance, Jack went on, you would say someone was a *Bolechower krikher,* it meant *crawler.*

Krowler.

Why? I asked.

Because you had to crawl around—there were so many streets and neighborhoods! He smiled, amused by this memory.

So many neighborhoods? I repeated. I was confused, since I've always thought of Bolechow as tiny. When we had been there, my brothers and sister and I, it seemed to consist of little more than the Rynek, the big square; the road leading in from Striy to the north; and the road leading out toward the cemetery. As is would turn out, we had seen very little of the town. There was in fact much more.

Sure, Jack said. For instance, he explained, there was a nice area of Bolechow—he was looking at a photograph as he said this, one of the snapshots from our Ukraine trip two years earlier—which we called the German Colony. There was a German Colony, an Italian Colony. There was a neighborhood called *Bolechow Ruski.*

Matt and I both looked at each other and laughed at the thought of there being "colonies" in this tiny shtetl, and Jack laughed, too.

Yeah, we were big-time Charlies! he crowed. The way he pronounced *Charlies,* as if it were spelled "chollies," reminded me so vividly of my grandfather that for a minute I couldn't say anything.

Jack went on. Take Lwów, he said. It was called *Lemberger pipick.* He grinned.

Pipick? Pipick is the Yiddish word for navel.

Yes, he said. Because it had a square, a *rynek,* right in the middle, it was like a belly button! Dolina you called *Dolina hoise. Hoise,* it's a pair of pants. Because it had only two streets, it looked like a pair of pants!

He stopped for a moment. I had long known the names of these towns, and had for a long time thought of them as nothing more than destinations, as places matched to certain dates, or certain people on my family tree. Now, suddenly, they seemed to have some life, because I could imagine them through the eyes of people who had lived there, who had these silly, affectionate nicknames for them.

At the moment that Jack was explaining about *Dolina hoise,* the doorbell rang and Mrs. Grossbard walked in.

SHE WAS NOT what I expected. Tiny but ramrod-straight, her auburn hair, with its expensive copper highlights, swept back in an impeccable and clearly expensive coiffure, she exuded an air that was at once crisp and distant. She was wearing dark colors that highlighted her brilliant hair: a black silk blouse, a violet sweater. Large gold earrings adorned her long lobes. Jack kissed her on each cheek as she strode in.

This is Daniel Mendelsohn, he said, pointing me out; and then, pointing to Matt, he smiled and said, And this is also Mr. Mendelsohn.

I'm so pleased to meet you, I said. My mother is Frydka's cousin.

Yes, she said, walking past me and seating herself at the table, where she immediately picked up some photographs, I *know.* Unsmiling, she abruptly started looking through the pictures Matt had taken during our trip to Ukraine: an ancient crone in L'viv, leaning out of a doorway in which you can just make out a groove for the mezuzah that had once been affixed there; an old man in the little square in Bolechow, holding a goat by a leash.

As I stood there trying to think of what to say, I noticed that the air of gentle reminiscence that had characterized the first fifteen minutes of this strange reunion had become charged. Clearly I wasn't the only one whom Meg Grossbard put on edge. I wondered what private histories, dating sixty years back, lay beneath the polite greetings being uttered by the others at that moment. Six months later, I would find out.

Because I was already a little afraid of her—this woman on whom I had to depend to rescue Frydka from total obscurity, and yet who was clearly already resistant in some undefinable but palpable way—I found myself instinctively trying to appease her, the way that, when I was a boy, I would try to appease my grandfather's fourth and last wife, that difficult and unsmiling woman with the tattoo on her arm, of whom we were all afraid. So when Mrs. Grossbard turned to me, pulling a photograph from a plastic bag and handing it to me, a posed studio shot of Frydka in which the pretty, long-dead girl is wearing a babushka and very barely smiling, an image I had never seen before and which looks strikingly like my mother—when Mrs. Grossbard turned to me and said, That is Frydka Jäger, I stupidly replied, as if to confirm something she considered important, That's my mother's cousin. She looked at me, not smiling, and said, Yes I know, she was my girlfriend, with just the barest, proprietary emphasis on the word "my."

She returned to her bag. I have only a few group photos of Frydka, she said. She explained that they weren't hers. They had belonged, she said, to a girlfriend of hers and Frydka's, a young woman called Pepi Diamant.

Di-AH-mant.

She perished, but her album survived, Mrs. Grossbard said, tonelessly. I found her album after the war, when I came back to Bolechow, and I took some—her pictures, my pictures, Frydka's pictures.

I knew that what she meant was: pictures of Pepi, pictures of Meg, pictures of Frydka. (Pepi's nickname, it became clear that afternoon, had been Pepci, pronounced *PEP-shuh*.) Oddly, Meg did not offer any of these miraculously preserved photos to me to look at just yet. I could just barely glimpse, through the plastic, snapshots of groups of girls: in summer frocks, posed in front of garden gates; in swimming costumes at the water's edge; in wasp-waisted winter jackets, standing on skis.

Across the table, Boris Goldsmith, squeezed between Jack Greene and Bob Grunschlag, was looking through more photographs; they were all clearly waiting for the group interview to begin. Ignoring them, Mrs. Grossbard went on. She said, I saw Frydka for the last time—this was when we were still able to walk around freely—in February 'forty-two. The last time . . .

Her voice trailed off. Suddenly she stopped short and looked right at me for the first time. You look very Aryan, she said, slightly accusingly.

I was taken aback. I do? I said, half in amusement.

Yes, Meg shot back. It's very important, you know. We have a little thing about it, all of us. Because someone who looked like you had a chance to live.

I was unable to think of any adequate response to this, so instead I took out a photograph that had belonged to my grandfather, a picture in which Shmiel, white-haired and tired-looking, and Ester, stout and big-bosomed in a print dress, stand protectively on either side of Bronia, who looks to be about ten. I put the photograph on the table in front of Meg Grossbard, and she picked it up tenderly. For the first time the hardness, the resistance, seemed to dissolve, and Meg Grossbard, nodding softly, said quietly, Yes. That was her parents.

And—also for the first time—she smiled.

MUCH ELSE WAS to happen that day, a great deal would be learned about Shmiel and his family; but when I think about our strange journey to Australia, it is that moment I dwell on. How casually we rely on photographs, really; how lazy we have become because of them. What does your mother look like? someone will want to know; and you'll say, Wait, I'll show you, and run to a drawer or an album and say, Here she is. But what if you had no photographs of your mother, or anyone in your family—indeed, even of yourself before a certain age? How would you explain what she, they, you, looked like? I never really thought about this until I talked to Meg Grossbard that Sunday afternoon, and realized how casual, even thoughtless I was being, traveling around the world talking to these survivors, who had survived with literally nothing but themselves, and showing them the rich store of photographs that my family had owned for years, all those photographs I had stared at and, later, dreamed about when I was growing up, images of faces that, for me, had no real emotional meaning at all in and of themselves, but which to the people to whom I was now showing them had the power to recall, suddenly, the world and the life from which they'd been torn so long ago. How stupid, how insensitive I had been. At the moment Mrs. Grossbard said *That was her parents,* I realized that she wasn't merely confirming the identity of the people in the photograph; I realized that what she was saying, in a way, was that she was laying eyes on faces she hadn't seen, hadn't dreamed of being able to see, in sixty years, faces that could summon her own lost girlhood to her. *These were the parents of my friend.* I imagined that it must seem unfair to her to have this young American man intervene in her life, suddenly, fanning out photographs of people he never knew as if they were cards in a deck and asking her to pick one, photographs of her girlfriend's parents, when she had no photographs of her own parents to look at. And so the picture that I showed her that Sunday, a picture I'd seen countless times since I was a boy, brought home to me for the first time the strangeness of my relationship to the people I was interviewing, people who were rich in memories but poor in keepsakes, whereas I was so rich in the keepsakes but had no memories to go with them.

The significance of pictures—the way in which an image that is, essentially, entertainment for one person can unexpectedly be profoundly emotional, even traumatic for another—is the subject of one of the most famous passages in all of classical literature. In Vergil's epic poem, the *Aeneid,* a poem not without significance for survivors of cataclysmic annihilations, the hero, Aeneas, is a young Trojan prince, one of the few survivors of the destruction of Troy (the Trojan War being the subject of Homer's *Iliad,* with its swirling, ringlike anecdotes). His city destroyed, his civilization in ruins, virtually all of his friends and relatives murdered, Aeneas travels the world seeking a place to settle and begin again. That place would, eventually, be Rome, the city that he founds; but before the traumatized Aeneas gets to Rome, he stops first at a city called Carthage, in North Africa, which (as we learn in Book I of the *Aeneid*) was itself founded by a hunted, desperate exile: a woman called Dido, with whom Aeneas will soon fall in love and, later, abandon, breaking her heart. When Aeneas and a companion first arrive in the bustling new town, they stroll around admiring its newly erected buildings and monuments. Suddenly, in a magnificent new temple, the two men stop dead in their tracks in front of a mural that is decorated with pictures of the Trojan War. For the Carthaginians, the war is just a decorative motif, something to adorn the walls of their new temple; for Aeneas, of course, it means much more, and as he stands looking at this picture, which is a picture of his life, he bursts into tears and utters a tormented line of Latin that would become so famous, so much a part of the fabric of Western civilization, that it turns up, really, everywhere: as the name of a musical group and the title of a musical work; as the name of Web sites and blogspots, of a science-fiction fantasy novel, the title of a newspaper story, of a scholarly book. What Aeneas says, as he looks at the worst moment of his life decorating the wall of a shrine in a city of people who do not know him and had no part in the war that destroyed his family and his city, is this: *sunt lacrimae rerum,* "There are tears in things."

This, in any event, is the line that came to my mind when Meg said, *Those were her parents,* and which would continue to come to my mind whenever I was confronted with the awful discrepancy between what certain images and stories meant for me, who was not there and for whom, therefore, the images and stories could never be more than interesting or edifying or fiercely "moving" (in the way that you say a book or a film is "moving"); and what they meant for the people I was talking to, for whom those images and stories were, really, their *lives.* In my mind, that Latin half-line became a kind of caption for the poignantly unbridgeable distances created by time. They were there, and we were not. *There are tears in things;* but we all cry for different reasons.

SHE PERISHED, BUT her album survived. As Mrs. Grossbard said this, with the slightest accent of irony, a tone I came to recognize as characteristic over the next few days, I was reminded of a story about photographs and their survival that Mrs. Begley had told me once during one of my visits to her place. She'd been trying to describe to me what she had once looked like, and what her mother had looked like, too. This was the visit during which she'd told me how she'd tried to rescue her parents and in-laws, only to see their bodies being carted away as she arrived at the rendezvous.

A real Rebecca, she had said, a real Jewish beauty. How can I explain?

At this, she took her stick in one hand and, bracing the other arm against the arm of her straight-backed chair, rose slowly to her feet. Painstakingly, she moved toward her bedroom and without saying anything beckoned to me to follow. She stopped in front of a dresser. Out in the living room, I had noticed many times, there were dozens of photographs of her son, his children, their children, pictures that crammed every available shelf and table-top. In here, in the bedroom, on top of the spotless dresser, were a handful of very old-looking photographs. One by one, she picked them up and, passing each one briefly into my hands before taking it back and carefully replacing it on the dresser, told me who the subject was of each: her mother, her father, to be honest I can't remember now because that day, in 2002, I knew I'd have many opportunities to look at them and enquire about them and hence didn't look at them intently enough or listen to her meticulously enough, and now when I try to summon them to mind I have a vague impression of a picture of an attractive woman in a fur stole, and a very, very old picture of a distinguished, unsmiling old man in black who could have been a rabbi, or perhaps was merely wearing one of the round, vaguely Oriental caps that adult men of a certain vintage and era used to wear as a matter of course.

But I did listen with great interest to the story of how she came to repossess these ancient family photographs from her girlhood in Rzeszów and Kraków, since I had wondered how it was that she'd managed to keep them after she'd fled her comfortable house on Third of May Street, the house that had then been appropriated for use as Gestapo headquarters. Had she hidden them somehow on her person, I asked after she put the last photograph neatly back in its place, had she concealed them in the lining of a coat, for instance, as she fled, disguised, with her small child in tow, from hiding place to hiding place, alias to alias?

Mrs. Begley looked at me. *Achhh,* she said, Of course not, do you think I was crazy? I'll tell you what happened.

We slowly made our way back to the living room. She lowered herself again into the chair, and then she told me the story: how, after the war was over, after she'd been reunited with her husband, the big doctor from Stryj who, like so many doctors, was taken east when the Soviets retreated in 1941, she was contacted by someone who'd come to live in her former house, the house I had tried and failed to locate the summer before.

He told me he had found a bunch of my photographs, she said, and if I wanted them, I could send money to such-and-such an address.

She grimaced, although her expression was not without some humor.

So I did it for a while, I would send money and he would send a photo, two photos.

I didn't say anything. I was trying to imagine how much I would pay to ransom my past.

But finally my husband got angry, he was sick of it, and I stopped.

She paused for a moment as her eyes lighted on the shelves of pictures of Louis and his family.

And you see that now I have many pictures, she said.

AT JACK GREENE'S, the picture of Shmiel, Ester, and Bronia started to loosen tongues, and the conversation about my lost great-uncle and his family became, suddenly, boisterous and somewhat disorderly. For so many years, we had known nothing about them, which was frustrating. Now I found myself frustrated in quite the opposite way, because I wasn't able to hear everything at once. Not knowing whom I should talk to first, where to put the microphone of my tape recorder, half-hearing scraps of conversations coming from all sides, I turned to Matt with an anguished expression, as these four old Bolechowers chattered to one another, and I said, I'm losing all this.

Jack Greene was saying, I remember the Jägers, I remember Shmiel Jäger, I remember Itzhak Jäger—you know he went to Palestine in the 1930s?

Yes, I said, I knew. Itzhak, Shmiel's brother, the brother who, my mother told me at some point, was the sibling to whom her father had been closest, the one he'd loved the most, Itzhak who had been dragged with his two small children from Bolechow to the Middle East by his ardent Zionist wife. On the opposite side of the table, Boris Goldsmith was smiling and trying to make himself heard.

I remember, Boris said, he had the first radio in town. It was *big*—raising both hands he sketched a big box—with a big aerial.

The *r* of "aerial" was lodged high up in back of his throat, where the uvula hangs—precisely where my grandfather would have placed it.

It was very high, the aerial, Boris said. You couldn't hear it, even . . . He also had the first telephone.

The first radio, the first telephone. *A big fish in a small pond.* As Boris told this story, which I prized because it fit an idea of Shmiel that I already had in mind, fragments of another story about appliances and status glimmered at the edges of my memory, although it wasn't until I returned home and called my mother that I recalled precisely what it had been. *My father bought Uncle Itzhak and Aunt Miriam the first refrigerator anyone had in Haifa,* my mother said over the phone. *They didn't have a refrigerator, and when they finally got electric lines through to this place where they lived, my father thought they should have a fridge, and he had one sent over. Itzhak and Miriam were the talk of the town!* But that afternoon in Australia, I couldn't remember this story.

So you knew him pretty well? I asked Boris Goldsmith.

I knew him very well!

And then I couldn't think of anything to say. This was the strangeness of this trip: here I was at last, talking to people who had known them well, very well even, and I had no idea where to begin. I felt like someone confronted with a locked door who is handed a very large bunch of keys. I realized, then, how ill-prepared I had been. How do you find out who someone was, really?

How do you describe a personality, a life? Fumbling, embarrassed, I turned to Boris Goldsmith.

So what kind of person was he? I asked.

Boris seemed taken aback.

He was an ordinary person, he said, slowly. He was a butcher. He had two trucks. He used to go from Bolechow to Lwów.

A butcher, the trucks, Lwów. This I knew, or could have guessed. I felt helpless.

And you knew Ester? I said, fumbling.

Oh yes . . . I used to come very often there. It was just across the street. I used to live there before he moved in there . . .

He had lived just across the street from them! I remembered, at that moment, how precious the moment had been, eighteen months earlier, when we'd met Olga and Pyotr and she had said, *Znayu, znayu, I knew them, I knew them.* I hadn't dreamed, then, that we'd ever get any closer. And now here I was, and all I could think of to ask was, Do you remember when he moved in?

Boris shook his head apologetically and said, I don't remember. It was a long, long time ago.

The way he said *a long, long time ago* was the way you might begin, or maybe end, a fairy tale. The room went quiet. Boris started talking again.

The house was there, he said. When he moved in he started to rebuild. He made it different. Then he bought two trucks, Studebakers. He was an expediter, he had a partner, his name was Schindler.

I shot Matt a look. He flashed a grin at me, but said nothing.

Boris went on, When the Russians came in 'thirty-nine, they took away his trucks, and then he was going in the country and buying cattles for the government.

Cattles. My grandfather would have said it like this: *kettles.*

Buying cattle for the government? I asked. This was interesting: I'd always wondered what became of Shmiel during the two years of Soviet rule, between 1939 and 1941.

Bob interjected: For the government, because he was then an employee of the government.

He was an employee of the government! Boris agreed, loudly. Yes, the Communists!

It was only later on that I read the testimony of a survivor who'd written about the Soviet years: the liquidation and subsequent nationalization of all businesses; the unbearably high taxes, the disintegration of the Polish złoty and, hence, the sudden evaporation of all liquid wealth, the queues in the few stores that had goods. The sudden, late-night deportations to Siberia of "bourgeois counter-revolutionaries"—a blessing, as it turned out, in disguise. I read this and tried to imagine what *going into the country and buying cattles for the government* must have meant for Shmiel, who'd given up a life in the United States, all those years ago, to rebuild his family's fortunes. The liquidation of the old family business, the seizure of the two Studebaker trucks, the appropriation by some minor Soviet official of the duties that had once belonged to the leader of the butchers' cartel, and, finally, assignment to a humiliatingly menial job—although it was, at least, a job related to the business he had known so well. It wasn't, in fact, until Boris said *going into the country and buying cattles for the government* that I had ever really thought of Shmiel as a butcher, as someone whose livelihood resided in animals, as had the livelihood of generations of his family. When I was a child and my grandfather would come to visit, he would, at some point during his stay, take me and, sometimes, my mother as well and drive my mother's station wagon to the local shopping center where, nestled between a barbershop and a pharmacy, there was a kosher butcher store. This store, narrow and always unnervingly cold because of the low open cases that ran down one side and were filled with frozen plastic-wrapped packages of stuffed derma and liver, was run by a pair of brothers with whom, once we got there, my grandfather would spend a good deal of time chatting in Yiddish. I often wondered, then, why we almost always left the store without actually buying anything, and it was only when Boris said *he was going into the country and buying cattles for the government* that I realized that my grandfather used to go there not only to hear the sound of Yiddish, but to talk about meat, about his family business.

SOMETHING OCCURRED TO me as Boris was talking. If Shmiel had, at some point, moved into a house across the street from Boris Goldsmith, then the house we had visited in Bolechow, the ancestral Jäger house on lot # 141, where Stefan and Ulyana now lived, was not, as I had assumed, the one in which Shmiel and his family had lived, and from which they had gone, however they had gone, to their deaths. Of this I wanted to be sure, and so I continued to question Boris.

So when he moved in he already had the four girls—?

Boris looked surprised. He had *three* girls, he said. I just remember *three* girls.

Well, I said, there were four, but—

I don't think there were four. I don't think so . . .

Boris picked up the picture of Shmiel, Ester, and Bronia, which by then had circled the table and come to his place. I picked up some other photos and, leaning across the table, pointed.

Lorka, Frydka, Ruchele, and Bronia, I said. At the opposite end of the table Meg Grossbard suddenly sat up.

And Bronia! she said. Yes! She smiled.

But Boris was unpersuaded. I just remember three of them, he insisted. I am positive he had just three daughters.

At this point Sarah Greene smiled and said, Well, they know better, they were their family!

Everyone laughed. I was afraid that in insisting on what I knew to be the truth, I had offended Boris by suggesting that his memory was faulty.

Boris, for his part, abandoned the daughters and said, a little testily, He was a butcher. I don't remember his relations.

Do you remember he had a brother who went to Palestine? I asked.

I don't know his brother, Boris said crisply. Just that he once had a *family*.

To change the subject, I asked everybody if there had been other Jägers in Bolechow. My grandfather had said that he had cousins who had lived in town, when he was a boy—Jäger cousins, I assumed, who had been related to his aunt Sima, the one whose headstone I had so improbably come across in the Bolechow cemetery.

That's what I asked Jack just now, Mrs. Grossbard said, turning in my direction. There were Jägers in the *rynek*. They were uncles of Dusia Zimmerman . . . they were her mother's brothers. Her mother was a Jäger. They had a sweet shop, a *cukierna*.

She turned to Jack and, in Polish, asked him how to render *cukierna* in English. Sarah Greene said, A coffeehouse?

Meg held up a manicured hand. No, no, no, no, she said.

This quadruple *no* was, as I would learn during the course of the day, a habit of hers when she was irritated by the inaccuracies of others. Her voice was tight and humorless.

Not a coffeehouse, I'm sorry, she said. We didn't have *coffeehouses*.

Everyone laughed, and whether it was at Meg's irritation, or at the absurdity that a little shtetl like Bolechow offered the likes of a coffeehouse, I was unable to tell.

I knew Frydka all my life, Meg told me. The last time I saw her was in 'forty-one when we could still walk the streets. And then I don't know what happened to her. I have no idea. But Lorka I met in January or February 'forty-two, in another girlfriend's place, because there was her boyfriend.

I am used to the twists and turns of English syntax when it's filtered through Polish, but I wasn't sure who "her" referred to.

Whose boyfriend was there? I asked Meg.

Lorka's boyfriend, she replied. Yulek Zimmerman was his name. That was the last time I saw her, because Yulek had a younger sister that we were friends with, me and Frydka.

She explained: Early in 1942, before the Jews of Bolechow were no longer permitted to walk the streets, Meg had gone to this Zimmerman house to see her friend Dusia Zimmerman, and when she got there Dusia's older brother, Yulek, was there, with Lorka Jäger, his girlfriend.

So she had a boyfriend, I thought.

As Meg lingered over this story, which she would tell me again a few days later, when I finally got to visit with her and old Mr. Grossbard—not, as it turned out, without some difficulty—I tried to think of why the name *Zimmerman* was ringing a bell. And then I remembered: on our last day in Bolechow a year and a half earlier, some old women had told us that they didn't know anyone called Jäger but they'd known a family called Zimmerman; but I hadn't wanted to stop and talk to them because people called Zimmerman had nothing to do with us.

I ASKED MEG, So you knew her since you were a small girl? Meaning Frydka.

Oh yes, we grew up together.

So did you know the other sisters at all?

She made a face. Of course, she said. The little one I didn't know so much because she was small, but the others . . .

Her voice trailed off and she smiled sadly. I was very often at their place, she said after a moment. They were lovely, they were friendly. It was a very lovely home. Very warm, very friendly.

After a moment she added, It was one story, but spacious. It was painted white, I recall.

Again I was bewildered and frustrated—angry with myself, in a way. She had known them so well, and I couldn't begin to think what kinds of questions might tease, from out of her memory, a living sense of what this vanished family had been like. I asked Mrs. Grossbard about Ester. We knew nothing whatsoever about her, I told her.

I mean—she shrugged—how would you like me to describe her? She was hospitable, she was friendly, and . . . I mean . . . I can't tell you any more, because life . . .

Everyone was silent for a moment, and then Sarah Greene intervened with a laugh. She said, She was probably like all the other Jewish mothers!

Meg reacted. I had noticed, by now, that she didn't like other people to have the last word; like everyone—like me, too, of course—she wanted control of her own story.

No, no, no, no, she said. She was very friendly, she had a cheerful personality. The father I haven't seen very much because he was seldom at home, but the mother, she was always at home.

Like all the other Jewish mothers gave me an idea. What if I started thinking about them as if they were just ordinary people instead of sepia icons? I decided to try to provoke Mrs. Grossbard.

You know, I said to her, you knew these girls when they were girls but also when they were teenagers. So did they have good relationships with the parents, did they complain about them?

She seemed confused, as if she couldn't quite grasp what I was after.

Look, she said to me, slowly, we were very young when the war broke out . . .

Yes, I thought, I know. The Polish State Archives had sent me a copy of Frydka's birth certificate. October 22, 1922. She was not quite seventeen when the war started, not quite nineteen when the Soviets retreated and the Germans came. Twenty-one, probably, when she died—if it was true that she had gone into the forest to join the Babij partisans in 1943, which of course there was no way of knowing with any certainty. I knew they had all been young when the war broke out, these girls, but I had a very faint sense, the instant when Meg retreated from talking about Frydka as a teenager, that she was doing so because the subject of Frydka as a teenager might lead to another subject that she was even less willing to discuss.

As it turned out, I was right.

Just then Bob Grunschlag interrupted. Who would dare to complain against their parents?! he said, grinning.

Everyone laughed. As people chuckled, I overheard Meg talking across the table to Jack in a low voice. She was saying: I don't recall exactly when Frydka—she was with Tadzio Szymanski? She was with Tadzio?

Between my ignorance of Polish personal names, at that point, and the way she pronounced those last four words, which to my ear sounded like *she wass wiss stadziu,* it was impossible for me to tell exactly what the name was.

I asked who was this Stadzio or Tadzio Szymanski.

No, no, no, no, Meg immediately said. Her voice was firm; she must have been a formidable young woman, I thought. Then she adjusted her tone, lightening her voice to make it seem that this was someone of no great significance.

Frydka was friendly with someone, you wouldn't know, but Jack would know. Meg looked, at that moment, right past Bob, to whom she said, *You know nothing.*

Then Jack turned to Meg and said, correcting her, *Ciszko* Szymanski.

Meg nodded Yes. Ciszko, she repeated.

To my ear it sounded like *Chissko.* Again I asked what they were talking about.

No, no, no, no. Nothing.

Nothing?

Jack said, I was trying to remember some boy, some non-Jewish boy.

Meg looked irritated.

Somebody was going out with a non-Jewish boy? I asked.

Now wait, Meg said. No, no, no, no. This is not to be in the records.

Jack laughed and pointed at me. See, he said, you're learning some things here!

Everyone laughed except Meg. I had the feeling, which was, as often happens with these intuitions, at once vague but unmistakable, that I had tripped onto an old, controversial piece of gossip.

Meg looked at me and said, You know that American comedy, where he says "I know NUSSSSink"? Of course I knew: *Hogan's Heroes,* the jolly Nazi POW-camp sitcom from the Sixties, one of whose characters was the obese Sergeant Schultz, who although he invariably was a party to the adorable antics of the American POWs, would always insist to his *Kommandant* that he was innocent, that he hadn't seen anything. *I know NUSS-ink!* he would cry, a line always played for laughs.

Well, Meg went on, when I'd nodded that yes, I knew that American comedy, I know *nussss-ink!*

But this wasn't television. This wasn't a comedy. The story that she wanted to keep from me was the whole reason I'd flown nine thousand miles to talk to her.

So Frydka liked this boy and he wasn't Jewish, I persisted.

I don't know, I wasn't there, Meg said.

It would have been a big deal, no? I said.

Bob, gleeful at having an opportunity to tease her, leaned in again. It would have been a *very* big deal, he said. This drew a sour smile from Meg.

That's an understatement. The understatement of the year, she murmured. But still she refused to confirm, in so many words, that Frydka Jäger had liked this Polish Catholic boy a lifetime ago, when such a romance would have been a very big deal; although now who really cared? My brother Andrew's wife isn't Jewish; Matt's wife is Greek Orthodox. I wondered, for a split second during this exchange, what he was thinking about this revelation.

Meg stonewalled. I don't know, I didn't witness it.

I'm not asking you to *witness* it, I said, half joking. But she was your best friend, she must have been confiding in you?

Meg sighed. No, no, this was happening during the war. Not before. Heavens forbid!

I made a mental note of how she said *Heavens,* plural.

Nothing like this could have happened before the war, she explained.

This, of course, was as good as an admission. At that moment, Frydka, who until now had been a child's face on a photograph or two, began to assume an emotional form, to have a story. So she had liked some Polish boy, I thought to myself with a smile, and he had liked her back.

And thinking that this was the story, a story that even as I heard it there, for the first time, I was preparing in my mind for subsequent retellings to my mother, her cousins, my siblings, when I got home, I leaned back in my chair and decided to change the subject for a while before I really alienated Mrs. Grossbard, who was looking unhappy. It was just then that Jack, leaning in from the end of the table and raising his voice, said, Let me tell you something. That boy lost his life because of Frydka.

Wait, I said. I'm sorry?

Jack lowered his voice. Everyone else at the table had stopped talking and turned to him. He looked at me and started talking again. Pausing for emphasis between each word, he went on, and what he said was this:

The. Boy. Lost. His. Life. Because. Of. Her.

There was a moment's silence.

What do you mean? I said.

Well, you see, he began, these three girls were in Babij, the partisan group, because three Polish boys befriended them. Three Bolechower girls. Frydka, the other one was Dunka Schwartz, and the third one was . . . the sister of the two boys who survived with the Babijs, Ratenbach.

I had no idea who these people were, but I didn't interrupt. I wanted him to go on.

These three boys befriended the girls, he went on, they helped the girls to get to the forest where were the Babij. It was a forest near Dolina, there were about four hundred Jews who were part of the partisans.

I nodded: he'd begun to tell me this story a year ago, on the phone.

Then of course we went to the forest ourselves, he went on, Bob and my father and I. So we lost track. When we came back, we were told that these three boys were—

He gestured vigorously with the flat of his right hand toward the side of the table, as if to demarcate a certain geographical area over *there*.

—were brought out in a field in Bolechow, he went on, and were shot.

Because they helped the girls, I said.

Because they helped the girls, he repeated.

And I thought, Now this is a story.

As it turned out, I wouldn't get the rest of the story of Frydka and Ciszko until I had traveled further: to Israel, to Stockholm, to Copenhagen. That afternoon, in Sydney, we didn't return to the subject of Frydka and Ciszko Szymanski, because it was clear that Mrs. Grossbard wasn't going to talk anymore if we pressed the subject. So instead I asked them all to clarify the chronology of the Nazi occupation.

What was the day the Germans arrived? I said.

People were making indecisive noises when Meg said, more to herself than to any of us, The first of July, 'forty-one. I saw the first patrols, I saw them coming.

She added that three weeks later Hungarian fascist units arrived and stayed perhaps two months.

No, Jack interrupted; it was just a few weeks and then the Slovaks came.

Bob said he didn't remember any Germans until September. Jack replied that "officially" the Germans entered on July 1 but they were preceded by the Hungarian units, who came through the mountains and stayed "a few weeks."

The dates were relatively unimportant to me. What was the first thing that happened? I asked. I was trying to paint a mental picture of the onset of the horrors, in order to be able to place Shmiel in it, somewhere. What had they seen, what had it been like?

The first thing that happened, Jack said, was that the Ukrainians came and they started to kill Jews. Whoever had, you know, an account to settle—

Bob cut in. You know, if you had something with the Jews, you killed them. I'll give you an example. After the Soviets retreated, that summer of 'forty-one, a lot of Jewish boys who'd been conscripted by the Russians had made their way home to Bolechow—they'd been drafted into the Russian army and were returning home. So the Ukrainians were standing on the bridge looking into the returning soldiers' eyes as they came back, and if they thought someone was a Jew, they threw him down from the bridge into the river. And as it was a river with big boulders and so forth, you can imagine what happened.

I nodded, although of course I couldn't really imagine, having never witnessed anything like what he was describing.

The reference to the river, the river beside which Frydka, at least, had frolicked—for by now, Meg had taken out and shown me all the snapshots from Pepci Diamant's album, the snapshots of the girls on skis, the girls lined up in front of someone's house, the girls in their swimming suits, peering comically out from behind the bushes at the water's edge, staring into the camera as they snacked, their hair tied up in kerchiefs—triggered a long-forgotten memory. Once before, I knew, the Sukiel River, which flowed through Bolechow and in which my grandfather, as a boy, had fished for mountain trout, had become a place of terror. When I was growing up my grandfather used to tell a story about Bolechow during the First World War. Because the town was right on the front between the Austrian and Russian armies, he would begin, it was constantly being bombarded, and at the onset of these bombardments he and his brothers and sisters—all except Shmiel, who was already away at the front, fighting for his emperor—would run into the woods outside of town for safety. Since, he would go on, sometimes these bombardments took place, terrifyingly, at night, his mother would make the children tie the laces of their shoes together and hang their shoes around their necks before they went to bed, so that if they had to run, they'd know where their shoes were. One night (he would say) the bombing began, but because my grandfather hadn't listened to his mother—and this, naturally, was the point of my grandfather's story; that you should always listen to your mother—because he hadn't tied his shoes around his neck, he couldn't find them when the bombs started going off, and as he and Ruchel and Susha and Itzhak and Yidl and Neche and their mother dashed out of the house and down the road toward the cover of the trees, they had to cross a branch of this river, the Sukiel; and because the bombs were going off in the water, the water was scalding and he burned his feet.

One of these bombardments lasted for nearly a week, he sometimes added, and to illustrate this point he told another story. Once, after they had been trapped in the forest for many days because of one of these bombardments, terrified to go back to the town, he and his family and a group of other Bolechowers had been reduced to hunting and killing a doe and eating the meat in the woods. When he said this, he gave me a significant look, and I knew what he meant: an animal that was killed in a hunt could not be kosher. My grandfather came from a long line, generations in fact, of Jewish butchers; in the woods, they must have known what they were doing. *But if life is at stake, God forgives!* he would say at this point . . .

So he had burned his feet in the boiling water of the Sukiel, that night. But this wasn't the end of the story. After pausing for effect, he would go on. *A boy I went to school with was boiled to death in the river that night.* Even now, as I hear, in my mind, the way he said the word *boiled,* I shiver. Who knows if it was true? *When we came back to town a few days later*, he would say, ending this tale, *half of the house was gone.*

I thought of this as Jack and Bob remembered how the Ukrainians, when the bad days first started, threw Jews into the river. Or (Jack added) sometimes they took the Jews alongside the river and just shot them.

You remember Gartenberg was shot? he said, looking at Bob.

Bob nodded, That's right.

Roight.

It was under the bridge, Jack went on.

Those were the first things, Bob said.

NOW, FOR THE first time, I got a clear picture of the first Aktion. I needed to know about it in as much detail as possible. This is when Ruchele had been killed.

The first *German* Aktion, Bob began, wanting me to understand the difference between the Nazis' organized killing events and the random, private vendettas of certain Ukrainians, those who'd lived with their Jewish neighbors, the gentle old Ukrainian woman had told me in Bolechow, *like a big family*, was on the twenty-eighth of October 1941.

As he said this Meg nodded, looking pensively down at the table. Then, slowly and distinctly, she said, It was a Tuesday.

Bob went on. They took somewhere between seven hundred and—

Jack and Meg interrupted him simultaneously. A thousand, they both said.

—A thousand, Bob said. And they kept them for about thirty-six hours in Dom Katolicki, the Catholic community center, and they kept them there while the Germans were drinking on the podium and the Jews had to kneel down on the floor and they got drunk and they'd shoot a lot in the crowd. And anyway after thirty-six hours they took them out in trucks and drove them out of town and to Taniawa Field and they already had the big hole dug up, and they shot them all.

This is what Bob told me that Sunday, my grandfather's birthday, when Matt and I met with all the Bolechowers. When I spoke to him alone a few days later, he said, Now I remember seven hundred and twenty, but all the others say it was a thousand. I believe they had a board across the hole and they shot them on the board. Machine guns, I don't know. Everybody remembers slightly different, it all depends on what you heard and what you remember.

How, I wanted to know, did they round up the people for this Aktion? I remembered my family's stories, that Shmiel had been on some kind of list.

Bob said, The Germans were going around with Ukrainian policemen, because at first they had a list. On the list, he explained, were the names of prominent Bolechower Jews: doctors, lawyers, businessmen. The idea was to demoralize the town by eliminating the leading citizens.

How, I asked, did the Germans come to assemble the list—how did they know who was who? The Germans, of course, were new to the area: unfamiliar with Bolechow and its inhabitants.

Bob replied that the local Ukrainians went with the German officers, pointing out who was who and who lived where. I believe there were 140 or 160
on the list, he said, and if the people were not at home, like my father, they
just started to gather people on the streets.

They had a list, and Shmiel was on it, my cousin Elkana had told me, once; from
whom he had learned this, it is impossible, now, to know. This must surely be
the same list that Jack was now talking about. And yet I was fairly sure that
Shmiel himself wasn't taken in the first Aktion. Aunt Miriam in Israel had written, long ago, that she had heard that Shmiel wasn't killed until 1944, along
with one of the girls, after they had joined the partisans; my brother Matt had
run into that man at the Holocaust survivors gathering, the one who had once
used the dead Shmiel's name, apparently a practice of certain partisans. And
Jack, in our first conversation over the phone, a year before, had told me that as
far as he knew only Ruchele had been taken in this action. So I concluded that
Shmiel, if he had been on that list (*very likely,* Jack said), had been away from
home that day, when the Germans and the Ukrainians had come knocking.

People in Bolechów take me for a rich man, he had boasted in one of his letters.
Perhaps they had, and in the end it had done him no favors.

On the day we talked with all of them, I wanted to know how Ruchele had
come to be taken.

Bad luck, Jack said, musingly. You see, there were four girls who were very
close friends. There was Ruchele and three others. Out of the four girls, three
perished that day. I figure they must have met up somewhere—that they had
made an arrangement to meet, and they got caught and taken away.

As he spoke I thought of the picture of Ruchele that I had: a big, wide-
grinned blond girl with the wavy Mittelmark hair she'd inherited from her
grandmother, the same hair I had as a teenager. A nice girl, a sweet girl, a
"placid" girl, Jack had told me. In October 1941 she was sixteen . . .

BUT THAT COMES later. Now I wanted to know what she was like, this
girl whom the seventy-eight-year-old man I was now talking to had dated
for a year and a half, sixty-four years before. Boris, when I'd asked him what
Shmiel had been like, had said *he was a butcher:* my fault, I knew, for not having prepared the right kinds of questions, not having been able to foresee how
hopeless it was to try to get a sense of what someone might have been like by
simply asking, *What was he like?* Of course, maybe he didn't have that much to
say, anyway: if someone asked me, now, to describe certain of the neighbors

who'd lived across the street from me forty years ago, I'm not sure I'd have much to say except *He was an engineer, they were very nice.* So what, really, could I expect? And Mrs. Grossbard, who I knew had much more vivid memories, had begun by being too protective of her memories of Frydka to share them freely; this, I knew, was the reason for the stiffness, the withholding quality I had sensed from the beginning. And ever since the subject of Frydka and Ciszko Szymanski had come up, she'd shut like a door in my face, suspicious of my motives, rightly leery that my desire for a story, for some kind of drama to animate the otherwise unknowable lives of these people, would take the Frydka she had known and reduce her to a stick figure, a cipher.

So I had failed thus far to reanimate the lost. But Jack, I felt strongly, would be able to grasp what I wanted; it was just a matter of finding the right moment to talk. Jack, who can be forceful in conversation, is nonetheless rather courtly in an old-fashioned way. He never interrupts, and was quick to apologize whenever he realized he'd gotten a name or a date wrong. (Since Mrs. Grossbard never, to my knowledge, got anything wrong, I never had the opportunity to see her apologize.) This unassuming quality, I guessed, made him reluctant to go on at great length about his relationship with Ruchele during the group meeting, and so I arranged to talk to him in private the following afternoon, at his place. The house was quiet—Sarah had gone out, leaving some cake and coffee behind—and the conversation was easy.

His memories of Ruchele, he told me, went back to when they were both perhaps just fourteen, when he used to see her at the nightly meetings of the Hanoar HaZioni, the Zionist organization. He said to me, It met every evening. It was groups of ages, so I was in a group of boys my age, and she was in a group of girls her age.

He pronounced *girls* like "GEH-earls." During the Thirties, the meetings of the Hanoar were where Bolechow's Jewish teenagers did most of their socializing, apparently. Jack went on: In Europe the main meal was lunchtime. So in the evening you ate sandwiches, and after that you went to the Hanoar. I would say that during the winter the meetings lasted between say, five-thirty till ten in the evening, in summer from eight, or from seven-thirty, until ten. Every evening, and on Saturday from lunchtime till night. Look, I traveled each day by train to school, to the high school in Stryj, I had to study, it was a crammed day. But that Hanoar club was the pleasant part of it. We played together, we danced together, the horas, and the lectures, and so on. I must have known the Jäger girls from before, but I remember them definitely from then.

Matt asked, What did she look like?

Jack smiled and, after a moment, said, She was blond, and I liked blondes. She was a beautiful girl, she had long hair, you know, how do you call that—

(he gestured with one hand at the back of his neck and made twirling motions with his fingers)

—they were plaited. She had, I think, green eyes, and in one of them (here he held a thumb and forefinger up to his eye a quarter of an inch apart and squinted) she had a brown quarter in it.

Listen, he finally said, she was my puppy love, as they called it, my love, and I was wrapped up in it.

How did they meet, we wanted to know.

Jack told us a funny story. I wasn't the first boy, he explained. There was a guy a year older than me, he also traveled to school in Stryj, and he used to go out with her. Mundzio Artman. He was a very religious boy and didn't go to school on Saturday to Stryj—he'd go on Friday, and stayed over the weekend so he could come back on Saturday night. So he asked me, "Look here, you look after her on Saturdays." Which I did! She cooled off to him and I became involved. I was fourteen, thirteen maybe, and she was the same age.

So when you were dating a girl in Bolechow in the late Thirties, we asked, what did you do?

We'd meet mostly at the Hanoar, and wherever the boys were not separated from the girls, we did everything together. We discussed, we talked. Needless to say she was more mature than I. I realized that later. You see, I didn't like school. The studies, well, I wasn't gifted on studies!

He chuckled with good-humored self-deprecation. When he said *on studies,* I smiled. Years after this conversation took place, Mrs. Begley's son mentioned that the hardest part of learning English was the prepositions.

I remember when, Jack went on, at the end of the year, I got my report card. Ruchele was there in the train, or maybe in the school, to check up how I performed. And I don't want to tell you her disappointment when she saw it! And I think eventually she cooled off a little . . .

Matt was gleeful. She wanted a doctor! he joked. I was gleeful for a different reason. I loved *more mature than I.* It gave this girl, of whom a single photograph now exists, a certain presence. I thought to myself, So she had certain ideas of what her boyfriend should be like; had, perhaps, an elevated sense of herself. She was, after all, a Jäger.

I asked Jack whether Ruchele herself had been a good student.

Jack smiled sadly and said, That I don't know. But I must assume that Frydka was the smartest because she went to high school and the others didn't. Possibly the parents decided only Frydka should go to high school and not her. Maybe Ruchele was a good student but Shmiel couldn't afford the high school at that time.

He paused. The fees were high, he said, as if trying to excuse Shmiel for not sending Ruchele to the high school. Plus the traveling, he added, plus the books, plus the uniforms . . .

The uniforms I had, by now, seen. Among the photos that Meg had taken out of the carefully folded plastic bag, the day before, was a very early one—it's dated 1936, the girls would have been fourteen—of Meg, Frydka, and Pepci Diamant, standing alongside a fence on a winter's day. All three are wearing heavy, dark winter coats, double-breasted, belted, fur-collared; on their feet are low boots, and they're wearing school berets. Their faces are young and soft; Frydka's is just losing its baby fat. Her face seemed to me to be older here than it is in another picture that Meg had shown me, a snapshot that belonged to Pepci (*who perished,* Meg said a second time as she showed me this picture, *although her photo album survived*), in which Frydka is lying on her tummy with her right arm crooked in front of her; she's resting her chin on the back of her right hand, while with her left hand she holds open (as it happens) a photo album. She looks rather self-consciously off to the right, her eyes turned upward. There is something stagey about the photo, something actress-y; she's a young girl, still, but already she's posing. In this picture her cheeks are still round, whereas in the other photos that Meg had brought—the snapshot of Frydka, dated 1940, in which she wears a kerchief, babushka-style, and stares pensively out of the picture field at you, dark-eyed and quiet; the group photos in which Meg, Frydka, and their perished friend Pepci Diamant are skiing, swimming, posing—in these, Frydka is already a terrific-looking young woman: tall, dark, fine-boned, with an amused gleam in her eye.

So Ruchele didn't go to Stryj to high school, Jack was saying. At the time she was going to seventh grade in public school, and then she started learning dressmaking.

I didn't mention it to Jack at the time, but I knew all this from Shmiel's letters, such as the one in which he wrote

> *I'm very isolated here and dear Ester has untrustworthy siblings, I have nothing to do with them whatsoever, imagine that they didn't want to help Lorka learn how to be a photographer.*
> *Not that I have to tell you, my dear ones, what even strangers say, which is that I have the best and most distinguished children in Bolechów; what good does it do*

me? Darling Frydka has finished high school, it cost me a fortune and where is one
supposed to find a job for her? Darling Ruchaly finished grade 7 with distinction, I
spent $25 for her and now she's been learning to be a dressmaker for the past year . . .

Frydka used to go to the high school in Stryj on the train, Jack was saying.
And she was a tall girl, I remember, you know, the girls—

He put a hand out and said, Wait, I'll bring a bag.

As I looked on, bemused, he hurried out of his living room and returned a few
seconds later with a battered old briefcase, so that he could do a proper imper-
sonation of the long-dead Frydka hurrying off the train with her schoolbag.

You see, he now continued, Everyone carried their bags like that—he
walked a few steps, holding the briefcase low at his side, as if it were loaded
heavily—because they were loaded with books. But Frydka was a tall girl, an
energetic girl, and she used to walk like *that*.

Thrusting the bookbag to his chest and bracing it with one arm, he strode
purposefully forward, imitating Frydka.

He said, She was always one of the first to come down from the train each
day, and she used to carry it like that.

But Frydka must wait. Now, I wanted to know about Ruchele, this girl
who, however placid she may have been, nonetheless had a certain spirit,
knew what kind of boy she wanted to go out with: an overachiever, maybe,
like her father.

So how long did you go out with her? I asked Jack.

A year and a half, two years, he replied.

What do you remember of her parents? I asked. Did you see them often?

Jack made an amused face. Of course! Remember, you knew *everyone*. It
was a little shtetl. I knew the parents, I knew the sisters. But I didn't speak to
them, didn't talk to them. . . . Everyone had a nickname.

The day before he had been telling me about the nicknames of the towns;
now he was telling me about the nicknames of the townspeople.

Jack suddenly said, The *król*! I had an aunt, my mother's sister, she called
Shmiel Jäger the *król*—the king. I think she must have been very fond of him.

It was difficult for me to think of Shmiel as someone people had emotions
about other than grief.

Jack went on, smiling to himself, She talked about him. The king this, the king
that. The *król*. It must have been—well, his appearance: he was the head of the
butchers' cartel, you know there was a butchers' cartel, and he was the boss. It
was kosher meat, of course, and every Jewish home had it that could afford it.

I thought to myself how happy my grandfather would have been, to hear this Bolechower boy talking about Shmiel like this.

You see, Jack told me, My father was very well-to-do, but he never dreamt of a car, even a horse and cart. But Shmiel Jäger . . . In Bolechow there were only two cars, and one of them belonged to Shmiel Jäger.

But I didn't want to talk about Shmiel just yet, either; I had to finish, first, with Ruchele. I took out the picture of her that had belonged to my Aunt Sylvia, a picture I'd mailed to Jack long before I met him, after we'd talked on the phone; a photograph from his past, not mine, which I had sent to him without ever thinking what its impact on him could possibly be.

He picked it up tenderly and smiled.

Yes, you sent me. That's how she looked, she was a beautiful girl. You can see the smile. Beautiful smile. That's how she looked in 'thirty-nine. She had a beautiful fur coat—not a full fur, just the collar.

Unconsciously, he patted his lapel.

When was the last time you saw her? we asked.

The last time I saw her was Yom Kippur in 1941, he said. We were praying outside of the *shtiebl,* Jack went on.

Shtiebl was a word I hadn't heard in years: a little shul, a little prayer-house, usually in a basement, in part of another structure; perhaps in some disdain, my grandfather used to call the Lubavitch synagogue he attended at the end of his life a *shtiebl,* the little place on Eighth Street in Miami Beach, which he attended not because he liked Hasidim, which in fact he didn't, but because it was the only shul within walking distance from his apartment building, the building where, eventually, he killed himself.

We were praying outside of the *shtiebl,* Jack was saying, and the backyard of the *shtiebl* bordered on the backyard of a girlfriend of hers, Durst. Yetta Durst. And I saw Ruchele there.

I thought, not for the first time, Every single name he mentions in passing was a person, a someone, a life. Maybe Yetta Durst had had a cousin, an uncle in New York. Maybe it would be possible for the child or grandchild of that person, a man or a woman of forty or so, to begin a search for the lost Yetta Durst, a search that would, eventually, take him or her to Australia, where he would talk to Jack Greene. . . .

Yetta Durst, Jack repeated, remembering. As he pronounced the name again I detected the tiniest whiff of satisfaction: he was glad he had remembered her name.

And so I saw Ruchele there and I remember I was praying and she came, it was outside, I prayed outside and she was playing in the backyard with that girl . . . or maybe she knew I'd be there.

Matthew asked, And what did you say to her?

Not much, Jack said, after a moment.

He was pensive.

I don't remember . . . We hadn't broken up but it had cooled off. I was still very keen, but she wasn't. I personally think she felt that she needed someone more mature. That's what girls are more interested in. That was Yom Kippur 1941. That was the last time I saw her. And then you know, four weeks later was the Aktion. She got killed four weeks later, Jack said.

IT WAS, IN a strange way, odd to be reminded of her death just then. I felt like I was just getting to know her.

I have often tried to imagine what might have happened to her, although every time I do, I realize how limited my resources are. How much can we know about the past, and those who disappeared from it? We can read the books and talk to those who were there. We can look at photographs. We can go to the places where these people lived, where these things happened. Someone can tell us, it happened on such-and-such a day, I think she went to meet some friends, she was a blonde.

But all this is, inevitably, approximate. I have been to Bolechow, but the town is now so physically transformed—many buildings vanished or altered beyond recognition, the bustle of the 1930s eroded to nothing after sixty years of Soviet stagnation and poverty—that the Bolechow I visited in 2001 bears only an imperfect resemblance to the place Ruchele had to walk through in the hours before her death. And even if (say) a photograph of the town existed today that had been taken on October 28, 1941, the day Ruchele was seized, could such a photo give me a precise sense of what she saw as she walked to the Dom Katolicki? Not really. (We don't, of course, even know which route she took, whether she kept her head bowed or looked up trying to get one last glance; we don't even know if she *knew* that this would be her last walk through the town.) So there is the problem of visualization. And what about the other senses? Bolechow, we know, had a particular smell, because of the chemicals used at the many tanneries—over a hundred in number, we are told. So as Ruchele walked to her death that day, did she smell the tangy smell of Bolechow? What is the smell of a thousand terrified people being herded to their deaths? What is the smell of a room in which a thousand terrified people have been kept for a day and a half, deprived of toilets, a room in which the stove has been lighted, a room in which perhaps a few dozen people have been shot to death, a woman has gone into labor? I will never know. And what is the noise that they make? A witness might have written or said, People were screaming and crying, the piano was being played, but the worst screaming I have ever heard in my life was, I am fairly certain, the screaming of my younger brother Matt on a day nearly forty years ago when I broke his arm, and to be honest I can't really remember the *sound* of it, I merely remember that he was screaming; and the worst crying I have ever heard was the weeping at a funeral of a friend who died too young, but my suspicion is that the quality of the sound of screaming made by young boys who have been injured, however severely, is not the quality of the sound of screaming made by (say) middle-aged men who have had their eyes cut out, or have been forced to sit on hot stoves; and, by the same token, the sound of perhaps sixty people weeping at a funeral is not the same as that of a thousand people weeping in fear for their lives. It is, indeed, likely that if you were to read a description of what went on during the two days of the first Aktion in Bolechow, the images and sounds you would supply to yourself, mentally, would be images and sounds you've acquired from films or television, which is to say images and sounds produced by people who have been paid to reconstruct, to the best of *their* ability—based on whatever reading, visiting, and looking they have done, extrapolated from whatever experiences they may have had—what such events might have looked or sounded like, although that, too, is just an approximation, ultimately.

So there is, too, the problem of the other senses.

You might say, Well, these details aren't the important things. And it's true that we know certain *kinds* of things that happened, and that these are important to know and remember. But part of my aim, since I first began to pursue what could be known about my lost relatives, had been to try to learn whatever scraps of details about them might still be knowable, what they looked like, what their personalities were like, and yes, how they died, if anyone could still tell me that; and yet the more I talked to people, the more I was aware of how much simply can't be known, partly because the thing—the color of her dress, the exact path she took—was never witnessed and is, therefore, unknowable now, and partly because memory itself, of those things that were witnessed, can play tricks, can elide what is too painful or be trimmed to fit a pattern that we happen to like.

I think it is important to be aware of this even as we try to *envision* what happened to Ruchele and the others, which we really cannot do.

What might have happened, then, that day? Although things were tense and frightening by October 1941, there had been no organized mass killings yet. And so Ruchele had (possibly) made a plan, that Tuesday, to meet up with some of her girlfriends. She leaves the single-story, white-painted house, maybe promising Ester, her mother, a stout and friendly woman, that she wouldn't be long. She goes down Dlugosa toward the Rynek. Perhaps she catches sight of her girlfriends and waves to them, walks toward them. And then, suddenly, the Ukrainians, the Germans, dogs barking, some strange-looking officers shouting to go that way, along with the others, to come this way. The three school friends are frightened, but at least they are together. Now they are walking with a big crowd, toward the Dom Katolicki, where they used to go on dates to the movies.

And yet the mind halts again, for it is useless to pretend that I can imagine the suffering of Ruchele Jäger during the next day and a half. Even if I have some idea of what happened, during those thirty-six hours, there is no way to reconstruct what she herself went through. For one thing, no one who survived saw her. (Decades earlier, my mother had been told that the girls had been *raped and killed by the Nazis*. Had Ruchele been raped in the Dom Katolicki? Impossible to know, now.) For another, too little remains of her personality to know, to even begin to imagine, what her state of mind might have been even for a second of those hours.

Still. Even if I assume that Ruchele herself was not beaten, raped, or killed during the thirty-six hours in which she and a thousand other people were held in the Dom Katolicki, certainly it is possible to have some broad notion of what it would have been like, as a sixteen-year-old, perhaps overly sheltered girl of a certain era, to witness other people being killed, tortured, raped, shot. To watch, for instance—an incident Jack mentioned to us when we talked to him alone—as the rabbi you have known since you were a young child has his eyes cut out, has a cross cut into his chest, and is then forced to dance naked with another terrified young woman . . .

How do we know what happened there?

Olga told us what she had heard, when we were in Bolechow: the human pyramid.

Jack told us about the cross that was cut into the rabbi's chest, a thing he cannot have witnessed. (I had asked him, during that conversation, how he knew for sure that Ruchele had perished in this particular Aktion. Had he seen her being taken? I stupidly questioned. He laughed grimly. *If I would have seen her, I would have been dead too!* So how did he know? Because *afterwards*, he said, a little impatiently, she was *missing*.)

Bob Grunschlag later told me that, incredible as it sounds, on the day the first Aktion started, after his mother had been taken from her house and his older brother pulled from where he and Jack and Bob had been hiding in a hayloft—Bob and Jack weren't discovered, although the searchers' pitchfork came within inches of Bob's face, he told me—he'd eventually emerged from the hiding place and sneaked under cover of darkness to the Dom Katolicki to see what was going on there. The D.K., he and the other called it, pronouncing it like this: *day-kah.*

The rumors, he said, were that they were taking the Jews who had been rounded up to some work place. And as it was the end of October it was already winter, so I thought we'd better take for Mother some woolen things, so the maid packed them up. We had heard by then where they were being held, in the D.K., the clubhouse. So I went there.

But Bob was spotted by some Ukrainian boys—there was a big crowd of Ukrainians hanging around outside the building, craning for a look inside (among them a boy who would grow up to be a man whom I interviewed two years after this conversation with Bob)—and ran back home.

The woolens, in any event, were unnecessary.

So Bob, although he had gone there to look, hadn't actually seen what was going on. How, then, did they know—how did the stories leak out?

Bob explained to me that a neighbor of theirs, Mrs. Friedmann, had miraculously survived, after a Ukrainian woman persuaded the Germans to free her. She got out and she came to our place twenty-four or thirty-six hours later, Bob said, and she told us what happened. She saw my mother inside, she saw my brother. You see, they took my mother first, so she didn't know my brother was there also, until Mrs. Friedmann pointed out to her that her oldest boy was there, too.

He stopped talking, and I didn't speak for a moment. I was thinking, as he must have been, too, how much happier his mother would have been not to know that her eldest son, Gedalje—who was surely named for his father's father, the same Gedalje Grunschlag whose name proudly appears in the 1891 Galicia Business Directory—was also waiting to die in the D.K.

After a moment, Jack added, It was the hall I went to with Ruchele maybe eight months earlier to see the movies.

ABOUT SOME THINGS, then, we learned from Mrs. Friedmann. And it might seem to be enough, in order to at least suggest the horror that my cousin Ruchele Jäger experienced during the last thirty-six hours of her life, to know what Mrs. Friedmann told the Grünschlags and what the Grünschlags later remembered and subsequently told me and certain others. The rabbi with the cross cut into his chest, the obscenity of the blinded rabbi forced to dance onstage with the naked girl as someone played the piano, this same blinded, mutilated rabbi immersed, finally, in the sewage of the D.K. outhouse.

But it is possible to learn in still greater detail what went on in the Catholic community center. The following is a translation of a document that I obtained from Yad Vashem in the summer of 2003, a few months after I visited Australia, when I went to Israel to interview certain other "ex-Bolechowers" (as they like to call themselves) whom I'd found out about from my Australians. The document, in Polish, is a transcription of the testimony of a certain Rebeka Mondschein, which was given on the twentieth of August 1946, in Katowice, Poland, where Mrs. Mondschein had moved after the war. On that date, when the stories were still fresh, still rich with all the details that time has since stripped away, she was twenty-seven years old. What she said about the first Aktion was this:

On Tuesday 28 October 1941 at 10 am, two cars arrived from Stanisławów, they drove up to the town hall. In one car were Gestapo men in black shirts. In the other were Ukrainians in yellow shirts and berets with shovels on them. The latter immediately drove to Taniawa to dig one large grave. From the city hall in a half hour a Ukrainian was assigned to each Gestapo man and these pairs went with a list set by city hall for the town.

The list consisted of the wealthiest and most intelligent Jews. The Gestapo men were wearing battle uniforms. The people thought that they were collecting for a workers' brigade. After two hours they were indeed taken according to the list. On the list were: Rabbis Landau and Horowitz; Dr Blumental; Landes, Isaak; Feder, Ajzyk; Frydman, Markus; Dr Leon Frydman; Chief Dogilewski, his daughter jumped out a moving car though four months pregnant and escaped. It was 160 people in all.

The director of the Gestapo, the notorious Krüger, arrived from Stanisławów. He played around in the town hall for half an hour and then left. The action was coordinated by Gestapo Officer Schindler. The militia was also taken. At

12 o'clock, they started taking people from their houses and the streets. Near houses where a Gestapo man left, a crowd of Ukrainians arrived, who poured into the house to rob it after the Jews were led to the town square. The Gestapo men, Ukrainian militia members and innumerable young Ukrainian civilians, among them ten year old boys, chased them through the town. They sent the Jews to the Dom Katolicki on Wołoski Field. They all had to fall to their knees and keep their faces to the ground. Jews who thought they were being taken away for work took a few warm things with them, rucksacks and valuable things. At the entrance to the Dom Katolicki, a Gestapo man ordered them to give up all valuable things and money on pain of death. Money was found on the wife of Abeg Zimerman, who had to undress like everybody else in the hall. She was shot right there. There were more such incidents. After an escape attempt through a window, indeed the only such attempt, Ajzyk Feder was shot.

Nine hundred people were packed into the hall. People were stacked on one another. Many suffocated. They were killed in the hall, shot or simply hit over the head with clubs and sticks, right there in the hall.

Isaac Landes had such a completely crushed head, that later, when 29 corpses murdered in the Dom Katolicki were taken to the cemetery and his son, Dr David Landes, examined all of them, he didn't recognise him. People were beaten without any reason; for example, Gestapo man Schindler threw a chair in the face of Cyli Blumental and shattered her face, for amusement, in excess. The rabbis were especially targeted. Rabbi Horowitz's body was literally chopped and shredded. Rabbi Landau was ordered by one of the Gestapo men to stand naked on a chair and declaim a speech in praise of Germany. When he said that Germany is great, the Gestapo man beat him with a rubber stick, shouting "You're lying!" After that he shouted, "Where is your God?" In the hall in the centre of the crowd the wife of Beni Halpern started to give birth and at the same time she was bewildered and started shouting. A Gestapo man shot at her, but only injured her, so he got her with a second. She lay there until 30 October. The chemist Kimmelman also died there in the hall. Completely naked, Szancia Reisler, the wife of Friedmann the lawyer, had to dance naked on naked bodies. At midday, the Rabbis were led out from the hall and there is no trace of them. It is said that they were thrown into the sewer.

The people were kept in this way from 28 to 29 October without food or water until 16.00. At 16.00, they were all taken by car to the woods in Taniawa, 8–10 km from Bolechów. About 800 people were shot there. There was a board over a ditch onto which people were forced and they were shot and fell into the grave; some were badly injured others only just slightly. Ducio Schindler escaped from there in the evening. He climbed a tree and waited out the whole execution and *filling in of the grave. He told us everything. On the next day, 30 October 1941, Commissioner Köhler ordered the Judenrat [the all-Jewish governing council, appointed by the Nazi authorities to act as intermediaries between the Germans and the Jewish community and to carry out their orders] to clean up the hall of the Dom Katolicki, to take the 29 bodies to the cemetery.*

The Gestapo demanded payment for the ammunition expended. The Judenrat had to pay. Beyond that, they forced them to pay 3 kg. of granular coffee for labour expenses.

So now it is possible to know what happened, even if it is difficult to reconstruct with any certainty what happened to Ruchele. She was picked up, most likely, sometime after noon on Tuesday, the twenty-eighth of October, as she walked the streets of her hometown with her girlfriends. She was then herded toward the Dom Katolicki, and there probably witnessed certain of the events described above—although we must keep in mind that the Jews who were forced onto the floor of the D.K. that afternoon were told to keep their heads down, and that those who got up off the floor were often shot dead on the spot, so maybe it's better, instead of saying that Ruchele *witnessed* some of what happened, to say that she mostly *heard* shots, screams, shouts, taunts, the piano playing, the footfalls of the awkwardly dancing feet on the stage.

It is possible (to go on) that the sixteen-year-old Ruchele was killed there, as we know some people were. It is, indeed, possible that she was the naked girl on the stage, with whom the rabbi, his eyes running blood, was forced to dance, or forced to lie on top of. I prefer not to think so. Then again, if she survived those thirty-six hours, as some did not, we know that at around four o'clock on the afternoon of October 29, a Wednesday, after spending the previous day, night, and morning in a state of terror that it would be foolish to try to imagine; after weeping with thirst and hunger and, undoubtedly, soiling herself with her own urine, for nobody can go a day and a half without relieving herself, she was then taken, exhausted, hungry, terrified, filthy with her own bodily fluids, something it is hard, perhaps even embarrassing to think about, a disgusting, deeply shaming experience for any adult, but a possibility I must consider, as I try to imagine what happened to her; she was taken to Taniawa—whether she walked the few kilometers or was put in a truck, it is impossible to know—and there, after waiting in even greater terror while watching group after group of her neighbors, people she'd seen around the little town her whole life long (well: sixteen years) line up on a plank and fall into the pit: after watching this, she took her inevitable turn, walked naked onto the plank—with what thoughts it is impossible to know, although it would be difficult not to imagine that she was thinking, in those last moments, of her mother and father and sisters, of home; but perhaps (*you're a sentimental person,* Mrs. Begley had once told me, in part dismissively and in part indulgently), perhaps for the most fleeting moment, she thought of Jakob Grünschlag, the boy whom she'd dated for a year and a half, his dark hair and eager smile—and standing on the plank, or perhaps at the edge of the freshly dug pit, with the bodies beneath her and the cold October air above, waited. The cold October air: we know that she was naked by this point, and between the weather and the terror, surely she was shivering. Again and again, as she waited her turn—unless she was the first?—the sounds of machine-gun fire rang out. (This was not the death that people came, in time, to hope for, if it was their bad luck to be caught. *The shot to the back of the neck, what did they call it in German—the "mercy shot"?* Mrs. Grossbard had asked no one in particular, the day all the Bolechowers gathered. She made a gun with her hand and pointed to the back of her own neck. *I can't think of it. When I am upset I can't remember things.*)

So: the rattling bursts of gunfire, the cold, the shivering. At some point it was her turn, she walked with the others onto the plank. Likely this plank had some give, perhaps it bounced a little as they lined up: an incongruously playful motion. Then another burst of fire. Did she hear it? Was the fervent activity of her mind at this moment such that she didn't really hear; or, by contrast, were her ears exquisitely attuned, waiting? We cannot know. We know only that her soft, sixteen-year-old body—which with any luck was lifeless at this point, although we know that some were still alive when they fell with a wet thud onto the warm and bleeding, excrement-smeared bodies of their fellow townsfolk—fell into the grave, and that is the last we see of her; although we have, of course, not really seen her at all.

AND ALL THIS happened most likely because she had left her house and gone for a walk to meet her little group, the three school friends, late the previous morning.

Only one-sixth of the Jewish population perished that day, Jack told us. (Only.) But three-quarters of those four girls perished that day.

I noticed, not for the first time, that the verb Jack invariably uses of those who were killed is *perish,* which, to my ear, lent a slightly elevated, perhaps biblical flavor to his conversation when he would discuss those who did not survive the war. *Kill* and *dead* are Germanic words; the clipped finality of those brief monosyllables—in German as in English, *Tod* as well as *dead*—leâves, as it were, no room for argument. *Perish,* on the other hand, from the Latin verb *pereo,* the literal meaning of which is "to pass through," feels more ample; it always suggests to me a realm of possibilities far beyond the mere fact of death—a feeling that's confirmed by a glance at the entry in the rather old Latin dictionary I own: *To pass away, come to nothing, vanish, disappear, be lost; To pass away, be destroyed, perish; To perish, lose life, die . . . To be lost, fail, be wasted, be spent in vain; To be lost, be ruined, be undone.* Given what I know, now, after talking to all the Bolechowers now alive, I have come, myself, to prefer *perish* over all other verbs, when I speak of those who died.

Three-quarters of those four girls perished that day, Jack had said.

And so you knew, I said.

He paused for a moment.

Well, he said, *they* knew . . . I remember. Father was in Judenrat—my father was a member of the Judenrat, so I asked him what happened to the Jäger family, so he told me, One girl perished. And then I found out it was Ruchele.

This he told me when all of the Bolechowers were gathered at his dining table. The next day, when Matt and I returned to Jack's home to interview him alone, he told me a slightly different version of this story.

The Aktion took place on the Tuesday, he said. And Tuesday night my father arrived home. He was in the Judenrat. They had taken away Mother from home, but my father was away in the Judenrat. He thought they'd take him, so he ran away and arrived that night to our home. So you know, I don't know whether that evening or the next morning, I started to ask him, Whom did they take? I asked, What about the Jägers? And he said, One of the Jägers' girls. So I asked, Which one? And he didn't know, he didn't know or he wouldn't tell me—I don't even know if they knew I was dating her. And two or three days later they sent me to my aunt's house—you know, I took it bad, losing my mother and my brother.

I couldn't think of anything to say.

So I went to stay with my aunt for a few days. So I remember in the evening—maybe in the afternoon, maybe in the evening, at night—I came to ask, One of the Jäger girls they took—which one? And they said, Ruchele. So it hit me again. I didn't sleep that night, I remember my aunt didn't know why, she thought that I was still . . . after the death of my mother . . .

He fell silent for a moment, then went on.

I remember every hour, every hour and a half, my aunt came into the room where I was in bed and said, You're still not asleep, you're still not asleep? At the time I was thinking of Ruchele, because it was a new shock.

What Shmiel and Ester and their three remaining daughters, for whom the fate of Ruchele was, until then, the greatest catastrophe of their lives, went through in the days following the first Aktion in Bolechow will never be known. (Although we do know that Shmiel, who was still alive in 1941, would have had to contribute money when the Judenrat ordered a collection of funds early in November of that year, which meant that, however indirectly, he had to pay for the bullet or bullets that had ended his third daughter's life.) But now I do know this: that very briefly, a long time ago in the house of Jack Greene's aunt, Ruchele had mattered very much to someone else, and when I considered this, as Jack went on talking to me, I was happy.

You see, I had known one of the girls perished, he repeated, but I didn't know which one.

This, as it turned out, was the last thing anybody ever said to me about Ruchele Jäger.

The murder of innocent children is a notorious problem that arises in the text of parashat Noach. Parashat Bereishit, *a tale ostensibly about Creation, ends with God's disgusted awareness that "the wickedness of man was great upon the earth," a realization that leads him—there has been much excited comment on this notion—*

to "regret" having made humankind to begin with. ("What could this mean?" Friedman asks. "If God knows the future, how could God regret something once it has happened?") The deity's melancholy mood lasts only a little while, as we know, since immediately afterward he declares that he will "dissolve" mankind, animals, birds, and all creeping things.

The cause of God's ire, the nature of the sin that elicits his disgust, is described at the beginning of Noach. The earth, as God becomes aware in Genesis 6:11, has been corrupted (vatishacheth); it was corrupted (nish'chathah)—the word recurs immediately in the following verse—because all flesh had corrupted its way (hish'chith).What exactly is the nature of this "corruption"? Rashi notes that the consonantal root of the Hebrew verb that recurs so strikingly often in these verses, sh-ch-th, denotes idolatry (it's the verb used in Deuteronomy 4:16, when God warns his people against making graven images lest they become corrupt), and even more suggests gross sexual immorality. He glosses "all flesh had corrupted its way" as follows: "Even domestic animals, beasts, and birds had relations with those which were not of their species."

The nature of the corruption, then, has to do with the wayward mixing of categories that are meant to remain distinct—a preoccupation of this particular religion, as becomes increasingly clear throughout the Torah, from that original act of cosmic Creation, described as a process of separation and distinction, to the rigorous insistence, in later books such as Leviticus, on the separation of kinds and species of things, for instance the segregation of dairy products from meat products, of the towels with the red stripes from the towels with the blue stripes. And indeed when instructing Noah on the construction, outfitting, and loading of the Ark, God reminds him that the pairs of animals with which he will eventually restock the earth (that second act of Creation) must be "each according to its kind"—a specification that Rashi explains thus: "Those who cleaved to their own species, and did not corrupt their way."

The punishment for this particular brand of corruption, appropriately enough, reflects the nature of the crime. For the Flood that God unleashes has the effect of blurring the distinctions between things: as the waters rise, the ocean engulfs the dry land, and the mountains and distinguishing features of the landscape all disappear; when they do eventually reappear—as they had first appeared at the beginning of parashat Bereishit, when God first separated the water from the land—we are meant to feel it, surely, as a second Creation. This linkage between the crime and the punishment, another instance of the preoccupation in Noach with the way in which opposites are secretly connected, perhaps, is made evident in a striking verbal feature of the text: for the word that God uses when he says "I am about to destroy" all flesh is mash'chitham, which, like the words for "corrupt," is derived from the same sh-ch-th root. In Noach, the punishment literally fits the crime.

Given the Torah's obsessive preoccupation with segregation, separation, distinction, and purity, what is striking about the tale of God's dissatisfaction with his Creation, and his decision to cause a Flood that will obliterate it, is his determination to destroy "all flesh." The word "all" raises some difficult issues, implying as it does that at least some innocents will perish in the disaster. For presumably we can imagine that included in the designation "all flesh" there are, for instance, small children, or even babies—a category of person unlikely to have been engaging in interspecies miscegenation. Surprisingly, since he shows great humaneness elsewhere, Friedman shows no interest in the disturbing implication that God could be capable of killing innocents; he lingers instead on Noah's "purity" and lack of "blemish" in a way intended to show how broad-minded the authors of this tale were. ("And it is important that a story composed by Jews emphasized the virtue of someone who is not a Jew . . ."; and indeed, this very passage has been adduced in certain debates to support the notion that there could be a category of people called Righteous Gentiles, i.e., non-Jews who tried to save Jews during the Second World War—people, presumably, like Ciszko Szymanski, about whom, in time, I would come to learn a great deal.) Rashi, on the other hand, wrestles, albeit briefly, with the dark implications of Noach. His sole comment on the phrase "the end of all flesh" is that "wherever you find promiscuity, catastrophe comes to the world and kills [both] good and bad." This seems to imply either that the very sin denoted by sh-ch-th taints all who are even remotely connected to it, even the passive victims of (say) miscegenation; or that it is the guilty, through their indiscriminate sinning, who bring the punishment on the innocent as well—an interpretation that has the virtue of deflecting blame from God.

None of this, it must be said, seems very satisfying when you abandon the abstractions of the commentators and pause to wonder what, say, the extinction of the life of a small child might look or sound like, by drowning or indeed otherwise. Even after pondering Rashi's commentary, it is hard not to feel, given the way that the Torah frets about maintaining distinctions between things, that the indiscriminate annihilation of the innocent along with the guilty in the Flood story is uncharacteristically sloppy and disturbingly—well, un-kosher. But then, perhaps in certain instances—when executing plans on a gigantic scale, for instance, plans for the reconfiguration of the whole world—the ability to keep all the details in mind, to make certain kinds of distinctions, becomes counterproductive.

DID ANYBODY KNOW for certain when Shmiel and Ester perished? I asked an hour and a half or so into our conversation on the day of the group meeting. By then I had already adopted Jack's word, *perish*.

Meg said she thought it was in the second Aktion.

Jack said, Yes, that's what I think, in the second Aktion. I didn't see them after that. He then added, But I'm not sure.

I asked if anyone had seen them between the first and second Aktions.

After the first Aktion, Bob said, of course, you know, life was changed. We had to wear the armbands.

I nodded. Among Meg's snapshots was a remarkable one that had all too obviously been taken during this period: Pepci Diamant walking down a street with another girl—Meg had identified her as one of the *Flüchtling*, the refugees from surrounding the area who'd poured into the town as the Germans stomped across Poland—both of them wearing the white armband with the blue Star of David. In this snapshot, both young women are smiling. I wondered who had taken it; and wondered, too, what Pepci Diamant had been thinking when she pasted it into her photo album, which, as we know, would survive her.

Jack said, After the first Aktion, you didn't go—you didn't come in the street. There was an allotted time you could only appear, an hour or two each day.

The Judenrat, Bob went on, had to provide people for work and so forth, and that's how it went on. And of course—

(I wondered why he said *of course* like this, and assumed that maybe he meant, simply, the bad luck of the Jews)

—at the same time a flood started.

A flood? I asked. For a moment I thought he was being metaphorical. *A flood of woes, a flood of troubles*, something like that.

But no: it was a real flood. It was raining a lot, Bob said, and took everything off the fields, so suddenly food became very expensive. There was hunger. By the time we got to the spring of 1942 a lot of Jewish people were dying—and not one or two a week but daily. Just of starvation.

I thought of Shmiel and Ester, the surviving three daughters, living in anguish and terror in the white-painted house. In his letters to my grandfather, to his cousin Joe Mittelmark, to Aunt Jeanette and her husband, he had constantly complained about money, the expenses of sending the girls to school, the fact that he didn't have enough money to get his truck out of the shop. Now, by—say—Passover of 1942, there was no work at all, of course, and people were starving. How do people live, I had wondered, when there was no longer any economy? They didn't; they starved.

Meg said, softly, Everyone talked about the hunger, after the first Aktion. I used to *dream* about bread. Not cake: *bread*.

Matt asked, I know this is going to sound silly, stupid, but I mean—can I ask something?

Of course, everyone said.

Matt wanted to know what it felt like, what the atmosphere in town was like, during those days after the first Aktion. I had started to notice that whereas I was preoccupied with learning what had happened, the events themselves, and in what order, it was Matt who always asked how it had all felt.

I mean, he said, here were people, members of your families had been killed, it was obviously awful. So when you saw one another in the street, during that time, you'd run into someone during the time you were allowed to go outside, what did you say, did you say to someone, "I'm so sorry, I heard about your mother," did you talk about it?

It would never have occurred to me to ask any of this.

Meg said, There was only one topic of conversation.

Jack laughed humorlessly and said, No, three.

Meg didn't laugh, but she picked up Jack's cue.

Yes, she said, *three*: food, food, and food.

AS THE FOUR survivors talked about the period between the two big Aktions, I tried to reconcile what I was hearing with what I'd previously been told. Aunt Miriam—who, writing to me thirty years before, had had access to survivors who were long dead by the time I started asking my questions, but who may well have had greater intimacy with and more vivid memories of what had happened to my relatives—had thought that Ester and two of the girls perished in 1942; that, clearly, would have been the second Aktion. The older girl, she had written to me, had joined the partisans and died with them: this, clearly, was Lorka, and as far as the Sydney survivors knew, this much was true. But Miriam had heard that Shmiel and another girl had perished in 1944, whereas the Sydney group was fairly certain that Shmiel, Ester, and Bronia, the youngest, were taken in the second Aktion.

Perhaps, I thought, what had happened was this: Lorka had wound up in the forests with the partisans, most likely the Babij, as everyone agreed. As to the others, Miriam had heard that Ester and two of the girls had died in 1942, whereas the truth was that Ester and two of the girls had died *by* 1942: Ruchele in October 1941, during the first Aktion, and Ester and Bronia in September 1942, during the second. And maybe Frydka had indeed died in 1944, as Miriam had heard—*after* having joined the partisans, as everyone else now said she had. (Everyone, at any rate, agreed that she was still alive in 1943, before the final liquidations took place.)

That left only Shmiel, who, whatever had happened to him by 1944, was by then what must have seemed eons apart from the world of 1939, when he wrote the letters through which, I strongly felt, his voice could still be heard: proud, desperate, hectoring, bitter, hopeful, exhausted, confused. What, I tried to figure out as I listened to the Australians, had happened to Uncle Shmiel?

Jack said that he thought he'd been taken in the second Aktion, since no one had seen him afterward. But then, as Meg had reminded me, you couldn't walk the streets after the second Aktion: many people hadn't been seen after the second Aktion, but that didn't necessarily mean they weren't still alive. And yet if Shmiel had survived the second Aktion, then Frydka, whom Jack saw regularly after that—since she would often visit his house, which had been converted into one of the *Lager,* the group living spaces for forced laborers—would surely have said as much at some point, and he likely would have remembered. But Jack's impression, even after seeing a lot of Frydka as late as November 1942, when everyone was in one *Lager* or another—because if you weren't you were either dead or in hiding or had been transferred to the ghetto in Stryj—was that Shmiel had perished in September 1942, along with his wife and youngest daughter. So maybe Aunt Miriam's information had been wrong. Perhaps it had been wishful thinking. (And indeed, as Bob would remind me when I met with him privately a few days after the group meeting, all throughout the occupation people simply disappeared, not necessarily during one of the organized Aktionen. *There were random people imprisoned, taken away*, he told me, *for instance the father of Shlomo Adler was taken away, and because his mother chased after him, they took her as well, with his uncle.*) So perhaps Shmiel did go in the second Aktion, or perhaps he simply disappeared one day. Perhaps that elderly partisan in Washington, D.C., had been deluded. Perhaps he had taken the name of another Shmiel Jäger.

The more Jack and the other Bolechowers in Sydney talked, that afternoon, the more convinced I was that Shmiel had indeed gone with Ester and Bronia, in the second Aktion, which was the worst of all.

WHEN DID THE second Aktion start? I asked them.

Bob said, In August 'forty-two.

Meg said, slowly and emphatically, *September*. September the fourth, the fifth, and the sixth.

That's right, Jack said.

Sorry! Bob said.

So Shmiel and Ester and Bronia went in that Aktion, I repeated.

It must have been the second Aktion, everybody said, because after that nobody had seen any of the Jägers except for Frydka and Lorka, who had already been working at one of the industrial camps in town, which is likely why they survived past the second Aktion.

They were in the *Fassfabrik*, the barrel factory, Jack said, together with the Adlers.

Of these Adlers, I knew, two had survived, two cousins: Shlomo and Josef Adler, both now living in Israel. Shlomo, I knew by now, was the self-appointed leader of the ex-Bolechowers, writing e-mails, organizing annual reunions in Israel of the town's survivors. He was the youngest of all the survivors; after the murders of his parents he'd gone into hiding with Josef, when he was just thirteen. The other Bolechowers, I would learn, made affectionate jokes about Shlomo's intense emotional investment in the dwindling little circle of Bolechow survivors, but to me it made a certain kind of sense: it was surely a way of staying connected to his parents, whom he'd lost so young. Shlomo, at any rate, had become in a way the official voice of what remained of Jewish Bolechow; it was he who had written my older brother, Andrew, after he'd seen the videotape of our trip to Bolechow, which Elkana, my cousin in Israel, had shown around; it was Shlomo who'd told us not to bother putting up some kind of monument because, he insisted, the Ukrainians would steal the bricks, the stone.

That was in the fall of 2001. In the summer of 2002, the summer that Bob Grunschlag had passed through New York City and stopped to meet me over iced tea in my apartment, I got a call from Shlomo Adler, who said he was going to be in New York, too, and that he wanted very much to meet. One hot afternoon, he came to my place, where my parents had also come, eager to meet this man, a man of their own generation, who had known my mother's relatives in Bolechow. We met, introductions were made; Shlomo loudly, proudly, recited a line of Latin poetry—of Vergil, I think it was—when he was told I was a classicist, something he'd learned in a Bolechow schoolroom a lifetime ago. He no longer knew what it meant. We all sat down. While I was showing him pictures from our 2001 trip to Bolechow, he paused before the picture of the town hall, the *ratusz*, the Magistrat. *This is where the second Akcja happened*, he said, pointing at the picture, using the Polish word for Aktion. Shlomo is a big-seeming man, with the solid build of a truck driver; he has a keen, hawkish face and talks with tremendous animation, the kind of person who will thrust a forefinger in the direction of your face when he wants to make a point. He is not someone whose bad side you'd want to be on, I thought that afternoon when we met. So I was surprised, that same afternoon, when, as he let his finger rest on the picture of the town hall, the place beside which the Jäger family butcher store stood for many generations until there were no Jägers left, the place where half of Bolechower Jews still living after the first Aktion, some twenty-five hundred people in all, were forced to gather during the first few days of September 1942, and from which, after much random killing in the courtyard of the *ratusz* had decreased that number by perhaps five hundred people, were forced to the train station and loaded onto the cars to Belzec—I was surprised, as this big, burly man pointed to Matt's picture of the quaint-looking building, when his finger and then his whole hand, then his entire arm, began to shake so violently that my mother said, It's all right, I'm going to get you a glass of water, which she did, and after a few minutes Shlomo quieted down and said, I'm sorry, bad things happened there . . .

So Frydka and Lorka had been in the *Fassfabrik* together with the Adlers, Jack was saying. But that was after the second Aktion. By then, they were likely the only surviving members of my family in Bolechow.

WHENEVER IT HAPPENED, everyone in Jack's dining room agreed that the second Aktion was by far the most horrific and devastating thing that would happen to the Jews of Bolechow.

Why was this so? Because between the late summer and early autumn of

1941, when the first Aktion had taken place, soon after the Nazis invaded eastern Poland, and the late summer of 1942, when the second Aktion took place, the aims and methods of the German overlords of the occupied territories, the so-called *Generalgouvernement,* had shifted. Throughout the occupied eastern territories, in the late summer and autumn of 1941, the special SS formations, known as *Einsatzgruppen*, that had been detailed to kill the Jews of the occupied towns and cities did so more or less in the way that the Germans and their Ukrainian helpers had killed the thousand or so Jews who had perished in the first Aktion in Bolechow: they took them to forests and ravines or cemeteries, remote places where pits had been obligingly dug by, often, the locals, and they shot them there. But this method of eliminating Jews was proving to be too traumatic to the members of the *Einsatzgruppen,* it turned out. In what is considered to be the authoritative volume on the extermination camps of eastern Poland—the so-called Operation Reinhard death camps, Treblinka, Sobibor, and Belzec—the author, Yitzhak Arad, explains that "the prolonged exposure of members of the *Einsatzgruppen* to the murder of women, children, and the elderly produced a cumulative psychological effect upon some of them and even caused mental breakdowns." In support of this contention, which after all is well known by now, he cites an eyewitness report concerning a visit by Reichsführer Heinrich Himmler to Minsk in the late summer of 1941, where Himmler got to witness the shootings of a hundred or so Jews— a tenth of the number, it's perhaps worth remembering, of those killed in the first Aktion in Bolechow:

As the firing started, Himmler became more and more nervous. At each volley, he looked down at the ground. . . . The other witness was Obergruppenführer von dem Bach-Zelewski. . . . Von dem Bach addressed Himmler: "Reichsführer, those were only a hundred. . . . Look at the eyes of the men in this commando, how deeply shaken they are. These men are finished."

Arad notes, in quoting this passage, that the word he translates as "finished" is *fertig,* which as we know can also mean "ready," as when my grandfather would say, looking at his fourth wife, the one who had been in Auschwitz, as they packed for another summer's visit to Bad Gastein, the Austrian spa she would so mysteriously insist on visiting each year, *Also, fertig?* So, ready?

Because the unfortunate SS men were *fertig,* finished, by the grueling demands of their tasks late in the summer of 1941, another method of solving the Jewish question had to be found. This turned out to be the gas chambers.

Arad cites the evidence given by Rudolf Höss, the commandant of Auschwitz, at his Nuremberg trial:

> In the summer of 1941, I cannot remember the exact date, I was suddenly sum-
> moned to the Reichsführer SS Himmler, who received me without his adjutant
> being present. Himmler said, "The Führer has ordered that the Jewish question be
> solved once and for all and that we, the SS, are to implement that order. The exist-
> ing extermination centers in the East are not in a position to carry out the large
> Aktionen which are anticipated . . ."
>
> Shortly afterwards, Eichmann came to Auschwitz and disclosed to me the plans
> for the operations as they affected the various countries concerned. We discussed
> ways and means of carrying out the extermination. It could be done only by gas-
> sing, as it would have been absolutely impossible to dispose, by shooting, of the
> large numbers of people that were expected, and it would have placed too heavy
> a burden on the SS men who had to carry it out, especially because of the women
> and children among the victims . . .

Out of consideration for the nerves of the SS, it was decided at the Wannsee
conference, held on January 20, 1942, that the Jews of the *Generalgouvernement*,
numbering (according to German estimates) some 2,284,000 people, were to
be liquidated first, by gassing in specially designed death camps: Treblinka, Belzec, Sobibor. This operation was eventually christened Operation Reinhard, to
honor the memory of Reinhard Heydrich, who had been appointed Protector
of Bohemia and Moravia by Hitler and who was assassinated in Prague in May
1942. Heydrich, we are told, had a passion for the violin.

All this is a matter of historical record. I only mention these few documentary details in order to explain why the second Aktion in Bolechow, the
Aktion in which Shmiel, Ester, and Bronia were taken, according to the Sydney Bolechowers, was so different from, so much bigger and more violent
than, the first.

The second Aktion in Bolechow was so different because it was part of
Operation Reinhard.

THE SECOND AKTION was the biggest Aktion, Bob said. It was over two
thousand people.

Next to him, not looking at him but intoning the words slowly and distinctly, Meg said, Two and a half.

They took them to Belzec, Bob went on.

Yes, Meg said.

They were taken out to Belzec, which was an extermination camp, Bob said.

I knew this, of course. *My Little Town of Belz*.

Fairly nearby, no? I asked, prompting.

Well, Bob said, you know, a hundred fifty, a hundred sixty kilometers. It was just past Lwów, you know.

And this was in September 'forty-two?

They remember September, I remember August, Bob said, slyly.

Bob! Jack interjected. It was in the book that the German historian has written.

I can only tell you what I remember, Bob replied mildly. I don't know what the historian says.

I secretly enjoyed Bob Grunschlag's tenacity in the face of his older brother's insistence—and, even more, in the face of Meg's opposition; something about it underscored a quality I thought I'd perceived in Bob himself, something feisty, something sunburned and leathery after years on Bondi Beach. The younger sibling's contentiousness, maybe. Although I was fairly sure, in fact, that he was wrong in this instance, his refusal to trust blindly in the historian's printed words was something I shared, knowing as I did how easily it is to make even innocent mistakes—the eye that travels down to the wrong line when transcribing an entry from a faded piece of paper—let alone the more compromised kinds of errors we so often make, the mind that misremembers even fresh information because of the need to make certain random scraps of data into part of the stories we have been brought up to tell ourselves about the world, and which for that reason we cherish.

It is, of course, important to distinguish between kinds of errors—to agree on the important things, as Bob would later put it. But even so, small errors, when we become aware of them, have the effect of unsettling us, however easily they are explained away, forgiven; inevitably, they make us wonder what other mistakes, however well we can envision the circumstances in which they came to be made, however insignificant they are, really, might lurk in the stories and, even more, in the texts on which we so often blindly rely for the "facts." Yitzhak Arad's book, for instance, contains an appendix, labeled appendix A, which provides, county by county, the details of the deportations to Belzec of Polish Jews in Operation Reinhard during the late summer and autumn of 1942. When I first added this book to my library of books about the Holocaust, the library that owed much, in the beginning, to my brother Andrew's recommendations (*Masters of Death* is a must-read, he'd told me, and so I got it, because I am after all a younger sibling, too), I leafed through this lengthy and rigorously organized appendix, searching for the name *Bolechow*. There I read that in the county of Stryj, in the town of Bolechow, two thousand Jews had been deported, which of course I knew, for this information tallies with the various reports of survivors of and witnesses to the second Aktion. But Arad's table also gives the dates of the mass deportations as August 3–6, 1942. This, naturally, is what Bob remembered, although Meg emphatically stated that the second Aktion occurred on the fourth, fifth, and sixth of *September*; and as we shall see in a moment, another survivor had recorded, just four years after the Aktion took place, that it had taken place on the third, fourth, and fifth of September. To my mind, the preponderance of the evidence suggests that the big Aktion took place during those early September days, and I suppose that Arad's "August" was merely an error (easy enough to make, given the vast number of entries he was recording for "September"). Because I grew up hearing stories, because I've spent so many years searching in archives and know (for instance) that an entry that says "Kornbuch" must really have designated a woman called Kornblüh, because I have talked to so many survivors, as I've said, I'm not uneasy about this disparity between oral and written testimonies, between the date someone might give you when you're conducting an interview and the information listed on a table in the authoritative book. After all, if you were to go online right now to the Yad Vashem Web site and search the central database of Shoah Victims' Names for "Jäger" from Bolechow, you would learn—or, rather, think that you were learning—that there had been a young woman named Lorka Jejger about whom the following statement was true:

> *Lorka Jejger was born in Bolchow, Poland in 1918 to Shmuel and Ester. She was single. Prior to WWII she lived in Bolechow, Poland. During the war was in Bolechow, Poland. Lorka died in 1941 in Bolechow, Poland. This information is based on a Page of Testimony submitted on 22/05/1957 by her cousin, a Shoah survivor.*

Whereas, in fact, not a single element of this entry in the Yad Vashem database is accurate, since (as we know from her birth certificate) Lorka was born on May 21, 1920, and she was, according to several eyewitness accounts, alive at least as late as the winter of 1942. And I might add that virtually all of the information provided by the same important source, the central data-base at Yad Vashem, for "Shmuel Yeger" (or "Ieger") and "Ester Jeger" (and the three daughters the database attributes to them: "Lorka Jejger," "Frida Yeger," and "Rachel Jejger") is demonstrably wrong, from the spelling of their names to the names of their parents ("Shmuel Ieger was born in Bolechov, Poland in 1895 to Elkana and Yona," an error which, I thought when I first read this, eradicates my great-grandmother Taube Mittelmark from history, and with her the sibling tensions that may well have resulted in Shmiel's decision to leave New York in 1914 and return to Bolechow, a decision to which his presence in this error-filled archive is attributable) to the years in which they were born and died. But unless, like me, you had a vested interest in the few facts that can still be known about them, you'd never know that the information about these six people that you were so happy to be able to find in the Yad Vashem database was almost completely incorrect, and you'd never be the wiser.

So I am used to the discrepancies between the facts and the "record," and don't get very upset by them. But I can see how they might be unsettling to some people.

Anyway, as Bob now reminded me, on the big things everyone agreed. Bad things happened during the second Aktion.

BOB TOLD ME later that he and Jack and their father had survived the sec-ond Aktion because his father, the head of the Judenrat, had had warnings; and because after the first Aktion, they'd built a hiding place.

We were hidden, he told me when we spoke together in private, because we had a false wall in the stable. That was built by a Jewish carpenter after the first Aktion. You see we already knew there'd be another Aktion. We knew already because a few weeks before that there were Aktions in different towns in the whole area. And the day before the Bolechow Aktion, the second, Father came in and said, "Tomorrow it's starting." So we went in the hiding place during the night, or the early hours of the morning, before the whole thing started in the street. They went into houses, house by house, catching Jews in the streets, in the fields. Then they herded them to the railway station and packed them onto the cattle trucks and took them to Belzec. And Belzec was an extermination camp—*just* an extermination camp.

He knew I knew what that meant. At Belzec, you got off the train and went into the gas chambers.

The going into the houses, the catching Jews in the streets, in the fields: the

Grünschlags had witnessed none of this, of course. I remembered Jack saying, *If I would have witnessed it I would have been dead, too.* And yet, because of a particular accident of geography, the concealed Grünschlags did have knowledge of certain things that transpired during the three days that the second Aktion lasted.

We *heard* them leading them to the train, Bob said, because we lived in the street leading to the train station. As you walk along Dolinska Street, you turned right to go to the train station. And they were leading them along that street, to the cattle cars. So we heard the turmoil, the cries and the yells, and so forth. That ended and we came out of hiding, and you can imagine what the mood was.

No, actually: I couldn't. And can't. I have tried many times to imagine, to envision the experience of Uncle Shmiel and Ester and Bronia as they were taken or pushed or dragged from the white-painted, single-story house on Dlugosa Street, the house that Shmiel had fixed up when he first moved in, and were then forced to walk the short distance to the courtyard of the town hall— forced to walk that short distance and then waited there for days until they were made once again to walk, this time to the train station. Residing in the minds of both Jack and Bob are concrete memories of the sounds, the wailing and moaning and screams made by the two thousand Bolechow Jews who survived the first few days of the Aktion and made it to the train station; but these memories, and those sounds, are impossible for me to imagine since I have never heard the sound that is made by two thousand people being marched to their deaths.

And yet while it is important to avoid the temptation to ventriloquize, to "imagine" and then "describe" something for which there is simply no parallel in our experience of life, it is possible at least to learn some of what transpired during those three days in September, the three days of that second Aktion, since eyewitness reports have come down to us. These descriptions will of course never allow us to "know what Shmiel, Ester, and Bronia experienced," since there is simply no way of reconstructing their subjective experiences, but it does permit us to construct a mental picture—a blurry one, to be sure—of certain things that were *done to them,* or rather were *likely* done to them, since we know that these things were done to others like them during the same event. I can look through the available sources and compare them, collate them, and from that arrive at a likely version of what probably happened to Uncle Shmiel, his wife, and their daughter in the days leading up to their deaths; but of course I will never know.

Of the various witness statements given by some of the forty-eight Bolechowers who survived the Nazi occupation, I randomly selected one given on the fifth of July 1946, by a certain Matylda Gelernter, thirty-eight years of age—born, therefore, the same year in which Meg's brother-in-law had been born, the same year in which my mother's aunt Jeanette had been born in Bolechow, too. She made the deposition in Katowice about what had happened in the town during the second Aktion:

On the 3rd, 4th and 5th of September 1942, the second action in Bolechów took place without a list: Men, women and children were caught in their houses, attics, hiding places. About 660 children were taken. People were killed in the town square in Bolechów and in the streets. The action lasted from before evening on Wednesday until Saturday. On Friday it was said that the action was already over. People decided to come out of hiding but the action started up again on Saturday and on that one day more people were killed than in the preceding days. The Germans and Ukrainians preyed especially on the children. They took the children by their legs and bashed their heads on the edge of the sidewalks, whilst they laughed and tried to kill them with one blow. Others threw children from the height of the first floor, so a child fell on the brick pavement until it was just pulp. The Gestapo men bragged that they killed 600 children and the Ukrainian Matowiecki (from Rozdoły near Żydaczowy) proudly guessed that he had killed 96 Jews himself, mostly children.

On Saturday the corpses were gathered, thrown onto wagons, children into bags and brought to a cemetery and this time thrown into one pit. Concerning the fact that this action was to take place, Backenroth, a member of the Bolechów Judenrat who came from Wełdzirz, telephoned from Drohobycz. He said that we should expect "guests" on Thursday. But the Ukrainians of Bolechów themselves, not waiting for the Gestapo, started to capture and kill Jews before evening. My father, my child (not quite two years old) and I ran to the house of a Ukrainian we knew who had said at one time that he would let us in. But he didn't let us in. We returned home and hid ourselves in a niche in our house. The child was crying and wanted to drink, but didn't cry out because it was accustomed to this from the previous actions. Even when they shot a certain Jewess in front of the door of our hiding place, the child was frightened but kept quiet.

In the attic of the house next door my mother, brother and sister-in-law were hiding with a few-month-old baby. When Gestapo men and Ukrainians appeared in the neighbour's attic, they wanted to escape so they climbed down the stairs from the attic but it turned out that Gestapo men and Ukrainians were sitting in the room getting drunk on cherry brandy, which they had found in the basement. They were so occupied with the brandy that they didn't notice the people coming down, who immediately stepped back up into the attic. But the child started to cry. My sister-in-law didn't have any breast milk or anything else that she could use to quiet the child. She covered it with a pillow and it turns out that the child suffocated.

A large number of the Jews worked in factories at that time. But they were taken from the factories, led to the town square and here they were sorted near the town hall. The most talented according to the advice of the foremen of the factories were released and the rest were kept in custody. Soon they were killed in the town square and the streets. The walls and pavements were literally splashed in blood. After the action, the house walls and pavements were cleaned with the taps of the town hall.

A terrible episode happened with Mrs Grynberg. The Ukrainians and Germans, who had broken into her house, found her giving birth. The weeping and entreaties of bystanders didn't help and she was taken from her home in a nightshirt and dragged into the square in front of the town hall. There, when the birth pangs started, she was dragged onto a dumpster in the yard of the town hall with a crowd of Ukrainians present, who cracked jokes and jeered and watched the pain of childbirth and she gave birth to a child. The child was immediately torn from her arms along with its umbilical cord and thrown——It was trampled by the crowd and she was stood on her feet as blood poured out of her with bleeding bits hanging and she stood that way for a few hours by the wall of the town hall, afterwards she went with all the others to the train station where they loaded her into a carriage in a train to Bełzec.

In the night after the action, the Ukrainians went looking for places to rob. They went barefoot. Among other things they tried the outer lock of the niche where we were hiding and enclosed. Our hearts stopped beating, we died. My child already made no noise. In the action——September 1942——which lasted three days, 600–700 children were killed and 800–900 adults. The approximately 70-year-old Krasel Streifer was also shot in her bed then, because she couldn't walk. My mother-in-law Jenta Gelernter, age 71, also died then. She was taken out of bed in a nightshirt; they didn't allow her to put anything else on. They shot her near the town hall because she couldn't walk quickly. The rest of the Jews who had been captured, approximately 2,000, were taken to Bełzec. During the trip, Stern escaped from the train. She told us that more people had escaped like that. She continued to explain that once at a station along the way,

I don't remember where, hot steam was let into the car and people were burned, started to faint and choke. People were terribly tormented by thirst, especially pitiful was the children's situation, starving and dying of thirst. There were incidents of sating thirst with urine. Mrs Stern leapt out of the car leaving behind her four-year-old daughter. That same Mrs Stern had been caught in her shelter, which had been revealed by the crying and moaning of her two-year-old child. When they heard that Germans and Ukrainians were near the shelter, people started yelling at Mrs Stern that her child would give them away. Then she covered the child with a pillow and when the shelter was found anyway, the child turned out to be suffocated.

Ukrainian Siczowcy [paramilitary units assisting the SS] specially brought from Drohobycz helped with the second action.

During the march to the train station in Bolechów for the transport to Bełzec, they had to sing, particularly the song "My Little Town of Belz." Whoever didn't take part in the singing was beaten bloody on the shoulders and head with rifle butts.

So that is one sketch of the kinds of things that happened during the second Aktion, a tiny part of Operation Reinhard—one aim of which, the records show, was to make the *Generalgouvernement* completely *Judenrein,* Jew-free, in time for the tenth anniversary of Hitler's rise to power in 1933, although another, perhaps larger aim was to spare SS men the psychological trauma of having to shoot children of my mother's cousin Bronia's age, or to shoot heavy-set women, *very warm, very friendly* women, like Aunt Ester, although presumably it wouldn't have been all that traumatic to shoot a forty-seven-year-old man such as Uncle Shmiel, a man who, after all, had once borne arms himself, fighting for his emperor. I have often wondered, since Jack Greene first called me and I began to be able to focus my mental picture of Ruchele Jäger's death—and since I began reading more deeply in the literature about Operation Reinhard—whether whoever it was who actually killed her, who operated the machine gun perched at some distance from the plank on the open pit, felt any psychological trauma, although I know that the odds are heavily against it. But it's important to try to think about this, about the moment of the shooting, because although we've become used to thinking of the killing in terms of "operations" and *Aktionen* and chambers, which are abstract-sounding terms, there was (and this is easier to envision in the case of the shooting, where the link between the hand that squeezes the trigger and the bullets, and the targets, and the resulting deaths, seems so clear, so direct) always a single person who actually did it, and this I think is as important, in its way, to try to envision—I almost said "remember"—as it is to attempt to salvage something of the personality or appearance of a single victim, of some sixteen-year-old girl whom you knew absolutely nothing about until you began to travel vast distances to talk to people who knew her.

So that, as I was saying, was one picture of what the second Aktion looked like, give or take.

But before I come to the deaths of Shmiel, Ester, and Bronia, it seems only fair to try to imagine them as they were when they were living.

SHMIEL, OF COURSE, we know a little by this point. Indeed after talking to Jack and the others I feel I can envision him quite clearly, for instance, on that day in the 1930s when one of the pictures I know so well was taken: walking through the center of town—you call it the Ringplatz, if you are, as he is, old enough to have been born a subject of Emperor Franz Josef; it's the Rynek to his children, the four beautiful girls who were born after the big war and who are, therefore, Polish, and think of themselves as wholly Polish until it becomes clear that they were wrong—there he is, walking through the Ringplatz, the Rynek, on his way to the shop, the head of the butchers' cartel, somehow always taller than you recall, well dressed in a three-piece suit such as the one he wears in the picture I have, dated 1930, in which he strides purposefully on a city sidewalk. So I can see him in my mind's eye, wearing a suit like that; or, perhaps, a suit like the one he's wearing in that picture he sent as a remembrance of his forty-fourth birthday in April 1939, the one in which he's posing with his drivers, two brothers, next to one of his trucks, the well-off merchant with his cigar and his gold watch-fob. I can see him. There he is, tall (as his second daughter Frydka was tall, too), prosperous, a tiny bit self-important, perhaps, moving in no great hurry since he wants to stop and greet everyone with that slightly lordly manner so many in his family have, a leftover from more prosperous times, as if he were indeed the *król,* the king, which is what some people, half-affectionate and half-mocking, secretly call him, and of course he knows it, everyone in this small town knows everything about everyone, but he doesn't mind. His vanity is, if anything, secretly flattered: after all, he is the one who chose to stay in this town, when he could easily have gone elsewhere, precisely because he wanted to be a *macher, a big fish in a small pond.* And so why not enjoy being called the *król,* whatever the tones of voice of those who were calling you that? There he is, then, walking, being a big shot, a man who liked to be noticed, who enjoys being a somebody in the town, a person who very likely thought, until the very end, that returning to Bolechow from New York was the best decision he'd ever made.

Later on things became difficult, and to this difficult period belongs the Shmiel of the letters, a vivid if perhaps slightly less appealing figure than the earlier, more grandiose figure, a middle-aged and prematurely white-haired businessman and the brother, cousin, *mishpuchah* to his many correspondents in New York, with whom he was reduced, as time went on, to pleading, hectoring, cajoling rather desperately and, it must be said, a little pathetically as he tried to find a way to preserve his family or, indeed, even a small part of it, the children, even one daughter, *the dear Lorka*. (Why her? Because she was the oldest? Because she was the favorite? Impossible to know, now.)

Still, at least it's possible to hear Shmiel's voice, through the letters. Of Ester very little remains, now—at least in part because years ago, in my grandfather's, or somebody's, apartment in Miami Beach, I didn't want to talk to the scary Minnie Spieler, who only thirty years later I realized was Ester's sister, since I'd never thought her interesting enough even to ask about. Having now talked to every person still alive who had the opportunity to see and know Aunt Ester, however obliquely, I can report that almost nothing is left of this woman, apart from a handful of snapshots and the fact that she was very warm and friendly. (A woman, I can't help thinking as I contemplate the annihilation of her life—*annihilation* may seem at first excessive, but I merely use it here in its fullest etymological sense, *to reduce to nothing*—who would, in the normal course of things, have died of, say, colon cancer in a hospital in Lwów in, perhaps, 1973, at the age of seventy-seven, although that is impossible to imagine, because she died so young and so long ago that she seems to belong wholly to the past, seems to have no claim on the present. And yet there's no reason, apart from the obvious one, that she shouldn't have been someone I knew, someone like all those other mysterious old people who'd appear at family events when I was growing up; just as the four girls, who will always be young, ought to have been the middle-aged "Polish cousins" whom we'd have visited in, say, the mid-1970s, my siblings and I, some summer. When I mentioned this strange notion to my brother Andrew, he paused for a moment and said, Yeah, it makes you realize that the Holocaust wasn't something that simply happened, but is an event that's *still* happening.)

There is, then, very little that remains on the face of the wide world today— a face I've looked at often from above, during the trips I made to find something out about her—of what Aunt Ester had been during the forty-six years she lived, before she disappeared from sight during the first few days of September 1942. *She was very warm, very friendly*, Meg had said, on the day we'd all gathered in Jack and Sarah Greene's apartment. A few days later, when, after a great deal of hectoring and cajoling on my part, Meg finally consented to meet with me and talk to me one-on-one, in her brother-in-law's apartment, I asked her to try to give me a sense of how a very warm, very friendly Bolechower housewife might have spent her time, in the days before the war changed everything.

Meg paused for a moment as she thought.

In winter, she said, the nights were very long. They used to play cards at our place, my father with his friends. And the ladies used to crochet and knit. Mostly embroider. That was the pastime. The parents used to play also bridge and chess.

The Jäger house was always very clean, she said, a little bit later on.

And then, toward the end of our conversation, she repeated what she'd said a few days earlier about the long-dead mother of her close friend, Frydka Jäger. *Her mother was very pleasant,* she said. *She had a cheerful personality, her mother did,* she said—although I should add that when, during this second and final conversation with Meg, she brought up Ester's personality (which, I can now say with certainty, will always lack the telling detail, the vivid anecdote: who among us won't remember the mothers of our high school friends as being friendly, and cheerful?)—it was to make a point about Frydka, her friend.

Frydka was like her mother, Meg said that day. Lorka was a little bit more— she was different.

How was she different? I pressed.

Meg paused.

She looked different, she *was* different.

But *how* different? I felt desperate to have one small fragment of Lorka's personality, something concrete, something that would rescue her from the generic.

How shall I describe it? Meg said, spreading her hands in exasperation. Then she said, Her personality was different. She was different from Frydka. They looked different. They didn't even look like sisters. Ruchele looked more like Frydka. But Lorka looked . . . different.

I ended up changing the subject. What, really, can you say about a person?

So it was very hard to know what Ester had been like. Perhaps she had played cards with friends on a winter's night, or crocheted or knit; certainly she kept a tidy house. And she clearly had a pleasant disposition. She was *very warm, very friendly, cheerful*. But this impression I have of her personality derives at least in part from the fact that an elderly woman who had once been a teenager in Bolechow was making a point about somebody else.

And about Bronia? Precious little of the youngest of Shmiel's daughters, the youngest of my mother's cousins, remains in the world now, either. The problem, in a way, was that she was too young: only ten when the war broke out, not quite thirteen when the second Aktion ended her life, she was too young to be a candidate for forced labor, which had the effect of prolonging some people's lives, in some cases long enough to die in subsequent actions, in other cases long enough to make the decision to flee to the Babij camp, which was also eventually destroyed, and in still other cases long enough to make the decision to go into hiding, as Jack and Bob and the others had done, which is how they survived. For all of this, Bronia was simply too young, and it is simply as an ordinary young girl that the few people who could remember anything about her in 2003 recalled her, and hence it is as an ordinary girl I must now describe her, too.

I remember Bronia, Jack told me, at the end of his much longer narrative about Ruchele. She was a little kid, I would see her in the street and I would say, "Hallo, Bronia!"

The way he says *hallo* instead of *hello* moved me; there was something so cheerful and everyday about it, something a little bit dated. The word itself— although it is, of course, just an English translation of whatever Jack had once said to Bronia in Polish, decades ago—was like an emissary from a lost moment in history. I smiled.

Jack smiled, too. She was four years younger, she was Bob's age. She was ten when the war broke out. Ruchele was born in 'twenty-five, I think it was September 'twenty-five, and Bronia, as far as I remember, was born in 'twenty-nine. She would be playing in the backyard, I'd stay by the fence and say "Hallo, Bronia." She was a sweet girl, still very childlike. You could see her mind was still on playing, on games.

Perhaps it was this childish sweetness that had made Meg, on the day all the Bolechowers had met, smile at the mere mention of Bronia's name, when I had handed around the picture of her, a pretty girl standing between her parents, that day. *And Bronia!* she had said, her face brightening for a moment. And yet when I talked to her in private, a few days later, she was frustrated that she couldn't really remember anything about Bronia—not even having stopped to say hello to her in the streets.

The youngest one I can't recall, Meg said slowly, as she sat in her brother-in-law's living room. Bronia. I was digging in my memory, trying, but I can't . . . Lorka I saw, because I saw her growing up together, and Ruchele was around the house. But Bronia I just can't—there are no recollections, I can't tell you why. She was just a baby.

She paused for a second. When you went to the house she'd be there, when you showed me the photo I knew it was her. But I just can't . . . Her voice trailed off.

So that was Bronia. In that one clear picture I have of her, from 1939, when she was most likely ten years old, she is wearing a dark-colored pinafore, low white socks, and Mary Janes. She is smiling. Her parents, who unlike her would have been reading the newspapers, aren't.

AND THAT, AS far as I knew, once I had spoken to all the Australians, was who they had been.

Maybe what had happened to them was something like this:

On whichever day it was—the third, the fourth, the fifth of September 1942—there came, mostly likely, the crashing at the door. (I cannot imagine that the Germans, with their Ukrainian guides, knocked: perhaps they smashed the butts of their rifles on the door of the white-painted house.) For whatever reason—most likely because they are already at work at the *Fassfabrik*—Lorka and Frydka aren't in the house; and so it is Shmiel, Ester, and Bronia who are moved along (beaten? grabbed? knocked about with the rifle butts that had knocked against the door? Impossible to know) from the house and into the street, where so many others, weeping, screaming, terrified, are gathered and being forced in the direction of the Magistrat, the *ratusz,* the city hall besides which the Jäger family store has stood for generations.

In the courtyard behind the city hall they are made to wait, with the twenty-five hundred others, and as I contemplate this scene, I have to entertain the possibility that one or even more of the three, it could have been all three, even, don't survive this waiting period. For instance, maybe Bronia was one of the ninety-six Jews whom the boastful Ukrainian single-handedly killed during that time, most of whom, as we know, were children. Maybe this girl was thrown from an upper story onto the pavement below; maybe she was spun round and round by a Ukrainian policeman by the legs until her head was crushed, splattering the matter of her brain, the matter that, so mysteriously, had once constituted the personality that no one, sixty-one years later, can recollect in any detail, against the corner of the city hall itself. Or maybe Ester, a large woman by then, had moved too slowly when they banged against the door of the white-painted house, or maybe she was sick in bed that day and, either out of impatience or just for fun, either the German or the Ukrainian who had come to collect them shot the fat, sick woman there, on the spot, in her bed.

Or maybe one of the Ukrainians who were helping with the Aktion that day recognized Shmiel Jäger in the crowd, and maybe this Ukrainian was (as, for instance, the father of old Olga, whom we'd met in Bolechow, had once been) a butcher, too, a member of that little cartel of local butchers, and maybe this Ukrainian butcher had long resented Shmiel, the big-shot Jew who had lorded it over people in the way that he had, and maybe, because of that, this Ukrainian, when he recognized Shmiel, came over to him and beat him for a while with his pistol or the butt of his rifle, or simply shot him in the head.

(Or, worse, not in the head. You *begged* to fall into the hands of the Germans, Meg told me on the day she finally allowed me to speak to her in private, *believe me*. The Germans had what they called the mercy bullet, the *Gnadekugel*—she had finally remembered the word—but the Ukrainians would shoot you in the stomach, and it would be maybe forty-eight hours before you died. A horrible, slow death.)

But maybe not. Maybe, somehow, my mother's aunt and uncle and child-like cousin survived the gathering process. In which case, we know, they would have been marched, after the days of terror in the courtyard of the city hall, the hours of screams and beatings and the crushing of children's skulls, of watching Mrs. Grynberg standing dazed with the bloody bits hanging from between her legs, marched across town to the train station, past the house with the false wall behind which the young Jack and Bob were, at that very moment, hiding—and perhaps here Shmiel, as dazed as he was, looked up and recognized the house of Moses Grünschlag, a man of his generation whom he certainly knew, another preoccupied businessman who rarely went to shul and who had siblings in America who, like Shmiel's brother, might at that moment have been bringing their annual summer holiday in Far Rockaway, New York, to a melancholy end—hiding and listening to the weeping and cries and groaning (indeed, to the *singing*) of which some small part, one sound, might have come from the throats of Shmiel and Ester and Bronia; and then forced, at some point, to get up into the cattle car.

Since by the time I talked to those four in Sydney that day I had already been to Bolechow, I was able, if not to imagine what any of this could actually have felt like for them, at least to envision the backdrop for this suffering, to see in my mind's eye the buildings they passed during their final walk through the streets of the town. From the courtyard of the Magistrat they would have walked straight down Dolinska, the street that leads south in the direction, ultimately, of Dolina; after a couple of hundred yards they would have made the left turn onto the Bahnstrasse, the rather long, dusty road, perhaps a half mile long, that leads to the railway station. I have made this trip myself, by now. It made me tired.

And afterward? Of their long final journey, the day or days on the train, in the suffocatingly cramped freight car, it is possible to know certain details from Matylda Gelernter's witness statement, which I obtained after I flew to Israel and drove to Jerusalem one day: details that themselves had been conveyed to Mrs. Gelernter by the woman she refers to only as "Stern," the woman who first was compelled to suffocate her two-year-old in the hiding place in which she had been concealed, and then, after being torn from that hiding place and forced to board the cattle car, left another child behind—perhaps one of the children who had slaked its thirst with its own urine—when she somehow managed to jump from the train, which is how we know, today, some of what went on in the same train that took Shmiel and Ester and Bronia to Belzec.

In trying to reconstruct what the final days or day of my three relatives might have been like, I have to entertain the probability that "Stern" described to Matylda Gelernter what it had been like inside the freight cars in far greater detail than Gelernter conveyed in her statement, and that Gelernter abbreviated her own description because she hadn't actually been there and, after all, the focus of her testimony was to relate things of which she had personal knowledge. With this in mind, I have consulted other sources about the conditions inside the freight cars to the Operation Reinhard camps, during the late summer of 1942. I will not paraphrase these sources, will not "describe" what it was like, but instead will let the survivor's account, cited by Arad, speak for itself:

> Over 100 people were packed into our car. . . . It is impossible to describe the tragic situation in our airless, closed freight car. It was one big toilet. Everyone tried to push his way to a small air aperture. Everyone was lying on the floor. I also lay down. I found a crack in the floorboards into which I pushed my nose in order to get a little air. The stink in the car was unbearable. People were defecating in all four corners of the car. . . . The situation inside the car was becoming worse. Water. We begged the railroad workers. We would pay them well. Some paid 500 and 1000 złotys for a small cup of water. . . . I paid 500 złotys (more

than half the money I had) for a cup of water—about half a liter. As I began to
drink, a woman, whose child had fainted, attacked me. I drank; I couldn't take
the cup from my lips. The woman bit deep into my hand—with all her strength
she wanted to force me to leave her a little water. I paid no attention to the pain.
I would have undergone any pain on earth for a little more water. But I did leave
a few drops at the bottom of the cup, and I watched the child drink. The situation
in the car was deteriorating. It was only seven in the morning, but the sun was
already heating the car. The men removed their shirts and lay half naked. Some
of the women, too, took off their dresses and lay in their undergarments. People
lay on the floor, gasping and shuddering as if feverish, their heads lolling, labor-
ing to get some air into their lungs. Some were in complete despair and no lon-
ger moved.

This account, together with the account of "Stern" as relayed by Matylda Gelernter, suggests why whatever we see in museums, the artifacts and the evidence, can give us only the dimmest comprehension of what the event itself
was like; why we must be careful when we try to envision "what it was like."
It is possible today, for instance, to walk around inside a vintage cattle car in
a museum, but it is perhaps important to recall, in the age of "reality" entertainments, that simply being in that enclosed, boxlike space—an unpleasant
enough experience, as I well know, for some people—is not the same as being
in that space after you've had to smother your toddler to death and to drink
your own urine in desperation, experiences that the visitors to such exhibits
are unlikely to have recently undergone.

It may be, in any event, that Shmiel, Ester, and Bronia did not survive the
journey in the freight car. If they did, however, what would have then happened to them would have been something like this (as we know from the
statements of the few who survived, and from the testimony of those perpe-
trators who were later brought to justice):

Upon arrival, the trains stopped at the spur inside the Belzec camp. Within
minutes of arriving ("three to five minutes," one Polish locomotive driver
later recalled), the cars were emptied of their freight of dead and living Jews.
Gasping, dazed, smeared with their own and others' filth, Shmiel, Ester, and
Bronia would have stumbled out of the car into the "reception area." Here,
they may well have heard a German officer, perhaps even the commandant
of the camp, Wirth, give his usual speech: that they had been brought here
for "transfer" only and that, for reasons of hygiene, they had to be bathed and
disinfected before being moved to their next destination. Whether Shmiel

or Ester believed this, it is of course impossible to know; but knowing how ready he had been, just three years earlier, to believe that a letter to President "Rosiwelt" might help him and his family to get to America, I will entertain the possibility that, like most people, he was reluctant to believe that the worst would happen, and so he may well have been one of those Jews who, as we know from the testimony of one of the officers who served under Wirth, actually applauded Wirth after he gave his speech to the dazed and shit-encrusted Jews on the railway siding at Belzec, the speech in which he assured them that their valuables, which they had been told to deposit on a counter, would be returned to them after the disinfection treatment. It is possible, although by no means certain, that Shmiel's eyes alighted for a moment, that day, on the sign that read:

Attention!
Complete removal of clothing!
All personal belongings, except money, jewelry, documents and certificates, must be left on the ground. Money, jewelry and documents must be kept until being deposited at the window. Shoes must be collected and tied in pairs and put in the place indicated.

Maybe he saw this sign, and maybe its tone—not, when you think of it, all that different from the tone of similar signs in the swimming pools and shower rooms of bath spas throughout Europe, spas like the one in Jaremcze where Shmiel's father, thirty years earlier, had dropped dead—had reassured him.

In any event, if things were proceeding normally, that day in early September 1942, which we now know was the period of the most intense "resettlement" activity at Belzec, Shmiel was at this point separated from his wife and daughter, and was brought to the undressing barracks. (The men were gassed first.) There is no question that he took off his filthy clothes; perhaps they included the dark coat and tattersall shirt he is wearing in the final photograph that we have of him, a tiny square on the back of which he has written *Dezember 1939*, which is therefore the only surviving relic of his life during the Soviet occupation. In it, he looks very old. . . . He was, as we know, very tall, and perhaps he had been beaten on the way to the Bolechow railway station; it is more than likely that, as he stopped to take off his shoes and socks, he was in considerable physical pain; and of course, then there was the shock, and now the horror of separation from Ester and Bronia. (Had he even been able to say good-bye to them? Maybe they were somehow separated in the cattle car, maybe they had been placed in different cars, back in Bolechow.) On the other hand, being the sort of person he was, maybe the fact that he was now in an organized and orderly institutional setting was something he hoped was a good sign. Maybe, he thought to himself, the terror of the gathering in the courtyard of the city hall, of the march across the town to the waiting train, and then the train itself, had been the worst of it.

From the undressing barracks, the naked Shmiel Jäger, whom we must pause to remember was, at this point, a tall man with blue eyes and a full head of white hair, was now herded through the relatively narrow passageway known as the *Schlauch,* the "Tube," a passageway about two meters wide and a few dozen meters long. Partly fenced with boards and surrounded by barbed wire, the Tube connected the reception areas at Belzec, in Camp 1, with the gas chambers and burial pits, in Camp 2. It is difficult to believe that my grandfather's brother, a fastidious man, did not try, by cupping and lowering his hands (which, if they were like my grandfather's hands, and mine, were squarish and dusted with dark hair), to cover his private parts as he half-walked, half-trotted along the *Schlauch.*

By September 1942, when Shmiel and Ester and Bronia were, I then thought, almost certainly gassed—there was almost no chance that this middle-aged man, who already looked old for his years, or his fat wife or young childlike daughter would have been selected for one of the work details, the groups of Jewish prisoners who cleaned out the chambers or buried the bodies after the gassing—Belzec's old wooden gas chambers had been demolished and replaced by a bigger and much more solid building of gray concrete. After traversing the Tube, Shmiel approached this building and then shuffled up the three steps that led into it, which were about a meter wide and in front of which stood a big pot of flowers and a sign that said BADE UND INHALATIONSRAÜME, Bath and Inhalation Rooms. Passing inside this solid new building, he would have seen before him a dark corridor, a meter and a half wide, on either side of which are the doors to the Bath and Inhalation Rooms.

It is possible that he still believed, even now, that these really were Bath and Inhalation Rooms. Into one of them he walked. The rooms had, as one German who helped operate this camp later recalled, a "friendly, bright appearance," and were painted either yellow or gray, something institutional and unthreatening. The ceilings were fairly low—two meters, which for a man of Shmiel's height must have been ever so slightly claustrophobia-inducing—but perhaps even now he didn't register this, even now thought that he was going to be getting a disinfectant shower. There were, after all, showerheads protruding from the ceiling. If he saw the removable door at the back of the Inhalation Room, which was across the room from the door he just came through and was, in fact, the door through which, ten minutes later, his body would be dragged, he probably thought nothing of it.

After this, though, after Uncle Shmiel is squeezed into this low-ceilinged, yellow-painted, friendly, warm-looking shower chamber, after it fills with nineteen-hundred and ninety-nine other Jews, it will surely be harder for him to think that he'll be getting a disinfection treatment, and at that point the gas comes on, and I will not try to imagine it, because he is in there alone, and neither I nor anyone else (except the nineteen-hundred and ninety-nine or so others who did go with him) can go there with him . . . Or, I should say, with them, since within a short time Ester and little Bronia will walk up the same steps, enter one of the rooms, make the same journey. (Unlike Shmiel, they had stopped first in the haircutting barrack where the *Friseurs,* the barbers, shaved off their dark hair.)

So we cannot go there with them. All I think I can say, now, with any degree of certainty, is that in one of those rooms, on a particular moment of a particular day in September 1942, although the moment and the day will never be known, the lives of my uncle Shmiel and his family, of Samuel Jäger, my grandfather's brother, the heir to and rebuilder of the business that the cautious matrimonial interminglings of those generations of Jägers and Kornblühs had been designed to enhance, a man who wrote a certain number of letters between January and December 1939, a woman who was very warm, very friendly, a forty-seven-year-old father of four girls, a natty dresser and a bit of a big shot, too, in the small town where his family has lived, it seems, forever, a young girl who was still very much a baby, to whom a seventy-eight-year-old man living in Sydney, Australia, will recall that he once said *Hallo, Bronia!* over a fence, a man, a woman, a child who have been forced, by this point, to live with the knowledge that their third daughter, her older sister, a sixteen-year-old girl whom the father had named to perpetuate the memory of his darling sister who had died, it would one day be intoned, *a week before her wedding,* was shot to death at the edge of an open pit; an uncle, aunt, and cousin who at that moment, the moment at which he and then they hear, perhaps, the strange hiss begin, have a niece and a cousin whom they have never met but whom he has mentioned, politely, in a few of those letters (*I say goodbye to you and kiss you, and also dear Gerty and the dear child, from me and also from my darling wife and children to you and all the siblings too*), a niece who lives in the Bronx, New York, a pretty blond eleven-year-old with braces who, in the first week of September 1942, has just entered the sixth grade (just as her future husband, then thirteen, so much of whose family would be lost to narrative, was just entering the eighth grade, where he played with a boy whom everyone called Billy Ehrenreich, which was not his real name but after all he lived upstairs with the Ehrenreichs, a refugee from Germany who would sometimes say to my father that he had had four sisters from whom he'd been separated and whom, he said, he'd "lost," a word that my father, just a boy then, couldn't quite understand)—in that room, they had eventually to breathe the poisoned air, and after a period of minutes the lives of Shmiel Jäger, Ester Schneelicht Jäger, and Bronia Jäger, lives that will, many years hence, amount to a collection of a few photographs and a few sentences about them, *She called him the król, the king, she was very warm, very friendly, she was just a baby, playing with her toys,* these lives, and many other things that were true about them but which now can also never be known, came to an end.

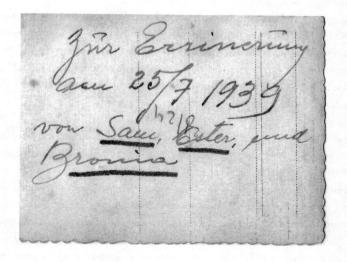

SO THAT WAS the second Aktion, which Bob and Jack Greene survived, because they had hidden themselves successfully, as Shmiel and his wife and daughter had not, if they had hidden themselves at all: a possibility that—so we thought, in Australia—it was impossible to confirm. Why had the Grünschlags been able to hide so successfully in the tiny space behind the false wall in the stable, and others not? Bob told us a story, and of all the stories we would hear on that trip, this is the one that affected my softhearted brother the most—perhaps because, unlike the other horrors we have heard about, which simply, and in my view rightly, defy any attempts, however well meaning, to identify with them, this story was about something small enough, homely enough, for even the innocent members of my and Matt's generation to grasp.

By the time of the second Aktion, Bob said, I had to get rid of my dog. Believe me, that was the hardest thing I ever had to do. You have no idea. I had him from birth, I used to take him to bed with me to sleep with me, and of course the bed would be wet in the morning and they didn't know if he did it or I did it!

He had to take this dog away and get rid of it, he went on, lest it bark and give them away, once they were in hiding behind the false wall. At the time we first heard it, Matt, who loves dogs, was very upset by this story; and since then this is the tale he will tell, when he talks about our trip to Australia that spring and wants you to understand the emotional horror of what people went through: this small boy had had to kill his dog.

I think it moved him so much precisely because it *is* so small. For some reason, the horror of a boy having to kill his beloved pet is easier to apprehend, to absorb and make real, than are other horrors. The horror, say, of having to kill your own child, lest its noise give you and the others away. But of course, when Bob Grunschlag first told us this story, we hadn't yet read Mrs. Gelernter's witness statement.

The vessel in which Noah and his family, along with numerous other examples of unblemished living things, were saved, has been an object of persistent fascination through history. What is intriguing about this famous vehicle of salvation is the strangeness of the Hebrew word used to denote the object we commonly render as "ark." Friedman rightly, to my mind, complains of this by-now unavoidable translation, for what the feminine noun tebah *properly connotes is, in fact, a "box." This is certainly the implication we get from the text's description of the ark: it is rectangular, there is no keel or rudder or sail, it is completely enclosed on all sides. It is moving to read Friedman's feeling comments about this strangely blank object, in which the lack of any features we normally associate with a seagoing vessel makes for a poignant image: "in such a vessel," he writes, "the humans and animals are utterly helpless, cast about in the waters without any control over their fate. To appreciate the image that this narrative sets before us, we must picture this helpless box of life tossed about in a violent universe that is breaking at its seams." This picture of infantile helplessness is, in its way, appropriate, since the only other object in the Torah that is referred to as a* tebah *is, in fact, the woven wicker container in which the infant Moses is secreted in order to escape yet another of the Torah's examples of an attempt at total annihilation: the Egyptian pharaoh's decree that the firstborn of Israel shall die. Like Noah's ark, Moses's basket is a humble, man-made object, totally enclosed, sealed with pitch, and no doubt utterly and frighteningly dark inside—a box whose passive occupant must, simply, take his chances.*

The image of such a box as a place of refuge in a world that is breaking apart at the seams comes naturally enough to mind when considering stories like the one that Jack Greene and his brother Bob told me in Australia—stories in which salvation, in times of terror, was possible only for those who had constructed dark, boxlike hiding places: for instance, the tiny space behind the false wall that Moses Grünschlag had built in a stable for himself and his two remaining sons, the underground dugout in the forest to which, eventually, those three and a few others escaped and where they hid for a year, until the latter-day pharaoh was defeated. In these modern-day arks, too, the humans were utterly helpless, without any control over their fates, passive inhabitants of darkened spaces from which, eventually, they too would emerge, like Noah, like Moses, blinking into the light.

And yet, perhaps because of the subtle but insistent way that parashat Noach *has of connecting things to their opposites, creation to destruction, destruction to rebirth, earthen figurines to muddy messes, sulfurous waters to sulfurous gopher wood, the boxes in which the forty-eight Jews of Bolechow were, ultimately, saved (to say nothing of how many other containers whose occupants were not so lucky, a figure impossible to know because there is no one to tell those stories) inevitably bring to mind certain other boxlike structures that were, in the latter-day narrative about the decree that the people of Israel must die, instruments not of salvation but of annihilation. Yes, there were the hiding places, the concealed, dark compartments in which the occupants could only listen and hope; but there were also the cattle cars, with their cargoes of storm-tossed humans; there were also the gas chambers.*

Those were boxes, too. Those, too, were arks.

THAT, THEN, HAD been the second Aktion, in early September 1942, in which—or so everyone sitting at Jack and Sarah's table thought—Shmiel, Ester, and Bronia had perished. Of this family of six, of whom there is only one extant photograph in which they all appear together, dated August 1934, in which Shmiel is shockingly unshaven and unkempt, an anomaly explained by the fact that he is (as the inscription on the back explains) in mourning for his mother, my great-grandmother Taube, who had died the month before: seven unsmiling faces that I now recognize as those of Shmiel, Ester, Ester's brother Bruno, Bronia, Ruchele, Lorka, and dark-eyed Frydka, part of whose face is cut off by the edge of the picture—of this family of six, for whom there never was a period of formal mourning such as the one they were observing when that picture was taken, two were left by October 1942.

They ended up in the *Fassfabrik,* Jack had been saying, the barrel factory, Lorka and also Frydka, together with the Adlers. And we were associated with that firm as well, he said—meaning he and his surviving family: his father, Bob.

It was after the second Aktion, Jack explained, that people were assigned to the work camps. There were a few tanneries, he said, a sawmill, a barrel factory. And they dominated certain places where they were converted into camps, *Lager,* to live in, from which they'd go to work, and then each night they'd return there. Our father proceeded to convert our house into a *Lager* house. And in that house there were living some twenty-odd people.

Everyone was in a work camp? I said.

Anyone who wasn't a worker, Jack replied, went to the ghetto in Stryj.

This, everyone said at the same time, was not a place you wanted to end up. But by 1943, it was clear that the "useful workers" were going to be killed as well. It was in '43 that those who were thinking clearly began to make plans to escape.

So when did he think that Frydka and Lorka had fled and joined the partisans? I wanted to know.

'Forty-three, Jack said.

Mrs. Grossbard interjected. 'Forty-three? she said, musing. Not 'forty-two?

'Forty-three, Jack repeated, emphatically.

Turning toward me, he went on: Frydka used to come to our *Lager,* our camp, almost every evening. She was in the *Fassfabrik* as an accountant. The chief accountant had gotten sick, he had kidney problems. So when that accountant, Samuels was his name, Shymek Samuels, when he got sick, he stayed in our *Lager,* which was considered a better *Lager.* So she used to come and visit him almost daily.

She and Lorka were in the *Lager* next to the *Fassfabrik,* where the Adlers lived, Jack added.

When he said this, I thought immediately of several things. First, that at least by 1943 Frydka and Lorka were living in the same place, which (I imagined) must have been a comfort. Second, Frydka, who in 1943 was twenty-one, must have been a sweet-natured young woman, to come visit this sick accountant, Samuels, even though merely to move around the streets of

Bolechow at that time was, as Meg Grossbard made clear, to take your life in your hands. (We were *outside the law,* she said, trying to get me to understand what this meant. *Anybody could kill us.*) And third, finally, that this, in the end, was what her education at the commercial high school in Stryj had gotten her, this girl with the purposeful walk, this tall young woman who, Meg would let slip, used to take the train to a local spa called Morszyn with Meg and Pepci Diamant, when they were teenagers, and sneak into the dances that would be held there, dances they were technically too young to attend, this vivacious girl whose dark good looks had snared a blond Polish Catholic boy, dooming them both, although I wouldn't know the details of that story for many months. This is what her costly education at the commercial high school had won Frydka: a few extra months as an accountant in the forced labor camp.

By now, long into our conversation at Jack and Sarah Greene's that day, a good while after the sounds of clinking plates and the gurgle of pouring coffee had ceased, only Frydka and Lorka were left. Their departure into the thick woods outside of Bolechow is the last time that anyone would ever see them.

So what was the thing that made people decide to escape into the forest? I asked.

After November 'forty-two we went into the *Lager,* Jack repeated. Everyone had a letter, either an *R,* which stood for *Rüstung,* munitions, or a *W,* which stood for *Wirtschaft,* economy.

At this point Meg and Bob began to argue about what *W* stood for: she thought it must be *Wehrmacht,* but he insisted it had to be *Wirtschaft* since, he argued, there was no substantive distinction between *Rüstung* and *Wehrmacht.*

As far as I was concerned, the question of what *W* had stood for was beside the point. The point is that in March 1943, all of the *W* workers, about three hundred people, were taken to the Jewish cemetery and shot in a mass grave. This was one of the "little" Aktions to which Jack had referred earlier; this was the Aktion that the old woman Olga whom we'd met in Ukraine had witnessed from her living-room window. At this point, Jack said, it became clear that even the "useful" laborers were not so crucial after all.

Yes, Meg said, slowly. Exactly sixty years ago. All my girlfriends were gone.

Bob said, All the *W*'s were exterminated.

Clearly, I thought to myself, it hadn't mattered to the Germans what the *W* stood for either, in the end.

And the *R*'s, Bob went on, were left till August 'forty-three.

Jack suddenly said, I'm reminded that there was another Aktion. They had taken the Jews who didn't go to the camps to Stryj. In March 1943, for some odd reason, they brought some ninety or a hundred people, Bolechower people, *back* from the Stryj ghetto to Bolechow. Among these was our uncle, Dovcie Ehrmann. And within twenty-four, forty-eight hours they took them into the cemetery and killed them.

Sorry, Jack, that I don't remember at all, Bob said.

I can't help it, Jack replied, it took place.

I know, I know. I know the *W*'s were in the camp there, in Adler's compound, they were taken in March of 'forty-three . . .

So then maybe it was April, Jack conceded. But they were taken, some ninety or one hundred people.

March, April: Whichever it was, by then Frydka and Lorka were, as far as these people remembered, no longer in Bolechow. Separately or together, possibly with the help of that certain Polish boy, the two sisters had managed to get away from Bolechow. They disappeared from sight, and nobody ever saw either of them again.

Or so we then thought.

This was the last that anyone in Sydney, that day, could tell me about any of the Jägers. It was also, as it happened, the last thing we talked about. Suddenly, the energy had gone out of the conversation. Everyone, and not only the elderly people there, was exhausted, spent.

ACTUALLY, THIS ISN'T quite true. The last person to speak that afternoon was Boris Goldsmith, who had remained quiet for most of this discussion, since he had not been there during the war, had not seen what the others had seen, or heard about. It was this that he suddenly wanted to make clear to me, just as the conversation was winding down.

I can't tell you anything, he said, looking at me and spreading his big hands apart, because I hadn't been there, I was in the army. In the Russian army.

I know, I said, in what I hoped was a reassuring tone of voice. But then, wanting to make him feel valuable, wanting to include him in the conversation as he had not been included in the events I had just been hearing about, I added, So what happened after the war was over. You went back?

Boris laughed and shook his head. No, he said, I didn't go back, because I found someone when I was in a hospital in the Caucasus—he pronounced it

COW-cass-ooss—and there I met somebody. Somebody in French uniform, and I went to him, and he looked like a Jewish person.

The idea that this Jew from a tiny town in Poland could have met somebody familiar-looking and sympathetic thousands of miles from home, deep in the Caucasus, struck me as so improbable as to be funny, and I grinned. There was, indeed, something the slightest bit humorous about the way Boris Goldsmith was telling this story, as if it were the opening of a joke. I could, in fact, imagine my grandfather starting one of his stories in just this way. *So think of it: there I was, in the Caucasus, in the middle of nowhere, and who should walk in but a Jew dressed up in a French uniform . . .*

He looked like a Jewish person, Boris went on, and so I went to him and I asked him, What, what's to be done, go back to Bolechow?

So what did he say, I asked, right on cue, just the way I would have done with my grandfather.

And then Boris told me what the Jew in the French uniform had told him, during that improbable meeting.

Boris said, *He told me forget it, there's nobody left.*

3

AND THE TOPS OF THE MOUNTAINS APPEARED ONCE AGAIN

T HAT HAD BEEN on Sunday, March 23, 2003, my grandfather's birthday. After Boris said, *He told me forget it, there's nobody left,* everyone had
slowly gotten to their feet, Jack and Bob and Meg and Boris, and one by one
the guests said their good-byes and went home. Jack insisted on driving Matt
and me back to our hotel. As I was getting out of his car, he suddenly leaned
toward the open door and said, out of the blue, Of course I remember Shmiel
Jäger—he wasn't someone you'd forget!

It was the next day, Monday, that Matt and I went back to Jack's place to
interview him privately; it was on Monday that he told us so much about
Ruchele. As I've mentioned, he had started to talk about Frydka—*she would
hold her bag like THIS!*—but, he said, if we really wanted to know about
Frydka, we should talk to Meg. So after those few hours with Jack at his place,
that Monday afternoon while Matt and I were walking around downtown
Sydney, the brightness and vivacity of whose buildings, the warmth of whose
late-summer weather, the attractiveness and easy friendliness of whose shop
clerks and taxi drivers and passersby were, during that visit, almost physically difficult to emerge into, after the darkness of the stories we had come
to hear, stories that indeed—like those of Jack and Bob—inevitably became
stories of enclosure, concealment, subterranean fixity; as we walked around
this city, I stopped at a phone booth and dialed the number of Meg's brother-
in-law's apartment to ask her yet again if she would consent to give me a one-
on-one interview.

I say "again" because, as everyone was leaving the day before, I had mentioned to them that I'd be wanting to talk to everyone individually, and everyone nodded yes, that would be OK. Except for Meg, who shook her head.

Sorry, she said. That's all I remember, I can't help you anymore.

Besides, she added as she picked up her leather pocketbook, she had to look after her brother-in-law, who was very frail, and with whom she wanted to spend some time before she flew back to Melbourne at the end of the week.

So I wasn't hopeful, when I dialed the strange, eight-digit number Jack had given me. The phone rang.

Hallo, Meg said.

Hi Mrs. Grossbard, I said, my heart thudding in my chest the way it had done years earlier when I'd called my grandfather's sister, Sylvia, whom we'd been raised, in a way, to fear, and told her I wanted to interview her about the family history, which is when she replied, *I'm not telling you the day I was born because it would have been better if I'd never been born* . . . Hi, I said to her, and then said again that I hoped she'd had time to think about it and had decided she'd let us talk with her before we flew back the twenty-two hours to New York.

Her voice on the other end of the line was more weary than angry.

I can't help you, I told you I don't remember anything else, she said; although we both knew this was a lie.

Because I was on the phone rather than facing her in person, I summoned the courage to be persistent. Oh come on, I said, all we want to do is talk to you.

What's the use? she said on the other end of the line, as much to herself as to me. Nobody knows, nobody cares. It will all die with us anyway.

I suddenly realized that she wanted to be convinced. So I said, Mrs. Grossbard, I think you're wrong. That's the whole reason we came here, to talk to you all, to hear the stories, to write them down. I want to *preserve* what you remember, that's the whole point.

It will only die if you don't talk to us, I added after a little pause.

Well, she said. There was dead air for a minute, and then she said, If I see you it must be in a restaurant, my brother-in-law is ill here, I can't have people over.

Fine, I said. We don't care. We'll meet you anywhere, just say where. Silently, I was miming VICTORY for Matt.

Yeah! he said.

OK, Meg said, I will meet you tomorrow, Wednesday. Telephone me tonight, we'll fix the time.

Great! I said. Thank you *so* much!

Later that evening, I phoned Meg again from our hotel room. She had clearly had time to think about our meeting.

She said, So I have decided, we will meet here, at Salamon's, for lunch.

Great! I said. I flashed Matt a V-for-victory sign as he peered at the TV news. The first American soldier had been killed in the new war.

But I can't prepare anything for you, Meg added.

That's fine, I said.

Perhaps I'll make sandwiches, she said.

We love sandwiches, I cooed.

So you should come around noon, she said. She gave me Mr. Grossbard's address, adding firmly that we wouldn't be able to talk to him, as he was too frail to get out of bed. I clenched my teeth and said that was all right, we understood. I got ready to hang up the phone.

There's one more thing, which I will insist on, she said, her voice tightening.

What? I asked.

And then she told me what her conditions for speaking to me one-on-one would be.

First: she wouldn't discuss anything about the war, because it was too painful. You know, she said, I never speak about the Holocaust. My son is a bookworm, he begs me to write it all down, and now that I'm coming to the end, I think sometimes perhaps I will. But I can't—I just can't bring myself to go through it.

OK, I said. I promised I wouldn't question her about the war itself.

She went on. She preferred not to talk about her own life at all, and would only entertain general questions about life in Bolechow during the prewar years, during her girlhood and early adolescence. She would be happy to share what memories she had about the Jäger family, but about her own family she preferred not to speak. If she did, for whatever reason, mention anything about certain experiences she herself had undergone during the war, they were to be considered off the record and I was not to make reference to them in the book she knew I would be writing someday.

Clenching my jaw, I said, OK.

So you still want to interview me? Meg asked, and this time I had a feeling she was smiling her bitter smile.

Sure, I said. Perhaps, I was already thinking to myself, she'd change her mind when we came, when we took out all our recording equipment, the digital video camera, Matt's tripods and umbrellas, the tapes, everything.

There was one more thing, Meg said.

I knew before she opened her mouth what it was going to be.

She said, I won't answer any questions about Ciszko Szymanski.

WHICH IS WHY, although Matt and I spent, as it turned out, nearly four hours with Meg, hours during which, apparently having forgotten her own strictures, she talked at length not only about what she remembered about my family but also about the war, about other people she remembered, terrible stories, often, I can't write any of it down.

I don't want my life in your book, she told me. One day I am going to write my own book. Yes, you will see, I will.

Both she and I knew, even as she said it, that she would never write a book of her own, but despite my frustration over not being able to include some of what she told me that day, stories and anecdotes that could, possibly, shed light on what it was like to go through the war in Bolechow, I understood perfectly what she was afraid of, why she wouldn't let her tales enter my book. She knew that the minute she allowed me to start telling her stories, they would become my stories.

So I can't tell you what she said during our interview. But I can say that when we arrived at Salamon Grossbard's tiny, slightly musty apartment in downtown Sydney, we did not find sandwiches waiting for us. A small table in the old man's kitchen had been carefully set, and four silver chafing dishes were simmering away. Meg, who was now smiling broadly for the first time, ushered us into the kitchen.

Now I must tell you, she announced, that I've prepared a lunch that your grandfather would *adore*.

I blinked. OK, I said, a little warily.

Everything from Bolechow! she announced, waving her arm at the chafing dishes. A *déjeuner à la Bolechow!* Then she looked at me cautiously and said, But I wasn't sure if—what nationality was your grandmother?

Russian, I said. I thought of the little shack in Odessa, burned to the ground, of the teenaged girl "walking across Europe." Oh, I thought, I have stories I could tell you, too.

Ah, Russian, Meg said, pausing for a moment. And your father?

My father's father was from Riga, in Latvia, I said. *He was born on the boat.*

He was a twin. He, too, traveled great distances in order to fashion a new life, to rein-vent himself far from the past; he, too, like his father, like my great-grandmother, like my grandfather, had come very far in order to be able to make their lives, the one to tell his stories, the other to keep silent.

And his mother was from Kraków, I added, playing the Galicianer card.

Ah, from Kraków, Meg said, satisfied. Do you know what kasha is?

Kasha! I said, we *love* kasha! My grandmother used to make my grand-father plates of hot kasha—buckwheat grains that are first boiled and then fried with onions, served with bowtie-shaped noodles—which he would eat, the way he'd eat farina or oatmeal, with great precision, starting at the edge of the bowl and working toward the middle. *That way you don't burn your mouth*, he'd say to me, as he blew carefully at the little mound of kasha in his spoon.

Do you know what pierogis are? Meg went on.

Of course, we said, we *love* pierogis! On the evening of the day the four of us had arrived in Poland, the evening before we went to Auschwitz, at the beginning of our trip to Ukraine, Alex Dunai had taken us to a "traditional" Polish restaurant. There, after spooning a dumpling into his mouth, Matt had looked at us and said, This isn't Polish food, it's *Jewish* food!

You know what is a *gołąki*? she asked, delighted. *Gawumpkee*. I thought of Mrs. Wilk, walking with her heavy-hipped tread up the shallow steps to my parents' house all those years, carrying, sometimes, the enormous jars of stuffed cabbages. Of course we knew.

Yes, I said, we certainly knew what a *gołąki* was.

Ah! Meg exclaimed, you do! And you see, I thought, to be on the safe side—I thought maybe they don't like this food, I bought a barbequed chicken to be safe. After all you're *second*-generation American.

She said the word *second* with the barest suggestion of disdain.

You know, she went on, because there are very few people from our parts left who know about this food, very few survivors from Galicia. Because them, those from the west, they put in the camps, and so there were more chances of surviving, but us they finished in the mass graves.

It was hard to remember we were talking about food.

And then, shuffling slowly into the kitchen, leaning on a walker and wear-ing natty pajamas the color of which my grandfather, who spent his entire working life in a business that produced ornate braids and trimmings, and who talked about colors with the relish with which other people talk about ice-cream flavors, would certainly have called *French Blue,* came Mr. Grossbard.

In a high, papery voice he introduced himself to us, told us how pleased he was that we were working on this project, and sat down to his lunch.

At first, I was so surprised that I couldn't think of anything to say.

It's self-serve, Meg told us, please help yourselves. I had a feeling that she was enjoying the fact that she'd surprised us.

I sat down next to Mr. Grossbard and turned on my tape recorder.

My goodness, Matt said. I haven't seen food like this since I was a kid!

Remember, I said to Meg, my mind racing, we're Bolechowers, too, from way back.

Bolechow, it was a nice town, Mr. Grossbard said. A happy town. There were twelve thousand people, three different cultures. Three thousand Jews, six thousand Poles, three thousand Ukrainians.

He was talking about his childhood, the years when my grandfather still lived there.

So here he was. Over his French blue pajamas he was wearing a robe of a color I think you could have called *claret*. The very wide frames of his thick glasses accentuated a sense that his thin face was entirely vertical. There were tufts of white hair on the sides of his head, with a few wisps on top neatly brushed back from the middle of his crown. Perhaps it was his very great age that caused me to think of those desiccated faces of Egyptian or Mesoamerican mummies as I looked at him, faces that also give the impression that everything extraneous has been stripped away over the course of time: there was nothing there but high, almost Incan cheekbones, the hooked, aristocratic nose, the wide, intelligent mouth, the ancient dewlaps hanging at his throat. And yet all this was somehow softened by a pair of wide, large, almost comical ears, which gave him a wizardlike air at times. When he spoke, in a voice so eroded that it was more like a whisper, he would sometimes lean forward, when making a point, and emphatically smack both hands on his bony thighs; at other times, he would lean slightly backward while spreading his upstretched hands apart, the way a fisherman will describe the size of a prize catch, as if he were measuring something: time past, his life. The walker that he kept at his side had about it an almost ceremonial air, as if it were an emblem of some obscure religious or political power. As he talked, he would sometimes knead his right hand repeatedly with his left, a gesture that had an agitated air.

It was a nice town, he said again.

I know, I said.

Bon appétit! he said.

I'm so happy, Meg said.

AND THAT IS all I can tell you. After lunch was over, we repaired to the living room, where, for hours, she talked, and where her brother-in-law talked, too, to my delight, about growing up in Bolechow during World War I, about the house on Dlugosa Street in Bolechow that he was born in and eventually inherited and lived in with the wife and child who did not, like him, survive, Dlugosa, the street onto which Shmiel Jäger had moved, at some point in the 1930s, with his wife and four daughters (*the butcher? he was a very tall, a strong man, a very nice man, of course I knew him, very often we crossed each other's paths, the children I don't remember so well*); about how, when he volunteered for the Polish army when war broke out in 1939, he had been turned away because he was Jewish. (And I was an engineer, and they *needed* engineers! he exclaimed, laughing with surprising heartiness for a person who had lived nearly a century. He paused for a moment and then cried, *That was Poland!*) Although I can't tell you in any great detail about what was said that day, I can tell you that I was happy that, for whatever reason, Meg had had a change of heart, and talked to us about a great deal, and that her brother-in-law had been strong enough that day to put on his robe and walk so painstakingly down the hall and sit with us for a few hours.

Just before we adjourned from the lunch table, Mr. Grossbard leaned in to me and said, in his reedy voice, Bolechow was a place with three cultures, and we all got along.

I nodded.

It was a *human* place, he said.

I nodded again.

It was a human place, he repeated, where there was no anti-Semitism.

He pronounced it, *antisemi-TIS-m.*

No anti-Semitism? I asked. Sentimental I may be, but still, I know the dangers of false nostalgia.

Well, there was, but everyone needed everyone else, you see. A Pole needed the Jew for shops, a Jew needed a Pole for offices. Ukrainians, they lived in the surrounding area but they brought food and timber every market day, every Monday.

This I knew. *And every Kol Nidre, the Ukrainian woodsman would get so frightened, because the town was so quiet and the mountains were so dark, that he would come down from the mountain and stay that night, that one night each year, with a Jewish family, he was so afraid of Yom Kippur.*

So there was the Ukrainians, Mr. Grossbard said. And each needed the other: after market day was over, the Ukrainians went to drink the beer at the Jewish hotels. And it was Jewish beer! And the Ukrainians brought the timber for the houses. And the Jews had the center of Bolechow, they lived above the businesses, or close by. And all the shops were Jewish. So they respected each other. It was a respect, the attitude.

He talked about the parks, when he was a boy, the orchestra concerts and the promenades, the ladies with their parasols walking among the trees.

I listened in silence, the way I used to listen.

Now the Germans did quite badly by my family, you know.

I nodded. The wife killed, the child killed.

But in *my* family, he went on, the ones we never could forgive were the French.

He sat back in his chair and nodded, slowly chewing a pierogi.

The French? I repeated, not quite making the connection. I looked across the table at Matt, who grinned. Our father doesn't like the French, who, he would say with a sneer, never won a war but always had great undergrounds. Had Mr. Grossbard, in his wanderings after the Holocaust, been ill treated by the French? Was his mind wandering? Keeping my face politely blank, I said again, You never forgave the French?

Mr. Grossbard leaned toward me again, wagging his finger.

Yes, he said, the *French*.

He paused for emphasis, and then he said:

You know, my father never *did* get over the Dreyfus Affair.

In parashat Noach, after God instructs Noah in how to build an ark, he gives detailed orders about what Noah must bring into the ark; for we must remember that no breathing thing will survive the awful annihilation. "Everything that is in the earth shall expire," God says. Noah will go, of course; and with him his sons, his wife, and his sons' wives. (The specific order—first men, then women, rather than, as one might expect, the elder couple followed by the younger couples—is an indication that separation between the sexes was maintained on Noah's ark. "From this," Rashi observed, "we learn that they were forbidden to have relations.") And then, famously, the animals and birds: not two of each, as is commonly thought, but at least two of each, so as to ensure the possibility of future propagation of every species; of "pure" species— i.e., those suitable for sacrifice—seven pairs were brought, presumably so that the proper ritual sacrifices might still be observed after debarkation without imperiling those species' future.

The description of the Flood itself lives up to the slowly building anticipation we feel as we read about the preparations for it: the founts of the earth and the windows of heaven opened, the rains poured down for forty days—the length of time, Rashi helpfully points out, that it takes for the fetus to form after conception (divine payback, he goes on to remark, for God's having been troubled to fashion the fetuses of the corrupt)—and for one hundred and fifty days the waters remained on the earth, rising until they covered the mountains themselves. It would be difficult to imagine a detail more effective than this last one (well, at least in biblical times, when the scale of things was smaller than it is today) in suggesting the extent of the obliteration that God accomplished with the Flood—not merely the destruction of life, but the erasure of the landscape itself, the swift and sudden elimination of every familiar landmark, of every familiar thing.

It is this that puts me in mind of something that we are not told in parashat Noach. Perhaps because I've spent the past few years listening to stories of people who had to leave certain places in a great hurry, and because, moreover, Rashi at least is alert to the fact that Noah, whatever his close relationship with God, waited until the last minute to get on the ark, a detail that led Rashi to conclude that Noah, like the others of the Generation of the Flood, "was one of those of little faith, he did not believe the flood would really come until the waters were upon him"—I often wonder whether Noah and his family brought anything else with them, besides the animals, some memento, perhaps, of the lives they had before the world was completely wiped clean. Since the text makes no mention of this, I must assume that they did not, and as a result I can't help thinking that this awful deprivation gave flavor to the joy with which Noah greeted the appearance of the olive sprig in the beak of the famous dove. We know, of course, what the immediate significance of the branch was, but I can't help thinking that seeing the green leaf—a sudden, vivid, specific reminder of the world he'd left behind—must have felt, to him, like a reprieve from another kind of oblivion altogether.

IT WAS LATER that afternoon that we met with Bob Grunschlag. This was also the day that Matt had selected for a photo shoot on the beach.

Why on the beach? I had asked, a little irritated, when he announced that he wanted to drive down to Bondi Beach with Jack and Bob and have them get their feet wet a little for his portrait of the two brothers from Bolechow who had survived. Didn't he know these were quite elderly people? I didn't want to push them too hard. I needed their goodwill.

Look, he said, you do what you do, and let me do what I know how to do. My job is playing bad cop to people until they reach the breaking point. I need a picture that says "Australia," otherwise why did I come?

Fine, I said.

So late in the afternoon of the following day, after we'd had our long lunch with Meg and Mr. Grossbard, we drove to Bob's apartment, which is right on the beach, and talked to him for a while, much to the satisfaction of Jack, who had wanted to make sure that his little brother, who hadn't really known the Jäger girls, was getting some attention, too.

Good boy, good boy, Jack had said, patting me on the shoulder affectionately when I told him we were in fact going to devote an interview to Bob.

Well, I said, I'm an older brother, too. I know how these things are.

But I didn't, really. It would be another trip or two before I got close to Matt, started feeling protective toward him.

On the beach, Matt shepherded Bob and Jack into the surf and then, having decided there was no other way to get the shot he wanted, suddenly took off his own wet shoes and, turning to me, thrust them into my hands. He waded knee-deep in the early evening surf and started opening the cases that hung from his neck. He kept glancing worriedly up at the sky. Our conversation with Bob had gone on a little bit longer than he'd liked; the sun was starting to sink.

I only shoot with available light, he said.

I only talk to available people, I cracked.

Jack and Bob laughed. They were in a good humor; they didn't have to be pushed. A little bit further, Matt said, waving at the brothers without looking up from the viewfinder of his boxy old Hasselblad. The brothers happily rolled up their trousers a little further, too. I heard the distinctive and by now familiar noise of the shutter on Matt's camera opening and closing: not so much a *click* as a *k-shonck*. Since there was nothing for me to do here, I began to amble off. Let him do his thing, I thought.

But just as I was about to go for a little stroll, I noticed that a small crowd of surfers had begun to gather behind where Matt had taken his stand, shooting picture after picture. *K-shonck, k-shonck.* It was seven in the evening by now and the light was failing fast, and I could tell from the frown Matt wore that he still didn't feel he had *the picture;* what was in front of him, evidently, didn't quite match the image he had in his head. Well, I thought, I know what that's like. Suddenly I saw him wading through the foamy water and approaching a dark-haired, white-toothed surfer. The sound of the surf was too loud for me to hear anything they were saying; it was like watching a pantomime. Matt waved his arm at the surfer, who couldn't have been more than twenty, and then pointed to Jack and Bob, and then made a little inverted V with his forefinger and middle finger and used them to make little walking motions back and forth. *Dolina hoise,* I thought. The surfer cracked a huge smile, then, and nodded. Lifting his board, he started walking back and forth behind Bob and Jack as the two brothers put their arms around each other's shoulders. Matt began squeezing the shutter, over and over. He was smiling now. He was doing his thing.

And, as it turned out, I got to do mine, too. As the grinning surfer boy tried to look nonchalant as he walked back and forth behind the real subjects of the picture, some of his friends started circling around me: two other boys, one blond, quite tall and serious-faced, the other dark and grinning, and a big, wide-grinned blond girl. Who were these two old men? they wanted to know. Were they famous? Were they our parents? Was this guy a fashion photographer? What were they doing here?

I looked across at the two old men from Bolechow, and then looked up at these Australian kids. They were so enormous, so tall. They exuded health and goodwill. None of them could be older than nineteen. They looked genuinely interested. The girl was cocking her head to one side, expectantly.

Well, I said. It's a long story.

The girl grinned and gestured to the boy whom Matt had conscripted for his picture. Hey, he's our mate, she said. We have to wait for him anyway.

OK, I said.

How on earth to begin?

Well, I began, My grandfather came from this little town in Poland . . .

The next evening, Meg flew back to Melbourne.

That afternoon, she had invited everyone to lunch at a fancy restaurant downtown: Jack, Sarah, Bob, Boris, Matt, me. She was in a buoyant mood, suddenly. Something had shifted, during our long conversation together the previous day; she had decided we were all right. (She made you *lunch?* Jack had exclaimed the previous night, when I'd called to report on our interview with Meg.) I only wish I could tell you what she said. I only wish you could see her face, how expressive it is, the wit, the mournful humor that plays across it sometimes, how a world-weary irony can give way suddenly and devastatingly to a sadness I can't begin to understand, the way it did when, at the end of that afternoon, Matt asked her to hold a photograph of her old friend Frydka as he shot her portrait, and just as the shutter clicked some memory washed over her and, as the final picture, which you will never see, clearly shows, she closed her eyes in grief, so that the picture that resulted shows the seamed face of an elegant if diminutive woman who is holding, in her immaculately manicured hand, a snapshot of a dreamy-looking, self-serious young girl whose eyes are wide open, although of course it is the old woman's eyes who are open, now, while those of the girl closed forever sixty years ago.

During our final lunch, her face was animated, and her humor good. As we all met in front of the restaurant, she walked toward me.

What, no kiss on the cheek? she said, presenting it flirtatiously. I grinned and pecked her on the cheek. She turned to Sarah Greene, who was laughing, and grew expansive.

I can't think about it, it's amazing, she said. First of all that I am alive, after so long, and then that I meet cousins of my girlfriends. I still can't believe it, that I'm standing here with the cousins of Frydka. It hasn't sunk in, really. I can't believe it.

I knew what she was talking about: the strangeness of suddenly being able to pick up threads long since abandoned, threads you'd never have guessed existed anymore. (*Doktor Begleiter? He was a very big doctor!*) You are now my family, she had told my mother the day before, when after the interview was over I called my parents' house on Long Island so that this woman and her lost friend's cousin could make contact. You are my relatives, now.

We turned to go into the restaurant, and, growing bold, I said I only wished there were others like her.

What? she said, staring at me with mock ferocity. You don't know? Sure there are others who knew them.

I looked at Matt and took my pen and notepad out of my bag.

Who? I said.

She smiled with satisfaction and started talking. One friend of Frydka, her name was Dyzia Lew, she's going now by Mrs. Rybek. She married a Russian. After the war I said, I'm going to the West. And she said, what for, there's 350 million beggars in the Soviet Union, two more won't matter. But I went to the West, and she stayed behind. And then she went to Israel, and she met Shlomo. His sister was my girlfriend, she added.

The others? I said, writing as I spoke: DYZIA LEV? LOEW?

And there is one in Stockholm, Meg said. Her name is Klara Schoenfeld, no, sorry, Schoenfeld was her maiden name. Her husband was the one who escaped, the only one who escaped on the way to the execution in the cemetery. His name was Jakob Freilich. Klara Freilich is her name, she's in Stockholm. She wasn't so close to us, we were on friendly terms but she didn't go to high school. But sure, she knew Frydka.

I grinned and turned to my brother.

What do you say, Matt, I said, loudly enough for her to hear, since I wanted her to approve of us, to believe how serious we were. We'll go to Stockholm?

Meg's eyes widened.

What, really? she said. I can give you the address.

She took the pen and pad out of my hand and, after searching through her bag, started writing. She tore off a sheet and handed me a piece of paper on which she'd written, in an old-fashioned hand, KLARA FREILICH, and then the address, the visual oddness of whose spelling and letters, which I contemplated in the strong sunlight of a New South Wales early autumn afternoon, already spoke of very distant places, further travels. EDESTAVÖGEN, she had written, a name that meant absolutely nothing to me. SVEDEN, she had written, a kind of misspelling I had stopped even noticing long ago because I was so used to the orthography of Jews from Bolechow. *This is the public school I attended. Sitting down is my dear brother* SHMIEL *in the Austrian Army, this picture was taking in 1916.* Well, I thought, maybe we will go to "Sveden."

What else do you want to know? Meg said, her voice growing noticeably lighter as I put the square of paper on which she had written EDESTAVÖGEN in my pocket. I'll tell you everything you want to know.

She smoothed a strand of copper hair that had flown upward in the warm summery breeze, and smiled faintly. No, I won't tell you everything. Some things cannot be told.

That's OK, I said, although I was already thinking that at least one of these others, whose names I had never heard before, was bound to tell me about Frydka and Ciszko Szymanski.

And? I asked.

Reinharz! Jack said to Meg. He should talk to them.

Who is Reinharz? I asked.

It's two people, a couple who survived, I'm sure they knew Shmiel and the others.

Just as my grandfather would have done, Jack pronounced it *surwived*.

And? I said.

Also you should go to Tel Aviv, Meg said, there is Klara Heller. She was Lorka's friend.

Lorka's friend? For some reason, I had never imagined her as having any— never imagined, in any case, that there would be any left. LORKA FRIEND!! → CLARA HELLER → ISRAEL, I wrote in my pad.

It's enough for you? Meg said, reaching out her arm to herd everyone into the restaurant at last.

It's enough, I said. We went into the restaurant.

Three months later, we flew to Israel.

PART FOUR

Lech Lecha,

or,

Go Forth!

(June 2003–February 2004)

BUT THE DISADVANTAGE WITH SOURCES, HOWEVER
TRUTHFUL THEY TRY TO BE, IS THEIR LACK OF PRECISION
IN MATTERS OF DETAIL AND THEIR IMPASSIONED ACCOUNT
OF EVENTS . . . THE PROLIFERATION OF SECONDARY AND
TERTIARY SOURCES, SOME COPIED, OTHERS CARELESSLY
TRANSMITTED, SOME REPEATED FROM HEARSAY, OTHERS WHO
CHANGED DETAILS IN GOOD OR BAD FAITH, SOME FREELY
INTERPRETED, OTHERS RECTIFIED, SOME PROPAGATED WITH
TOTAL INDIFFERENCE, OTHERS PROCLAIMED AS THE ONE,
ETERNAL AND IRREPLACEABLE TRUTH, THE LAST OF THESE
THE MOST SUSPECT OF ALL.

José Saramago,
The History of the Siege of Lisbon

Parashat Noach, *that terrible tale of extermination, is in many ways a story about water. By contrast, the next weekly reading in the Torah,* parashat Lech Lecha, *is very much preoccupied with dry land. Like* Noach, *it is, in a way, also a narrative about traveling, with the difference that the landscape (or seascape) through which the characters in the earlier* parashah *must travel is mysterious and unknowable, whereas the heroes of* Lech Lecha—*Noah's distant descendant Abram, a Chaldean from the city of Ur, and his family, the first worshippers of the Hebrew God—move through spaces that are described in careful detail: their appearance, dimensions, their unfamiliar inhabitants. Indeed, it's possible to see* Lech Lecha *as the first travelogue, a story that takes its hero from his "homeland, birthplace, and father's house" to the land of wonders in which he and his people will henceforth live.*

This preoccupation with land and territory is not accidental: for as is well-known, Lech Lecha *is the* parashah *in which God explicitly names his covenant with Abram: "Go out from your land, your birthplace, your father's house," God says to Abram, "to the place that I will show you. I will make you into a big nation, and I'll bless you and make your name great. And be a blessing! And all the families of the earth will be blessed through you." (Friedman, whose translation this is, is not the first commentator to point out that it's never made clear just what the nature of this blessing, this benefit to the whole human race, will be.) For this reason,* Lech Lecha *is, among other things, the most obviously political of all the early* parashot: *again and again, it introduces into the ongoing narrative of the human race advertisements, announcements, and warnings intended to legitimize the claims of the people of Abram to a specific patch of land. The name of that square mileage was Canaan. From the moment Abram arrives in this land, we feel that trouble lies ahead, for as the text is unembarrassed to acknowledge, "the*

Canaanite was in the land then," too. Still, God makes his promise, and keeps reiterating it throughout Lech Lecha: "I will give this land to your seed." The coordinates of the property to be shifted thus from the Canaanites to the people of Abram—the details of the transfer are not worked out in the text of God's promise—are carefully spelled out: as far as the place of Shechem, as far as the oak of Moreh, Beth El to the east and Ai to the west, the Negev, and so forth.

The text's increasing specificity about land mirrors a grander narrowing process, nicely analyzed by Friedman in his commentary: the first eleven chapters of Genesis, he writes—that is, Bereishit and Noach—are about the relationship between God and the entire human community. That relationship clearly soured, with the result that after ten generations God destroyed humanity except for Noah's family. (This is the first "narrowing.") After another ten generations, God focuses on one of Noah's descendants, Abram. (The second "narrowing.") The rest of the Bible will, essentially, be a story told in exhaustive detail about that one virtuous man's family as it struggles to maintain a hold on the property God has promised them.

I myself have no interest in the territorial aspect and political implications of Lech Lecha, although it goes without saying that the promises cited in this parashah have been often cited for political purposes, even (as incredible as it may seem to secular people, for whom the Torah is nothing more than a work of literature) today. To be sure, certain more general themes of this parashah are intriguing for someone like me, a person deeply interested in the rich and complex culture of certain now-vanished civilizations, such as the culture of pre–World War I Austria-Hungary, or the multilayered urban life of interwar Polish cities like Lwów. Not the least of these themes is the way in which different groups of people can either coexist in a certain place or (more often) try to expel each other from it. Another might be this: what it means to feel at home in a country in which you are, by rights, a stranger, and yet to which you've been told you have a profound and inalienable claim.

But what interests me far more about this parashah, however interesting its implied commentary about territory and culture may be, are, as usual, certain details of the diction and narrative, the sorts of things that are of interest to (say) bookish adolescents and library-bound scholars rather than to prime ministers. For instance, the very title of this parashah is itself the object of no little controversy. The first word of the Hebrew title, lech, means "go"; it is the strange usage of the second word, lecha, that has confused commentators. The sense of lecha is something like "for yourself": but what, exactly, does "Go for yourself" mean? As Friedman points out, it's been translated as "Get you" or "Go you"; he himself, disdaining what he calls "clumsy English," simply writes "Go," while another new translation offers "Go forth," which has a nice archaic ring. Rashi lingers, as usual, on this problem. He suggests in the end that "for yourself" has a twofold implication: "for your pleasure" and "for your benefit." Why does God promise Abram pleasure and benefit? Because, Rashi goes on to note, the awesome travels to which Abram commits himself will have terrible costs. Such extensive journeying, he notes, results in three negative things: loss of reproduction (because it is improper for couples to engage in marital relations when they are guests in another's home, and Abram and his wife, Sarai, won't have a home of their own until the end of their travels); loss of money (this hardly needs explanation, even today); and loss of reputation—this latter, because in each new place that Abram comes to, he must work to reestablish his own reputation for goodness from scratch.

It is, the text implies, as a compensation for the losses involved in traveling the world over that God promises Abram great rewards: his name will be great, he will be blessed ("blessing," as Rashi points out, being a word that suggests material goods, too), his progeny will be as numberless as the dust or the stars. He will, in time, have sons of his own: first Ishmael, by the Egyptian slave-woman Hagar, and then Isaac, by his lawful wife, Sarah. (More politics.) Even his name will grow, by a single syllable: halfway through parashat Lech Lecha, God declares that Abram's name will henceforth be "Abraham."

Perhaps it is because I am a classicist that, as I read this parashah, a tale of a man who sets out on a great journey through strange lands filled with unexpected friends and terrible foes, lands both highly civilized and violently primitive, of a man who enjoys the special protection of a god who guides him without, however, making things too easy, a tale, in the end, about a man's desperate struggle to get to his home—as I read this, I think less about Hebrews and more about Greeks. I think about Homer's Odyssey. In that epic poem, the hero also endures dreadful adventures and confusing travels in order to reach home, and in it, too, he is rewarded for his hardships by the gods: by the end of the poem, he has acquired material goods, power, family. What surprises me is that in comparison to his Greek counterpart, the biblical patriarch—indeed, Lech Lecha itself—seems bizarrely uninterested in the lands through which he passes, bizarrely incurious about the cultures he encounters (and, of course, eventually displaces); it occurs to me that the difference between Abraham and Odysseus is the difference between a dangerous and terrifying emigration and a return to the home one already knows. For whatever reasons, in any event, the Odyssey emphasizes something to which Lech Lecha seems indifferent, which is that there is another and greater reward to be gained from journeying all over the world and observing new lands, new cultures, new civilizations, from coming into contact for the first time with different kinds of people and customs: knowledge. Knowledge, then, is another blessing that increases the farther you go.

Or sometimes not. For anyone who's traveled extensively knows that, although you may think you know what you're looking for and where you're going when you first set out, what you learn along the way is often quite surprising.

THE PROMISED LAND

(Summer)

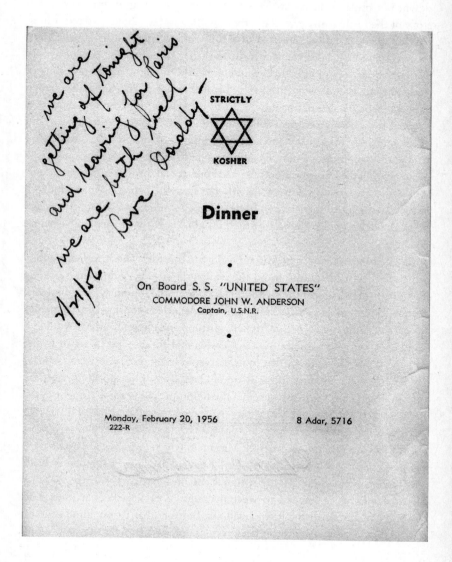

I T WAS MY grandfather's fault that I had always avoided going to Israel.
It wasn't that he didn't love Israel. He did, and he told many stories about it. There was, to begin with, the story, by now almost a myth, of his brother's journey to Palestine in the 1930s. "Just in the nick of time!" we would say in unison, whenever my grandfather would tell about his older brother's fabulous and prescient emigration a mere five years before the world locked down, not quite realizing, as we said it, that by reacting in this way to the story of the brother my grandfather was willing to talk about (the one whose Hebrew name, Yitzhak, or Itzhak, we pronounced the Yiddish way: *ITZ-ik*), we were alluding, however tacitly, to the fate of the brother that he would not talk about. My grandfather would explain to me how, at the prodding of Aunt Miriam, that fervent Zionist, his brother Itzhak, too, had finally escaped from Bolechow's gravitational field, from the pull of the past, the attraction exerted by so many centuries of family connections and family stories, and made a new life for himself and his small children, my mother's cousins, who would grow up to take a new, Israeli name, with the result that the only Jäger of my grandfather's generation who had sons ended up with sons and grandsons and, now, great-grandsons who do not have the name *Jäger;* and indeed, in the case of more than a few of Uncle Itzhak's numerous descendants, as I learned when I finally did go to Israel, do not know that their family's name was once Jäger.

So Uncle Itzhak and Aunt Miriam had gone to Israel. There, we knew, they had settled, just in time to avoid the conflagration that consumed everyone else. There they had had their children and, later, the innumerable grandchildren with the odd names that sounded, to us American cousins, like the names of characters in science-fiction movies, guttural and clipped and oddly lulling: Rami and Nomi and Gil and Gal and Tzakhi and Re'ut. And there, in Israel, they did the kinds of things that to my ear sounded at once exotic and, since I had been brought up on a different kind of family story, unappealing: lived on communes in drab houses, worked in the fields, picked oranges, fought in the endless wars, got married very young, were fruitful and multiplied. Every six months or so, when I was growing up, we would get another flimsy, almost transparent aerogramme from Aunt Miriam in which (against the postal rules; but then, she was a fiery socialist) shiny Kodacolor prints of someone's wedding had been enclosed, and what struck me, in those days, was the fact that these Israelis never seemed to wear neckties or even jackets at important family events. A small thing, you will say, but one that to my mind seemed obscurely to confirm the fact that these people weren't, in the end, really

Jägers. For to me, when I was a boy, it seemed obvious that being a Jäger, like being Jewish, had much to do with traits I associated with my grandfather: a dressiness, a formality (which in religious terms meant a strict Orthodoxy, and in secular terms might translate into the fact that you never traveled in anything but a suit and tie), a severity of attitude, things that clearly had much to do with Europe and, as far as I could tell, nothing to do with a place in the middle of the desert.

But as it happened, my grandfather loved Israel deeply, had loved it from the very beginning. He—and later on, after he was dead, my mother—liked to tell the story of how, during the United Nations vote on Israeli statehood in 1947, he sat on the windowsill of his apartment in the Bronx listening anxiously to the radio broadcast of the voting, and how as each member nation voted Yay or Nay, he would make a meticulous notation on a sheet of paper, keeping a careful tally. And then, when the vote was in, how he exclaimed, how they cried!

Before this new country was even a decade old, there took place the storied trip in the great ocean liner that, in such pointed contrast to the first time my grandfather crossed the Atlantic in a boat, that unimaginably difficult, strange, and terrifying voyage, took him and my grandmother across the ocean in great luxury, this time not to Europe but to the more ancient place, which was now new again. In February 1956, my grandfather, having retired quite early after selling the business he had co-opted from the Mittelmarks and turned into a company that bore his name, JAEGER, took my grandmother and boarded the SS *United States*, the ship that would take them to Itzhak and Miriam. The ship was renowned above all for its swiftness, which hardly surprises me: for how could my grandfather, who had last laid eyes on his brother Itzhak more than thirty-five years before, wait even one unnecessary extra day to see him now?

Just as there were stories about the luxurious crossing, the menus and passengers lists that my grandfather, and then my mother, carefully preserved in plastic bags so that when, twenty years after that trip, I looked at them, they seemed quite new—just as there were stories about the crossing, about the sleek elegance of the ultramodern ship, the opulence and variety of the strictly kosher food they were served, the endless entertainments on board, so there was a story about the moment of that long-awaited reunion. For when the great boat docked, my grandfather grew impatient with the long lines at the customs area and, having glimpsed his brother in the crowd across the vast room, took my grandmother by the hand and pushed through the lines of Israeli customs agents and immigration officials, telling them, in that way he had, *I haven't seen my brother in thirty years and you're not going to stop me now! So arrest me!*

And that is how my grandfather came to Israel. There, in this brand-new country that was, simultaneously, a very old place, he and my grandmother spent a full year. My mother still will tell you that during that period, when ordinary people did not casually make transatlantic phone calls, her father called her twice from Israel: once when he and my grandmother arrived, and once on my mother's birthday. But then, being in a foreign country didn't stop my grandfather from being himself, from being a person who liked to make big gestures—from being a Jäger. Because he himself had a flawless instinct for the appropriate gesture, whether sentimental or comical (*Now Marlene, first you'd better stop crying because you know how lousy you look when you cry . . .*), he tended to arouse, in people who appreciated this about him, a similar desire to make grand gestures for his benefit. For instance: my grandfather always loved birds. When I was growing up and he would come to stay with us during the summers, we would pick him up at Kennedy Airport, and of all the luggage that he carried, the many suitcases and the special briefcase for his pills, the only thing that he would insist on carrying himself, after my father, exasperated perhaps but silent, had lugged everything else to the car, was the large, round-topped cage of Shloimeleh, the canary. *Solomon.* Why was the bird called Shloimeleh? I asked him one July morning when I was fifteen, and he was dictating to me (because I could type, because I was so interested in his family, because it would have upset my mother too much for him to ask her to do it, because I was happy to have any time alone with him) that long list of instructions for what needed to happen on his death, an event that he thought about often but good-naturedly, the way you might think about a visit, far in the future but certain nonetheless, from a childhood friend with whom, you knew, the conversation would soon run out.

Should I die on a Saturday or a Friday night,

(he made me type)

please don't move my body until Saturday night after sunset. The Chewra Kadishu should do my last rite, not the funeral parlor. Give them for that one hundred dollars. Make sure and order a Jewish man to sit with me that night, and to say Thilim. Now send immediately one-hundred and fifty dollars to <u>Beth Joseph Zvi</u>,

Jerusalem, Israel, attention Mr. Davidowitz to say Kaddish for me for the full year. My name is <u>Abraham ben Elkana</u>. *Please use my big tallis for burial.*

Why was the bird called Shloimeleh? he repeated, when he had signed this document with the blue fountain pen he liked to use. *Why else? Because it's the smartest bird I ever talked to.*

It was because my grandfather loved birds so much that his brother Itzhak, whom he loved so much and who clearly loved him, too, built for him, when he and my grandmother spent that year in Israel, a pigeon coop atop their house, so that my grandfather could sit and look at the pigeons each dusk as the day faded.

There were other stories about that trip to Israel, stories in which my grandfather emerged, rather typically, as the quick-witted or grandiose hero. For instance, there was the story about how, when my grandmother ran out of insulin, her husband didn't bother with anything so mundane as pharmacies or hospitals but instead phoned the American consulate and got them to take him in a motor launch to an American warship that lay harbored nearby, where there was known to be a supply of insulin. (You know *him,* my mother added, when retelling me this tale recently. He was afraid of *no one.*) Or the one about how he took the orphans in a certain asylum under his wing, and would walk to this orphan asylum—only now, long after any answer is possible, do I ask myself, Whose children were they?—he would walk to this orphan asylum and take the children for walks in the park and give them candy. The orphan asylum was his favorite thing, my mother reminisced the other day, when I was asking her about her father's trip to Israel and certain other things. Which is why that's the one I still send money to. Beth David Zvi. She giggled and went on, I remember he told me, *When I kick the bucket, every yahrzeit and every holiday, every yontiv, you should send them a little money. But you know, those Jews, they'll take you for everything you got! So just send them a little at a time!* She paused for a moment and then added, unnecessarily, So that's what I did.

So my grandfather continued to be himself, during the year he spent in Israel. What is odd, given how much my grandfather talked about his great journey to Israel, and his long stay there, is that I knew very little of Itzhak himself when I was growing up. Long after my grandfather jumped into the cool water of the swimming pool at 1100 West Avenue in Miami Beach, I realized I had no notion of what Itzhak's personality was like, what dramas had filled his life, apart from the drama of having had the foresight to leave Bolechow, impelled by his fervent wife's ideologies; it was always as if it was enough for us to know simply that he was the One Who Had Been Smart Enough to Leave Just in the Nick of Time. About Itzhak I knew exactly two specific things. One of these I learned from Elkana, when I finally went to Israel: that like my grandfather, his father had a certain jokey nonsensical expression that he'd smilingly use as a reply whenever his small children (and, later, grandchildren) asked him for money to buy an ice cream or a candy: *What do you think I am, grafpototski?* I myself had no idea what *grafpototski* could possibly mean, when my grandfather offered this silly-sounding response to my pleas for a nickel or a quarter, but it sounded funny; and of course by the time I was studying German, years later, and learned that *Graf* is the German word for the aristocratic title "count," I had forgotten all about this nonsense phrase of my grandfather's.

So that was one thing I knew about Uncle Itzhak, long after he and my grandfather had died. It was from my mother that I got the other vivid flash of what Itzhak's personality might have been like. My mother used to tell me that like his brother, my grandfather, her Uncle Itzhak had had a good sense of humor. Certainly the one photo I have of him (besides the small photograph of him taken in the 1920s, bearing a couple of official-looking stamps, perhaps for a passport, a photo in which he is slender and looking off a bit dreamily to his left, smiling to himself in a preoccupied way) shows a solid, fleshy middle-aged man grinning with an apparently perennial good humor. (Well, I think now: look how lucky he'd been.) My mother would recall how, when she was a young woman, she would dutifully write letters to this uncle whom she'd never met, and when addressing them would carefully copy out the address her father had given her: ITZHAK YAGER, at such-and-such address in Kiryiat Hayim, ISRAEL.

My mother laughed about this, recently. I remember (she said) Uncle Itzhak would write back to me, "Where is the *respect?* You write ITZHAK YAGER on the envelope. You should write *MISTER* ITZHAK YAGER!!"

We giggled—but what I was thinking was this: what the joke was about, really, what the humor depended on, was a certain elevated and imperious sense of self, of who he was in the world.

Which, as we know, was also something that ran in her father's family.

So that was the first trip to Israel by a member of my family. There are a number of photographs from this trip: not just those my grandfather took as they boarded the ship at the West Side Piers in New York City, the photos of my mother and her mother and aunts and uncle standing in the stateroom before the whistle blew, but photos of my grandparents in Israel, too. There they are on board the ship, arm in arm one sunny day in the middle of the ocean, a picture taken by some unknowable person in which my grandmother is wearing a white sundress looking happy and even healthy, which she was not; another of her, wearing the same dress, sitting pensive on a wooden deck chair; there they are in Israel, posing in front of Greco-Roman ruins with a very young Elkana, or being driven in a horse-drawn taxi on a palm-shaded street in, I think, Tel Aviv. A favorite of mine shows my grandmother, my Nana, walking on an unpaved road beside a Bedouin, who's sitting on a donkey and leading a camel: on the back of this one, my grandfather wrote *1957 in Israel, Grandma with a camel and an ARAB*. I love this picture because I often think, now, of how difficult my grandmother's life was, what with her diabetes (*every day she had to boil those awful needles in a shissl,* my mother recently recalled, using—strangely, it seemed to me—the Yiddish word for *pot,* a word I'm used to hearing in discussions about *kasha* and *gołąki*) and what with living with my grandfather; and when I see that picture of her with the camel, I'm happy to think that she, who'd had the most meager of educations, who'd been so terribly poor as a girl, had had a little adventure. As I've said, there was a time when I loved no one so much as I loved my grandmother, perhaps because she told no stories, was merely her warm and softly smiling self, was silent and undemanding as she let me play with her earrings while we sat on the front step; and the fact that she has been dead for forty years does not make me any less protective.

There is one more picture, a photo of a small group of people who are standing far from the camera lens, perhaps on a pavement, an image it took me years to decipher. This was partly because it's somewhat blurry and the faces are impossible to make out, partly because of the strange angle from which it was taken: an odd diagonal line cuts across the bottom left of the picture. Only recently did I realize that my grandfather took this picture on the day he left Israel, indeed at the moment he was going up the gangplank of the ship that took him and my grandmother back home, after their year in Israel; it was, I saw, the gangplank's railing that slices diagonally across the left side of the photo. Only after I understood what that angled bar was could I see that the small group standing below was Uncle Itzhak and his family, waiting on the dock for my grandparents to sail away.

IT WOULD BE nearly twenty years before anyone else in my family visited the Israeli cousins, and another thirty years after that, exactly, before I myself went, although as I have said what I was interested in was not Israel but Bolechow. But during those twenty years, Israel made itself felt. Occasionally, as those years passed, we would have Israeli visitors to the house, people who to my young mind were interestingly exotic and, for that reason above all, worth attending to. There was, for instance, a certain woman, somewhat younger than my parents, called Yona—another one of those mysteriously curt Israeli names, the clipped, stripped-down syllables of which seemed to me, then, to represent some essential quality of Israel itself: pared down, small, necessarily practical, impatient with sentimental ornament. This Yona would occasionally appear at our house alone, but more often would come with my grandfather who was, for a short time in the mid-1960s, "between wives," as I once overheard someone say, before I knew what it really meant—the minds of children being quite literal, I envisioned my grandfather squished between my dead Nana and some other woman—and before I understood the underlying disdain of the comment. It was this overheard remark, perhaps, that made me wonder once, to my mother as she heated a pan filled with the tiny baby peas that were the only peas my grandfather would eat, whether Yona was going to marry Grandpa.

Yona! my mother laughed, shaking her head. No, silly, Yona is our *cousin!*

Since my mother is an only child, I had learned by then that when she talked about "cousins"—as when she talked about certain "aunts" and "uncles"—she was referring to relatives of mine whose connection to me and my siblings was, in fact, fairly remote—if indeed they were related to us at all. So I took it on faith that this youngish woman, attractive in a remote way, her black hair piled in a bouffant above her languid face, was connected to my Jaeger family somehow, and that I must be nice to her. I wanted to be nice to her anyway, since as young as I was I sensed that the attention she paid to me then was special. Such blue eyes he has! she would tell my mother, rather intensely. And indeed she was quite serious. Only my grandfather, as far as anyone knew, could make her laugh, my grandfather who would teasingly call her *Yona geblonah!* and tell scandalous stories to her in languages I did not, then, understand. But then my grandfather married the first of the three wives who succeeded my grandmother, and instead of Yona there would come to our house in the summers first Rose and then Alice and then, finally, Ray, *Raya* with the tattoo on her forearm, *Raya* who would always take care to occupy my father's chair at the head of the table every night and then feign surprise when he'd stand next to her, looking down expectantly at the beginning of the meal, *Raya* who, when she finally ate, would hunch over her plate as if fearful, even now, that someone would take away her food; and maybe it was because of all those wives that we somehow lost track of Yona, who by the end of the 1960s had stopped visiting us on Long Island, and we never saw her again.

Also in the 1960s we had our first visit from Elkana. He was, then, young, dark, rather dashing; his ability to get the local police department to fly him over our house in a helicopter seemed, to me, to be a reflection of his importance in the world, of his glamour. Elkana wasn't a very tall man—no Jäger was, or so I thought until I learned better—but he had an expansive and commanding presence, much as my grandfather had had. It was both jarring and pleasing to me to see this familiar personality now worn by someone else, translated, on this younger, subtle, and foxy face, with its amused eyes and dashing mustache, into something vaguely exotic. When he came to visit us, sometimes alone and sometimes with his beautiful wife, Ruthie, who, we had already heard, wide-eyed, had never cut her hair, and who would let me watch her, sometimes, as she coiled her amazing blond braids around her head each morning in our blue-tiled bathroom, Elkana would promise us that if we would only come to Israel, he would make things easy for us, wonderful, first-class.

With me, he would say (*wiss me*), you won't have to do anything (*anyssing*) but get off the plane—no customs, no immigration, no passport controls, *nussing*. Just leave *everyssing* up to me! His voice, when he spoke, was even, amused, authoritative, spiced with the English-speaking Israeli's citrus vowels and thickly buzzing consonants. *Dehniel*, he would call me. *All ze best!* he would say when parting or hanging up the telephone.

In 1973, soon after my bar mitzvah, my parents finally took him up on his invitation. I was happy they were going: my grandfather and Ray were going to babysit for us five kids while my mother and father were gone. Let them have Israel; I had my grandfather.

My parents had been planning this trip for a long time, because my grandfather had always wanted my mother to meet his brother, his adored brother whom he loved best of all. In the fall of 1972, which is when the plans for my bar mitzvah the following April were getting under way, my parents were also beginning to plan their first trip abroad, the long-postponed, long-awaited trip to Israel. But in December of that year, Uncle Itzhak died. Born with the century, he was seventy-two. It was a devastating blow to my mother to have come so close to meeting this storied relative—a mere four months would have made all the difference—and then to be denied, forever, the possibility of connecting to him. A couple of months after his death, close family friends happened to be traveling in Israel and, because they were close friends, then, ended up spending some time with Elkana there. They returned to Long Island from this trip with a precious cargo: among the many slides that they'd taken during their trip, a few were of Itzhak's gravestone. One night, not too long before my parents themselves went to Israel, we set up the slide projector in our living room and there, on the immaculate white-painted walls of our house, there appeared what was to be my first-ever glimpse of the name "Jäger" as it looks when spelled out in Hebrew characters on a gravestone— a sight I would not see again for nearly thirty years, when in the overgrown cemetery in Bolechow we so unexpectedly came across the tombstone of my grandfather's and Itzhak's distant cousin, Chaya Sima Jäger, née Kasczka.

On the wall of my parents' living room, vastly enlarged, what you saw was this:

יעגער

It was soon after my bar mitzvah, the occasion on which my voice so humiliatingly broke on the final few words of my *haftarah*, that my parents flew to Tel Aviv. From this trip there are, of course, many stories. My mother likes to tell, for instance, about how, just as Elkana had promised years before, she and my father were spared the arduous line at customs and were, instead, whisked away in a waiting car; about the instantaneous affection between my cerebral father and old Aunt Miriam, the multilingual intellectual whose fiery Zionism, we knew, had been responsible for saving her family; about the secret nighttime trips to Arab neighborhoods where the restaurants were unequaled, the late nights out in cosmopolitan Tel Aviv with friends. (It was shocking for me to hear this, since—my curiosity having never been engaged enough to read very much—I still thought of the entire country as a sea of brand-new two-story concrete apartment blocks.) And she would talk about how they then went to Haifa, where Aunt Miriam and her other child lived, Elkana's sister, Bruria: Miriam upstairs and Bruria and her family downstairs, and about how as different groups of friends and relatives, some belonging to Miriam and some to Bruria, would come by to visit the American cousins, my mother would, like a character in a farce, race up and down the stairs, up and down all day, in order to make sure that she'd spent enough time with each group of relatives. One detail in particular snared my interest. Oh, *Daniel,* my mother said, when she and my father called from Israel very quickly to see how we were all doing, you should see Aunt Miriam's photo album! She has Aunt Jeanette's wedding picture, it's the one I lost, she's in a gown made entirely of lace that the Mittelmarks bought for her. She's so *beautiful.* As she said this, it seemed both odd and thrilling to me to think that these far-off relatives had photographs of *my* family.

And there was, most famous of all the stories, the tale of my mother's attempt to explain what cholesterol was to a group of distant cousins, in the only common language they all (more or less) spoke, which was Yiddish. My mother still loves to tell this story, and even now I can't help smile as I hear her repeating it, as she did just the other day:

And so I said, Es iss azoy, di cholesterol iss di schmutz, und dass cholesterol luz di blit nisht arayngeyhen!

And then the cousins suddenly looked at me and said, Ahhhh, DUSS iss di cholesterol!

And yet although I love this story, what interested me about it the last time she told it was a detail that she had either never mentioned before, or one that I'd merely let slip because I hadn't been interested in it: that the cousins to whom she was striving so mightily to describe the latest American health obsession were "Jägers from Germany." Who were they, exactly? I asked my mother recently, when she was reminiscing about that trip to Israel. I thought I might know: my grandfather, years earlier, had told me that one of his father's brothers had settled in Germany, and another in England, but beyond that he knew nothing. And now, it seemed that in 1973 there had been Jäger cousins from Germany in Israel.

Who were they? I repeated. But thirty years later, my mother couldn't remember.

The tantalizing but frustrating appearance of those lost Jäger cousins reminds me of why I never wanted to go to Israel for so long. When I grew up at my grandfather's knee, listening to his stories and, later, writing them down and entering information on index cards and (later still) in computer programs, it seemed to me that what our family meant, where its value lay, was inseparable from its long history in Europe, a history that my grandfather tried so hard, I now realize, to convey to me through the many stories he told. Of course I knew, abstractly, intellectually, what Israel was supposed to mean, historically and religiously and politically, both for Jews in general and, of course, for my family. (*He left just in the nick of time!*) And I knew, moreover—I, who even as a child was interested in ancient Greece and Rome, would spend my free time building models of ancient temples—that Israel, the place itself, boasted a history that, like that of Greece or Rome, went back millennia, and boasted ancient ruins of every provenance, too. But I still had little interest in going there, as if the newness of my relatives' presence there was a consideration that outweighed the ancientness of the place's history—a history in which my family had had no part, until thirty years earlier, whereas its history in Europe, in Austria-Hungary, in Poland, in Bolechow, I knew, went back to that distant time when the Jägers first came to Bolechow, which, I also knew, was when the Jews themselves had first come, centuries ago. I had no more interest in visiting my Israeli relatives than someone interested in the American Civil War would have in visiting my family in their split-level house on Long Island.

And so it was because my grandfather seduced me with enticing stories that were always about the distant past, when I was still young enough to believe everything he told me, that I had no interest in Israel, that brand-new place. Indeed, it was because of my grandfather, I now see, that I would spend so much of my life researching the distant past, not just his ancient family history, *the same family living in the same house for four hundred years, a family of prosperous merchants and clever businessmen, a family who knew who they were in the world because they had lived for so long in the same place,* but other, even more ancient histories, the histories of the Greeks and Romans, which, although seemingly so different from the history of these Austro-Hungarian Jews, also told their comic and, more often, their tragic tales, their stories of wars and ruin, of young maidens sacrificed for the good of their families, of brothers locked in deadly struggles, of generations of a given family destined, it seemed, to repeat the same dreadful mistakes over and over again.

It was from my grandfather that I developed my taste for what is old, and because of that, I never wanted to go to Israel until I learned that in Israel, as late as the year 2003, there lived a handful of Bolechowers.

I ARRIVED IN Israel on June 26, a Thursday.

Or, I should say, we arrived. Matt hadn't been able to come with me on this trip, because in May of that year he had had his first child, and couldn't get away; we were already talking of a return trip later on, maybe, when I'd go back to Israel and he'd come with me to shoot the survivors I'd be seeing there, the five Bolechowers now living in Israel whom Shlomo Adler had arranged for me to meet. Apart from Shlomo himself there was Anna Heller Stern, *who was Lorka's friend;* she lived now in Kfar Saba, a suburb of Tel Aviv where my mother's cousin Elkana lived, too. (*You should come already to Israel,* Elkana had told me years ago, in his knowing and throaty voice, the voice of someone used to giving orders and being obeyed, of someone who just *knows,* a Jäger voice. *And you should come already and meet the family,* he told me years before I ever dreamed of going to Bolechow, of writing a book. And, knowing how to bait the hook, he had added, *Also there's a woman here who was Lorka's friend, you'll talk to her.* It was in this same voice that he'd said, over the phone, about a year before I finally did go to Israel, after I'd sent him the immense printout of the Jäger family tree that I'd generated from the new genealogy software I'd bought, the family tree that now went back to the birth, in 1746, of my distant ancestress Scheindl Jäger, a document so large I had to mail it in a tube, since when fully extended it covered most of my living-room floor— it was in this same voice that he'd told me, after I'd called to find out if he'd had a chance to look at it, *Yes, it's very impressive, a very good research you made. But there are mistakes—I'll tell you when you come to Israel.*)

So there was Anna Heller Stern.

And there were, of course, Shlomo and his cousin Josef Adler who, as young boys, had been hidden by that Ukrainian peasant, and for this reason were the only ones of their families to survive. And there was, too, the Reinharz couple, Solomon and Malcia, who now lived in Beer Sheva, far to the south of Tel Aviv, a couple who were newly married in 1941, Shlomo had told me in one of the many e-mails we'd exchanged before I finally went. He'd told me that during the terrible roundup for the second Aktion, this Reinharz pair had somehow broken free and had hidden for a long time in the space between the ceiling and the roof of a building that was to become an amusement hall for the German occupiers—a *casino*, as Shlomo called it.

We would interview them, too, Shlomo assured me. He had arranged everything, he said. He would drive me himself. I thanked him, gratefully. For neither the first nor last time in what has become a long and complicated friendship with this big bear of a man, a man whose broad and incisive gestures and emotional voice have left their traces on every videotape I have of my trip to Israel, gestures and intonations I hear even when reading his e-mails, now, I sensed that behind Shlomo's offers of assistance, the tremendous energy of his communications, his enthusiasm, there lay the shadow of something else, more personal to him: his own need to stay connected to Bolechow, to his lost childhood and lost life.

So those, I agreed with Matt, were the people we would have to come back and visit again, at whatever point in the future Matt felt he could leave his new child, the latest addition to the family that, officially at least, began in 1746 with the birth of Scheindl Jäger.

But still, I wasn't alone on this trip. I was traveling with a friend; a friend despite the fact, one that I never think of, really, that she is a woman of my mother's generation; a friend who is, like me, a classicist—indeed, a specialist above all in Greek tragedy, a genre that (as I am sure even Rashi would agree) has never been surpassed for the concision and elegance with which it ponders and portrays the disastrous collisions of accident and fate, of the individual will and the larger, seemingly random forces of History: those luminous and scalding points in time where men confront the inscrutable will of the Divine and must decide who is responsible for the enormities visited upon them. When I was in my twenties I went to graduate school to do a doctorate in Classics, went specifically to the university where Froma, this woman who is now my friend, taught, because I had been so electrified by the articles of hers that I'd read in scholarly journals, articles in which the style of the writing, sinuous, allusive, complex, brilliantly layered, almost *woven,* perfectly mirrored the characteristics of the texts she sought to illuminate, texts that themselves made their subtle and beautiful meanings felt by means of complex interweavings, delicate but persistent allusions, small things that culminated in large and stirring comments about the way things work. I read these articles, when I was twenty-two and twenty-three, and I wanted to know her; and so went to where she was. Now she is so familiar to me, but I still remember the impression she made when I first entered her office, with its notorious metastasizing piles of books and masses of papers; several long brown cigarettes of different lengths were burning down in chunky glass ashtrays, forgotten. She was surprisingly (to me) small, and whereas I had expected someone who looked severe—I was still young enough to confuse brilliance with severity, then—there she was, disarmingly accessible, with her round, alert face, the feathery light-brown hair, close-cropped, and of course the famous clothes, the velvets and leathers in complicated hues, the Cubist bags with latches in unexpected places. We talked for only a few minutes that day when I first visited her, and at the end of our conversation she fixed me with one of those sudden, intense gazes of hers and said, in her low, slightly gravelly voice, But of course you must come here, it would be an *embarras de richesses!*

Still, it must be said that her mind is far vaster than mine, synthesizes material more creatively and daringly, sees possibilities where I (who grew up after all in a house run according to *the Mittelmarks' German mania for order,* as my mother liked to say) see only messes, only problems. *Your* problem, Froma said to me once when I was halfway through my dissertation on Greek tragedy and had come to what I'd thought was a hopeless impasse, until she showed me that it was a passageway, Your problem, she said—she was holding one of the long brown cigarettes with one hand, staring at me, as she does when her mind is occupied with a problem, with her head cocked slightly to one side, oblivious to the fact that two inches of ash were about to drop into her lap; the other hand, heavy with rings, was toying with one of the large, artisanal pieces of metal-and-enamel jewelry she favors—your problem, she repeated, is that you see the complexity as the problem, and not the solution.

It was only after I went to study with her that I learned that she, too, had a profound interest in the fate of the Jews during World War II. Typically, her interest was higher, more far-ranging, at once more abstract and more searching than mine. The granddaughter of two rabbis, themselves the products of the high intellectual culture of Vilna ("the Jerusalem of the North," as it was called, although I have been there and can tell you that very little remains) and the daughter of serious Reconstructionist Jews, she, unlike me, had had a rigorous Jewish education: read and spoke Hebrew fluently, knew Jewish and Hebrew religion and law and literature intimately, as I had never cared to, until now. As a profoundly Jewish person and, in a way, as a person who had devoted her professional life to the nature of tragedy, how could she not, in the end, become obsessed by the Holocaust?

Whereas for me, as we know, it was a family affair, something much smaller. I wanted to know what happened to Uncle Shmiel and the others; she wanted to know what happened to everybody. And not only that. Even today, long after she first started pointing me in the direction of multivolume works on Nazi medical experiments and documentary films on the partisans of Vilna and dozens, hundreds of other documents and films and books, things I simply don't have the time to absorb, and which leave me wondering, even now, at the enormous energy of mind that allows her to read and see and digest it all; years after those beginnings, she still hungers after information that will help her formulate answers to still larger questions: how it happened and, a question for which there can never be an answer any one person can grasp, why it happened.

Anyway, this is why, years after I had ceased to be her student, formally speaking, years after she had helped me through my thesis on Greek tragedy, I was still learning from her, still being pushed to see the problem as the solution.

AND SO FROMA, too, became part of the search for the lost, and now, in the summer of 2003, we were traveling together. We had met in Prague, where she was finishing up a tour of Holocaust-related sites. What did we see in Prague? We saw Josefov, the ancient Jewish quarter, with its tiny, almost subterranean synagogues with their cool walls perspiring against the summer heat, the crooked street filled with blond tourists dutifully consulting guidebooks and impulsively buying postcards (THE PINCHUS SYNAGOGUE IN JEWISH PRAGUE); we saw the opulent Islamic-inspired interior decoration of the yellow-and-white-painted Spanish Synagogue, built in 1868 on the site of what had been the oldest shul in Prague, and now restored for the admiring eyes of tourists in all of its riotous, polychrome dazzle; we saw, in the Old Jewish Cemetery, the lavishly sculpted and ornamented tomb of Rabbi Judah ben Loew Bezalel, who died at eighty-four in 1609 and who is the man who is said to have created the Golem from the mud of the Vltava River as a defense against the bitter anti-Semites in the court of the Habsburg emperor Rudolf II. By a curious coincidence, the Golem was called Yossel—"Joey," in Yiddish—the same nickname that, three centuries later, the grateful Jews of towns like Bolechow gave to Rudolf's descendant, Franz Josef I, in affectionate gratitude for his benevolence to the Jews. As you leave this cemetery, you can buy little statuettes of the earlier Yossel, an early if primitive response to the persecution of the Jews of the city.

What else did we see? We saw objects that were far more artful than the Yossel statuettes: the thousands of fabulous carved and sculpted and engraved and embossed cups and vessels and ritual objects of every description that can be found in the permanent exhibition of European Judaica that is located on the upper floor of the Spanish Synagogue, the part that had once been the women's gallery, when there were still Jews in Prague to pray in the synagogues through which I and hundreds of other tourists reverently walked, that fine summer day. By a curious coincidence, this collection of Torah crowns and ceremonial tapers and goblets and medallions owes its richness (although this information is not prominently noted in the exhibition itself) to the fact that Hitler had designated Prague as the location of the Museum of an Extinct People he planned to have built, so that Aryans might, presumably, gawk at them in years to come. And indeed the riches of at least one-hundred and fifty-three communities from the region around Prague were duly transported to the city in 1942 for evaluation and sorting, although the Nazis' museum of the Jewish people was never built, which is why these ornate and opulent pieces may now be admired by tourists today as they pass through this quarter of Prague before returning to their hotels to start thinking about where to get some dinner.

So we saw all that, before we returned to our own hotel looking for dinner; for after all, as interested—as obsessed, even—as we may be in the past, we live in the present, and the business of living must be attended to. Still, the past has odd ways of catching up with you. It was in Prague that the first of what I thought, then, as a bizarre series of coincidences took place. On the evening before Froma and I were to go to Terezin—the "model" concentration camp, located not far from the city, which had once been shown to visiting Red Cross officials as an example of German humanity to its interned Jews, subversives, and other prisoners—she and I were taking the elevator to the top floor of our hotel, where there was a bar that, our hotel guide informed us, boasted a fabulous view of the city. A few floors before we reached this marvelous aerie, the elevator stopped and a well-dressed, not particularly old man got in. He had, I noticed, a few large gold rings and a very expensive watch. As often happens in this situation, there was an awkward, smiling silence as the doors closed and the elevator began to rise again. Suddenly this white-haired, vigorous-looking man turned to us rather casually and—nodding as if in agreement, as if what he was about to say were the continuation of a conversation the three of us had been having all along—said, *Yes, I was in BabiYar.*

The next morning we got on an immense, air-conditioned motor coach for the hour-long drive to the last camp that Froma's group was visiting on its grim tour. The Czechs call the place Terezín, but its name, when it was founded under a much earlier regime, and also under the Nazi occupation, was Theresienstadt, "City of Theresia": which is to say, the city of Maria Theresia, the great Habsburg empress of the eighteenth century, the Victoria of Mitteleuropa. It was thus named because the fortress town of Theresienstadt, completed in 1780, the year the queen died, was part of a network of walled and armored fortress towns constructed during and just after the reign of this plump, domineering woman for the protection of the vast Habsburg dominion, a multicultural patchwork of countries and provinces and principalities that finally disintegrated after a Serb nationalist called Gavrilo Princip (who was clearly not happy to be part of this patchwork) assassinated Maria Theresia's descendant, Archduke Franz Ferdinand, the heir to the throne of the by-now ancient Franz Josef, *Yossele,* on a June day in 1914, thereby triggering the first of the declarations and ultimatums that led, as rapidly, predictably, and inevitably as a snaking row of dominoes will collapse, to the outbreak of the First World War. And I must say that, when I visited the camp and the various museums now located on the site on that drizzly day in June 2003, as Froma and I walked through the reconstructed barracks and the ghetto museum, lingered over the poignant display of artwork done by children in the camp during the Nazi years, the thing that moved me most, that had the most profound resonance for me, was the realization that in one of the old cells of this onetime fortress prison—a tiny, thick-walled chamber that I entered briefly before I was overcome, as I often am (for instance in elevators and small underground spaces) by claustrophobia—Gavrilo Princip himself had been incarcerated after he killed the archduke. He died there not long afterward. I stood there, strangely moved by this unexpected and very concrete reminder of the crime that triggered the first tremendous slaughter of the century, and as I did so I felt embarrassed that it was this, more than anything, that had affected me in more than a generic or abstract way. It was only after I'd stood there for a while and thought about it that I realized that the reason I was so moved was that this trace of Gavrilo Princip and his crime, unsought by me or anyone else who was visiting that day, all of whom were avid for Holocaust-related information, had allowed me to leapfrog back in time to my grandfather's Austro-Hungarian childhood and adolescence, the vanished moment when the worst political disaster that had ever befallen Bolechow's Jews was, in fact, the assassination of their beloved emperor's heir and the onset of the war, that, they were sure, would be the worst they'd ever see.

So we saw Theresienstadt, too. From the Theresienstadt Web site you can send your friends electronic postcards bearing the greeting ARBEIT MACHT FREI; the postcard that I mailed to Mrs. Begley from Prague was simply a cheery photograph of Josefov, the quaint old quarter that is now a tourist destination. *Prague is beautiful*, I wrote, *today we went to the Jewish quarter. No Jews in sight.* Given her slightly sour sense of humor, I suspected she'd enjoy the grim joke, and I was right. *Very funny,* she told me with mock disapproval when I visited her soon after returning from my monthlong trip to Prague, Vienna, Tel Aviv, Vilnius, and Riga. We were sitting in her apartment as I retailed my various adventures. She brandished the postcards I'd sent. *You see? I got all your cards.* She motioned for Ella to pour me some more iced tea; it was warm in her living room because, although it was the end of July, she'd turned off the air conditioner. *I can't hear when that thing is on*, she said, glaring at the appliance from the high-backed reproduction bergère she liked to sit in, at the corner of the living room, a chair that looked, I always thought, vaguely like a throne, although that might have less to do with the chair itself than with her posture, which was, until only very recently, ramrod straight: she would perch at the edge of the seat, sometimes holding a cane to lean on, and look at me levelly with her hooded, appraising eye, and listen to my stories, only occasionally shaking her head a little and sighing that I was too sentimental, or gesturing angrily at some flowers I'd brought, which Ella had placed on the coffee table and which Mrs. Begley waved away with a gnarled hand as a waste of money I could have been spending on my children. *How are the children?* was always the first question she'd shoot at me, after she'd taken her throne-like seat next to a bookcase crowded with photographs of her child and his children. *The child, the child, everyone told me I must save the child,* she had wept one day, fairly early on in our relationship, the day on which she told me how guilty she felt for not having been able to save anyone else. On this particular day three years later, the day I visited to regale her with stories of my Central European odyssey, I drank my iced tea while she smiled humorlessly and said, *No Jews, I can imagine. We're all here or in the grave.*

FROM A FILTHY and depressing Soviet-era train station in Prague, where the decrepit and aggressive old man who wouldn't stop bothering us turned out to be a porter offering his services, we took the four-hour train trip to Vienna, a city that I love, not least because it figures, however slightly, in certain family stories. (*My father,* my grandfather used to tell me, *would go once a year even to Vienna, for his business, and oh the treats he would bring back for us, the toys, the sweets!*) Vienna was a city that Froma had not seen before, and I was eager to show her its grandiose beauties, the epically scaled baroque and Beaux-Arts buildings whose always slightly outsized details, the inflated cornices and overwrought moldings, were once a symbol of an excessive imperial self-confidence, and now can seem almost embarrassing, given that the empire for which these ornaments were designed has vanished—the way in which, say, an older female relative who has gotten absurdly overdressed for a casual occasion might embarrass you. And yet I love Vienna, perhaps because the tenacity with which it clings to discarded formalities of another era reminds me of certain former Austrians I myself have known.

What did we see in Vienna? We saw many of the things I love, not the least of which, since my enthusiasm for tombs is not at all limited to Jewish tombs, is the Kaisergruft, the imperial Habsburg crypt, a cool underground space that reminded me, the first time I visited some years ago, of a wine cellar, although instead of casks and bottles waiting under the low vaulted ceilings there were sarcophagi in bronze and stone, writhing with statues and crowned skulls, whispering Latin inscriptions to anyone who cared to look. Naturally the largest of the monuments is that of Maria Theresia herself who, in life-size bronze, raises herself up on one arm from the lid of her own enormous coffin, her face wreathed in an ecstatic smile, although whether the ecstasy is due to the anticipation of eternal life, or to the fact that her much-loved husband, Stephen of Lorraine, is similarly elevating himself opposite her, I can never quite determine. We saw the Kaisergruft, where Franz Josef himself lies in a sleek marble sarcophagus in the center of a soberly restrained chamber ringed with subtle sconces, the emperor between his beautiful doomed wife, Elisabeth, herself the victim of an assassin, and his romantic son, Rudolf, the crown prince who killed himself in a suicide pact with his teenaged mistress at a royal hunting lodge called Mayerling in January 1889, a fact that, among other things, makes me wonder about certain family stories, for instance the one my grandfather's unhappy sister Sylvia used to tell about how, as a small child, she saw this same crown prince ride up the steps of a palace in Lemberg (as she would have called it) on a white horse, wearing a blue uniform, since Sylvia herself wasn't born until 1898, which is to say nine years after Rudolf committed the act that would make him so romantically famous.

So we saw all that. But as I've said, Froma has a hungry mind. *My feeling is,* she told me later, when I asked why, as we traveled together, she was always saying *Let's go back and take one last look,* why she always pushed to see more sights, to ask more questions, to wring out of her travels far more than I ever would, *My feeling is, you may never pass this way again, so you have to squeeze everything out of it.* Froma was not, at any rate, content with dead Habsburgs; she was particularly interested to see sites of Jewish interest. And here again I am forced to admit that because of my own history, the influence of my family and its stories, my emotions were engaged by one site in particular that might not be of great interest to most others. For it wasn't until our last day in Vienna, after we'd visited the Jewish museum in the Dorotheergasse (where you can learn, as I did, that soon after the first Jews arrived in the city, in the late 1100s, the first pogrom took place, in which sixteen Jews were killed, an act to which the pope gave his blessing); after we'd gone to see the new museum in the ancient Judenplatz, *Jew Square* (under which, we were told, archaeologists have discovered the remains of the city's early synagogue, destroyed in 1420, the year in which, on the twenty-third of May, the duke ordered that the Jews of Vienna be either imprisoned or expelled and their property confiscated; these remains, however, cannot be that extensive since the stones from the demolished synagogue were used for the construction of city's University); after we'd examined the Memorial to Austrian Holocaust Victims designed by the British artist Rachel Whiteread, which takes the form of a concrete cube representing a library of seven thousand volumes whose doors are permanently locked and whose books cannot be read, the base of which gives the names of places where nearly seventy thousand Viennese Jews were eliminated—after we saw all this, we went on our last day to the Zentralfriedhof, the great Central Cemetery of the city. We went there because Froma had been particularly interested to locate the original gravesite of that nineteenth-century Zionist pioneer, Theodor Herzl, "the father of modern Israel," who died in Vienna in 1904, at the age of forty-four (and whose remains had, in fact, been transferred in 1949 to the newly founded state of Israel: a gesture that makes sense when you keep in mind the fact that graves, gravesites, memorials, and monuments are of no use to the dead but mean a great deal to the living). We consulted one of the innumerable maps and guidebooks that Froma likes to acquire when she travels—I, less inquisitive and more passive, prefer to amble around and run into things—and made our plans.

The tram ride from central Vienna to the Zentralfriedhof takes a good twenty minutes, and the cemetery is so gigantic that there is a different tram stop for each of its various gates; the distance between gates (by which of course I mean not simply the space but also the *time* it takes to get from one to another) is not at all inconsiderable. We began at Gate 1, which is the gate to the "Old" Jewish Section of the cemetery, and strode into a thicket of graves that was, that summer, still somewhat overgrown, although a recent outcry about the sorry state of the once-great necropolis had resulted in a much-touted restoration effort. But after wandering for nearly an hour among the elaborate and neglected gravestones and monuments, memorials to people whom there is nobody anymore to remember, since for the most part the descendants of these nineteenth-century grandees had themselves vanished off the face of the earth, it became clear that we were in the wrong place. And so, after walking twenty minutes to the central section, we walked another twenty minutes to get to Gate 4, where the New Jewish Section is located. I myself had little interest in Herzl or his grave since, as I have said, Israel was at that point still a place about which I felt indifferent. But I did find myself overwhelmed by what we found in the New Jewish Section.

Or, I should say, what we didn't find. Eyes wide, we passed through the extremely attractive, rather Art Deco gateway of this new part of the Zentral-friedhof, a gateway whose repeated motif of stylized, vaguely Moorish arches was repeated, on a gigantic scale, in the dome of the New Jewish Section's Zeremonienhalle, the Ceremonial Hall of the cemetery's burial society. (This society is known, in Hebrew, as the *Chevra Kadisha,* and traditionally it is the members of the *Chevra Kadisha* in a given Jewish community who wash and prepare Jewish bodies for burial: the rite that had been specified by my grandfather in the instructions he dictated to me, that summer morning.) The Vienna cemetery's Zeremonienhalle complex, I later learned, had been designed and built between 1926 and 1928 by the prolific Hungarian-born Viennese Jewish architect Ignaz Reiser, every one of whose public buildings, from the 1912–1914 synagogue on a street called Enzersdorferstrasse to the Zeremonienhalle itself, is listed, in the German-language architectural refer-ence I consulted after seeing this remarkable cemetery complex, as *zerstört:* "destroyed." As we moved past the Zeremonienhalle, which I did not then realize was a restoration, a reconstruction of an edifice that had been sav-aged on the evening of November 8, 1938, and walked to the burial ground itself, the sight that greeted us was one largely of emptiness. For of the vast plot of land that had been bought by the Jews of Vienna in the 1920s for the new section of the cemetery, once the old section had become overcrowded with the dead of this flourishing community, only a relatively small portion was filled with graves. Next to those graves (almost none of which, Froma and I noticed as we walked around, dates to later than the early 1930s) an enormous expanse of empty land stretched out. We stared at this for a while until we realized that the New Jewish Section was largely empty because all of the Jews who, in the normal course of things, would have been buried there had, in fact, died in ways they hadn't foreseen, and if they'd been buried at all, had been buried in other, less attractive graves not of their choosing. When we think of the terrible damage that results from certain kinds of wartime destruction, we normally think of the emptiness of places that had once been filled with life: houses and shops and cafés and parks and museums, and so forth. I'd spent a great deal of time in graveyards, but even so it had never occurred to me, until that afternoon in the Zentralfriedhof, that cemeteries, too, can be bereft.

This, at any rate, is what Froma's search for the grave of the great Zionist Theodor Herzl had led us to. We never did find the grave itself, although I suspect that only Froma was unhappy about that, since for me what we'd seen, or rather not seen, in the New Jewish Section had been enough.

From Vienna I sent Mrs. Begley a postcard of opulent Habsburg palaces. *Vienna is still beautiful,* I wrote, *but no Jews—not even dead ones.* She had liked that one, too.

It was on the day after our visit to the Zentralfriedhof that we left for the land that Herzl fathered.

IN THE APARTMENT of Anna Heller Stern, *who was Lorka's friend,* it was cool and shadowy. The window shades were lowered against a summer sun so strong that it felt almost fluorescent. The furnishings were comfortable but few: a low sofa, a couple of contemporary chairs grouped around a low table. What with the sparseness of the room's contents and the coolness of the bare floors and the almost subaqueous shade, the overall impression I had, on walking through the door of Anna's apartment, was of the pleasant relief I've sometimes felt when, to escape from the heat of a summer afternoon on a day spent copying down inscriptions in neglected cemeteries, I have taken refuge in some once-grand and now-forgotten family's mausoleum.

Like her apartment, Anna herself seemed at once friendly and slightly reserved. She smiled warmly and shook my hand firmly when Shlomo introduced us, but there was also a sense about her of something very slightly wary, as if somewhere in her apartment, or perhaps in her, there was something she might not, after all, want you to know about. When she answered the door, a slightly pear-shaped woman with a tentative, pretty face and the delicate complexion and faintly ginger hair of someone who avoids the sun, she was wearing a sleeveless white blouse and a narrow gray skirt that reached the tops of her knees. As with my grandmothers, the heavy flesh on her upper arms was both plump and sleek, like a dough that has been kneaded for a long time. With one of these arms, Anna Stern gestured for Shlomo and me to come into the apartment, and we sat down. Anna sat opposite Shlomo, and I sat down on the sofa, where I spread out my tape recorder, tapes, videocamera, file folders, and the one extant photograph of Lorka that we possess, that group shot of the family during their mourning for Shmiel's mother in 1934, which I planned to show her during the interview.

Shlomo was speaking to Anna in Yiddish, and my ears pricked up when I heard him say *Di ferlorene*. The Lost.

He is writing a book about his family, Shlomo explained to her as we took our seats. On the low table Anna had laid out plates, cups, napkins. There was a tray of carefully sliced cakes and pastries that could easily have fed fifteen people. Smiling, Anna gently pushed the tray toward me, beckoning for me to eat. Shlomo went on, It is called *The Lost. Di ferlorene*.

Di ferlorene, Anna repeated, nodding, as if this title required no explanation.

Di ferlorene. I wasn't sure exactly how it was decided that this interview would be conducted in Yiddish. I had expected to be hearing the soft, susurrous sounds of Polish, the language that both Anna and Shlomo had grown up speaking in Bolechow in the interwar period, the language into which Meg Grossbard had often lapsed, during the group interview in Sydney, pretending that it was a slip on her part, although I suspected then, and suspect even more today, now that I know her better, that she did so in order to remind me, subtly, that this was her life, her story, a story from which I, *a second-generation American,* as she liked to point out, was inevitably excluded, except perhaps as a latecomer, a mere observer. Alternatively, I had thought that they might be speaking Hebrew, the language of the country in which these two former Poles now lived, until Shlomo explained to me that Anna had moved to Israel fairly recently from South America, where she'd gone after the war with her husband.

She left Poland in 1947, Shlomo said to me in English. She was twenty-six. And she lived forty-two years in Argentina. She is only in Israel for the past few years.

At the sound of the word *Argentina,* Anna smiled and picked up a Spanish newspaper that was lying on a side table and nodded at me. *Ikh red keyn Ebreyish,* she said to me in Yiddish. *I speak no Hebrew.*

This was fine with me; neither did I, I who had learned by rote my *haftarah,* and for that reason had no idea that I was singing about the purgation of the Jewish community; I who for a long time had no interest in deciphering Hebrew texts, texts that I found out almost too late could illuminate family secrets and family lies. But I was only too happy to hear, as I had never expected to hear again after my grandfather died, Yiddish falling from the lips of a Bolechower. Yiddish was the language of Europe, of the Old Country; its moist, rich sounds curl around my memories, familiar yet mysterious, the way that Hebrew letters undulate on a piece of paper or stone. My mother spoke it with her parents; her parents spoke it with each other; her uncles and aunts spoke it among themselves and with their husbands and wives, and—so my mother told me, when I was trying to remember the other day just how much Yiddish was spoken in my family once, but of course not anymore, since almost everyone who knew it has died—her older cousin Marilyn, Jeanette's daughter, spoke it as a child with her grandmother, her father's mother, the dreaded Tante. Yiddish was the language my mother spoke with her father when she didn't want us to know the nature of whatever drama or crisis or gossip they were discussing. (*Ober mayn frayndine hut gezugt azoy,* she would say with a frown as she talked on the phone with him, gesturing with a pursed face that he could not, of course, see, toward the house of a neighbor she had quarreled with and soon would not be speaking to: *but my girlfriend said that . . .*) Yiddish was the language of the punch lines of my grandfather's jokes.

This is why, when Shlomo asked if it would be all right to conduct this interview in Yiddish, of course I said yes. I was longing to hear Yiddish again.

Yaw, I said in her direction, and she smiled. She put the Spanish paper back down, turned to Shlomo, and spoke in a Yiddish too rapid for me to understand. He waited for her to finish, nodded at her, and turning to me he said, In Argentina she started living again. In Argentina she understood that she was a human being again.

I nodded, and then I said, Let's begin.

For the sake of the record, I said, I wanted to ask her to tell me the name she was born with, her parents' names, the names of her family in Bolechow. I liked to begin this way, because it was easy.

Ikh? she repeated. Me? *Ikh hiess Chaya, jetz hayss ich Anna.* I was called Chaya, now I'm called Anna. Where, I wondered, was the "Klara Heller" Meg Grossbard had told me to find in Israel? Without translating for Anna, Shlomo explained to me that when she was a girl in Bolechow she'd been called Klara, but to honor the Ukrainian priest who'd saved her life by giving her false baptismal papers, she'd kept the name he made up for her even after the war was over: *Anna.*

And her family? I asked, gently coaching her through this easy part.

She looked at me and splayed the fingers on one hand, reserving the thumb. *Vir zaynen geveyn fier kinder,* she said. We were four children. She tapped her forefinger: number one. *A shvester, Ester Heller—*

On the second syllable of *Ester* her voice suddenly became ragged with tears and she put both hands to her face. Turning to Shlomo, she said in Yiddish— this I could understand—

You see? Already I can't go on.

LATER ON DURING this conversation in the shady, cool apartment, I would learn how the sister was taken in the second Aktion—an event that Anna, hiding in a hayloft, witnessed, watching the two thousand Jews of Bolechow make their way to the train station, singing "Mayn Shtetele Belz," a memory so painful to Anna as she recalled it that morning in her apartment that she covered her face with her hands once more at the recollection—learned how Ester Heller had died, how the two brothers and the parents died, another family of six that was destroyed; but that came later. At the beginning of our discussion, when the cakes were still largely untouched, Anna politely tried to connect whatever information she was giving me to my family.

Ikh verd den Detzember dray und achzig yuhr, she told me. In December I'll be eighty-three years old. She added, Lorka was a few months older than I.

Oh? I said, although I knew this must be true, because Lorka's birth certificate says *21 May 1920.* I wanted to know how she remembered that so vividly.

Anna smiled. *Vayss farvuss ikh vayss?* You know why I know? Because in first grade I was the smallest and the youngest! With Lorka I went to school until the seventh grade. From six years old till thirteen. Understand? *Fershteyss?*

I nodded back. *Ikh fershteyeh,* I said.

Anna started talking about the Jägers. Her memories came in no particular order. I didn't interrupt, because I was as interested in her chain of thought as in the memories themselves.

Shmiel Jäger had a truck, he used to take things to Lemberg, Anna said, using the old, old name for Lwów. And he would bring goods back from Lemberg. . . . They were a very nice family, a nice woman . . .

I am always interested to know more about Ester. Did she have clear memories of Ester, Shmiel's wife? I asked.

Anna smiled. *Sie veyhn a feine froh, a gitte mamma, a gitte balabustah. Vuss noch ken ikh vissen?* She was a fine wife, a good mom, a good housewife. What else could I know?

She said something to Shlomo, who turned to me.

She was a child, he said, what happened in their house she doesn't know. She said the mother was an excellent wife, the house was very clean, and the children were clean-dressed, the children were clothed very nicely.

Anna turned to me. *Di zeyst?* she declared. *Lorkas familyeh kenn ikh besser als Malka Grossbard!*

See? I know Lorka's family better than Meg Grossbard does!

She said something to Shlomo, who explained to me that her mother's brother, a Mr. Zwiebel, was a neighbor of Shmiel Jäger. He was living next to him, Shlomo said. So Anna (he went on) used to come see her uncle, and for that reason she used to see Lorka all the time, not just in school.

To prove this, perhaps, Anna shared an early memory. I remember, she said, that when the first strawberries came out each year they would be on sale first in Lemberg. So your uncle Shmiel Jäger used to bring them from Lemberg to Bolechow, because they weren't available in Bolechow yet. So Lorka would call for me at home the day the strawberries came and say, *Come, take some of the new strawberries!*

I caught, suddenly and powerfully, a whiff of something, a trace, as unmistakable but elusive, of a certain rhythm of living, now invisible and unimaginable.

Shmiel and his trucks: everyone seemed to remember that. What kind of man was Shmiel, I wanted to know.

Anna gave a little smile and tapped her ear. *Er var a bissl toip!* He was a little deaf!

Deaf? I repeated, and she said,

Yes! Toip! Toip!

I was silent. Then I asked, Does she remember any of the other girls?

Di kleynste, she started to say, the youngest—

Bronia, I prodded. I was excited at the thought that finally someone might be able to tell us something about Bronia. Bronia, who had disappeared into the Bath and Inhalation Rooms sixty years before; Bronia, who had the bad luck to be so young when she was taken, and because nobody that young was a useful worker, almost nobody that young—her friends, her schoolmates—had survived, which is why so little of her is left today to know about.

Bronia? I said again. But Anna shook her head and said, *Ruchele var di kleynste.*

Ruchele? I asked, startled. Anna nodded emphatically, but I didn't pursue it.

Which is why, when she went on to tell me that *di kleynste,* the smallest one, was a very solid girl, very sensitive, very delicate, that she belonged to a group of children who were all of them very polite and very gentle—a description, I knew, that fit well with Jack's description of Ruchele—I couldn't be sure if I'd ever learn anything about Bronia.

I HAVE SOME pictures to show you, I said to Anna.

To trigger her memories, I'd brought my folder of old family photographs, the ones I'd brought to Sydney, too. But after Sydney—after Boris Goldsmith had squinted at that tiny 1939 picture of Shmiel, Ester, and Bronia and said, with a sigh, *I can't make it out*—I'd learned my lesson, and had greatly enlarged all the pictures I had. Now, even the smallest snapshot in my collection had grown to the size of a standard piece of printer paper: Shmiel's careworn face, in that final photograph from *Dezember 1939,* was almost life-size. As I handled the folder one of the enlargements inside slid onto the table: the 1936 photo of Frydka, Meg Grossbard, and Pepci Diamant in their fur-lined school over-coats and berets.

Duss iss Frydka mit Malka Grossbard und Pepci Diamant, I said. This is Frydka with Malka Grossbard and Pepci Diamant. Anna immediately pointed to Meg's face and, like someone taking a winning trick in a card game, gathered up the picture and said, Malka! Then she said, *Frydka var zeyer sheyn*—zeyer *sheyn!*

Frydka was very pretty—*very* pretty!

As she said this, Anna made an admiring gesture, a universal expression of wonderment: hands to cheeks, eyes raised heavenward. We had come to talk about Lorka, whom no one else had known well, but it didn't surprise me that we had gotten onto the subject of Frydka, a girl who was so beautiful, a girl for whom a boy had given his life, the kind of girl, I had already sensed, to whom stories and myths naturally clung.

I want to tell you a fact, Anna said, looking at this picture of the fourteen-year-old Frydka, and she started talking. Shlomo listened and then turned to me. He said, She said that Frydka should live today, be alive today. She was a modern woman, but she was living in the wrong time!

What did she mean? I asked.

Because the way she was living in that time, in a small shtetl, she was criti-cized! She was, you know, *free!*

Criticized? I said, while I thought to myself: What *was* it about her? Even then, they were talking about her. Even then, she was the center of the story.

Anna nodded. She should have lived fifty years later, she said again. Lorka, she went on, was quiet, serious, and had only one *sympatia*—

(later, I looked up *sympatia* in a Polish dictionary: *flame,* it said, and there was something about how old-fashioned *flame* sounded to my ears that moved me, when I recalled Anna talking about Lorka and her *sympatia*)

—one *sympatia* at a time. She had somebody that she liked, a brother of Mrs. Halpern. So she dated him . . . Bumo Halpern.

Really? I said. This caught me by surprise. I explained to them that in Syd-ney, Meg Grossbard had insisted that Lorka's boyfriend had been her dis-tant cousin—my distant cousin—Yulek Zimmerman. Anna shook her head emphatically and said, *Bumo Halpern.*

OK, I said. Anyway.

Shlomo went on: Anna said that Lorka behaved, she behaved honestly and she didn't—she had a sympathy to one man and she never betrayed him.

Betrayed.

And Frydka? I asked, knowing in advance what the answer would be.

Anna beamed at me, and shaking her head as if the memory still amused her, and waving her fingers in the air, she said, *Frydka var geveyn a*—

(she paused and, not finding the correct word in Yiddish, shifted to Spanish)

—*sie's geveyn a picaflor!*

Frydka was a hummingbird!

Shlomo beamed as he translated this, enjoying the image; then added one of his own. Yes! He nodded, smiling: he remembered her, too. She was a butterfly! he cried. Going from flower to flower!

At this point, between Anna and Shlomo, a great deal of Yiddish buzzed and gurgled. Shlomo slapped his thigh and laughed.

She told me two stories, he said. One: about Frydka she can say that she and some friends were once going over to Russki Bolechow. Now there was a guy who was renting a room there, they were curious about him. So they knocked on the door, and who was there when it opened? Frydka!

I grinned. *A butterfly!* Well, I thought, who could blame her? I'd seen the pictures from Pepci Diamant's albums. Frydka the moody teenager, mooning at her open photo album; Frydka on a brilliantly sunny day in a white dress and those open-toe shoes, squinting into the camera, tall and leggy; Frydka clowning in the bushes by the Sukiel River; Frydka scowling at the camera with her fingers to her finely carved lips, a pose nobody likes to be caught in, snacking on something delicious that her mother had prepared for her, a meal that turned to dust a lifetime ago. You could, I thought, get a crush on this girl.

Anna excused herself to answer the phone, which had rung quite loudly at the end of this story, and while she was gone I talked about Frydka with Shlomo, who had worked in the *Fassfabrik* with her.

You know, I said to him, I could tell from the pictures what Frydka was like, you could tell she thought she was a movie star—

Shlomo nodded and pointed a thick finger at me in that *Aha, I told you so!* way that he has. And I am telling *you,* he said, that I think that I saw her myself in the *Fassfabrik,* because there were two beautiful girls in the *Fassfabrik,* which we already, youngsters, were aware of—because I was twelve and a half years till thirteen and a half, till thirteen actually, in that place—so I remember we saw, probably one was Frydka and another one was Rita, Rita was a girl of a refugee family which came to Bolechow. A *Flüchtling,* a beautiful girl. And the other one was Frydka. And I remember the two girls represented the women in the *Fassfabrik*. I remember, we would say, *if somebody was beautiful, it was Frydka and Rita!*

Anna returned to the armchair. Did I want water, a soft drink, a Coke? Yes, I said, Coke would be great. While she was in the kitchen Shlomo went on with Anna's second story about Frydka the butterfly, a story from darker times.

It's a little bit difficult to translate! he said, laughing loudly. He said: Anna said that during the war, when people were working in the factories, most of the girls worked outside. But Frydka, because she, you know, because she was free in such a way . . . she arranged for herself that she was working inside! In the camp, in the *Lager,* in the barrel factory . . .

Well, I said, half-amused even as I spoke by my own reflexive impulse to protect the reputation of my long-dead cousin, We know from what Jack Greene told us, and from Shmiel's letters, that Frydka had gone to a commercial high school to learn to be a bookkeeper. (*Darling Frydka has finished high school,* Shmiel had written, *it cost me a fortune and where is one supposed to find a job for her?* And again: *Frydka has finished with the Commercial School in Stryj, she still has one more school to deal with; I'd like to have her learn a trade as I see fit, as today one is nothing without a trade . . .*) And so, I went on, maybe that's why she worked inside the camp building? After all, I thought to myself, hadn't Jack said that she'd worked as a bookkeeper in the *Fassfabrik?*

Anna came back with a large bottle of Coke and put it down on the table. Shlomo relayed my objection to her. Anna shook her head, smiling broadly, and told him something.

She said no, Shlomo explained, Frydka didn't work in an office, she didn't do bookkeeping then, she worked at a machine. He turned once more to Anna and then turned back to me. He said, I told her that I sat next to Frydka inside that building and it was not so nice, it was very hard inside, but Anna said to me just now, No, no, it was nicer than working outside in the freezing winter!

Ess var shreklikh kalt! Anna said to me, knowing I wouldn't need a translation. It was horribly cold!

I remembered my endless conversations with Andrew, years earlier, in which we'd wonder how my grandfather would have fared, had he too been trapped in Bolechow during the war; about whether his wonderful ability to finagle what he wanted, to sweet-talk his way into and out of things, was unique to him, or was the expression of some characteristic that had once flourished in our family but seemed (for this was the unspoken feeling that lay behind our interest) to have died out. Now Shlomo had said, not without admiration: *She arranged for herself to be working inside!*

She should have lived today! Anna repeated.

I smiled. Yes, I thought, this was definitely a girl you could get a crush on.

I WANTED TO return to the pictures, to the one photograph of her friend Lorka that we had. But just as I was reaching into the folder to pull out the enlargement of that group picture, now just under seventy years old, Anna said something to Shlomo. I heard the names *Shmiel* and *Frydka*. Would we always be talking about Frydka? I thought.

Then Shlomo said, *Aha!*

He turned to me. She said (he told me) that she heard, somewhere, probably that Frydka and Shmiel were hidden somewhere and somebody gave them up and they were killed.

Frydka and Shmiel? I repeated, stupidly. Anna looked at me; it was clear she could tell that I had heard a different story. She nodded, looking at me, and went on.

Zey zent behalten bay a lererin . . .

Shlomo listened and then translated, although I was able to make out the story. He said, They were captured at the home of a schoolteacher. It was a teacher who learned them how to make drawings.

An art teacher, I said.

Yes, he said. An art teacher. A Polish woman.

Did she know the name of this teacher? I asked. I wanted something concrete, something specific that would pin the story down.

Anna talked more to Shlomo, who shook his head. No. But as they went on talking, I heard a name I knew well: *Ciszko Szymanski*. I looked up, wide-eyed. For anyone who spends too much time in archives, doing research about obscure events that have long since faded from the memories of everyone except, maybe, a very few old people, it is gratifying to have independent confirmation of the stories you're pursuing. So she, too, had heard the story about Ciszko Szymanski. Anna smiled and nodded, and said something to Shlomo.

She says Ciszko Szymanski was Frydka's boyfriend, Shlomo said.

I told Shlomo to tell her that Meg Grossbard in Sydney wouldn't tell us anything—I turned to Anna and said *gurnisht!*, Nothing!, and she smiled—because Ciszko wasn't Jewish. Shlomo translated this for Anna, who turned to me and made an incredulous expression, frowning and spreading her arms wide, as if to say, *Who could possibly care anymore?*

I told her that we had heard from Jack Greene that Ciszko Szymanski was executed for having tried to help Frydka. She clearly understood what I was saying, because before I was finished speaking she looked at me and said, in Yiddish, Yes, that's what I heard.

It was at that point that she leaned across the low table toward me, that way a woman might lean over to confide a bit of gossip to a girlfriend, and said something very quickly. The tension between the intimacy of her gesture and the strangeness of having to wait for Shlomo to translate struck me, at that moment, as significant: it seemed like a symbol for everything I was feeling that day—the strangeness at having to process, all at once, impossible distances of time and language and memory, together with the immediacy and vividness of the small but moving fragments I was hearing, just then, about my long-dead relations. *Come, take some strawberries! He was deaf! A butterfly!*

Shlomo listened to what Anna said, as she leaned over so confidingly, and then turned to me.

Shlomo said, She said that when they were caught, Ciszko said, *If you kill her, then you should kill me too!*

For a moment nobody said anything. I knew, of course, that Frydka had inspired much more than a crush: *That boy paid with his life for it,* Jack had said in Sydney. But it was something, now, to overhear the fervor, the youthful bravado, of this lost boy's words. *If you kill her, then you should kill me too!* And they did kill him; that much everyone agreed on, although it would be two years before I found out exactly how.

I said, How does she know all this?

Shlomo and Anna talked, and then he said to me, She heard this from her cousin, he was in Kfar Saba but now he's in Haifa. He had been in Russia but he came back and he was living in Bolechow right after the war. He was one of those who built the memorial at Taniawa. So he knew a lot—how, what, where things happened. They spoke, you know, the ones who came back spoke after the war, right after the war, they spoke to the Ukrainians.

Shlomo paused and said, just to me, There were so many things that I didn't ask—that *I* didn't ask. You know, I'm wondering. Today I want to know more things than I wanted to know then.

He took a breath and then returned to the subject of Anna's cousin, who had heard about Ciszko Szymanski's last words. So, Shlomo said, speaking of this cousin, he knew, he knew a lot, and this is what he heard.

What happened to the cousin? I asked. I was suddenly excited: if he were in Haifa, I could take the train up there, talk to him, perhaps there were other details he might remember.

There was a rather prolonged exchange with Anna. Shlomo turned to me. He said, She says his mind is not clear anymore. She said that he was talking recently to her on the telephone and he said to Anna, "I just talked to my cousin," and she said, "Which cousin?" and he said "Anna," and she said, "*I am Anna.*"

So: I wouldn't be talking to the cousin.

During all this, I suppose that my emotions were pretty transparent: the moving detail about the fate of Ciszko and Frydka (if it was true), and, even more in a way, the fact that there was an important variant of the story I had heard in Australia, of the story about Shmiel's fate that had been told to me by the four Sydney Bolechowers, who were absolutely convinced that Shmiel had been taken, with his wife and youngest daughter—really the youngest—in the second Aktion, and had perished at Belzec. It took me a moment to sort through the feelings that this sudden shift in my assumptions had produced. On the one hand, it was disconcerting; I was beginning to become aware of how fragile each story I heard really was. (*Look,* someone would tell me, much later, *how does anyone who survived know for sure? It's just what someone told them. They weren't there. If they survived, they were already in hiding when it happened.* . . .) On the other, I felt the strange exhilaration you can feel when faced with a particularly challenging mystery story, or crossword. What *had* happened to Uncle Shmiel, then?

My face must have betrayed my feelings. *Du sehst?* Anna said, her gentle eyes on my face, that soft, private smile hovering around her lips. *Ich veyss alles.*

You see? I know everything.

FINALLY, WE GOT down to looking at the picture of Lorka.

I have a picture of Lorka, I told her. It was Lorka I had come to find out about, although most of our conversation, most of the vivid memories, had ended up being about Frydka. I wondered, briefly, if there had been some sibling rivalry between Lorka, the responsible older sister, the one who was so faithful and true, and her wild (or so I thought) younger sister, whose personality seemed more real to me, more concrete and vivid, with each story I heard about her.

Pictures fun Lorka? Anna said, eagerly. She went into the bedroom to get her glasses. When she returned, I triumphantly held up the sixty-nine-year-old photograph. There they were again, frozen in their mourning for my great-grandmother: Shmiel, Ester, Ester's brother Bruno Schneelicht, and four girls who were, I was now certain, the nine-year-old Ruchele, the five-year-old Bronia, the fourteen-year-old Lorka—the tall one standing at the back, crouching to get into the picture, with her long, shy, somewhat serious face, not at all unattractive, but not nearly as vivaciously pretty as Frydka's—and, half cut off by the edge of the picture frame, Frydka, aged twelve.

Anna held up the picture with both hands and looked at it for a moment. Confidently, she pointed to Ester and said, *duss ist di mitter fun Lorka,* and I said, Yes, this is Lorka's mother. Anna looked up at me and, making a negating movement with the flat of her hand, said, Ester was not from Bolechow, she was from Stryj. From my own research I knew this statement was true, but I was moved to see that she knew this small fact, something she'd gleaned from some childish conversation that took place seventy years ago and had, mysteriously, retained a lifetime later. I nodded and said, Stryj, and she smiled and said to me, So you know!

She returned to the picture and said, as she scrutinized it with a frown, *Di kinder, zi kenn ikh nokh nikht.*

The children, I don't recognize them anymore.

I pointed out Lorka to her with my finger. She pulled the picture back toward her and, looking at it intently, asked what year it had been taken. Nineteen thirty-four, I said. I know this for a fact. *Zur Erinnerung an den ersten Monat wo ich nach unser gottseligen Mutter trauerte. Bolechów in August 1934. Sam.* As a souvenir of the first month of my mourning for our blessed mother, Bolechow, August 1934. Sam. My great-grandmother, Taube Mittelmark Jager, died on July 27, 1934. Taube. Years ago, when I was a child, a family moved into the house next door, and when my mother met the wife, whose name was Toby, my mother smiled and said, My grandmother's name was Taube. It means "dove."

From this photo, taken to commemorate the first month of mourning for this delicate-boned, indeed rather dovelike woman, whose face stares out with the exact same expression of sadness in all of the photos we still have of her, Anna turned away and looked at Shlomo emphatically.

What did she say? I asked Shlomo, getting nervous.

She said, I don't think this is Lorka. She said she sees Lorka in her mind, and this is not Lorka.

He turned back to her for confirmation. *Nayn?* Anna made a clucking sound three times with her tongue, *no no no*. Then she turned to me and said, in Yiddish, Who told you this is Lorka?

Mayn zeyde, I said, a little hesitantly. *My grandfather*. He was the one who had let me pore over the albums from which all these photos had come, three decades ago; he was the one who had told me everything I knew about the family history, *his* family history, the stories and jokes and dramas, the names that went with the unsmiling faces in those old pictures. Of course it was Lorka, I thought; there are four girls there, and clearly the one I had pointed to was the oldest.

Mayn zeyde, I repeated, more confidently.

Anna smiled her sad smile at me, but was firm. *Dayn zeyde hut zi gekeynt?* she said.

Your grandfather knew her?

What could I say?

I said, No.

THE DISCUSSION OF what Lorka looked like seemed to trigger an important memory in Anna, who suddenly became quite emotional. Her voice thickened, as she turned first to me and then to Shlomo, speaking heatedly, gesturing with her hands: pointing, lifting them up as if to call God to witness, and, finally, circling her own torso, as if in an embrace. Finally she stopped talking, and looked at me expectantly, waiting for Shlomo to translate.

Ah, Shlomo said, you see? You remember that I told you that everybody was for himself, egotistic?

I remembered: the day before, when I had interviewed him, when he had told me how he and his cousin Josef had hidden, after the rest of their families had been killed, and had survived together; had told me how, because his mother was so *frum,* so devout, she had abandoned her hiding place in order to make Pesach, Passover, and had been caught and taken away, how he had tried to go with her, and how, to spare him the sight of whatever might happen to her, she had sent her little boy back to their house to fetch her some warm socks, and when he'd run and gotten them and then returned to where she'd been, she was gone—when Shlomo was telling me all this, the day before, he'd said that one of the things that the Occupation did to people was to make them secretive, even with friends and loved ones. People who were planning to go into hiding, he'd said, with a look that was both knowing and mournful, knew that their chances of survival were better if as few people as possible knew what they were planning. I didn't even try to imagine what it would have been like to have to practice this kind of passive deceit with people you loved—people who, you must have known, would die if they weren't making plans like the ones you were keeping from them.

You see? Shlomo said again, that day we were talking to Anna Heller Stern. Nobody wanted to tell, nobody who was going to hide! And she was a close friend of Lorka, they were working in the *Fassfabrik* together. Anna told me that on the day that she knew she was going to escape, they were walking, on the way to work in the factory. And she told me that she suddenly said to Lorka, *Lorka, let's embrace each other, give each other a kiss, because God knows when we will see each other again.*

That was the last she saw of Lorka.

We were all silent for a few moments. Then I asked, When was this? Shlomo and Anna talked for a minute, and then he said, It was in November of 'forty-two.

He added: In 'forty-two she left Bolechow and was hiding. She said she knows about what happened to Lorka, how she escaped and how she was with the Babij, and then she was probably killed. She said she heard about Frydka, she heard about Frydka and Shmiel, that they were together in hiding. But she doesn't know how exactly Lorka was killed or Frydka.

She says she doesn't even know what happened to her *own* family, he added.

It was this last remark that made me refrain from asking any more questions. But I now knew this: November 1942 was the last time anyone now alive saw Lorka; which is to say, saw a face that I will never know.

BY THIS TIME the tray on the table was filled with crumbs, and the glasses of Coke were sweating. We'd been talking for an hour and a half or so, and I felt that Anna had told us as much as she could that morning about my family. I thought to myself, What if, in forty years, somebody came to my apartment and asked me what I remembered of a boy who'd grown up nearby, a boy who'd gone to elementary school with me? Of Danny Wasserman, say, the blond boy who lived across the street from me when I was growing up, a boy who was a little older than I was, whose blond hair I remember, now, along with the fact that he liked sports, that he was tall, a nice boy; what could I tell them? So I was grateful to Anna Heller Stern, that morning. I was grateful for the story of the strawberries, just as I was slightly, oddly excited to find out that I still didn't know what, precisely, had happened to Shmiel, and bitterly upset to think that the girl in the photograph was not, in fact, Lorka—and who better to know than this woman, who had known her for so long?—which meant that there was no image that existed anywhere, anymore, of this young woman.

As it turned out, this was not to be the final shock, the final disappointment, the final necessary readjustment to the family story.

Because we were tired, because I thought we'd gotten everything we could reasonably hope for, given how emotional all this was for Anna, that morning, I was starting to think about moving the conversation to an end. And anyway, I had to get ready for the enormous family reunion Elkana was planning for that afternoon, the gathering at which "all the cousins" were going to be present to meet this unknown American relative who was, they had been told, writing a book about the *mishpuchah*. So I asked a question that I thought would help wrap up our long discussion.

Did she remember any other Jägers in Bolechow? I asked. Having talked to the Sydney group three months earlier, I knew about the distant Jäger cousins who owned the *cukierna,* the Jäger brothers, one of whom was named Wiktor, the son (I was sure) of the Chaya Sima Jäger whose gravestone Matt had, so improbably, seen from the window of Alex's car that day, the Wiktor whose sister was the mother of Yulek Zimmerman, the boy who, until today, I'd thought had been Lorka's only boyfriend. Maybe she would know about that, I thought.

Instead, while she was talking to Shlomo, she mentioned something about

Yitzhak Jäger. Uncle Itzhak! It was strange to think that there were people here in Israel who remembered him from his Bolechow days, before he—or rather, Aunt Miriam—had the foresight to get out.

She talked a little while and then Shlomo turned to me and said, Itzhak Jäger had a butchery, but not in the Rynek—

(the Rynek was where the store had stood in my grandfather's day, I knew, and Shlomo knew that I knew that: I had the picture from the Yizkor book, a picture of one side of the Rynek with the town hall building and, just across from it, a low building under which my grandfather had drawn an arrow to identify where his family's store had been)

—not in the Rynek, Shlomo was saying, but opposite the mill. It was there. And from this store he must run away from Bolechow.

Knowing by now about the difficulties of working in several languages at once, I said, You mean he left the store when he left Bolechow?

Shlomo shook his head.

I said, You mean he didn't want to be there? I was confused.

Shlomo looked at me.

He must *run away*, he said.

I said, Why was . . . what does that *mean*?

Anna was watching this exchange, and said to Shlomo, *Er vill vissn?*

He wants to know?

Shlomo turned to me and said for her, although I didn't need the translation, You really want to know?

And I said, *Yes*.

At this point Anna launched into a long story. I knew it would be long from the way she took a breath, from the rhythms of her Yiddish sentences, those ripe vowels and gurgling consonants that unraveled across the room like thick wool from a spool. She talked for a few minutes, sitting at the edge of her chair and looking from Shlomo to me. When she had finished, she sat all the way back in her chair with the sigh of someone who's finished a difficult job.

Shlomo said: OK. They were customers of Itzhak Jäger's butchery. (Anna's family, he meant.) So there was a time when Itzhak built himself a nice house, not far from Shmiel, and they had a big celery.

Cellar, I said.

A big cellar, yes. And she said that there was a certain time, one year, you couldn't get veal meat. No no no—you couldn't get veal.

I wasn't quite following this. You couldn't get veal, he'd said. Why? I wondered aloud if there had perhaps been some blight on the cattle, slightly embarrassed, for reasons I still can't quite isolate, at the thought that this ridiculous, old-fashioned, biblical word, "blight," might have occurred to me because I was now in Israel. He said maybe that was it; maybe the cows weren't calving that year.

Shlomo continued with the story. Suddenly, he said, one woman came to another woman and saw in her kitchen that she had veal. So she asked, *Where did you get the veal meat?* and the other woman said, *By Itzhak Jäger.*

Because I grew up hearing Yiddish, I know that his *by* was the word *bay*, the same as the German *bei*, "at the home of," like the French *chez*. *Zey zent behalten bay a lererin.* They were captured at the home of a schoolteacher. *Bay Itzhak Jäger.* At Itzhak Jäger's place.

Bay Itzhak Jäger, he repeated.

Bay Itzhak Jäger, I repeated.

Shlomo said, So the information came from one to another, one to another—it was a small city. So everyone was buying veal meat from Itzhak Jäger. And then they found out *how* he was getting veal meat—that he used to go out deep in the country and buy a young calf, and then he would take the calf in his cellar to kill it by himself, and so he had veal meat to sell.

Even if you didn't come from a long line of kosher butchers, as I had, you'd know what this meant. Because the calf hadn't been killed by a *shochet,* a ritual slaughterer, it wasn't kosher.

Shlomo was watching my face, and nodded. He said, loudly, So! It was not kosher! He was beaming with the excitement of this story, which he had been too young at the time, perhaps not even born yet, to know about. He went on, A professional person must do it to kill it kosher! So the rabbis, so the rabbis of Bolechow put a sign saying that this store is not kosher, is not selling kosher meat! And all the religious women had to break all the dishes in their home. And it was a big scandal!

He added, on his own, You know, kosher meat used to cost double what other meat cost. So this is how Itzhak could build his big new house with this!

I didn't say anything for a while. Then I asked, What year was this? Shlomo asked Anna, and then said, She was about ten years old.

Nineteen thirty, I thought. Just before Itzhak came to Palestine. *Just in the nick of time! She was a Zionist!*

I thought that was the end of it, when suddenly Shlomo rose forcefully from his seat and cried out.

You *see?* he said, excitedly, You *see?* You see? I want to tell you a very important thing.

I had no idea what he was going to say.

Shlomo looked at me. He said, barely controlling his emotion, I want to tell you something very important. My mother was a *frum,* a religious woman. She was in hiding because she had information that the Germans wanted to take her. But she came *out* of hiding to make Pesach, because of God!

Shlomo took a deep breath. As with many big men who are also unafraid to show their emotions, he seemed somehow to inflate, to get bigger, as he spoke, his voice trembling.

He said, And she came out, and she was killed.

He looked at me meaningfully, and I knew, then, exactly what he was going to say. I said, Shlomo, I know what you're going to say.

But it was as if he didn't hear me. He looked at me, pointing his big finger right at me, and he went on. He said, For being *frum,* my mother was killed! And Itzhak Jäger did a thing that was *against the religion completely*! So God saved him, he sent him away to Palestina! You understand?

I understood. I thought of my grandfather, years earlier, saying about another meal of unkosher meat, *But if life is at stake, God forgives!* But he had eaten that meat to stay alive; this was different. I couldn't think of anything to say. Instead, I listened as Shlomo translated what he'd just said to me for Anna. The second time around he was no less agitated.

Itzhak hut gemakht a zakh duss iss kegn Gott, Shlomo cried out, again.

Itzhak did a thing that is against God.

Unt Gott hut ihm gerattet!

And God saved him!

At this point, Anna, who I suppose had had many years to ponder certain ironies of history, to think about how, or indeed whether, God intervened in human affairs, interrupted Shlomo, shaking her head with that smile she had, which this time mixed with its usual sadness a certain weary amusement. She gestured vaguely heavenward.

Vuss, kegn Gott? she said, admonishing him. *Kegn di* rabbunim!

I didn't need Shlomo to translate this. What she had said was, What, "against God"? Against the *Rabbis.*

If life is at stake, God forgives!

SOON AFTERWARD, SHLOMO dropped me off at Elkana's sleek apartment complex for the festive family reunion. My mother's cousin was expansive over the gigantic late-afternoon lunch, served in the dining hall of the complex. After the twenty-five or so cousins, second cousins, first cousins once-and twice-removed, third cousins, the Ramis and Nomis and Pninas and Re'uts and Gals and Tzakhis had been laughingly introduced (those strange, truncated Israeli names again!: sitting there, I remembered how we'd laugh and say YONA YONA YONA when we were little and my grandfather would come with that dark-haired young Israeli woman, until he started coming with those other women); after the bashful smiles and mute nods and grins, after all these people had taken their seats, Elkana rose to his feet and made a toast of welcome. Embarrassed because I couldn't reply in Hebrew, I smiled stupidly and nodded to everyone. In English, I said I was happy to be in Israel and finally meeting the whole *mishpuchah*. Thoughtfully, Elkana had put me next to his sister's granddaughters, young women in their late twenties who both spoke fluent English. We got to talking and after a while started sharing family gossip and comparing family secrets. *In this family?* Gal said incredulously at one point, in response to something I'd asked. *Are you kidding?* She looked at Ravit and started laughing. I grinned and said, *Yeah, lots of us, too.* At the other end of the table, Elkana had kept his son Rami's son, Tzakhi, a darkly handsome young man who was by now nearly thirty, at his side. *Rami,* a nickname for Abraham: my grandfather. *Tzakhi,* the diminutive of Itzhak. Rami was off in the Far East somewhere; like his father, he was a somebody. Elkana was holding forth in front of his grandson. The papers had said that the search was on for the deposed leader of Iraq; Elkana, who although he was long retired still had the sleek aura of someone who had special access to rarefied information in high places, nodded his head in my direction and said, with a certain largesse, *You will find him in Tikrit, I'm telling you. That is where his home is, his people.* To my right was Ruthie, her braids now a mixture of straw-blond and white; she was translating, as fast as she could, whenever I tried to communicate with the others, whenever she thought it was worth repeating. It was in this fashion that I learned that most of the younger people there were unaware of the fact that this large and buoyant family had come from a place called Bolechow, and that their name had once been יעגר.

Abram's initial encounter with a foreign culture is not, at first glance, terribly successful. Relatively early in parashat *Lech Lecha, we're told that although God had led Abram to Canaan, the territory that had been promised, there was, soon afterward, a famine in that land that caused Abram to flee with his family into Egypt, a land of plenty. Before arriving in Egypt, Abram hatches a plan. She is a beautiful woman, he tells Sarai, and because of that the Egyptians will want to abduct her and kill him; accordingly he instructs her to tell a lie and say that Abram is not her husband, but her brother. This* way, Abram tells her, "it will go well with me for your sake, and I may live on account of you." As it turns out, the former part of Abram's prediction is borne out: the moment they arrive in Egypt, Pharaoh's officers praise her beauty to the king, after which "she was taken to the Pharaoh's house." And indeed it did go well for Abram, who was rewarded for his lie with "flocks and cattle and donkeys and slaves and maidservants and camels." Abundant blessings indeed.

As to the second part of Abram's nervous prediction—that the Egyptians would have killed him if they'd known he was Sarai's husband—there is no evidence to support this, and indeed the text suggests that the opposite, if anything, would have been true. After Sarai is taken into Pharaoh's house (and we are not told what transpires there), God afflicts Egypt with "severe plagues" as punishment for what we must assume is Pharaoh's (unwitting) insult to a married couple. In a passage remarkable for what it doesn't tell us, Pharaoh himself deduces, presumably from the nature of the plagues, which is left unspecified, that he's being punished for taking Sarai as his wife when she is, in fact, a married woman, and angrily summons Abram. "What is this you've done to me?" he cries. "Why did you not tell me that she is your wife? Why did you say, 'She is my sister' so that I'd take her as my wife? Now here is your wife, take her and go!" Abram does go, we are told at Genesis 13:1, "up from Egypt," loaded down with his booty: livestock and silver and gold.

Much of the scholarly commentary on this peculiar detour in Abram's far-flung travels has been on the way in which the episode, which features a confrontation with Pharaoh, punishing plagues on Egypt, the Egyptian king's anger at the man of God, and the king's impatient order for this Hebrew to "go!" out of Egypt with his family and "all that he had," is a self-conscious foreshadowing of the later and central episode narrated in Exodus. And there has, of course, been much discussion of Abram's strange plan, based as it is on an assumption about Egyptian behavior that is never actually borne out by what transpires; in particular, what looks to many commentators as the deliberate prostitution of his wife, coupled with an instruction to lie, has made many scholars of this passage uneasy, and many have taken pains to exculpate Abram. "He cannot be faulted for choosing to put Sarah in a compromising position," Friedman writes, "because, in his understanding, Sarah would be taken either way." Still, there is something unpalatable about the patriarch's behavior. Friedman, the California-based modern, is willing to entertain the notion that perhaps Abram "is not perfect," but Rashi suggests that Abram was not interested in the gifts per se, but—aware that the episode in which he was now an actor was merely the forerunner of a grander biblical drama—was eager for his future progeny in Exodus to leave Egypt similarly laden with gifts.

These and other attempts at exculpating the father of all Jews cannot help but appear rather flimsy to me, now. I think of the story often, the man and his wife and family, the homeland from which they are forced to flee during a time of crisis. The exploitation of a lie for (there is no other word for it) self-enrichment, the use of the wife to provide a kind of cover story for an escape that became, however improbably, a vehicle for self-enrichment, for the propagation of a successful new progeny in the new land. I think of these, and I think that whoever wrote parashat Lech Lecha knew something about the way people can behave in troubled times.

ON SUNDAY, THE twenty-ninth of June, Shlomo picked me up at the Tel Aviv Hilton, which, because of the six-month-old war and the threat of increased terrorism that was one of its inevitable by-products, was rather empty. At the famous breakfast smorgasbord, about which Froma had excitedly told me, the fabulous spread with its many kinds of lox and smoked fishes, the giant electric juicer engorged with intensely colored Israeli oranges, the cheeses and herring and bagels and breads, six or seven people were wandering around that morning. I leafed through the papers. A fifteen-year-old terrorist had killed an Israeli telephone repairman. Israelis were skeptical about a cease-fire that had been announced by Hamas and the Islamic Jihad. A naval commando had been killed during an Israeli crackdown on Hamas. Leon Uris, the author of *Exodus*, had died. I put down the papers and drank my orange juice.

Soon afterward, at ten o'clock sharp, Shlomo navigated the security checkpoint at the entrance to the hotel and pulled up in front of the vast, vacant lobby. He had eagerly offered to drive me the two hours or so south, deep into the desert, to talk to Solomon and Malcia Reinharz. We needed to get there at around lunchtime, Shlomo had told me, per the couple's request.

The husband don't like to take too much time away from work, Shlomo explained.

Work? I repeated, incredulously. Based on what Shlomo had told me, this Mr. Reinharz must be nearly ninety.

Sure, Shlomo said, grinning broadly. They have now a shoe store for over fifty years, they are still working there.

What I thought was, At least their memories must be good.

As we drove out of Tel Aviv, down through Jaffa—where Elkana had taken me for dinner, on the night I arrived, in an unprepossessing Arab restaurant where the food was extraordinary and where he chatted in Arabic with the owner, his old friend—and then out onto a highway that soon was nothing more than a thin line cutting through a great deal of sand, Shlomo and I talked. Not since my grandfather had died had I felt so at liberty to indulge my desire to ask questions about Bolechow. We discussed with excitement the revelations of the day before; in particular, Anna's insistence that Frydka had been in hiding with Shmiel—a version of events that owed no small part of its appeal to the fact that it dovetailed with the version that Aunt Miriam had heard, so many years before. Once again, I felt the urgency behind Shlomo's enthusiasm, the energy that irradiated every new fact related to Bolechow, even if it was a fact about a family that was not his. It was he, after all, who had made himself the head of the "ex-Bolechowers," who would be gathering in the autumn, as they always did, for their annual reunion. It was Shlomo who enjoyed telling me about famous people who had their origins in Bolechow or the surrounding area.

You know who is Krauthammer, the American journalist? he asked me.

Yes, I said, I did.

A Bolechower family! Shlomo cried triumphantly.

No kidding, I said.

He asked me if maybe this Krauthammer had gotten in touch with me when the article I'd written about our trip to Bolechow in 2001 had appeared.

No, I said, smiling, he hadn't. I told him, however, that another well-known figure in American publishing, a man whose father had been born in Stryj, had contacted me after he'd heard about my first trip to Ukraine, two years earlier. *Wieseltier,* I said, when Shlomo asked me the name.

Ah! he said, I think yes, there was a family Wieseltier in Bolechow too.

I nodded and explained that this famous editor, Wieseltier, who lived in Washington, D.C., had told me that he knew for a fact that his mother's family, called Backenroth, were connected to Bolechow, and that he also thought he had had relatives on his father's side who had lived in Bolechow before the war, although he didn't know their names. He had thought that maybe they owned a bakery, as his father had done in Stryj. Shlomo nodded again, and we agreed that *Wieseltier* was a rare name, not the kind you'd be likely to confuse with something else, or forget altogether. *Of course I knew Wieseltier,* Mrs. Begley had told me after I'd returned from Ukraine, *he had the bakery. I knew the father,* she added, knowing that I was likely to know of the son from an entirely different context. Then she had pushed a white bone china platter across the tablecloth toward me and said, *Take another cookie, you think I'm going to eat them?*

Look! Shlomo suddenly cried. He pointed out the window at a figure walking beside a camel. *Bedouins!*

We're certainly not in Bolechow, I joked. I thought of my grandmother in 1956, *with a camel and an Arab.*

He asked me to tell him in more detail about the interviews I'd done in Australia. As I told him, as best I could remember, about each of the long conversations I'd had with everybody, he would nod slowly, relishing each story, each fact, although of course they were stories and facts that he himself knew well by now. At one point I asked if he'd ever heard the story that my mother had somehow heard, all those years ago: that her cousins had been raped before they'd been killed. *They had four beautiful girls, they raped them all and killed them.* Where had she heard this? I used to wonder; but when I finally asked my mother she said, I can't remember anymore, there were so many terrible stories, I used to have nightmares. So as Shlomo and I drove toward Beer Sheva I asked him what he might know, might have heard. No one in Australia had had any specifics, I told him as the desert sizzled around us. He grimaced a little and shrugged sorrowfully. So many terrible things happened during the Aktionen, Shlomo said, it could be possible, sure. Could be. But to know for sure, it's impossible as far as I know.

I nodded but didn't say anything. Maybe it was better not to know some things.

After a pause he said, You know that also Regnier was there in Australia? Anatol Regnier was the author of *Damals in Bolechow,* the book that told the story of how Shlomo and his cousin Josef, how Jack and Bob and the rest, had survived. I thought of Meg Grossbard, telling me how strange she had found it that a German had called her one day, asking to talk about Bolechow; and of how she had refused to talk to him, refused to let her story be written down.

Yes, I replied to Shlomo, I know he was there. And then, continuing the unspoken thought that had risen in my mind, I said, half smiling, It's different to write the story of people who survived, because there's someone to interview, and they can tell you these amazing stories. As I said these words I thought of Mrs. Begley, who had once looked coldly at me and said, *If you didn't have an amazing story, you didn't survive.*

My problem, I went on to Shlomo, is that I want to write the story of people who didn't survive. People who had no story, anymore.

Shlomo nodded and said, Aha, I see. He kept driving. You know, he said after a while, this Regnier, he's a German, but he married a famous Israeli singer, a very big star, Nehama Hendel.

I apologized, said that I had never heard of her.

She's very big in Israel, he told me. But she died a few years ago.

It suddenly occurred to me to ask Shlomo a question that had been on my mind for some time. My grandfather, I told him, used to sing me two songs when I was a little boy; I wondered if maybe they were songs from his own youth, songs his father or mother had sung to him. Bolechower songs.

How did they go? Shlomo asked.

Well, I said, somewhat embarrassed, the first one he used to sing to us at bedtime. And it was true: when we were little and my grandfather would be visiting, he'd sometimes come into our rooms when we were being put to bed and would sing this song, a song whose lyrics alone will, no doubt, seem quite odd, seem very flat on the page, much more so than, say, the lyrics of "Mayn Shtetele Belz," "My Little Town of Belz," which after all are rather sentimental. If I wanted to convey what was so special about the song my grandfather used to sing to us, I would have to do much more than transcribe the lyrics:

> *Oh why did you hit my Daniel,*
> *My Daniel did nothing to you.*
> *Next time you hit my Daniel,*
> *I'll call a policeman on you!*
> *Hoo hoo!*

I might, for instance, try to transcribe it slightly differently, so that it would be possible to get a sense of the rhythm of this song, which to me, when I was a child, was both soothing (because it was, ultimately, a promise of protection and retribution) and frightening (because it raised the incomprehensible notion that someone would want to hit me, a child). That transcription might look like this:

> *Oh WHY did you HI-it my DAN-iel,*
> *My DAN-iel did nothing to YOU.*
> *Next TIME you HI-it my DAN-iel,*
> *I'll CALL a po-LICE-man on YOU!*
> *hoo-HOO!*

But of course, even then there would be no way to convey the particular inflections of my grandfather's almost vanished voice. (I say *almost vanished*, because my grandfather killed himself before the advent of videorecorders, and hence the only recording we have of his voice is the cassette tape I made of him in the summer of 1974 when he told us the story of how he'd run out of his house during a Russian attack without his shoes. Voices are among the things that vanish first, in the case of people who lived before a certain moment in the evolution of technology: no one will ever know, now, what Shmiel and his family sounded like.) To convey more than just the lyrics of this song, which I have sung, rather self-consciously, to my own children now, although I doubt they will sing it to theirs, I would have to try to approximate that special Bolechower pronunciation, like this:

> Oh VAH-EE did you HI-itt my DEHN-iel,
> My DEHN-iel ditt nuttink to YOU.
> Next TIME you HI-itt my DEHN-iel,
> ehl KOLL a poLICEman on YOU!
> hoo-HOO!

And even then there is the tune, the sad, sepia, minor-key inflections that made me wonder, briefly, whether this was a translation of some old song of his childhood. Quite recently I asked my brother Andrew, who plays the piano so well, whether he remembered this tune of my grandfather's, and when he said, *Of course I do,* I asked him to transcribe it for me. A week or so later I opened the file that he sent me and grinned when I saw that he'd titled it *Oh Why Did You Hit My Andrew*. When I mentioned this to him, he said, quite genuinely, It never occurred to me that he sang it to anyone else.

So I sang this song to Shlomo, as we drove south into the desert toward the Reinharz apartment, and he shook his head and said, No, I can't say I have ever heard such a song.

I was disappointed. But there was another song I wanted to know about, another rather melancholy song, and perhaps it was because it was so sad that I, who know so little about popular music, thought it, too, might be a song from my grandfather's lost childhood as the son of a family of butchers in a town a hundred years and four thousand miles away. I sang it, too, to Shlomo in the car:

> I wish, I wish, I wish in vain
> I wish I were sixteen again.
> Sixteen again I'll never be
> Till apples will grow on a cherry tree!

I didn't bother putting in the accent this time: *vish,* my grandfather had said. *I vish in wain. Till ehpples vill grrohh* . . . Shlomo listened and made an apologetic face. I have never heard this song before neither, he said.

Oh well, I said. It's no big deal. It's just a song.

I looked out the window; the desert had turned into buildings.

Aha! Shlomo pointed. We are in Beer Sheva.

Oh Why Did You Hit My Andrew

Abraham Jaeger

WEARING A SLEEVELESS housedress covered with cheery flowers in various shades of blue, Malcia Reinharz was waiting for us on the landing in front of her door. As we walked up the concrete steps toward her she smiled broadly, exposing even rows of teeth. Hallo! she said in English. The voice was deep and had a pleasantly grained texture, like a clarinet. Her hair was pale auburn, and her long, full-cheeked, humorous face was almost girlishly animated.

Hallo Malcia! Shlomo said. He had told me that Malcia spoke good English; her husband did not, but Shlomo would translate for him. We walked inside. The apartment was darkened against the afternoon sun. Toward the rear, in front of windows whose shades had been drawn, was a cluster of comfortable furniture; at the front, just past the door, was a small dining table. Sitting at the table, his back to the kitchen wall, was Mr. Reinharz. I liked his face: oddly youthful, grave but friendly. He had the pleasingly old-fashioned look of a well-to-do farmer: he had on a crisp tan shirt, dark trousers, suspenders, and a tan golfer's cap. He rose to shake our hands. Then Malcia gestured to us to sit down.

Please, Malcia said. First we will talk a bit, and then we will eat, it's all right?

It's all right, I said. Perfect.

The three of them chatted for a few minutes in Yiddish as I set up my tape recorder and video camera. Shlomo was explaining what would be happening; they nodded as he spoke. Then I was ready. When I talked, I tried to look at both of them, but since I knew that Malcia could understand me better than her husband did—and because there was something so appealing, so deliciously soft and available about her, qualities my mother's mother had once had—I found myself speaking to her more. Still, I noticed how, during our long conversation that day, she and her husband would look at each other as we all talked, as if silently to confirm whatever they were being asked or whatever she was telling me for the two of them.

All right, I said, I'm going to start asking.

She nodded.

We didn't know anything about Shmiel, or the wife, or the children, I said. So I'm going all over the world and talking to everyone who knew Shmiel, and from those conversations I'm trying to bring back something of Shmiel and the family. Because all we ever knew until now is that they were killed.

She closed her eyes. *I* know, she said.

And we want to know something better than that, I said.

Malcia nodded again and said, Oh, I know, I know them very well.

I was struck by the way she kept using the present tense when speaking of these dead: *I know. I know them very well.*

She said, Ask what you want. What you need.

OK, I said.

We started to talk. She told me that her family were all Bolechowers. Would she tell me what year she was born? I asked. She burst into a wide grin and said, *I was born in Hungaria! In 1919!* She seemed amused by the idea that I felt awkward about asking her how old she was. She explained, then, that she'd been born in Hungary while her parents were briefly staying there, but that they'd soon returned to the town and that, from the age of three months, she'd lived there. With her parents, she said, and her sister Gina, and her two brothers, David and Herman. She said, And nobody is living. I have only a picture of my younger brother.

She told me that she was married in 1940. *Who today is married for such a long time, sixty-three years? Nobody!* She burst out laughing and waved her hand, as if to dismiss the protestations of anyone who'd been married less than sixty-three years.

So you knew the Jägers when you were growing up? I asked.

I knew them very well, she replied, switching now into the past tense. It was Shmiel Jäger with his wife, she was a pretty wife. With pretty legs!

Wiss pretty lecks.

Malcia touched her heart with her left hand and then made a gesture of connoisseurship, like a maître d' describing a particularly tasty specialty of the house.

Oh! she had legs—I have not *seen* such legs!

I smiled, and so did Shlomo.

And two pretty daughters, she went on. Lorka too had pretty legs!

She also? Shlomo asked, amused.

Yes. Malcia nodded.

I was more interested in another detail. *Two pretty daughters.* Everyone, it seemed, had a different memory of how many children Shmiel and Ester had had.

You knew only two of the girls? I asked.

Only two? As we talked, Malcia would listen silently and patiently, like an attentive student, with a grave expression on her long and alert face; but often as soon as I'd finished speaking her face would instantly register some strong reaction. Now, she was making an exaggerated face of incredulity.

There were four, I said.

Malcia looked at me. *Four?!* Four children he had?

I named them all. Lorka. Frydka. Ruchele. Bronia.

Four girls? she repeated. I showed her, then, the picture of Shmiel, Ester, and Bronia, but all she said was, *Ja,* Shmiel Jäger.

She put the picture down on the table and said, simply, *Ai, Gott.*

I know only that the oldest was Lorka, she continued after a moment, and the younger was Frydka. And we were often in touch. With Lorka—of course. She was a *pretty* girl. And Frydka, she was a bit higher from Lorka.

She placed one hand high in the air and I realized she meant *taller.* I let her keep talking. To me, all of this was much more than charming: as much as we'd learned thus far, still every scrap, every detail was precious. Ester had pretty legs. Frydka was taller than Lorka. We hadn't known it before; now it was part of their story. *Frydka was a very tall girl, taller than her older sister,* I'd tell my family when I got back home . . .

Then she said, She was a heavy one, Frydka. A fighter, a *fighter.*

Here we go again, I thought to myself; it always ends up being about Frydka. A fighter? I said. What do you mean by that?

Malcia took a sip of wine. *Ja.* She was so *robust!*

She pronounced it ro-BOOST! and as she said it she put up two arms in a pugnacious pose, like a prizefighter.

Robust, I repeated. Well, I thought, she *was* a fighter.

But Lorka, Malcia went on, unaware of my preoccupations, was pretty. And she had two legs—!

Her voice trailed off and she looked heavenward, as if calling God to witness.

I showed her the picture of the whole family in 1934, the picture in which they were mourning for my great-grandmother, Taube. *It means a dove.* Suddenly Malcia looked up at me, beaming at some memory.

Shmiel Jäger was *hiresh!* Because I expected her to lapse into Yiddish or German whenever she couldn't find an English word, I was confused, until I realized she was speaking Hebrew. As she said this word, *hiresh,* she pointed helpfully to her ear, much as my mother used to gesture and point when she spoke on the phone to my grandfather in Yiddish, which is how I learned much of my Yiddish.

Toip, Shlomo said. Deaf!

I know, I said.

You must to speak to him *very* loud, Malcia went on. Perhaps it was the vividness of this memory that made her slide, once again, into the present tense.

And he was a tall man? I prodded.

Yes, he was tall—a very nice man. *And*—he loved his wife! Malcia again made the face of someone calling God to witness. *Au au au au!* she exclaimed. He loved her *so* much!

I didn't say anything. It is, after all, possible to keep referring to your wife as *die liebe Ester,* "dear Ester," out of habit or obligation; but now we knew. *He loved his wife!* If their children's friends knew it, I thought, they must have been demonstrative with each other, this loving couple, Shmiel and Ester.

I showed her another picture.

Ya, duss ist Shmiel Jäger. She sighed. Shmiel Jäger, a very pretty man he was. A pretty man, a very handsome man!

Then she reached her hand into the air and said, *High!*

MALCIA MADE SURE that we all had wine in our glasses and went on reminiscing. I looked at the bottle. MURFATLER PINOT NOIR, the label said.

I used to go with my mother to buy meat in his shop, she said. And he gived my mother the bestest meat that he had! Together they were saying *Du,* because they went together in school.

After a moment I realized what she meant: that her mother and my great-uncle had used the informal German "you" instead of the formal. They were, after all, old school friends.

So you would have been close in age to Lorka, I said. She was maybe one year younger.

Yes, yes. We were not in the same class, but in the same school—there was not another school in Bolechow!

So did you play together?

Yes, yes, Malcia said. Then she hesitated for a moment and added, But she was—every time she was—

Groping for the word she wanted, she turned to Shlomo. *Es tat ihr immer leid,* she said, laughing impishly. In German it would have meant, *She was always hurt, always sorry.*

Insulted? Shlomo ventured.

Still giggling, Malcia said in Yiddish, *Zi is immer geveyn mit a hoch Nase.*

A high nose? I'd never heard the expression.

Ah! Ah! Shlomo said. He turned and looked right at me. She says she kept herself, you know—as "somebody." He took a finger and with it lifted up the tip of his nose in a universal gesture of snootiness.

Why was that? I asked Malcia.

She made a deprecatory face. Well, she knows that she was pretty, that she has a good home, good parents . . .

What exactly was the reputation of the family? I asked, and at that she launched into a story. There was a charitable organization that her father had founded, she said, called Yad Charuzim, The Hand of the Diligent. She laughed. When my father was the president, she said, I would tell everyone, *My father is the president!* I grinned, and she added that Shmiel had been the president at one point, too. This explained, at long last, a photograph I'd seen years before in the Bolechow Yizkor book. In the bottom of the two photographs that appeared on page 282, my grandfather had written, were his two brothers Shmiel and Itzhak. In it, Shmiel is sitting, dressed in a dinner jacket with a wing-collar shirt and black bow tie, at the center of a large group of well-dressed men; sitting on the floor was Itzhak, holding up one end of a sign that must have borne the name of whatever club this was, but in the reproduction the only letters visible in the photograph are C H A. At that moment Malcia said something quickly to Shlomo, who left the table and went to a pile of papers. A moment later he returned and handed me a photocopy, on

A-1 paper, that had clearly been made from the original of the image so fault-
ily reproduced in the *Sefer HaZikaron LeKedoshei Bolechow*. The original, it now
turned out, belonged to Malcia. On the photocopy the placard that Itzhak is
holding is quite legible:

ZAŁOZYCIELE
19   JAD   28
CHARUZIM
BOLECHOW

FOUNDERS OF THE YAD CHARUZIM, 1928, BOLECHOW.

Malcia pointed to a face I knew well: handsome, aloof, sporting an impeccably trimmed toothbrush mustache that (I can't help thinking) he thought
would make him look older, more dignified. He was only thirty-three. Itzhak,
by contrast, looks the faintest bit amused.

Here, she was saying, now in this picture is Shmiel Jäger the president. And
this is my father.

She pointed to a dignified-looking man with pale eyes and a goatee sitting in
the same row as Shmiel. And this is Kessler the carpenter, she went on.

Once again, I was both moved and pained by the thought that each of these
people had a family, a story; and that somewhere, somebody who was interested in, say, the Kessler family might be saying, *And wasn't that one Jäger the
expediter, in the middle, he had the trucks? And isn't that his brother, who had the
butcher store, you remember the story . . . ?*

Yes, Lorka had a good home, a good family, Malcia said, making a little
shrug as her voice trailed off. I thought again of Shmiel and his letters to my
grandfather.

> *Not that I have to tell <u>you</u>, my dear ones, what even strangers say, which is that I
> have the best and most distinguished children in Bolechów . . .*

Or,

> *People in Bolechów take me for a rich man (since I pay enormous taxes), and
> anyone who needs anything comes to Samuel Jäger. I have a lot of influence here*

and I've had preferential treatment everywhere, and so I have to present myself well everywhere. Indeed I spend time with the better class of people, I've been everywhere in town as an honored guest, and I'm continually traveling.

Hoch Nase, I said. Malcia grinned and nodded, and I had no reason to disbelieve her. Everything, I thought, fit perfectly.

At that point, Malcia served lunch, and we talked for a while of happier things.

LATER ON, WHEN we'd finished the enormous meal that she'd prepared, Malcia said, And after, what happened in the Occupation, you know? I noticed that Shumek—Shlomo often called Solomon Reinharz by this Polish nickname—wasn't making any move to return to work.

I did know, by this point—or thought I knew—but as I'd done in Sydney,

I asked her to remember for me what had happened and when. This time, though, I tried to think more like Matt. I asked her not just what had happened, but what people were thinking and feeling and saying.

I said, When you knew that the Germans were coming, in the summer of 'forty-one, what were people saying before the Germans actually got there—what idea did people have of what it was going to be?

Shumek and Malcia exchanged glances. She said, We knew, we knew, we knew. The first night that the Russians were out of Bolechow, our Ukrainer, our *goyim,* killed one hundred and twenty Jews and throwed them in the water.

I nodded. I remembered Jack and Bob in Sydney, saying, *The first thing that happened was that the Ukrainians came and they started to kill Jews. You know, if you had something with the Jews, you killed them.*

But what were people expecting from the Germans? I asked. How much did they know at that point? Exchanging a look with her husband, she said with a bitter little laugh, *Alle gloybten duss di doytscher wirdn uns tzvingen in a fabrik.* Everyone thought the Germans were going to force us into a factory.

At that point I asked what people had known, in general, about the Germans' plans for the Jews of Europe when the war started.

Malcia said, again, We knew, we knew, we knew. In 'thirty-nine all the people, all the Jews, they went from Poland—this was the Polish *gouvernement*—and they run away.

She suddenly put both hands to her face, remembering something. Oh! she said. And if you had seen the people with the small baggages, and the families—

Meg Grossbard, too, had remembered seeing hordes of Jews, together with certain Poles, fleeing for their lives eastward and southward, toward the Soviet half of Poland, toward Hungary, driving and riding and walking as fast as they could after the Germans started bombing Warsaw that day in September 1939. Bolechow, Meg explained to me, was the last town before the frontier with Hungary; thousands of refugees had passed through the town as they sought shelter. Many, indeed, had simply stayed in Bolechow. The *Flüchtling,* they were called; those who were fleeing. Better to be under Soviet rule than under the Nazis.

As if reading my thought, Malcia said, They run away to *us.* Not only from Poland, but from Czechoslovakia, from Austria. Because they knew we stayed under the Russian *gouvernement.* She shook her head again as she remembered and said, This picture I cannot forget.

Shlomo suddenly interrupted at this point.

Malcia, he said, you are a few years older than I. And you saw the pictures—the refugees—

Oh, the refugees! she said, covering her face with her hands once more.

And you remember that it was two years of quiet, from 1939 until 1941, Shlomo went on. And then you remember that people knew the Germans were coming.

Malcia nodded, and Shlomo said with that emphasis he has, *So why we didn't run away as those refugees ran away?*

Malcia smiled humorlessly. Why, why? Ahhhh . . . *Because you cannot leave a home!* How can you leave a *home*?!

How can you leave a home? I remembered, then, something else in Shmiel's letters—how, as time passed, he kept oscillating between desperate fantasies of escape and proud refusals to leave. He would write to President Roosevelt, he wrote; he'd sell whatever he could, anything to get them out; to get the girls out; to get one of the girls out. *The dear Lorka.* And yet, often in the same letter, he'd change his mind. *But I emphasize here to you all that I do not want to leave here without something to live on—conversely, I have, thank God, everything that I need. . . . I know now that I wouldn't be able to get such a life very fast in America.* I'd wondered, once, about these extravagant shifts of mood, but of course, that was years ago, when I was a teenager and young man, before I had a life, a house, children. Often, when I talk to certain people about the Holocaust, about what I've discovered about my great-uncle's letters, his too-late realization that the world was locking down around him, his tardy efforts to escape, I find that those who have the benefit of history, of hindsight, say what Shlomo had just now said—although Shlomo's furious question was motivated by grief, not the complacent goodwill that comes of considering historical crises from the comfort of one's own safe life. *You wonder why they didn't read the writing on the wall,* people like to say. But as I've grown older, I don't wonder that much, really. I don't wonder, and nor, I saw, did Malcia.

How can you leave a home?!

Malcia got up to do something in the kitchen; we still hadn't had dessert! she'd cried. While she was there, Shumek and Shlomo were speaking rapidly in Yiddish about other wartime memories. I tried to listen, but they were talking too fast. At one point, I heard Shlomo ask Shumek something about *di Yiddishpolizianten*, the Jewish militia that was conscripted in each town and forced, often, to do the occupiers' dirty work: rounding up a certain number of people, say, or locating this or that Jew and taking him or her somewhere from which there would be no return. I had read, and now heard, that the Jewish police were often feared and detested by the people with whom they'd once lived as neighbors and friends. Anna Heller Stern had visibly reacted, two days earlier, when the subject of the Jewish police had come up. *I was more afraid of them than anybody*, she had said. But even as she'd done so, I thought to myself: If I thought I could save my family by joining the Jewish police, would I? I thought of my children and refused to make judgments.

Anyway, as Shumek was now saying to Shlomo, the Jewish police were themselves hardly indispensable. *Und vuss hut zey getin? Zey hutten zi alle geloysht.*

And what did they do? They liquidated them all.

It was in this context that Shlomo asked about the fates of two such policemen whom he'd known. They were speaking rapidly, and I didn't catch the names.

Er is oykh geloysht geveyn? Shlomo asked. *He also was liquidated?*

Shumek at that moment was wearing a gentle, somewhat resigned expression. *Yaw, er oykh.*

At that point, Malcia entered with an enormous cake and, having listened to what her husband and Shlomo were talking about for a moment, turned to us and said, That's enough. I don't want to talk about *mishugenah tzayten* and *mishugenah menshen.*

Crazy times and crazy people.

She added, Who wants a nice cup of tea now?

SO ABOUT THE Occupation you already know, Malcia was saying, after we'd eaten the dessert and had sat back, exhausted, in our chairs. As I'd done at Meg's *déjeuner à la Bolechow* in Sydney, I thought, Soon there will be nobody left who cooks this food.

Well, I said, we don't *really* know. I mean, we know what happened in general, but we don't know anything *specific* about what happened to them. I didn't want to feed her any information; I wanted to see what she knew, unprodded.

The Jägers, she said. What happened to them happened to everybody. She sighed.

But immediately afterward she said, And Frydka, she has a relation with the son of a Polish man, the neighbor.

Frydka again, I thought. What I said was, *Ciszko Szymanski.*

She nodded. And there was somebody that—

She turned to Shlomo for the word she wanted and said something to him.

Someone who denunciated them, Shlomo said.

Denounced, I said.

Yes. Malcia nodded again.

Frydka. After the conversation with Anna Stern, I doubted I could learn anything new; certainly nothing more dramatic and moving than *If you kill her, you should kill me too!* Still, I wanted to proceed in an orderly way.

All right, I said, I want to go slowly here.

But Malcia was remembering things, and pressed ahead with her story.

They denunciated them, and they found her, and she was pregnant.

Pregnant? I said. I sat up straight and looked at her.

Pregnant? Malcia asked Shlomo, making sure it was the right word.

He nodded. It was the right word. Pregnant.

I said, Wait, I want to go back just one minute. Frydka was with the Polish boy, Ciszko Szymanski. They were going together, he liked her?

Malcia said something to Shlomo, who turned to me and said, She says he saved her, he tried to hide her.

Malcia nodded and resumed speaking to me in English. To hide her, she said. And they lived together.

I wasn't sure I understood; I wanted more specifics. They lived together where?

Malcia said, In his, his house.

He was hiding her in his *house*? I said, startled. This had never occurred to me.

Malcia nodded, more to herself than to me. She said, Yes. And they found them, they found them and she was pregnant. So they told me.

Shlomo, reading my thoughts, cut in. Tell me, he said to Malcia, and her father, Shmiel, was not there?

She shook her head slowly and emphatically: No.

He loved her very much, she went on, and he said her he want to hide her. He like her very much and she like him. And it was for her a, how we say, a *mazel*. And he hide her but, there was bad people that knew that they . . .

Her voice trailed off. She looked pensive. Shlomo said, to me, So part of the story was true. Somebody gave up Frydka.

Part of the story, I thought. And why did we think it was true? Because somebody else, somebody who hadn't been there either when it happened, somebody who had hidden successfully and who'd also only heard about what happened to Frydka after the war was over, had heard it from somebody else, who'd heard it from someone else; and because a certain detail from that thirdhand story now dovetailed with a detail that Malcia had heard from someone who'd heard it from someone else. *Frydka had been hidden and betrayed.* But what about Shmiel, now? I felt like I was walking on quicksand.

Betrayed her, Malcia said. Yes.

And we have no idea who that was? I said.

Malcia was matter-of-fact. She spread her hands. The neighbors. *Ukrainer.*

I was still trying to adjust to this new version: no Shmiel, no nameless Polish schoolteacher, just Frydka and Ciszko. Shlomo must have read my thoughts, because he looked at me and then turned to Malcia and said, Because, you see, we heard a story that Frydka and Lorka went to Babij.

Malcia made a very strong face of negation—of disdain even. No, no!

OK, I said. So then the last that we know of Frydka is that she was hiding with him, and someone denounced them—

Malcia nodded. They killed her and he, too. I saw his mother after the war.

His mother? This was interesting. I asked, And what did she say?

Malcia looked amused. What does she say? She said, *He was a stupid boy!*

She gave me a subtle and complicated look. She said, He paid with his life, this.

I wanted to keep pressing for more details. So you ran into Mrs. Szymanska after the war—

We did not come to her, she came to us. We had a store after the war in Breslau—

Wrocław? I asked. "Breslau," I knew, is the old German name for what is now Wrocław, just as "Lemberg" is the old name for L'viv. Froma and I, exhausted from too much walking in Prague, had once disintegrated into tearful laughter over the difference between how the word looks to an English-speaker's eyes, and how it's actually pronounced: *Vrotzwohf.* It was only later that I learned how certain Polish letters are pronounced.

Malcia nodded and grinned. Yes, *Wrocław.* She remembered the address where she'd lived, then. *Rynek sześć. Ringplatz sechs.* Market Square 6. Resuming the story about Ciszko Szymanski's mother, she said, And she came in, she knew that we had a shop. Everybody looks for a face that he knows. Because she wanted to see us. She wept, she cried and we talked together.

Malcia looked at me and, as if to explain the emotion she was recalling, said, People from Bolechow.

Then she said, She talked about the son. She told how *stupid he was!*

Malcia shouted the word *stupid* as Mrs. Szymanska had once done. She went on: He gave his life for this girl. But he loved her *very* much.

Like mother, like daughter, I thought.

She looked at me firmly. She said, And for her it was a *mitziyeh,* you know what it is a *mitziyeh?*

I shook my head no, and she gestured, as she liked to do, with her right hand, thumb and first two fingers squeezed together, the way you might do when you want to indicate that a recipe needs a pinch of salt.

Shlomo said, A *mitziyeh*—it's something, something, you know, something special.

(Later on, I looked up *mitziyeh* in the 1938 Hebrew-English dictionary that I inherited from my grandfather, and learned that it means this: *a finding, a discovery; a thing found; a precious thing.* It was interesting to learn, further, that it is connected to the verb *mâtzâh,* which means *to find out, guess; to find; to come upon, meet, discover; to befall, happen.* What kind of culture was this culture of the Hebrews, I wondered when I looked this up months after my interview with the Reinharzes that day, a culture in which the notions of *coming upon* and *meeting* and *discovering* were inextricably linked to the idea of *preciousness?)*

Malcia nodded very vigorously and cried out, To stay alive! To stay alive! Who has such a *mazel?* Who has such luck?

I thought, then, of something my mother had said to me in Sydney, after she'd finished talking to Jack Greene on my cell phone. *Why didn't my family survive?* she had said, her voice filled with tears. *Even just one of them?* After I'd hung up, I had repeated this to Jack, who'd said, *Look, it was just a matter of luck, that's it.* Now, as I listened to Shlomo and Malcia, it occurred to me that although she'd died, in the end, Frydka had still been lucky. She had lived that much longer, after all; had had someone who wanted desperately to save her, someone who died for her. A *mitziyeh,* a *mazel* only seems strange if you're thinking about things in hindsight, which is a luxury that Frydka and Ciszko did not have.

Shlomo said to me, Who knew that somebody would betray them?

I WANT TO get the chronology straight, I said again, although this time I was referring to one Jew in particular: to Frydka. Now at that point she was living in one of the *Lager,* right? And then—

Look, Malcia said. We could work till *Juni* 'forty-three.

July! Shlomo exclaimed. Not June, July!

And after, the Germans said that now they are building a new *Lager* and everybody will be saved. But they just wanted to take everybody in one *Lager.* And that was the end.

I nodded. Jack had already told me how those who'd fallen for the Germans' ruse had all been locked in the new camp and killed. Guns, he had said. Fire.

But at that point, I went on, instead of going in this *Lager,* Szymanski hid Frydka in his house?

Malcia nodded. *Yes.*

So Szymanski was hiding her in his house, and this was after June 'forty-three.

Another nod.

July, Shlomo said.

July 'forty-three, I said. And so at some point after July 'forty-three she was hiding in his house.

(Again, I wanted specifics.)

And does anybody know where was his house?

As had occasionally happened before, I noticed that my syntax had vaguely changed, now that I was speaking with Bolechowers.

I know where, Malcia said. Not far from Frydka's house. It was on the beginning of the street—

I took out the map of Bolechow that Shlomo had sent me. Malcia looked at it and asked where Dlugosa Street was. Then she pointed with a little cry of victory.

Yes! Here was the Jägers and here—

(she pointed to a spot on the same street but the opposite side)

—was the Szymanskis, at the beginning of the street.

So he lived on the corner, down the street, I said. That was where she'd been hiding. That was the place. I knew the story by now; now I wanted a *place,* a spot to stand on, if I ever went back to Bolechow.

Shlomo, Solomon, and Malcia were talking in Yiddish and German about the liquidation of the *Lagers* in the late summer of 1943—which is to say, the liquidation of the town, since by that time the only Jews left who weren't in hiding were those in the last *Lager.* By that point, I knew, the Reinharzes were hiding, immobile but alert, in the German officers' recreation hall, the *Kasino,* right in the middle of town.

Am vier und zwanzigsten August, Malcia was saying, in German now. *Dann is meine schwester gegangen: und jeden Schuss haben wir gehört.*

On the twenty-fourth of August. That's when my sister went. And we heard every shot.

They were in hiding, Shlomo explained to me, although I knew the story.

Malcia nodded and said to me, in English, And every, every—

She turned to Shlomo. *Unt yayden shuss hub' ikh getzuhlt.*

Yiddish, again. I understood. *And I counted every shot.*

She turned to me but continued in Yiddish. *Noyn hindert shiess hub' ikh getzuhlt.*

Nine hundred shots I counted.

She paused and said, in English now, And after they came to the *Kasino* to wash their hands and to *drink!* I was right there, I saw them! They washed the hands and they went to *drink!*

Shlomo, who was as obviously moved as I was at the image of the two hidden Jews, cramped in their tiny hideout, unable to see but counting, counting, one after the other, the shots that were ending the lives of their friends and neighbors, turned to Malcia and said, And you knew what was happening?

Malcia pointed with her forefinger to her temple. She said, We *imagined.*

I, TOO, WAS imagining at that moment. We had arrived around noon, and it was now nearly three; I had much to think about. It wasn't just the new and sensational additions to Frydka's story—*she was pregnant with his child, he was hiding her in his house*—although these, like the sounds of the shots that Shumek and Malcia had heard that day, could not be ignored; they demanded, if anything, an effort of the imagination that couldn't help but add to the story I wanted to be able to tell. *They were lovers, they were deeply in love, these were desperate times, they were sleeping together, she was pregnant. He loved her that much— enough to endanger not only himself, but his entire family.* Well, I thought, *Good for her.* Good for *them.* I'm glad she knew a profound love, before she died. To hell with what Meg Grossbard thinks; to hell with *I know nussink, I see nussink!*

And yet as important as this was, it was those other, smaller, less sensational details that I was thinking of when Malcia said *We imagined.* Here, too, there was much of interest to be extrapolated. *He loved her so much! She had such pretty legs!* These, too, were facts; these, too, might tell a little story. Perhaps it was her legs he'd first noticed, that day in 1918 when they'd met for the first time as adults, she a pretty twenty-three-year-old with her family's regular features and solemn face, he an energetic young man, something of a war hero, determined to revive his father's business. Perhaps he had seen her playing with her girlfriends, in the peaceful summer of 1919, down by the banks of the Sukiel, the place where their daughter would one day cavort with her girlfriends, just a few years before nearly all of them were raped or shot or gassed. Perhaps it was that small thing that had triggered their romance, a romance that had never, as we now know, ended. *He loved her so much—au au au au!*

It was while I was thinking about this business of imagining, of extracting the story from the small, concrete thing, that I realized that Malcia and Shlomo were reminiscing, after our huge lunch, about certain foods they used to eat, and which fewer and fewer people now knew how to cook. *Ahhh, bulbowenik!* Shlomo exclaimed. Shumek rolled his eyes in appreciation, and the other two started explaining to me what it was: a dish of grated potatoes and eggs that you baked and—

Wait! Malcia exclaimed. I think she was relieved not to be talking about the past anymore, after all this time. You'll sit here a little while, and I'll make it for you!

I gave Shlomo a look. We had to be back in Tel Aviv by seven, I reminded him, since a friend whom I'd met in the States, a philosophy professor at the University of Tel Aviv, was expecting me for dinner.

Shlomo smiled broadly and said something to Malcia, who shook her head impatiently. It's nothing, it won't take no time at all, he said.

I thought, Why not? This, too, was part of the story; and after all, it hadn't often been the case that some abstract aspect of the lost civilization of Bolechow could so easily be made concrete. I grinned and nodded. OK, I said, let's cook.

Malcia took me into the kitchen so I could watch. We grated potatoes, we beat eggs, we poured them into a baking dish. We sat for forty-five minutes while it baked. We took it out of the oven to cool. While it cooled, I thought to myself that we had just eaten an enormous lunch with lots of wine; I suspected that I was about to be taken to an enormous dinner.

Still, I'd been raised in a certain kind of home, and I knew what to do. I sat down at the table and ate. It was delicious. Malcia beamed. *It's a real Bolechower dish!* she said.

Only after I'd had seconds did we finally get up to go.

SHLOMO AND I went back down the concrete stairs of the Reinharzes' building to the parking lot. What with the impromptu cooking lesson, and then the tasting of the *bulbowenik,* we'd ended up staying much longer than we had thought we would. The sun, low on the horizon, was mellow, and when we got into Shlomo's car we opened the windows. Shlomo was preoccupied, at first, with finding our way back to the highway from the apartment house on Rambam Street—a street, I was happy to notice, that was named after the great twelfth-century Jewish scholar and philosopher Maimonides (the acronym of whose Hebrew name, Rabbi Moses ben Maimon, is RMBM). Rambam was a Spanish-born Jew whose family fled the anti-Jewish persecutions of the Muslim ruler of Spain and came, eventually, to Egypt, which is how Maimonides ended up becoming the esteemed servant of the enlightened sultan in Cairo. He is the scholar who, along with Rashi, is the most widely admired and studied of all Jewish intellectuals. The rationalist views expressed in his masterwork, *The Guide for the Perplexed*—and, it's hard not to think, the enormous renown that Rambam enjoyed—so enraged certain rival rabbis in France that they denounced him to the French Inquisition, while (by contrast) his death was mourned throughout Cairo for three full days by Muslims. Where do you live, and what are your loyalties? *parashat Lech Lecha* asks; and no wonder.

As we navigated our way out of the Israeli street named for this remarkable man, we talked enthusiastically about our long interview with the Reinharzes.

So she was *pregnant*, I said to Shlomo as he peered at the street signs.

Well, it's what she says, he replied. But it's very interesting, no?

I nodded. Very interesting. I had gone to Australia not even knowing what stories we'd hear, and now it seemed I had a real drama on my hands. I wondered what Meg would say, if I decided to share this latest detail with her.

Soon we were out of the city and racing back toward Tel Aviv. We must have both been feeling depleted, after such a long day; I didn't mind at all when, after some minutes of companionable silence, he flicked on the radio. A female voice was singing, and it took me a moment to realize that she was singing not in Hebrew, but in English. The tune was familiar, but at first I didn't recognize the song for what it was because the verse was unfamiliar to me. I had only known the refrain, it now turned out. The woman's voice had become the voice of a young girl, a girl who was narrating the story of her own death. She had died, she sang, for love of a boy who would not love her back. Then the voice slid into the refrain:

I wish I wish
I wish in vain
I wish I was

a maid again
but a maid again
I ne'er can be
till apples grow
on an ivy tree

I sat up, sputtering, and turned to Shlomo. This is the song! I finally shouted, This is the song! The one I was telling you about on the way here this morning. The song my grandfather sang!

We both listened as the voice came to the last verse, which caught my attention, perhaps because *dying for love* was much on my mind that hot early evening:

Oh, make my grave
large, wide and deep
put a marble stone
at my head and feet
and in the middle
a turtle dove
so the world may know
I died of love.

How on earth, I thought as I wrote these words down—something about the grave, the stone, the *dove* moved me, and made me want to remember this lyric—did my grandfather come across this song? Why had he learned it?

The song was over, and the radio announcer said something in rapid Hebrew. Shlomo said, It's an Irish song.

How had Grandpa learned this? I thought again. *And why?*

Then Shlomo grinned even more broadly.

You know something else? he said. Something it's another coincidence?

I shook my head no. I couldn't imagine anything more uncanny than what had already happened.

Shlomo looked at me and said, You know who it is singing? It's Nehama Hendel, the wife of Regnier, the one who wrote the Bolechow book.

I suppose my face was legible. Shlomo exhaled heavily, gestured broadly with his hand in a way that took in both the radio/cassette player of his car and the desert, and said, You see? You *see*? Israel is a country of miracles!

Not being a believer in miracles, I simply smiled and nodded silently. Then, when I got back to the Hilton, I did an Internet search for the following cluster of words: I WISH I WISH I WISH IN VAIN. Instantly, dozens of citations appeared on my screen, which is why it was a matter of just a minute or two before I learned the name of the song my grandfather had always sung to me when I was a child, a song that I'd always assumed was a song from his youth but that, I now realized, he must have learned at some unknowable point after he'd left Bolechow forever, and that must have touched him profoundly none-theless for reasons I can only now guess at, among which may have been, sim-ply, its title, a title that I'd never have known if I hadn't come to Israel, and which was *The Butcher Boy.*

THAT WAS SUNDAY. On Tuesday I had scheduled an interview with Shlomo's cousin Josef, who indeed came to my hotel room that day, a wiry, fit, military-looking man in his seventies, handsome and unsmiling, and in a steady and unsentimental voice talked for ninety minutes, more or less without interrup-tion, about the fate of Bolechow's Jews. I listened carefully, although it was a story I knew well by then, not only from my previous interviews but from the crisply informative chapters in the Bolechow Yizkor book about the war years, which had been written by Josef Adler himself. There was something about his demeanor that made me want his approval: perhaps it was his crisply creased tan pants and fresh khaki-colored short-sleeved shirt, which seemed impressively military to my eyes. When we sat down in the narrow hotel arm-chairs that I'd clustered around the desk, Josef Adler acknowledged right away that he hadn't known my own family particularly well; but he wanted to make sure I knew what had happened. I nodded and let him speak. The arrival of the Germans. The first Aktion. The second Aktion. The *Lager.* The *Fassfabrik.* The final liquidation in '43. The remarkable details of how he and Shlomo, two young boys, had survived. How he had come to Israel; how important Israel was. As he made this last point, this soft-spoken but emphatic and rigorous man, I felt ashamed of my long-standing lack of interest in modern-day Israel; I wondered if every American Jew traveling in Israel ended up, at some point, feeling like a draft dodger. When Josef was leaving, I thanked him fervently for driving all the way to Tel Aviv from Haifa, which he had insisted was no problem when we made the appointment to meet a few days earlier. It's very important what you're doing, he told me as we shook hands at the door of my room. It's very important that people know what happened.

But that, as I've said, wouldn't be until Tuesday. On Monday, we stayed in Tel Aviv. Froma, who'd been busy seeing relatives since we arrived in Israel, wanted me to see the Beth Hatefutsoth, the Museum of the Jewish Disapora, which is located on the starkly modern campus of Tel Aviv University. There's tons to see there, she told me, We should get there early. We got there on a blazing late morning, just after the museum opened. The scattering of palm trees in front of the museum building itself did little to alleviate the almost aggressive monumentality of the building.

Inside the cavernous entrance hall it was cool. We paid our entrance fee and began to walk through the permanent exhibition, which begins with a repro-duction of a bas-relief from the so-called Arch of Titus in Rome, which depicts the triumphant return home of the Roman legions who conquered Judaea in A.D. 70 and destroyed the Second Temple. On it, you can see what is recogniz-ably a menorah, the great candelabrum used in the Temple, being borne away on the shoulders of sturdy Romans. This is a rather somber introduction to what the museum literature describes as its founder's desire "to emphasize the pos-itive and creative aspects of the Diaspora experience." The latter are far more noticeable as you pass by the bas-relief and enter the exhibition proper. As with the Zentralfriedhof in Vienna, your experience of the Beth Hatefutsoth is orga-nized around a series of "gates," although in this case the gates are metaphori-cal: The Gate of the Family, the Gate of the Community, the Gate of Faith, the Gate of Culture, and so on. We passed through them, looking. I was particularly enthralled, as we walked through the various gates, by the splendidly large and astoundingly detailed scale models and dioramas with which the creators of the Beth Hatefutsoth have sought to evoke various aspects of Jewish life throughout the centuries of the Jews' wandering. There are, for instance, remarkable models of synagogues throughout the world, from the eighteenth-century double syna-gogue of Kaifeng, China, which to my uneducated eye looked indistinguishable from any other Chinese building I'd ever seen, with its upward-curved eaves and slender painted columns, to the Tempio Israelitico in Florence, a grandiose domed Moorish affair that reminded me of something, as I stood there—some other doll-like restoration of a great Jewish place of worship for the edification of attentive if not necessarily Jewish visitors—until I realized that what I was thinking of was the Spanish Synagogue in Prague.

There was, too, a beautifully detailed re-creation in miniature of the Great Synagogue of Vilna, in Lithuania, which was built in 1573, around the time that Jews first arrived in Bolechow, and consisted of a vast complex of schools, yeshivas, and places for prayer—which was only fitting, when you think about

it, given that the Jerusalem of the North at one time boasted three hundred and thirty-three scholars who claimed to be able to recite the Talmud by heart—a vast complex that was destroyed in 1942, the same year that most of the Jews of Bolechow disappeared.

(After Froma and I left Israel, we flew, as it happened, to Vilnius, as it is now called, and it was toward the end of the week we were there, seeking out the few remaining traces of this greatest city of European Jewish scholarship, that we visited the tomb of the famous Vilna Gaon, a man so renowned for his learning during his lifetime in the eighteenth century that congregations from as far away as Portugal would anxiously but patiently wait for years to receive his responses to their questions about scripture or law. And it was while we stood at the grave of this great man that our guide informed us that in this tomb were also buried the bones of a Polish Catholic, the scion of an enormously rich and aristocratic family, a count, a *Graf*, who, under the Gaon's tutelage, converted to Judaism and for that reason had been burned at the stake by the Catholic authorities. We politely scrutinized the Polish inscription on the tomb, and I read the name of this *Graf* aloud rather haltingly, pronouncing it phonetically. Poetahkee? I said, a bit tentatively, and the guide smiled and said No, no, the *c* is like a *ts*, it's pronounced *Pototski*.)

To me, even more wonderful than the models were the equally detailed and beautiful dioramas, such as the one to be found in the section of the permanent exhibition called "Among the Nations," which depicts the great tenth-century A.D. Babylonian sage Saadia Gaon holding forth in the palace of the caliph in Baghdad. Standing beneath the ornate and beautiful vaults of the palace, draped in a white robe, the tiny figure of the gaon has his left arm extended, as if making an important rhetorical point. And no wonder: the career of this remarkably learned man, who was Egyptian by birth—his real name, Said al-Fayyumi, hints at his origins in the Fayum in Upper Egypt—and became the star of the Babylonian gaonate, was peppered with important doctrinal, cultural, and intellectual controversies. Before he was forty, Saadia had brilliantly quashed an attempt by his archrival, Aaron ben Meir, the gaon of the Jewish community in the territory of Palestine, to challenge the authority of the Babylonian gaonate; the Palestinian's efforts to introduce a new calendar soon disintegrated. Saadia also struggled against the widespread assimilation of the Arabic-speaking Babylonian Jews, a suave elite to whom the enlightened rationalism of the Greek philosophers, reintroduced through translations into Arabic, was proving seductive. In his groundbreaking work *Kitab al-'amanat wa-l-'i'tiqadat,* "Book of the Articles of Faith and Doctrines of Dogma" (now better known, for reasons that will be obvious, by the title of its Hebrew translation, *Emunoth ve-Deoth,* "Beliefs and Opinions"), Saadia—much influenced by the Motazilites, the rationalist dogmatists of Islam—for the first time laid out a systematic explanation of Jewish thought and dogma. Written in an elegant Arabic bound to appeal to his cosmopolitan audience, Saadia stressed the rational aspect of Judaism and suggested that the Torah had an intellectual appeal not at all different from the writings of the increasingly popular Greeks. As part of his project of clarification and elucidation of Jewish texts for the tastes of his assimilated, Arab-speaking fellow Jews, he also translated the Bible into Arabic, and added to it a lucid and appealing commentary: an achievement of enormous importance.

It occurred to me, as I learned all this, that to me, part of the appeal of Jews like Rambam and Saadia Gaon was their immense cosmopolitanism, which was in turn a reflection of the richly layered imperial cultures in which they lived. Cultures in which, say, Arab-speaking Jews wrote treatises meant to combat the popular intellectual appeal of ancient Greek philosophers; cultures not that different, in their way, from the richly layered one in which my grandfather grew up, another imperial culture in which Jewishness was, for a while, one of many vivid strands woven into a complicated but beautiful pattern, a pattern that is now, as we know, in tatters. It will seem odd, but when I read about Saadia, I thought of my grandfather, who of course was not a man of immense learning or great intellectual subtlety, but who was an Orthodox European Jew who spoke seven languages and who, even after the Second World War, would go to Bad Gastein in the heart of Austria to take the waters, because that was what you did if you were a certain kind of European person, a subject of a certain vanished empire. Two years after Froma and I walked through the Beth Hatefutsoth, ogling the diorama of Saadia Gaon, we sat in a café in L'viv talking avidly about the remarkable richness of that city's pre-war culture, in which Jews and Poles and Austrians and Ukrainians had coexisted, in which Ukrainian priests would lunch regularly at a certain famous gefilte fish restaurant cheek by jowl with Polish bureaucrats and Jewish merchants. Now it's just completely *homogenous*, Froma said, rather forlornly, perhaps even with a tinge of disapproval, as she looked at the slender and quite pretty blond Ukrainian women walking up the avenue, past Beaux-Arts and Secession buildings that had been built, a hundred years earlier, by Austrians. I looked at her and said, mischievously, I know, it's like having a country only of Jews. She gave me a look and I took another swallow of my Ukrainian beer, which was called L'VIVSKAYA.

To return to the tenth century A.D.: the most vital struggle that Saadia conducted during his scholarly career was his ongoing attacks on the sect known as the Karaites. Starting in the ninth century A.D., these "People of the Scripture" distinguished themselves from mainstream rabbinic Judaism in important ways: unlike most Jews, they do not regard the immense body of oral law to have been handed down, along with the written law, by God, but instead see it as merely the work of sages and teachers, and thus subject to the errors of any human teaching. As a result of this rejection of rabbinic interpretation, which is after all the basis of all contemporary Jewish practice, certain Karaite practices differ importantly from those of mainstream Jews. Karaites, for instance, will not light candles on the Sabbath, a practice universal among all other Jews. (Nor will they engage in sexual intercourse on the Sabbath, although other Jews believe that the Sabbath is particularly propitious for that activity.) Because of these and many other errors, Saadia argued in the three treatises that he devoted to refuting Karaite belief (grouped under the title *Kitab al-Rudd*, "Book of Refutation") that the Karaites were not, essentially, Jewish at all. This is interesting for a number of reasons, not the least of which is that, twelve centuries after Saadia made this argument, the leaders of the Karaite community themselves argued as much before the Nazi authorities in 1934, and—gesticulating, perhaps, in the same heated way that the Beth Hatefutsoth figurine gesticulates—persuaded the Reich Agency for the Investigation of Families that they were not, in fact, Jewish, and therefore ought to be exempt from Nazi racial laws; which is why the admittedly small population of Karaites in Eastern Europe, for instance the community in the town of Halych, which is, today, perhaps an hour's drive from Bolechow, were left unharmed while the Jews around them were vanishing off the face of the earth.

IT TOOK A great deal of time, that morning in Tel Aviv, to absorb all this and so much more; we hadn't gotten through more than two-thirds of the museum when we realized it was already two-thirty and we hadn't eaten lunch. So we left the museum and, after emerging into the bleaching sunlight, found a chic little café on the grounds of the university campus. As we sat under an awning and devoured our *pappardelle* and *insalate,* it became clear that Froma, as usual, wanted to cram more activity into the day.

After lunch, she said, let's go back. Come. How can we leave here before we've finished with the museum?

I shook my head, smiling. After all these years, I was familiar with her insatiability, and like to tease her about it, sometimes—just as she likes to tease me back about how lazy and incurious I can be.

Froma, I said, I've had *enough.* I kept smiling, although I had every intention of winning this little skirmish. The day before, the trip to Beer Sheva, had been a long and tiring one; the weather was annihilatingly hot, and tomorrow, Tuesday, our last day in Israel, I had still more interviews to do. I wanted to rest. I wanted to swim in the Mediterranean, which lay, green and glassy, in back of my hotel. Besides, I've always found myself resisting when a certain kind of woman, someone my mother's age, some authoritative older woman to whom I feel both indulgent and obliged, says, *Let's go back*.

What I said, however, was that I needed time to be by myself and absorb what I'd gotten thus far, to go over my notes, and so forth.

But, *Daniel,* Froma said, waving a little black olive in my direction, you haven't even *seen* the genealogy section! She was appalled by my lack of enthusiasm. When we'd first entered the museum, we'd been told that there was a genealogy database upstairs—a room with computers on which you could, for instance, enter your family's name and see what information appeared. Trying to seduce me into going back up the hill and into the huge museum with her, Froma argued that we had no idea what undiscovered troves of information about the lost Bolechow Jägers might be in those machines. I crankily replied that whatever information was on those computers was just the information that my own relatives had entered, however many years ago; and that frankly, I knew more than they did.

But of course, in the end, she won. She has always been pushing me to go further, think harder; even though I knew there'd be no reward, this time, it seemed petty not to accompany her back inside, if she wanted it so badly. Besides, I thought to myself, it was now nearly three-fifteen; the museum closed at four. Whatever happened couldn't last too long.

We finished our lunch, walked back, and went upstairs. The place already had the feel of a public space that was emptying out for the day; as we passed by various office doors, we heard the unmistakable desultory noises of collegial leave-taking. The genealogy room, for instance, was empty when we got there, except for two women in, I guessed, their sixties, who were clearly employees and not visitors: they were standing at the front of the room and chatting familiarly with each other in Hebrew when we walked in. I stood in the little entryway and Froma said, Go, tell them why you're here, maybe you'll find something.

Before I had a chance to open my mouth, the one who seemed to be in charge, a serious-looking woman with a face that was both sweet and somewhat aloof, said to me, in English, I'm sorry, we're just about to close.

Oh, I said. Of course I was relieved.

It doesn't make sense, she went on, for you to rent the computer to research, you pay for an hour at a time and we close at four, it's only a few minutes from now.

For Froma's sake I tried to act disappointed. I nodded sadly.

The woman, smiling very faintly, looked at me in a vaguely maternal way and said, So you came a long way to Tel Aviv?

New York, I said.

From New York? It's far! She looked at me and then, relenting imperceptibly, said, OK, listen, you tell me one name from your family, I'll put it in the computer, we'll see quickly what comes up.

Wonderful! Froma said. She stood close to the door, leaning on a little railing, but motioned me to move closer.

I think, now, that the reason I said *Mendelsohn* at that moment, instead of *Jäger*, was in part a childish resistance to Froma's enthusiasm, to her insistence that we *go back for another look*, her confidence that my investigation would somehow be furthered by coming to this place, which I knew it would not. I had come to Israel to research my mother's family, not my father's; but out of some irrational spite, when this woman asked me for a name to enter into the system, I said *Mendelsohn*. When you grow up in a house of rigorous, even maniacal orderliness, you can find a certain deep satisfaction in rebellion.

Mendelsohn! the woman said to me, smiling faintly. She turned to her colleague and said something quickly in Hebrew, and they both laughed. So as not to appear rude, she turned back to me and explained that they were laughing over the fact that there were plenty of Mendelsohns in their database.

It's a famous Jewish name! she said to me.

I know, I said.

While she did things on the computer, she half turned toward where I was standing, still at the entrance, and said, You know, I used to know Mendelsohns, but they didn't live in New York City. They lived on Long Island.

Froma and I exchanged an amused glance, and I said, Really? I was born on Long Island.

Oh? the woman said. So where on Long Island?

Old Bethpage, I said, with a little challenging grin. Nobody knows Old Bethpage; it's too small. *Five Towns,* people will say, knowingly, when you tell them you're from Long Island. *The Hamptons.* But Old Bethpage was nowhere, a tiny needle in an immense haystack.

She smiled, then. She said, What was your father's name?

I said, Jay.

She paused and looked at me.

Then she said, And your mother's name is Marlene, no? And there are three boys, no? Andrew, Daniel, and Matthew.

Froma and I were no longer smiling. Her mouth was, literally, open.

I blinked and said, Who *are* you? Whoever it was, she hadn't been in touch with our family for a long time, was unaware that my mother had had two more children after Matt.

The woman smiled again. It wasn't the impersonally polite smile she'd offered when I first arrived, nor the slightly warmer smile she'd given me when we first began talking. Her smile was, now, both sweet and slightly melancholy, slightly resigned, the smile of someone who is used to things working out in a certain way. I had the distinct if irrational impression, for a second, that she'd somehow been expecting this to happen.

She said, I am Yona.

THE FOLLOWING AFTERNOON, on a brilliantly sunny and quite windy day, Yona and I walked along the beach near my hotel. I was still reeling from the improbability of our meeting the way we did, after so many years. And I was, too, still thinking about the peculiar coincidences that, as we learned while Yona talked in the entryway to the Genealogy Section, had always linked my family to hers.

After the initial shock, the exclaiming and embraces, she'd said to me, You know why I'm called Yona?

No, I said.

She smiled faintly. Well you see, it has to do with your grandfather and my parents. In Bolechow, before even the First World War, Avrumche—

(throughout this conversation, she called my grandfather by his Yiddish nickname)

—Avrumche your grandfather was the closest friend of my mother and father, when they were all growing up together, children together.

I had never heard this before. So that's why he was so close to her, I thought.

Yona nodded. Yes, she said, you see they grew up as next-door neighbors. And my mother and your great-grandmother Taube knew each other, they were very close friends. So when my mother was giving birth to me (Yona touched her own chest, briefly), she was dreaming about her friend, your great-grandmother. And so she named me after her!

A look of comprehension broke over Froma's features. She had been watching this whole thing unfold, stock-still. Froma said to me, Yona in Hebrew means "dove."

Yona looked at me, then, and said, Why are you here in Israel?

I smiled and said, Wait till I tell you.

That evening, I'd called my mother from the Hilton and told her what had happened. Like me, she was amazed, almost tearful. *Yona geblonah,* my father used to call her! my mother had said, emotional as always when it came to anything that brought back memories of my grandfather. And yet Yona herself seemed oddly matter-of-fact about what seemed to me to be an astounding coincidence; when we talked about it the next day, as we ambled along the boardwalk, it was again as if she had half-expected something of the sort to occur.

The strong breeze clipped her words. Well, she said, in that low voice, Israel is a—

Country of miracles? I said, half-joking, thinking of what Shlomo had proudly exclaimed as we were driving way from Beer Sheva.

Yona looked at me with her sweet, slightly crooked, slightly melancholy smile. No, it's just a small country, that's all. You'd be surprised. Things like that can happen here.

We strolled for a while and finally found a nondescript little restaurant to sit down in, facing the ocean. The water was flecked with small whitecaps. She ordered very little; I ordered a salad and a Diet Coke.

It's all you're having? she said, giving me a look that was at once curious and amused. Eat more! You're not eating anything!

I smiled and shook my head. We started to talk about family history. She had said there was a lot she could tell me about the Jägers of Bolechow.

Since hearing the story about how she'd been named, I asked her if she'd ever heard anything about my great-grandmother Taube's personality—*something specific,* I said.

Oh, she was a *personlikhkayt,* a personality, a very good woman, Yona said after a minute, remembering whatever it was she'd heard from her own parents, years ago. She was so honest, so . . . good.

Well, I thought to myself, what had I expected? She had died years before Yona was born; and besides, what can you really say about someone? *She was so good, she had such pretty legs. He died for her.*

For my parents, your grandfather was something special, Yona went on. My parents used to say, *Avrumche, he's not a friend, he's like a brother.*

I was so used to thinking of my grandfather as a Jäger above all, as a member and then head of his difficult, anxious, self-dramatizing, and tragedy-ridden family, that it came as a small shock to hear that he had had close friends, had had relationships with people outside of the family, friends in whom he'd inspired such loyalty and affection.

Yona nodded. Nowadays, you can't understand this kind of friendship, she said, looking at me steadily.

I nodded. Although I didn't know precisely what she meant, I wasn't surprised to hear that Bolechower friendships, friendships forged in a lost civilization in a lost empire before the First World War had even begun, were, like everything else about Bolechow, irretrievable.

She smiled suddenly. Your grandfather was a *vitzer,* you know what a *vitzer* is?

I nodded again; I knew. A man who could tell a joke, someone who could spin a funny story. I thought of my Aunt Ida who peed in her pants, one Thanksgiving a half century ago; I thought of the way my grandmother would say, *Oh,* Abie!

Your family lived on the Schustergasse, she said. *Shoemaker Street.* This small detail interested me; I had been to the house, but hadn't known what the street was called. SCHUSTERGASSE, I wrote on the back of the paper place mat.

She gave me a look. You're taking notes?

I nodded. It's for the family history! There was about her soft-spokenness something defensive, I thought; she liked her privacy. She made a face, but kept talking. She told me about her father, whose name was Sholem, and who in 1916 had gone to Vienna to find work in order to support his family. It did him some good; he was very fond of music. Her family had a store where they sold bread, things like that. The times were hard, she said.

I smiled. What else do you remember your parents saying about my grandfather's family? I asked. I wondered if anyone had ever talked about my grandfather's father, that well-heeled, goatee-sporting, homburg-wearing gentleman who'd died one day at a spa, setting in motion the disasters that would send my grandfather to New York, send Shmiel to New York and then back to Bolechow, and send me, eventually, here.

Yona shook her head. About Elkune Jäger she knew nothing.

But I can tell you that your grandfather's family was always very poor, she said.

Poor? I looked at her. Very poor? *Always?*

She nodded. Yes, she said. I remember my father saying that when he was a child and his family would take him to a resort in Poland, Zakopane, he felt badly because Avrumche was too poor to come along.

I thought for a moment, and said, Well, I knew that things were bad after my great-grandfather died, and then the war came—

She shook her head, then shrugged and said, Anyway, when they were *little*.

I thought of my grandfather's stories. I thought of his description of his father, the prosperous businessman, the little bottles of Tokay he would bring to Vienna. I thought of his descriptions of the Ukrainian maid he had had, growing up, of the cook who had baked each child his own little challah, for Friday nights. I thought of him telling how his father had such great influence in the town. It wasn't that I disbelieved these tales, necessarily. But as Yona talked about how desperately poor my grandfather's childhood had been, I started to wonder, once again, how much of my grandfather's stories were based on fact, and how much they were the projections of his vivid and yearning imagination. It's no surprise if a small boy who's barely ten when his father dies enlarges, over time, the memory of that father, gives the lost father an allure, a stature, a wealth that he might not actually have possessed, because during the terrible times through which this boy must now live, this enhanced memory—which will become ossified, over the years, into facts, into the stories he tells others, like me—allows the boy to think better of himself. *We were something, once,* this boy tells himself, *we were somebody special.* The hard times, if anything, now seem to the boy like a test of that mettle, that innate quality of superiority that his dead father, receding increasingly into the past, once had, and of which the wealth, the status, the esteem with which the boy, now grown up and a successful businessman himself, retroactively endows the memory of the dead father, when he talks about him in later years, was, after all, merely the outward expression. Sometimes the stories we tell are narratives of what happened; sometimes, they are the image of what we wish had happened, the unconscious justifications of the lives we've ended up living. *We were rich, we had maids. She was a Zionist, he was my favorite.* Only in stories, after all, do things turn out neatly, and only in stories does every small detail fit neatly into place. If they fit too neatly, after all, we are likely not to trust them.

I was thinking about all this, was starting to wonder just who and what my family had really been, when the check came. Yona insisted on paying; after a few ritual protests, I allowed her to. It was around two o'clock in the afternoon by now, and the sun was amazingly strong. I squinted.

You always had such blue eyes, she told me, looking evenly at my face as we waited for the waiter to return with her change. I smiled and didn't say anything. It was when we were parting, a few minutes later, and had started to exchange phone numbers and current addresses and e-mail contacts, that I actually blushed.

Yona, I said awkwardly, as I started to write her name on a napkin, this is so embarrassing.

She gave me a quizzical look.

YONA was all I'd been able to write on the napkin. I looked at her and said, I just realized that in all these years, I don't know what your family name is.

She smiled her little smile and shrugged a little and said, *Wieseltier*.

That was in the summer. Late in the fall, I came back to Tel Aviv with Matt, so he could take pictures—of Yona, of all the others. But Israel would be our second stop. First, we flew to Stockholm.

The tale of Abram's wanderings as he made his way to the Promised Land is a story that's preoccupied with increase: increase of territory, of descendants, of wealth. (And, presumably, of knowledge, too.) Abram's burgeoning wealth, following his advantageous stay in Egypt, ultimately causes a rift between his employees and those of his nephew, Lot, and in order to avoid conflict Abram and Lot agree to split up and occupy different territories, the nephew claiming the plain to the east of the Jordan (a plain occupied, disastrously, by the cities of Sodom and Gomorrah), and the uncle claiming the land to its west. But increases of other kinds preoccupy Abram even after he is comfortably settled

in the land toward which he was told to "go for himself." After all, God repeatedly promises him that he will be fruitful and his offspring will be as innumerable as the dust and stars; and yet Sarai, his beautiful wife, has failed to conceive. So among the plenty there is, too, dearth. Abram, aware of this paradox, bitterly lashes out, at one point, wondering what good his vast wealth is when strangers will inherit it. The problem is solved (seemingly) when Sarai offers her Egyptian-born slave woman, Hagar, to Abram, that she herself, Sarai, "might be built up through her." Abram obliges—although not without some resultant marital tension—and Ishmael is born. Thirteen years later, when Abraham (as his name has by then become) is ninety-nine and Sarah (whose name also changed) is eighty-nine, God announces that in the next year, she will give birth to a son. Not surprisingly, this announcement evokes from Abraham a certain incredulity, and he falls, literally, on his face and laughs. In due course, the child is indeed born, and the Hebrew name that is given to this child fittingly recalls his father's reaction to the news of his conception: the name means "he laughed," which in Hebrew is Yitzhak.

The unique dynamic of Lech Lecha is, indeed, one of movement between opposites: increase and lack, activity and stasis, barrenness and fertility, and—as is always the case with tales of adventurous travels—solitude and crowds, the loneliness of the traveler, on the one hand, and the multitudinous bustle of the places he sees but cannot belong to, on the other. To my mind, this constant tension between opposing forces, this tortured and expressive dynamic (which seems, I often think, a metaphor for the way in which we always want more, want to add to ourselves and grow as we move through our lives, even as we fear that that very addition and increase will make us into something that is not recognizably ourselves, will make us lose our own past) is most concisely and elegantly expressed toward the end of Lech Lecha, when God promises the nearly centenarian Abram that he will indeed be fruitful and multiply. As a symbol of his new status as the father of great nations, Abram will be the beneficiary of another increase: his name will gain a syllable and become "Abraham." The name of his wife, too, will undergo a change, from Sarai to "Sarah." Various explanations of the significance of the name change have been offered; Rashi goes to no little trouble, for instance, to explain how the Hebrew Avraham can, in fact, be construed in the way God wants it to be construed, which is as a contraction of Av-hamon, "father of multitudes." The r in Avraham, not present in Av-hamon, presents a problem, although Rashi as usual solves this with considerable ingenuity. Similarly, much thought is devoted by Rashi to what happens to the final i in Sarai, once she becomes Sarah—since once a letter has been part of the name of a righteous person, it is an insult to the letter itself to remove it. (No worry: the final letter in the Hebrew spelling of Sarai was, we're told, later added to the name of the hero Hoshea, who was thereby reborn as Joshua.)

As ingenious and indeed satisfying as this is, I find myself agreeing with another commentator (not Friedman, who passes over the name-change passage in silence), who argues that the significance of the name-enhancement process lies less in what the names might actually mean but in the larger sense that, as he accepts the covenant with God, Abram must have a new name, just as monarchs assume a throne name on their accession. The significance of the name change is, in this reading, more psychological than philological. This makes perfect sense to me, who by now have become all too familiar with the checkered careers that names can have: how there can be a certain yearning to change the name, and in so doing to signal a necessary break with the life one has led; and yet how crucial it can be that the name be recognizable, too, because it's not always clear what parts of the past will turn out to be worth saving.

2

SWEDEN / ISRAEL AGAIN

(Autumn)

*A*CCCHH, *IT'S MESHUGA, no?*

It was early afternoon on a Sunday in December, and Mrs. Begley was telling me how crazy she thought my upcoming travel plans were. At the end of the month she'd be having a birthday, and I'd be returning from a trip that would zigzag from New York to London to Stockholm to London to Tel Aviv to London and back to New York. As she shook her head, half-amused and half-disdainful, I tried to explain that our erratic itinerary, the exhausting juggling of continents and climates, was all because of Dyzia Lew. As I made my futile case I had little notion of how meshuga that trip would turn out to be, what with the awful blizzard, the half-day delays, the canceled flights, the missed connections in strange airports; and then, worst of all, the almost comical series of misunderstandings about the lady from Minsk, the futile transatlantic flights to places she'd just left.

It had started with a phone call I received in November, four months after I returned from Israel.

Until that point, I'd thought we had two more trips to make: first, a northerly trip in the first week of December—the earliest Matt could get free—

which would include Stockholm, where Klara Freilich lived, and then Minsk, where Dyzia Lew lived. Then we'd go home and, perhaps a month or so later, we'd fly to Israel for a week so that Matt would be able to shoot portraits of the Bolechowers whom I'd met during the summer, when he hadn't been able to come with me.

And then, I thought, we'd be finished.

But early in November Shlomo called me with bad news. Dyzia, he said, was very ill with some circulatory disease, sufficiently ill that she'd just flown from Belarus to Israel to receive treatment there. So there was no point in going to Belarus, Shlomo said. If anything, he went on, we must come to Israel sooner rather than later, since frankly there was no way to know how long . . . His voice trailed off. As Shlomo told me all this I thought, Here it is at last: Time catching up with us. I had known, of course, since the night that Jack Greene called me out of the blue and I decided, as he talked, that I would have to go to meet the few remaining Bolechowers in the world, that the people I needed to talk to were quite elderly; I'd always understood that someone might die before we got to them. But it was one thing to be aware of that theoretical possibility, and another to be confronted with the chilly reality of a particular woman's being so ill that I might, now, never get to meet her and probe her memory.

I said to Shlomo, If she's that sick, maybe I should interview her over the phone soon, now? The earliest that Matt and I could get to Israel to see her was that first week in December; I supposed we could postpone Stockholm and simply go directly to meet Dyzia in Tel Aviv, but now, in the light of Shlomo's dire news, even the three weeks until December seemed like a dangerously long time to wait. Shlomo agreed, and said he'd talk to Dyzia and set up a time for me to call when he could be at her hospital bedside to act as translator. A few days later, he e-mailed me to say that everything was settled, that he'd be sitting at Dyzia's side in the hospital at four-thirty in the afternoon, Tel Aviv time, on the following Sunday, and that that was when I should call to talk to Dyzia Lew.

Sunday the ninth? I asked.

Yes, he said, Sunday the ninth.

Now as it happened, Sunday the ninth of November that year was going to be a full day for me, a day rich with family feeling and rich, too, with thoughts about the past, since it was the day of the big celebration that my brothers and sister and I were going to be holding in New York City in honor of my parents' fiftieth, "golden" wedding anniversary. It was a date, then, of small and rather local significance for one particular family of seven people, unless you take into account the fact that November 9 marks another anniversary, an anniversary not of gold but, you might say, of crystal, one that, I suppose, is of equally great if somewhat oblique significance for my family, since in 2003 November 9 also marked the sixty-fifth anniversary of *Kristallnacht*. On that night in 1938 there began a vast nationwide pogrom throughout Germany and Austria, organized by the Nazi Party: two days of terror during which marauding gangs of Nazi youth (and adults) roamed the streets of Jewish neighborhoods, looting Jewish homes and businesses, beating and often murdering Jews, and of course breaking the windows of innumerable buildings. I say "of course," because it is to the billions of shards of millions of broken glass windowpanes that the term *Kristallnacht,* "Crystal Night"—a term first coined at a meeting of the Nazi high command a few days after the event, the same meeting at which it was announced that Hitler had demanded "that the Jewish question be now, once and for all, coordinated and solved one way or another"—owes its grotesque glitter. Although the damage resulting from Crystal Night was enormous (although at least by later standards, the loss of life was negligible)—nearly a hundred Jews killed, seventy-five hundred Jewish businesses destroyed, over a hundred synagogues and holy places destroyed, among them, as we know, every single one of the religious edifices designed by the Hungarian-born architect Ignaz Reiser, designer of the Zeremonienhalle of the New Jewish Section of Vienna's grand Zentralfriedhof— the real significance of that particular ninth of November, the reason it is a date that had, that year, a double significance for my family, was that *Kristallnacht* is now generally accepted as the event that marks the beginning of the Holocaust proper. And indeed, although the cities of Germany and Austria were distant in every conceivable way from the shtetls of what was then eastern Poland, it is possible to see a resemblance, what you might call a sibling resemblance, between what happened on *Kristallnacht* in famous places like Worms and Lübeck and Ulm and Kiel and Munich and Koblenz and Berlin and Stettin (the latter being the city from which my great-grandfather Itzig Mendelsohn and his family, including twin two-year-old sons, had departed in 1892 for New York), in places like Vienna and Linz and Innsbruck and Klagenfurt and Graz and Salzburg, "city of Mozart," and what happened a little later on in tiny places like Bolechow. For instance, in November 1938 the Jews of Germany were fined a billion marks to pay for the damage that had been done on that night of crystal, which is to say, the Jews were fined to reimburse the Nazis for the damage that the Jews had suffered (and indeed, even the six million marks—a relatively small number, compared to a billion—that insurance companies paid for the broken windows were diverted into the Reich's treasury). These grotesque accounting practices of November 1938 were not at all dissimilar to those we observe being put into practice in November 1941, when the Jews of Bolechow were forced to reimburse the Germans for the cost of the bullets that had killed Jews.

On the ninth of November, then, a date that in 2003 was a day of rejoicing in my family, I called the number that Shlomo had given me and talked to the ailing Dyzia Lew.

Hello, Shlomo said into his cell phone. He was sitting next to Dyzia, he told me; she was ready. His voice echoed slightly into the phone.

You want to talk to her? he asked.

Well, I can't, I said, she doesn't speak English.

But don't you want to record her voice? he said. By now, Shlomo understood my passion for concrete things.

Well, I can't right now, I said, maybe next month when I'm there. By way of introduction, I told Shlomo to tell Dyzia that one of the reasons I wanted to talk to her so urgently was that Meg Grossbard had said that Dyzia had belonged to this group of girls that knew the Jäger girls.

Yes, Shlomo replied, I told her all that and she was starting to tell me that she knew all the girls, the Jäger girls, and she knows that Lorka was the elder one, and Frydka was in the middle, and she knows of the other one—Fania? She says she remembers only three, he went on.

I grinned to myself and said, There were four. Lorka, Frydka, Ruchele, and Bronia. *Bronia,* I repeated—although, I thought, who was I to be correcting what this woman recalled, I who still have a piece of paper on which, in the 1970s, I'd made a list that reads as follows: LORCA FRIEDKA RUCHATZ BRONIA?

Bronia, niye Fania, I could hear Shlomo telling Dyzia, whose face I tried to imagine as I waited for everything I said, and some things I hadn't said, to be translated a continent away into Polish.

She says maybe, maybe yes, Shlomo said into his cell phone.

I laughed out loud; by now, Shlomo knew why. And ask her which was the one she knew the best, I said.

A low buzz of Polish, then: *Frydka.*

I asked him to ask her if she had any memories of the parents, if she remembered them in any way.

No, Shlomo said after a moment of Polish. She don't remember them at all.

I said, If she knew Frydka the best, what does she remember best about her personality? What was she like? We heard she was a very lively girl, she liked the boys—is that true?

He exchanged a few words with Dyzia.

She was very beautiful, he said. Beautiful eyes. She said that Meg Grossbard knows her eyes, Frydka's eyes, that they were beautiful. She said that Frydka was not such a, you know, an easy girl. She was beautiful, young, the youngsters were crazy after her.

More Polish.

She said in März 'forty-two Frydka was working at the barrel factory. *March 1942.*

I was on the same factory, Shlomo went on, I was at the same factory but I don't remember if it was true.

This surprised me. But he *had* to remember, I thought: it was he, sitting in Anna Heller Stern's living room, who'd told me that story, the story about how everyone used to say that there were two good-looking girls in the *Fass-fabrik,* and that one of them was Frydka Jäger.

Maybe, I thought, his "I don't remember if it was true" referred to *März* 'forty-two.

Shlomo continued. Dyzia worked then in the bureau where they supplied work, the *Arbeitsamt* they called it in German. She said she remembers in 1942, one day was a nice day, Frydka came to the *Arbeitsamt.* It was lunchtime, so she came from the barrel factory to visit her in the *Arbeitsamt.* She said that she remembers a guy named Altmann that talked to Frydka in that *Arbeitsamt.* She said again that she had a lot of friends but she was not an easy—

Not an easy person? I interjected, perhaps a little too quickly. My curiosity had been piqued by the thought that I was going to be hearing something new about her personality, something more than *there were three girls, she was the younger, she had beautiful eyes.* I told Shlomo, Ask her what does she mean when she says she was a difficult person.

Shlomo paused and then saw my misunderstanding. No, not that, not a difficult *person.* No, she means, for the boys, it was not easy to *get* her.

I said, Oh I see—although I wondered, in that case, just what *picaflor* had referred to. Trying to hold that story together, I prodded a little. But she liked the boys? I said.

A moment in Polish, then: Yes, she liked the boys, the boys liked her, but it was not easy to *get* her.

I felt relieved. I said, Tell her if she had to compare Lorka with Frydka, what was the difference in their personalities?

They spoke in Polish, then Shlomo said, She didn't know Lorka so well, but people used to say that Lorka was, you know, she was easier than Frydka.

Easier than Frydka? I remembered how adamant Anna had been about Lorka's fidelity to her one boyfriend, Halpern—although, then again, the fact that Anna thought Lorka's sole boyfriend had been this Halpern fellow, whereas Meg had told me that there was no question that it had been Yulek Zimmerman, should itself have suggested how fragile these perceptions, these stories could be.

She was easier than Frydka. I said, You mean with boys?

With boys, yes. She says before the war she and her friends of her age were too young to start flirting with boys. But they would look up to Lorka and take her example.

Ah, I said, I see; although of course I didn't. I said to him, Tell her that Anna Heller said Frydka was like a butterfly with the boys . . .

They talked and Shlomo said, Because she was so beautiful, so it was not a problem for her to flirt with each of the boys. She says that with respect to boys, she was selfish, Frydka. She wanted them only for her!

She was selfish with the boys, she wanted them all to herself, but she wasn't "easy." Six thousand miles from Dyzia Lew's hospital bed I sighed and thought, Well, why not? I had known girls like that in high school, girls who toyed with boys until one day they fell hard for one specific boy, and that was that. I thought, Nothing will ever be known about the relationship between Frydka and Ciszko: what had brought them together, what its substance and character was, what they had done together and talked about: Nothing. But it doesn't seem unreasonable to surmise, at least, that for him, it was serious enough to risk his life for, and that for her—possibly—it was serious enough for her to have given herself to him, to have become pregnant with his child. Hearing Shlomo report Dyzia's impressions to me, *she wasn't easy, she wanted them all for herself,* I realized that these two apparently contradictory details were, in fact, the bare bones of a certain story: a story of a willful and beautiful teenager, rather tall and perhaps a little bit spoiled, a girl whose flighty and egotistical personality, subjected to the tremendous and crushing pressures of war, to the unimaginable forces of hardship and suffering and grief under the Occupation, had metamorphosed into something heroic and brilliant, the way that a lump of ordinary carbon can, under the right pressure, be transformed into a diamond. But of course, we will never know.

I said: I just now want to talk more about the war time. What does she remember specifically about Frydka during the war? How and when did she see her? When was the last time that she remembers seeing her?

They talked for a while and Shlomo said, OK, this was the last time—when Frydka came to her at lunchtime when she was the *Arbeitsamt*. That was the last time she saw Frydka.

I asked her again what year that was. She don't remember, she thinks it was 'forty-two. She thinks it was before the second Aktion. Frydka was free at lunchtime so she came to see her, and this Altmann.

I remembered Anna Heller Stern's story of how she and some friends had gone once to see some young man who'd taken a room in Bolechow, and when they got to his place, Frydka answered the door. I smiled to myself and said, She came *with* this Altmann?

No, Shlomo said, she came to *see* this Altmann.

I smiled again and said, finally, Now ask her if she knows anything about Ciszko Szymanski and Frydka.

They talked for some little while in Polish.

She said that Frydka told her *then* about Ciszko Szymanski, and she knew that Ciszko Szymanski was in love with Frydka. She said that she knows from rumors that people said that when she was taken, he was taken, too.

It wasn't until that moment that the fact that everything we thought we knew about the love affair between Frydka and Ciszko was based on hearsay, on rumors and stories and conversations that had taken place after the war was over, really came home to me. Now, on November 9, 2003, this short sentence, *she said that Frydka told her* then *about Ciszko Szymanski,* became for me like one of those "wormholes" which, we are told by scientists, penetrate the fabric of the universe, allowing sudden and miraculous jumps in space and time. *Frydka told her* then *about Ciszko* gave me the same feeling that Mr. Grossbard's *He never got over the Dreyfus affair!* had given me eight months earlier, in Sydney: a sense that a single human memory can catapult you to a specific and now irretrievable point in space and time, and that once that single human being, that memory, disappears, the point to which it was able to hurl you also disappears, in a way. Of course Frydka must have confided to her friends about the affair at the time it was happening; but now here was the friend, and here, sixty years later, was the confidence that had been made, retrieved from the past and casually held out for my contemplation, the thing itself, not some thirdhand piece of gossip eroded and misshapen by years of handling. At that moment I imagined Frydka whispering excitedly to Dyzia, perhaps on the day Frydka had come to the *Arbeitsamt*—although of course it needn't have been that day, it needn't have been excited, it could have been dreamy, it could have been anything, since Dyzia didn't remember what the exact words had been.

She said that she knows from rumors that people said that when she was taken, he was taken, too. I thought of what Anna Heller Stern had remembered: *If you kill her, then kill me, too.*

What does she remember about Ciszko Szymanski? I asked.

She remembers a little bit. He was middle height. He liked to drink, he liked to play around! Shlomo laughed, and in my mind I drew a picture of a bruiser with a solid build, a prankster, the kind of solid blond teenager I myself would have avoided in high school, never guessing how softhearted, how sentimental he could get about a certain girl, how unimaginably heroic he would turn out to be, in the end, long after I'd dismissed him as a cretin.

From Shlomo's phone there suddenly came the noise of a small commotion: people entering the room, talking back and forth. Shlomo said, And I think we will have to make it short now, because they come to change the beds and everything, and we must move. Do you have a quick question?

A quick question? *Christ,* I thought. I said, Well, Shlomo, you know because you were there when we heard, that someone said Frydka was pregnant by Szymanski . . .

Shlomo knew where I was going with this.

Wait, wait a second, he said, I'll ask her.

They talked for a moment, and then he said, She was pregnant, she said.

I felt a little surge—not quite satisfaction, but an obscure pleasure in the fact that this particular story seemed to be true after all. Some of the pleasure stemmed from what Mrs. Begley would call my *sentimental* imagination; some, on the other hand, came from the realization that this confirmation of the rumor about Frydka's pregnancy was bound to discomfit Meg Grossbard, who in Sydney had said to me, imperiously, *I know nussink!*

I was thinking this when Shlomo added the following:

She says, She was pregnant, but not from Ciszko Szymanski.

AFTER A MOMENT I blinked and said, *What?*

Shlomo made a noise not unlike a chuckle. People talk about this, he explained, but she don't know from whom she heard it. But she's not sure if this is true. She thinks that they changed it, that they changed it from the name of Pepci Diamant—you know she was my cousin—and maybe they talked about Pepci Diamant and they made a mixture after so many years, and you don't know the truth, who was who. You understand?

No, I didn't understand; in fact, I had no idea what he was talking about. It wasn't until four weeks later, when we were sitting once again in Anna Heller Stern's darkened apartment in Kfar Saba, that he told me the whole story: that Pepci Diamant, who was a cousin of his, had been raped, he thought, by a member of the Ukrainian police, and that, while visibly pregnant, she was killed during the same "small" Aktion in 1943 in which his sister, Miriam, had been killed—the Aktion at the Bolechow Jewish cemetery that Olga and Pyotr had witnessed, the one in which the few remaining Jews of the town had been marched along the Schustergasse and while they did so had called out to their onetime neighbors, *Farewell, we won't be seeing you again.* It was at the end of this later telling of the Pepci Diamant story that Shlomo had added, It was maybe the one who raped her—the policeman who shot her there that day.

Now, as Shlomo talked to me hurriedly that morning of November 9, I was able, more or less, to piece together what he was talking about: that only Pepci Diamant had been pregnant, and that somehow, over time, the detail of the pregnancy had found its way into the story of another Jewish girl, the story of Frydka Jäger. What was clear, at the time I talked to Shlomo and Dyzia Lew—what both he and Dyzia were obviously anxious to *make* clear, in that conversation—was how easy it was for such things to get garbled in transmission.

You know, Shlomo said, in a small city . . . *somebody* was pregnant. The question was who. Was it Frydka or was it Pepci Diamant? You know, it was smoke, but who? Where? There was smoke, *maybe* there was a fire, but nobody knows.

I understood the English expression he was groping for: *Where there's smoke, there's fire.* But I wanted to know where the fire was, and who had set it; and all I was getting was smoke.

A few minutes later, we said our good-byes. Shlomo pointedly asked me if I wanted him to take a picture of Dyzia right there in the hospital. What he meant was, there might not be a picture to take by the time Matt and I arrived in Israel. I said yes. But this sotto voce transaction had made me feel guilty. So just before I got off the phone, I said, emphatically, Tell her I'll see her next month, and we'll get to talk more.

We flew to Israel exactly a month later, on the ninth of December. When we arrived on the morning of the tenth, Dyzia wasn't there.

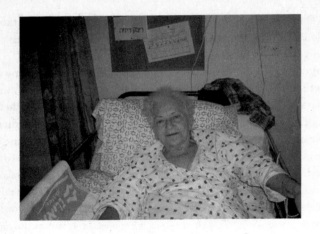

BUT THAT CAME later. First we went to Stockholm where, because it was winter, the light was scarce and the days were eerily short, as if time itself were being squeezed out of shape.

We arrived in Sweden at nearly one in the morning on a night whose absolute, literally crystalline purity—the air was so cold we could feel the tiny needles of frozen condensation on our cheeks—was all the more dazzling since we'd left New York during the worst blizzard to hit the city in a decade: a furious snowstorm that caused us to sit for nine hours on the runway at JFK, looking on with no little anxiety as the deicers sprayed the wings of our plane, anxiety that didn't decrease even after we took off for Heathrow, since by that time we knew that we'd missed our connecting flight to Stockholm and were beginning to wonder whether there'd be any connections at all by the time we arrived. Through all this I found myself preoccupied with Matt, who I knew was a nervous flyer, and who thought I wasn't looking when, at the moment of our unpleasantly bumpy takeoff, he took from his pocket a photograph, one of his own, of his six-month-old daughter and furtively kissed it, as if it were an icon. The furtiveness affected me as much as his worshipful treatment of the little icon had: the worship, because it was such a pure expression of paternal love, an emotion I'd been thinking about a great deal since my trip to Israel, and the furtiveness, because it reminded me that our improbable partnership in the search for Uncle Shmiel was still only beginning to erode the years of estrangement between me and Matt, the years of not much to say and no easy way to say it. There are many ways to lose your relatives, I thought; war is only one of them. In the photograph that Matt kissed when he thought I wasn't looking (and would kiss again, during other takeoffs), his daughter, my niece, is dressed for a Halloween party in a green felt costume designed to make her look like a pea in a pod.

So we arrived very late at the first stop of our autumn trip, exhausted, cold, sodden, and vaguely depressed. The day that we'd entirely missed because we arrived sixteen hours late—Friday the fifth of December—was, luckily, the day we had planned to spend walking around the city and seeing the sights; our first interview with Klara was scheduled for Saturday. It is because we missed Friday that, for the most part, we missed seeing the city's sights, and that what we know of the city remains limited to what we saw out of the windows of our taxi as we sped to meet Klara Freilich on Saturday, and what we encountered when, on Sunday and again on Monday, we met with her again. Blue and gray and white, with accents of red brick; turrets and spires and solid apartment blocks; water everywhere. We glanced at all this and chatted with the Polish-English interpreter whom I'd engaged in advance through the hotel concierge: a Polish-born woman in, I thought, her late forties, who'd lived in Stockholm now for many years. Ewa was handsome-looking, with a strong, intelligent profile and very short, very dark hair, the kind of head you associate with Roman coinage. As the taxi drove further into the suburbs of Stockholm on that overcast Saturday morning, we explained to Ewa what our project was, who Klara was, and what we were hoping to learn.

The bell of a streetcar clanged somewhere, made louder, it seemed, by the coldness of the air. Ewa looked at us and smiled. This was a very interesting project for her, she said, since she herself was Jewish. A nice coincidence! we said, although by that point I was no longer as surprised by coincidences as I might once have been. Ewa told us a little about herself. She said that it wasn't until she'd left Poland and married the son of an Orthodox rabbi that she knew anything much about being Jewish.

My father was a Communist and my mother was not, she explained. So I didn't know a thing about religion or Jewishness before we went to Israel. I was in a synagogue for the first time when I was married in Göteborg, in Sweden.

The driver checked the piece of paper on which we'd written the address that Meg had given us. Bandhagen seemed to consist of huge blocks of inoffensive modernistic apartment buildings; unless you lived there, I thought, it would be impossible to find your own place. As the taxi crept around the streets, Matt and I smiled and said, almost simultaneously, that we knew how Ewa felt: that we hadn't thought much about Jewishness, either, until we'd started this project.

The car stopped. We were there.

Klara Freilich was waiting for us in the small entrance hall of her apartment, which was, Matt and I immediately noticed, filled with shoes carefully lined up against one wall. *The Bolechow shoe thing!* he said to me with his sudden, wide, dimpled grin. I looked at Klara, who extended her hand toward me. She was dressed with the care and slightly exaggerated stylishness that you often find in old women who have been very pretty in their youth. Although it was lunchtime, she looked like she was going out to dinner: an elegant black wool pantsuit, a double string of pearls. Her hair was jet black, and her lipstick an electric red. She was rather petite. As she looked cautiously from me to Matt, her eyes glistened behind huge, gold-plated glasses, the lenses of which, I couldn't help noticing, were tinted a pale rose. Her face was round, its appeal enhanced rather than diminished by a witty, slightly squashed nose. Her son Marek, a big man with a solid handshake and a wide, Slavic face, stepped forward to make the introductions in English, and we all shook hands and nodded and smiled in the slightly exaggerated way you resort to when language fails. Klara said something to Marek and with a semi-apologetic laugh he asked us if we minded taking off our shoes. All the snow and slush! he said, by way of explanation. Matt and I grinned to each other and Matt said, No problem! Our mother makes us do the same thing! Marek laughed and said he was very interested to hear what *his* mother would say, since she and her late husband had rarely talked about their prewar lives to him or his siblings. He said he'd tried to get his teenaged children to come today, because he thought it was so important that they learn about their heritage. But they hadn't.

We went through a curtained passageway into a living room–dining room area. Against one wall, a glass-fronted credenza with three shelves was neatly filled with bric-a-brac that reinforced the sense I'd begun to get that Klara was someone who liked fine and pretty things. On the top shelf, a crowd of glass and porcelain figurines glittered: apart from one tall cupid, nearly all of these were tiny statues of ballerinas, pirouetting, tracing arabesques, arms extended, legs extended, leaning forward, standing upright in attitudes of charm and ease. On the second shelf there was a good deal of silver: a squat pitcher, a tall ewer, some champagne *coupes*. On the bottom shelf I glimpsed a group of rather dainty porcelain figurines: a flirtatious eighteenth-century couple in elegant clothing, forever leaning toward each other over a porcelain card table; a seated milkmaid: figurines not unlike those that had once graced the credenzas and tabletops of my own grandmothers' apartments, which as often as not were likely to feature reproductions of Gainsborough's *Blue Boy* as part of the decor, figurines whose appeal to these aging middle-class New York Jewish ladies, I have to surmise, lay in the fantasy of leisured gentility that they projected, which was the antithesis of the lives these ladies themselves had led. In Klara's apartment, a few framed prints hung above a sofa, and a low table nearby supported a thriving plant and a silver candelabrum that held five red candles. At the far end of the room there was a small dining area featuring a table and a number of chairs, and it was there that Klara motioned for us to sit and eat and talk.

It was clear from the start that she was nervous. To put her at her ease, I said I wanted to start with some basics: for instance, what year she was born. Nineteen twenty-three, she answered, and then she asked, Why did I want to know? As we talked, I noticed that she twisted the rings on her fingers, and looked often from me and Matt to Ewa.

She was the eldest of four children, she went on, a sister and two brothers. She smiled faintly as she named them. *Józek, Władek, Amalia Rosalia.* Her maiden name was Schoenfeld, her father was an engineer in one of the local leather factories. In a little talkative rush, like a student taking an exam she hopes to get over with, she said, You want to know what year my parents died? They were very young when they died. Killed by the Germans. Leon and Rachel.

She stopped and talked to Ewa for a minute. Ewa turned to me and said that Klara had a statement that she'd prepared, and instead of talking like this she would prefer to read the statement. So you'll know everything, she added.

I said, I'm really more interested in just having a conversation. I don't want her to study. Tell her it's just two Bolechowers sitting at the table.

Ewa relayed this and Klara smiled a little.

I asked what she remembered about the Jäger girls. After all, Meg had sent us here because, she said, Klara had been one of their group. How many daughters did she remember? I asked.

Ewa talked to Klara and then said to me, There were two.

I smiled and said nothing.

Ewa went on. She only knew Frydka and the only way she knew them was that she would go to the store to buy some meat. But otherwise they had no contact, really. She was young, and she had different girlfriends from her. She can tell you what she heard. She can only tell you that Frydka was taken by Ciszko Szymanski, and he wanted to save her. Somebody of course told the Germans that he was trying to hide her, and the Germans came of course and murdered him and her. But when and where she doesn't know.

I noted the two *of course*'s and asked, a little bit later, What was Ciszko like?

Ewa said, She knew him by sight. He was quite large, everybody was afraid of him. Because he was a big guy, a strong guy, well-built. He was also the son of a butcher.

Matt grinned and said, They came together over meat! and everybody chuckled. Not for the first time, I wondered what *had* brought them together. Impossible to know.

Klara said, I don't know why they met and how. Well, he liked her. She was a beautiful girl.

I said to Ewa, Tell her we heard two different stories, and I'd be interested to know which one she heard. The first was that he took her into the woods to try to get her to the partisans, and the other was that he was hiding her himself.

Ewa translated the question and Klara shrugged expressively and smiled more broadly than she had before, a smile of resignation. Could be, Ewa said after they'd exchanged a few words. Well, she thinks that the second—the other one, with the attic, and somebody told the Germans—is most close to the truth. The first one, about the partisans, she never heard about it. But she just *doesn't* want to say anything either way.

She just doesn't want to say anything either way ended up being the theme of that first day with Klara, who over and over again, as we talked, seemed afraid to commit herself to any kind of definitive statement. Although frustrating for us, this was, I realized, admirable in its way. More than anyone else we'd spoken to, Klara emphasized that afternoon that anything anybody claimed to know about the fates of Shmiel and his family was, at best, hearsay. I was struck by how anxious she seemed lest something that could, in time, turn out to be inaccurate be attributed to her. At one point I said, Explain to her that we're not *holding* her to anything, I just want to get at this . . . *cloud* of information.

Well, I don't remember a lot, Klara said to Ewa. It's very, very hard.

It's fine, I said, and tried to give Klara a reassuring look. I decided, then, that for the rest of this interview, we'd talk only about innocuous things. I said, So she said she knew her by sight, then, a girl around town?

The two Polish women talked, and Ewa turned to me again. She was tall, and very nice looking, a good-looking woman.

In English Klara said, *Very nice! Very nice!* She smiled at me and Matt. We smiled back.

Then she said something else to Ewa, who suddenly looked intrigued.

It was a good camouflage, she said.

I said, What do you mean?

Ewa exchanged a few words with Klara and then said, First of all, the nose.

Klara made a little gesture with her hand to her face to indicate a small, turned-up nose.

Ewa said, The nose, a little bit like *that*. And she was light, and she had a quite Slavic face—not dark like mine, not dark like Klara. Well, in Poland, you could say she's Polish.

Camouflage, she had said. I thought of what Meg had said to me, in the first minutes of our meeting in Sydney. *You look very Aryan. Somebody who looked like you had a chance to live.*

Ewa listened to Klara and said, She wasn't—she didn't look like a *Jew*.

Then she looked at me and asked if that was what Meg Grossbard had said, too.

AT THIS POINT I wanted to make Klara comfortable. Although I'd reassured her that we didn't have to talk about the Occupation, she seemed very eager to read her prepared statement. It occurred to me that the written words of the statement were comforting to her, a feeling I myself, who had so hopefully ordered so many documents from so many archives over the years, was familiar with. That was fine with us, I said. Klara reached for something that lay on the table, picked up a piece of paper, and peered at it through her tinted glasses. She began to read, one sentence at a time, as Ewa translated.

Klara Freilich said:

I was born in Bolechow on the twenty-third of August 1923, and I went to school in Stryj, to high school, the *Handelschule*.

She said, In 1939 the hard life for Jews started, when the Germans came to our town. When they started to shoot and bombard our town I ran into the woods together with my parents and family.

She said, In 1940 the Russians came, and the Germans left. The Russians stayed in our town until 1941.

She said, I married in May 1941 during the Russian era in our town.

She said, In June 1941 the Germans came again and then the real Holocaust of the Jews started in our town. Because of our town's industry, like the leather industry, they took the younger Jews and put them in a special place—

(she said *barak*, which I surmised was the Polish word for *Lager*)

—and the older ones were taken to Stryj.

She said, That's why I and my husband stayed in this place for the young people, and we started to work in this leather industry and we were producing glue.

She said, Every day we went to our job together with the German police and the Ukrainian police and they were beating us and harassing us every day.

Klara took a deep breath at this point and went on, In December 1943 we ran away to the woods but it was impossible to stay there because Germans and Ukrainian police knew about it and tried to take people back.

She said, Accidentally, we met a fellow from a nearby village and he was so kind that he took us with him to this village. But I have to underline that this fellow was half-Polish, half-Ukrainian.

She said, His name was Nikolai Krekhovyetsky from Gerynia.

She said, This fellow built for us a place under the floor, like a bunker. It was under the barn where the cows were.

She said, The conditions of our life in this bunker are simply impossible to tell.

At this point Klara looked up from her paper and said, Why do I have to tell you a lot? Do you want me to tell you?

We told her to tell us whatever she wanted.

Klara let the paper drop to the table and spoke to Ewa for a few minutes, and then Ewa said to us: She says that every day, almost every day, the Germans and the Ukrainians came and wanted to find the Jews because they knew that he was hiding Jews. And they found other Jews, but not Klara and her husband. It was Klara and her husband and her husband's brother, and another guy, a boy from this village.

Perhaps because I was listening to all this with Matt at my side, I was particularly moved to think that the two brothers had figured out a way to stay together all that time (another brother hadn't survived, we later learned): first in Bolechow itself, where they'd managed to linger in the forced-labor details until the last possible moment; and then in the hideout. I was about to ask Klara about this brother of Yankel Freilich—she hadn't even told me his name—but she was eager to get through her narrative.

She doesn't want to tell you everything because it is a too-long story, Ewa said.

Klara went back to her paper. She read:

And besides those people in this bunker we had the company of mice, rats, and other things.

She said, In this horrible state we survived until the war was over.

She said, I have to tell you that in 1942 the Germans killed my parents, and my sister, and my brothers.

After a moment I told Ewa, Ask her if that was the second Aktion.

They talked, and Ewa said, It was the last Aktion. Her father survived that long thanks to the fact that he was a professional specialist, so the Germans needed him. And she says that later on, it doesn't matter, it's not important.

Soon after this, Klara suddenly interrupted as I was saying something to Ewa and talked to her in a rush of Polish. Ewa listened and then translated. Klara, she said, had just had a vivid memory of something that had happened during the first Aktion, when Klara and her family were trying to conceal themselves during the roundup. They were at home, Ewa said. They were staying with some Poles, a man named Szymanski, he had a tannery.

Szymanski? But this man had a tannery, and Ciszko's father, I had always heard, was a butcher who had a little delicatessen attached to his house. Well, I thought: Szymanski was a very common name.

And she went outside in order to beat a carpet, Ewa went on, but this guy, maybe it was Szymanski, shouted at her, Listen Klara, the Germans are coming, hide! So she went to this place in the house where they kept wood. The walls weren't built very tightly, so she could see out. And she remembered, just now, that one German was standing outside and looked right at her, but didn't see her. And a German shepherd dog was with him, the Nazis always had them—and she was sitting on a piece of wood on the floor and they were looking at her, the German and the German shepherd, and she was looking right at them but they didn't see her.

Klara leaned back in her chair and told Ewa she had to take a break.

AFTER A WHILE Klara got up and served an enormous lunch. Gefilte fish, borscht, cold poached salmon in raisin sauce, delicious bread. Yes, she said, smiling, the bread was homemade, too, although she'd had to make it the day before, because she didn't have enough time today. As an accompaniment, she served vodka in little glasses, and kept making sure that everyone's glass was filled. She made a joke in Polish, and Ewa, smiling, translated it: Fish like to swim, so you have to have some vodka with it!

During lunch, we were careful to talk only about pleasant things: how exciting and interesting our previous travels had been, how much we'd enjoyed meeting the other Bolechowers. We talked about Meg, about Jack and Bob. Jack Greene had been her brother's friend, Klara said. She smiled when we mentioned Shlomo's name: everybody, it seemed, was familiar with the "king of the Bolechowers." She used to go to Israel often, she said, because her daughter, who had since died of cancer, had lived there. We talked about the Israeli Bolechowers. She didn't seem to know the Reinharzes, and so I told her their remarkable tale of survival, hidden above the ceiling of the German officers' club. She had arranged once to meet Anna Heller Stern at one point when she was in Israel, she said, but Anna had gotten sick, and had canceled.

Because Klara now seemed more relaxed, I gently prodded her about her memories of life in Bolechow before the war. Anything, I said, anything at all, in no particular order. Were her parents very religious, for instance?

Her parents hadn't been particularly observant, she said after a minute, although of course they'd observed the big holidays, Pesach, Rosh Hashanah, Yom Kippur. They'd go to the big synagogue on the Rynek, the one that eventually became a club for Ukrainian leather workers, only on Rosh Hashanah and Yom Kippur. Matt gave me a look that said, *Just like us,* and I nodded. I asked Klara if she remembered what foods her mother would cook on holidays. Challah, she said; *gefilte fisch,* she said. *Tsimmes,* she remembered, smiling at the thought of that savory New Year's dish of meat, sweet potatoes, carrots, and prunes. *My mother sometimes put honey in it,* my own mother used to say of this dish, *Honey!* and I would think, with the special, protective tenderness that to this day I reserve only for my dead grandmother, my mother's mother, Nana, *All that work for a dish she couldn't eat.*

We ate Klara's savory food and she talked about the commercial high school that she and Frydka had attended, how classes had run from eight in the morning till two in the afternoon, how many and difficult were the courses they'd taken. All different subjects! she exclaimed. Ukrainian, Polish, mathematics, natural sciences, physics, geography, history. What they ate in Bolechow, when she was a girl: always fish on Friday nights, carp or trout; otherwise, chicken or meat or even turkey. Her mother had been a wonderful cook, she said: but then, how could she possibly say her mother *hadn't* been a good cook! She talked about how she and the other teenagers would go to the Hanoar HaZioni after school; how there'd been an eight o'clock curfew for teenagers in the town, in the prewar years. How, come to think of it, Frydka Jäger hadn't been one of the girls who went regularly to the Hanoar meetings. About the movies she would see as a girl, at the cinema in the Dom Katolicki. I still remember silent movies! she said, almost boastfully. Charlie Chaplin! Gary Cooper! Ramon Novarro! People said how he was so good-looking!

Klara offered me yet another piece of gefilte fish. I said I couldn't, I'd already had two pieces.

Who's counting? she said.

She talked about how she used to ski in the hills outside of Bolechow, how they'd played volleyball in school, how she had played Ping-Pong. (Matt and I exchanged a swift look: *Ping-Pong!?*) She remembered the school uniforms: berets for the girls, caps for the boys. Every school had a different color, she said. She talked about the homework she and her friends had to get through before the Hanoar meetings.

What do you expect? she said suddenly. People lived as *usual,* it was business as *usual,* we tried to get good marks in school because it was important to our parents, and that was all! Life as *usual!*

She talked about her wedding day, during the Soviet years. It was May, she said, a beautiful morning. She wore a light-blue dress with a dark-blue coat, and a little hat on her head. And suddenly, snow and rain! They took a carriage drawn by horses to a restaurant in the Rynek; they invited their wedding guests to this restaurant. But Klara couldn't take part in the wedding dinner because she had a temperature. I was sick, she said to us, nodding at the recollection of this strange day of joy and snow and fever.

Who was there? I asked, wanting her to relax with these happy memories.

My friends, she said, my husband's friends, my family, my brothers, my sister. At the rabbi's it was just the family, and then the dinner was all the friends and family. But it was only a very modest dinner since I was sick.

What was the name of the rabbi? I asked. Did she remember? Klara thought for a moment and then she cried, Perlov! Perlov! She beamed and said, Now I remember! It's a miracle!

I wondered if other miracles might happen. As Klara got up again to get the dessert, returning after a few moments with an enormous coffee cake, I asked her if she remembered anything else about the Jägers. The butcher shop to which she'd go to buy meat, for instance: Did she remember that there were two Jäger brothers? She thought for a moment and then cried out, Yes! Yes! Now I remember. I was a little girl. There were two Jägers, one had a butcher shop and the other was Fryda's father—

(*Fryda*, she had said: the name on the birth certificate, not *Frydka*, the nickname; for some reason, this tiny, insignificant variation seemed to add a dimension to her recollection, seemed to make the girl I knew only as Frydka more real)

—my mother would send me to one of the Jäger brothers to buy meat, but I would go to another one because it was nearer to our house. Was one of them religious? The owner of this little shop?

Then, suddenly, she made an *aha!* face. *Tak, tak. Skandal!*

She said something to Ewa, who turned to me with a look that was half-querying, half-amused. She said, The religious Jews started to boycott this shop?

BY THIS POINT it was, quite abruptly, darker outside, and what with the heaviness of the meal and the disappearance of daylight, the mood of the room seemed to grow heavier and darker, too. Marek, I'd noticed, had listened carefully and courteously as his mother spoke about the days of her girlhood and teenage years, the normal, *life as usual* years before the war started, and as we ate our dessert and coffee he started to talk to me from the other side of the table, as Ewa and Klara talked softly to each other in Polish. It was clear there was something on his mind, and I could tell how frustrated he was at not having more fluent English. But I helped and prompted him now and then, and in the end understood everything he said.

I asked him how much he already knew of what he'd heard.

Not much, he said. Mostly I talked to my father. My mother told me about it sometimes. Now I'm asking more because I want to know for my children. He told me he had two children, Jonathan and Sarah, eighteen and twelve. How much of this are they aware of? I asked. Marek shook his head. Five percent, he said. They know they were survivors, they were at a farmer's under the floor, eleven months, and that's all. I listened to him and decided that I liked him: his frank and eager interest, his openness in talking about difficult things to a total stranger. He looked, I suddenly realized, like a handsomer Bob Hoskins, and this unbidden association somehow strengthened the impression I had that he was a very decent person. We talked a while about how, as we got older, further away from the past, the past paradoxically had become more important to us. He said, My father, for him it was very important to be Jewish but he never taught us to be Jewish. I never had Jewish friends in Poland, but he pointed to me that I am Jewish, too—I must be strong, I must be the best.

I nodded sympathetically.

I wanted my children to come today for this reason, Marek told me. He said that his father had very rarely talked about the past, only on Yom Kippur, and then only "a few words." But nothing *deep,* he added. I wanted to tell my son about my family, Marek went on, not only my wife's family—

(his wife was Polish, he'd told me)

—but it's so difficult. When you came here today, my mother wanted to remember the dates. I tried to tell her *dates* are not important, it's not the dates, but how was it to *be* there, what was it like, who was my grandfather—not his profession, but his *personality*. She cannot understand that you want to know about trivial things, like what was the school like, the teachers. This is so difficult to explain.

I was very moved by this. So much of what he'd said, after all, dovetailed with my own yearning, over so many years, to learn the small things, the tiny details that, I told myself, could bring the dead back to life. At this point Matt, who when we were growing up would often say heated, emotional things that, at the time, would embarrass me, so naked were the feelings that prompted them—things like, Racists should just *die!* or, People who do that to animals should just be *killed!*—Matt said, vehemently, A lot of people want to know how they died, but not how they *lived!*

Continuing his thought, Marek nodded and said, People think it's not important if someone was a happy man, or not a happy man. But this *is* important. Because after the Holocaust, those things disappeared.

Soon after this, we got up to leave. As I sometimes would do at the end of these interviews, I asked Ewa to ask Klara what her best memories of Bolechow were. Ewa spoke to Klara and Klara, listening, made a wistful face. Then she said something brief to Ewa.

What Klara had said was, *The bad memories have erased the good.*

WE TALKED TO Klara the next day, too, after Matt had taken some photos of her in a little square paved with cobblestones. It has to say "Stockholm," he'd said to me the night before as we lay in our adjoining beds, softly discussing the long and, I felt, oddly thwarted conversation we'd had with Klara. She had told us a lot, I knew, but somehow I had the impression that she was keeping something back, which I had not had when talking with the others, except perhaps, at the beginning, with Meg. As I listened to Matt saying that his picture *had to say Stockholm,* I grinned, but took care not to let him see. Not having had time to explore Stockholm, after all—our day for being tourists had melted away as we waited on the runway at JFK—neither one of us could be quite sure just what Stockholm "said." Cobblestones, with water in the background, seemed reasonable.

So the next day, the second day, we met Klara and Marek and Ewa at a spot that Marek had suggested, and walked for a bit. For her official photograph, Klara had put on a chic snakeskin jacket with padded shoulders. She was looking much happier today, as she posed in front of the small obelisk that stood at the center of the cobblestone-paved square, and flirted with the camera. It was bitter cold and gray outside, and rather damp; from time to time the sun seemed to be trying to find a way through the thin, weary-looking clouds, only to retreat after a few minutes. After twenty minutes or so of posing and picture-taking, we gratefully ducked into a coffee shop just off the little square. It was appealingly dark and warm inside, and a fire was burning. We all ordered cappuccinos.

Marek had wanted to talk about his father the day before, and now he did. My father was from another side of Bolechow, he explained, from the poor side. He went only to the fourth class—fourth grade. He had to go to work early in his life.

Before I'd left for Sweden, I'd checked once again in the 1891 Galicia Business Directory online at www.jewishgen.org. EFRAIM FREILICH, the database read: *HADERN- UND KNOCHESHANDLER.* Rag-and-bones man. Yes: the other side of Bolechow.

With a soft look on his broad face, Marek went on talking about his father, who had died long before I ever dreamed of finding out what happened to Uncle Shmiel. Marek said, He was . . . he was very *special*. Very, very special. He helped a lot of Jewish people after the war. Every Jew knows him here! He gave money to a lot of people. It was amazing: when he died—and he was here in Sweden only a very short time, because I brought him here to the hospital from Poland—when he died it was one hundred people here.

I realized he meant, at the funeral.

He said, It was amazing.

From the counter of the café came the sound of milk being foamed. Klara and Ewa were talking softly, and Ewa turned to me and Matt to explain that they were discussing a news report about some recent anti-Israeli feeling in Sweden. She said that a bookstore that sold openly anti-Semitic pamphlets and newspapers and books had opened near a church where, during the war, refugee Jews had been given shelter.

Klara shook her head and said, *Skandal!*

The mention of newspapers reminded me of a question about everyday life that I'd meant to ask Klara. Were the papers in Bolechow mostly in Polish?

Mostly, she said. Her parents spoke Yiddish and Polish at home. Also a little Ukrainian.

Ukrainian reminded me of another question: When Jewish people had household help, were the maids usually Ukrainian? *The maid betrayed them,* I'd heard someone saying a lifetime ago, before I knew anything at all.

Yes, Klara said, Ukrainians.

I thought suddenly of my grandfather teasing my mother's stout cleaning lady, Mrs. Wilk, with his dirty jokes in Polish, and this led me to a further thought. Was there some kind of castle near Bolechow, I asked, that had once belonged to a Polish count?

No, she said, she couldn't remember any such place.

I heard my grandfather's voice saying, *They were hiding in a kessle.*

Then: Did she ever hear about Graf Potocki?

Yes! Klara said. But he wasn't from Bolechow!

I smiled and told the story I'd heard in Vilna, about the Potocki who'd been burned at the stake by the Church after he converted to Judaism.

In Bolechow, Klara said emphatically, a Jew who converted to become a Christian was put out of the community!

She turned to Ewa and told a longish story. Ewa listened, nodding, and then said, There was one family that she knew, a Jewish family who lived either in Gerynia or another place, not a town, but a village. In this family there were two sons. One son fell in love with a Ukrainian girl, and the mother of this boy wanted him of course to leave this girl, so the family moved away to Bolechow. But love overcame everything! So he stayed and converted to the Ukrainian Orthodox Church. And he was expelled from the family and the community—the Jewish community—and everyone in Bolechow would point out the mother, saying "That's the mother of the convert!"

She told this story, and as she did so I realized that I was very tense, because I was worrying about Matt, wondering, as Klara said *the mother of this boy wanted him of course to leave this girl—of course!*—what my brother, who'd fallen in love and married a Greek Orthodox girl, was thinking as he listened, too. I thought of my grandfather, who in many letters, and then in his will, had written, *If any of my children or grandchildren go outside the Jewish faith, they should not benefit from one penny of my hard-earned money.* From the Old Country he had brought over more than just his accent, his stories. Every person, in the end, is a person of a specific time, a specific place, and from that there is no escaping, however far he may travel.

But Matt said nothing.

MAREK GOT UP to leave; he had to get to work. We shook hands and said we'd see him the next day, since he'd told us that he was going to try to get his son, Jonathan, to join him and his mother and us for lunch somewhere. Earlier, he'd confided to me the reason why Jonathan hadn't come the day before. Klara and her grandson had, it turned out, quarreled just before we arrived: he'd apparently told her that he was very busy with schoolwork and wouldn't be able to stay for the whole afternoon, and taking offense at this perceived lack of interest, she had told him that if he couldn't spare time for the whole story, he shouldn't bother to come at all. They are very close, Marek said, but both very proud! Now, Klara's son, Jonathan's father, was playing the middle man, to reconcile them in time for Jonathan to meet us before we flew off to Israel.

I was hoping that Jonathan could join us for a different reason. His English, Marek had told me, was excellent, and I was hoping that Klara might open up more if she were talking to her grandchild. *They are very close,* Marek had said.

Marek left. I asked what I thought of as a Matt question, a question about feelings, not facts. I told Ewa, Ask her how she felt yesterday after the interview.

Ewa translated the question and then listened as Klara spoke. Ewa said, Well, she says she was nervous and couldn't sleep, so she took some pills. She couldn't concentrate. She said she hasn't always been stable in her nerves.

Every time she experienced something new, she went to doctors, to psychiatrists, and so on. And everyone told her she had to just lay quietly. But her husband had cancer for fifteen years, and then her daughter. A beautiful girl, she died. The problem is that from time to time she can't remember the very bad things, because she doesn't *want* to remember. She says she never talked to her children about these things. Her husband maybe talked about this when he was alive, but she went through such horrible things that are not to be—

Ewa, who had been translating all of this as Klara spoke, listened for the end of the sentence; but Klara's voice had trailed off. Then she resumed talking. A lot of people went away, to hiding, but me and my husband were the longest time in this place where they kept all the Jews, the *Arbeitslager,* after the others went—we ran away to the woods much later after Dyzia and Meg and the others.

We nodded and tried to make the sympathy we felt for her plain on our faces. Ewa said, But she says it was really nice to meet you, and she will call Meg and tell her how nice it was to meet you.

None of the other survivors we'd met had talked this openly about the psychological anguish they'd experienced as a result of their wartime experiences, and I wanted to say something that would make Klara feel good. I said to Ewa, Tell her we're very grateful, tell her every little thing is meaningful and important to us. Like when she told us what Ciszko Szymanski looked like . . .

As Ewa translated this, Klara interrupted. Did Meg tell you what Ciszko looked like? she wanted to know.

Matt and I exchanged broad grins, and I launched into the story of how Meg had refused to talk about Ciszko. I explained Meg's joke: *I know nussink! I see nussink!* Matt laughed out loud as I finished the story. I was struck by how eager Klara seemed to know what we'd learned from Meg, and whether the information we'd gotten from Meg dovetailed with the information she was giving us.

Klara said, I do not know much about him, just that he wanted to save her. And he died because of it. So why doesn't she want to talk about it? She paused for a moment, and then said, Meg is very careful with every word. Dyzia, Dyzia Lew, a school friend of mine, my best friend, she is very sick now, this woman is very open and will talk to you.

I said, Yes, we're going to talk to her on Thursday. I turned to Matt and said, That's good to know, about Dyzia Lew.

Klara said, When you see her tell her I wish her well, and I wish her a long, long life.

It wasn't until the next day, at a noisy Italian restaurant with her handsome teenaged grandson at her side, that Klara finally told her story.

It was clear from the moment we arrived that Jonathan's presence both soothed and buoyed Klara. She was animated and talkative, and over lunch she readily agreed to tell us about the whole of her experiences during the Occupation, which she did slowly, waiting for Jonathan, at whom she gazed adoringly, to translate each sentence. And so as we sat at a big round table, Klara talked: about the bombing when the Germans invaded in the summer of '41, the first Aktion, the terrifying, silent encounter with the German and the German shepherd as she and her family hid from the Ukrainians and Germans who were looking for victims. How she and her husband, Jakub, *Yankel*, had planned almost from the beginning to escape; the terrible months in the work camp, waiting for the right moment. How he had run away from Bolechow first, to the tiny village of Gerynia, how frightened she had been when, the next day, she followed him. The hiding place that they'd had to abandon when the wife of the farmer who was concealing them expelled them, fearing—not unreasonably—for her own life, for the lives of her own family. The second hiding place, under the floor of the barn.

What did the hiding place look like? I asked. Ever since Sydney, ever since the story of Frydka and Ciszko had first threaded itself into my imagination, I had wondered what the physical reality of these hiding places had been like. Since I would never know for sure where Frydka—and, perhaps, Shmiel, too—had been hiding, I was eager to have a picture, some concrete particulars, of what it could have been like, at least. Klara talked for a minute or two, trying to explain the layout of the hiding place in which she'd lived for nearly a year under the earth. Suddenly, she snatched a paper napkin off the table and took a pen from her son and drew a map, which she thrust toward me as she started explaining.

That is the stable, Marek translated. And that's the opening to the basement. That's the basement. From the basement you could go under the stable, under the floor. It was like a secret door. In the corner was a secret door that went to the cellar underneath. There were four people there.

Marek paused, and Klara said in English, I, my husband, my husband's brother, my husband's friend. Again I opened my mouth to ask about this brother—I still didn't know his name—but Klara started talking again in rapid Polish.

When they wanted to sleep, Marek said, one of them had to stand up because there was only room for three to lie down.

I have a terrible fear of small, enclosed spaces; I shuddered. OK, I asked after a moment, so they're in the cellar, but what are they talking about, what are they discussing, planning, during all those months?

Jonathan relayed the question, and Klara then told what seemed like an involved story, and when she finished talking Jonathan turned to me.

The farmer's wife brought them the food, he said. They were very nice people. They had two daughters, one of them was Hanushka. And they were seven and nine years old. Both of them went to school. In secret my grandmother was teaching the older daughter mathematics and such. But it created a problem, because soon the girl knew a lot more than the other students, and the teacher started asking questions.

I thought, Even generosity could be deadly.

Jonathan went on, But the girl's father was very intelligent. He told the teacher that they had an uncle who was staying with them, and it was he who had been teaching the girl.

He added, This girl would run to the forest and bring them blueberries, blackberries.

I thought, *The first strawberries of the season!* but what I said was, Was she ever concerned that these two small children knew about them? Was she worried that they would give them away?

Jonathan talked to Klara, and then turned to me and said, No, no, no. She really loved those two girls. She wasn't afraid.

Then she said something else, and he said, She tried to write to them after the war, but she never got a response.

Klara went on talking and talking. She said they had remained in their cramped underground lair until the Soviets liberated the area in the summer of 1944. She said they were like animals, they lived like animals, *with* animals. She said she couldn't find the words to say how it feels to live in a hole in the ground with rats running around for all those months. She said it was a miracle they survived, because you could be killed at any second: if it wasn't the Germans, it was the Ukrainians.

Klara then talked about how it felt to return to Bolechow after the Soviets had liberated the town, how she and other survivors had found their way to a house in town—she thought it might have been Meg Grossbard's house—and shared their stories there. (How many people is she talking about? I asked, twenty? thirty? and Klara said, Maybe ten.) How she had tried to work in a hospital just after the war, but she was too weak to carry things. How she hadn't stayed long in Bolechow after the liberation, because, she said, I had lost everything, everything was lost. So she and her husband had left forever and, against all odds, had prospered in Poland, even under the Communist regime; and then had come here, to Sweden.

When her story was finished, I asked Jonathan how he felt, now that he knew the whole tale. He said, I think it's kind of astonishing—I didn't know that they were such a long period of time and that it was so complicated. In my mind it was like they were in hiding and then they came out. I didn't, I didn't . . . I didn't think about all these small *details*.

I nodded and said, Details is what we want so badly, too.

Matt said, Imagine living in a place the size of your *shower stall* for eighteen months—it's hard to comprehend.

Jonathan nodded. I knew some things, he said, but I didn't know just how horrible it was.

I said, Well, I'm sure we haven't even heard the most horrible. Whatever she tells us, I'm sure there's a lot that's much worse.

At that very moment, Marek leaned over and said something in a low, confiding voice to me and Matt. We listened as he spoke and then I said, Oh, my God.

SO KLARA'S STORY had, in the end, been told. Watching her look at Jonathan, I had no illusions that her decision to narrate everything that had happened to her in the order it had happened—or almost everything—was for my benefit. It was, all too clearly, for Jonathan: for this bright and serious youth who had told me, as we were seating ourselves around the large round table at the beginning of that meal, that he knew too little about what his grandmother had been through in her life. In his near-fluent and almost unaccented English, he had said, I just know fragments, not the whole picture.

So we had gone to Sweden, as we had promised an incredulous Meg we were willing to do. And yet we still had only had fragments of a picture that, it was starting to appear, would never be whole. *She just doesn't want to say anything either way*, Ewa had said, when we'd asked Klara which of the two entirely incompatible stories about Frydka was more likely to be true, the one in which she'd run to the partisans or the one in which Ciszko had been hiding her. *She thinks that the second—the other one, with the attic, and somebody told the Germans—is most close to the truth. The first one, about the partisans, she never heard about it.*

It wasn't until a year after I'd returned to New York from that trip, one night when I was watching the videotape of this interview for the third or fourth time, that I realized that I'd never said anything about an attic.

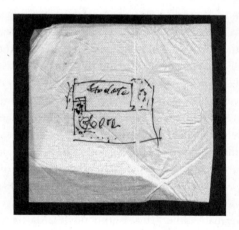

BECAUSE I NEVER like having to go back and revisit places I've just been, it may have been the fact that I'd recently been in Israel; or perhaps it was the grueling trip to Stockholm; or perhaps it was Klara's unexpected, frank acknowledgment of the psychological suffering she'd endured in her life; or perhaps, even, it was the sense, after we'd talked to her three days running, that there was not much left to be learned; perhaps it was any or all of these that gave to our week in Israel an aura of melancholy.

There was something else, too, which we couldn't know about until we landed at Ben Gurion Airport and had checked into our hotel. After Matt and I had settled into our rooms, the first thing I did was to call Shlomo: I wanted to confirm our various appointments over the next few days, which as usual he had very helpfully arranged. It was in the course of doing so that he told me that Dyzia Lew had flown back to Belarus only days before.

What? I was furious, but tried not to show it. We'd scheduled this entire trip to coincide with Dyzia's stay in Israel.

What happened? I asked, attempting to control my voice.

The treatment wasn't working, Shlomo told me. So she went back.

He didn't have to say, To die. Anyway, it wasn't Shlomo's fault; there was nothing to do but carry on. So I held my tongue, and we went over the itinerary he'd organized. But a certain sadness now clung to this trip more tightly than ever.

It was there when we went back to Beer Sheva to photograph Shumek and Malcia Reinharz. Once again, Malcia had prepared an enormous meal; once again, we sat talking and she smiled and spoke her forceful if broken English and thrust more food on us. Once again, Malcia shared her memories, this time for Matt's sake: that Shmiel had been *toip,* deaf, that Ester had had *two such pretty legs!* That there had been only two girls, as far as she knew, and that they were a nice family, a handsome family. But this time it was as if she, too, were feeling depleted: her mood was far more pensive now than it had been when I'd interviewed her in June, and she tended, this time, to finish her sentences with a little sigh. She continued reminiscing, bringing out the memories in no particular order. She recalled the card games her parents had played: Rummy, Sixty-Six, something called *Der Rote König,* the Red King. The movies they used to go see on Saturday afternoons, when they'd sit in the more expensive seats, in the third row, with the lawyer Dr. Reifeisen who was nearsighted and who, I knew, although not from Malcia, had hanged himself from a beam in his office soon after the Germans came. Greta Garbo movies, Malcia remembered; Jeanette MacDonald! She remembered Bruckenstein's, the restaurant that was owned by a pianist who was blind and who, during the first Aktion, in the Dom Katolicki, was ordered to play sprightly tunes on a piano that had been placed on the little stage while the Gestapo men put out the eyes of Rabbi Landau and forced the other rabbi who was there, Horowitz, to get up on that stage and lie naked atop some terrified naked girl as my mother's cousin Ruchele lay cowering and listening, hours before her short life came to an end. She recalled how she and the other Bolechowers used to walk everywhere, as far as Morszyn, far into the woods where they would gather . . . *Erdbeeren?*—

Strawberries, I said.

Strawberries, she said, enunciating the word slowly, *und Blaubeeren*—

Blueberries, I said.

Blueberries, Malcia said. Strawberries and blueberries and *every*berries! She burst out laughing at her own joke, and then suddenly became wistful again. Oh, it was nice, it was nice. It was a *life*. It was, and it will never be again.

Sixteen again I'll never be, till apples will grow on a cherry tree.

It was at this point that Shumek Reinharz said he wanted to show us something that maybe Matt would want to photograph. He got up slowly from the dining table to fetch something from his bedroom. Malcia went into the kitchen and returned with an enormous apple strudel she'd been baking. Matt did something with his camera, and I took advantage of the lull in the conversation to boast to Malcia that Matt had just been named one of the top ten wedding photographers in the country. She made delighted noises, and then Shumek returned and held out a bunch of yellowed papers to me. I took them carefully, almost gingerly: I know how fragile old paper can be. One, roughly the size of a passport, had a swastika on the front and said, in block letters, PASSIERSCHEIN. It was, I immediately recognized, the safe-passage document that had allowed him, as a "useful worker," to walk the streets of Bolechow without getting killed. Inside there was a big letter *W*, and I remembered what Jack and Bob had told me in Sydney, how the work force had been divided into *R*'s and *W*'s; and remembered, too, how Bob and Meg had bickered about what *W* stood for. I handled this piece of paper and Shumek looked at me and said, *Wehrmacht! Wehrmacht!* and pointed at his chest. It was odd and exhilarating to handle a concrete object connected to what had been, until then, a story. I remembered that day in Ukraine, two years earlier, when Matt had glimpsed the tombstone on which the name JÄGER was written, and which turned out to be the tombstone of my grandfather's relative Sima Jäger, whom I'd known about for years from my Internet research but who hadn't seemed quite real until that moment.

I handed the *Passierschein* to Matt, who positioned it on the table and took a few pictures of it. But it was the next document Shumek handed me that caused to descend once again the sadness that seemed to adhere to this Israel trip. Every year, Shumek explained through Malcia, in order to continue receiving reparations from the German government, he had to present this document. I scanned the German print on the piece of paper. It said that he, Solomon Reinharz, had endured certain privations and losses during the Nazi occupation of Bolechow, and that as a result he suffered from ongoing *Panik, Angst, Spannung.*

I turned to Matt and translated. *Panic, Fear, Tension.*

Malcia said, Every year he must present this certificate, to prove that he is alive!

Matt flashed his wide grin and said, Ask him how does he prove that he's alive!

Everybody laughed, but there lurked behind the joke an unfunny and complicated history, and we all knew it. Soon afterward, the eighty-nine-year-old Shumek drove us all to the shoe store that he and Malcia had run since 1950, and Matt started taking pictures.

The sadness still clung two days later, when we went to Haifa to take pictures of Josef Adler.

We'd spent the earlier part of that Saturday at another giant family reunion at Elkana's place, a lunch party at which, it seemed, even more first and second and third cousins had shown up than the last time. This time Elkana's sister, Bruria, had come from Haifa. She turned out to be a fine-boned woman who wore her dark hair in a pageboy; she had brought from her home her mother's fabled photo album, the one over which, thirty years earlier during my parents' only trip to Israel, my mother had exclaimed, crying, *Oh, Daniel, you should see the pictures Aunt Miriam has, Aunt Jeanette's wedding picture, her dress is made completely of lace!* And yet now, sitting in Elkana's living room, I looked through this fabled object at last and soon realized that nearly every picture in it, with the exception of that wedding photo (a photograph that, of course, could never even begin to suggest the tragedies and dramas that had resulted in that particular wedding) was merely a copy of a picture that we had back home in New York. It was obvious that Shmiel had sent identical copies of the various photographs taken of his family over the years to all his siblings, precisely the way that I and my own siblings do. To this disappointment was added the dismay I felt as I leafed through a number of quite old-looking, frayed photographs that I did not recognize, photographs that bore no labels or inscriptions of any kind, including a very ancient one of an Edwardian-looking man who, I wildly thought, could be my great-grandfather Elkune Jäger. When I held these mysterious images up to Bruria, whose English is as limited as my spoken Hebrew is, she shook her head sadly and made a little shrug. So all these, I thought, looking at the mute faces, all these are utterly lost, impossible to know.

I realized, too, as I looked through Aunt Miriam's famous album, that my grandfather had owned many more pictures of Shmiel's family than, it seemed, Uncle Itzhak had owned. It occurred to me that there were two possible reasons for this: first, that because Uncle Itzhak had lived and worked so closely with Uncle Shmiel, he didn't need to have souvenirs of his older brother; or, alternatively, that because Uncle Itzhak left for Palestine under a cloud of *skandal!*, the two brothers didn't communicate afterward. As I sat on Elkana's sofa wondering about this, a line from one of Shmiel's letters came back to me: *What does dear Isak write to you from Palestine?* It had never occurred to me, until now, why Shmiel, in Poland, had to ask for news of Itzhak, in Palestine, from my grandfather, who was in New York. Then again, Shmiel calls Itzhak *der lieber Isak,* "dear Itzhak," so how estranged from him could he really have been? Impossible to know.

After we'd finished with the album, we went into the big communal dining room and ate. Once again, the meal began with a toast by Elkana, who slowly got to his feet and, looking at me with his narrowed pasha's eyes, that amused and knowing look with which he would make his pronouncements about politics, delivered with a certain self-confident swagger that I recognized from my childhood, or would bid you farewell—*They will find him in Tikrit! All ze best!*——raised an eyebrow as he raised his glass and said, *L'chaim and here's to Dehniel's book, he must finish it already and zen come back to Israel just to visit us and not always to interview!* Once again, two dozen or so people, with most of whom I had almost nothing in common, not geography or language or politics or personality, apart from a certain set of genes that were, even as we sat there, being diluted with each new generation, sat down to an enormous meal of fried whitefish and *chulent* and *tsimmes* and *kasha varnishkes,* the kind of food, my cousin Gal leaned over and told me, that young Israelis refer to as "Polish," not because it is in fact Polish but because "Polish" is the word they use, with the tiniest flicker of a perhaps dismissive irony, to refer to the mores and manners of what, in my family, is referred to as "the Old Country," which is to say nearly all of Jewish Europe from Germany to Siberia. *Oh sometimes she's just so Polish!* this same cousin said, affectionately, of her overprotective mother, who is my second cousin Anat: the granddaughter of Itzhak, *Isaac,* as I am the grandson of Avrumche, *Abraham.*

It was Anat and her husband, Yossi, in fact, who, after this big reunion had ended in flurries of hugs and kisses, some genuine, some merely polite, drove us from Tel Aviv to Haifa, where Josef Adler was waiting for us. As we drove north away from Elkana's, where after lunch Matt had paused to take some pictures of the family, *the family,* Matt and I talked about the Dyzia Lew disaster and whether it was possible, or even desirable at that point, to fly to Minsk to interview her.

Well, I did already interview her, I said, trying to convince myself as much as him. Is there really a *point*? She already told me that she didn't know them that well, that she didn't know Shmiel or Ester at all, that she only knew Frydka but wasn't close to her. And frankly that story about Frydka being pregnant by someone *else* doesn't fill me with confidence, I have to say. So is this woman really worth schlepping to *Minsk*?

I added, after a moment, From what I hear, Belarus makes Ukraine look like *Paris*.

We pulled up in front of Josef Adler's house on a quiet street on a hill in Haifa. A lone child played by a parking sign; a cool evening wind pushed an empty paper coffee cup across the street. A few months earlier, Josef had mentioned to me on the phone, when I'd called to get his address, that there had been a terrible suicide bombing in this very neighborhood. A bus had been blown up. But now it was quiet. Apart from the child, there wasn't a soul on the street. That week, I'd noticed that the newspapers and televisions were free of violence; the big story in the papers just then was about the attempts by the descendants of the Wertheim family, once the richest Jews of Berlin, to get reparations for the vast holdings that had been seized by the Nazis, including the land on which a new office complex for the German Bundestag, the Parliament, which had been dedicated on the day we'd arrived in Tel Aviv, had been built. BUNDESTAG'S SHAKY FOUNDATIONS, read the headline in *Haaretz* on the day we met with Josef Adler.

We went to the front door, where Josef was waiting. Once again, he was dressed with an almost military neatness. But this time—partly because of the fact that he was in his own comfortable home, and partly because of the presence of his wife, Ilana, a slim, good-looking brunette who looked far younger than her age and whose voice had, as do the voices of many Israeli women, a certain appealing bitterness to its timbre, a note like the rind of an orange—this time he seemed more relaxed, more expansive than he had six months earlier, when he had retailed for me, crisply and with a scholar's dispassion, the history of Bolechow under the Occupation. After introductions were made, we all sat down around a low table and Ilana brought out a pot of coffee and an enormous brass platter heaped with nuts and fruits: oranges, dates, figs. We drank the bitter coffee and ate the fruit and talked.

For the wife's sake, I described once again what our project was, and what we had hoped to achieve. Because there was something about this couple that appealed to me, I wanted to say something that would please her, and would be true. After talking for maybe twenty minutes about the Bolechow project, I said, I must tell you I was very happy I spoke to Mr. Adler the last time I was here. I went on, saying how impressed I had been, on my last trip, that her husband had taken the trouble to drive all the way from Haifa to my hotel room in Tel Aviv to talk to me. I said how important it was for people to be so forthcoming, so generous with their memories. I described how, in some cases, it took more than one interview to establish a rapport with people. I smiled and described how we'd called Meg Grossbard every day when we were in Sydney, trying to persuade her to talk to us, and then how lovely and excited she'd been when we finally got to her brother-in-law's little apartment. And even then, I added, she was very reluctant to say anything about the war, anything at all about her family.

Josef looked at me from across the low table and said, She had a good reason for that.

Matt and I exchanged confused looks and Matt said, What was the reason for that?

In an even voice Josef said, Her brother was a member of the Jewish police, and he had not such a good reputation for that.

Matt and I exchanged looks. *I know nussink,* Meg had joked. *I see nussink.* I thought of Anna Heller Stern who, during my last visit, had said that she was more afraid of the Jewish police than of anyone; thought, too, how much easier it is, often, to be cruel to those with whom we are truly intimate, the ones we know too well. Cain and Abel, I'd thought as I listened to Anna. Siblings. I thought, Maybe Ciszko Szymanski wasn't the only thing Meg didn't want to remember.

What was his name? we both asked simultaneously.

Lonek, Josef said.

Not such a good reputation?

Josef was philosophical. Well, you know, today it's very hard to judge such things.

I made an emphatic gesture. I'm not *judging*! I judge *no* one, I said. And it was true. Because it is *impossible to know* certain things, because I will never experience the pressures that people experienced during the war years, the unimaginable choices that had to be made, because of all this, I refuse to judge. Still, there was this new thought, as I sat there eating sweet dates and figs: All those years of knowing nothing about Shmiel and all the rest had provoked in me a terrific yearning to know, to have facts and dates and details; and yet it had never occurred to me that the facts and dates and details I learned might add up to something more than entries in a chart or elements in a story—that they might one day force me to judge people.

I said, I want to emphasize my business is not judging. I judge no one. I can't be in 1942, I don't know what it was like, people did what they did, they were under unimaginable pressure and stress.

Josef said, It's complicated. There were some Jewish police who were good, and some were bad.

I said, Of course it's complicated.

Josef sighed and said, With Lonek Ellenbogen—

(Meg's maiden name, I knew, had been Ellenbogen, which in German means *elbow,* a name that might strike you as the most bizarre surname imaginable were it not for the fact that, as even a cursory search through the Jewish Records Index–Poland database on jewishgen reveals, a name that was just as common was Katzenellenbogen, *cat's elbow*)

—with Lonek it was like this. We were in this forced labor camp, Shlomo and myself. Shlomo's cousin, Moishele, he was brought from the Stryj ghetto. He met with us. But the day they decided to liquidate the Stryj ghetto—in

Stryj—they also arrested people who had been sent *from* Stryj to work in the labor camp in *Bolechow.*

In Sydney, months before, Jack Greene had told me a story about Dolina, my great-grandmother's hometown, a place whose World War II monument today, because it was erected by the Soviets, makes no mention that the people lying in the mass grave behind what used to be the town's synagogue—today it is a Baptist church—were Jews. Even after there were several Aktionen in Bolechow, he'd said, his voice still filled with a certain bemusement, even after two years, when the Germans had killed four, five times in Bolechow, the Jews of Dolina weren't touched. This, Jack told me, had confused and enraged Bolechow's surviving Jews, who thought that maybe the Dolina Judenrat was doing something right that the Bolechow Judenrat wasn't. And then, Jack reminisced, one night the Germans came and liquidated the whole town of Dolina all at once. The whole town! That's the German . . . procedure, logic, I don't know what to call it. Now, in Haifa, listening to Josef Adler talk about the Stryj Aktion, I thought, Here it was too: liquidating the Jews of Stryj didn't mean merely killing the Jews who happened to be *in* Stryj. German logic.

So, Josef went on, anyway Lonek came with the Germans, the barracks were surrounded by SS and Jewish police, and Lonek entered and he recognized Moishele. He said, Moishele, you must come. And Moishele said, Have pity on me, you *know* me. Lonek said, You have to go, it's your duty to go.

Josef gave me a look. You see, Lonek was convinced that somehow he's doing some kind of very important duty that he had to comply with. It was their duty to execute their own . . . And Moishele was taken away to the Rynek and they shot him.

We listened in complete silence. Then Matt said, What happened to her brother, to Lonek?

Josef said, He was also killed in the cemetery. He tried to run away, but I don't remember if it was the same day or it was later. No, it was later. I only heard about it. First they had to arrest them, and then they conducted them along Shevska Street, Schustergasse, and they had a kind of military discipline, they were arranged in rows . . . His voice trailed off, and then he said, Ah, it was strange.

In Ukraine, Olga had told us, *They marched them two by two up this street to the cemetery. The sound of the shooting went on so long that my mother took down her old sewing machine . . .*

And Lonek Ellenbogen, he tried to escape, he tried to climb the wall of the cemetery—the wall doesn't exist anymore—and he was shot. And someone told Shlomo how it happened.

He finished, and Matt, articulating my own unspoken thought, said, But if you were Jewish police, perhaps—even naively—you thought, If I am Jewish police I will get better treatment?

It's complicated, Josef said again. Anyway, after so many years, after all Meg is not responsible.

I thought of Meg, her pride, her riveting acuity, the oscillation between tenderness and steeliness, and for a moment I could have wept. She had surely always known of the stories that we were hearing today for the first time, and just as surely, I now saw, she was terrified we'd find out. Terrified that we'd judge her brother, a boy in his—what? twenties? late teens?—who'd buckled under pressures that no American or Australian kid of nineteen or twenty-two today could even begin to conceive of. He had swaggered, had thought he was doing something important when he refused to let an old friend escape. She had been terrified that we'd judge him. No, I thought: Terrified that we'd judge *her*. I shook my head and said to Josef, No, no. I'm just trying to understand psychologically—Meg remembered many things, but anything about her in the war—nothing! How she survived, what her story was: nothing. It's like a black hole.

Ilana, who had remained silent throughout her husband's narrative, and through my response, spoke softly from her seat. She said, And I think time has nothing to do with it, because we don't forget.

I looked across the table. There was something about this dark and thoughtful woman that I found very appealing: the opinions she expressed seemed to me complicated in just the right degree, a fine balance of unsentimental rigor and a softening humanity. As if to confirm my silent appraisal, at that moment Ilana Adler said, rather heatedly, extending an arm as if to embrace the whole of our conversation that evening, *What is memory?* What is *memory?* Memory is what you remember. No, you change the story, you "remember." A story, not a fact. Where are the facts? There is the memory, there is the truth—you don't know, *never*.

Soon it was time for us to leave for the train station. Matt, as usual, was worrying about the fading daylight, and so we finished our coffees and went outside, where he took some pictures of Josef standing by the parking sign, whose Hebrew warning, I thought to myself with a smile, certainly "said Israel." Then we got into Josef's car. As we pulled up at the intersection of two streets called *Freud* and *Wallenberg*, Josef turned to me and said, apropos of nothing we'd been talking about, a sentence that could have been an explanation, a justification, I'm not really sure, It isn't enough to be nice to people. In Bolechow we were nice to people, and it didn't do us any good.

INTENSIFIED AND DARKENED, now, by unpleasant revelations, the gloom clung still when we went to our final destination the next day, the cool and darkened apartment of Anna Heller Stern: another exhausted and melancholy return to a place I'd already been.

Once again, she had prepared an elaborate tray of cakes and cookies; once again, she hovered, making sure we had enough Coke, enough iced tea. Once again, she told us what she remembered about Shmiel and Ester and the girls. Once again, she related what she'd heard about Frydka and Ciszko. This time, however, since both Dyzia and Klara had offered recollections of Ciszko as well as of Frydka, we prompted Anna to try to remember what the Polish boy had been like.

Yes, she said, of course she remembered him. He was heavy, not too *high,* and blond. *Blaue augen.*

Solidly built, I guessed was what she meant; medium height, and blue eyes. That much, all three women agreed on.

He was hiding somewhere, she added, unprompted, but probably not in his own house: his mother would have killed him! she said. He was bringing her food, she said. And then somebody denounced them. This is what she'd heard, at least.

So she told us everything once again. She shared, too, her own remarkable story of hiding, a hiding that was, unlike Frydka's, successful. Once again she showed the picture of the Polish priest who had saved her life by making false papers for her. Once again she showed us the false baptismal certificate, the one that had given her the name *Anna,* which she'd kept ever since. Matt took a picture of the document. ANNA KUCHARUK, it said.

I noticed that the date of birth given on the certificate had just passed, and smiling I said I was sorry to have missed the big day, if that was indeed her real birthday. Anna said yes, that was her real birthday, in fact; she'd just turned eighty-three. Happy Birthday! we all said.

Matt wanted to know what she planned to do with all these documents. Would they go to Yad Vashem? he asked.

Anna talked to Shlomo, who said to us, Yes, everything.

Then, becoming animated in that outsized way that he has, Shlomo started speaking heatedly to us, gesturing with both hands and biting into the English words. I myself gave all to the Holocaust Museum in Washington, I have almost no originals, he said. You know, I think . . . I think, what was the reason for my survival. What was it? Why people elder than I, smarter than I, more educated than I didn't survive, but I survived?

Surwived.

Shlomo took a breath and then said, more slowly: I think it is two reasons: one, that I take my revenge. And the second is to tell, to tell whoever wants to hear the story of what happened.

We nodded. He went on.

For years, he said, I believed that this life was not real life—that I would look up and there would be my family. *I didn't want to bring children into this world.* When I was married I *did not want* to have children! The main change started, I think, after the trek I made in 'ninety-six to Bolechow, with Jack and Bob and the rest. When I saw, when I saw that nothing, nothing is left, not our houses, nothing was left of our factories, nothing was left even of the garden with the pool . . . OK, I thought, this is it: I cannot return. The past cannot return. I had to admit it. So I started writing.

Matt and I nodded, and I said I certainly understood. Shlomo turned to

Anna and translated all of what he'd told us into Yiddish, and she said something briefly.

Shlomo looked at us. She said that her husband used to say that whoever came through the Holocaust and says that he is completely normal, he's lying. It's not true.

Anna spoke again briefly in Yiddish.

She says for years she's under treatment for psychiatrist, Shlomo said. Her children know that they grow up in a home which is not a happy home. You know, in a sad home, the parents cannot be happy, because they have this background. And they understood.

I looked at Anna and tried to show how sympathetic we were to her. I was struck again by the fact that all of the people I'd talked to last time and who had shared with me, then, so many stories, so many facts, were now suddenly offering, for the first time, these acknowledgments of their struggles with mental anguish, with fear and panic and anxiety.

I said, Well I'm sure, of course. Not a happy home.

Mrs. Begley's son once said of his mother, *Something in her had been broken,* and when he said this I had thought, The ones who were killed were not the only ones who'd been lost.

Anna spoke a third time, slowly enough so that this time I didn't need Shlomo to translate. *Will fargessen, zol nisht fargessen, kann nisht fargessen.*

You want to forget, but you shouldn't forget, you cannot forget.

I nodded and explained to her that this was exactly why we were doing this project, going all over the world and finding the remaining Bolechowers so that we could glean from them every scrap, every nugget of information about my family.

She asked us where else we had been. I told her I'd been many places, and not only places where there were Bolechowers, but other places too, places that would help me get a feel for what had happened. Not only Australia but Vienna and Prague; not only Tel Aviv but Latvia, where I met the one remaining Jew in a small town outside of Riga, a man named, as it happened, Mendelsohn—although because the Mendelsohns in my family had never talked, because there were so few stories, so few concrete details about my father's family, those Mendelsohns who came in 1892 from Riga, I had no way of knowing whether I was related to this Jew of Riga named Mendelsohn. (This Mendelsohn was a craggy white-haired man who, although he was nearly ninety, towered over me, and who went into his bedroom, after we asked him how he dealt with whatever anti-Semitism might be left there, now that there was only one Jew left to hate, and came back brandishing a shotgun.) Not only Beer Sheva but Lithuania, where the death pits in the Ponar forest, where the Jews of Vilna once picnicked, hold a hundred thousand of those same Jews, lying now under the lawns they'd once sat upon in pleasure. This return to Israel, I told Anna, was our final trip, now that we'd been to Sweden to see Klara Freilich.

Anna looked at me, and then looked at Shlomo. Klara Freilich, she said, musingly. *KLAAhh-ra FREIIII-lich.* The way you might say, *Ahh-HAAAhhhh.*

Shlomo nodded and said, *Yankeles froh.* Yankel's wife.

Anna said, *Yaw. Fun Yankele vill ikh nisht reydn.*

About Yankel I don't want to speak.

I looked at her, startled. *Farvuss nisht?* I said. Why not?

She looked at me hard. *Farvuss? Vayl er geveyn in di yiddisheh Militz.*

I thought I'd heard right, but Shlomo's translation left no room for doubt.

Her husband was a *Yiddish poliziant,* he said, looking at me severely. She said she doesn't want to speak about him because he was a Jewish policeman. And one *Akcja,* Aktion, was led by the Jewish police.

Matt and I stared at each other. I knew we had the same thought: it was like a replay of Haifa. Now, as my mind raced, certain things Klara had said—and certain things she had, I now realized, not said—started to come back to me. For instance, that they had left for their hiding place unusually late, much later than everyone else. For instance, that all throughout her narrative, that last day, of the war years, she'd never actually talked about her late husband, had merely let it be assumed that whatever was happening to her had been happening to him, too. The dreadful anxiety in the work camp, the tense waiting for the night of departure. Fumbling, I said, So when the Jewish police were part of these actions, they were just as—doing everything that . . . ?

Shlomo said, with startling loud emphasis, They *came,* they took you *away,* if you had any money you gave them *money,* they led you *away.* They believed that everybody *else* will be killed, but *they* will be left.

I thought of what Marek had said about his father, how generous and good he had been. I remembered what Josef Adler had said the night before: some were bad, and some were good. It was complicated. At that moment, I chose to believe that Yankel Freilich had been one of the good ones. With this in mind, I turned to Shlomo. Let me ask you this, I said. How did you *become* a Jewish police? I mean, could you say no?

Shlomo shot me a reproachful, mirthless half-smile. You couldn't say no, no. Some of them volunteered, and some of them were forced. But who was "forced"?

I said, Who knows? But I'm saying that—

(What I wanted to say was this: that if I thought I could save my new wife, and myself, by being in the Jewish police, by enjoying whatever tawdry perquisites they received in return for being the ones who rounded up their fellow Jews, would I do it? Yes, I might.)

Shlomo interrupted me. But we had two leaders of Judenrat, they *hanged* themselves, in Bolechow.

I nodded. I know, I said. Reifeisen—

Reifeisen and Schindler, Shlomo said.

His point, I could see, was that there were some whose moral repugnance at what they were being forced to do had led them to make other choices. But who was I to judge? Anyway, Yankel was long in his grave, his generosity to his fellow Jews after the war, at any rate, a matter of record. Right now I felt protective of Klara, who, I had by now come to know, had once been forced to endure an unimaginable horror, and whose almost girlish flirtatiousness, her porcelain ballerinas and bucolic paintings and poignant dressing up and taste for fancy clothes and nice jewelry, I now thought, were perhaps a kind of superficial recompense, a flimsy reparation, for the things that still haunted her. So I chose to believe that her Yankel had been one of the good Jewish policemen.

Anna said something to Shlomo, who after a moment turned to me and translated. She says, He can be ashamed how they behaved, the *treatment*.

Then Shlomo said, I have for you a story, a private story, but this cannot be in your book, you have to turn off the tape recorder.

I turned off the tape recorder. He started talking.

It was not long afterward, just as we were about to leave Anna's apartment, that a certain memory came suddenly to Shlomo and changed everything.

We'd been talking about Dusia Zimmerman, the girl whose brother, at least according to Meg Grossbard, had been Lorka's boyfriend during the Occupation . . . although now that we'd heard about Mr. Halpern, now that we'd heard Lorka had been *easier* than the others remembered, who knew? Yulek Zimmerman had perished, Shlomo was saying, but his sister had survived. He told me a remarkable story. After the war, she had married a Belgian to whom she had not revealed she was Jewish until many years after their marriage. But it was well known that she refused to talk to anyone, clung to her privacy tenaciously.

Well, I joked, at least we wouldn't have to go to Belgium. It was enough that we'd just been to Sweden, had made this crazy trip from New York to London and London to Stockholm and Stockholm back to London and then London to Tel Aviv!

And, I thought, it was enough that we followed Dyzia Lew on a wild-goose chase to Israel.

At that moment Shlomo literally slapped his hand to his forehead. *Ooooh!!!* he exclaimed, Oh!!! I forgot!!! You were in *Scandinavia*! In Copenhagen lives a man from Bolechow. Oy oy oy oy oy!

I said, Who? Maybe, I thought, he's not important.

But Shlomo, recovering himself, just said, You know what? We will talk. We will phone him later from my place.

After this photo session with Anna, we were supposed to go to Shlomo's for a festive lunch prepared by his wife, Ester, a solid, round-faced woman who spoke little English but whose warmth and generosity, despite the language barrier, permeated her few words of English the way that the smells of the delicious foods she roasted and fried and baked each time I visited filled her small kitchen. It was Ester who had said to me, inclining her head toward her husband as the three of us sat down to the gigantic lunch she'd prepared for my first visit to Israel, *Bolechow, Bolechow, Bolechow!* and made a face of affectionate exasperation as she ladled out *kneydlakh*.

Now, in Anna Stern's living room, I said again, Who is it? Who lives in Copenhagen?

Shlomo excitedly talked to Anna in Yiddish for a while. I heard *Malcia Lewenwirths onkel*. I heard, *Akegn der D.K. D.K.* Pronounced *day-kah*. The Dom Katolicki. Across from the D.K.

Der haus akegn di D.K. The house across from the D.K.

I listened, getting impatient. So who *is* this man in Copenhagen, Shlomo?

He told me that there was another Bolechower whom he had completely forgotten to tell me about, a much older man named Adam Kulberg, who'd lived in the neighborhood of the Dom Katolicki. It hadn't occurred to him to mention this man to me before, he said, because Kulberg had gone east into the Soviet Union just before the Germans arrived. For this reason, he wouldn't be able to tell us anything about what had happened to the Jägers. He hadn't been there. He wouldn't know.

I thought, Nobody else was really "there," either, nobody else had actually seen what happened to them; but they all had stories. I thought, We were in *Sweden,* for God's sake: it would have been so easy to stop in Denmark on this trip. But I looked at Shlomo and saw how mortified he was, and thought, Who am I to complain about inconvenience, to these people? So what I said was, Well maybe we should call him from your place, we'll find out if he knows anything, maybe it's not even worth schlepping there.

Shlomo looked relieved. I will phone him, he said. In five, ten minutes you will ask him your questions.

I said, How old is he? Maybe his memory was gone, I thought, wildly. It could well be that there was no point in being upset in the first place.

Shlomo said, Oh, elder than she. He nodded in Anna's direction—she was sitting on the sofa, posing for Matt—and then he said, Oh, how did I forget, how I forgot?!

THERE IS A room in Shlomo Adler's apartment in Kfar Saba that I privately think to myself as *Bolechow World Headquarters.* It is a smallish room that was intended to be a bedroom, but is all too clearly an office. Everywhere you look, papers spill from boxes crammed onto shelves, and loose-leaf notebooks are stacked one on top of another: dominating the room, sitting atop a smallish desk that it dwarfs, is a large beige computer monitor. It is from this room that Shlomo does his Internet research and Web browsing, and keeps track of the other Bolechowers, sending them e-mails and letters, occasionally sending out his *samizdat* newsletters and, most important, the yearly reminders that go out not only to the survivors themselves but to their relatives and friends and, indeed, anyone who might have anything to do with Bolechow, which is to say people like me, about the annual Bolechow memorial service that he organizes.

It was to this room that we rushed as soon as we got to Shlomo's place, once we'd said good-bye to Anna. Shlomo sat down heavily in the desk chair and, putting on the reading glasses that hang, with an incongruous daintiness, from a cord around his neck, looked through some papers for a minute or two. Then he said, Aha, and lifted the receiver of the phone, which he cradled between his neck and shoulder. I picked my way among the papers, and near a bookcase against the wall found a place to stand while he made the call.

Even at a distance of a few feet, I could hear the tinny burble of a phone ringing somewhere far away through the receiver that Shlomo was holding; he must have had the volume turned up very high. Then Shlomo started talking animatedly in Polish. I heard him say *Pan Kulberg*. I heard him say *Anna Heller*, then *Klara Heller*. I heard him say *Bolechowa*. I heard him say *Jägerach*. I heard him say *Frydka Jäger, Lorka Jäger*. He said a lot more that I had no way of understanding.

Standing there, waiting for Shlomo to translate whatever this man Kulberg was saying, I remembered how, months earlier, on a late summer afternoon when Matt had come up to New York to take a portrait of Mrs. Begley and we'd sat in her living room discussing our various trips and what we'd found out, I'd mentioned that by this point I thought it might be a good idea to learn some Polish. Sitting in her thronelike chair in front of the dormant air conditioner, Mrs. Begley made a face. *Accchhhh,* she said, letting a dismissive hand flap onto the arm of the chair. *It's too difficult for you, don't bother!* She pushed more iced tea on Matt, to whom, I'd noticed, she had taken a fancy. To my surprise, she had readily acquiesced when he said he thought he'd get a more atmospheric photo if we took it in her bedroom, which meant that she had to get out of her throne and, leaning on her cane, make her painstaking and painful way through the living room. Why the bedroom? I thought, suppressing a surge of irritation at my brother. In the bedroom was her walker, and the hard, unflattering light from a window that was only lightly curtained. She would look like an old lady, I thought; in the elegant striped blouse she'd put on that day, she'd look like a prisoner of old age, and, although of course I knew that she was extremely old—she would turn ninety-three in December—I never thought of Mrs. Begley as an old lady. I thought of her, in some strange way, as someone who had survived so much that there was no reason she wouldn't survive time itself.

But Matt, I realized, was different, and saw a different woman than the one I had come to depend on so much, and for this reason, maybe, wanted a portrait of her sitting in her striped blouse on the lonely expanse of her big bed.

And because she liked him—partly because he is a big, good-looking man with beautiful yellow eyes and a wide, unpredictable, ingratiating grin, and partly because, as she had once told me, his moody picture of a solitary old Jew sitting in the grand synagogue in L'viv, which he'd taken on our first trip two years ago, had brought back to her wonderful memories of her girl-hood in the lost world, the holidays, the meals, the way her father had car-ried her on his shoulders in shul on Simchat Torah so she could see what was happening—because she had decided to like him, she uncomplainingly got up from her chair in the living room and went to the bedroom and sat on the bed, and there he took the picture that, when he sent a copy to her, she declared the best picture ever taken of her.

From that point on, whenever I talked to Mrs. Begley, she'd end the con-versation by saying something like this: How is that brother of yours, the one who's so much better-looking than you are? And she would chuckle her mirthless chuckle.

For instance: a few months after Matt took the picture, Mrs. Begley called to ask me how my Yom Kippur fast had been. It was a nice *yontiff,* I said, we had a good fast and my mother had made a lavish break-fast.

She sighed heavily. It's nice to hear those terms. They are familiar to me, but they won't be long in this world.

Then she said, Give my best to your brother and tell him he's much better-looking than you; and hung up the phone.

Six months after that, she called me on my birthday, which always falls around Passover. I told her about the big family seder we were all going to be attending on Long Island. Because her son happened to be abroad just then, I invited her, as I had sometimes done in the past, to come out and celebrate with my family and our friends, although I knew that she'd pooh-pooh the idea, as indeed she had done in the past.

Accchhh, she said, sighing dramatically. (I envisioned her right hand, spotted and thin, flapping in disdain.) Once I would have gone, but my knees are bad, I can't walk, I don't feel well at all. But it's nice you should ask.

It was pointless to argue, so I said nothing.

She added, I always maintained a nice Jewish home, not that it did me any good.

There was a pause. Listen, she said—often, she would signal the end of a topic, or an entire conversation, with a brusque *Listen*—Listen, give my best to your mother and father and say hello especially to your brother. You know, he's a lot nicer-looking than you are. Ha!

Six months later, it was Yom Kippur again. On the afternoon of Kol Nidre, the evening service that marks the beginning of the holiday—the name *Kol Nidre* meaning "all vows," since the ritual begins with a prayer on behalf of the congregation that all vows, obligations, oaths, and anathemas undertaken by its members from one Yom Kippur to the next might be absolved and nullified and made void, a prayer that began as a necessary corrective to the vehemence with which (as one source puts it) "Jews and Orientals" used to take oaths in ancient days, although this yearning for absolution from oaths took on profound new meaning for Jews, if not for other Orientals, during the years of the Spanish Inquisition, when Jews were regularly forced to formally abjure their faith and swear fealty to Catholicism (although, perhaps inevitably, the existence of the Kol Nidre prayer was long cited by anti-Semites as proof that the oath of a Jew could not be trusted, a curious if by no means rare kind of *logic*)—on the afternoon of Kol Nidre, Mrs. Begley called to ask me *exactly* what time sundown would be. While I checked an online Jewish calendar Web site that scrupulously gives the exact moment of sunup and sundown to the tenth of a second, I asked how she was feeling.

Not *vell,* she replied heavily. We chatted while I looked at the Web site, and I told her that I was thinking of going back to L'viv and Bolechow, that maybe that would give me an idea about how to finish my book.

Write fast, she said. Or I won't be around to read it.

Then she asked me again what time sundown was, and when I'd told her again she said, All right, so tell your family to have a good fast . . . especially your brother, the *handsome* one.

I sat in my apartment, holding the receiver, and grinned. This was the point at which she usually liked to hang up on me, but this time there was a little silence on the other end of the line, and I was afraid she was going to ask me for a third time what time sundown was. But what she said was, And I'll tell you something: I love you! How do you like that? To be loved by a ninety-three-year-old woman! Ha!

She gave her sour little laugh and hung up on me before I had a chance to tell her that I loved her, too. I had wanted to do so for a long time—I, who over the years of my childhood and adolescence had signed dozens of letters to my own grandparents *Love, your grandson, Daniel,* but could not remember having ever said *I love you* to any of them when it wasn't merely a mechanical response—but for a long time had refrained, because I knew she'd laugh and say I was just being *sentimental,* just as she'd said, so dismissively, that I'd never learn Polish.

I NEVER DID LEARN POLISH. Now, in Israel, in December, as Shlomo spoke loudly with this strange man in Copenhagen, I listened uncomprehendingly to the sibilant sounds that crackled out of the receiver that Shlomo gripped tightly, the noises that were being made by a man who (I admit it) for a moment I'd hoped might be too frail or forgetful to require, now, yet another transatlantic journey. Shlomo turned to me and, cupping a hand over the mouthpiece, said, The Jägers—who else was there?

I said, Shmiel.

I heard him say, *Shmiel Jäger.*

Then Shlomo listened for a long time as a firm, thin voice on the other end spoke.

Shlomo looked over the rim of his glasses at me, with an expression that said, If you were mad before because I forgot to tell you about Adam Kulberg, you won't be mad because of what I'm about to tell you now.

He said, His father was related to the Jägers but he don't know how. He remembers *everything.*

Shlomo talked more to Kulberg. I heard him say, *Ruchel . . . tak tak tak tak tak, tak. Tak. Brat? Wolf?*

He cupped his hand over the phone again and said, His youngest brother, named Wolf, was living *at Shmiel's house!*

I said, Living in Shmiel's *house?*

Shlomo beamed, as if he were responsible for Kulberg's brother's address. Living in Shmiel's house! And he knows they are related but he don't know how, but he remembers *all* the daughters!

I thought, *Related?* I couldn't imagine how, couldn't imagine what relation this man, of whom I'd never heard, could be to us. Racking my brains, mentally flipping through the dozens, hundreds of names and facts I'd accumulated since 1973 when I first became obsessed with gathering and sorting everything that could be known about my family, I said, What was his mother's maiden name?

They talked for a moment and then Shlomo said, Friedler, she was not from Bolechow, not from Bolechow. She was from Rozniatów.

Rozniatów? As far as I knew, we had no relatives, even by marriage, in the little village just a few miles from Bolechow.

At that moment Matt, who'd been in the living room doing things with his camera, walked into Bolechow World Headquarters. I turned to him and said, I'm going to have a heart attack because of this. This guy's brother lived with Shmiel. He knows *all* of them.

Matt raised one of his fine brows in amusement and said, Where's he live?

Copenhagen! I said in a tight voice, not without exasperation. I thought again how easy it would have been to go from Sweden to Denmark, before coming to Israel.

At that moment I overheard Shlomo saying, *Tak, Frydka i Ciszko Szymanski . . . Shmiela Jägera. Ah, nu?*

I turned from Matt to Shlomo. What did he say just now?

Shlomo nodded excitedly. He said, He tells me the story about the teacher that kept Frydka! He knows that Ciszko was killed together with Frydka. In Bolechow. This is a story he heard after the war.

They talked some more in Polish. Shlomo turned to me, raising his eyebrows high.

He said, He remembers the name of the art teacher who hid them!

He paused for effect and then said, The name of the teacher was Szedlak!

Shedlak? I pronounced it the way it sounded to me

Shlomo nodded, beaming. He knew what this news was worth. Yes. *Szedlak.*

I turned to Matt and said, I guess we're going to Denmark.

Soon afterward, we finished talking to Adam Kulberg, to whom, after a brief, frantic consultation with our datebooks, we promised we'd come in February. Then we ate Ester's epic lunch, rolling our eyes in mute appreciation of the many courses she brought out. We ate and ate, and talked about the remarkable new discovery, this man whom nobody had told us about, and finally got up to leave. It was our last day in Tel Aviv; the next day, we were going to Jerusalem, partly to do some innocent sightseeing at last, and partly because I wanted to go to Yad Vashem. Yona Wieseltier had a friend there who, she said, would help me get copies of all the witness statements that had been made by survivors from Bolechow after the war. We got up from the table, kissed Ester good-bye, and went into the hallway, where Shlomo pushed the button for the elevator. As we got into the tiny lift, a neighbor of Shlomo's was getting out. He said something excitedly to Shlomo in Hebrew.

Shlomo turned to us, beaming, and said, They captured Saddam Hussein!

Matt said, This is amazing! He told Shlomo that we'd come home from our first trip for this project, our Ukraine trip, just before 9/11, and then had gone to Australia on the day the war started. And now, Matt said, on our last trip—

I shot him an amused look.

Matt grinned. Well, on what we *thought* was our last trip, they got Saddam Hussein!

Something occurred to me and I said, Where did they find him?

Shlomo spoke briefly with the neighbor.

Shlomo said, They found him in Tikrit.

3

DENMARK

(Winter)

WE SPENT TWO days in Denmark, in mid-winter: a trip that, until quite recently, we really did think would be the last of our travels.

Because we flew out of New York on a Thursday night late in February, arrived on Friday morning, and left on Sunday afternoon, I can tell you relatively little about Copenhagen. For most of Friday afternoon and evening, and then again for nearly all of Saturday, we talked to Adam Kulberg, mostly in the apartment of his daughter, Alena, an art historian with whom, perhaps because like me she is an academic, but possibly because we have other things in common, blood being the least of them, I felt an immediate bond; but also—so that Matt could get a picture that "said" Copenhagen—in a beautiful park in the center of the city, in an allée of tall, funereal trees where, as we stood there, snow began gently to fall. Because we were in that city for such a short time, and because we spent nearly all of that time with Adam and Alena, we can tell you very little about Copenhagen, which was, I felt, a shame, since Denmark stands alone among the nations of Europe as a country with a remarkable record of mostly quiet but stunningly effective resistance to the Nazi anti-Jewish policies, the most spectacular example of which was the successful smuggling, in a single night, of nearly all of the country's eight thousand Jews in small boats to Sweden, with (according to one book I consulted) only four hundred and sixty-four Jews deported to Theresienstadt, a place I did have time to visit. Four hundred and sixty-four out of eight thousand means that six percent of Denmark's Jews perished in the Holocaust, which, although it looks like a cruelly high figure, in purely statistical terms pales in comparison to the figures to be calculated in a place like, say, Bolechow, of whose six thousand Jews—not terribly fewer than the Jewish population of the entire nation of Denmark—there were forty-eight survivors in 1944, which is to say that ninety-nine-point-two percent of the place's Jews were killed. But we had little time to explore Copenhagen, let alone to search out whatever traces of its wartime history there might be. Indeed, you could say that a minor irony of the various trips that Matt and I took in search of Uncle Shmiel and the others is that the only artifact of the famous rescue of Denmark's Jews that we ever saw was not in Denmark but rather in Israel, where one of the tiny little boats that were used to ferry the eight thousand Danish Jews across the water to safety in Sweden is lovingly preserved at Yad Vashem—where, among other things, I did in fact obtain copies of a number of the witness statements that were taken just after the war was over from the few Bolechower Jews who survived, including the statement that ends its description of the behavior of the Jewish police with the following sentence:

Finally, these following four are those who acted miserably in the book of the Jews of Bolechów: Izio Schmer, Henek Kopel, Elo Feintuch ('der bejder'), Lonek Ellenbogen.

Next to this typewritten list there was a handwritten addendum: *And Freilich (Jakub's brother).*

Still, it's true that during the couple of hours Matt and I had free prior to our first meeting with Adam we did wander in the neighborhood around our hotel, which is why, if someone were to say "Copenhagen" to either one of us today, certain images might come to our minds, for instance an image of an elegant little palace with a beautiful cobblestone courtyard through which soldiers in bright, toylike outfits regularly paraded. Or the image of a narrow street of orderly, low-ceilinged early-nineteenth-century houses, one of which turned out to be an antiques shop in which Matt and I spent perhaps half an hour or so after descending the few stone steps to the front door, and in which there hung, among collections of eighteenth-century books and dark old paintings and pewter vessels, an enormous framed copy of the front page of the Thursday, January 13, 1898, edition of the French newspaper *L'Aurore,* on which gigantic black letters shouted the notorious indictment *J'ACCUSE!* But for the most part, the images that come to mind are of the inside of Alena's apartment—and of course the images that her father's astounding narrative would conjure, images like something out of a fairy tale, or a myth. As we sat in the elegant apartment of Adam's daughter, listening to her handsome and dignified and absolutely clear-minded father talk, first over a dinner that stretched late into the evening, then over a lunch that became yet another dinner over the course of an entire day, it became almost difficult at points to remember that we'd come to hear what he had to say about the Jägers, so remarkable, so improbable, so Homeric was the story he had to tell.

Which is not to say that we didn't get what we had come for.

We came to interview Adam on Friday afternoon, a few hours after we flew in. Alena Marchwinski opened the door. An attractive, intense-looking woman in her early fifties, she was wearing her dark hair pulled severely back, and had dressed casually but elegantly in a black open-necked sweater and black slacks. She introduced us to her family, who had crowded into the entrance hall of the apartment to meet us: her husband, Władyslaw, who goes by Władek and who is a concert violinist; their daughter, Alma, a girl of perhaps twelve with a dreamy face and a soft smile; and her parents. I looked at Adam Kulberg, this man who might be my relative. He had the face of a Mayan king: rectangular, a craggy nose, the kind of face that is suited for sculpture. His eyes, though, were gentle as he looked back at me, smiling. He had a full head of snow-white hair that was brushed, like his daughter's, straight back from his high forehead to reveal the strong features. For this special occasion he had donned a dark gray suit over a lighter gray sweater that had slender vertical white stripes; this formality, together with the slicked-back hair and the fact that the points of his open white collar rested neatly above the collar of his sweater, gave this eighty-three-year-old man a curiously fashionable aura.

Our plan was to conduct an interview first and then have our meal. In her spacious living room Alena had set up a small glass-and-steel table in front of the divan where I sat down. On the table she'd placed an assortment of drinks: Evian, sparkling water, fruit juices in small bottles. An entire wall to my left was filled with carefully organized books of the sort that scholars accumulate: multivolume sets of reference works, thick tomes. Catty-corner to it was a wall of large windows. On the sill of the window nearest to us a simple vase held a profusion of flowers. Below another of these windows, slightly off to the right of the group, Adam's wife, Zofia, a very pretty woman with soft white hair, the short cut of which revealed large pearl earrings, was sitting on a small, tufted, Edwardian-looking leather sofa. She was wearing a dark skirted suit with a white blouse and satin jabot at her throat. That night, and then the next day, she smiled often and lovingly as Adam spoke. She had a wide, beatific smile, which it was clear her granddaughter had inherited, and she used it often.

Alena and her father sat down next to each other and directly across from me as I checked my recording equipment, she lounging comfortably in a dark-stained wicker armchair, he sitting erect in one of the dining table chairs that had been brought in for him. Behind them, through a large window, the weak but plentiful afternoon light streamed in. To my right sat Alena's husband, a tall, handsome, reserved man who looked Nordic despite the fact that he, like his wife and in-laws, was born in Poland and had, like his in-laws, like the

Freilichs, like Ewa, like many Jews who had stayed in Poland after the war was over, left for Scandinavia in the late Sixties. Władek listened quietly as his wife and father-in-law talked, intervening only to translate for Adam whenever Alena left the sitting room to check on dinner. Throughout our long visit, Alena often smoked, with an un-American lack of apology or self-consciousness. Now, after everyone had settled into chairs and sofas, she lighted a cigarette and we began to chat.

For a few minutes we discussed the progress of the war, which was a sensitive subject just then if you were an American traveling in Europe, where the war was not popular—although, to be sure, the subject was not as sensitive as it would become eight weeks later, after the revelations about prisoner abuse by American soldiers, a subject I would have liked to be able to discuss with Adam Kulberg and the others, in fact. The reason I would have liked to bring this subject up was this: among the abuses said to have taken place was a certain bizarre humiliation that took the form of forcing the naked prisoners to climb on top of each other in order to form a living pyramid. When I first read about this in the papers, two months after I returned from Copenhagen, I was struck forcefully by this detail, since I remembered of course the detail, one of the first we ever learned about the Nazi torture of Bolechow's Jews, that Olga in Bolechow had told us about, that August day in 2001: how, during the first Aktion, the Germans and Ukrainians had forced naked Jews in the Dom Katolicki to climb on top of one another, forming a human pyramid with the rabbi at the top. What was it, I wondered when I read about Abu Ghraib, what was this impulse to degrade that took the specific form of building pyramids with human flesh? But after a while it occurred to me that this particular type of degradation was a perfect if perverted symbol of the abandonment of civilized values; since after all the impulse to pile one thing atop another, the impulse to build, the impulse—spread across continents and civilizations—to build pyramids, whether in Egypt or Peru, can be seen as the earliest expression of the mysterious human instinct to create, to make something out of nothing, to be civilized. I, who had once spent so much time reading about the Egyptians, sat and read the newspaper on an April morning in 2004 and looked at the fuzzy photograph of the ungainly naked human pyramid, which for all we know was how certain Jews in the Dom Katolicki looked on October 28, 1941, and thought, There it all was, contained in this small triangle: the best of human instincts and the worst, the heights of civilization and the depths of bestiality, the making of something out of nothing and the making of nothing out of something. Pyramids of stone, pyramids of flesh.

But that came later. Now, at Alena's flat, we turned our attention to another war, to the past.

First, we found out we were cousins.

Since the day of the phone conversation in Israel that had brought us here, I'd been eager to figure out what the relationship could have been between our families: after returning from our last trip, I'd thoroughly searched through all my genealogical records and could still find no connection between the Jägers of Bolechow and the Friedlers from Rozniatów, Adam's mother's family. I asked if his father's family had been Bolechowers for a long time, and after Alena translated the question, Adam waved a hand behind his left shoulder, beckoning backward. She didn't need to translate that: Yes, a long time. He said he'd known the Jägers from his earliest childhood, and counted out on his thumb, forefinger, and middle finger the names of the Jägers he knew of: *Shmiel. Itzhak.* Someone called *Y'chiel*, perhaps one of the cousins. He knew the wife, Ester, he said: she was beautiful, good-looking. He smiled.

I asked how many girls he thought there were.

Alena talked to her father for a minute and then said, He knew that there were four, but he only knew personally two: and the name of the ones he knew was Lorka—he thinks she was the oldest—and Frydka. They were both good-looking, but they were different. One was light, blond, and the other was dark.

Matt, who was holding the video camera, looked over and shot me a huge smile, which I returned. Adam Kulberg was the first person we'd talked to who knew how many girls there had been. Irrationally, perhaps, this gave him a kind of instant authority in my eyes. It was our last trip. I wanted to believe every word he said.

He said something to Alena, who said to me, He said that he always knew that his family were connected, like a family relation, with the Jägers. He always knew that it was a connection, but he never knew what *kind* of connection.

I had an idea. What was his father's business? I asked. They spoke for a minute or two and Alena said, He had a butcher shop, and over a period of time he eventually had three butcher shops. They were in the center of the town, but one of the shops was not a kosher shop, and this shop was in front of the salt mine, the *salina*. The other shop was just beside the house, and the street address was Szewczenki 2 3, and it was just opposite the Dom Katolicki.

Akegn di DK, across from the DK, Anna Heller Stern and Shlomo had said, that day in her apartment when Shlomo had smacked his hand against his forehead and said, *How did I forget? How I forgot?*

I said, Well, that's the connection. You know, the Jägers were also butchers.

They talked. Alena took a drag on her cigarette, exhaled, and said, He knows where was the butcher shop of Shmiel, next to the Magistrat. Five meters from the Magistrat, he said.

I nodded. In my mind's eye I saw a piece of stationery from the PARKER-JAEGER COMPANY, which had been carefully tucked long ago into a book with a faded blue cloth binding. *67—Bottom. Our store, Left.*

Beside the Magistrat, Alena repeated, Shmiel had the butcher shop. During the 1930s, she went on, translating her father's memories, Shmiel had bought a truck and had started shipping his meat to Lwów, to other Jewish butchers. He had a reputation for being very good in business. He was very clever, very clever in business. And—she listened while her father added something—he was rather well known in the city, in the town.

I smiled but didn't interrupt.

Adam now explained that his uncle, his father's brother, had been Shmiel's driver. His name was Wolf Kulberg. Alena said, And not only did he work for Shmiel but they were living there, in Shmiel's house!

He lived in Shmiel's house?

Adam gestured with his hands, sketching a floor plan. Alena said, To the house of Shmiel they built an extension. So he was living, the brother of his father was living in the extension. And he brought his wife from Lwów, and he rented this room from Shmiel, and lived there with his wife and daughter.

It seemed clear to me at this point that this was the family connection between the Jägers and the Kulbergs that Adam had remembered from his childhood; this would explain why he'd spent time around Shmiel's house, as a boy, and had consequently known them so well: Shmiel the big fish in the small pond, pretty Ester, the daughters—not two, not three, but *four*—of whom he remembered Lorka and Frydka so clearly. The one fair, the other dark.

Adam seemed to be reading my thoughts, and said something to Alena. She said, But if we're connected to the Jägers, he says it's not this, it's because they are *family*, the Jägers and the Kulbergs.

Her father corrected her and she listened for a moment and then said, No, not Kulbergs—Kornblühs.

Adam looked at me and said, *Kornblüh!*

Kornblühs! I repeated excitedly. We're related to them!

No! Alena said, incredulous. He also! His grandmother was a Kornblüh. Ryfka Kornblüh was the mother of his father.

I said, Well that's how we're related. My grandfather's grandmother was a Kornblüh. Neche Kornblüh. She came from a family of butchers, too.

Adam and Zofia watched this exchange, smiling tentatively. Now Alena translated it for her parents, and as she spoke they beamed. Adam talked for a while to his daughter, who nodded occasionally and then told me a story. Ryfka Kornblüh, she said, she lived . . . well, *there* was the Magistrat and *then* the Russian church, and *just* in the neighborhood of the Russian church she was living. He talks about her *very* often. They had a place in the market, with vegetables. And she had sixteen—no, *seventeen* grandchildren! So the grandchildren, when they met, would always make jokes that when they visited her they got the spoiled vegetables—the leftovers. Not that it was true! She died before the war, but her husband died very young. My father is named after him, his name was Abraham Kulberg.

Adam said something. Alena said, But he says that his grandfather when he was born was registered as an illegitimate child, with the mother's, not the father's, name—Abraham Kornblüh, not Abraham Kulberg.

Of course I thought, at that moment, of another document I was familiar with from long ago: the 1847 birth certificate of my grandfather's uncle Ire Jäger. *Der Zuname der unehel. Kindes Mutter ist Kornblüh. The surname of the illegitimate child's mother is Kornblüh.* I asked Alena to tell her father that, by a curious coincidence, in our family, too, there had been this business with "illegitimate" children; and in our case, too, the mother had been a Kornblüh.

So we are related! Alena said, smiling.

I looked at her, at her father, the room, the book-lined walls, not so different from my own apartment. I thought, If you were making this up, it would seem too pat: the man we nearly missed hearing about, the trip we nearly didn't make, the instant sense of connection that we had felt with this family, a university professor and a musician, a family with whom my own family in the States, a family of writers and journalists and filmmakers, of pianists and harpsichordists and, long ago, of violinmakers, had so much in common. And then the discovery, also almost accidental, that this family *were* our family.

I looked at Alena and her father.

We're cousins! I replied.

ON THAT SAME night, after we'd moved from the sitting room to the dining-room table, on which the roast duck that Alena had prepared was now waiting, Adam told us what he knew about Frydka and Ciszko.

He said he knew the Szymanskis very well, that they'd lived in the same neighborhood as the Jägers. Alena paused, and Adam then related an anecdote I'd heard before: that the Szymanskis, who had always been known for having friendly relations with the town's Jews, were known for the excellent Polish sausage they made. Now, as Adam put it, To eat not kosher, or ham, it was a terrible thing!——

(Oh, yes, I thought, we knew)

——a terrible thing. But in the Szymanski shop there was a special room where the Jews would come and, in secret, try a piece of bread with ham.

Adam laughed as he told the story, and Matt said, A secret place!

Szymanskis, a secret place. I asked, What did Ciszko look like?

Adam said that Ciszko had been very big, quite strong. Not tall, but not small either. He had a very good relationship with the Jewish kids in town, Adam said. He didn't wonder that it was Ciszko who'd tried to save Frydka.

I asked Alena to ask her father exactly which story he'd heard. Then I said, No, ask him first *how* he heard it.

Immediately after the war, Adam said, at the very beginning, everybody was hungry for information. So people searched for information, for stories. He said that somebody from Bolechow had made an appointment for the Bolechowers to meet in Katowice after the war, at the beginning of 1946.

It was there, Adam said, that everybody was talking about what had happened to the people they'd known, swapping the stories they'd heard, and this is when he'd first heard the story about Frydka and Shmiel and Ciszko. With an apologetic smile, he added that he didn't remember who he'd heard it from.

But Meg Grossbard had been at that meeting, he added.

I said to Alena, Tell him that Meg isn't telling the story.

Alena gave me a puzzled look and said, She doesn't remember?

I explained to her about Meg, how in Australia she'd refused to talk about it.

I told her something that had happened more recently, only last month, two weeks after I'd returned from Israel . . .

THE PHONE HAD rung late one evening in my apartment in New York: it was Meg. The connection wasn't terribly good, but even so I could hear the tightness in her voice.

I have to come to Frydka's defense, she announced after we'd said hello. She went on, There is nobody to defend her now.

I immediately saw what was going on. Somehow she'd found out that I'd heard the story that Frydka was pregnant.

They're only stories, Meg said. They can't be proved. Just write the *facts*.

I told her that I, too, was interested in facts, of course, that we had started out on this long series of journeys because we wanted to find the facts. But I said that because of what we'd heard on our trips, I'd also become extremely interested in stories, in the way that the stories multiplied and gave birth to other stories, and that even if these stories weren't true, they were interesting because of what they revealed about the people who told them. What they revealed about the people who told them, I said, was also part of the facts, the historical record.

I said, Some stories aren't the *whole story*.

Meg said, And what is behind these stories? I can tell you lots of stories of what is behind these stories. There are personal grudges. If someone didn't like your family, they told a story.

It was as if she were reading my thoughts, which at that moment had nothing to do with the information that she claimed to find so scandalous: that Frydka had been pregnant with Ciszko's child. But of course I didn't say anything.

She said, And how did they know she was pregnant? Who saw her? Who *saw* her? If somebody knew about it, she knew it, and Ciszko knew it, and that would be all.

In Anna Heller Stern's apartment, Shlomo had told me a story about a man he'd known from another town who'd been a member of the Jewish police in that town. He did not behave nicely (Shlomo had said) but had started his life over, had joined the Polish army. Apparently during the time this former Jewish policeman was in hiding, after he'd run away from the Jewish police, run away from this town to save himself, he'd written down an account of everything he'd seen.

He wrote them when he was hiding in a cellar, Shlomo had said. Very, very strong words! *Very*. It says only things that *he* saw, things that *they* saw that nobody else saw, nobody was able to see. He described some things that were *horrible*.

I thought of this and wanted to say to Meg that a Jewish policeman could have seen that Frydka was pregnant, on the day she was dragged from her hiding place in the house of the art teacher, Mrs. Szedlak (or, as Adam also referred to her, Szedlakowa); but of course I couldn't, now, bring up the subject of Jewish police. So I said nothing.

Meg said, If people talk, it's just orally. But when you see the written word, it's different.

I said, I know.

. . . So Meg wasn't going to share the story, I now told Alena with a wry smile, as we sat in her dining room in Copenhagen.

Matt said, But what was the story he heard?

Adam and Alena talked for a while. She said, He heard that Ciszko tried to help her. And the idea was that Frydka and her papa should hide by Szedlakowa.

"Her papa" had a strong effect on me, for some reason, and for a moment I couldn't say anything. It's all he'd been, in the end, all and everything: somebody's papa, a dad. I thought this, and then I registered her use of the word *by*. "By Szedlakowa." *Zey zent behalten bay a lererin.*

Alena said, She was a teacher. Then she said, disconcertingly, I'm so sorry, it's a cliché!——

I had no idea what she was talking about.

It's a cliché, but I have to go check the oven! I grinned with relief and Alena got out of her chair and darted off to check on the dessert. While she was gone, her mother spoke up, and in halting but forceful English finished translating what Adam had said.

And they was together, Frydka with Ciszko, by the teacher Szedlakowa. Somebody say this to the Germans, and Germany killed both Frydka and Ciszko. He hear, but if the story is true or not he cannot say.

Germany, she had said, although I knew she meant *Germans*. Well, I thought: either way.

She was hiding in the house of this teacher?

Yes, in the house, Zofia said.

I nodded and said, So the story is that this woman had Frydka in her house, and also Ciszko?

Alena took her seat again and said, Yes. No. He said Ciszko was only visiting Frydka, and bringing her things, food, whatever, but he was not staying there, he hid her there. What happened to that Szedlakowa, my father does not know. He only knows that they killed her and Ciszko.

Alena passed me a platter and, leaning toward me, said, It's a heroic story!

As we all started eating dessert, she turned to me and said, But how will you tell it? Before I had a chance to answer, she told me about some friends she had in New York, people her age, whose family had stories—*terrible stories,* she said—about the war. Now these people had a child, Alena went on, a daughter in her early twenties, who'd just taken her degree in literature, and who had written her thesis about her grandmother, the one who'd suffered those terrible things. Alena said that this young woman had given her the thesis to read, and while reading it she had been struck by something.

She said, It was like what she was interested in was not so much the story of her grandmother but how to *tell* the story of her grandmother—how to be the storyteller.

I thought of my grandfather and said that, yes, it was a very interesting problem.

She described how caught up in the thesis she'd become, against her initial expectations. With great animation she said, I felt that when I was reading it, like in the end, it got closer and closer to the important things, the things about the war. At first it was as if she was telling a common story, a story everybody could tell, but it got narrower and narrower.

After a moment I said yes, that's how my grandfather used to tell stories. The long windup, all that background, all those Chinese boxes; and then, suddenly, the swift and expert slide into the finale, the finish line where the connections between all the details you'd learned along the way, the seemingly irrelevant facts and subsidiary anecdotes he'd lingered over at the beginning, suddenly became clear.

I said to Alena, I know, I know. This girl she knows, I thought, must be very clever. So many people know these horrible stories by now, after all; what more was there to say? How to tell them? One way, I supposed, was to get narrower and narrower toward the end, the way my grandfather did.

At that moment Alena said, Narrower, yes. It's always the small things. It makes it like life. The most interesting thing is always the details.

I said to Alena, It's a very tricky, a tricky problem. But, I went on, the story we learned on this trip was a far more dramatic story than anything we could have dreamed of, when we first started looking for information. It's a story that would, as we say in English, tell itself.

To myself I thought that this was a bit of a lie: here we were at the end of all our travels, and still I had no definitive story to tell. The finale was still lacking, the one thing that would lock it into place, account for all the discrepant versions: Ciszko hid her, a schoolteacher hid her, she was pregnant, she was pregnant by someone but not by Ciszko. I know nussink, I see nussink. But even as I thought this I also thought, For whose benefit, exactly, is the wholeness that I want so desperately? The dead need no stories: that is the fantasy of the living, who unlike the dead feel guilt. Even if they did need stories, surely *my* dead, Shmiel and Ester and the girls, had much more of a story now, and far, far more details, than anyone could have dreamed of even two years ago; surely that counted for something, if as some people think the dead need to be appeased. But of course I don't believe this: the dead lie in their graves, in the cemeteries or the forests or roadside ditches, and all this is of no interest to them, since they have, now, no interests of any kind at all. It is we, the living, who need the details, the stories, because what the dead no longer care about, mere fragments, a picture that will never be whole, will drive the living mad. Literally mad. My grandfather had a nervous breakdown in middle age, not too long after that day in 1946 when my mother came home from school and found him sobbing with his head in his arms at the kitchen table of their apartment in the Bronx, a letter like none other he had received from Bolechow in all those years of writing back and forth to Shmiel—a correspondence of which we have, after all, only one half, and of which the other half could have consisted of letters saying *Dear Brother, We have tried everything but cannot come up with the money, but we will not give up*, or then again *Why don't you ask Ester's brothers first?*: an incompleteness that, while I would never claim that it's driven me mad, has kept me up on certain nights. My grandfather had a nervous breakdown when he was not much older than I am now, and I'm not so sure anymore that it was about business pressures, as I have heard, just as I am no longer completely certain that when he killed himself, that Friday the thirteenth in Miami Beach, it was only a cancer that was eating away at him.

I thought all this but what I said was, yes, a heroic story! We never could have imagined where it would take us! (I meant *geographically,* and implied *emotionally*. But I also thought, *morally,* since I'd now seen how these facts and stories could force you, almost against your will, to judge people.) For instance, I said to Alena, we were now trying to find relatives of Ciszko Szymanski, although as she well knew, Szymanski was a common name in Poland. Laughing, I told them how, leafing through the program of a ballet performance I'd attended a few months earlier, I'd noticed that one of the dancers was named Szymanska, and that she came from Wrocław, where we knew Ciszko's mother had gone after the war; and how I'd raced backstage and accosted this slender blond girl, who couldn't have been more than twenty-five, and started spilling the entire story of Frydka and Ciszko until I realized I was being ridiculous.

Everybody chuckled, and Alena said, They were in Wrocław?

We told her to tell her father the story we'd heard from Malcia Reinharz, about how Ciszko's mother had bewailed her young son's foolishness. *How stupid he was!*

Matt said, He did a good thing! And his family was upset with him for doing a good thing! I looked at him with a sudden stab of affection. It was the same furious, outraged purity that he'd had in high school.

And yet, as I remembered Malcia's anecdote, I remembered Josef Adler saying, It was *complicated*. I thought of Mrs. Szymanski's outburst, and then thought of stories we'd just heard in Stockholm, heard in Israel. If it was impossible, grotesque, for us, for me or Matt or anyone of our idle generation, to sit in judgment on the emotions of these Jews whose stories we'd been hearing, maybe it was also impossible to sit in judgment on Mrs. Szymanski, who had cried out *How stupid he was!* when she recalled how he had died for a Jewish girl.

Well, I murmured, she lost her *child*.

Matt was indignant. But he acted like a human *being*!

ONCE AGAIN, WE made ourselves comfortable around Alena's table. We showed Adam some more photographs. Shmiel and Ester on their wedding day, surrounded by hydrangeas. Shmiel with his fur-collared coat. The three girls in the white lace dresses. Frydka in her scarf; Ruchele with her wavy, Mittelmark hair. Shmiel standing in front of one of his trucks with Ester and her brother Bumek Schneelicht.

Adam picked up this blurry snapshot, in which Shmiel was already white-haired, looking far more than his forty-five years but smiling and thrusting his hands into his overcoat pockets with a self-confident, proprietary air, and said, *To jest Shmiel*. This is Shmiel. He turned and said something to his daughter, who said to me, This is Shmiel as he remembers him. He says he would recognize Shmiel Jäger anywhere.

I like to think, now, that it was because of Matt's presence that, when I showed this man these particular pictures, I took care to ask him about the feelings they evoked in him.

I said to Alena, Ask him how does it feel to see these faces that he hasn't seen in such a long time.

She translated this into Polish, and Adam took off his glasses carefully and thought for a moment. Then he smiled gently and said, I am thinking, and I am going back to the past. I feel like I am on my way to heaven.

Every Bolechower we had talked to until that night had survived by not moving: by staying perfectly still for days and weeks and months in attics, in haylofts, in cellars, in secret compartments, in holes dug into the forest floor, and in the strangest, most confining prison of all, the fragile prison of a false identity. The last story of survival we were to hear was, like a story you might hear in an epic poem, a Greek myth, a story of perpetual movement, of ceaseless wandering.

On the day of his twentieth birthday, Adam Kulberg left Bolechow. He told us that night that he'd always had what he thought of as an "instinct for information," and his instinct, after the Germans started surging through eastern Poland on the twentieth of June, was to leave his hometown and travel east into the Soviet Union with the retreating Russians. He had no job that summer; he was young, he was restless. There had been stories from towns farther away, stories of Jews being shot in cemeteries. Few people believed the stories, but still, he told us, he had his *instinct*. He tried to persuade his parents that the whole family should leave—his mother and father, himself, his three sisters Chana, Perla, and Sala, girls who were roughly the age of Shmiel's daughters Frydka, Ruchele, and Bronia. But his father, who hated the Russians, resisted. As his son argued with him, Salamon Kulberg said *No*. He gave Adam his blessing, but refused to budge. We are born here, the father said. Here is our house, and here we will stay.

How can you leave a home? Malcia Reinharz had exclaimed in Beer Sheva.

On his twentieth birthday, Adam said good-bye to his family, kissing each of them in turn as they lined up in the kitchen. As he turned to leave, he impetuously grabbed three photographs. He has them still. In one of them, his youngest sister, Sala, is wearing a watch that, as he realized on his millionth scrutiny of this rare relic of what his life had been, although he had coveted it for a long time and bought it with money he'd painstakingly saved, he had nonetheless let his sister wear.

So maybe I am a good brother after all! he said to Matt and me with a little smile, when he told us about this picture. He produced the photograph in question, so worn by now that the lost girl's features are all but unimaginable to anyone but Adam himself.

Adam left his father's house—which he would see again just after the war, a little bit older and transformed by his remarkable travels, although the house itself when he saw it again was, he later said to me, utterly unchanged; it was as if somebody had been cooking a meal, had been interrupted, and was planning to come back in a few minutes, which for all we know may well have been the case—he left this house, which would remain almost unchanged even though everything else would change, or at least ninety-nine-point-two percent of everything else, and started walking east. He was accompanied, at first, by two friends who had also had an instinct to leave. One was called Ignacy Taub; the surname, I know, means *dove*. The other was a boy named Zimmerman, but after a few days on the dusty road to Russia this Zimmerman boy started crying and said he missed his family, and so he turned back and went home. The next, and perhaps last, time that a boy named Zimmerman appears in the narrative of Bolechow is when, in the winter of 1942, Meg Grossbard expressed surprise, during a clandestine visit to the place where her friend Dusia Zimmerman lived, on seeing that Lorka Jäger had taken up with Dusia's brother Yulek Zimmerman, a boy that Meg would never have guessed might be Lorka's type. Yulek Zimmerman was killed in a "small" action that took place in 1943.

So Bumo—as we now must call him, since he was traveling with a friend and all of his friends called him not Adam but *Bumo*—so Bumo Kulberg and Ignacy Taub started walking. They kept to the smaller roads and every day walked farther east, making sure to keep an eye out for the other traffic: if they saw Russian troops, they knew they were, for the most part, safe. They kept walking and walking, and after a while their course took a southerly turn. They had hit upon a plan: they would walk to Palestine, taking a route through the Caucasus, then south to Iran, and then through Iran, where they would turn westward and penetrate into Palestine.

Palestine? you might exclaim, as Matt and I did when we heard the beginning of Adam's tale. Adam smiled self-deprecatingly. We were young, he said.

After three months, sometimes hitching rides, sometimes jumping on trains, Bumo and Ignacy reached the Caucasus, where they paused and worked for a while at a tobacco farm. It was very hard work, but they were strong and young and, he had to admit, the weather was wonderful. The trees were heavy with fruit, they didn't go hungry. At the collective farm they had a room with two beds. Everything was spotless. The walls were immaculate, whitewashed. They were even paid a little bit. The place was beautiful, remote. A place where they had many horses, Adam remembered as he spoke. Famous for Cossacks.

They were in Groznyy. In three months, Bumo and Ignacy had walked from Poland to Chechnya. Although it seemed incredible that there was a war going on—the beautiful weather, the fruit, the clean beds and hard, decent work—Bumo's pillow was wet with tears every night. He missed his family, and he realized, now, that he was very far from home. At night, he would take out his three photographs and talk to them.

SOON THEY HEARD that the Germans were coming, and after talking it over the two youths decided that since they hadn't stayed at home in Bolechow to wait for the Germans to come, they weren't going to stay in Groznyy, either, however improbably idyllic it was. The local people and their fellow workers on the collective were sad to see them go: they were good workers, and everyone else was in the army. But the boys were firm. They took their back pay and started walking again. Sometimes they traveled by train. The surroundings were beautiful, Adam recalled. Like a *Kurort*. A spa. The two young men continued heading east through these breathtakingly lovely spots toward the Caspian Sea.

It was around the time Bumo and Ignacy were traveling through the tiny Soviet

Socialist Republic of Daghestan that Ruchele Jäger was made to stand naked on a plank that had been laid over a hastily dug ditch in a place called Taniawa.

In Makhachkala, the big port city of Daghestan that lies on the western shore of the vast Caspian Sea, Bumo and Ignacy found thousands of war refugees. It was very difficult to get food; nobody had any money. Despite these conditions, Adam and Ignacy, with little more than the clothes on their backs, and, of course, the three precious photographs, gaped at the exotic locals, whose everyday wear included enormous swords.

Sabers! Big swords! They were allowed to wear them! Bumo exclaimed. Even now, he shook his head in disbelief.

The city of Makhachkala was, Bumo thought, very beautiful, built like a cascade that dropped gradually into the sea. For three or four weeks they lingered there, waiting for a chance to get on a boat that would take them across the sea; they would continue heading east. The wait seemed endless. Soviet military personnel and their families had priority, thousands of women and children also fleeing east. Bumo and Ignacy spent hours and days loitering around the harbor, waiting to get on a ship. Finally they decided that in the event that only one of them could go, he should do so, and then wait on the other side until his friend joined him. This is what happened. Bumo went first, illegally. It took two days in unbearably crowded conditions to reach the other side, the port city of Krasnovodsk in Turkmenistan. The temperature was forty-five degrees Celsius—one hundred thirteen degrees Fahrenheit. It was, he said, like the Sahara. Krasnovodsk was known as the city without water, because the water in the Caspian Sea is salt water. Undrinkable. So water was rationed.

At around the time that Bumo was exploring the brutally hot city without water, Frydka Jäger somehow managed to get herself a place working inside the barrel factory, which wasn't a bad thing, given how severe the Carpathian winter was.

In Krasnovodsk, Frydka's distant cousin Bumo Kulberg got himself a job in the harbor as a longshoreman, hauling things off of ships, and waited for Ignacy Taub to appear.

After a month, Ignacy came. Although both of them could have had jobs in Krasnovodsk, they kept moving. It was too hot, and there were problems with the water. They knew that the most important thing was to stay healthy. So they decided to go farther, to Ashgabat, on the Turkmeni-Iranian border. They sneaked onto trains and in that manner passed through the terrible Kara-Kum Desert in Central Turkmenistan, a place so barren that the few train stations they saw had not names, but numbers.

THE CENTRAL ASIAN DESERT

THEY ARRIVED AT Ashgabat in the evening. Here again, even this far, there were refugees everywhere: Ukrainians, White Russians. At the station people asked where they were going, might they be able to be of assistance; but of course Bumo and Ignacy knew that they couldn't reveal that they wanted to pass through Iran to Palestine. And so they said nothing. Ashgabat was only fourteen kilometers from the Iranian border.

It was now early in 1942. As the two Bolechow boys hovered tantalizingly close to the land of the Peacock Throne, terrified even to mention where they yearned to go, a nineteen-year-old girl who would grow up to be Meg Grossbard laid eyes on Lorka Jäger for the last time at the home of their mutual friend Dusia Zimmerman, who herself, in time, would come to know something about the wisdom of total discretion.

In Ashgabat, news of the larger world was scarce. Soviet radio was useless propaganda, and listening to the BBC was a dangerous crime. The two boys loitered and eventually found a place to stay. As it happened, the day after they found lodgings they met somebody from Poland who was working in a barbershop. He had some information. Ashgabat, this Polish man said, was closed because of its proximity to the Iranian border; there was no use trying to go any farther. Bumo himself had seen the soldiers regularly patrolling the borders, but still he and Ignacy tried. They started walking from Ashgabat toward Iran. After a few hours, a border patrol stopped them. They were told that they had to turn back; surprisingly, they were treated rather gently. The border soldiers bought tickets for the two Bolechow boys and said to them, You are not allowed to be here.

So they kept going. Throughout the year of 1942, the boys made their way northeast, cutting through the width of Turkmenistan, through the Kara-Kum Desert and across the Amu Darya River into Uzbekistan. At around the time Bumo Kulberg and Ignacy Taub were crossing the Amu Darya, Ester Jäger and her thirteen-year-old daughter Bronia were being shoved into the cattle car that would take them to Belzec, where they would expire in a gas chamber and where, immediately after their deaths, the mouths, vaginas, and rectums of their corpses would be pried open and searched for valuables before the bodies were thrown in a pit, only to be exhumed months later—at about the time that Bumo and Ignacy were ogling the sights of the legendary Silk Road city of Samarkand—and incinerated, after it was felt that this was a more advisable means of disposal for those two bodies and the six hundred thousand other Jewish bodies that had been buried along with them.

A few months later Bumo and Ignacy were nearing Tashkent, and it was at about this time that the young woman who was born Chaya Heller but who, because of the courageous goodness of a priest in Lublin, Poland, would one day be called Anna Heller Stern, turned to her school friend Lorka Jäger and said, *Come, give me a kiss, who knows when we will see each other again?*

By the beginning of 1943, when the *W*'s were liquidated in Bolechow, Ester and Bronia's onetime neighbors were in Tashkent, in the far eastern corner of Uzbekistan. At the time, it was the largest city in Central Asia, a city of two million people. Some time later, around the time the *R*'s were being liquidated, Bumo, traveling alone, reached Frunze—the present-day Bishkek—the capital of Kyrgyzstan.

It was very interesting! Adam exclaimed. He grinned modestly, as if to say, Anyone would have done the same. He said, I was twenty-one years old!

Did he ever think of how amazing all this was while it was happening? I asked.

Alma talked to her father. No, she said. He says it was his fate.

Wait, Matt said. Why was Bumo traveling *alone* in Frunze?

Because, he explained, he and Ignacy, like all the other travelers and refugees who surged through the cities of Central Asia during the war, were in the habit of stopping in the bazaar of each city and town they passed through, to ask for news of the world and look for the friendly faces of foreigners like themselves. And in one of these bazaars, in one of these places, Ignacy Taub had run into his family from Bolechow.

This is a true story, Adam said.

I didn't doubt that it was. I thought of the man in the elevator in Prague, on the day Froma and I came back from Theresienstadt, who had turned to us and said, out of the blue, *Yes, I was in Babi Yar.* The woman in Beth Hatefutsoth who had turned out to be Yona. The woman in a flea market in New York City who, one summer day as she was trying to sell me a piece of fabric, cocked her head to one side and suddenly said to me, You lost someone in the Holocaust, didn't you? I thought of Shlomo, asking me in the car on the way to Beer Sheva, Have you ever heard from a Bolechower, a famous American journalist called Kraut-hammer? and my saying No, I had only heard from a famous American editor named Wieseltier; and then Yona turning to me and saying her name was *Wieseltier.* Maybe there were no coincidences, I thought. Or perhaps it was just a statistical issue. Maybe there were so many Jewish ghosts that you were bound, in the end, to run into one.

FINE-LOOKING SARTS IN OLD TASHKENT

After he said good-bye to Ignacy, in this bazaar in Kyrgyzstan, Adam said, he met two people from Bolechow. He didn't remember in which city he said good-bye to Ignacy, but it was midway through 1943, which is to say when the last of the Jews of Bolechow were being liquidated; and he knew it was at the Chinese border. Another way of putting this is to say that by the time that Bumo Kulberg, a Jewish youth from a small town in Poland, reached China, there were no Jews left in Bolechow, apart from those who were living in cellars and attics and haylofts and holes dug into forest floors. Among these hidden Jews, at least for a little while, were, we think, Shmiel and Frydka Jäger.

With his two new Bolechower friends—one of whom, I may as well mention, was named Naphtali Krauthammer—Bumo had heard that at some distance from where they then were there was a camp for refugees from Poland, located in a place on the northern border of Uzbekistan called Tokmok. At this point Bumo had decided that he wanted to make contact with Poles, because now, after his original plan to reach Palestine had been thwarted, he was eager to find out where he could find the Anders Army, the Polish battalion that had been formed in 1941, after the Germans turned on the Soviet Union and Stalin realized that the many Poles who were then languishing in Soviet jails would be put to better use fighting Germans. The exploits of this unit were already legendary, and Bumo had heard that a captain in the Tokmok refugee camp was planning to go to Iran to join the Anders Army.

Travel from Frunze to Tokmok was, however, difficult. There were no easy roads, and the terrain was mountainous; some peaks were as high as five or six thousand meters. From one dwelling to another, the grown-up Bumo recalled, it was several kilometers. They weren't even houses: they were *yurts,* the portable dwellings, made of felt and saplings, long used by the nomads of the Central Asian steppes. As Bumo and Naphtali and Abraham walked toward Tokmok there was a violent sandstorm, and they were forced to take refuge in a *yurt* inhabited by a young couple with a small child. These kindly local people offered food to the three strange-looking men: a kind of pastalike dough that had been filled with lamb. It was delicious.

At about the time that Bumo was relishing this savory meal, Ciszko Szymanski, as I later found out, was shouting, *If you kill her, then you should kill me, too!*

And they did.

THE YOUNG COUPLE offered the three men a place to sleep. They gave them mattresslike rolls to put next to the oven: the place of honor. It was dreadfully hot during the day, but bitter cold at night. The next day the Uzbek nomads showed them the way they needed to go: across a river called Chu. Off they went. When they came to the place it was filled with other refugees. The three Bolechow men found employment with a veterinarian who lived in a beautiful house with a garden and a sauna. A garden! They worked in the garden. Soon it became clear that the rumor they'd heard about the captain who could lead them to the Anders Army was empty. Although the three of them lived relatively well and had plenty of food to eat, a typhus epidemic broke out in the camp. A quarantine was imposed. After the quarantine was lifted, the three decided to leave. They went to another place they'd heard of, called Antonufka, where there was another camp for Poles. When they arrived, it was clear that the camp was run on a military model. There were military tents. The people who took refuge there earned their keep by doing hard work in stone quarries. Discipline was strict: every morning there was a reveille. Bumo soon realized that here, too, there seemed to be little chance of finding someone who could help him make contact with the Anders Army. The people who ran the camp said that anyone who wanted to work had permission to return to Frunze; it was all right to leave. So Bumo went back to Frunze and got work in a factory that manufactured farm equipment. The boss of the company was a lawyer from Kraków named Ravner. He was married to a beautiful Uzbek woman and with her had had two children.

As Adam Kulberg told this story on a snowy night early in 2004 in Denmark, I thought of another story of an unlikely marriage I'd once heard, about that Jew named Shmiel Jäger from Dolina who'd married an Uzbek woman and had children with her who, as far as anyone knows, still live in Uzbekistan with their children and grandchildren, all of whom have a certain gene that, most likely, is a gene remotely connected to certain genes that I and my brothers and sister all have.

It was here, in Frunze, that Bumo became ill for the first time. Realizing one night that he probably had appendicitis, he walked to the hospital, where an emergency surgery was performed on him. Because supplies were limited, Bumo received only a local anesthetic for this procedure, which is why he was able to watch as they cut him open and removed his bursting appendix. As he went into the operating room Bumo entrusted his most valuable possessions—most valuable not merely because they were, at that point, his only possessions—to a kindly nurse who had offered to take care of them if anything happened to him. For it was still true that even now, he talked to the photographs of his family every night. The kindly woman took the pictures and, as she promised she would, stored them carefully until he was well enough to leave. The woman was German, the wife of a Russian officer.

After he recovered, Bumo Kulberg was determined to find an army unit, any army unit, with which he could fight. With the other two men he began retracing his fantastic steps. From Frunze they journeyed westward, back to Tashkent. It was here that Bumo rested for a while. For ten months, he worked at a Soviet champagne factory in Tashkent.

A Soviet champagne factory in Tashkent?! Matt and I both exclaimed at the same time, laughing. Well, why not? We had drunk Soviet champagne in Nina's cramped living room in Bolechow as her husband had played "Yesterday" on his rickety piano, had drunk it and had been incredulous that there was even such a thing as Soviet champagne.

Finally, Bumo heard the news that he'd been longing for: some local people told him that they knew where he could apply to join the Polish regiment. He applied. Two weeks later, he was on a train from Tashkent to Moscow to a place called Divovo on the Oka River, where the unit was being trained, and where he happened to run into Amir Sapirstein, a famous thief from Bolechow. The young recruits lived in a vast forest. Their heads were shaved. Discipline was severe. Late in 1943, at which point Shumek and Malcia Reinharz and Jack Greene and his brother and father and Anna Heller Stern and Klara and Yankel Freilich and Josef and Shlomo Adler and Dyzia Lew were all sealed tightly and silently into their hiding places, Bumo Kulberg, in a forest by the Oka River, watched as three other young men who, like him, had thought that they wanted to become fighters against the Germans, but unlike him had tried to desert, were executed in a clearing in the wood. One was a Jew from Warsaw. It was so cold that the faces of the three bound men, who begged the commander for their lives at that point and promised they would fight for Poland, were, Adam remembered, the color of violets.

In December Bumo was heading west toward the front. They stopped in Kiev. Berdetsov. They kept going west. They entered Polish territory. The weeks went by. He was in Lublin where, unbeknownst to him, his former neighbor Chaya Heller was pretending each day to be a Catholic girl called Anna Kucharuk; he was in Majdanek. A mere four kilometers from the center of Lublin, Majdanek was a camp that had begun life as an SS-run POW camp at around the time the first Aktion was taking place in Bolechow, but six months later became the site of killing operations that lasted until July 1944, by which time three hundred sixty thousand Jews, Poles, and prisoners of war had been gassed there. In Majdanek, Bumo found, everything had been burned; the Germans were covering their tracks. When he and the others got there, the crematoria were still hot. Bumo walked through the camp and saw, he said, *mountains of suitcases, mountains of photographs* that had once been keepsakes of the lives of Jews and were now indecipherable rubbish. For reasons he couldn't quite explain, he took a few photographs and saved them.

He kept going. From September 1944 until January 1945 he sat with his army across the Vistula from Warsaw doing nothing, although the Soviet army, with its little Polish regiments, was supposed to be the ally of the Poles of Warsaw who were attempting to rise against the Germans; doing nothing because Stalin, who was already considering the postwar picture, wasn't interested in having a brave and active Polish resistance around after Germany had been crushed. It was at this time that Bumo Kulberg became an officer. After the Warsaw Uprising had been stomped to nothing, his army ground ahead into German territory. From April 15 to 16, 1945, Bumo fought in the offensive against Berlin. In some tiny part because Bumo Kulberg, a boy from Bolechow, was fighting there, Berlin fell.

And so the war in Europe was over, and with it the Holocaust. What had begun the night of November 9, 1938, on *Kristallnacht*, had finally come to an end. Bumo Kulberg was not quite twenty-four years old. In Bolechow, the number of Jews who had emerged from their attics and cellars and chicken coops and forest bunkers was precisely forty-eight.

Nearly sixty years later, the old man who young Bumo would become finished telling this story by saying, I am not the only one, there were thousands of Jews fighting in all the armies of the world.

He paused and added, So I do not feel that I am something exceptional.

DURING ALL THIS time, during all these adventures, Bumo had no idea what had become of his family. He had traveled and traveled, had walked across a good part of Asia, always thinking about his mother and father and Chana and Perla and Sala, but never knowing what had happened. As he sat with the Soviet army outside of Warsaw through the late months of 1944, this thought possessed him. He wrote a letter to a Polish family he knew well in Bolechow, called Kendelski, who had been his neighbors before he'd left town and begun his journey. He addressed the letter to Bronia Kendelska, but it was from her sister Maria that he finally received a reply, as Berlin fell.

Adam Kulberg has this letter still, and that evening in Copenhagen he took it carefully in his hands and read it aloud to me and Matt. He would read a sentence or a phrase, and then Alena would translate, occasionally offering commentary at points where she thought it necessary.

The letter sounded like this:

> Dear Bumo
>   In answer to your letter,
>   I would like to tell you

that in the first Aktion
the 28th of October '41
the Germans killed
all your sisters.
And in the last Aktion
in Autumn '43
they killed your parents.
In Bolechow is only forty people of your faith left.
In your house is living
Kubrychtowa
who took the house even during the German occupation.

(Alena stopped for a moment and said, This Kubrychtowa woman claimed that the house was the property of her parents! Then she went on reading.)

By us, a lot of changes.
You cannot describe them.
Sister Bronia——my sister Bronia——
together with my mother
are in Rzeszów.
Of the Israelites——

("*Israelites,*" Alena interrupted, I must say to you that in Polish when you say "Israelites," it sounds very curious, like you don't want to mention the word *Jews.* So you say Israelites)——

Of the Israelites
the only people that are left
are the son of Salka Eisenstein,
Hafter, Grünschlag, Kahane, Mondschein,
and a lot of others
that I don't know—the names are not known to me.
Try to come
so you will know a lot of things.
I am ending then.
Greetings,
Regards,
Kendelska Maria, Bolechów 7 December '44.

That was the end of the letter. Adam stopped reading and Alena stopped translating. There was a little silence. Then she said, It's the letter that changed my father's life, you know?

We remained silent. Adam said something to Alena, who then said to us, He says that in first years after the war, whenever he was going somewhere by train, he would always watch all the faces because he always thought, Maybe I will recognize somebody, somebody from my family.

Adam watched her translate this and said after a moment, I always look at the few pictures of them, and every night I say good night to the family, the Bolechow family.

Alena paused and then said to me, *I* am saying this to you: my father is living with those people every day, they are very real and very alive for him. Looking at the pictures, every night, saying good-bye to them.

I, who had spent three years searching for people I could never know, said nothing. Matt said, Let me take his picture holding the letter.

Adam got up slowly, and they went over to the window. Once again I heard the *k-shonck* of the shutter of his Hasselblad. Then they returned to the table, and it was time for us to go. We'd spent far more time talking about Adam's adventures than about Uncle Shmiel; but in the end it didn't seem to matter. There were no more stories to tell.

As we were getting up from the table and gathering our things, I had the feeling that there was something I wasn't remembering. Just as we got to the door, I thought of what it was.

Ask your father, I turned and told Alena, if he wanted someone who was reading my book to know something about Bolechow, one thing that should be remembered, what would it be?

She relayed the question to her father, and after she stopped speaking a faint smile played on his lips. Then he said something slowly, three cadenced phrases in Polish that he recited in an almost ecclesiastical rhythm. Alena listened to her father and then looked up at me and translated the answer, an answer, I thought, that was worthy of someone who had seen more of the vast world than any Homeric hero.

She said, He says, There were the Egyptians with their pyramids. There were the Incas of Peru. And there was the Jews of Bolechow.

We flew home the next day. As it happened, it was February 29: a day that mostly doesn't exist, a day that, like a ghost ship in a story, materializes out of nothingness only to disappear again before you've had a chance to grasp what it is; a day outside of time itself.

Lech Lecha, *the* parashah *that relates in great detail the exhausting and depleting travels that Abram, later Abraham, the father of the Jewish people, had to undertake in order to reach the land that God has promised to him—travels that, we learn, include harrowing and violent encounters with the battling chieftains of the territories among which Abraham and his kin must one day dwell, places like Sodom and Gomorrah, places where terrible wickedness dwells—this* parashah, *so filled with movement and turmoil and violence, ends on an uncharacteristic note of stillness. One day, when Abraham is ninety-nine years old and has still not fathered a son by his wife, Sarah, God appears to him and announces two important pieces of news. First, God declares that he has decided to establish a convenant with Abraham and his descendants, to whom God promises vast tracts of land in an eternal possession. And second, he announces to the old man, who thus far has only produced a son by his Egyptian serving-woman Hagar, that Sarah will bear a child in the next year. The boy, as we know, is born, and the name that God gives him is, as we also know, Yitzhak, "He laughed."*

In the context of these promises, which must indeed have seemed incredible, it is worth pausing to consider a detail of God's speech to Abraham. When God first speaks to his prophet, he says, "I am El Shaddai"—the first time that this peculiar epithet appears in the Torah. For some scholars—although not for Friedman, who, seeing a connection between the Hebrew shaddai and the Akkadian sadu, "mountains," dismisses the epithet as meaning nothing more than "the One of the Mountain"—the name has considerable symbolic meaning. Rashi explains the words at some length, for instance. For the medieval Frenchman, "I am El Shaddai" means "I am he that there is in My Divinity enough for every creature": which is to say, the name contains an implicit guarantee that the Deity can keep the promises he makes. One further gloss on this passage—Be'er BaSadeh, taking a leaf from the midrashic commentator Bereishit Rabbah—explains further the reason that such a guarantee is necessary: Abraham feared that circumcision, which God will demand as a sign of his new people's commitment to him, would dangerously isolate him from the rest of humankind, and hence God had to reassure him. In Bereishit Rabbah 46:3, we are told that Abram said, "Before I entered into this bris people came to me. Will they really continue to come to me after I enter the bris?" This is why God, at the moment he makes his promises and, as we shall see, demands the establishment of the ritual of bris in return, declares himself to be "enough." This "enough" is, therefore, what we may call a "positive" use of the word, and therefore quite different in sense from the rather wry way in which another Abraham, my grandfather, liked to use it. For instance: whenever he would hear that So-and-So, typically an aged cousin of the branch of the family he shunned, had died at some vast old age, he would nod his handsome head a little and say, Nu? Genug is genug! Enough is enough! He would make this grim little joke often as he took me around the family plot at Mount Judah and pointedly recite the ages at which his sisters had died—twenty-six, thirty-five—and then steer me a few steps away to the bronze footstones of his first cousins Elsie Mittelmark, who died at eighty-four in 1973, and her sister Bertha, who died at ninety-two in 1982, more than three times as old as her cousin Ray, Ruchele, had been when she had died a week before her wedding. Genug is genug!

At any rate, God makes these extravagant promises to Abraham, and whatever the name he uses at that moment may mean, his fulfillment of his promises suggests that his power is, at least according to this text, "enough" to fulfill them.

Promises work both ways, and as I have mentioned, in return for the promise of protection and abundance that he makes to Abraham, God requires a permanent sign of the bond between him and the chosen people, a symbol that will be cut into the flesh itself. Hence the last event that is narrated in parashat Lech Lecha is a rather curious one: a mass circumcision that takes place just before Yitzhak, whom of course we know as Isaac, is born. After God's appearance as El Shaddai, Abraham took his thirteen-year-old son Ishmael and all of his household and all of his slaves, both those who were born into slavery and those who were purchased, and circumcised them all. This circumcision, of course, is the visible and inalterable sign of God's covenant with the Hebrew people—this same visibility, this same inalterability later being one of the reasons that you are more likely to hear stories about women who, like Anna Heller Stern, were able to pretend, because of a lucky accident of genetics, that they belong to non—chosen peoples when the chosen one was being eradicated from the face of the earth, than you are to hear about men, since even when the men were, say, blond and blue-eyed, their flesh was marked by the covenant that was established by God with his chosen people, as narrated at the conclusion of parashat Lech Lecha. In my experience, at least, the men either hid, like Bob and Jack and the others, or fled, like Bumo Kulberg, who was named for his grandfather Abraham—a man whose name was both Kulberg and Kornblüh; Bumo Kulberg, who, in the fullness of time, had his child, a girl, who in time had her own daughter, a girl whose first name, Alma, means "soul," and whose last name, as it happens, is not the name of her father, but the name of her mother's father, Kulberg, since there is no one else left to carry this name forward into the future. It is, at least in part, the profound emotion behind the decision to embrace that particular inheritance that led Adam Kulberg's daughter to say, at the end of our first night with him, The best thing that happened to my father is Alma. It's like——all the pain and unhappiness, Alma makes it good again. He says he is living for Alma.

At any rate, a famous question about the conclusion of Lech Lecha is this: Why does God wait until Abraham is ninety-nine years old before he establishes the mark of the covenant for him and his household and descendants? After all, as Friedman puts it in his modern-day commentary, "God has known Abraham for years" by this point: "Why not command it at the beginning of the relationship?" Friedman then goes on to answer his rhetorical question in a way that I find persuasive, I who know the Torah less intimately than I know the Odyssey, a story of an epic struggle to attain home that withholds the satisfaction of a family reunion from its hero not for the moment of homecoming itself, but for the aftermath of many trials and tests by means of which he proves that he deserves that reunion. Why does the moment of circumcision, the moment at which a new kind of family is created, come so late in Genesis's narrative? Friedman asks. Because, he answers, the circumcision is only a sign of the covenant.

So why not make the covenant itself right at the beginning? he persists.

Because, the rabbi tells us, Abraham has to endure many trials to show that he deserves the covenant. This, it occurs to me, is as much a narrative as an ethical consideration. For if parashat Lech Lecha fails to convey the effort, the struggle that must be endured over time, by which Abraham earns the covenant, the climactic gesture will feel flat and anticlimactic: we will not feel, as we are meant to, the finalizing impact of the scene of mass circumcision, that visible and inalterable sign that Abraham is unique in the world, that he and his people have been singled out for something special, have been chosen.

HOME AGAIN

(A False Ending)

FOR A LONG time, I thought this was the end of our travels, and the end of the story.

After we returned from Denmark, and I began to think back on all the trips we'd made and all the stories we'd heard, a phrase of Alena's kept ringing in my mind. *It was like what she was interested in was not so much the story of her grandmother but how to* tell *the story of her grandmother,* she had said that night. *How to be the storyteller.* Here again, it occurred to me, was the unique problem that faces my generation, the generation of those who had been, say, seven or eight years old during the mid-1960s, the generation of the grandchildren of those who'd been adults when it all happened; a problem that will face no other generation in history. We are just close enough to those who were there that we feel an obligation to the facts as we know them; but we are also just far enough away, at this point, to worry about our own role in the transmission of those facts, now that the people to whom those facts happened have mostly slipped away. I thought of this; and saw that, after the tens of thousands of miles that Matt and I had traveled over the past year, a year of almost solid journeying, what we had, in a way, was a story about the problems of proximity and distance.

On the one hand, we had learned so much, so many facts, a great many details, as a result of getting close to those who had been there, who had themselves been close to the event itself. And even this information, these facts, would have disappeared had we not arrived in time to cull from those people what was important to us—would have disappeared because the protagonists of our story, Shmiel, Ester, the girls, four girls whose names we now know, were, inevitably, the secondary characters in the stories of those who had survived. In the tales we'd heard in Australia and Israel and Sweden and Denmark, the Jägers could be nothing more than the friends, the neighbors, the schoolmates, but not the mothers, the fathers, the sisters, the brothers, the ones you never stop thinking about. This is why, if we hadn't found the few remaining Bolechowers, Shmiel and his family would have become that much more lost, as, over time, the heirs of those who did survive recalled and recorded what was important to *them*——to the Greenes and Grunschlags and Goldsmiths and Grossbards and Adlers and Reinharzes and Freilichs and Kulbergs——and, inevitably, allowed the rest to disappear, the names of the neighbors and friends and schoolmates of those original survivors, names that would stop having significance as time passed, just as I have allowed to fall by the wayside names that I have heard as I searched for the Jägers, names that weren't central to *my* story.

To be alive is to have a story to tell. To be alive is precisely to be the hero, the center of a life story. When you can be nothing more than a minor character in somebody else's tale, it means that you are truly dead.

Still, I know well that it's possible for even secondary characters to have a shadow existence, possible for walk-ons to persist into the present, assuming that someone wants to tell their story. Who would my grandfather be now, if I hadn't sat at his feet when I was a boy and learned by heart the stories that he told me?——stories that are of course all about him, in one sense, and in that sense are pleasurable to hear merely in the way it can give pleasure to know an interesting thing, which is the pleasure of knowledge, of the scholar; but, in another sense, are about what it means to be a member of a certain family, and in that sense have a larger worth to a greater number of people, and for that reason are surely worth preserving.

So the trips that we took brought us into proximity with a past that, like the people who inhabited that past, we thought we had lost forever; and from that past, about those people, we rescued so many facts. What had we learned, after all of that traveling? *He was deaf, she had pretty legs, she was friendly, he was clever, one girl was aloof, or possibly easy, one liked the boys, or perhaps played hard to get. She was a butterfly! He had two trucks, he brought the first strawberries, she kept a spotless house, he was a bigshot, they played cards, the ladies crocheted, she was snooty, hoch Nase! She was a good wife, a good mother, a good housewife: what else is there to say? They called him "the king," she carried her books like this, her eyes were blue but had a brown quarter here, they went to the movies, they went skiing, they played volleyball, they played basketball, they played Ping-Pong! He had the first radio, the aerial was so high, only two men in Bolechow owned cars, and one of them was him. They went to shul, or didn't, or only went on High Holidays; they davened, they made tsimmes on New Year's, they sneaked into that Polish butcher's place and ate sausages in secret! He loved his wife so much, au au au au au!*

It was a nice family, a fine family.

It was a life, it was a life.

We had learned all that, which we had never known before—because just as the survivors, the people who had seen these things and remembered them, began to die away, we learned where they were and we got close to them and heard what they had to say.

We learned all that, and of course we learned their stories as well, the storytellers' stories; and so that will become part of our story, too. The hiding places, the bunker, the attic, the rats, the forest, the false birth records, the barns. And there is the story of the present: the people we met and talked to, their families, the food we ate, the relationships that were formed now, today, against odds of 99.2 to 1. And from all the traveling, all that getting close, I found something else, too: a brother whom I'd never really known before, a deep-feeling and soft-hearted man, an artist who says little and sees much, and worries more than I do about feelings, a man whose arm I broke once because, at least in part, he had a name of which I was jealous.

So there is proximity, and all that it brings you.

And the rest? For although we got close to those who were there, there was also the problem of distance. A physical distance, first of all, at the time it was all happening, a spatial difference between where the survivors were and where our lost were: different houses at first, then different *Lager,* and, finally, different hiding places. After a certain point, it was simply impossible to know what was happening to other people. There was, too, a kind of psychological distance: when you are the protagonist of a life story that has become, of necessity, a tale of animal survival, there is little room for digressions, for looping, leisurely rings of further narratives about other people. And now, even more, there has intervened that other kind of distance, the distance of the six decades between then and now, a crevice that has opened up between the happening and the telling, a void into which so much has fallen.

Because so much time had passed and so much had disappeared, there were only tantalizing fragments: fragments that, now that we had talked to everyone and there were no more fragments to find, were finite in number, and could never, it was now clear, quite come together to make a whole picture. *The blond boy who wasn't Jewish—he loved her so much, too. She went to meet some friends, I think. She was taken to that place and after a day and a half she stood naked on a plank and was shot. She listened as the piano played, as the man was made to sit on the hot stove. She was raped. She may have been raped: could be. The first Aktion was in October. It would have been cold. They were taken and put on a cattle car and went into the gas chambers, that was in the second Aktion. It was in September. It was in August. It was the mother, the father, the youngest. It was the mother and the daughter. She worked*

in the barrel factory, she found herself a place inside, when everyone else was in the cold!
She was still alive in 'forty-one, she was still alive in 'forty-two, she was with Zimmer-
man and no one saw her again. No, she was with Halpern, she was very loyal to her
sympatia, she was easy, who knows? She was with the Babij, she was killed with them
in 'forty-three, who can say, the last person to see her left in 'forty-two. She came to the
Arbeitsamt one day, she talked to a girl called Lew and a man called Altmann. She was
embraced as her friend said, Come, give me a kiss. They sat for three days in that court-
yard and watched as children were thrown from windows, as Mrs. Grynberg stood there,
dazed, with the bloody bits hanging from between her legs. She fled to the Babij with
her sister. She stayed in town. He loved her so much. He hid her in his house. Zey zent
behalten bay a lererin. *A Polish teacher was hiding her in her house. She was preg-*
nant. A Polish schoolteacher was hiding them in her house. She was pregnant by some-
one, but not by Ciszko. The maid betrayed them, a neighbor saw them. She was alone, she
was with her father. It was Ciszko, it was an art teacher. A woman. Sedlak. Shedlak. Ser-
lak. Szedlak. Szedlakowna. Szedlakowa. No one knows where she lived.

Impossible to tell.

Long ago, I had begun my search hoping to know how they had died,
because I wanted a date to put on a chart, because I thought my grandfather,
who when I was a boy used to take me to graveyards where he would talk
to the dead, my grandfather whom I knew to be flawed but had adored anyway, who had had breakdowns, who had committed suicide, might rest a little
easier—a sentimental notion, I am aware—if I could finally give an answer to
the question that, when I asked it of him, he would merely repeat to me with
a shrug and a shake of his head that said he would not talk about it: *What hap-*
pened to Uncle Shmiel? He would retreat into an uncharacteristic silence, then,
and I told myself that one day I would find the answer: that it was *here,* it was
then; that now we knew, could go to a place where we could put a rock on
a grave and talk to him, to Shmiel, too. We had gone to learn precisely how
and where and when he had died, they had died; and had, for the most part,
failed. But in failing we'd realized, almost accidentally, that until we went
nobody had ever thought to ask about what can't be put on a chart: how they
had lived, who they were. By the time we returned from Copenhagen, I was
aware of this irony—that in the end, we'd learned far more about what we
hadn't been looking for than about what we'd set out to find. But of course, so
much of our journeying had been like that.

So it was distance, I thought when I was done with all my travels, that in
the end would always prevent me from telling the kind of story I had hoped
to be able to tell: A story that had a beginning, a middle, and an end. A story

that, like my grandfather's stories, began with all the time in the world, and then speeded up as the lineaments became clear, the characters and personalities and plot, and ended with something memorable, a punch line or a tragedy that you'd always remember. We had learned so much more than we'd dreamed possible, but when all was said and done I couldn't tell the whole story, couldn't rescue *that* for them, or for my grandfather, or for me.

And yet, for some time after that final trip to Denmark, as I brooded over this problem of proximity and distance, of what happened and how it becomes a story, I would think of Alena's little tale about the young woman who was writing about her grandmother. On the one hand there was the grandmother, the person to whom the *terrible things* had happened, and who could sit not three feet from a person like her granddaughter, or like me, an interested younger person, and tell her story. On the other hand there was the granddaughter, who *because* of distance, the passage of years and the failure of memories, would inevitably have to fill in the gaps in order to make the raw data into a story. I realized that what Alena had told me that night could be read as a kind of fable about the eternal conflict between what happened and the *story* of what happened, a fable that hints at the inevitable triumph of the storyteller even as it warns of the dangers inherent in that triumph. To become a story, the details of what happened to the grandmother, what happened in real time, in real history, to a real person, would have to be subordinated to the overall outline that already existed, for whatever idiosyncratic reasons of personality and preference and taste, in the mind of her granddaughter—the way that the small stones or tesserae used by ancient Greek and Roman artisans were set into grout or cement according to a design of the artist's invention, a design without which (the artist would tell you) the tesserae themselves—which could be glittering semiprecious stones, onyx or quartz or jasper, or merely homely bits of local stone—were nothing, in the end, but attractive bits of rock.

Another way of saying this is that *proximity* brings you closer to *what happened,* is responsible for the facts we glean, the artifacts we possess, the verbatim quotations of what people said; but *distance* is what makes possible the story of what happened, is precisely what gives someone the freedom to organize and shape those bits into a pleasing and coherent whole—to, for example, take three separate quotations, made by one person over the course of three nights, and string them together because when strung together in this fashion they create a dramatic effect far more powerful than they could possibly make if you were to encounter them in three successive chapters of a book.

For a long time, after we'd gone on the last of our trips, this notion of the triumph of distance, of the storyteller, seemed to me to be an attractive and interesting one. And why not? I am the heir of my grandfather who (people used to joke when I was a little boy) could go to the grocery store to buy a quart of milk and come back with an amazing and dramatic story to tell. If you are a certain kind of person from a certain kind of family, you don't need much to make a story.

It was for this reason that, when I came back from Denmark and looked at my dozens of videotapes, took stock of all the stories we'd heard even as I acknowledged that we hadn't gotten the whole of the story we'd hoped for, I considered it all and I thought, It's enough. I thought, *Genug is genug.*

I thought, We're finished.

PART FIVE

Vayeira,

or,

The Tree in the Garden

(July 8, 2005)

. . . IN THE STATE OF MIND IN WHICH SOMEONE "OBSERVES,"
HE IS FAR BELOW THE LEVEL AT WHICH HE FINDS HIMSELF
WHEN HE CREATES.

Marcel Proust,
In Search of Lost Time
(Within a Budding Grove)

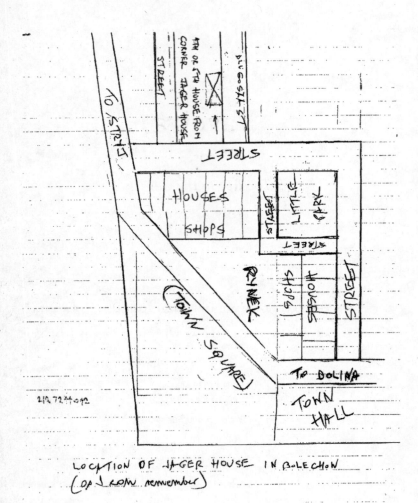

LOCATION OF JAGER HOUSE IN BOLECHOW
(OJ from remember)

Mrs. Begley's funeral took place on a cold, bright Tuesday morning, late in December. She had died on a Saturday, two days shy of her ninety-fourth birthday. She had, as usual, been right: I hadn't written fast enough.

For months she hadn't been well. *Not vell, not vell at all,* she would snap back wearily whenever I was foolish enough to begin one of our phone conversations with a mechanical *How are you?* By then, I knew the answer. Although she had begun to seem frailer, her mind, as far as I could tell, was intact. She listened intently as I kept her up to date on my travels, my research, my writing; she was warmly, almost disconcertingly sympathetic when I told her, one afternoon as we talked on the phone, that I'd just had word that Dyzia Lew had died in Belarus; that we wouldn't be going to Minsk, ever. *We are all going, one by one,* she said, tonelessly. She continued to read the *Times* and the *New York Review of Books* cover to cover, and throughout 2004 she called me frequently to comment on this or that piece I'd written. A month before she died, we talked over the phone for some time about the Greek playwrights, and again she told a story that she'd first told me on the January day nearly five years earlier when I had come nervously to her house and she had poured me the first of so many cups of tea. The story was this: that, soon after the war was over in Poland, the first cultural event to take place was a performance of Sophocles' *Antigone*. As we both knew well, *Antigone* is a play about an individual who bravely stands up to authoritarian rule and dies for it. But there are other forms of resistance that are unthinkable in Greek tragedy; for instance, surviving. Now, whenever I teach

Greek tragedy, I tell both stories: about *Antigone* in Poland after the war, and about Mrs. Begley, who had hidden, and had survived.

The Greeks, she sighed heavily into the phone, the Greeks, the theater, I used to know them all, I used to go to see everything.

But her body was failing her, I knew, although as usual I refused to think about the ending, about where that failure would finally lead. Her knees bothered her, she would say each time we talked, each time I visited her on upper Lexington Avenue, where she no longer came to the door to greet me but instead would be waiting, enthroned in the chair by the silent air conditioner, or seated at the dining-room table, in the chair nearest the kitchen door, waiting with the platters of smoked salmon, of bread, of serried pastries. What does it matter if I'm stuck here? she chuckled grimly into the phone in mid-August of her last year, when a blackout had cut the power to New York City, I can't move anyway! From my apartment on Seventy-first Street I had rung her apartment on Ninety-fourth Street, to check in and make sure she didn't need anything. My electric phone was, like everyone else's, dead, but I'd dug an old telephone out of my closet, a massive black 1950s model that I'd bought on a whim at the flea market. This phone had no need of electricity, nor, I knew, did the ancient model that Mrs. Begley used. As I laboriously dialed the numbers, letting the dial rotate back with each digit to its resting point, a process that made a sound I hadn't heard for years now, a sound that revived in me memories of my mother on the old rotary phone in the kitchen gesturing with her blond head in the direction of the neighbor's house; as I dialed her number, I knew I'd get through to her. Her voice, when she answered, sounded surprisingly full of fun, as if the excitement of the citywide crisis were a relief from the stale news of her own failing health. She told me that, yes, she was all right, that, no, I didn't need to bring her anything.

I looked out my window at the darkened buildings to the east of my neighborhood and, toying with the heavy receiver, said, We're probably the only two people in New York City who are able to have a phone conversation!

You know why? she muttered. Because only we have such telephones! Because we both like *old things*! Ha!

So she had knee problems. Or she had deficiencies of sodium, or calcium, maybe it was potassium, I can't even remember the names of the chemicals that ran too thickly or thinly in her blood. But I knew that one of these deficiencies was causing her a problem that enraged and frustrated her, which was an odd kind of aphasia. She'd be in the middle of a conversation and would suddenly look helpless and angry and say, *Ecchhh, I can't think of that thing I want to say, you know what it is,* and sometimes I did and sometimes I didn't but either way I would say, It's all right, Mrs. Begley, it's not important. Two words, I noticed, that had not vanished from her vocabulary in the summer and then autumn months just before she died were *sentimental* and *better-looking.*

And then she got pneumonia, and then she was better, and then she was worse, and then she died.

Inside the funeral chapel on Madison Avenue, at the front of a modest room lined with plain, polished wooden pews, the plain pine coffin, as is the custom, was waiting. Seated in these pews there were perhaps twenty people: apart from the family it was mostly friends of her son, and a smattering of people who, like me, against all odds, were her friends, too. In the little antechamber where we gathered before the service began, a tiny, tiny old woman, as shrunken as some tribal idol, was sitting on a settee, dressed with a surprising chic: jaunty fedora, tailored suit, a jabot, huge glasses. Only her outlandish shoes, with thick, sporty soles, seemed out of place. She looked like she was a hundred, and as it turned out, she nearly was. Louis's wife steered me over and introduced her. This lady had been Mrs. Begley's neighbor in Stryj, Anka said. The old woman looked up at me with hugely magnified eyes and, peering at me, said, *I have known Louis since he was a baby! Now I am the last one!*

But for once, I wasn't interested in talking to an old Jewish lady, and I just nodded and left soon afterward to take my seat, carefully avoiding contact with the other guests. The last time I had buried a Jew from a town in Galicia, it had been my grandfather, and what with the emotion and the family and my mother crying, it had gone by in a strange accelerated flash. I had been twenty. This time, I was in my forties. I knew what I was losing.

While the brief service went on, I took out the snapshot I'd taken four years earlier, on the day of the festive lunch she'd given after I came back from Ukraine. In it, she's sitting at her dining-room table, her elegant, thickly veined hand resting on the cloth, staring a little warily at the camera, her good eye half-open, the long Central European face aloof and weary, but not unfriendly. As her son spoke—*But something in her had been broken,* he said at one point; that much I remember—and then her grandchildren and, finally, her great-granddaughter, a soulful, dark-haired teenager with a full mouth and dream-filled eyes who, I am convinced, looks remarkably like her great-grandmother must have looked, and indeed on the night I first laid eyes on this girl, which was the same night I met Mrs. Begley and she laughed at me and said, *Bo-LEH-khoof!*, on the first night I saw this girl I said, *Oh! You look so much like your great-grandmother!* which for all I know may, in thirty years, be the beginning of some other book—as the Begley children and grand-children and great-grandchild spoke, I took out this photograph and looked at it and ran a finger across it, just as my mother had done, stroking a casual (but, for that reason, more authentic) photograph of her father, that June day in 1980 when they lowered the plain pine box into the earth of Mount Judah Cemetery, had stroked it and said over and over again, as a rabbi who had never met my grandfather went through the ritual by rote, and there-fore had no way of conveying anything significant, any authenticating detail, about the person whose body he was committing to the earth, You have to say how funny he was, he was so *funny!*

That had been a quarter century earlier. Now it was time to bury Mrs. Beg-ley, who had given me a second chance to know someone of my grandfather's culture and time, to ask the questions I didn't know how to ask when I was twenty. The service was over, and the room gradually emptied. I lingered after there was no one left, not even the ancient crone who had once been a young, fresh-faced housewife in a city far away who had, I suppose, once cooed over her neighbor's new baby and said, *Ludwik, Ludwik!* as she stroked the plasti-cene infant flesh. I felt awkward: partly because it seemed strange to leave her alone there in the high-ceilinged institutional room; and also because I knew that when I walked out the broad doorway into the hallway where the family had formed a line and were shaking hands with the guests, I would never see her again. I started to walk to the door, but something stopped me, a hesita-tion so strong it felt like a physical force, like a firm hand being placed on my shoulder, and I turned back to look. Not caring who saw me or how foolish I looked, I walked briskly down the center aisle to the coffin and stood in front of it. I laid my hand on the unvarnished wood, blemished with its dark knots the way that an aged hand is blemished with its liver spots, and gently ran it back and forth for a moment, the way you might stroke the arm of a very old person, at once gingerly and reassuringly.

I said, I really loved you, Mrs. Begley. I'm going to miss you a lot.

Then I turned around and walked to the door. I stopped and turned back for one last look—I am, after all, a *sentimental* person—and then I walked away, and that was the last time we talked.

Although it is not the end of Genesis, parashat Vayeira, *which takes its name from the* divine manifestation to Abraham with which it begins—And He Appeared—*pro-* vides, to my mind, a fitting and satisfying conclusion, at once dramatically riveting and morally searing, to the narrative that arcs through the first few parashot *of the Hebrew* Bible. Those readings trace the evolution of the Chosen People, narrowing its focus with increasing intensity as the text proceeds: beginning with the momentous, grand, wide- angle drama of the creation of all of Creation itself, every species and kind of living thing, and then proceeding, as it were through a series of ever smaller Chinese boxes, to the story of one species, mankind, then to the story of one specific family, and finally to the story of one specific man, a man whom God chose out, Abraham, the first Jew. This story of Abraham and his relationship with God, whom Abraham was the first human to acknowledge as the object of a proper religious awe, comes to an end in parashat Vayeira, which itself culminates in two famous and harrowing tales.

The first, the story of God's destruction of Sodom and Gomorrah, recapitulates themes that occur earlier in Genesis, while exploring more profoundly the moral implications of being chosen. There is, to begin with, another instance of divine annihilation: God's decision to destroy a not insignificant number of human beings—the entire populations of two metropolises—as a punishment for their wickedness, an event that will inevitably call to mind his earlier decision, described in Noach, to destroy all of humanity with the exception of Noah and his immediate family. That decision raised flickering concerns about the possibility that innocent humans might have been destroyed along with the guilty ones—a moral problem that will be fully confronted at last in the Sodom and Gomorrah story. Furthermore, because it presents a stark confrontation between those chosen by God and the non-chosen, and indeed between what it means to have chosen goodness and what it means to have chosen wickedness, parashat Vayeira may be thought of as presenting to the reader yet another—perhaps the final and most refined—in the series of acts of distinguishing so memorably described at the beginning of Genesis. For as we know, the act of distinguishing is the hallmark of creation itself.

These and other repetitions of earlier themes and motifs persuade me that parashat Vayeira is intended to feel like a culmination, a summing up. This cyclical quality of the text applies not only to large themes, but also to passing details. For instance: in this reading we learn that, after the destruction of the twin cities of the plain, as Sodom and Gomorrah are often called, Abraham moves on with Sarah to the Negev, to the city of Gerar. Here, exactly as he had once done in Egypt, the patriarch pretends that his wife is his sister, with the result that, exactly as we saw before, the king of the place takes her into his household, only to be stopped from touching her by the hand of God himself, who gives the king a warning in a dream. Precisely what designs this king, Abimelek, may have had on the ninety-year-old Sarah are unclear, but the recurrent motif of the patriarch's lie about his wife, however contrived it feels at this point, is surely meant to bring us back, at the exact point at which the story of this couple's wanderings comes to a close (for Sarah dies at the beginning of the very next parashah) to a recollection of how those wanderings began. Certain kinds of manipulations of the truth are irresistible if what one wants to create is a story with a satisfying shape.

So there is Sodom and Gomorrah. The second of the climactic stories told in parashat Vayeira, the story of Abraham's intended sacrifice of Isaac, nicely suggests—because it involves a father's relationship with his young son as well as his relationship with his own divine parent—the way in which every single person constitutes within himself a bridge between the past and the future; and by introducing Isaac at last as a full-fledged character in the narrative, this story also lays the narrative foundation for the story of Abraham's descendants, which will take readers to the end of the Hebrew Bible itself. The latter, however, will not concern us here, since, as I have said, at the time I briefly studied the Torah when I was a young adult and before I turned once again to the Greeks, I only got as far as parashat Vayeira, and so it is there that we shall stop.

I will return to the individual stories later, but here it seems worth trying to interpret one of the best known moments in Vayeira, if only because the two commentaries I have sought out to illuminate these texts, the ancient and the modern, Rashi and Friedman, seem to me to fail to elucidate the meaning of this strange and famous incident (which is, however, minor enough not to be of concern to us later when considering the larger moral implications of the two stories I have alluded to). I refer here to the well-known story of Lot's wife—of how, even as she and her husband and two daughters are being rescued from the doomed city by the intervention of God's angel, are being physically dragged away from their home by the heavenly beings, the wife of Lot violates the angel's express command not to turn back and look at the city during their flight, and for that transgression is turned into a pillar of salt.

Shockingly, at least to me, Friedman has nothing whatsoever to say about this riveting moment—perhaps because he's saving his exegetical ammunition for where it's really needed, which is the far more troubling story of Abraham's willingness to kill his own child. Nor does Rashi's explication seem to me, for once, to be persuasive. The medieval French scholar begins by explaining the angel's order not to "look back" as a punishment of sorts: he glosses the text's "Do not look behind you" by suggesting that, since Lot and his family had sinned in precisely the way that the inhabitants of the twin cities sinned, and since they are being saved only because of their relationship to Abraham, that good prophet, they have no right to witness the punishment of the doomed from the comfortable vantage point of their escape route. "You do not deserve to see their punishment while you are being saved" is how the Frenchman puts it. As for the fate of Lot's wife, Rashi explains the bizarre detail of her metamorphosis from human being into mineral by saying that she "had sinned with salt" and hence "was stricken with salt." This "sinned with salt" is a reference to a midrashic tradition that Lot's wife had begrudged the traditional gesture of giving salt to guests. (The same tradition also holds that later, on the pretext of borrowing salt from her neighbors, Lot's wife reported her foreign-born husband's actions to the Sodomite authorities— a reminder that, unlike her husband, she is, presumably, a native Sodomite.)

As ingenious as this explanation is, it seems to me to miss entirely the emotional significance of the text—its beautiful, and beautifully economical, evocation of certain difficult feelings that most ordinary people, at least, are all too familiar with: searing regret for the pasts we must abandon, tragic longing for what must be left behind. Perhaps because I am a classicist, I was struck, as I read Rashi's explication of this passage, by how little attention is paid, how little appreciation is devoted by the Jewish text and its Jewish commentators to what seems to me to be the obvious question that arises in the story of Sodom and Gomorrah, the question of the value of beauty and pleasure. Abraham, we must not forget, was born in a city but has spent most of his life as a nomad, as parashat Lech Lecha makes clear; perhaps by now he has forgotten the pleasures of urbanity. But Lot's wife is deeply attached to her city— Rashi identifies it as a "metropolis," in fact—and we may imagine that this is because, like all great metropolises, the one we encounter in parashat Vayeira undoubtedly offered its share of beauty, of rarefied and complicated pleasures, among which, indeed, may have been the very vices for which it was eventually punished. Still, perhaps that's the pagan, the Hellenist in me talking. (Rabbi Friedman, by contrast, cannot bring himself even to contemplate that what the people of Sodom intend to do to the two male angels, as they crowd around Lot's house at the beginning of this narrative, is to rape them, an interpretation blandly accepted by Rashi, who blithely points out that if the Sodomites hadn't wanted sexual pleasure from the angels, Lot wouldn't have suggested, as he rather startlingly does, that the Sodomites take his two daughters as substitutes. But then, Rashi was French.)

It is this temperamental failure to understand Sodom in its own context, as an ancient metropolis of the Near East, as a site of sophisticated, even decadent delights and hyper-civilized beauties, that results in the commentator's inability to see the true meaning of the two crucial elements of this story: the angel's command to Lot's family not to turn and look back at the city they are fleeing, and the transformation of Lot's wife into a pillar of salt. For if you see Sodom as beautiful—which it will seem to be all the more so, no doubt, for having to be abandoned and lost forever, precisely the way in which, say, relatives who are dead are always somehow more beautiful and good than those who still live—then it seems clear that Lot and his family are commanded not to look back at it not as a punishment, but for a practical reason: because regret for what we have lost, for the pasts we have to abandon, often poisons any attempts to make a new life, which is what Lot and his family now must do, as Noah and his family once had to do, as indeed all those who survive awful annihilations must somehow do. This explanation, in turn, helps explain the form that the punishment of Lot's wife took—if indeed it was a punishment to begin with, which I personally do not believe it was, since to me it seems far more like a natural process, the inevitable outcome of her character. For those who are compelled by their natures always to be looking back at what has been, rather than forward into the future, the great danger is tears, the unstoppable weeping that the Greeks, if not the author of Genesis, knew was not only a pain but a narcotic pleasure, too: a mournful contemplation so flawless, so crystalline, that it can, in the end, immobilize you.

OH, DANIEL, DON'T go *back*! my mother said to me one night a few months after Mrs. Begley's funeral.

I had called to mine her memory a little bit. At that point I was thinking a lot about my grandfather's trip to Israel in 1956, and so I had asked her, a few days before, if she wouldn't mind going into the family files and finding certain photographs that I thought might be helpful—not, of course, helpful in jogging my memory, since the event had taken place long before I was born, but helpful in providing a visual counterpart to the stories I'd so often heard. Because of her *meticulous German blood,* she had told me to call back in a few days; by then, she said, she'd have had the chance to carefully unwrap the albums from what, since I was eight, I had thought of as their mummy wrappings. Now, as I talked to her on the phone one summer day about a month ago, she told me that she had unwrapped them all, and as we spoke on the phone she was describing various pictures, separating the ones I wanted from the ones that didn't sound interesting.

Here was Nana, she said, sitting on a deck chair on the liner, she looked so *healthy* that year; here was her mother at the bon voyage party in their stateroom, smiling good-naturedly with one arm around her sister-in-law, Aunt Sylvia, who as usual was looking disappointed, and the other around Minnie Spieler, who, true to her bohemian legend, was daringly wearing a man's suit and tie. Here were other pictures, mixed into the ISRAEL TRIP SS UNITED STATES album, pictures that, my mother observed as a puzzled annoyance crept into her voice, didn't belong there. Her mother's only brother, Jack, the handsome blond bachelor whom her father didn't like (because, I said to myself as she talked, he was *competition*), here was her mother's older sister, the unstable one who toward the end of her life wouldn't bathe because she was convinced the Russians had put electrodes in her hairdo, a story that used to make us shriek with laughter when we were kids; the same older sister, indeed, who had tried to stop my grandfather from marrying my grandmother. This was a story I'd known by heart since I was ten years old, a staple of my grandfather's after-dinner repertoire: how Pauline had broken the engagement three times because, she insisted, her baby sister, a bona fide American girl born in New York City, shouldn't marry beneath her, marry an immigrant, a greenhorn, *grinhorn*. But love conquered all! my grandfather would joke; and years later, when he had done well for himself, had acquired the Mittelmarks' factory and had greatly prospered, this same Pauline had come up to him one night at some seder or another, some event at which my grandmother made her famous soups and the desserts that she could not eat, and said, You know something, Abe? You were always my favorite brother-in-law! To which my grandfather, not missing a beat, replied, *Ahhh, Pauline—so now I'm a Yenkee Doohddle Dehndee!*

And what's more, it was true. Nobody pledged the Pledge of Allegiance more loudly than he, put out a bigger flag on Memorial Day, gave out more ice-cream cones on the Fourth of July. He had traveled far for this.

So my mother retold these stories as she looked through her folders, which, it is possible, she likes to label and arrange so neatly because, a hundred years before we had this conversation, a matchmaker in Bolechow had chosen for the young widower Elkune Jäger a girl from Dolina called Taube Ryfka Mittelmark, *Mittelmark*, a family whose German blood expressed itself, they liked to say, in a taste for orderliness, the way that certain genes will express themselves in a straight nose or blue eyes or a tendency to develop cancer of the colon. It was while my mother was leafing through her neatly filed pictures that I mentioned to her that I'd decided to return to Ukraine, to Bolekhiv. (*Bolekhiv*, as I must henceforth call it, since I know now that I will never return there, never again go back, and for that reason—and the fact that, having gone back that one last time, I know at last that there is, now, truly nothing left to see, nothing left of *Bolechow*—I am willing, finally, to allow it to take its place in the present.) I told her that although I didn't enjoy the thought of yet another trip—a trip, moreover, to somewhere we'd already been, where we'd already talked to people and seen what there was to see—I now thought that going back might be an interesting way to bring to an end the search that had started so long ago. I told her that I wanted to go back, in part, because I thought that more than anything else, a return to Bolekhiv would give me a sense of an ending; I thought that however much we'd never know, it would be satisfying to contrast this second and final trip with the first one we'd made: to walk again the confusingly twisting streets of the town once more, but armed, this time, with so much more information than we had had the first time we went, four years earlier, when we had known nothing at all except six names. This time, I had my notes, my tapes, the stories I'd heard, the descriptions, the maps that Jack and Shlomo had meticulously drawn and faxed to me, all the data that I'd culled over four years, which would now allow me to stride confidently around my family's town saying *This is Dlugosa, the street where they lived, here, five meters from the Magistrat, was where the store was, here was the school, there was the Hanoar building, here was the Dom Katolicki, that is the road to Taniawa, here was the Szymanski store, here is the road that leads to the train station, those are the tracks to Belzec.* This time, we knew something, even if it wasn't all we'd hoped to know. I thought I might end, I told my mother, by contrasting the total ignorance of our first trip with the partial knowledge of this final trip. By saying, There is more and more distance as time goes by, but just in the nick of time, we got close enough to know a few knowable things. By saying, There will never be certainty, never be a *date,* a *place:* but see how much we learned. An ending that showed how close we'd gotten, but also how far we'd always be.

So I told my mother all this, and she sighed. Do you really have to go back? she fretted. Haven't you and Matthew already *been* everywhere? She made that little clicking noise she makes when she resigns herself to the fact that you're making a bad decision: a double *tch, tch* formed by striking the front part of the tongue against the upper palate. I supposed, as she made this familiar sound, that she had gotten it from her mother, who had gotten it from her mother, and so on, a thread stretching all the way back to Russia, to the nineteenth and eighteenth and seventeenth centuries, to Odessa in the sixteenth century and then beyond that, past the beginning of the modern era; a thread that spooled backward from the June afternoon in 2005 on which my mother told me not to go back, past the day of her wedding in Manhattan in 1953, of her parents' wedding on the Lower East Side in 1928, of Elkune Jäger's second wedding in Bolechow in 1894 and of his parents' wedding in the same small town in 1846; past the day on which the architect Ignaz Reiser saw in his mind's eye a certain shape that would later become the shape of the Moorish-style arches of the gate of the Zeremonienhalle of the New Jewish Section of the Vienna Central Cemetery, past the day on which an Austrian official in a hamlet called Dolina wrote the words *The mother of this illegitimate child is named* . . . , past the day on which Ber Birkenthal decided to commit his memories to paper in his elegant Hebrew, past the unknowable day on which a nameless Slav had raped a Jewess in a village near Odessa, thereby introducing a gene for a certain color of hair and eyes into the makeup of a family that would eventually be called *Cushman;* past all this, backward in time, spooling continuously, past the Sunday in 1943 when the first transport of Jews left the railway station in Salonica, the Wednesday in 1941 when the first Aktion in Bolechow ended in a field called Taniawa, the Friday in March at the beginning of the High Renaissance when Ferdinand and Isabella of Spain signed the Edict of Expulsion of the Jews, the Thursday in May 1420 when Duke Albrecht V expelled the Jews from Vienna, the Friday in 1306 when Philip the Fair drove the Jews out of France and assumed title to the loans owed to them by his fellow Christians, the Tuesday in 1290 on which Edward I expelled the Jews from England, back through the Middle Ages, past Saadia Gaon making his learned arguments before the caliph in Baghdad, past the moment at which the first of the Karaites decided he was not a Jew like the others; and back even farther, this tiny insignificant tic that, from daughter to mother, had created a thread, a path that you could, theoretically, follow as surely as it is possible to follow the trail left by the special DNA that exists in a certain organ that is present in every human cell, an organ called the mitochondrion, DNA unlike the DNA of every other part of every other cell, since this mitochondrial DNA is transmitted unchanged only from the mother to her child, unmixed, as is all other DNA, with the DNA of the father, and hence provides an unbroken chain of DNA from the present to the remotest imaginable past, only through the line of the mother. Perhaps, I wondered as I heard my mother make her disapproving *tch,* perhaps this little sound went back through eons of time to some dark-haired, black-eyed, hawk-nosed woman in a long-vanished city called Ur, a woman who had made this noise one afternoon when her son Abram announced that he was leaving home on a trip from which he might never return.

Yes, I said to my mother, that day when she sifted through the Israel pictures for me, I *really* do need to go.

Then, to appease her, I told her that I'd arranged to do a travel article about L'viv for a magazine I write for. This way, I said, the journey would be worth it, even if the Bolekhiv portion of it turned out to be a failure.

My mother made that sound again. I could hear the rustle of paper in the background, as she carefully folded the pictures and menus and passenger lists back into their envelopes, their plastic baggies, their cartons.

All right, she said, But after this trip, *genug is genug,* OK?

I know, I said. I *know.*

She said, Good. All right, darling, I'm hanging. Good-bye and good luck.

This had always been her and her father's ritual telephonic valediction to each other, which now she used with us. But before she actually put down the receiver, she said something else, something that took me by surprise.

She said, My family ruined their *lives* by always looking at the past, and I don't want you to *be* like that.

On the Fourth of July, I flew to Ukraine.

AGAIN, I WAS traveling with Froma. Of all the once-great cities of Jewish Eastern Europe, L'viv, Lwów, Lemberg was the one she hadn't been to. I knew she wanted to see it (It'll be *just like last time!* she cried when I called to ask her if she wanted to come, and I grinned and thought, *Not very likely*); I knew, too, that I didn't want to make this trip alone. It was the middle of the summer, and Matt was overwhelmed with weddings, with studio portrait work. There was no way he could accompany me.

I just don't have any weekend free until September, he told me when I called to ask whether he wanted to get a few final photos of the town. These days, what with discussing the photos for the book and sharing news of the various Bolechowers, I talked to Matt more or less every day: a thing I'd never have predicted, five years before. It's OK, I said, you already got the Bolechow pictures last time, we can use those. Don't worry about it. But I hung up with a kind of pang. I'd gotten used to him being there on the long flights, always offering me the aisle seat, grinning over *New Yorker* cartoons, which he loved to describe out loud rather than let me look at them; secretly adoring his pea-in-a-pod idol.

So this time, on the last of all the last trips, it would be me and Froma again.

There would also, eventually, be a third. My friend Lane, a photographer, was planning to join us in L'viv halfway through our week there. A vivid, dark-haired North Carolinian who had lived for years in New York, she had been working for several years on a photo essay about "sites of genocide." Since I'd first met her, nearly five years earlier, I had been hearing about her trips to Rwanda, Darfur, Cambodia, Bosnia, an ever-lengthening list that suggested, as she liked to say, that NEVER AGAIN was an empty slogan. So Lane had been to all those places. Her problem, she told me, was that she hadn't figured out her approach to the Holocaust yet. Auschwitz, she feared, had become a visual cliché—*It lets you off the hook,* was how she put it to me one night over supper at her place, as I leafed through the pictures she'd taken. I thought of the woman who'd said, *If I don't get an Evian I'm going to* pass out, of the cattle car you can ride in the Holocaust Museum, of the ARBEIT MACHT FREI electronic postcards you can get at the online Terezín Museum. Yes, I said, I agree. I added, If I go back to Bolekhiv, you should come with me. If you're interested in sites of genocide, there's a lot to see around there. As I said this I thought of Taniawa, which by then was on the list of places whose locations I now knew.

So Lane would meet us in L'viv. Froma and I planned to arrive on a Tuesday and would spend the better part of our week there looking at the city, to gather information and experiences for the travel article I was going to be writing, and Lane would come on Saturday, at which point we'd drive to Bolekhiv, take some pictures, and then drive to all the neighboring towns, to places that had once been called Dolina and Drohobycz and Stryj and Kalusz and Rozniatów and Halych and Rohatyn and Stanislawów, those places and all the others, each one of which had its own Taniawa, its own mass grave and monument. We'd spend Saturday and Sunday driving around and seeing the ruins of Jewish Galicia, and then I'd go home, once and for all.

Alex met us at the airport, beaming. He'd grown bigger, more affectionately bearlike, since the last time I'd seen him. By now, of course, we knew each other well, and this time, after he'd jostled his way to the front of the packed reception area at the tiny L'viv airport, he wasn't standing with a piece of cardboard that said MENDELSOHN but threw his massive arms around me and gave me a hug that knocked the breath out of me. I grinned at him: I was glad to be seeing him again. One of the things that rescued this trip to L'viv from feeling like the kind of emotionally draining "going back" that I disliked was the prospect of spending a lot of time with Alex. I considered him to be a friend, and as such I thought I could talk frankly with him about certain issues that had arisen during the course of my research, not the least of these being the difficult issue of the nature of Jewish-Ukrainian relations, both before and after the war. When I'd written an article about our first trip to L'viv three years earlier, I had wanted to contrast the refrain I'd always heard from my grandfather—*the Germans were bad, the Poles were worse, the Ukrainians were the worst of all* (and how, anyway, did he know? what had *he* heard?)—with the reception we had received everywhere we'd gone in Ukraine, the unhesitating warmth and generosity and friendliness that every Ukrainian we'd encountered had shown us. It seemed to me that the discrepancy had something to do with specifics of history, and something to do more generally with time. No doubt because I stand wholly outside of the event, it is possible for me to think that certain things that some, even many, Ukrainians did during the war were the products of specific historical circumstances, and it is difficult for me to believe that Ukrainian atrocities against Jews in 1942 are any more a natural expression of the essential Ukrainian character than, say, Serbian atrocities against Bosnian Muslims in 1992 are a natural expression of some essential Serbian characteristic. So I am, perhaps naively, unwilling to condemn "Ukrainians" in general, although I know that many Ukrainians committed atrocities. I am, however, willing to believe in other generalizations, for instance that seething resentment by a class of people who both have been and perceive themselves to be an underclass, particularly when those people have recently suffered unspeakable oppression—one example of which would be,

say, Stalin's intentional starvation of between five and seven million Ukrainians in 1932 and 1933, which for Ukrainians is the galvanizing national tragedy
just as the Holocaust is the galvanizing national tragedy for Jews—that seething resentment of such a class of people will, under the right combination of
circumstances, explode into bestial savagery against those whom they hold
responsible for their suffering, however unjustly. And as I know, it is easiest to
hold responsible those to whom you live in closest intimacy.

More generally, I thought that the difference between *and the Ukrainians
were the worst* and what we found when my siblings and I went to Ukraine
and were treated so well by Ukrainians who knew we were Jews was clearly
related to the subject I was interested in, which was how much gets lost as a
result of the passage of time. To me, it seemed obvious that cultural habits and
attitudes are also eroded over time, and even if it was once true that a seething
anti-Semitism had raged throughout the Ukrainian populations of places like
Bolechow, I wanted to believe that this was no longer the case—that I had no
more reason to be fearful while traveling in Ukraine than I have when I travel
in Germany, although some of my survivors had warned me that I should. *Be
very careful when you go back there,* Meg had told me as we were about to leave
Australia. Why, I asked, you think they still hate Jews? She looked at me wearily and said, *That's an understatement.*

And indeed certain survivors to whom I'd described my friendship with
Alex and, more generally, our pleasant reception by Ukrainians, had dismissed it all with a bitter laugh, or worse, saying the Ukrainians today had
only been nice to us because we were Americans, because they thought
we had money to give them. *You weren't there, you didn't see,* someone told
me when I protested that the Ukrainians I'd met and talked to had been so
warm, so welcoming, so nice to us; and what could I reply, I who believe it
is impossible to draw facile analogies between the kinds of experience that I
and others of my class and geography and generation are likely to have, and
certain kinds of experiences that certain people had during the war? When
certain of my survivors would shake their heads at me and tell me that I
could know nothing of Ukrainians based on my experiences, it would occur
to me that perhaps they were right: perhaps too many variables had changed,
perhaps it was *impossible to know,* just as you can know nothing of what it was
like to be on a transport to Belzec in the summer of 1942 by riding the cattle car ride at the United States Holocaust Museum in Washington. I, more
than most, knew too well the roots of this bitter, generalized animosity to
Ukrainians—after all, the survivors I had spoken with had seen with their

own eyes the Jewish babies impaled on Ukrainian pitchforks and thrown out of windows and smashed against walls by Ukrainians and stomped underfoot by Ukrainians, as Mrs. Grynberg's newborn had been stomped moments after she delivered it, the umbilical cord still hanging from between her legs; they, not I, had witnessed a sheer, almost animal savagery so ferocious that, as has been recorded, there were times when the Nazis themselves had to restrain the Ukrainians. They had seen this, and I had not seen, would never see, anything like it. Still, it must be said that this unwillingness to believe anything good of Ukrainians struck me as irrational, too, since every survivor I talked to had been saved by a Ukrainian. I did not say this to them at the time, but it seemed to me that Jews more than others should be wary of condemning entire populations out of hand.

So I talked about all this with Alex, during my visit, openly and frankly. Because he is a historian by training, as I am a classicist, he tries to see things in their complexity, and is leery of generalizations, just as I like to see things through the lens of Greek tragedy, which teaches us, among other things, that real tragedy is never a straightforward confrontation between Good and Evil, but is, rather, much more exquisitely and much more agonizingly, a conflict between two irreconcilable views of the world. The tragedy of certain areas of Eastern Europe between, say, 1939 and 1944 was, in this sense, a true tragedy, since—as I have mentioned earlier—the Jews of eastern Poland, who knew they would suffer unimaginably if they came under Nazi rule, viewed the Soviets as liberators in 1939, when eastern Poland was ceded, temporarily it turned out, to the Soviet Union; whereas the Ukrainians of eastern Poland, who had suffered unimaginably under Soviet oppression during the 1920s and 1930s, viewed the cession of eastern Poland to the Soviet Union in 1939 as a national disaster, and saw the Nazis as liberators in 1941, when the Germans invaded and took control. This is not, of course, a formula that can explain everything, the pitchforked babies or the umbilical cords: but it is at least more complex, and therefore more likely to be accurate, than the formula that simply dismisses all Ukrainians, always, as *the worst*. Alex and I talked about this kind of thing often during our visit, and in the end he shrugged and sighed and said, echoing other people I'd talked to over the past few years, Look, some people were good, and some people were bad.

But that came later. At the airport, on the day of my return to L'viv, I hugged Alex back and introduced him to Froma. I asked about his wife, Natalie, about his studious son, Andriy, whom Alex always refers to as Andrew in my presence, and his round-faced daughter, Natalie, both of whom would be much bigger now than when I'd last seen them at the lavish farewell dinner Alex had held for my brothers and sister and me at their apartment. Everything was great! Alex said. Everyone is great! He refused to let us carry anything, even a computer bag, as we emerged from the bizarre little airport building into the bright sunlight. Sitting at the curb was the blue VW Passat. No! he said, when I made a theatrical gesture of recognition on seeing the car. This isn't the same car you knew before, it's the same kind but a different one, newer. Same, but different!

We sped off to the hotel. It was either then, or at some point later on, that he laughed his ringing laugh and said, You won't believe it, but Andrew has taught himself to read Yiddish!

THAT WAS ON Tuesday. On Friday, we would drive to Bolekhiv.

It was good to spend some time in L'viv. The first time I'd gone to this city, I'd been so anxious about what we'd find in Bolekhiv that I hadn't paid a great deal of attention to the sightseeing we did before and after we went to my family's town. This time, I like to think we saw everything.

Many places of historical interest with respect to the city's now-vanished Jewish life have not, I should point out, vanished, but are simply what you might call *the same, but different*. A good example of this is a plump and pleasant if somewhat eccentric building—it has little turrets—that stands at Number 27, T. Shevchenko Prospekt, and is now called the Desertniy Bar. To certain people it is far better known, however, as the Szkocka Café, the Scottish Café, which in its previous life stood on an avenue called Akademichna— an appropriate enough name, given that the café was the meeting place for a famous and influential group of mathematicians known as the Lwów School. The Lwów School was dominated by the Polish mathematician Stefan Banach, who did seminal work in an area called functional analysis, and who, with another Lwów mathematician, Hugo Steinhaus, founded in 1929 the journal *Studia Mathematica*, "Mathematical Studies," which along with the Warsaw-based *Fundamenta Mathematicae* ("Foundations of Mathematics") became one of the premier journals of the lively and important Polish mathematical scene during the interwar period. It is the liveliness of the Lwów School that brings us back to the Scottish Café, since the café was a favorite meeting place of the members of that group. It was Banach who bought the large notebook, later an object of legend, in which, over the course of animated conversation accompanied by many coffees, thorny problems were written down, and answers eventually entered as well. At the end of each gathering this note-book would be left with the headwaiter who, when the group returned on another night, would bring it out of the secret hiding place to which it would be returned as soon as they'd left once again.

The Lwów School and that lively and important Polish mathematical scene would never recover from the devastating effects of the Nazi occupa-tion, which decimated the ranks of the Polish professoriat, Catholics and Jews alike. As it happens, both Banach and Steinhaus survived the war, although each suffered horrible deprivations. Banach, a Pole who was born not far from Kraków in 1892 and was, therefore, of the same generation as Uncle Shmiel, and who, because he was an illegitimate child, bore the surname of his mother rather than his father (a thing that as we know could happen even to legitimate children), was arrested by the Nazis at one point, and, stripped of the august standing he had enjoyed before the war, was put to work in an infectious diseases laboratory where, for the duration of the Occupation, the great mathematician spent his days feeding the lice that were to be used in experiments. He outlived the war by three weeks, dying of lung cancer in August 1945. Steinhaus, born a few years earlier than his colleague, was Jew-ish, which meant that when the Nazis came he had more to worry about than lice. He went into hiding and suffered severe privations, hunger not being the least of them, although it is said of him that, as one biographer has put it, *even then his sharp restless mind was at work on a multitude of ideas and projects*— in which he was not unlike Klara Freilich, who as we know was also thinking about mathematics while she huddled under the ground with the rats. In any event, when the war was over Steinhaus moved, as Ciszko Szymanski's family had, to Wrocław, and died there at the age of eighty-five in 1972, having man-aged, I should add, to rescue and preserve the Scottish Café notebook, which was subsequently published. The rescue of the book may be thought of as a symbol, since Steinhaus is in fact often credited with helping Polish mathe-matics to rise from its ashes after the devastation wreaked by the war on Pol-ish university and intellectual life.

It happens that I have just had the chance to handle a curious artifact of this particular aspect of the wartime devastation. I originally went to the Scottish Café—or rather, the Desertniy Bar—because my father is a mathematician, and when we all went to L'viv the first time he was eager for us to visit this famous place, which is in its way a shrine for mathematicians, a group of people not nec-essarily known for the intensity of their devotion to shrines. But most of what I know about the Lwów School I owe to my godfather, my father's close Italian friend whose real name is Edward but whom we have always called by the affectionate nickname *Nino,* who for many years was a professor of mathematics at a university on Long Island, the man who was the only person we knew who would reach up and pluck apples from the tree in my parents' yard and eat them, back when I was a child and wondering why the Tree of Knowledge was a *tree.* By a curious coincidence, one of Nino's areas of expertise is functional analysis, the area opened up long ago by the Lwów School, and it was Nino who tried to explain to me, when I was visiting him after my final trip to Ukraine and telling him of what we'd found there, what exactly functional analysis is. A lot of what he told me was too difficult for me to understand. But I was fascinated to hear him say that he himself had used functional analysis to study problems in something called optimization theory. Since I had liked the name *optimization theory,* I asked him in an e-mail I wrote after I got back home to try to explain what that was, and he immediately replied:

> *optimization is the study of maxima and minima in different guises. two quick examples, the first classical, attributed to Dido, the second from the sputnik era:*

> *1) what closed surface of given area encloses the maximum volume ? (Dido: what planar figure of given perimeter encloses the greatest area. answer: the circle)*

> *2) what flight path does a rocket take to minimize the time to rendezvous between two points in different orbits?*

Reading this, I was moved to see that a name familiar to me from Latin literature had, strangely, become the symbol of a famous mathematical problem. In Vergil's *Aeneid,* we are told a certain story relating to the queen of Carthage, Dido—the woman with whom Aeneas falls in love, only to abandon her later on, an act that eventually brings about her suicide. The story has to do with how Dido came to found her city, Carthage. Exiled from her native land, Dido wandered far and wide seeking a place to settle. After she landed in North Africa, a local king struck a strange bargain with her: he agreed to grant her and her followers just as much territory as could be enclosed by the hide of an ox. Dido's ingenious response to this cruelly stingy offer was to cut an oxhide into thin strips and, making these strips into one long cord, to make that cord into the perimeter of an enormous circle: the territory of the future Carthage, which eventually became a great city, the city in which Aeneas would later so unexpectedly come across a painting of his own life, causing him to burst into tears.

This is why, when mathematicians refer to "Dido's problem," they are worrying about this: how to find the maximum area for a figure with a given perimeter; although when classicists refer to Dido's problem they are probably more concerned with the fact that after she was forced from her home and had to flee for her life, after she had built for herself a new and prosperous existence, she still ended up—for all her cleverness, for all she'd done to survive—a suicide, a woman whose new life was no life because her heart had been broken.

In any case, when I first read Nino's e-mail I wasn't sure what all of it meant, but—since I had just returned from that particular trip—the problems of how to get closed surfaces to enclose maximum volumes, and of how to minimize the time it takes to reach rendezvous points, had been much in my thoughts, although of course in a different context, and I suppose that's why Nino's answer pricked my interest.

It was while I was at Nino's house that, in talking about the Lwów School, he mentioned that he had several volumes of both *Studia Mathematica* and *Fundamenta Mathematicae,* and it was in one of the latter that he pointed out to me the memorial issue of 1945, which began with a black-bordered list of the dozens of former contributors to that publication who had been killed in the war, a list that went a long way toward suggesting to me just how difficult Hugo Steinhaus's project of reanimating Polish mathematics had been. When we think about great devastations, about what gets lost as a result of the decimation of entire populations of people, the million and a half Armenians slaughtered by the Turks in 1916, the five to seven million Ukrainians starved to death by Stalin between 1932 and 1933, the six million Jews killed in the Holocaust, the two million Cambodians killed by Pol Pot's regime in the 1970s, and so forth, we tend, naturally, to think first of the people themselves, the families that will cease existing, the children that will never be born; and then of the homely things with which most of us are familiar, the houses and mementoes and photographs that, because those people no longer exist, will stop having any meaning at all. But there is this, too: the thoughts that will never be thought, the discoveries that will never be made, the art that will never be created. The problems, written in a book somewhere, a book that will outlive the people who wrote down the problems, that will never be solved.

Anyway, I've been to the Scottish Café in L'viv. It is, you could say, the same, but different; which is also one way of describing L'viv today, which, with its renovations and new construction and rising tourism, may be said to be old and new at the same time, to be *rising out of its ashes,* at least in certain respects, at least in cases when there are ashes still left to rise out of.

BOLEKHIV, TOO, WAS the same, but different.

Once again, Alex had stopped the car at the crest of the hill beyond which it was possible to see the little town nestled in its valley, the hill where four years earlier Matt had paused to take a picture. Here we are in Bolechow again, I announced, a shade ruefully, to Alex and Froma. But this time, when we drove down into the town, over the little stone bridge that squats over the thin and insignificant trickle that the Sukiel River has become, past what used to be Bruckenstein's Restaurant, the place seemed transformed. Before, on the overcast, drizzly afternoon of our first visit, the town had seemed deserted; the gray sense of desolation that hung in the wet air that Sunday had seemed, somehow, like another piece of damning evidence, as if the place itself were perpetually on trial and the weather and mood were witnesses for the prosecution. Now, on a brilliant and cloudless late morning, Bolekhiv was alive with activity: cars buzzed noisily around the square, construction sites clanged and buzzed and sputtered, mothers were pushing strollers, and the place was alive with the colors of many newly painted buildings. Meg Grossbard's house, of which she'd given me a photo, and which she had asked me to take a look at—this was in the afternoon after the lunch at her brother-in-law's, when, as Matt and I stood outside the apartment building waiting for a cab, Meg had insisted that if we were foolish enough ever to return to Ukraine (cannibals!), we must not tell anyone that she was living in Australia; and, reacting to my amazed expression, went on, they killed the rest of my family, why wouldn't they want to kill me too?—Meg Grossbard's house, I saw, had been painted a bubble-gum pink.

When we got out of the Passat, Froma looked around and said, I wonder whether all these people are curious about us.

This time, too, I realized that the last time we'd come, we'd only really seen half of the Rynek. Armed with the map Jack had faxed me the week before I left, I started navigating as Froma and Alex trailed behind. There was the house where my grandfather had been born, the plum trees sagging with fruit; there was the Little Park with its lime trees. We stopped at the Magistrat, and I now pointed to the exact location where Shmiel's store had stood. I took out a Xerox of the photograph from the Bolechow Yizkor book, the one that my grandfather had long ago captioned OUR STORE, and showed it to Froma and Alex for comparison. They nodded and smiled. We found the Dom Katolicki, now a meetinghouse for Jehovah's Witnesses, a solid-looking, ugly, two-story box of a building with square windows and a corrugated tin roof, which sits in the middle of a residential block down the street from what I now knew used to be called the Polish Church. Once again, as is so often the case when I've finally stood in front of buildings the physical appearance of which does not—and couldn't possibly—suggest the saturated histories of the events that have occurred within them, I felt a vague disappointment, a sense of flatness. It was difficult for me to connect this stolid little structure in front of me with the many and vivid and terrible stories I had heard about it. It wasn't until several weeks later, when I was back home in New York looking at the photos from this trip, that I noticed that large metal letters of a distinctly contemporary design had been affixed to the front of this decrepit structure, just under the undulating tin roofline. KIHO, the Cyrillic letters said on the left side of the building; TEATP, they said on the right. *Cinema. Theater.*

That is when I realized they were still showing movies there.

Perhaps because I was enjoying my knowledge, enjoying the confidence that my maps and interviews had given me, and perhaps, simply, because of the beautiful weather, I was in a buoyant mood. The contrast between this confident and sunny visit and the one we'd made in 2001 couldn't have been greater. For once, I told myself, I'd found exactly what I was looking for.

In a matter of only a few minutes, it began to be clear I was wrong.

IT STARTED BECAUSE we couldn't find the one thing I'd wanted more than anything else to find, which was Shmiel's house. In Australia, Boris Goldsmith had told us that Shmiel hadn't lived in the house that he and his siblings had been born in, House Number 141, the address given on those hundred certificates of birth and death Alex had sent me years ago, but had moved in the Thirties to a big new house on Dlugosa Street. Over time, Jack and the others, in Australia and Europe and Israel, had confirmed this and had drawn maps for me pinpointing the location of the street—just across the street from the Little Park—and of the house itself, four houses down on the right as you enter the street. But four (and even five, and six) houses down the street that more or less corresponded to Dlugosa Street on Jack's map, which was called Russka, there was an enormous, very long and very ancient-looking barn that occupied what looked like several lots. It seemed clear there had never been a house there. We started wandering down the street, farther away from the Little Park. This ambling around the town was, I had to admit, a lot more pleasant than it had been before, when Andrew and Matt and Jen and I had trudged through the rain and the mud. It wasn't yet eleven in the morning, and the air was already quite warm. Our footsteps crunched aridly in the dirt and gravel of the street. Every house, it seemed, had a long back garden filled with apple and plum and quince trees. Dogs barked lazily. Alex stopped a woman, a young woman, and asked whether she knew of some old person who lived nearby who could tell us the location of the street that was once called *Dlugosa*. They chatted for a minute, and Alex made a motion with his arm, beckoning for me and Froma to turn back. We must walk this way, back toward the park, he said. There is an old man who lives in the beginning of the street.

The woman led us to the house and pointed. A thickset man with a Slavic face and a full head of white hair combed straight away from a low, suntanned forehead was sitting in a kind of motorized wheelchair in the yard in front of the house; still, when he saw us coming he rose to his feet. He and Alex started talking. He didn't seem to know anything about Dlugosa Street. Alex gave a quick wink, and had started to tilt his head to the side with a *let's get out of here* gesture—a tic I'd come to recognize as his sign that we were wasting our time and should be moving on—when the old man in the chair loudly saluted someone who was coming down the street from the direction we'd just come from. We turned to look. *Stepan*, the old man said. This Stepan ambled up to us and shook hands firmly with everyone. He had on a blue-and-gray-plaid workman's shirt and an old-fashioned cap. When he spoke, you could hear the sound of a faint sloshing, almost a buzzing. He had no front teeth, which did not prevent him from smiling very often. His skin was as brown and weathered as saddle leather.

Alex repeated what he'd just told the other man. We were looking for Dlugosa Street, he said. We were looking for the house of this American's great-uncle, a Jew who had lived in Bolekhiv, in Bolechow, before the war. Shmiel Jäger.

Jäger! Stepan exclaimed. He started talking rapidly to Alex.

Alex, whose broad face was already red from the sun and beaded with perspiration, beamed more brightly. He looked at me and said, He says his father was a driver for Shmiel Jäger!

Oh *really*? I said. But here, I realized, was another contrast between 2001 and 2005. In 2001, Jen and I had lowered our heads and wept simply because we'd found someone who'd known of Shmiel and his family, without actually knowing them: that's how impossible it had seemed, then, that there might still be people in the world who could remember them. But now I'd talked to so many people, people who really knew them. This is why I listened to what Stepan had to say with interest, but not excitement.

Jäger, tak, Stepan was saying. As he talked, Alex gave a running translation.

Jäger had a truck. In this truck he would move goods between Bolechow and Lwów. His father would drive the truck. And he, Jäger, would sometimes tell the father to take a couple of horses to help him to pull the truck up a hill, because sometimes it was very overloaded and sometimes would get stuck! Very big horses, German horses, the kind they used to use in the war to pull cannons.

Oh really? I said again. By this time a few other people had gathered around to hear what was going on: a middle-aged woman in a housedress, and two younger women in jeans and tight-fitting T-shirts.

They were, in fact, curious about us.

He used to go to Lwów, Alex went on, translating for Stepan, and if something broke he would be very upset, it would be ruined! He had his shop somewhere near the center, a place where three new houses were built since. Not far from the Ratusz, opposite the Magistrat. Across the street.

Yes, I said.

And so Stepan stood there talking for a while, and told us many things. He remembered the Szymanskis, a Polish family. They had a house with a kind of tavern inside, you could eat good sausages there. The house was now gone. He knew nothing more about the Szymanskis. He remembered the Grünschlags; they had a lumber store. He remembered a family called Zimmerman. He and the other old man remembered the Ellenbogens; they had a shop on the Rynek. He remembered some Jews who had been taken to Siberia in 1940: Landes. He remembered the names of people I'd never heard of: Blumenthal, Kelhoffer. He remembered Eli Rosenberg, who had returned to Bolechow and lived there long after the war was over. He remembered that during the Occupation, all the Jews were killed. He remembered certain specific things from the war years, too, for instance the day he had been helping his father with some job not far from the Rynek and shooting had erupted. Bullets everywhere, *pchoo! pchoo! pchoo!* Stepan said, making little bullet noises. *Down! Down!* his father had shouted at him, and they lay on the grass to avoid the bullets. Who was being shot? we asked. Probably Jews, he said. He saw once how the Jews were being led down the road as Nazis with rolled-up sleeves stood with machine guns. And a couple of local guys (Alex translated), who were not in uniform, were helping them. There was also a Jewish police militia organized by the Nazis, and the Jewish police knew everybody.

So these Jews were led to the place at the end of the town, near Taniawa. Yes, he knew where Taniawa was, his father was one of the men who had helped to make the monument. They used to mow grass up there.

Good, I said, we're going there. I'd heard that it was so overgrown that it was impossible to find anymore; clearly this Stepan was the ideal person to help us find it. (And we did go there, later that day, after an hour's search in a forest so opulent with chest-high wildflowers that being there was like being in a fairy tale, and I turned to Alex and said, the way my mother would have said it, But it's so *beautiful,* this place!, and he smiled grimly and said, It was *always* in a beautiful place. Finally, with the help of a youngish man who lived nearby—not so young, though, that he was too young to have had a father who'd been there on the day it happened, and had gone home to tell his children about the rows and rows of Jews who'd been lined up there and shot—with his help we found it and we stood there by the little concrete obelisks, this man and Alex and Froma and Stepan and I, and there was a moment of silence. I felt a little bit foolish. Then I took out the enlargement of the picture of Ruchele and said, I'm not sure, but I think we just need to think for a moment about this girl, a sixteen-year-old girl. Her life. And this is where she died, in this place, right here. I passed around the picture, and everyone took it in turn and looked at it and nodded sadly. Then we left.)

So Stepan stood there in Russka Street and as we encircled him he told us what he remembered. Froma wanted to know what the feelings of the Ukrainians had been during the occupation. Everyone was always afraid, Stepan said, and at that moment the other man, the man with the fierce face and the mane of white hair, who had remained silent throughout our conversation, stepped up. Of course everyone was afraid, he said. Then he told a story. A Ukrainian named Medvid—it means "bear"—had hidden a Jewish family. They were discovered, and the Nazis came and killed not only this man, Medvid, and his entire family, hanged them all, including small children, but they also killed everyone in the whole area whose name was Medvid.

German logic, I could hear Jack saying. That order, that surface formality with no rational or moral content.

The old man went on. So after that, he said, nobody even tried to help anymore. Or almost nobody.

I thought of Ciszko Szymanski. I thought of all the survivors I'd talked to, nearly all of whom had been hidden by Ukrainians. I thought of the Szedlak woman, whoever she had been. For some strange reason, people had, in fact, continued helping. When Alex, of his own accord, asked Stepan whether he knew stories of people who had turned in Jews to the authorities, Stepan said, I don't know people like that. There were good people, and there were bad people. I listened and thought, Yes. There were Szymanski and Szedlak; and there were the pitchforks, there was the neighbor who betrayed them. When all is said and done, it was as simple, and as mysterious, as that.

In the end we talked for about forty minutes, standing there in the sun as Alex got redder and redder. The one thing that nobody seemed to know was exactly where Dlugosa Street was. Stepan scratched his chin and frowned, then shook his head. *Dlugosa Dlugosa Dlugosa.* No. But he could tell us, however, that during the Stalin years, everyone who lived in the street on which we were now standing, on Russka Street, was deported to Siberia because they had houses with tin roofs, and tin roofs meant that you were bourgeois, counterrevolutionary. His own family, he added with the broad, cavernous smile of a toddler, had been spared when this irrational (but, we knew, by no means uncommonly irrational) decimation took place, because their house had a roof made of thatch: a proletarian roof.

He talked and we listened. He said something to Alex, who turned to us and said, He said you should talk to a woman who lives in the . . . the German Colony—?

Yes, I said, I knew about it, it was up past the bridge. Jack had told me.

—the German Colony, her brother was also a driver for Shmiel, maybe she knows more.

OK, I said.

And he says even more you should talk to a very old man named Prokopiv, he works in the church now. He is so old, maybe he will know more than anyone.

OK, I said.

Do you want to go there? Alex asked. He knew we'd come here today for a specific purpose, to have the experience I needed to write about: to see the places about which I now knew so much, to walk, as much as anyone today can do so, in their steps. He knew, because we'd e-mailed and talked to each other so much over the past years, and knew me so well at this point, that I didn't want to spend time culling stories that were, by this point, stories of a variety with which I was by now familiar, stories I already knew.

No, I said, it's OK, why not? I thought to myself, These stories were charming: the dray horses, the stuck truck. A few more couldn't hurt.

We all got in the blue car, Alex and Froma and Stepan and I, and drove to Prokopiv's house.

If only because of the magnitude of the punishment that they suffer, it is curious that the sin for which the inhabitants of the luxurious cities of Sodom and Gomorrah are exterminated is never actually named, much less described in detail in parashat Vayeira. *Although there is, as we've seen, a strong implication that the sin is that of sexual transgression, involving practices well outside of the famous proscriptions given in Leviticus, a biblical text with which we are not concerned here, there is really nothing in the text that says why the cities must be destroyed: God merely announces to Abraham, more or less out of the blue, that the "outcry of Sodom and Gomorrah has become very great," and that their sin—unnamed—is "very grave." In defense of God, whose taste for total annihilation as well as for creation has by this point been well established in Genesis, Rashi lingers over the fact that God then announces that he will "descend" to take a look at the cities of the plain, in order to make sure that the "outcry" he has heard is in fact accurate. "This," the French sage declares, "has taught judges not to issue a verdict in capital cases except through seeing [them]," which is an attractive thought, although it is probably fair to say that modern legal intellects are more likely to linger over the fact that in this case, the condemned don't seem to have been informed of the charges against them— charges that, at least in the text that we have, are neither named nor, indeed, ever proved, which is worrisome when the accused is an entire population.*

There then ensues one of the strangest exchanges in the Torah's vast catalog of prickly dialogues between patriarchs and the Deity himself. As God's destructive angels head off to the evil cities, Abraham confronts God with a concern that any contemporary reader is likely to have as well. What worries Abraham is what has worried some commentators at other points when contemplating the wholesale ruthlessness of God's punishments (as, for instance, in the passage in Noach *that raises the faint possibility that innocents—children, say—might be drowned by the Flood): What if there are blameless people living in the cities that God has destined for inescapable extermination—as, given the magnitude of the obliteration, there are likely to be? What if, say, even fifty innocent people lived among the wicked of Sodom and Gomorrah? (Fifty, as we know—like forty-eight—being but a tiny fraction when you consider the population of an entire city.) Would it not, Abraham argues, be a sacrilege unto God himself to punish the innocent along with the wicked? Would it not be unjust? Should the judge of all the earth commit an injustice?*

God readily takes his prophet's point, and assures him that if there were only fifty good men in Sodom, he would spare the entire place ("the entire place," as Rashi pauses to explain, eager as he is to suggest that God is being unnecessarily generous, refers not only to Sodom but to the other cities of the plain, since Sodom is a "metropolis"). Perhaps worried by God's swift reply—nobody who has ever bargained feels safe when the other party agrees too readily to his terms—Abraham squeezes his Creator a bit, and tries to get him down to forty-five: would God spare Sodom (and the whole place), he asks, if there were only forty-five righteous people there? God agrees: forty-five. And so they continue, from forty-five to forty, from forty to thirty, from thirty to twenty, from twenty to ten. Abraham desists from his aggressive bargaining only after he gets God to promise that he won't destroy the greater Sodom area even if there are but ten righteous people in it. In the end the cities are destroyed, the luxuriant and decadent cities of the East, with all their people, the young, the old, the sick, the lame, even the newborn infant at his mother's breast, presumably, although here again the text is reticent with details, as unwilling to describe the punished as it was to describe the crime.

In a way, this story is irresistible to those who feel a lingering unease after the story of the Flood, with its faint suggestion that precisely that which Abraham later fears, the slaughter of the innocent along with the righteous, took place then. And yet for me, the fate of Sodom and Gomorrah—or rather, the deaths of the men, women, and children of those two cities, since I have learned by now that it is too easy to say that this or that city has been destroyed, when what you really mean is that all the people in the city have been killed—is troubling for another reason. Although I admire Abraham's acuity in the marketplace, I have always wondered why he should have stopped at the number ten. Friedman has almost nothing to say on the subject, and simply accepts God's verdict: "Since God knows the situation and its necessary outcome, why speak?" Rashi explains, rather ingeniously alluding to the Flood narrative, which is the prototype of this story, why ten is the number of each successive decrement in the bargaining process. (Because the number of those rescued in Noah's ark was eight, and eight plus Abraham plus God equals ten.) But neither commentator seems much troubled by the question that troubles me so much, which is this: Even if there were fewer than ten good Sodomites—even if, let's say, there were only one righteous person in the whole vast metropolis—wouldn't it be unjust to kill him along with the guilty? Or even this: As long as there is one good inhabitant of the country of the wicked, can we say that the entire nation is guilty?

THERE WAS NOBODY home at old Prokopiv's place, so after dropping Stepan at home, where his irate wife was waiting on the porch, hands on hips, wondering where he'd been all morning, we drove to the German Colony and found the address he'd given us for Mrs. Latyk, the old woman whose brother had worked for Uncle Shmiel.

As he likes to do, Alex knocked on a window rather than the door and in Ukrainian called out, Is anybody home? After a minute or two, a white-haired woman appeared at the chain-link gate that led to the tidy little backyard. Her deeply lined but animated face, the broad, surprisingly mobile features, the frank nose with its ski-slope tip, the strong white hair pulled carelessly back into a little bun, the vigorous, large hands that flapped and waved as she walked slowly to the gate, even the intense cornflower blue of her thin cotton housedress—all these projected a kind of solid trustworthiness. Alex talked to her briefly and at some point said *Shmiel Jäger,* and she nodded vigorously and said *Tak, tak,* and beckoned for us to come through the gate. As she motioned to us to sit down on some plastic chairs in a corner of her little shaded yard, she told us she had been born in 1919. No, she said, Stepan had been wrong: it was her uncle, she said, who'd been Shmiel's driver, not her brother. But yes, of course she remembered Shmiel Jäger. She didn't see him often herself, and so didn't remember the children—she thought there might have been a daughter—but sure, she remembered Jäger, he had a big truck. His drivers would drive this truck to Lwów and pick up all sorts of goods there, clothes and food and fruit—

Strawberries, I thought—

—and other things, and transport them to various places . . .

And so it went. We talked for about half an hour, and she shared with us what memories she had: homely things, everyday things. Things we'd heard. She knew that Jäger had lived somewhere near the Rynek, but the house wasn't there anymore; another house had been built on the site where his had been. Yes, her uncle had liked working for Jäger, she said. And Jäger had *loved* her uncle! They were close, not just a man and his worker. Jäger was known as a nice man, a generous man. People liked him. Her uncle's name? Stanislaw Latyk. *Stas,* she said. His children had long ago moved to America; if we wanted, she would give us their names and addresses. The son in particular, she thought, would remember a lot. I said yes, that would be nice, and thought to myself, Maybe they'd have charming stories to tell, too. ("And Jäger *loved* our father!") She brought out a piece of paper, and as I copied the address, she showed us snapshots of her uncle, the whole family. I promised I would call her cousins in the States when we got home, and soon after this, when we had shaken her firm hand warmly, we walked back to the Passat. Alex's instinct was right: we shouldn't waste too much more time on these interviews.

As it happened, I did phone the children of Stas Latyk a few weeks after we got back from that trip, although the stories they told me were not charming. When I talked to Lydia, the daughter, who now lives near New Haven, she gladly lingered over what memories she could summon, trying to help in whatever way she could. Yes, sure, she remembered Shmiel Jäger, she said: her father had been very friendly with him, they were close. During the war, she added, her father had his own big truck—he'd stopped working for Shmiel and gone into business for himself during the Thirties—and had somehow created a kind of hiding place out of one of this truck's huge fuel tanks, and in this hiding place he had smuggled Jews to safe spots, to other hiding places. (After I told her what I knew by then about Shmiel's fate, she said it may well have been her father who'd taken him to the Polish schoolteacher's house.) This, she added, had to have been before the day on which, during a roundup of Jews, her father had seen a German soldier brutally dragging a woman away from her child, and had gone up to this soldier and struck him in the face and said, *Shame on you.* For that, Stas was taken to a Gestapo cell and beaten for two days. When he finally came home, Lydia said, he was so unrecognizable that her mother fainted. Soon after that, fearing for his life, Stas Latyk had disappeared into the forest. Lydia and her mother and brother Mikhailo found out later that he'd joined up with the Russians at some point and returned after the war to Bolekhiv, but by then the rest of the family was in America, and for one reason or another, because of the way the world was then, because of other things, they never saw him again.

I also called Michael Latyk, as Stas's son Mikhailo is now called. He lives in Texas. He was very warm when I rang him out of the blue the day after I spoke to his sister, and said, yes, of course he'd be happy to share his memories of his father, the war, anything. He confirmed what Lydia had told me about his father's close friendship with Shmiel, adding only that, as he recalled quite clearly, the two men had often engaged in impromptu wrestling matches.

Wrestling matches? I couldn't wait to tell my mother.

What else did he remember? I asked. It was hard for him, he said: he was a boy, it was a very bad time, he saw terrible things. He was part of the crowd that gathered around the Dom Katolicki that night in October, he said: he had seen people being lined up against the wall and shot. There was the time one June day he'd been outside, picking and eating cherries off a tree, when suddenly he heard the sound of shooting and looked up to see a group of people being shot right there in the open. After that, he said, he hadn't been able to eat for three days. He had seen other things. A woman, six or seven months pregnant, wounded, asking for a doctor, a doctor. And then there was the time when, after one of the big *Aktionen*, he'd seen a boy of about his own age who'd been shot in the the right shoulder during the roundup—*No, wait,* it was the left shoulder, he could see it in his mind's eye—but had somehow survived. He remembered seeing this boy about four days later, sitting at the fence of a *Lager.* He was sitting under the fence, Michael recalled, all swollen with hunger, and he was taking—

His voice grew ragged and he began to weep. I'm sorry, I'm sorry, he said. I can't tell this.

It's OK, I said, the way I sometimes talk to my children. Just take your time, take a deep breath.

He took a breath and said, He was taking.

He broke down again. I could not imagine what the outcome of this story was going to be, but as I sat at my desk with the phone in my hand I realized that I was squeezing the receiver so hard my hands were wet.

Finally Michael Latyk in Texas in August 2005 took a deep breath and said, He was sitting all swollen with hunger, sitting by the fence, and he was taking the lice off his own body and eating them.

Then he said: I'm sorry, I can't talk about these things anymore.

I nodded and then remembered I was on the phone. Yes, I said quietly, OK, you've been so helpful, I appreciate so much what you've shared with me, I and my family appreciate it—

Suddenly he interrupted me. But there's one more thing I have to tell you, Michael said. You know that expression, "Eat a Balanced Diet"? Well, for the rest of my life, every time I hear that expression, I think of *that*.

I had kept my promise to Mrs. Latyk, and had called her cousins in the States.

WE FOUND THE old man Prokopiv just in time. As we pulled up in front of his house, he was walking briskly away from his front door toward town—on the way, as he later told us, to his job at the church, where he tidied up every day. The house was large and handsome, a generous wooden structure with a steeply pitched tin roof. It was painted brick red, and the frames of the windows were white. The impression it gave of being a barn was enhanced by the fact that it stood a little to the side of the street in the middle of a profusion of apple trees, and altogether it looked like something you might come across during a pleasant day of driving in the countryside. Prokopiv himself, whose first name was Vasyl, gave no hint of being ninety. His frame was tall and quite solid, and he had a handsome, oval head and a firm-fleshed face, almost completely unlined, except for two deep laugh lines on either side of his wide mouth. His puckish nose, like that of Mrs. Latyk, ended in a little ski jump, which gave him an incongruously boyish quality. Like Josef Adler on the day I'd met him, he was wearing a tan shirt with epaulettes. He looked about seventy. His handshake was crushing.

Because Prokopiv was clearly on his way to an appointment that he wanted to keep, Alex kept the introduction short. He said we were Americans, looking for people who may have known Jägers from Bolechow.

Prokopiv brought his left hand to his face as if in contemplation and spoke for a minute in Ukrainian.

He doesn't remember Jägers, Alex said.

What with the unexpected interviews with Stepan and Mrs. Latyk, and the hour we'd spent looking for Taniawa, it had been a long day by this point. The sun was hot. A little hastily, I said, No? OK.

Prokopiv said something else to Alex, which from its intonation I knew was a question. I was pretty sure I heard the word *zhid:* Jew.

Alex said *Tak,* Yes, and added a sentence, at which point Prokopiv threw back his handsome head and laughed, a laugh of recognition.

Alex said, I told him about the trucks, then he remembered immediately. *Tak tak.* Yes yes. He remembers. Shmiel Jäger. He was living in Russki Bolechow. He doesn't know where the street was. He knew the name, he didn't know them himself.

I said, OK, that's nice. Then I asked him to ask Prokopiv, who I knew was eager to get to church, if he recognized some other names: Szymanski, Grünschlag, Ellenbogen. He and Alex talked for a minute, and Alex again said, Yes, he knew those names. It was a small town. Everyone knew who everybody was.

OK, I said, so he remembers some names.

Alex nodded and made the *Let's leave* face, the *We're not going to get anything else from him* face. Yes, he said. All right then.

We thanked Prokopiv and he started on his way, and Alex and I turned toward the car.

Wait, Froma said.

We turned back.

She said, Don't you want to ask him something else?

I thought, Here we go again: the pushing, the reluctance to let go, the insistence on going back for one last look, one more question. I felt a twinge of exasperation, and not merely because I didn't want to turn back. At Taniawa, there had been a little scene between Froma and Alex. When we finally reached the site of the mass grave, idyllic and remote, Froma had commented that the Germans would never have found this spot without the help of local Ukrainians. Ever since she and I had been in Vilnius together, and had visited the mass grave in the Ponar forest, with its hundred thousand Jews sleeping their unquiet sleep beneath the picnicking grounds, we had returned almost obsessively to the issue of local collaboration. Many times since then we had discussed the mechanics of the killing, which so often would not have been possible without the help of local people, the people who knew who the Jews were, where they lived, where the fields in the forests were. Many people think of the Holocaust and think, *Germans.* Just recently, at a bat mitzvah I attended in New York (a ceremony of which my grandfather would have disapproved, but then, time changes even traditions), someone who had heard about my search for what happened to Shmiel, my many trips abroad, came up to me and said, Doesn't it make you feel uncomfortable around Germans? and I asked, You mean Germans in general? and then I laughed and shook my head and said, No, of course not; and then I added, And anyway, if I were the kind of person who thought that way, I'd be more afraid of Ukrainians than of Germans. Froma was particularly preoccupied with this issue, and at Taniawa she'd said, They never could have found this place without the Ukrainians, and Alex, who was hot and tired, had bristled a little and snapped back at Froma that what she had said was *impossible to know*—bristled not because he was a Ukrainian, since as a historian he is interested in facts, and is therefore acquainted with the stories of Ukrainian atrocities, just as he can tell you the facts of the great forced starvation, the Soviet soldiers who surrounded the towns and villages, one after another, and simply took out all the food and let the people die, which eventually they did, after they had eaten the mice, and the rats, and finally one another. It was because Alex was interested in facts that he bristled and said, I'm sorry, but how do you *know* that, there's just no evidence for that in *this* case, it was just an open field then, any place would have done, anybody driving down this *road* could have found a place like this or any other place, OK? It had been to quell this moment of tension that I'd spoken up, as we stood there in the green and leafy glade, and said, *I think we just need to think for a moment about this girl, a sixteen-year-old girl. Her life.*

It was because I had this uneasy scene in mind, and because I was afraid that Froma was going to bring up something about Ukrainian collaboration, that I responded to her question about our wanting to ask Prokopiv *something else* by saying, firmly, No, that's OK.

Froma persisted. Don't you want to ask him what he knows about when they took them?

Hmmm? I said, not wanting to get into it. We knew what had happened, by now. And clearly this Prokopiv didn't know my family. I thought it was time to finish up here, to take a few more pictures and leave.

What you asked the *others,* Froma went on. What happened when they took the Jews away?

Alex was perspiring heavily; a big man, he suffered more from the heat than we did. Even so, he repeated Froma's question in Ukrainian. Prokopiv talked for a while and said, yes, he remembered one time when some Jews were taken to where the brick factory used to be and they themselves dug up pits in that place, and they killed them and buried them there. There was a memorial of some kind at that place. And others were killed in the cemetery.

Where's this memorial? Froma asked.

He thinks it's in the forest, Alex said after a brief exchange. The Germans took them to this club that there used to be here, they were taken to the movie theater and then they took them to that place and killed them.

It was clear they were talking about the first Aktion, about Taniawa. This was a waste of time.

OK, I said, let's say thank you, and let's go.

But Froma said, Does he know of any that were *hidden?* What she was interested in was this: As we had stood in front of the Dom Katolicki that morning, we'd encountered a diminutive and very old woman who, after she'd stopped briefly to greet Stepan, had begun to talk to us, and while she talked had said that long ago she'd helped to hide a little Jewish girl named Rita. Then the woman had burst into tears and said, *The Jews never did anything and they killed them all anyway.* This had touched Froma, and it was clear that the story of Rita was much on her mind. So she said, now, Does he know of any that were hidden?

Alex, standing a few yards away with Prokopiv, gestured as if he couldn't hear. Loudly, I repeated the question. Does he know of any who were *hidden*?

Alex relayed the question. Giving up, I moved away from the car and walked back to Prokopiv.

Prokopiv gave a tight little smile of assent. Hidden, he said. Yes, I know.

Motioning with his head in the direction of the next street over, the old man started talking again. I heard what I thought was the name *Kopernika*. Copernicus? My Ukrainian was clearly no better than my Polish.

Alex listened and then translated.

He said, In Kopernika Street there were two Polish women who were schoolteachers. One of them was hiding two Jews. The Jews were taken and the teachers were killed.

STANDING THERE, IN the moment after old Prokopiv had said *two Polish women who were schoolteachers, one of them was hiding two Jews,* I understood for the first time in my life the expression *rooted to the ground.* I couldn't move. My ears were ringing. I heard my voice echoing in my head when I finally spoke. It is only because my digital voice recorder continued to run as I stood there speechless that I know I said, But this is the—it's the—

I tried to collect my thoughts. I said, Ask him was it a Polish *art* teacher? Because that's who was hiding my uncle and his daughter, an art teacher from the school, ask him—

It occurred to me that I still hadn't told Alex this part of the story. There was so much that we'd learned since I'd last seen him, so much for us to catch up on, and I'd been saving it all for the big dinner that he and Natalie were going to be hosting the next night, Saturday, after Lane arrived. I hadn't told him all of what I'd learned, hadn't yet told him about Frydka and Shmiel and Ciszko and Szedlak, because I didn't think it would matter, on this trip, today.

Ask him, I had said, barely knowing what I was saying. Alex started talking to Prokopiv, and I cleared my throat and said, Does he remember the *name* of this teacher? There could have been two teachers, I thought, after all there had to have been more than one teacher in this town, maybe another one was also hiding Jews. Maybe it wasn't the same one. Maybe it wasn't them. I had to be sure.

Alex asked the question. Prokopiv listened and then nodded twice, vigor-ously, and smiled broadly. His teeth were small and square.

He said, *Tak tak*.

He said, *Szedlakowa*.

He said something else, one sentence.

Alex looked at me. He said to me, He says she was killed right in the yard of her house.

I stood there and said to the old man, as if the force of my emotion at that moment could transcend the language barrier:

That was my uncle and his daughter. It *was*.

In the months that have passed since that afternoon, Froma has told me that when she tells the story of what we found during that trip, tells it to other people, she describes me, at the moment when Prokopiv uttered the name *Szedlakowa*, as having *melted*. And it's true that something snapped in me at that moment. I simply sank down and squatted there in the dust of the street and started to cry.

Partly it was this: the bizarre coincidence that of all the stories of *people who were hidden,* this man, whom we'd almost missed that day, whom we would never have talked to if we'd come five minutes later, whom we'd never have asked the right question if Froma hadn't once again pushed, demanded one more look, this man knew only one story of Jews who'd been hidden, which turned out to be the one story I was interested in, the story I'd spent the past four years tracking down and piecing together.

And partly it was this: that for a long time it seemed that there could never be real confirmation of that story, because everyone who'd told it to me, in all the various versions that they had heard, had been absent when it happened. Now I was talking to a Ukrainian, not a Jew, which is to say, someone who was there when it happened. Suddenly, it seemed less like a story than a fact. I had hit bedrock.

I crouched on the quiet street with my hand over my wet eyes, and when I finally looked up Prokopiv had come closer and was looking at me with an expression of deep, almost fatherly sympathy, the way a man might look at a child who had hurt himself.

Aiiiii, he said with a deep sigh. *Tak tak.* Yes yes. It felt like, *There there.*

Froma and Alex were silent for a while. After a while Froma asked softly, Everyone knew of it? Everyone knew this story?

Prokopiv gave a firm nod. Yes, yes, Alex said. Everybody knew. He says everyone was talking about it right when it happened.

Right when it happened. Not in 1946 in Katowice, not in 1950 in Israel, not in 2003 in Australia. It was this thought that reminded me that I had work to do, that I needed to get information now. My mind cleared, and I got to my feet.

I said, So he says there were *two* teachers? This was news to me.

The two Ukrainians talked for a while, the old man of ninety who had seen so much and the bearlike young man in his thirties who, for whatever mysterious reasons, taste or temperament or accident, had ended up devoting his working life to tracking the history of the Jews of Galicia. Alex said, Yes, these two teachers were two sisters, they were living together. And he thinks both of them were killed.

I asked, Does he remember what part of town these ladies lived in?

Alex talked to Prokopiv and then gave me an intense, private look.

He said, Sure he remembers. He will take us to the house, if we want.

The street was quiet. A little breeze ruffled the leaves of the apple trees.

I said, Yes. We want.

THE HOUSE THAT had once belonged to the Szedlak sisters, a low, single-story bungalow not unlike many of the houses you see in Bolekhiv, looked deserted when Prokopiv pointed it out to us as we drove him to the church. We dropped him there with effusive thanks.

During the ride, Froma had told Alex to ask the old man if he remembered the name of the *betrayer*. I myself was feeling so overwhelmed with the discovery of the Szedlak house that it hadn't occurred to me to ask. I couldn't imagine discovering anything else; it had felt like enough. But Alex, who was, I could tell, deeply affected emotionally by what was happening, was as eager to pursue this tack as Froma was. He talked for a while with Prokopiv, who shook his head sadly.

He doesn't know who betrayed them, Alex said as we drove the short way from the neighborhood of the Dom Katolicki to the Rynek, where the little gold-domed Ukrainian church stood, fifty paces from the house where my grandfather was born. Alex added, He says maybe *then* he knew. Yes, back then, people knew. . . . But it's such a long time.

The thought that perhaps Prokopiv was protecting someone flashed briefly through my mind, and when Froma spoke I knew she was thinking the same thing. She said, Everything that happened, happened because someone, an individual, made a decision. She and I had talked about this a great deal over the years. In Ponar she had expounded on a thought she'd framed before and would frame again: that the Holocaust is so big, the scale of it is so gigantic, so enormous, that it becomes easy to think of it as something mechanical. Anonymous. But everything that happened, happened because someone made a decision. To pull a trigger, to flip a switch, to close a cattle car door, to hide, to betray. It was with this consideration in mind—which to the record of historical facts, to the catalog of things that happened and could be witnessed, adds the invisible dimension of morality, of *judging* what happened—that she had asked *Who was the betrayer?* and had wondered, as I briefly had, whether Prokopiv's inability to come up with a name that everyone had once known was the result of a moral decision of his own just then, perhaps a decision not to bring judgment down today on some ill and ancient neighbor, rather than the inevitable consequence of the passage of so many years.

We drove back to the Szedlak house. Prokopiv had told us that there had once been a nice veranda at the front. There was no veranda now. The house presented its long side to the quiet street, a blank stucco expanse punctuated by three modest windows. It looked inscrutable. The door, it seemed, was on the far side, which you reached by going through a chain-link gate and up a little walkway into a courtyard. Toward the back of the courtyard was a little outbuilding, its sloping roof made of the same corrugated metal that the house was covered with. It had a door and a little window. I looked at it and thought, Too obvious. In the walkway that led from the street to the courtyard, two dogs, a little black terrier and a big German shepherd, lay looking up at us. They did not look particularly friendly.

Alex knocked on the window. In a moment, a haggard-looking woman emerged from the courtyard: squashed Slavic features, dyed black hair sticking up in tufts, a garish purple robe of some thin stuff wrapped hastily around her solid midriff. She could have been sixty, she could have been forty. The dogs started barking furiously. Froma and I waited by the gate in the street while Alex stood talking to the woman.

She says we can come into the courtyard, he said. But she don't know nothing, she came here in the seventies from Russia.

It's OK, I said, we just want to look at the courtyard. Prokopiv had said, They killed them in the yard. I wanted to see the place, stand in it, and leave.

We walked up the little walkway, the dogs scrambling round our feet and barking loudly. He said something to the woman and she yelled at the dogs, who retreated.

We walked around the little cement-paved area. The yard, Prokopiv had said. They killed them all right there. I handed the video camera to Alex and said, I can't deal with this now, do you mind doing the video? He nodded, expressively, and took it. The three of us walked around the tiny area for a bit. This is where they died, I thought. It didn't seem quite real. I said to Froma, I don't even know what to think. It's amazing to think it was here. I stood there shaking my head as I looked at the decrepit house, the tiny concrete court-yard, the sagging shed.

Whatever it was, it was not the *kessle* of a Polish count.

I looked at the shed again and a thought occurred to me. I said to Alex, Can we ask these people if we can just go in there? I wanted to see the inside of the house. Here, somewhere in this square footage of broken concrete, they had died. But somewhere inside the house, in there, they had been hiding, had been alive. Thirty years before, Aunt Miriam had written me a letter. *Onkel Schmil and 1 daughter Fridka the Germans killed them 1944 in Bolechow, so say me one man from Bolechow nobody know what is true.* Now we knew the truth. They had been here, somewhere right *here.* I wanted to see it.

Three other women, just as haggard as the first, their bare feet filthy, had gathered just inside the door. Alex said, I don't think we should stay long because they are alcohol addicts—very strong addicts.

We nodded. We navigated the narrow door. Two pairs of bony cats were copulating on a sofa. The place had the musty smell of stale alcohol and, I thought, urine. Inside there were a few small rooms: a little kitchen just past the door, beyond that a little living room with two sofas—on one of which, I realized after a moment, the inert body of a woman lay wrapped in blankets—and beyond that a dining room with a table and a few chairs. The walls of the dining room were painted bright yellow; a pretty stencil of green ivy leaves ran around the perimeter, just beneath the ceiling. Lace curtains hung at each window, and the walls were hung with inexpensive carpets in oriental patterns. Here and there you could see an icon, an old portrait photograph that had been tinted with pastels, and, bizarrely, some ancient posters of languid 1940s models in slinky lingerie. There was one more room off the dining room, and when I opened the double door to it I saw inside an enormously tall teenaged boy with severe and beautiful Slavic features. His hair was jet black and his skin was almost a pure white, as if he had no circulation. He looked at me with glazed and unseeing eyes. I shut the door and turned around. Alex had been standing behind me.

Not just alcohol, he said. Maybe drugs, too.

So this was the house. One story. Minus a poster or two, it was possible to imagine it as it had been then, neat as a pin, the lace curtains parted rather than drawn, the tiled stove near the kitchen, now cold, giving off the rich aromas of cooking food. I walked back and forth, reluctant to leave. My mind was racing. *Where could you hide someone, here?*

I said to Alex, OK, well.

Then I literally smacked my forehead with my hand. *Ask her,* I said, Ask her if there's a *basement*, any kind of *cellar*.

The woman had been following us as we paced the small rooms. I supposed she was worried that we would find her stash of booze and God knew what else. Alex spoke to her. Yes, he said, there is a room underneath.

The black-haired woman sighed heavily and gave a resigned little frown, as if she were long used to the impositions of strangers more powerful than she. She walked the few paces from the dining room back into the little living room. The three of us crowded behind her. The two sofas were about a yard apart from each other, a round woven rug between them. With a weary gesture, she dragged the rug away with her foot and jerked her head.

There, cut out of the floorboards, was a trapdoor. It was about two feet square, and had been cut out in such a way that the edges of two of its sides were flush with the edges of the boards. *Good camouflage,* I thought. A little metal ring that served as a handle was attached to one end. We all stood, staring at it, thinking the same thing.

I pointed to the square outline cut into the floorboards and turned to Alex and said, I can go in there?

Before Alex had a chance to translate, the woman nodded. She said something to Alex, who told me that this cellar was there when they moved here from southern Russia. Now they stored jars there: pickles, things like that. I bent over and pulled on the little ring and raised the door. It was surprisingly thick and heavy. I swung it upward and a smell escaped, the dank smell of earth and something else, the failed odor of disuse. One of the other women, sitting on the sofa opposite the one on which the inert woman lay, helpfully extended a hand in order to keep the door open. We all peered inside. For a moment all we could see was a pitch-black square. After a second or two, the outline of some shelves emerged, lined with bottles and jars. I walked around the opening and stood next to the raised door. Some new pine steps had been nailed into one side.

I looked up and said, I have to go down there. Alex, holding the video camera, nodded.

I crouched down and lowered my legs into the hole, searching for the step with my foot. I found it and started to descend, looking upward toward the light the whole time. As I've mentioned, I have a deathly fear of enclosed places, but couldn't and wouldn't bring myself to mention it now, under these circumstances. I thought of the cattle car at the Holocaust Museum. Maybe Shmiel had been as claustrophobic as I, I thought. Maybe it's genetic, who knows? At least I was going to climb back out of here and walk out of this place in broad daylight.

The hole was just that: a hole. I had descended maybe eight or nine feet and was at the bottom. Down here, there was no light, and even though the trap-door above my head was open, the space itself was steeped in a profound, inky black: I had to stretch out my hands to locate the walls, which turned out to be very close. I figured the space measured three feet on a side. Because I was deep underground, it was very cold, surprisingly cold. I fought back the panic and thought, This is horrible, it's like being in a—

Oh my God I am so *stupid*, I said to myself at that moment. A *kestl*, a *kestl*, not a *castle*. In the end, we get so much wrong not because we aren't paying attention but because time passes, things change, a grandson cannot be his grandfather, for all that he may try; because we can never be other than our-selves, imprisoned by our time and place and circumstances. However much we want to learn, to know, we can only ever see things with our own eyes and hear with our own ears, and how we interpret what we see and hear depends, ultimately, on who we are and what we already think we know, or want to know. *Kestl* is the Yiddish word for *box*. All those years ago I had listened to my grandfather talk, the one time he had offered me information about Shmiel's death, and I, listening to those plush vowels and thickened consonants, had heard what I'd wanted to hear, a story like a fairy tale, a tragic drama com-plete with a nobleman and a castle. But he hadn't, after all, been telling one of his own stories, a story based half on facts and half on fantasy, a story about Jews in a faraway land hiding in a castle. They had been hiding in some kind of *box*. He had, after all, known *something* all along, had heard some story whose details are now vanished; a story not so far from the truth, as it turned out. It had taken me all this, the years and the miles, had required that I come back and see the place with my own eyes before the fact, the material real-ity, allowed me to understand the words at last. They'd been hiding in a ter-ribly small and enclosed space, a space that someone, somewhere, must have once described as being like a kind of box, a *kestl*, and now I was standing in the box, and now I knew it all.

Shivering, I groped in my pocket for the camera Froma had given to me and blindly took a picture. The picture shows nothing, really: a blank wall garishly illuminated by a flashbulb. They had been here, hiding for weeks, months, nobody knew. But it had been *here*. I had always wanted specifics. Now I had found them.

I stayed there for a moment, because I thought it proper to pause and I wanted to collect my thoughts, which were racing in a million directions, and then I climbed out hastily. We stood there for a minute and took some pictures of the rooms, the rugs, the trapdoor, the sofas, the hiding place. Then there was nothing more to do. We thanked the women and left.

THERE ARE TWO further and extremely important pieces of information that came out of that return trip to Bolekhiv.

After we walked out of the house I asked Alex and Froma if they wouldn't mind if I called my parents on my cell phone: I had to tell them right then what had happened. Of course, they said, and I walked a little distance away from the Passat and punched in the number. Seven hours earlier in time, my father picked up the phone. I know exactly what I said to him that day, because I'd forgotten to turn off the voice recorder when we left the Szedlak house, and weeks later, after I'd returned home and was transcribing all of the voice files, I was startled when, at what I thought was the end of the *HIDING HOUSE!* file, I heard the sound of my own excited voice talking, although the recorded conversation is, like certain other family communications that have become part of this story, one-sided, since it is impossible in this record of the exchange to know what one of the parties is saying.

Dad? It's Dan, get Mom on the line.

[pause]

Momma

(I have no idea why I said this, it's a name I hadn't called her since I was four years old)

—*it's Daniel, I'm in Bolechow. I'm in Bolechow. Wait, you can't believe what just happened, you can't believe. What happened. We met an old man, and he took us to the house where Shmiel was hidden. . . . And I went in the house and I went in the hiding place, it's still there, it's like an underground . . . cellar and it's all there. And he remembered the whole thing, they were in the cellar and they denounced them and they took them out into the yard and they shot them. . . . Yes it's unbelievable, I was just in it. I just never thought in my life I would find the place. Yes, I took pictures, I took pictures. Anyway, it's just very . . . emotional and strange. I'm fine, I'm fine, we're going to go back to Lwów now. I just never even thought I would find this place, I just thought I was going here to get pictures. Anyway, call my brothers and sister and tell them this, I found the house, I found a person who took us to the house where they were hidden, and I went to the place where they actually died. OK, yes, I'll call again later, OK, I love you too, bye, bye.*

So that is how I described what we'd found to my parents. But the phone conversation in which I learned something from them came later, after we'd driven back to L'viv and had had a chance to talk about what had happened, to dissect the extraordinary emotions of the day. More composed than I'd been when I called on the cell phone, I rang my parents later that night from my hotel room. My father was out. Slowly, step by step, I recounted again the day's events to my mother.

It's a good thing Froma was there again! she exclaimed, Or you wouldn't have found it! It's just like how she got you to find Yona in Israel!

I smiled and said, Yes, it was. I had already considered the similarity between this remarkable discovery and that one. My mother said something else and I rolled my eyes and said, Yes, I had been sure to tell Froma thank you. In fact what Froma had replied, when I'd said *it was all because of you,* was interesting. For all of her intense energy, for all that she's unafraid to insert herself into situations, to push *harder,* as she likes to say, Froma, I've always observed, hates being the object of a certain kind of compliment, the center of a certain kind of adulatory fuss; and so, when I said *it was all because of you,* she'd made a face and said, Well, yes and no. I mean, what if it had been raining, what if nobody had been on the street when we started looking for the house, what if Stepan hadn't been there or old Prokopiv had left for the church ten minutes earlier? So it was me, but it was everything.

I listened to her and thought, Well. I thought of that afternoon in Israel, of the eerie coincidences that we'd experienced during this long search. The man in the Prague elevator. Yona. Shlomo flicking on the radio and the voice of Nehama Hendel singing "Sixteen Again I'll Never Be." Since I do not believe in the supernatural—when, a month later, a friend of mine said, I told your story to a psychic I know and she said, "The dead were leading you to them, they made sure that you found them," I just rolled my eyes and made the kind of face my father would have made—since I don't believe in the supernatural, I groped for an explanation, and what I concluded was this: That what we had achieved, what we had experienced, finally, during the course of all of our searching, was precisely what history is. On the one hand, there is always a vast series of random potentialities, the weather, the mood, the unknowable and infinite mass of things that go into the living of the life of a person or a people; and on the other hand, intersecting with this unimaginable and infinite universe of factors and possibilities, there is the irrevocable fact of individual personality and individual will, the fact that someone will do *x* but not *y,* the decision to do this rather than that, to make distinctions and thereby to *create,* to push a little bit *harder;* there is the hardwired impulse to go back for *one last look;* there is the thing that will make a person turn left rather than right, approach this woman in the street but not that man in order to ask a question about the location of a house or a road; there is the thing that makes you decide one night, as you are carrying a package of food to the hidden Jewish girl whom you love, that it is dark enough that you don't have to conceal the package under your coat; there is the impulse that causes the neighbor who sees the youth carrying the package to wonder, for the first time, why this boy comes every night to this street, that house; there are the whole vast histories of temperament and psychology in all their incalculable but ultimately concrete and knowable minutiae, the tiny things that make you decide to pursue a conversation with an old Ukrainian woman for precisely thirty-two minutes rather than, say, forty-seven minutes, with the result that you arrive at the house of an old Ukrainian man just as he is leaving for his job at a church, rather than a quarter of an hour later, at which point, because of a whole vast series of other factors and considerations, hunger, the hot sun, exhaustion, you may have decided that enough was enough, *genug is genug,* and let's just drive back to L'viv.

So there is the vast mass of things in the world and the act of creation that cuts through them, divides the things that might have happened from those that did. I did not and do not believe that the dead, that the long dead and disintegrated Shmiel and Frydka somehow reached out from the ether and pointed us, that day, to Bolekhiv and then Stepan and then Prokopiv and then the house and then the women and then the hiding place, the hole in the ground, the awful *box,* where they had once cowered in the cold and failed, finally, at their bid for survival. But I do believe in some things. I, to whom a friend had listened, quietly and sometimes in tears, one night in September 2001, when I'd just returned from our first trip to Ukraine and was telling the story of what we'd found there after all that time; had listened to me weeping and finally said, *I'm crying because my grandfather died two years ago and now it's too late to ask him anything;* I did and do believe, after all that I've seen and done, that if you project yourself into the mass of things, if you look for things, if you search, you will, by the very act of searching, make something happen that would not otherwise have happened, you will find *something,* even something small, something that will certainly be more than if you hadn't gone looking in the first place, if you hadn't asked your grandfather anything at all. I had finally learned the lesson taught me, years after they'd died, by Minnie Spieler and Herman the Barber. There are no miracles, no magical coincidences. There is only looking, and finally seeing, what was always there.

For everything, in time, gets lost: the lives of peoples now remote, the tantalizing yet ultimately vanished and largely unknowable lives of virtually all of the Greeks and Romans and Ottomans and Malays and Goths and Bengals and Sudanese who ever lived, the peoples of Ur and Kush, the lives of the Hittites and Philistines that will never be known, the lives of people more recent than that, the African slaves and the slave traders, the Boers and the Belgians, those who were slaughtered and those who died in bed, the Polish counts and the Jewish shopkeepers, the blond hair and eyebrows and small white teeth that someone once loved or desired of this or that boy or girl or man or woman who was one of the five million (or six or seven) Ukrainians starved to death by Stalin, and indeed the intangible things beyond the hair and teeth and brows, the smiles and frustrations and laughter and terror and loves and hunger of every one of those millions of Ukrainians, just as the hair of a Jewish girl or boy or man or woman that someone once loved, and the teeth and the brows, the smiles and frustrations and laughter and terror of the six million Jews killed in the Holocaust are now lost, or will soon be lost, because no number of books, however great, could ever document them all, even if they were to be written, which they won't and can't be; all that will be lost, too, their pretty legs and their deafness and the vigorous way they strode off a train with a pile of schoolbooks once, the secret family rituals and the recipes for cakes and stews and *gołąki,* the goodness and wickedness, the saviors and the betrayers, their saving and their betraying: most everything will be lost, eventually, as surely as most of what made up the lives of the Egyptians and Incas and Hittites has been lost. But for a little while some of that can be rescued, if only, faced with the vastness of all that there is and all that there ever was, somebody makes the decision to look back, to have one last look, to search for a while in the debris of the past and to see not only what was lost but what there is still to be found.

IT WAS, AS it happened, of backward glances that my mother ended up speaking that night that I called from the hotel.

Yes, I had said, echoing her words, It's a good thing Froma was there. Thank God she's always doing that thing that she does, that *Wait! There's one more thing! But we have to go back!* I laughed and shook my head, mimicking Froma.

My mother laughed, too, and said, suddenly serious, It's just like what happened that day my mother died.

(This is true.)

I said, What do you mean?

She said, Oh, Daniel, you remember, you loved her so much, you were there with me the whole day, the two of us.

My heart quickened a little and I said, No, I've just always had these confused sort of images.

I told her about the pattern of the waves on the tiles of the waiting room, the sound of her own voice saying something I couldn't or wouldn't remember, the sense of a yearning and a terror, the feeling of an obscure shame. The sound of water running.

Daniel, she said again. I can't believe you don't *remember.*

Then she started to tell me the whole story in order, the way I had just told her the story of our day in the place where her uncle had died. She told me that my grandmother had had some kind of abdominal blockage, and that when they'd done an exploratory surgery, a massive cancer was revealed in her colon. They closed her back up, my mother said, and said they'd have to do a colostomy, but before then she needed to get her strength back, needed to be nourished.

My mother went on in a rush. She said that my frantic grandfather had called her from Miami to tell her this and that they'd agreed that in a few days she would fly down and take care of her mother. But then, that same day, my grandmother, as the doctors like to say, just crashed. She went into a coma, and the day after that first phone call the doctor had called my mother and said, If you want to see your mother alive again, you need to get down here today. And so my mother had frantically entrusted Andrew and the newborn Eric to the next-door neighbor, and, her hair still wet from the shower, she'd gotten me and Matt ready for the plane trip.

You don't remember that Uncle Nino came in his car and drove us that day to the airport? she said.

I said, no, I didn't remember this.

My mother went on. She said that she'd called the hospital just before we left the house for the airport, and that by some miracle her mother had briefly surfaced again, and my mother had said to her mother, Don't worry, I'm coming. But by the time we got to Miami Beach, my grandmother had slipped into the sleep from which she would never awake, a coma that lasted over a week.

A week, ten days, I don't remember now. You don't remember we went every day to the hospital? my mother asked me from Long Island as I sat in a high-ceilinged room in L'viv, staring out the window as blond Ukrainians strolled and laughed in streets down which no Jews now walk.

No, I said.

Well, we did. And then the day she died, you and I spent the whole day there by her bed just sitting there. Oh, she loved you so much. And then it was the end of the day and we walked down the steps to the lobby. And then—this is what reminded me of Froma—suddenly something in me, like a voice, a feeling I had, *something,* something said I should go back. And so I leaned down and said to you, *Daniel, let's go back and look at Nana one more time,* and we went back up the steps. And when we got there, she was dead. The nurse was standing in the hall and she said, I'm sorry, your mother just passed. And I went in the room and I went on my knees by the bed and I said, Mama, Mama, don't leave me, don't leave me, I still need you.

As my mother talked I thought—I remembered—that this is what had filled me with shame: that before that day I always wanted to see my grandmother again, because it would be sweet to rub her arm back and forth, as we did while she lay there with her blue eyes open. But on that day I was tired; and there was something, too, about the urgency in my mother's voice when she leaned down and said *let's go back* that frightened me, that convinced me, for some reason, that my grandmother was already dead. I longed to go back and I was terrified of what I would see, I was confused, I was ashamed of my confusion, and didn't want to let my mother see either, the confusion or the shame.

And we cried, my mother was saying, and then we went into the bathroom and I washed my face and hands and I washed your face and hands, because you're always supposed to wash your hands when you've been with the dead.

I remembered: the running water. I remembered my grandfather, when we would come back from the cemetery all those years ago, saying, Run children upstairs and wash your hands now, you've been in the cemetery. *Vush your hents.*

You don't remember any of this? my mother repeated.

I said, Now I do.

A few weeks later, when I described this conversation to my friend, the one who'd talked to the psychic, she listened for a long time and when I finally finished speaking she said, It's so weird that you have this block about *turning back and having one last look.* Her voice isolated the words, made the phrase sound like an axiom, the final sentence of a fable.

I said, Why? It's not weird at all, that story explains it all! I was rather pleased with myself.

Donna, who is a poet, laughed and said, Oh, Daniel, it's so *obvious.* It's weird because you're a *classicist,* you're a family *historian.* You've spent your whole *life* looking back.

So there was that.

The second communication that came out of that afternoon in Bolekhiv was an e-mail I had from Alex about ten days after we flew back to New York, and it, too, changed the way I saw certain things.

Before we'd left, I had had an idea: maybe, I told Alex, he could return to Bolekhiv after we'd left, maybe a week or so after—long enough to give Prokopiv's memories time to steep, but not too long so that they'd fade once again—and ask him one more time if he could remember who the betrayer was. I thought—and because I felt completely comfortable with him, told Alex what I was thinking—that maybe if Prokopiv *were* keeping something back out of some desire to protect somebody, he might feel more comfortable talking just to Alex, Ukrainian to Ukrainian, without a cluster of anxious Jewish relatives hanging on to his every word. Alex said he'd been pretty sure that Prokopiv was being straight with us, but he agreed that now that the old man's memories had been churned up, perhaps the name might come to him after a few days.

And so, a week after we flew back to the States, he drove back down to Bolekhiv and found Prokopiv and talked to him. They talked for some time, he wrote me in a long e-mail after he got back home, and the old man still wasn't able to remember the name of the betrayer. He had gone through the names of everyone who'd lived on the block—for he himself, as a comment he made soon afterward subsequently revealed, had always lived in that neighborhood, and indeed could remember the names of families who'd lived there before the Germans came, for instance, the family of Kessler, a Jewish carpenter— and none of them had seemed to be the name of the person who, long ago, everyone in town knew had betrayed Szedlakowa.

In a sense, I was relieved: the hunt for the guilty party was, I felt by that point, almost a different story. We had gone looking for Shmiel and the others, for who they had been and how they had died, and we had come closer to concrete details than we'd ever dreamed possible. It was enough. If anything, I was less interested in the identity of the betrayer than I was, now, in the personality of this Mrs. Szedlak. For the saviors were, in their way, as inexplicable and mysterious to me as the betrayers. For some reason, perhaps because I knew she had been a schoolteacher, and—the force of mental habits and clichés being stronger than we like to admit, which is why, operating on unconscious assumptions about people, we often make serious mistakes in interpreting historical events unless we stay on our guard—I had, since the day in Anna Heller Stern's living room when she'd said *zey zent behalten bay a lererin*, always imagined a middle-aged woman who'd lived alone, perhaps a tall, thin woman with gray hair pulled back. Now I had been in this woman's house, and was more than a little curious about the person who had once lived there, this person who, whatever else we knew about her, had with her eyes wide open followed a rigorous morality, knowing it could cost her her life, which of course it had. *They killed them all right there in the yard*, Prokopiv had said. She had been Polish. I wondered if she had been a devout Catholic, as many saviors were. A devout spinster who divided her days between school and church.

It was for this reason that what Alex had to report about the would-be savior of Uncle Shmiel and Frydka was so interesting.

First, he wrote, Prokopiv had remembered one more detail about the day that the Szedlak hiding place had been discovered: he'd been walking home that day, in the neighborhood, and as he'd passed the schoolteacher's house he'd seen the bodies lying in the street, waiting to be carted to the mass grave in the Jewish cemetery where the bodies of people who'd been discovered and killed in this way were taken.

I read this and thought, At least they're in the Jewish cemetery, somewhere.

I kept reading the e-mail. I had asked him to ask Prokopiv whether he could recall hearing that one of the Jews who'd been discovered and killed that day had been pregnant. What Alex wrote next was this:

> Prokopiv didn't know that somebody hiding was pregnant. However, he said that the teacher who was hiding the Jews had an illegitimate child by the director of the school, Paryliak (or Parylak).

> However, Prokopiv doesn't know what happened to the child (a girl) when the mother was killed.

So I had been wrong once again. Whoever she'd been, she was not, it seemed, a pious middle-aged woman with a gray bun. When I read Alex's e-mail, I thought of Stepan's story of the Medvid family, of the whole family hanged in the Rynek, of every Medvid in the county killed as well. These public executions had been carried out for a purpose, and as we know the purpose was to discourage other people, people like Szymanski and Szedlak and all the others, from doing what they'd done anyway, for whatever mysterious reasons they had had: love, goodness, religious conviction. Whoever she was, whatever else may have been true of her—and I don't know at all whether I will ever find out more about her, although I have begun to search—whoever she was, this Szedlakowa woman was not a single woman with only one life at her disposal to risk for the sake of two Jews.

More than any other parashah *in Genesis, perhaps,* parashat Vayeira *is preoccupied with the implications of moral choices: in the Sodom and Gomorrah story we are meant to appreciate the consequences of the decision to follow wickedness, and in the tale with which this eventful* parashah *ends—the story of God's demand that Abraham sacrifice his only legitimate child—we are meant, I think, to appreciate the consequences of the other choice, the choice to follow the good.*

God's demand for human sacrifice, which as we are told at the very beginning of this remarkable passage is, at least for God, nothing more than a test of Abraham's devotion, is so repellent to the civilized mind that commentators have spilled oceans of ink explicating, analyzing, interpreting, and justifying it over the millennia. Friedman, for instance, devotes three full pages to his commentary on the sacrifice—striking in itself, when you consider that earlier, the text of the Sodom and Gomorrah story flows by uninterrupted by any kind of comment at all on his part—and provides an admirably lucid summary of the classic answers to the questions raised by the sacrifice. Rightly, it seems to me (from a purely literary, structural point of view), the modern rabbi focuses on the clearly intentional contrast between, on the one hand, Abraham's heated defense of the Sodomites, his attempt to bargain for the lives of the doomed cities, and, on the other, his utter silence in the face of God's demand, even more appalling in its way, that the patriarch kill his own human child. One possible explanation for this striking contrast, Friedman says, is that the mark of Abraham's personality throughout Genesis is obedience—the characterological explanation, which is satisfying as far as it goes, although it does not delve very deeply into the troubling question of whether Abraham's seemingly innate predilection for unquestioningly following orders is, in cases when those orders are themselves clearly immoral, worth exploring more. ("Commands," Friedman writes, "leave no room for discussion," a peculiar thing, at least to my mind, for a rabbi writing in the late twentieth century to assert with no further comment, even in the context of explicating a biblical text.) Friedman goes on to provide what we may call the rhetorical argument: the patriarch, he writes, is able to argue more persuasively (indeed, at all) on behalf of the wicked Sodomites precisely because he has no relationship to them: he cannot argue the justice or the injustice of the demand for his son's sacrifice precisely because he is so close to it. This, too, seems somehow unsatisfying at first glance, as if to be "biased" necessarily was the same thing as to be stupid. Third, Friedman suggests, intriguingly, that the outcome of the first of this parashah's two important morality tales, the tale of Sodom and Gomorrah, provides the key to Abraham's silence. The futility of Abraham's argument with God, he suggests, the fact that nothing came of his hard bargaining, that God always and already knew how bad the Sodomites were and how good Abraham is, are the reason Abraham knows not to argue when God requires a destruction that is infinitely more painful to Abraham than is the annihilation of the populations of several cities.

Rashi, too, goes to no little trouble to suggest that God's interest in having Abraham demonstrate (as of course we know he will do) that he is "God-fearing" has vast international and cosmic implications: it is necessary that Abraham's righteous obedience be demonstrated, he writes, so that God has something to answer Satan and the nations of the unbelievers when they demand to know what the cause of God's love for the tribe of Abraham could possibly be. "That they are God-fearing," is the answer that Abraham's willingness to cut the throat of his young son provides.

One of the interesting moral questions raised by the Sacrifice of Isaac—and, by *implication, by the* parashah *as a whole—is that the text's presentation of what it means to be a good person (i.e., Abraham, who is obedient to God even in extreme and confusing circumstances) is, in its way, as flat and unsatisfying, as cagey, as is its presentation of what it means to be a wicked person (i.e., a Sodomite, whatever that precisely means). In fact, all that the text of this* parashah *indicates is that goodness is obedience to God and wickedness is disobedience, as if morality were a superficially coherent structure of behavior that had no actual content—although, to take the examples from this particular weekly Torah reading, on the face of it what the Sodomites do, which may be depraved but doesn't, as far as we know, result in any dead bodies lying around, is a lot less awful than what God asks Abraham to do.*

On the other hand, what does seem to me valid about this last parashah *is that, whatever the validity of its larger moral investigation, it paints what I have finally come to see as an extremely accurate picture of the way that people behave in unimaginably extreme conditions. Which is to say, a picture of a blur, an image of something that remains, in the end, totally unknowable and completely mysterious: that some people simply choose to do evil and some choose to do good, even when, in both cases, they know that their choices will require dreadful sacrifices.*

THERE IS ONE final tale of returning, of going back for one last look, that I have to tell before I end this story.

The day after we discovered the hiding place was Saturday. Lane flew in to the L'viv airport that afternoon, and as Alex and I drove her back to the hotel, where Froma was waiting, poring over maps of the area in preparation for our sites-of-genocide excursions with Lane, we excitedly told her about our great discovery.

Lane jerked her delicate head up in one of those quick gestures that always makes me think of the adjective *birdlike* when I'm around her.

But that's *amazing,* she said. As the car careened around the opera house, where seventy years ago a young woman whose name was not yet *Frances* went to see the opera *Carmen,* Lane gestured expressively at one of her enormous, complicated-looking black canvas camera bags. But did you get *pictures?* she asked, good *pictures* for your *book?* When I told her that all we had was Froma's little digital camera, she made a grimace that was half disapproval and half disbelief. She said, We have to go *back.* We can go back, and I'll take good *pictures* for you.

Picshuhs, she said. *Booh-uhk.*

So on Sunday, we went back, and it was on this final visit—which really was the last trip that I took on Uncle Shmiel's behalf—that I made our last discovery, and ended our search.

Once again, we drove down the little hill into the sleepy town, which this time was dozing under angry-looking rain clouds. Once again, we sped into the town and through streets that now indeed seemed very familiar to us. Once again, Alex pulled up in front of the nondescript little house, where once again the black dog and the brown lay eyeing us in the walkway. Once again, he knocked on the window, and once more the black-haired woman came out. We explained that we hoped she'd let us in once again, since this time we had a better camera to take the photos we needed. I noticed that she seemed slightly more animated that day than she had been two days earlier. She nodded a few times, a bit wearily perhaps but with a faint smile, and motioned to us to go inside. Once again, we walked around the tiny rooms, opened the trapdoor; once again, shutters clicked. The only difference was that this time, I did not go down into the hiding place, the *kestl.* It had been enough.

As we emerged from the house once more, we noticed that this time, something else was different, too: a vigorous-looking young man—not the bloodless zombie I'd seen standing motionless in the bedroom on Friday—was hanging around the place, apparently the son of one of the women. Alex and he had an animated conversation and the man started gesturing over the fence. Alex said, He says that this house is actually divided into two parts.

Froma and Lane and I all peered over the fence, and noticed this time, as we had not two days earlier, that the one house straddled two yards.

Alex said, He says that there in the other half an old Russian woman lives, she came soon after the war, maybe she can tell us some more information.

I looked dubiously at Froma and Lane. Did they mind? I asked. Of course not, they said. That's what we came for!

We went back into the street and around the front of the house, down the street a ways, to the other side. Sure enough, there was an entrance here, too. Alex knocked and called out in Russian, and presently a rosy-cheeked woman with a bright child's face and improbably dark curly hair bustled out. Her dress was bright blue with big white polka dots. Alex talked to her and she insisted, in a warmly enthusiastic and high-pitched voice, that we come inside. As in some children's story, her half of the house was as immaculate and pretty as the other half was filthy and decrepit. The powerful aroma of baking peaches filled the little kitchen. We all sat down and, as she turned down the volume on the little portable cassette player that had been playing, at an astonishing volume, a tape of Russian church music, Alex explained why we had called on her. The rich, *shushing* sound of Russian filled the room. The woman was so lively, nodded so vigorously and spoke so ringingly, that it was hard not to want to embrace her. She was like a grandmother or a good witch in a folktale.

After a few moments of this back-and-forthing, Alex looked up at me. He was not smiling.

She says yes, she heard this story about the Jews being hidden, and the schoolteachers. She herself came in the 1950s, but she heard it. But she says she is pretty sure that these schoolteachers were both still alive after the war, and also that it was not in this house they lived, that it was in another house on this street.

We looked at each other blankly, in a kind of despair. I said, That can't be, I don't believe it.

I had been in that place, that cold place. It felt *right*.

We talked some more but it became clear to me after a while, as I read Alex's wide, fair face, that he wasn't getting anything more from her than what she'd already said. But it had been enough. Everything was in ruins. We were back to square one.

We all got up to leave. Alex said, She told me which house it is that she thinks it was in. A very old man lives there. She says he is deaf. Do you want to go?

I knew what he meant. He meant, Maybe we should quit while we're ahead.

I nodded grimly and said, Let's talk to this old man.

The four of us trudged down the street. Alex turned to me at one point and said, I don't want to hear this new story, I want this to have been over on Friday! and I gave a glum smile and said, That's exactly how I always feel.

Yes, he said. Now I know!

The house that the old woman had directed us to really did look like something out of the Brothers Grimm: a ramshackle, once-grand wooden house with impossible steep gables, its eaves and timber darkened by time, set back from the street a little ways. Here, too, Russian church music was blaring; although the front windows were forbiddingly closed up, you could hear it pouring out from the direction of the backyard. As a little drizzle began, we stomped to the backyard. The door was open. Alex shouted; there was no response. He shouted again, and finally we all just walked through the back door into the old man's house. The ceilings were cavernous, icons hung everywhere. We followed the sound of the music until we reached what had clearly once been the great room of the house, an enormous, once-elegant chamber in which, now, a deal table, on which an old-fashioned phonograph stood, was among the few furnishings. Next to the table the old man himself stood: a figure, appropriately enough for this place, out of a nineteenth-century woodcut, a gaunt, impossibly tall old man whose yellowed white hair hung limply down either side of his head. His deep eyes were ringed with black. He looked like Franz Liszt, I thought.

Alex approached the man and, heeding the old Russian woman's words, shouted directly into the man's face for a few minutes. Between the shouting, the icons, the smell of incense, and the music—and, now, the wild emotional letdown of the information we'd just received—the whole thing started to feel like a farce, and Froma and Lane and I tried to repress an incredulous giggle. After a few minutes of shouting, Alex turned to me with his *let's-get-out-of-here* expression. When we got outside into the relative quiet of the backyard, he said, This guy moved here in the 1970s, he doesn't know *nothing*.

So that was that. We started to walk toward the car. I was devastated: not two days ago I'd thought that I'd found the end of our story at last, and now it had vanished into smoke: the teacher's house, the hiding place, the courtyard where they'd been shot. *Once there was a veranda in front, but now it's gone.* It seemed that old Prokopiv wasn't as clear in his mind as we'd thought.

And then, just as we were getting into the car, Froma said, Wait, he wants us. We turned around and looked toward the other house, and the young man was waving his arms and beckoning for us to come back. We walked back to the house and he started talking to Alex. After a rapid exchange Alex brightened and said to us, He says that across the street on the other side is an old Polish woman, she has lived here all her life, she will know for sure the story, and which is the right house. She will *know*. He talked a little while longer to the young man, who pointed down the street and gave the address. The woman's name was Latyk—a common name in these parts; she was no relation of the other Mrs. Latyk.

Again, the knocking on the window; again, the tentative shouted greeting. The house was large, white, and immaculate. Peering around the fence we could see a generous yard. Out of this yard, in a few moments, a small, solid-looking woman with thick white hair and a canny, round face appeared. She was wearing a thin gray robe that she clutched tight with one hand, and I think now that it was the fact that she wasn't dressed for company that made her seem so wary as Alex explained what we were looking for. Almost immediately after he stopped talking her face relaxed and she nodded and smiled broadly.

She said, *Tak, tak! Tak. Tak, tak, tak!*

She spoke rapidly to Alex in Polish. Alex said to us, She knows the story! She knows the story, she knows that there were two teachers who were hiding Jews. She said the names of these two sisters were—

He listened, and she said, *Pani Emilia i Pani . . . mmm . . .*

She couldn't remember the name of the other woman, it was clear. Emilia and who? While she frowned, trying to remember, Alex went on. One escaped, the other was killed.

This Mrs. Latyk suddenly said, Hela! *Emilia i Hela!* She said something quickly to Alex.

Hela was killed. Emilia escaped.

For the second time in three days I said, Does she remember their family name?

Alex asked, and Mrs. Latyk said, emphatically, *Szedlakowa.*

Does she know the house? I asked. At least, I thought, we'll know either way.

Alex said, She will show us precisely where it is, sure.

Froma and Lane and I said, Thank you!

It was at that point that Alex made all the introductions. Pani Janina Latyk. Pan Daniel Mendelsohn. Pani Froma Zeitlin. Pani Lane Montgomery.

The woman, now smiling and relaxed, started speaking again.

I heard her say, *Szymanski.*

Wait, I said. Everybody was talking and I wanted quiet. Until now I had wanted simply to know which, finally, was the right house. Now she had said *Szymanski*. It was clear that she could tell us more.

Wait, wait, wait, I shouted.

Everyone stopped talking and I said to Alex, What was she saying just now?

They talked again for a minute and Alex said, There was this guy who was helping Jews to find places to be hidden.

I said, And his name was?

Mrs. Latyk said, *Czesław*.

My heart started thudding. Old Prokopiv had told us about the house, had known that a teacher named Szedlak was hiding Jews there. Long ago, I had heard this story for the first time in a living room in Kfar Saba, and had wondered ever since how all the versions could possibly be reconciled. *Ciszko was hiding her in his house. A Polish schoolteacher was hiding them both in her house.* Now we would see.

I said, Czesław who?

Mrs. Latyk said, Czesław—Ciszko, *Ciszko*!

The nickname. We all looked at one another. Again, Froma and Lane and Alex all started talking and asking questions at the same time. By now, they knew the stories as well as I did. It was exciting.

Wait, I said. I was suddenly perspiring, and again I heard that faint echo in my ears. I said, more calmly, Look, I have to conduct this interview in a *very* specific way. We cannot feed her any information, we cannot tell her what we want to hear, we cannot tell her what we already know. This is the *last* time any of us will ever be in this place, and after what we just went through I want to leave here with something *definite*. So let's just ask her what she knows and hear it out of her mouth. I want it to be *pure.*

I turned to Alex and said, OK, she said Czesław, she said Ciszko, before that she said Szymanski. What does she know about him, why does she mention the name?

They talked for a minute. Alex said, Because *he* found the place for them to *hide*. And he was bringing food to them also.

Froma and I stared at each other. Another woman, middle-aged and pleasant-faced, appeared out of the house: Mrs. Latyk's sister. The two women talked to Alex. He turned to me with a dubious expression. They are inviting you to the house, but I say that I'm sure we don't want to bother them . . .

I gave him a severe look and said, I want to go. I think that if we were sitting down, it would be better. Tell her this is extremely important to me and my family.

Alex talked and the woman nodded and we all went in the house.

For the next forty-five minutes, she told us the story as she knew it, and it's a story I can now tell although there's no point telling it again here, since it's a story the bits and pieces of which are already familiar to anyone who has read these pages. The difference is that as we listened to it coming from the lips of Mrs. Janina Latyk, a lifelong resident of Bolechow, a lifelong resident of Kopernika Street, a onetime neighbor of the sisters Szedlakowa, we all of us heard it for the first time from someone who was there, and who, because she was there, could tell us a story that accounted for all the bits and pieces that, until that day in July 2005, hadn't quite been able to gel into a coherent narrative, a story with a beginning and a middle and an end.

What she told us was this: that she'd been born in Bolechow in 1928, which is why she was about fifteen on the day in 1943 when she came home from doing errands in the town center and everybody on the street was talking. What they were saying was this: their neighbor Hela had been discovered hiding Jews in her house. Everybody was talking! Mrs. Latyk said. Yes, there had been the two Szedlakowa sisters, but one of them, Emilia, had become afraid and had left town—gone, somebody said at the time, to Boryslaw. So when they were betrayed, it was Hela who was killed. She was hiding the Jews in a basement somewhere in her house, a place under the ground. And the boy Ciszko Szymanski, who had found for them this hiding place to begin with, was bringing them food every night from his father's shop, he had a tannery but also a kind of shop in his house, people came there to buy meat, sausages. He loved this girl, this Jew, people said, so he found a hiding place for her and her father. But somebody saw him bringing the food every night to Szedlakowa's place, and got suspicious, and this person—a neighbor, probably, she couldn't remember—denounced him and Szedlakowa to the Gestapo. The Germans came and took the Jews to a spot by the end of the garden and shot them right there.

What exactly happened to Szymanski and Szedlakowa? we all asked. Jack Greene, ages ago by now, it seemed, had said he'd heard that they took him to a place in a field, *there,* and killed him. Now, Mrs. Latyk, who'd been there the day that it happened, said, He was killed in Stryj. And Hela was also taken to Stryj and they were hanged there together. But the Jews were shot on the spot.

Stryj, I thought: Mrs. Begley's little provincial city. This small detail, which

I'd never heard before, seemed to me to be the absolute proof of authenticity. Jews were outside the law, you could just kill them, shoot them, anywhere. But disobedient Poles could be made examples of. They likely took them to Stryj to make some terrifying show of them there before the executions that were a foregone conclusion.

And that was the story. Now, all the pieces fit: Ciszko *and* Szedlak, the Szymanski house *and* the Polish schoolteacher's house. It all made sense, now, and it was finally possible to see how what had really happened had, corrupted by distances both geographical and temporal—they weren't right *there,* they'd heard it two or three or ten years *later*—metamorphosed into the stories, the many stories, that we had heard by now.

We sat and talked for a while more: about the war years, the terror people felt, the anguish at seeing longtime neighbors disappear; and, too, the brutality of the years after the Soviets took over in 1945, the conditions of near starvation, the petty oppressions. Mrs. Latyk reminisced warmly about the years before the war, the years of a girlhood spent with Jewish and Ukrainian and Polish friends, years when there were, as far as she could say, no tensions, no hatreds, no animosities. It was a busy, happy town, she said, smiling faintly. I sat quietly and listened, partly because I was moved to hear a Polish woman born in 1928 utter the same words my grandfather, a Jewish man born in the same town in 1902, had repeated over and over to me ages ago, and partly because it was the least I could do for this kindly-faced woman whom we'd almost never met, whom we would have missed if we hadn't turned back that one last time when we thought that all was lost, and who had, finally, told me the story I had wanted to hear, from the beginning to the end, for a long time now.

ONE THING REMAINED now to be revealed to us by Janina Latyk, and I was nervous as I said, at the end of our long chat, Now can she show us what house it was?

She nodded. Before we left her house, I said to Alex, Please tell her my family lived in this town for three hundred years, and I'm honored and grateful to have her as a neighbor.

He translated my sentence and she smiled at me and brought a hand to her heart, then brought it back toward me. *Same to you,* Alex said.

We all left the house and walked slowly down the street. Mrs. Latyk stopped in front of the first house, the house we'd gone inside the first day we'd been here, the house with the trapdoor and the hiding place, and pointed.

I knew it, I thought. I had been inside, had been in the cold, cold place.

This is the house, Alex said. She says, If you want, she can show you the place where they killed them. The neighbor saw the whole thing, people knew about it.

I said, Yes.

THE DOOR TO the back garden was in the back of the Russian woman's half of the house, and she bustled and burbled as Alex told her why we'd come back. Beaming, she opened the gate for me. I stood at the fence and looked back toward the end of the garden, a long, long garden densely planted with rows of vegetables and vines that extended all the way back to the distant end of the property. Mrs. Latyk, standing next to me at the fence, pointed. At the end of the garden there was an ancient apple tree with a double trunk. She said something to Alex. He said to me, That is the place.

Slowly, I started walking back to the tree. The vegetables and vines and raspberry bushes grew so thickly along the barely visible furrows that it was sometimes hard to find a secure footing. After a few minutes, I reached the tree. Its bark was thick, and the place where the two thick trunks diverged was about as high as my shoulder. Every now and then a tiny drop of rain, little more than condensed mist, would splatter on a leaf. But I stayed dry.

I was standing in the place.

For a while I stood there, thinking. It is one thing to stand before a spot you have long thought about, a building or shrine or monument that you've seen in paintings or books or magazines, a place where, you think, you are expected to have certain kinds of feelings that, when the time comes to stand there, you either will or will not have: awe, rapture, terror, sorrow. It is another thing to be standing in a place of a different sort, a place that for a long time you thought was hypothetical, a place of which you might say *the place where it happened* and think, it was in a field, it was in a house, it was in a gas chamber, against a wall or on the street, but when you said those words to yourself it was not so much the *place* that seemed to matter as the *it,* the terrible thing that had been done, because you weren't really thinking of the place as anything but a kind of envelope, disposable, unimportant. Now I was standing in the place itself, and I had had no time to prepare. I confronted the place itself, the thing and not the idea of it.

For a long time I had thirsted after *specifics,* after *details,* had pushed the people I'd gone all over the world to talk to to remember more, to think harder, to give me the concrete thing that would make the story come alive. But that, I now saw, was the problem. I had wanted the details and the specifics for the *story,* and had not—as how could I not, I who never knew them, who had never had anything *but* stories?—really understood until now what it meant to be a *detail,* a specific. The word *specific* comes, as I well know, from the Latin word *species,* which means "appearance" or "form," and it is because each kind of thing has its own appearance or form that the word *species* is the word we used to describe consistent types of living things, the animals and plants that constitute Creation; it is because each type of living thing has its own appearance or form that, over numberless centuries, the word *species* gave birth to *specific,* which means, among other things, *"particular to a given individual."* As I stood in this most specific place of all, more specific even than the hiding place, that place in which Shmiel and Frydka experienced things, physical and emotional things I will never begin to understand, precisely because their experience was *specific* to them and not me, as I stood in this most specific of places I knew that I was standing in the place where they had died, where the life that I would never know had gone out of the bodies I had never seen, and precisely because I had never known or seen them I was reminded the more forcefully that they had been specific people with specific deaths, and those lives and deaths belonged to them, not me, no matter how gripping the story that may be told about them. There is so much that will always be *impossible to know,* but we do know that they were, once, themselves, *specific,* the subjects of their own lives and deaths, and not simply puppets to be manipulated for the purposes of a good story, for the memoirs and magical-realist novels and movies. There will be time enough for that, once I and everyone who ever knew everyone who ever knew them dies; since as we know, everything, in the end, gets lost.

So, in a way, at the very moment I had found them most specifically, I felt that I had to give them up again, let them be themselves, whatever that had been. It was bitter and it was sweet; and indeed, when, later, I would describe this moment to Jack Greene, to whom in a way I owed everything, he said to me, making an analogy to his own emotion on emerging from his hiding place so many years before, Yes, I know how it feels, it is a feeling of *accomplishment* but not a *happy* feeling. I had traveled far, had circled the planet and studied my Torah, and at the very end of my search I was standing, finally, in the place where everything begins: the tree in the garden, the tree of knowledge that, as I long ago learned, is something divided, something that because growth occurs only through the medium of time, brings both pleasure and, finally, sorrow.

I suppose it was concrete facts, specifics, that I was somehow trying to grasp when, out of some instinct that even today I can't quite identify, I reached down and thrust my hands into the earth at the base of the tree and filled my pockets with it. Then—since this is the tradition of the strange tribe to which, although parts of that tradition make no sense to me, I know I belong, because my grandfather once belonged to it—I groped around in the earth for a large stone, and when I found one, I put it in the crook where the branches of the tree met. This is their only monument, I thought, and so I'll leave a stone here. Then I turned and walked out of the garden, and soon after that we said good-bye and got into the car and left.

It was while we were driving away that I made the last of my many mistakes. I had promised myself that this time, when we left Bolekhiv, I would do something I'd meant to do years earlier, on our first trip to the town, because back then I'd thought that it would also be our last trip to this place, this little town, this bustling *shtetl*, this *happy* place, a place that *was and will never be again*: I had promised myself that as we drove out of the town and back up the little hill toward L'viv, I would turn around, as I somehow knew my grandfather had done on an October day eighty years before, turn around for the reason we always turn around to stare at what lies behind us, which is to make an impossible wish, a wish that nothing will be left behind, that we will carry the imprint of what is over and done with into the present and future. I told myself that I'd look through the back window and stare at the little town as it receded, because I wanted to be able to remember not only what the place looked like when you were arriving there, but what it looked like when you were leaving it forever.

But as Alex maneuvered the blue Passat out of the complicated little streets that an epoch ago had given the inhabitants of that place, very few of whom are left now, none of whom will be alive when I am Jack Greene's age, the nickname that nobody knows or cares about anymore, *Bolechower crawlers!*—as Alex navigated those twisty streets, we all started talking at once, telling the remarkable story of what we had found and where we had walked, and by the time I remembered to turn around and take that one last look, we had traveled too far, and Bolechow had slipped out of sight.

IN MEMORIAM

Frances BEGLEY, née HAUSER
Rzeszów 1910——New York 2004

Elkana EFRATI, né JÄGER
Bolechow 1928——Kfar Saba 2006

Josef FEUER
Bolechow 1920——Striy 2002

Boris GOLDSMITH
Bolechow 1913——Sydney 2005

Salamon GROSSBARD
Bolechow 1908——Sydney 2004

Bob GRUNSCHLAG
Bolechow 1929——Sydney 2005

Dyzia RYBAK, née LEW
Bolechow 1923——Minsk 2004

Solomon (Shumek) REINHARZ
Bolechow 1914——Beer Sheva 2005

POSTSCRIPT
(FEBRUARY 2007)

FOR A LONG TIME it had been my hope that, following the publication of this book in September 2006, new information about my six lost relatives might come to light—that some reader who, against all odds, had special knowledge of my family would get in touch with me. As it turned out, I didn't have long to wait.

Two months after *The Lost* was published in the United States, I received an e-mail from Yaacov Lozowick, the director of the Yad Vashem archive. He told me that he'd read the book and wanted to share his reaction. A friendly correspondence soon began. A month or so later, on New Year's Day 2007, I received an e-mail from Yaacov informing me that he had come across a reference to one of the Jägers in a vast mass of new material, much of it from the former Soviet Union, that had been uploaded to the Yad Vashem database only the day before. He sent me a link to the reference in question. As it turned out, exactly one line of one particular document in this mountain of newly available records—there are over 350,000—provides at last some concrete information about the fate of one of my relatives. Or, I should say, concrete information about one of them, and implicit information about another.

The record in question is part of a report delivered soon after the war was over to a body known as the Soviet State Extraordinary Commission for Ascertaining and Investigating the Crimes Committed by the German-Fascist Invaders and Their Accomplices. (I should say here that friend whom I asked to translate this document for me had this to say about the Russian word for "crimes" used in the title: "Note that the word for crime here has strong moral implications—different from, for instance, the 'crime' in *Crime and Punishment*, which is dispassionate/legal—and it would not be an overstatement to translate it as 'evil deeds' or 'villainies.'") This commission, created in 1942 by the Supreme Soviet and usually referred to as the ChGK (an acronym of its Russian name), was responsible for investigating German war crimes.

According to their own records, more than thirty thousand investigators took part in the project, interviewing the remaining residents of the ravaged, *Judenrein* towns and cities and documenting their stories; more than seven million Soviet citizens are said to have been interviewed. The twenty-seven vast digests that were condensed from this enormous trove of eyewitness material represented the bulk of the evidence presented by the Russians in the Nuremberg trials. One of the towns that was visited by the investigators for the Extraordinary Commission was Bolechow—or, as the Russians called it, Bolekhov.

Yaacov sent me three pages from the Bolekhov report. The first is the title page, and it reads as follows:

RECORD OF THE INVESTIGATION OF THE EVIL DEEDS OF THE GERMAN FASCISTS AND THEIR ACCOMPLICES IN THE BOLEKHOV DISTRICT OF THE STANISLAVOV REGION

The third page that Yaacov sent, which is actually the seventh and last page of the Bolekhov report, contains five signatures: the signatures of the chair of the investigating committee and the four other committee members. These handwritten names of Soviet bureaucrats, with their illegible flourishes, appear just below a vertical list of other names. These names, given in the standard Russian format *family name-first name-patronymic*, are all typed out in Cyrillic letters (like the letters that you can now see on the front of the building in Bolekhov that used be the Dom Catolicki, the ones that spell out CINEMA and THEATER). Before each of these names is a number, and after each there appears the following information, organized in columns: year of birth, sex, profession, date of shooting/roundup, and address. Some of the names on this list—which I can read because years ago I taught myself to read Russian characters, perhaps out of a desire to ingratiate myself with my grandfather's sour last wife, the one who had been Russian before Auschwitz made her a citizen of nowhere—are familiar to me now, because of the journeys I made and the people I talked to. I can, for instance, make out a Malka Abramovna Lew, who must be related to Dyzia Lew, although of course Dyzia cannot give me any information, ever again; I can make out a Dovid Israelevich Reifeisen, and assume he is connected to the attorney Reifeisen, who hanged himself before things got even worse. I even see someone with Meg Grossbard's maiden name, and wonder silently who he might be, although I am aware that I'll never know, now, because I no longer get late-night phone calls from Meg.

The last entry in this list is numbered *350*. When I first hastily looked over these pages, I was struck by the fact that none of the names provide an entry under the column header "profession." This anomaly, I soon realized, was due to the fact that the "year of birth" for nearly all of these three hundred and fifty people generally falls between the late 1920s and the early 1930s, and virtually every entry under "date of roundup/shooting" is given as 3/IX/1942; which is to say that all of the people on this list were children of between ten and fourteen years old. As I first read these names, these entries, it slowly dawned on me that what I was reading was a list of the Jewish children of Bolekhov who were murdered during the roundup that proceeded the "big" Second Aktion on the 3rd, 4th, and 5th of September 1942, the Aktion of which the survivors went in the cattle cars to Belzec. The Aktion in which, to the best knowledge of any of the people I talked to over the course of the five years of writing this book, my great-aunt Ester and her youngest daughter, Bronia, perished.

By an uncanny coincidence, Bronia is, in fact, the very first entry on this list, which begins on the second of Yaacov's pages: she is Number One. Her name is given as Bronia Samuelevna Yeger, and her address is given, correctly, as Dlugosa 9. The year of birth given on this document is 1929, which now provides an official confirmation of Jack Green's hunch that that was, indeed, the year she was born—the same year, as he told me in his living room in Australia now four years ago, in which his late brother Bob had been born. The date on which Bronia was "rounded up and shot" is given as the 3rd of September 1942.

And so, as the result of yet another fortuitous reaching out, another improbable contact made against all reasonable expectations, I now have this concrete fact to add to the small mound of facts I assembled: that Bronia, about whom all that anyone remembered was that she was *still a child, still busy with her toys*, was rounded up and shot to death during the dreadful first days of the Second Aktion in Bolekhov; and that when she died in this fashion, she was either thirteen years old, or just about to be thirteen years old. (We still do not know her birth date.) And so her very brief story now has, at least, a concrete enough beginning ("1929") and a very precise ending ("3/IX/1942").

I mentioned above that this new document provides us, too, with another kind of information—not concrete, but implicit. You see, at the end of all my travels and all my interviewing, when it seemed certain, at last, that Aunt Ester and Bronia had been taken in the Second Aktion, I had thought—sentimentally, to be sure—that during those final unimaginable hours, perhaps days, of their lives, the mother and the daughter had at least had *each other*: had made that journey together, had (perhaps) stood there, naked and afraid to be sure, but *together*, the mother's arms wrapped tight around the daughter as the fumes began to seep into the airtight room. But now, because of what some neighbor saw in 1942 and reported to the Soviet Commission a few years later, a small fact among the many millions of facts that made their way into the report delivered to the Soviet State Extraordinary Commission for Ascertaining and Investigating the Crimes Committed by the German-Fascist Invaders and Their Accomplices, we know that Bronia was killed during the roundup; a roundup famous for its brutal killings of children, as we also know. And because I know this concrete fact now, I am also forced to speculate about something that can never be proved, but which is almost a certainty: that whatever my Aunt Ester—Ester Jäger *née* Schneelicht, to give her her due, a forty-six-year-old mother of four, a matron of Bolekhov who was a good wife and fine homemaker, who very likely crocheted to pass the long winter nights, who *had two such pretty legs* and who once added a postscript to a desperate letter that made its way to New York, a postscript that somehow, somewhere got lost, which is why nothing of that woman's thoughts survives today—that whatever my Aunt Ester suffered during the dreadful ending to that life, she suffered alone.

AUTHOR'S NOTE

T HE EVENTS RECORDED in this book are true. All formal interviews were recorded on videotape, and nearly all other conversations, including telephone conversations, were either recorded by the author or reconstructed on the basis of notes taken by the author during those conversations. Some but by no means most of the dialogue recorded in these pages was edited for the sake of coherence and in order to avoid repetitions; occasionally, this editing has necessitated the chronological rearrangement of some remarks. Several names have been changed to protect the privacy of certain individuals, at their request.

Because this book is, among other things, the story of distant travels across many countries and continents where I was often speaking with people who themselves had migrated from country to country, a word about the use of language is in order. In cases where English was the language used in my interviews, I have reproduced the spoken English of my subjects, however awkward, since the habits of speech, accents, and forms of expression of the people I spoke with during my research are part of the culture, now almost vanished, that was to some extent the object of my search; I've treated the English of the translators I occasionally employed in the same way. I have generally transliterated Yiddish according to YIVO standards, except when those standards are at odds with my memory of certain pronunciations. Quotations from witness statements in Polish obtained from Yad Vashem are given here in an English translation commissioned for the purposes of this book.

With respect to place-names, for the most part I use present-day Polish and Ukrainian spellings when referring to towns and cities I visited, but— partly for the sake of historical accuracy, and partly to suggest the flavor of a lost era—I have resorted to older spellings in passages describing events that took place in the past. Hence, for example, I write about my trips to L'viv in 2001 and 2005, but refer at times to the Lwów School of mathematicians that flourished between the two world wars, since the Ukrainian city now known as L'viv was properly known during that period as Lwów, a Polish city. The one more or less consistent exception to this norm—a forgivable one, I hope—is my use of the old German spelling for the name of the town that atlases today give in its Ukrainian form, *Bolekhiv*, and which most of the people I interviewed referred to by its Polish name, *Bolechów*; but to which my family, who dwelled there for well over three centuries, has always referred as *Bolechow*—a habit I have found impossible to break.

ACKNOWLEDGMENTS

N o b o o k t h a t has been five years—indeed, more—in the making can have been written without the support and encouragement of many people, and it is a pleasure to mark here my gratitude to those who so richly deserve it.

This book is a book about family, and my greatest debt in every way is, and has always been, to mine: first and foremost to my parents, Marlene and Jay Mendelsohn, who encouraged my odd childhood enthusiasms ("Athena's table"; photography excursions to the cemetery) and who since then have unstintingly lavished their time, memories, and much else on me; and then to my siblings and in-laws, who, as these pages will have shown, were not only enthusiastic supporters of but active and ongoing participants in the Bolechow Project: Andrew Mendelsohn and Virginia Shea; Matt Mendelsohn and Maya Vastardis; Eric Mendelsohn; Jennifer Mendelsohn and Greg Abel.

It would be an injustice, however, not to mark especially my deepest gratitude to Matt above all, since he has been a full collaborator in this project from start to finish; the tale told in this book owes as much to him as it does to me, and not simply because so many of its pages give evidence of his extraordinary talent. If I say that he has a beautiful way of seeing things, I am referring to more than his professional eye; in the end, his profound humaneness made itself felt in the words as much as the pictures. Of all that I found during my search, he is the greatest treasure.

The Bolechowers whom I met and talked with over the course of two years are not, technically speaking, family, but by now it is very difficult not to think of them as such; there is no need to repeat their names here, since this entire book is a record of my gratitude to them for their superb and abundant hospitality, for their generosity with their time and with memories the sharing of which was not, I know, always a happy task. I do, however, want to mention here the names of certain other friends and relatives connected to the Bolechower group to whom I owe a debt of hospitality or friendship or both: Susannah Juni; Malka Lewenwirth; Debbie Greene in Sydney; and in Stockholm, our Mittelmark cousin, Renate Hallerby, and her husband, Nils, whose warmth and generosity were all too plain despite the brevity of the time we had together. Friends and relatives in Israel were constant and treasured sources of hospitality, encouragement, and enthusiasm, and I'm profoundly grateful to them. To Linda Zisquit in Jerusalem I owe a particular debt of thanks for her loving persistence in helping me find something small but crucial. At home, Allan and Karen Rechtschaffen and Marilyn Mittelmark Tepper shared many vital memories over a long and delightful "cousins" weekend, and Edward ("Nino") Beltrami guided me to an important insight.

It will be clear to anyone who has read this book that I have been the beneficiary of extraordinary hospitality in Bolekhiv, Ukraine, for which I am as grateful as I am for that shown me everywhere else. Of all the Ukrainians who have helped me, however, none has been as generous, eager, and, finally, as instrumental as Alex Dunai in L'viv, who for nearly ten years now has been my right-hand man in the project of which this book is the culmination. For his tireless efforts on our behalf, I am more grateful than I can say. He began as a valued colleague, and together with his family has become a valued friend.

Invaluable archival and technical assistance came, too, from a group of talented young people whose contribution I'm happy to note: Nicky Gottlieb, for his calendrical wizardry; Henryk Jaronowski, to whom I owe some crucial photographs; Arthur Dudney, without whose Polish translations I would have been lost; and my *benjamins,* Morris Doueck and Zack Woolfe: "from your students you will learn."

I am also deeply grateful to Ariel Kaminer at *The New York Times Magazine* for seeing my first writing on Bolechow so successfully into print.

A small circle of cherished friends close to home were crucial in seeing me through to the end of this long project: Chris Andersen, Glen Bowersock and Christopher Jones, István and Gloria Deák, Diane Feldman, Lise Funderburg and John Howard, Bob Gottlieb and Maria Tucci, Renée Guest, Jake Hurley, Lily Knezevich, Laura Miller, and Stephen Simcock. Donna Masini has been everything anyone could want in a best friend; Patti Hart was an invaluable support. Myrna and Ralph Langer, together with their extended family, have always provided a bedrock of affection and encouragement to me and mine, especially valued by me during this project; I'm particularly happy to have Karen Isaac as a supportive and loving IM correspondent. My debt to Froma Zeitlin, one that I am happy to continue acknowledging whenever possible, should be evident in these pages; this book quite literally couldn't have been written without her—and indeed without her husband, George, a generous host from days of old and, more recently, an indefatigable travel companion in Vienna, Israel, and Lithuania. My travels with Lane Montgomery have, it is safe to say, run the gamut of the comfort spectrum; I'm so grateful to her for her contribution to the second and very emotional journey that we took together. From the start of this project, Nancy Novogrod and her husband, John—who have listened to my tales of Galician travel (if not leisure) with a uniquely sympathetic ear—have been the sources of treasured friendship and encouragement. I am grateful to Nancy as well, wearing her editor's hat, for her forbearance and patience in letting me take time off from my obligations to her in order to complete this book; Bob Silvers at *The New York Review of Books* has also been enormously generous to me in this respect, as indeed he always has been in many others.

No friends, however, have been as vital to the writing of this book as have Louis and Anka Begley. It would be an understatement to say that they shared with me much that was so important; only a small part of it was a crucial week of hospitality during which I brought my work to an end.

That work has, from the start, been a terrifically pleasurable collaboration with my editor, Tim Duggan, and what merits it has are owed largely to him. His initial enthusiasm for the project, his patience as it grew in scope and size (and duration), his immaculate professionalism, the skill with which he balanced an acute editorial sensibility with a deep sensitivity to my aims, have made the writing of this book a joy to me and, in the end, an experience from which I've learned a great deal. For that I am thankful. I should add that not the least part of the pleasure of working with him has been the excellent help, unflaggingly cheerful and unfailingly efficient, given me by his assistant, Allison Lorentzen, to whom I'm also very grateful.

I will once again end where I began. I was just out of graduate school when Lydia Wills more or less scooped me up and pointed me in the right direction, and our professional collaboration has, ever since, brought me great pride and many satisfactions—as indeed has our friendship. It was she who knew all along that this book was the one I had to write, and she who made it happen in just the right way; for that reason it, like so much that I've accomplished, is as much hers as mine.

THOSE READERS WHO have gotten this far in the book will have become familiar with one of the dedicatees, Mrs. Frances Begley, née Franciszka Hauser, my feelings for whom will have been made clear in these pages. The other deserves to be commemorated by more than a mere name. Sarah Pettit was, at first, my editor, in the days when I first began writing; but she soon developed into a cherished friend, while continuing for a long time to be a supportive colleague. Her many extraordinary qualities—her intellectual brilliance, her editorial gusto and professional acumen, the superb taste, the wry humor that barely masked a sentimental, even poetic heart, her beauty and her passions—have been duly eulogized elsewhere, as befitting a person who achieved so much in the public world in so little time. Her death from lymphoma in January 2003, when she was thirty-six, was and continues to be a tragedy for a world much larger than that constituted by the circle of her intimate friends. I will say here only that she was the earliest and most enthusiastic champion of this book, and for me it is indeed an unhappy proof that *there are tears in things* that she cannot see the end result of a project whose birth she greeted with such selfless enthusiasm, at a time when a lack of interest in anything but her own condition would have been more than forgivable. She was, and will always be, my darling girl.